The Literature of
AMERICAN MUSIC

in Books and Folk Music Collections:

a fully annotated bibliography

by

DAVID HORN

The Scarecrow Press, Inc.

Metuchen, N.J.   1977

Library of Congress Cataloging in Publication Data

Horn, David, 1942-
 The literature of American music in books and folk
music collections.

 Includes index.
 1. Music, American--History and criticism--Bibliogra-
phy. 2. Music, American--Bibliography. I. Title.
ML120.U5H7   016.7817'73   76-13160
ISBN 0-8108-0996-6

To Gill

with love

PREFACE

For sheer diversity the music of the United States is not
equalled by that of any other country. It is (or should be) clearly
impossible to approach this body of music with just one set of critical baggage (though many have tried), and the literature in book
form is as diverse as the music itself. To the relatively uninitiated
this can be confusing, if not actually dangerous terrain, and even the
specialist, when he or she leaves the security of the domestic hearth
and ventures out into the world, can lose the way. In such situations
this book is intended to offer a map, a compass, and--occasionally
also--a rifle.

Towards the end of 1972 the American Arts Documentation
Centre at the University of Exeter published a short bibliography of
mine, called "The Literature of American Music: A Fully Annotated
Catalogue of Books and Song Collections in Exeter University Library." The present work is an outgrowth of that one, though it is
basically a wholly different book. Its scope extends beyond the confines of a single library's collection, increasing the total number of
items from 500 to 1,400, and although a number of the original annotations are included here unchanged, many more have been rewritten.

In a guide such as this it would be hard, if not impossible,
to attain comprehensive coverage (if any one doubts this, let him
look, for example, at the International Jazz Bibliography, and consider, for one thing, how to locate and consult some of the items
listed there). I have tried to include all English-language material
known to me that I judge to be of interest, whether that interest be
scholarly, historic or popular, with the addition of a representative
sample of books in languages other than English. Since a diet of

v

too many books designated "indispensable" eventually discourages the digestive processes I have sought to blend the important with the less important, even the inconsequential (though there are standards even for inconsequentiality), believing that only in that way can a rounded picture be obtained. I have tried to avoid a specific "terminus ad quem," but only a few items published later than August, 1975 have been included. There have, inevitably, been some books that I would like to have incorporated, but have failed, for one reason or another, to see. These are listed in the Appendix, where they will be found rubbing shoulders with items of a more minor interest (both seen and unseen) that I have encountered "serendipitously" in the course of the bibliographic wanderlust that has occupied much of the past few years. (The presence of the Appendix is not meant to imply that, taken with the main bibliography, the reader has a complete listing.) I hope that, in due course, it may be possible to bring out supplements to the present work. Anyone having information, suggestions or advice is invited to write to me at the University Library, Prince of Wales Road, Exeter, EX4 4PT, Devon, England.

By its very existence this book implies several more, for that is what it would take to cover the literature on the music of the United States that exists in periodical articles, which are not included here. Other areas of excluded material are: dissertations; serial publications (though I have included the first issue of some important recent series, and have also given space to some completed series that had short runs); fiction; popular song collections (except for a selection of historical anthologies with substantial linking narrative); all "art" music scores (which, for this purpose, includes 18th century tunebooks by William Billings and others); general reference works, such as the Dictionary of American Biography, Current Biography, large encyclopedias, and standard music reference works like Grove, Baker's and the International Cyclopedia; and, finally, the cultural background. This last area is omitted with some regret, particularly as I realize that, for black music especially, a knowledge of the social, historical and cultural background is important for a true appreciation of the music. To do justice to this enormous subject, however, would require another book, and so, in the case of black music, I have indicated some basic reference works and bibliographies, and confined myself to a small selection of social and cultural studies that give more than just passing mention to music.

The literature on jazz in book form is vast. In order to keep this section manageable and not to allow it to overshadow all others, I have had to be a little more selective than in other areas. For further information the reader is advised to consult the bibliographies listed under H.1.b.

As a glance at the Table of Contents will show, I have divided the book into a fairly large number of sections and sub-sections. This not only reflects the great variety of the subject, it also serves to indicate the relationships of various musical styles to each other. There is a limit, however, to the degree to which a book like this can point to historical patterns and stylistic families, and it is also important to realize that, in the nature of things, many books could equally well go in several places. The most important of these are cross-referenced in the text, but the subject index should be used for a complete picture of the literature on any one topic.

Users of this book may decide for themselves on the advantages or otherwise of its having been compiled in England. It is a situation which has not been without some practical drawbacks, and it was clear to me early on that a period of study in the United States would be required, to see material not available (apparently) in Great Britain. As Oscar Sonneck once remarked, "Unfortunately scientific enthusiasm does not always go hand in hand with a full purse," but I have been very fortunate in the assistance I have received. I am particularly grateful to the University of Exeter (who also granted me a period of leave of absence), the United States Information Service at the U.S. Embassy in London, and the Sir Ernest Cassel Educational Trust for the financial help they gave me, without which this book would not have been finished.

Many other people have helped me with books, advice, encouragement and hospitality, and I would like to express my thanks to them. In England: Judith R. Jamison, Cultural Affairs Officer at the U.S. Embassy; Graham S. Langley (British Institute of Jazz

vii

Studies); staff of the British Library Reference Division, and of the University of London Music Library; Reg Bristo, John R. T. Davies, Martin Power, Phil Evison, Denise and John Brinker. In Exeter: Dr. Mike Weaver and Dr. Mick Gidley (American Arts), the Librarian, J. F. Stirling, and many members of his staff; the Librarian of Exeter City Library, G. Hardy, and members of his staff.

In the United States: the staff of the Library and Museum of the Performing Arts, Lincoln Center, New York, particularly my good friend Richard Jackson of the Americana Division, Music Library; staff at the Library of Congress; AMS Press, Ascap, The Lynn Farnol Group; for hospitality in Washington, Carolyn and Bill Michaels; in Williamsburg, Sheila and Terry Meyers; and for unmatchable kindness during my stay in New York, Ilse and Eric Moon.

I would like to say a special word of thanks to Myra Crook for her considerable and much appreciated help with the typing of the manuscript, far exceeding the calls of friendship.

To Gill, my wife, I owe an immense debt of gratitude. Her name should really stand at the head of these acknowledgments, for without her huge contribution as chief typist, indexer, file clerk, checker, general collater of information and dispenser of encouragement and love, there would be no book. I'm sure she thinks marriage vows should be amended to allow would-be bibliographers to give notice of their intentions, but she has been wonderfully tolerant of all the muddle and attendant paraphernalia that go with a book such as this, and I am eternally grateful. To our children, Katherine and Robert, who have tolerated with a good grace so many stories unread and games unplayed, a sincere apology, and a promise to mend my ways.

David Horn

Exeter,
April, 1976

CONTENTS

A. GENERAL WORKS

1. Bibliography and Reference

a. Bibliographies of Music

See also nos. 8, 1150, 1156

1. HIXON, Donald L. Music in early America: a bibliography of
   music in Evans. Metuchen: Scarecrow Press, 1970. 607p.
   A key reference tool for the study of 17th and 18th century
American music, both sacred and secular, this is an index to music
listed in Charles Evans' American Bibliography (Chicago, 1903-1959,
14 vols.), and also in the Readex Corporation microprint edition,
Early American Imprints, 1639-1800 (New York, 1951-), which attempts to provide a microprint of every item in Evans. Hixon's
bibliography lists every item in Evans that contains musical notation;
this includes books, pamphlets, broadsides, sheet music and larger
collections, but omits music in periodicals, newspapers and serials.
The main bibliography is in two parts. Part 1 is an alphabetical
composer/editor listing of all musical items in Evans available in
the Readex microprint format up to the summer, 1970. There are
title entries for anonymous works, Evans serial numbers for each
item, and composer analytics for each piece in collections of secular music. Part 2 provides exactly the same kind of listing for material not yet available in microprint. Following is a collection of
biographical sketches of the composers in Parts 1 and 2, excluding
well-known Europeans. The usefulness of the book is further enhanced by three indexes: of composers and editors, of titles, and
of Evans numbers. The bibliographical citations omit elements of
descriptive cataloging (such as size, illustrations) and library locations in the U.S., all of which are given in Evans (and also in Sonneck and Upton, no. 2).

2. SONNECK, Oscar George Theodore. Bibliography of early secular American music. Washington: Printed for the author by
   H. L. McQueen, 1905. 194p.
   _____. A bibliography of early secular American music (18th
   century); revised and enlarged by William Treat Upton. Washington: Library of Congress, 1945. (Repr. New York: Da
   Capo, 1964). 616p.
   The credit for the vision that recognized the need for such a
monument of scholarship as this, and for the energy and zeal to set

1

it in motion, belongs exclusively to Sonneck, but the work in its present form owes a tremendous amount to the devoted labors of Upton, who, in the three years it took to revise Sonneck's original (Sonneck died in 1928), more than tripled its size until the total of items exceeded 3,000. Sonneck himself had seen and deplored the lack of interest in early American music, and recognized the futility of proceeding with scholarly researches until a sound bibliographical base had been laid. This he proceeded to do, very largely through the study of newspapers and magazines of the period covered (and later took splendid advantage of his own groundwork with his Early Concert Life in America, no. 210). Besides increasing the size of the book, Upton added numerous appendages: lists of articles and essays relating to music; of composers (with biographical sketches of all Americans); of songsters; of first lines; of American patriotic music; of opera librettos; of publishers, printers and engravers.

Sonneck's original plan, which Upton adhered to, was to make a "complete collection of titles of secular music and books, pamphlets, essays, etc." These were either issued by an American press prior to the 19th century (whether located in certain specified libraries or not) or written by native or naturalized Americans (whether extant in MS. or apparently neither published nor extant). The bibliography follows an alphabetical title arrangement, with complete bibliographical details, notes on form, text, etc., and library locations.

3. UNITED STATES INFORMATION AGENCY. Catalog of published concert music by American composers; selected, compiled and prepared by Music Branch, Information Service ... Washington, D.C., 1964. 175p.

_____. _____. Supplement no. 1, July 1965. Washington, 1965. 74p.

EAGON, Angelo. Catalog of published concert music by American composers. 2nd ed. Metuchen: Scarecrow Press, 1969. 348p.

_____. _____. First supplement. Metuchen: Scarecrow Press, 1971. 150p.

_____. _____. Second supplement. Metuchen: Scarecrow Press, 1974. 148p.

Eagon's most useful catalog is based on the two USIA volumes, and like them is a classified listing, covering native-born Americans and foreign-born composers naturalized before the age of 26, whose works are "generally available in some printed form for purchase" (foreword). Electronic music is not included. The six original groups are expanded to eight: voice, instrumental-solo, instrumental-ensemble, concert jazz, percussion, orchestra, opera, band. Arrangement is alphabetical by composer in each section, with abbreviations for publishers and full performance details (instrumentation etc.), including, for orchestral and band music, durations. The format of Eagon's two supplements is identical to that of his main volume. All have a key to publishers, an author and a composer index.

4. WOLFE, Richard J. Secular music in America, 1801-1825: a bibliography; introduction by Carleton Sprague Smith. New

York: New York Public Library, 1964. 3v.

This vast bibliography of over 10,000 items continues Sonneck-Upton (no. 2), and includes song sheets, instrumental works in sheet form, non-religious music in collections, sacred music in secular collections, and religious pieces by native composers in sheet music form. The works are listed in an alphabetical composer sequence (unlike the title sequence in Sonneck-Upton), with anonymous works under arranger, if given, or title. There are biographical notes for each native or naturalized American composer, followed by an alphabetical list of his published compositions, with full bibliographical details and locations in public or private collections. Indexes of titles, first lines, publishers, engravers and printers, plate and publishers' numbers and a general index complete one of the great reference works in American musicology.

b. Bibliographies of Music Literature

See also no. 14.

5. JACKSON, Richard. United States music: sources of bibliography and collective biography. Brooklyn: Institute for Studies in American Music, 1973. (I. S. A. M. Monographs, No. 1) 80p.

An admirable, accurate, and--by comparison with general bibliographic practice--animated guide that adheres closely to the field defined in its subtitle. Ninety books are listed and described, in four sections: reference works, historical studies, regional studies, and topical studies (folk music, black music as a genre, blues, ragtime, jazz, pop, church music, opera, women in music, and 20th century music). All the books selected are described as having "potentially useful features," even though they may not be considered of a very high standard, and the compiler's annotations, done with a refreshing lightness of touch, are at the same time succinctly informative and do not mince words when the occasion demands. Particularly useful are the lists, included in the annotations, of people for whom biographical information is given in the work concerned. These include complete lists of American musicians in Current Biography and the Dictionary of National Biography. Bibliographical citations are full, and are followed by references to reviews in numerous cases. There is also a good name index.

6. MEAD, Rita H. Doctoral dissertations in American music: a classified bibliography. Brooklyn: Institute for Studies in American Music, 1974. (I. S. A. M. Monographs, No. 3) 155p.

A most valuable and revealing compilation, listing "doctoral dissertations written in departments of music and other disciplines in American (and a few foreign) universities" from the 1890s to 1973. Working from titles or abstracts, the compiler includes all theses related to American music that have "historical or analytical significance." The 1,226 entries are arranged in six broad groups: reference and research materials; historical studies (with subdivisions for composers, performers and groups, genres--including opera, musical theater and jazz--area studies, education, theater, and socio-cultural studies); theory; ethnomusicology (racial and ethnic groups, and regions); organology; related fields. Each entry gives the author's name, full title, degree, institution, date of acceptance, and pagination. Microfilm number and location of abstract are added if available, and explanatory notes are occasionally supplied. No details of subsequent publication are given. There are author and subject indexes. It is noticeable how strong an imbalance has existed between concert and church music studies and those devoted to jazz and popular genres, which are not very strongly represented.

7. MUGRIDGE, Donald H. , and McCRUM, Blanche P. A guide to the study of the United States of America: representative books reflecting the development of American life and thought; prepared under the direction of Roy P. Basler. Washington: Library of Congress, 1960. 1193p.

Even when the manpower resources of the Library of Congress have been acknowledged, one cannot help but admire the industry necessary to produce this indispensable bibliography, which gives extensive annotations for 6,487 books, and mentions many others in passing. The thirty-two sections cover the whole range of American civilization including, for the background to music studies, society, intellectual and religious history, and entertainment. Music itself is found in two places: in chapter 24, "Folklore, Folk music, Folk art," which includes 35 books specifically on songs and ballads; and in chapter 25, "Music," in which there are 83 books in eleven categories (general histories, contemporary surveys, localities, religious music, popular music, jazz, orchestras and bands, opera, choirs, music education, and individual musicians). In their preamble to chapter 25 the compilers of this section (from the Music Division of the Library) comment that "the literature of American music is rather recent and rather scanty; save in the field of jazz and singers' autobiographies, the following pages list a considerable proportion of it." Even so, there are some surprising omissions (e. g. W. F. Allen's Slave Songs, E. F. Morneweck's Foster family chronicles, and the total lack of anything on Amerindian music). More significant, however, as far as music coverage is concerned, was the unfortunate timing of the volume (the terminal date was 1958), as the early 1960s saw the beginnings of an explosion in literature on American music, particularly on the vernacular tradition, which continues unabated.

8. SENDREY, Alfred. Bibliography of Jewish music. New York: Columbia University Press, 1951. (Repr. New York: Kraus, 1969). 404p.

This pioneer bibliography of 10,682 items is divided into two halves: literature and music. The first part contains a section on individuals (p. 141ff) that includes numerous Americans in its separate divisions for composers, instrumentalists, singers, conductors, opera managers and musicologists. Other, not very frequent references to literature on specifically American music are scattered among the various sections for Jewish musical life and history. While Part 1 includes Jewish composers of all types of music, including popular, Part 2 (which encompasses sacred and secular music) does not attempt to catalog all music by Jewish composers, but only music showing "obvious Jewish characteristics." There are name indexes to both parts.

9. SPILLER, Robert E., et al. Literary history of the United States. Editors: Robert E. Spiller, Willard Thorp, Thomas H. Johnson, Henry Seidel Canby. Volume 3. Bibliography. New York: Macmillan, 1948. 817p.
_____. _____. Bibliography supplement; edited by Richard M. Ludwig. New York: Macmillan, 1959. 268p.
_____. _____. Bibliography supplement II. New York: Macmillan, 1972. 366p.
Although it is principally a literary bibliography, this excellent work is a useful source for cultural materials, and contains numerous references to music. The basic design in four sections (Guide to Resources, Literature and Culture, Movements and Influences, and Individual Authors) is repeated in both Supplement I (covering the years 1948-58) and Supplement II (covering 1958-70). Most of the references to cultural and specifically musical works come in Section II (Literature and Culture). In the background section of the main volume and of each supplement there is a short entry under music (including art music and jazz); more informative are the ten pages devoted in the main volume to folk songs and ballads (general and regional studies and collections, Negro folklore, river songs and sea chanties, folklore of the lumberjack, folk plays, literary ballads, and bibliography); the supplements each have a shorter section up-dating this. An item in the main volume not repeated in the supplements is the section on hymns and hymn writing. The information is assembled and presented as a guide, with occasional defining or evaluative comments, rather than as a tabulated bibliography.

10. TOLZMANN, Don Heinrich, comp. German-Americana: a bibliography. Metuchen: Scarecrow Press, 1975. 384p.
This massive, 5,307-item bibliography includes a section specifically on German-American music (pp. 267-274). In it the compiler lists 127 books, articles and dissertations on concert, operatic and religious music from the 17th to the 20th century. Author index.

c. Biographical Dictionaries and Reference Works

11. CHENEY, Simeon Pease. The American singing book, contains more than 300 pages of a great variety of excellent sacred and secular music, old and new, for all purposes where such music is used. A valuable feature of the book is the biographical department, containing biographies of forty of the leading composers, book-makers, etc., of sacred music in America.... Boston: White, Smith, 1879. 320p.
This late 19th century tunebook, deliberately designed to hark back to the 18th century tunebooks of Billings, Read, etc., came out

in the wake of the revival of popular feeling for the music of the
singing schools (of which the Old Folks Concerts were the main man-
ifestation--see Kemp, no. 211). Its interest today lies more in its
"biographical department"--a highly unusual feature--with its biographies of 18th and 19th century New England composers, singers and
compilers. Of this section Cheney states "it certainly contains precisely the information I ever sought but never found in any book ...
Among [the musicians] were farmers, a great variety of mechanics,
inventors, preachers, lawyers, poets and warriors. This department has cost me much research and painstaking" (preface). Among
those credited with assisting him are John W. Moore, James A.
Johnson and George Hood. Each biography contains a "characteristic tune." The compilers seem to have drawn liberally on contemporary sources such as journals and correspondence. Among the 40
are Billings, Swan, Holyoke, Ingalls, Read, Hastings, Lowell Mason
and William Bradbury (i.e., though most are New England yeomen,
a few are included who cared little for the music of the singing
schools). (Cheney also compiled Brother Cheney's Collection of Old
Folks' Concert Music ... Boston, 1879.)

12. CLAGHORN, Charles Eugene. Biographical dictionary of Amer-
      ican music. West Nyack: Parker, 1973. 491p.
    The compiler aims to bring together in one work information
on individuals in all styles of American music, for which one would
normally be obliged to search through several specialist books. To
this end he provides entries for over 5,200 persons and groups from
the 17th century to the present day in one alphabetical sequence.
The coverage includes concert music, opera, church music, musical
theater and films, jazz, ragtime, folk song, country music, popular
song, rock and soul. Non-native Americans who lived and worked
for an extended time in America are included. All black artists are
designated as such. Entries give dates, brief biographical and career data, and selected works/recordings/performances, etc. Never
very long, they are kept deliberately short for noted individuals--
the information being available elsewhere.
    [Some comments are necessary. The attempt at comprehensive
stylistic coverage means that selection is inevitable, and this leads
to evaluative judgments; thus, jazz and concert music are well
represented, blues and early country music relatively poorly. The
decision to include many obscure figures, especially from the 19th
century, enhances the danger of unevenness: is it not insulting to
artists such as Blind Blake and Charlie Poole to exclude them,
while space is given, for example, to Charles Edward Horsley (1822-
1876), English-born organist? A smaller number of non-native
Americans would have alleviated this problem; many such individuals
are included, whom one would not look up in a book devoted to American music (e.g. Otto Klemperer, Gracie Fields).
    Undoubtedly, the information on lesser-known figures is valu-
able, but the greater detail accorded them, as against better known
figures, prompts the question: should they not have the field to
themselves? If Aaron Copland is restricted to a minuscule biography
and eight works, is there any point in including him at all?]

13. GROVE, Sir George. Dictionary of music and musicians.
       (2nd ed.) American supplement, being the sixth volume of
       the complete work; Waldo Selden Pratt, editor, Charles N.
       Boyd, associate editor. New York: Macmillan; Philadel-
       phia: Presser, 1920. 412p. illus.
       _____. _____. (3rd ed.) American supplement ... New ed.,
       new material. New York: Macmillan, 1928. 438p. illus.
     The wisdom of devoting a separate volume of the world-famous
international music encyclopedia to the music and musicians of one
country was doubted from the outset by the editors themselves (cf.
preface); nevertheless it was and is a useful work. The bulk of the
book is given over to "specific descriptive articles about leading individuals, organizations, institutions and interests," in much the
same pattern as the main encyclopedia. An unfamiliar feature of
the supplement, however, is the "chronological register" preceding
the main section. This is a group of short essays on five periods
of music in the United States from the colonial era to 1920, each
one followed by a set of biographical sketches of musicians from the
period. About 1,700 individuals appear altogether, of whom 800 or
so are foreign-born. All are cross-referenced in the main section,
which gives more extensive treatment to about 700, complete with
lists of works. In cases where an article appeared in the parent
work there is a cross-reference, and sometimes a supplementary
article. The whole work is conscientiously and objectively executed.
Critical opinions on the part of writers are avoided "except in general terms or in quoted form."

14. HISTORICAL RECORDS SURVEY. District of Columbia. Bio-
       bibliographical index of musicians in the United States of
       America since Colonial times. Washington: Music Section,
       Pan American Union, 1941. 439p. bibliog.
       _____. _____. 2nd ed. Washington, 1956. (Repr.
       New York: Da Capo, 1971). 439p. bibliog.
     Conceived by Keyes Porter in 1936, and supervised first by
him, then by Leonard Ellinwood, this valuable index contains bibliographic references for approximately 10,000 "persons who have contributed to the history of music in the United States." The references
are to 66 studies, histories and reference works--not all devoted entirely to American music--listed, with the symbols used to refer to
them, at the beginning of the book. Coverage is confined almost
entirely to the field of church and concert music, and includes (rather a high percentage of) foreign-born musicians mentioned in the
source books. Opera is particularly strongly represented. Music
teachers and administrators, writers, and instrument-makers are
also included. Several limitations on the usefulness of the book are
apparent: a) the index is in no way complete; b) as the introduction
admits, coverage of contemporaries is thin; c) jazz and popular music figures, and black musicians are not well covered. Each name
is followed by dates where known, nationality if foreign-born, musical occupation, a list of references to the bibliography, and,
where relevant, reference to the appendix, which contains a list of
books relating to individual persons in the index. The 2nd edition is
an uncorrected reprint of the 1st.

15. JONES, F. O., ed. A handbook of American music and mu-
    sicians, containing biographies of American musicians, and
    histories of the principal musical institutions, firms and
    societies. Canaseraga, N. Y.: F. O. Jones, 1886 (Repr.
    New York: Da Capo, 1971); Buffalo: C. W. Moulton, 1887.
    182p.

A highly regarded source of information on American musicians
and musical life up to the last 15 years of the 19th century. The
volume's slim appearance belies the treasure store inside. Arranged like an encyclopedia, it contains entries for persons (composers, performers, instrument-makers, teachers), societies and institutions, instruments, publishers, and selected individual musical
works. Composer entries often include independent critical summaries. Much biographical information was apparently obtained by
correspondence.

16. LAHEE, Henry C. Annals of music in America: a chrono-
    logical record of significant musical events, from 1640 to
    the present day, with comments on the various periods into
    which the work is divided. Boston: Marshall Jones, 1922.
    (Repr. New York: AMS Press, 1969). 298p.

"The object of this book is to give as complete a record as
possible of the beginning and progress of music in the United States
of America" (preface). What Lahee means in fact is that he provides a chronological list of what he deems to be significant events
in the field of "serious" musical activity, especially in New York
and New England. As such it is a valuable work, covering mainly
concert or stage performances of particular works (mainly European),
artistic debuts and the organization of societies, with some extra
data such as the birthdays of American composers and musicians.
The snag is the word "progress," which leads the author to omit all
but a few items he describes as being "of interest rather than of
educational progress," so one may discover the debut date of Madame Anna Bishop (Aug 4, 1847), but is not told that Stephen Foster's "Susanna" was first performed in public five weeks later in
Pittsburgh. There is an index of compositions, with dates and locations of performances.

17. MATTFELD, Julius. Variety music cavalcade, 1620-1960: a
    chronology of vocal and instrumental music popular in the
    United States; with an introduction by Abel Green. New
    York: Prentice-Hall, 1952. 637p.
    _____. Variety music cavalcade, 1620-1961 ... Rev. ed.
    Englewood Cliffs: Prentice-Hall, 1962. 713p.
    _____. Variety music cavalcade, 1620-1969 ... 3rd ed.
    Englewood Cliffs: Prentice-Hall, 1971. 766p.

This splendid compilation, which began life as a librarian's
card index, and its published career in the Variety Radio Directory
for 1938-1939, is first and foremost a chronological listing of a-
round 5,000 secular and religious songs, hymns, choral compositions,
instrumental and orchestral works that enjoyed a degree of popularity in America. The Colonial period is rather briefly covered, but
is followed by a year-by-year listing of items by title, with full de-

tails of author, composer, publisher and copyright date. The real
delight of the book comes with the additional information--the historical notes for each year on all manner of social, political and
artist events. Mattfeld died in 1968, and the additional information
in the 3rd edition is by Herm Schoenfeld. An appendix to this edition
lists some songs omitted earlier that later became standards. Title
index.

18.　SALESKI, Gdal. Famous musicians of Jewish origin. New
　　　　York: Bloch, 1949. 716p. illus.
　　　An "imposing array" of American musicians appears among
these biographical portraits of composers, conductors, violinists,
cellists, pianists, singers and others. Personal recollection plays
a significant role in the portraits, which, while being chiefly confined to the life and career of each subject, attempt to be more than
mere recitations of facts. Personality traits and general features
of a composer's music or a performer's art are also included.

19.　TURPIE, Mary C. , comp. American music for the study of
　　　　American civilization. I. Formal compositions. II. Folk
　　　　and popular songs. Minneapolis: Program in American
　　　　Studies, University of Minnesota, (1954). 91p. bibliog.
　　　Though this reference tool is now out-of-date the interesting
concept behind it could be re-explored. The compiler aims to provide students with a guide to music that provides some kind of commentary on American history and culture. The first section contains a selected list of 130 art music compositions chosen because
they develop native material (a number revealing strong links between America and Europe are also included). The compiler's
choice is restricted by the current availability of recordings. There
are very brief descriptions of each piece--a difficult task with some
not always very happy results. The second section lists about 350
English-language folk and popular songs reflecting "the activities,
the opinions and the emotions of ordinary Americans." The crisp
annotations (more successful here) draw attention to features relating to the overall theme of music as a mirror of civilization.
There are references to collections in which the songs appear, and
to LP recordings. An index draws together the topics covered.

2.　Histories*

20.　RITTER, Frederic Louis. Music in America. New York:
　　　　Scribner, 1883. 423p.
　　　　　　　. Music in England and music in America. Vol. 2.
　　　　Music in America. London: Reeves, 1884. 423p.
　　　　　　　. Music in America. New ed. New York: Scribner,
　　　　1890. (Repr. New York: Johnson, 1970; New York: Frank-
　　　　lin, 1973). 521p. bibliog. notes.

*This section is arranged chronologically.

Ritter's volume, the first attempt to view historically the course of music in America, is described by its author as intended "to place before the American musical student and sincere musical amateur, a faithful mirror of past musical life in the United States" (preface). Ritter (1834-1891) was an Alsatian who came to the U.S. in 1856. Though he considers first Puritan psalmody, and the composers of the late 18th and early 19th centuries, his focus of attention is firmly on the developments in musical activity in the cities in the 19th century--societies, performances of opera, oratorio and instrumental music, musical conventions, traveling orchestras. His yardstick is the degree of progress towards emulating Europe. A curious final chapter--curious to us today at least--denies the existence of folk music in white America ("the American landscape is silent ... the American country people are not in the possession of deep emotional power"--pp. 385, 387). Modern attitudes to Ritter's work are generally deprecating but one historian, Robert Stevenson, pointed to a redeeming feature: "Bad as was Ritter's pioneer history, at least he showed himself willing to examine some documents personally" (no. 43, p. 9). Its value today lies chiefly in the factual information on both organizations and lesser-known individuals. Eight music examples are given at the end, before the index.

21.   ELSON, Louis C.   The history of American music.   New York: Macmillan, 1904.   380p.   illus., bibliog.
_____.   _____.   Rev. ed.   New York: Macmillan, 1915. 387p.   illus., bibliog.
_____.   _____.   Rev. to 1925 by Arthur Elson.   New York: Macmillan, 1925.   (Repr. New York: Franklin, 1971).   423p.   illus., bibliog.
The treatment of history by compartmentalizing it into categories and paying attention to the march of time within, but not generally without, these compartments, has its conveniences, but overall historical perspective tends to be sacrificed. Elson's history proceeds for the most part by such a method. Following a preliminary account of "the religious beginnings of American music" he describes first the developments in organizations, orchestral life, societies and institutions, and opera. A chapter on folk music (divided equally between American Indian music and Stephen Foster, these two unaccustomed bedfellows being separated by a page on Negro folk music) and another on national and patriotic music act as a bridge to the central part of the book, which is a series of chapters describing the lives and works of 19th century composers-- "tone masters," orchestral composers, operatic, cantata and vocal composers, song composers, composers for the piano. There are also chapters on organists and choir leaders, women in music, musical criticism, and education. Thus Elson balances his history between musical life and musical creativity, with a slightly greater emphasis on the latter. One misses any sense of interest in popular currents for their own sake as intrinsic parts of America's music, but for informed comment on 19th century "serious" composition Elson is a useful work. The revisions both take the form of supplementary chapters (four in the 1925 edition), which are separately indexed. Besides the twelve full-page photogravures each edition contains over a hundred small illustrations.

22. HUBBARD, W. L., ed. History of American music; with introductions by George W. Chadwick and Frank Damrosch. Toledo: Irving Squire, 1908. (American History and Encyclopedia of Music, Vol. 4) 356p. illus., bibliog.

Hubbard's solution to the problems posed by trying to arrange all the forms of American music into one historical sequence is to abandon chronology and adopt a wholly categorical approach, beginning with Indian and Negro music (including spirituals and minstrelsy), thus giving these subjects an honor rarely conferred on them in histories of American music. Maintaining a catholic approach, Hubbard's other groups are: popular, patriotic and national, psalmody and church, education, concerts and oratorios, opera, instrumental, bands and orchestras, musicians, trades. Though he does not explore very deeply he is quite informative on trends and on particular people, and is as concerned with musical life as with musical creation. Chadwick's chapter is an essay on late 19th century composers (himself excluded), while Damrosch writes on music in public schools.

23. FARWELL, Arthur, and DARBY, W. Dermot, eds. Music in America; introduction by Arthur Farwell. New York: National Society of Music, 1915. (The Art of Music, ed. Daniel Gregory Mason, Vol. 4) 478p. illus., bibliog.

So much has happened in American music since the first general histories were written, and views of the colonial era have undergone such a profound revision that one tends to consult volumes like this one mainly for information on the 19th century. And it is there in plenty: various aspects of musical life surveyed by Darby (1885-1947), who bore the lion's share of the work; music education covered by M. M. M. (?); music of the classic period and music in a "lighter vein" by B. L. (Benjamin Lambord); the folk element by C. S. (César Saerchinger); and, most significant, around 40 composers of the later 19th and early 20th centuries in Arthur Farwell's two chapters. But beyond the factual level the book has more human personality than its predecessors, and a greater range of critical vision. On the one hand there is the almost perpetual twinkle in Darby's youthful Irish eye, viewing the musical activity of his newly adopted land with enjoyment and a European ironic detachment that avoids condescension. On the other hand there is Farwell, lending the book a sense of some higher significance in all the activity recorded in its pages, seeing American musical history in its broader sense as "appreciation, creation and administration." Where Darby is down-to-earth Farwell writes with vision, and the ability to step out of an age and view it historically. His chapters on "Romanticists and Neo-Romanticists" and "Nationalists, Eclectics and Ultra-moderns" combine factual detail with a perceptive critical assessment that almost intuitively relates people and events to a framework of creative American culture. Basic to his overall view, as he expounds it in his introduction, is the belief that, in 1915, "the past has consisted chiefly of a tasting of the musical art and traditions of the old world," that "the fruitage of our national musical life is still for the future." Index.

24. HOWARD, John Tasker. Our American music: three hundred years of it. New York: Crowell, 1931. 713p. illus., bibliog.
_____. . Rev. ed. New York: Crowell, 1939. 743p. illus., bibliog.
_____. . 3rd ed. New York: Crowell, 1946. 841p. illus., bibliog.
_____. . 3rd ed., with supplementary chapters by James Lyons. New York: Crowell, 1954. 841, 77p. illus., bibliog.
_____. Our American music: a comprehensive history from 1620 to the present. 4th ed. New York: Crowell, 1965. 944p. illus., bibliog.

Described by one critic as "highly respectable" in approach, and implying that America has "made aesthetic progress" (Carleton Sprague Smith, quoted by Chase, no. 25, p. xvii), this remains the most comprehensive survey of the development of the serious music tradition in America, and an indispensable source of information-- biographical and, to a lesser extent, critical--particularly on the 19th and early to mid-20th centuries. Less well covered are the popular and folk idioms. Howard is visibly less comfortable when discussing these, which he treats as appendages rather than as integral elements. His general approach to his sources is criticized by Stevenson (no. 43, p. 9), who remarks on his failure to consult original documents. Each successive edition adds and updates material on 20th century composers. By the 4th edition the bibliography (revised for this edition by Karl Kroeger) had reached a massive 75 pages. Index.

25. CHASE, Gilbert. America's music from the Pilgrims to the present. New York: McGraw-Hill, 1955. 733p. bibliog.
_____. . Rev. ed. New York: McGraw-Hill, 1966. 759p. bibliog., discog. note.

This fine history, both scholarly and readable, attempts "to understand, to describe, to illuminate, and evaluate, the vital processes and factors that have gone into the making of America's music" (Introduction). In three parts, which correspond very broadly to century divisions (1600-1800, 19th century, 20th century) the book analyzes in detail the various concurrent and intertwining trends in church, concert and vernacular music. This broadly conceived outline--it was the first major history to include as integral elements the various vernacular traditions of religious folk song, minstrelsy, ragtime, blues, jazz and musical theater--omits the secular Anglo-American folk tradition per se, and the early commercially recorded folk repertoire (early country, hillbilly, etc.). For the second edition the author left out the chapter on Indian tribal music that appeared in the first, revised considerably his view of post-New Orleans jazz, and included a new chapter on the scene in the art music field in the sixties. No mention is made of rock and roll or modern country music. Extensive use is made of music examples and bibliographical references. The bibliography in the revised edition is massive, and is arranged by chapters. There is a note on some significant record labels, and an index. (In a generous comment on Chase's book, Robert Stevenson remarked: "Not only is each chapter graced with many an apt quotation, but for felicity of phrase, perspicacious overall design, and sense of movement, Chase cannot be matched" (no. 43, p. 10).

26.   HOWARD, John Tasker, and BELLOWS, George Kent.   A short history of music in America.   New York: Crowell, 1957.
      470p.   illus. , bibliog. , discog.
      _____.   .   2nd ed.   New York: Crowell, 1967.
      496p.   illus. , bibliog. , discog.
      A wide-ranging survey for student and layman of the develop-
ment of American music from the songs of the Indians to the present, covering all major styles, with emphasis on the more significant
figures and events--particularly in the serious music tradition--and
placing these in their historical context.   The 20th century receives
the most attention, with a chapter on each decade and one, outside
the chronological arrangement, on folk music.   Within each decade
the outstanding stylistic developments are discussed alongside each
other--ragtime beside opera and the phonograph, early jazz beside
the symphony orchestra.   The discography is merely a list of works
that have been recorded, without details of performers or labels.
The bibliography in the 1967 edition updates that in Howard's history
(no. 24).

27.   MELLERS, Wilfrid.   Music in a new found land: themes and developments in the history of American music.   London: Barrie & Rockliff, 1964; New York: Knopf, 1965.   543p.
      illus. , bibliog. , discog.
      A highly illuminating, learned and enjoyable survey of selected
aspects of American music, especially 20th century developments, by
a noted English writer and composer, who succeeds well in balancing
--from the point of view of both space and understanding--art music
and the popular idioms.   Part 1 briefly surveys American music to
the 20th century, then devotes chapters to Ives, Ruggles and Harris,
Copland, Carter, Riegger and Sessions, Griffes, Cowell and Varèse,
Partch, Cage and Feldman, Barber and Thomson, Foss and the
younger composers.   The style and contribution of each is acutely
analyzed, with music examples.   Part 2 begins with 19th century
musical entertainment, discusses blues and ragtime, and the development of jazz from New Orleans to the 1960s (again, with examples).
The final chapters are concerned with the musical theater, in particular that of Gershwin, Bernstein and Blitzstein.   This second
part contains some outstanding writing on jazz and 20th century popular music.   The immense discography, by Kenneth Dommett, is arranged according to the chapters, and there are indexes of examples
and of literary quotations, plus a general index.

28.   RUBLOWSKY, John.   Music in America.   New York: Crowell-
      Collier; London: Collier-Macmillan, 1967.   185p.   illus. ,
      bibliog.
      To attempt to cover American music from the Puritans to the
1960s in 180 pages is to invite all kinds of disaster.   The one that
befalls Rublowsky is that limitations on the size of his canvas are
not reflected in a narrowing of the focus of his picture, with the

result that everything is hazy and rather distant, the rich and diversified colors of psalmody, Indian music, white and black folk song, Moravian music, minstrelsy, jazz, and the art music tradition looking anemic and unexciting. The book is, however, mainly intended as a historical digest for the high schools, and as such might serve as a preliminary introduction. Index.

29. EDWARDS, Arthur C., and MARROCCO, W. Thomas. Music in the United States. Dubuque: Brown, 1968. 179p. bibliog., discog.
A concise survey from the Pilgrim Fathers to the 1960s with special consideration given to the pre-20th century achievement. The authors' technique is to divide each chapter into sections, each with a heading, under the name of a person, a style, or a broader subject. Characteristics identifying distinctive styles, from psalmody to fasola and patriotic songs, are noted, with discussion of the influence of successive immigrating peoples and sects; there is consideration also of musical life, and of educational and academic aspects. Nationalistic and ethnic styles are identified, including ragtime, jazz, and blues, in the light of their use of nationalistic elements. The concluding chapters survey two divergent paths: the continuance of traditional styles, and the new techniques. The text includes music examples and references, and there is an index. The discography is arranged by chapters.

30. HITCHCOCK, H. Wiley. Music in the United States: a historical introduction. Englewood Cliffs: Prentice-Hall, 1969. (History of Music Series) 270p. bibliog. notes.
_____. _____. 2nd ed. Englewood Cliffs: Prentice-Hall, 1974. (History of Music Series) 286p. bibliog. notes.
A very useful survey, for the student and general reader, of the major currents in American music from the 17th century to date, concentrating on the 19th and 20th centuries, and taking into almost equal account religious, concert and popular (but not, usually, folk) music. Divided into three sections, the book begins with sacred and secular music up to 1820. The second section describes the main features of a divergence of the ways into a cultivated and a vernacular tradition--art and church music on the one hand, and popular religious music, minstrelsy, band music and ragtime on the other-- and concludes with a chapter on Ives. The third section describes the various directions taken by music since 1920 by period, including concert music, jazz and city blues, and musical theater. The final chapter examines interactions in the 1960s and '70s. In the second edition the author extends the discussions of music in the Colonial and Federal periods, and of 20th century popular music, and revises the section on recent trends. There are numerous music examples in the text, bibliographical notes after each chapter, and an index.

31. SABLOSKY, Irving. American music. Chicago: University of Chicago Press, 1969. 228p. bibliog., discog.
A historical study of the uniquely American interplay between musical cultures, concentrating on the converging and diverging trends, as Europeans and Africans reacted to the encounter with each other

in the New World. Encompassing a wide range of musical forms, the book proceeds historically from the Pilgrims to the 1960s, and is arranged in three main parts, entitled "New Beginnings," "Building and Searching," and "Emergence." There is a chronology of important dates, and both bibliography and discography take the form of suggested guidelines, arranged to correspond with the main divisions of the book. Index.

32. BORROFF, Edith. Music in Europe and the United States: a history. Englewood Cliffs: Prentice-Hall, 1971. 752p. illus. (some col.), bibliog. notes.

Borroff's history offers a framework for the development of "representative forms and stylistic definitions" of music for the general reader and student. Only a few representative composers from each of the author's six eras (spanning musical history from the ancient world to the present day) are discussed. While it might be thought excessive to devote one sixth of such a book to music in and of America, this bias--reflecting the growing interest in America in its musical history--allows musical developments and patterns in the U.S. to be seen in a world context. Thus, for example, the author includes in her third era (Baroque) a summary of music in the early New England colonies, and its transportation to the New World. Her approach is eminently catholic, and her outline of 19th and 20th century trends devotes much space to both popular and art music in America. The text is rich in contemporary quotations and in music examples. Though few individual composers are discussed there are several groups of biographical sketches. Index.

3. Miscellaneous Studies and Historiography

33. CHASE, Gilbert, ed. The American composer speaks: a historical anthology, 1770-1965. Baton Rouge: Louisiana State University Press, 1966. 318p. bibliog.

A very interesting collection of writings by 30 American composers from William Billings to Earle Brown, including such varied figures as A. P. Heinrich, Stephen Foster, Louis Moreau Gottschalk, William Walker, John Hill Hewitt, Edward MacDowell, Arthur Farwell, Henry F. Gilbert, Charles Ives, Jelly Roll Morton, Aaron Copland, Harry Partch, John Cage, Elliott Carter and Roger Sessions. The editor contributes an introduction, brief explanatory prefaces, and musings on the composer's place in the world. The bibliography lists general works, criticism of individual composers and sources. Index.

34. CRAWFORD, Richard. American studies and American musicology: a point of view and a case in point. Brooklyn: Institute for Studies in American Music, 1975. (I.S.A.M. Monographs, No. 4) 33p. bibliog.

The first of these two important papers is an interpretation of the style of American musicology as reflected in the study of American music, and of the implications of this for musicologists. Four traits exhibited by the scholar of American music are isolated and discussed: a recognition of values other than aesthetic; an acceptance of music on its own terms; responses that operate on many levels; and a sense of being a participant in the culture studied. Crawford argues for the necessity, for the historian of American music, of personal vernacular experience (vernacular is equated here with Proust's "what life communicates to us against our will"), and for the importance of his understanding his own musical taste. These two elements, amounting to a trust in the historian's own sensibility, are "precisely what imparts a rigor and a reality and a necessity to his observations" (p. 14). (Implications of this for foreign students of American music are not mentioned.) The second talk focuses on three areas of potential musical independence suggested by Billings in 1770--the American as composer, the type of music appropriate for sacred use, and the idiom of sacred music--showing how, in each case, the next 20-30 years witnessed, not a flowering of a vernacular tradition, but a withering, as attitudes to the American composer became increasingly apologetic, and there was a return to the European sacred repertory. All these processes represented the development, not of a cultured tradition, but of a distinctly reactionary one.

35. HOLLANDER, A. N. J. den, and SKARD, Sigmund, eds. American civilisation: an introduction. London: Longman, 1968. 523p. illus., bibliog.
This collection of essays, introducing the reader to basic aspects of American life and culture, includes a concise chronological survey of the major forms of American music, by H. Wiley Hitchcock. A section of the bibliography is also devoted to music.

36. KRUEGER, Karl. The musical heritage of the United States: the unknown portion. New York: Society for the Preservation of the American Musical Heritage, 1973. 237p. illus.
Karl Krueger's Society has performed a splendid service in its recordings of lesser known American music of the 18th, 19th and early 20th centuries. The sleeve notes to 49 of the Society's records (1958-1972) are given here in abridged form, following a historical section that includes short accounts of numerous 19th century composers, performers, writers and conductors. Index.

37. LIST, George, and ORREGO-SALAS, Juan, eds. Music in the Americas ... papers read at the First Inter-American Seminar of Composers and the Second Inter-American Conference on Ethnomusicology, held at Indiana University, April 24-28, 1965. Bloomington: Indiana Research Center in Anthropology, Folklore, and Linguistics, 1967. (Inter-American Music Monograph Series, No. 1) 257p. illus., bibliog.
Included in these conference papers are five of particular relevance to music in the U.S. Frank Gillis discusses, with music examples, the use of hot rhythm in the piano ragtime of Scott Joplin, James Scott and Joseph Lamb. Alan Merriam explores what music can tell us about the ethnological origins of a tribe (the Flathead

Indians). Bruno Nettl reviews aspects of folk music found in North American cities and their implications for acculturation. The present and future situation regarding state and private patronage of music in America is discussed by John Vincent, and Charles Seeger examines the links between traditional music and the composer in North America, and the need for a joining of forces to formulate a theory of music communication. Each paper has bibliographical references, but there is no index.

38. LOWENS, Irving. Music and musicians in early America. New York: Norton, 1964. 328p. illus., bibliogs.

An outstanding collection of 18 masterly essays on aspects of music in America from the 17th to the 19th century, reprinted with revisions from various journals. The text is divided into three sections: music, men, and miscellanea. In the first there are essays on the Bay Psalm Book, works by John Tufts, Andrew Law, Benjamin Carr, the Easy Instructor, and John Wyeth's Repository. The second section contains biographical portraits of, among others, Daniel Read, A. P. Heinrich, W. H. Fry and Louis Moreau Gottschalk. In the miscellany are essays on the fuging tune, music and transcendantalism, music and democracy, the James Warrington Collection of items relating to psalmody (see no. 185) and the church song tradition in America. Appendices give the text of Tufts' "Introduction," and checklists of editions of Little and Smith's Easy Instructor, and of articles on music in transcendentalist periodicals. There is a general index, and an index of titles.

39. MUSSULMAN, Joseph Agee. The uses of music: an introduction to music in contemporary American life. Englewood Cliffs: Prentice-Hall, 1974. 258p. illus., bibliog., discog.

The bewildering diversity of music in 20th century America frequently leaves traditional teaching approaches floundering, and the average person's critical responses confused. Mussulman's book is designed to offer a coherent way of understanding this diversity for both the student and the layman. He tackles the problem by first outlining basic musical principles--scale systems, timbre, etc.-- so that the reader is equipped to judge music as "sonorous design"; with this basic knowledge he is then introduced to various areas of musical usage in contemporary America, and encouraged to examine and assess the music in terms of its success in fulfilling the specific function for which it was created. The areas under discussion are: musical accomplishment in secondary schools, music as background to human activity ("mood" music), music in films, theater and ballet, ceremonial music, and music as entertainment. As well as discussing the practical aspects of these types of music Mussulman compares and contrasts each with art music with regard to style, function and creative process. Art music is also independently examined, with special reference to Ives and Copland. A look at international trends in contemporary art music concludes the text of the book, which also has listening guides, a chronology, a list of the examples in the three records accompanying the book, a bibliography of books and articles, and an index. There are numerous music examples in the text.

40.   REESE, Gustave, ed.   A birthday offering to Carl Engel.   New
      York: Schirmer, 1943. 233p. illus.
      The distinguished American career of Paris-born Carl Engel
(1883-1944) embraced music publishing, musicology, librarianship
and composition.   A composite portrait of him is provided by a
series of portraits by John Erskine (on Engel the man), Harold
Spivacke (on Engel the librarian, who succeeded Sonneck as head of
the Music Division at the Library of Congress in 1922), Norman
Peterkin (on Engel the composer), and Percy Lee Atherton (on Engel
in Boston, 1909-1922).   There is also a list of his literary and musical works.   Of the other essays four have a specifically American
interest.   There is a delightful, eloquent profile of Henry F. B.
Gilbert by Olin Downes, some extracts from the correspondence of
Charles Martin Loeffler, a piece on the poet Amy Lowell and music
by Willis Wager, and an account of Arthur Farwell's Wa-Wan Press
by Edward N. Waters in which numerous excerpts from Farwell's
letters to the author concerning the genesis and history of this unique
venture on behalf of the American composer are quoted, and which
also contains a complete catalog of Wa-Wan publications.

41.   ROURKE, Constance.   The roots of American culture, and oth-
      er essays; edited, with a preface by Van Wyck Brooks.   New
      York: Harcourt, Brace, 1942.   (Repr. Port Washington:
      Kennikat Press, 1965).   305p.
      A fundamental work for the understanding of American culture
and the role of music.   Left unfinished at the author's death (Miss
Rourke lived from 1885-1941), it is based on the conviction that this
culture sprang from indigenous experience, and expressed distinctive
native thought and feeling.   The 34-page essay on music and musical
life in the years following the Revolution ("Early American Music")
is a landmark in its identification of the wellsprings of American
musical culture in the popular, practical use of the art, springing
from the native soil.   The works of Hopkinson, Reinagle and others
were "mainly those of the dilettante.   The strong drift of public
taste lay in other directions: substantially in music it was practical"
(p. 168).   The author points to Andrew Adgate as a significant figure, whose projects, as against those of the promoters of smooth,
"pseudo-democratic" music, involved music "native in origin, primitive in character, rural in its main sources and mainly religious,
though not wholly so, in theme" (pp. 171-2).   Billings played an important part in this movement, and his role and sources are examined
also.   Other relevant essays include those on the Shakers and on
folklore.   Index.

42.   SONNECK, O. G.   Suum cuique: essays in music.   New York:
      Schirmer, 1916.   271p.
      The eminent music librarian, bibliographer, musicologist and
pioneer of the study of American music in the 20th century presents
here a collection of lucidly conceived articles and papers, originally
published in other sources between 1900 and 1913.   Several are on
American subjects: the musical side of Presidents Adams, Washington and Jefferson; the musical side of Benjamin Franklin; Edward
MacDowell's revisions of his original editions; the argument for and

against a National Conservatory; and the state of musical life in the United States in 1913. This last essay, which includes in its range the historiography of American music, the position of the American composer (including questions of expatriation in Europe, and the use of American vernacular materials) and the state of operatic production, is not only an interesting account from a historical point of view, but is also still a challenging one.

43. STEVENSON, Robert. Philosophies of American music history: a lecture ... Washington: Library of Congress, 1970. 18p. bibliog. notes.

In this interesting lecture, given at the Library of Congress in a series commemorating Louis Elson, Stevenson examines the ways in which the principal historians of American music have approached such questions as the establishing of temporal starting and finishing posts in the area covered, the selection of particular facets as being worthy of chronicle, the criteria for determining musical value, the importance attached to original sources, the type of audience envisaged for the history, and the presence or lack of a feeling of "progress." If we press him for his own philosophy, it would be one "that extended hospitality to all sorts and conditions of men," that began in Florida or New Mexico instead of Plymouth, that had Gottschalk as a wheel and Dwight as a spoke, that permitted the coexistence of Lowell Mason and Ned Rorem, the "Yellow Rose of Texas" and "Hora Novissima."

4. Women in Music

44. BARNES, Edwin N. C. American women in creative music. Washington: Music Education Publications, 1936. 44p. bibliog.

Short biographies of 90 women composers, with mention of their principal compositions. If there is an underlying logic to the apparently random arrangement, Barnes exercised the divine prerogative of making it difficult to discover. He evidently obtained his information both from printed sources and the ladies themselves (who seem in some cases to have had recourse to traditional diffidence regarding their dates of birth). A further list of 98 names from whom no response was received briefly states the type of music written, with one or two titles. There is an index, and a list of printed sources.

45. HIXON, Don L., and HENNESSEE, Don. Women in music: a biobibliography. Metuchen: Scarecrow Press, 1975. 347p.

The two-fold aim of this useful quick reference work is to provide an index to biographies of women musicians as they are found in a representative group of 48 important reference works, and to give with each entry sufficient information for identification purposes. Only two works devoted specifically to American music are indexed: Pavlakis (no. 369) and Reis (no. 291)--i.e., such works as the American supplement of Grove's Dictionary (no. 13) and Claghorn (no. 12) are absent. Nevertheless a large number of American women are included, Thompson's International Cyclopedia and the various editions of Baker's Biographical Dictionary being particularly fruitful sources. The entries for each individual give full name, place and date of birth (and death), field of activity, and the references to source books. At the end of the volume is a classified list in which the names are grouped by activity.

46. JONES, Hettie. Big star fallin' mama: five women in black music. New York: Viking Press, 1974. 150p.
The five singers in focus in this introductory volume are Ma Rainey, Bessie Smith, Mahalia Jackson, Billie Holiday and Aretha Franklin. There is a biographical sketch of each, with some general comments on their music. An introduction surveys the early development of the blues.

47. SMITH, Julia, comp. Directory of American women composers, with selected music for senior and junior clubs. Chicago: National Federation of Music Clubs, 1970. 51p.
An alphabetical list of the names of over 600 women composers, both dead and alive (250 more having been omitted because of insufficient documentation). The directory gives name, dates if deceased, address, professional affiliation (ASCAP, ACA, BMI), type of music composed, and publisher, or, alternatively, whether the music is in manuscript form. There is also a short classified list of selected music suitable for senior and junior programs.

48. WILLIAMS, Ora. American black women in the arts and social sciences: a bibliographic survey. Metuchen: Scarecrow Press, 1973. 141p. illus.
Clearly this is a timely volume, and though literature is its principal concern the music created by black American women is quite prominently featured. Primary material is catered for in a chapter listing musical compositions by black women in both art and popular music fields, with publishers and dates where known. Composers Margaret Bonds, Julia Perry, Florence B. Price and Philippa Duke Schuyler have full listings. This chapter also mentions LP recordings without making clear the criteria employed in selecting them (e.g., there are 18 LP's by Billie Holiday, but none featuring either Alberta Hunter or Ida Cox, both of whom appear on blues reissues). Further problems arise with secondary material-- or the lack of it--where the compiler's decision to include only works "edited or created by American black women" (pp. xvii-xviii) results in an incomplete bibliographic record for the individual concerned. With the exception of Philippa Schuyler (who is one of 15 black women singled out for special treatment in a chapter of individual bibliographies, which include secondary material), the only works about black women musicians listed are either autobiographies or are by other black women. The section for autobiography and biography includes books on Paul Robeson and Nat King Cole--but nothing on Bessie Smith. Potential users of the book might well not anticipate this kind of distinction. Index of names.

5. Vocal Music

a. Song

49. STEVENS, Denis, ed. A history of song. London: Hutchinson, 1960; New York: Norton, 1961. 491p. bibliog. notes.
This standard history includes a long, wide-ranging chapter on song in the U.S. by Hans Nathan, which begins with the New England composers of the late 18th century, discusses the Moravians, minstrelsy, early art song, MacDowell, early 20th century, Charles Ives and others, Chanler and Thomson, Barber, Diamond, Copland, Carter and others, and concludes with the popular song of Gershwin, etc. Indexes of names and titles.

50. UPTON, William Treat. Art-song in America: a study in the development of American music. Boston: Ditson, 1930. 279p.
_____. A supplement to Art-song in America, 1930-1938. Philadelphia: Ditson, 1938. 41p. (Repr. in one volume, New York: Johnson, 1969).
With a minimal amount of historical background ("skeletonized," Upton calls it) this book scrutinizes and assesses the songs of over 120 composers, from Francis Hopkinson to Charles Tomlinson Griffes (with a further 20 or so in the supplement). Some are considered only briefly, but others in detail and with an abundance of music examples. Index.

51. YERBURY, Grace D. Song in America: from early times to about 1850. Metuchen: Scarecrow Press, 1971. 305p. illus., bibliogs.
The span of time covered in this history of the early development of sacred and secular song is seen as dividing into two: a "period of reminiscence" of English styles, characterized by a tendency to simplification, and a "period of sentimental imitation" from about 1800 to 1850. Part I gives us a compressed survey of early psalmody, the music of the German immigrants, James Lyon, early schools of style in Philadelphia, New York and Boston, and the work of Benjamin Carr, who is seen as a turning point from the first era to the second. In Part II the author identifies and describes the features of four "schools" of song style, each centered round one composer (John Hill Hewitt, Oliver Shaw, George Bristow and Herrman Saroni). Into these groups are slotted a large number of early 19th century composers. The bibliographic material, a central feature of the book, is divided into five sections, one following Part I, and one following the account of each of the "schools." Items are arranged chronologically under each composer's name. The scholarship in the book is clear; lacking, perhaps, is a sense of fascination with the subject, and this makes for somewhat arid, uninspiring reading. Two songs by Saroni are given in an appendix, and there is an index.

b. Opera by Americans

See also no. 143. For Operatic Life see A. 7. c.

52. DRUMMOND, Andrew H. American opera librettos. Metuch-
        en: Scarecrow Press, 1973. 283p. bibliog.
    The particular concern of Drummond's study of the librettos
of forty American operas performed at the New York City Opera Co.
between 1948 and 1971 is their exploitation of the dramatic elements
of plot, characterization and literary style. A survey of the development of opera in America from the late 19th century to 1948--
with many quotations from contemporary criticism--precedes an examination of the way these dramatic elements have been identified
by dramatic theorists from Aristotle on. Taking the forty American
operas in turn, the author briefly discusses the dramatic elements
in each (nine are by Menotti), and illustrates how they were ap-
praised in contemporary reviews (particularly in the New York
Times). In his conclusion the author singles out those librettos
that exploit the dramatic elements most successfully. There is an
extensive bibliography of scores, books and articles, an appendix
listing the entire opera repertoire, 1948-1971, and another--of a-
bout a hundred pages--providing plot synopses of the forty operas
discussed. Index.

53. HIPSHER, Edward Ellsworth. American opera and its com-
        posers: a complete history of serious American opera,
        with a summary of the lighter forms which led up to its
        birth. Philadelphia: Presser, 1927. 408p. bibliog.
        _____   . (Expanded edition). Philadelphia:
        Presser, 1934. 478p.
    The accuracy of Hipsher's work has been questioned (see Rich-
ard Jackson, no. 5, p. 55), but it remains the only work of its
kind as yet devoted to 19th and early 20th century American opera
composers. In Hipsher's defense it may be said that he himself re-
gretted "certain data are not more complete," and referred to difficulties in obtaining information from composers. The bulk of the
book is not a history at all, but a series of biographical and, to a
lesser extent, critical portraits of the lives and operatic works of
119 composers (148 in the 1934 edition). These vary considerably
in depth of treatment; some are content with a brief note and description of the person's stage works, with dates, while others provide an account of each opera, with the cast of the first performance,
synopsis of the plot, and comments on salient features. Composers
added to the 1934 edition include George Antheil, Virgil Thomson
and Clarence Cameron White; there is also a short necrology. Index.

54. JOHNSON, H. Earle. Operas on American subjects. New
        York: Coleman-Ross, 1964. 125p. bibliog.
    Of the 400 or so operas listed here as having been inspired
by American (including Spanish American) subjects, a little under
half are by American composers. Coverage extends from the 17th
to the 20th century. The list is arranged by composer, and the

notes on each work give details of first performance, wherever known, with a brief description. Information on some works is extremely scanty, unfortunately. A subject breakdown provides groupings on such topics as Spanish America, Indians, Revolution, Civil War, Columbus, race relations. Title and general index.

55. McSPADDEN, J. Walker. Operas and musical comedies; enlarged ed. New York: Crowell, 1951. 637p.

McSpadden's earlier works in a similar vein, Opera Synopses and Light Opera and Musical Comedy, are incorporated in this book, and form the two main parts. Each is subarranged by country, and each has a section for the United States. In the first section 26 American opera plots are summarized, from Victor Herbert's "Natoma" (1911) to Gian Carlo Menotti's "The Consul" (1950), including, among others, operas by Horatio Parker, Charles W. Cadman, Deems Taylor, and Howard Hanson. Brief biographical details precede each composer's group of works. The second section provides the same categories of information for 77 musical comedies and light operas from Willard Spenser's "The Little Tycoon" (1886) to Frank Loesser's "Guys and Dolls" (1950).

6. Church Music

a. General Works

56. DAVISON, Archibald T. Protestant church music in America. Boston: Schirmer, 1933. 182p.

From a rigidly pro-European stance Davison makes a fiery attack on what he sees as the indifference, complacency and prejudice characteristic of prevalent attitudes to music in the Protestant churches of America. "Modern American Protestant church music," he says, "bears melancholy testimony to the superficial mental effort expended on it in the past" (p. 169). What he proposes is "music which, by its unfamiliarity and its absence of secular suggestion, is the primary property of the church"; by this he means plainsong, Bach chorales, Reformation anthems, Lutheran hymns, English anthems. He supplies a brief list of music fitting the ideal; no American music is admitted.

57. ELLINWOOD, Leonard. The history of American church music. New York: Morehouse-Gorham, 1953. (Repr. New York: Da Capo, 1970). 274p. illus., bibliog. notes.

A diligent, if somewhat dour, scholarly history ranging from 1494 to the mid-20th century, and centering on developments in Episcopalian practice in the East. There are three sections: the first, 1494-1820, includes summaries of music in New Spain, of psalmody, singing schools, fuging tunes, music outside the Puritan sphere, the first organs and bells, and the achievements of leading 18th century composers; the second, 1820-1920, includes accounts of the developments in choirs and their repertory, brief consideration of shape-note and gospel songs, description of the leading musical figures, and further information on the organ; the third considers the contemporary scene, including repertory changes, characteristics of the hymnal, and outstanding individual musicians. Accounts of oratorio societies are deliberately excluded, and hymnody discussed only where it "affected the main-stream of our church music." There is no discussion of the music or musical life of the black churches. The appendices contain a list of the organists of Trinity Parish, New York City, selected lists of musical repertory, biographies of around 80 American church musicians, and notes to the text. There is also an index.

58. GOULD, Nathaniel D. Church music in America, comprising its history and its peculiarities at different periods, with cursory remarks on its legitimate use and its abuse; with notices of the schools, composers, teachers and societies. Boston: A. N. Johnson, 1853. (Repr. New York: AMS Press, 1972). 240p.
            . History of church music in America; treating of its peculiarities at different periods; its legitimate use and its abuse; with criticisms, cursory remarks and notices relating to composers, teachers, schools, choirs, societies, conventions, books, etc. Boston: Gould & Lincoln, 1853. 240p.
        Gould (1781-1864) was prominent in music education, including singing schools, in New England ("even before Mason entered it," according to Elson, no. 21). His history is principally concerned with developments in the uses and character of sacred music in worship and education from the end of the Colonial era to the first decades of the 19th century. He views the post-Revolutionary years as "a dark age," and has little sympathy with the indigenous musical compositions of the time. Nevertheless he does give the most detailed account of the life of Billings to have appeared at the time, drawing for this on recollections of people who had personally known the composer, and recognized his importance. He also gives accounts of the use of Billings' music in schools and churches, the manner of teaching music in the late 18th century, the features of late 18th century church music, the progress of musical instruction at the turn of the century, instruments, and societies, and the effects of music. There is also an authoritative-sounding portrait of Andrew Law, with whose reforming ideas Gould is more in sympathy.

59. HARTLEY, Kenneth R. Bibliography of theses and dissertations in sacred music. Detroit: Information Co-ordinators, 1966. (Detroit Studies in Music Bibliography, No. 9) 127p.
        Among the 1,525 items listed here by institution are 114 on American subjects, including general, regional and period studies, and works on individuals, denominations, types (e.g., hymnody) and ethnic groups (e.g., Negroes). There are indexes of authors, composers and subjects.

60. HASTINGS, Thomas. The history of forty choirs. New York: Mason, 1854. 231p.

Drawn from Hastings' long career as a choir-master, these
"substantially true" incidents connected with forty unspecified choirs in
urban and rural areas in the North-East (mostly, one presumes, in
and around New York) give a good reflection of the state of
choral music in church in the first half of the 19th century, as seen
through the eyes of one of the leading lights in the movement to
Europeanization. Hastings' own preoccupations with the primary
claims of worship over aesthetics are made clear towards the end.
Reiterating a problem which had occupied minds back to John Cotton in 1647, he declares: "The office of praise connects aesthetic
considerations with devotional sentiments and purposes. We incline
to seize upon the former for the purpose of enjoyment, and treat
the latter as auxiliary concomitants. Let us reverse this order
of things. Let us give devotional considerations the highest place
... The question whether the praises of Zion shall become as sound-
ing brass or a tinkling cymbal ... is truly a momentous one. How
shall this question be decided? It is not a question of art" (pp. 230-
1).

61.   MESSITER, A. H.   A history of the choir and music of Trin-
        ity Church, New York, from its organization to the year
        1897.   New York: Edwin S. Gorham, 1906.   (Repr. New
        York: AMS Press, 1970).   324p.   illus.
A detailed record of the musical activity in a centrally important New York church and parish from 1698 to the year of the
author's retirement as music director.   Messiter claims in his introduction that "in church music Trinity Church has been the pioneer
... the history of Trinity Church music covers the history of church
music throughout the country" (psalmody, for one, having "not the
slightest artistic value").   The late 17th and the 18th centuries are
less thoroughly covered than the 19th.   A large proportion of the
book is devoted to the period (from 1839) covered by the careers of
three men as music directors--Edward Hodges, Henry Stephen Cut-
ler, and the author.   Information on choir members, composers,
and organs is included in the appendices.

62.   METCALF, Frank J.   American writers and compilers of
        sacred music.   New York: Abingdon Press, 1925.   (Repr.
        New York: Russell & Russell, 1967).   373p.   illus.
A pioneer work in its field and still doing good service, this
is a collection of highly informative, impartial biographical sketches
(often including plentiful bibliographical information also) that took
ten years to research.   Ninety-one individuals are included in the
four main, chronological parts, from John Tufts and Thomas Walter
(the only ones born before 1700) to Samuel A. Ward (1848-1903).
A fifth part, devoted to revivalist groups (Joseph Hillman et al.),
camp meeting music, and Washington hymnody and psalmody, contains rather briefer sketches of a further 45, plus a concluding portrait of Mathias Keller (1813-1875) of the "American hymn." Other
than Andrew Law and John Wyeth no shape-note compilers are included.   The original index is revised in the reprint edition.

63.   STEVENSON, Robert.   Protestant church music in America:

a short survey of men and movements from 1564 to the present. New York: Norton, 1966. 168p. illus., bibliog.

This excellent, concise survey, covering the period from the first Huguenots in Florida to date, includes the music of the Puritans, the Pennsylvania Germans, outstanding native-born composers of the 18th and 19th centuries, the musical life of the white South, Negro spirituals, and developments from 1850 to the 1960s. Major individuals are clearly set against the background of musical life and development. Stevenson's purpose is "to provide a compressed text for use in seminars, choir schools and colleges" (p. xi); although this results in the omission of some data there are plentiful bibliographical footnotes, making the book as a whole a minor miracle of densely packed information, a veritable goldmine--even if, on occasions, some hard quarrying is needed to remove the nuggets. The extensive bibliography is restricted to "such materials as are listed under ML in the Library of Congress system; or books outside the field of music that have nonetheless offered useful documentation" (p. xii). There are also musical examples in the text. Index.

64. WIENANDT, Elwyn A., and YOUNG, Robert H. The anthem in England and America. New York: Free Press; London: Collier-Macmillan, 1970. illus., bibliog.

Presenting their historical and critical information in a chronological narrative, the authors of this fine, scholarly study see it as one of their primary aims "to show that the English had an important field of choral activity outside the usually discussed cathedral tradition, and that it is from this parochial and Nonconformist practice that the American anthem first derived its patterns" (p. vi). Four of the ten chapters deal with America. Chapter 5 examines the situation before the American anthem emerged (the "regular singing" controversy of the 1720s) and describes the importation and development of the anthem in the second half of the 18th century (in particular through the work of Hopkinson, Lyon and Billings). In chapter 6 the successors of these pioneers are discussed--the "compilers and borrowers," from Daniel Bayley and Andrew Law to Lowell Mason and Thomas Hastings. With chapter 8 we move into the second half of the 19th century and encounter the rise of an American market for choral music, noting especially the choir magazines of Edward S. Lorenz (1854-1942) as well as the gospel songs, the minority cathedral style, and the popular anthem composers. Chapter 10 surveys the course of the anthem in America in the 20th century. There are 160 music examples in the text. Index.

b. Hymnody

65. BENSON, Louis F. The English hymn: its development and use in worship. London: Hodder and Stoughton, 1915. 624p. bibliog. notes.

This massive, epoch-making study--the first and best scholarly history of English-language hymnody--is still a basic tool in any examination of the American hymn. Benson's approach is based on a

view of the hymn as a vehicle of worship, not as literature (though
he is occasionally condescending towards rugged popular hymns).
His main source material is the vast number of hymnals, English
and American, many of which he was the first to uncover. The
first parts of his history deal with the evolution of the English hymn
from psalmody and devotional poetry, and early efforts in England to
introduce hymns into worship. The development of the American
hymn is traced (alongside the English) in five areas of study: (i) the
era of Isaac Watts--the gradual spread of his hymns in 18th century
America, and their association with the growth of the singing schools
and the work of Billings; (ii) the hymnody of American Methodism,
Wesleyan in inheritance, but having as its decisive influence the
camp meeting hymn--making American Methodism's principal contribution one of revivalist hymnody; (iii) the hymnody of the Evangelical
Revival--begun by Whitefield, and examined among Baptists, Presby-
terians, Congregationalists and the Dutch and German churches;
(iv) the literary hymn--offshoot of the Romantic movement, introduced by the Unitarians, driven to prominence by Henry Ward Beech-
er--against which is set the gospel hymn, child of the camp meetings,
taken to a high point by Sankey and Bliss; and (v) the influence of
the Oxford Movement. In conclusion Benson outlines some trends
in early 20th century hymnody. There is a 34-page index.

66.   FOOTE, Henry Wilder.   Three centuries of American hymnody.
        Cambridge, Mass.: Harvard University Press, 1940.
        (Repr. Hamden: Archon Books, 1968). 418p. bibliog.
        notes.
        Aiming to steer a middle course between the scholarship of
Benson (no. 65) and the commoner biographical/anecdotal approach,
Foote surveys psalmody and hymnody from 1640, concentrating on
texts rather than music, and examining the hymn as a changing expression of succeeding generations' religious thought and feeling.
He first gives an account of English psalmody up to the Ainsworth
Psalter, and examines New England psalmody in the Bay Psalm
Book and other compilations. An assessment of the Puritans' atti-
tude to music is followed by a detailed survey of the singing revival,
led by exponents of "regular singing." The rich German tradition
in Pennsylvania is examined before the narrative turns to the transition from psalmody to hymnody in the 18th century (the role of the
Wesleys, Whitefield and Samuel Davies, and the folk hymnody tradition), and the rapidly accelerating pace of development in the 19th
(Lowell Mason and others, the Unitarian contribution, the hymns of
Longfellow, Whittier, etc.). In the post-Civil War era Foote is
mildly disapproving of gospel hymnody, recognizes the beauty of
Negro spirituals, but is more at home back in the mainstream, which
he then surveys up to 1940. There are indexes of names and subjects, psalm books and hymn books, and first lines. The reprint
edition contains, as an appendix, a paper continuing the saga to 1952.

67.   MASON, Henry L., comp.   Hymn-tunes of Lowell Mason: a
        bibliography. Cambridge, Mass.: Harvard University Press,
        1944. 118p. illus.
        Among his many activities Lowell Mason was a prolific com-

poser and arranger of hymn-tunes, using them in his campaign to improve Protestant church music as he saw it. This catalog lists 1,697,487 of them arrangements and the remainder original. The work is divided into 14 separate listings. The first--to which all others refer--gives the publications in which his tunes appeared; the subsequent lists itemize the original tunes and the arrangements separately, the major ones grouping each by title and by date, while the supplementary ones include a list of the sources of the arrangements, and chronological lists of both original tunes and arrangements bearing biblical or religious names.

68. NINDE, Edward S. The story of the American hymn. New York: Abingdon Press, 1921. (Repr. New York: AMS Press, 1975). 429p. illus.

Though it begins with several chapters giving a general survey of psalmody in America to the end of the 18th century, including the "accommodation" of the hymns of Isaac Watts, the chief concern of this undemanding study is with the lives and hymn texts of 19th century hymn writers from John Leland and Oliver Holden to gospel song writers such as Robert Lowry and Philip P. Bliss. Anecdotal accounts of over 60 individuals, illustrated with textual excerpts and comments of a general, uncritical nature, are given in chronological sequence. Though they are arranged in small groups each portrait tends to be a water-tight compartment, with very little comparison or cross-reference. Among those featured in the longer accounts are Thomas Hastings, William A. Mecklenberg, William Cullen Bryant, Oliver Wendell Holmes, Leonard Bacon, John Greenleaf Whittier, Harriet Beecher Stowe, Julia Ward Howe, Ray Palmer, Fanny Crosby and Phillips Brooks. Music is mentioned only incidentally (as seems often to be the case with writing on hymnody). Despite his preference for sentiment over objective historical assessment Ninde's book is of interest, mainly because of the continued widespread popularity in worship in English-speaking Protestantism of the verses of these modest 19th century poets (a situation which makes one regret more the omission of the music, since it is at least doubtful if the hymns would show such power of survival without the accompanying tunes). There is a general index and an index of first lines.

69. STEVENSON, Arthur L. The story of Southern hymnology. Salem, Va.: the author, 1931. 187p. bibliog. notes.

Stevenson's study is not concerned with the recounting or interpretation of musical development in the hymn but with practicalities and controversies involved in the use of hymnals in Southern church life. In a historical account of denominational hymnbooks he pays particular attention to the genesis of the 1905 Methodist hymnal and to disagreements over its contents. Turning to the contemporary gospel hymns, he describes their popularity, the numbers of singing schools and the extent of commercialization, quoting from a lengthy attack on the hymns by a North Carolina professor, and trying also to discover some of the reasons for their powerful influence. A chapter is devoted to Sunday School hymns past and present, and another to a summary of present trends.

c.   Gospel Hymn

See also no. 605.

70.   BAXTER, Mrs. J. R. ("Ma"), and POLK, Videt.   Gospel song
        writers biography.   Dallas: Stamps-Baxter, 1971.   306p.
        illus.
      Biographical portraits of 102 white gospel song composers in
no very obvious order.   A few 19th century notables (Bliss, Sankey,
Lowell Mason, Fanny Crosby) are included, but coverage extends
principally to 20th century Southern composers.   A picture accompanies each of the biographies, which are of the "human interest"
type and mention few actual compositions.   Index.

71.   BURT, Jesse, and ALLEN, Duane.   The history of gospel mu-
        sic; foreword by Dottie Rambo.   Nashville: K & S Press,
        1971.   205p.
      Let's be frank.   Any resemblance between this assortment of
reminiscences, portraits and chatter, and the history (definitive, no
less) of gospel music is entirely fortuitous.   The authors do not
even define their area, though what interests them is mid-20th century Southern white religious music.   The only useful part is the
biographical directory, giving tabulated details on almost 200 individuals or groups.

72.   HALL, J. H.   Biography of gospel song and hymn writers.
        New York: Fleming H. Revell, 1914.   (Repr. New York:
        AMS Press, 1971).   419p.   illus.
      Perish the thought that the likes of Lowell Mason or Ira D.
Sankey ever need a character reference in the hymn writers' here-
after; in that unlikely event either would doubtless be happy to en-
trust the task to Jacob Henry Hall, whose biographical portraits of
76 notable 19th century hymn and evangelical gospel song writers
show him rather as a composite version of those three sagacious
Japanese monkeys.   For all that it is a valuable, often engaging
volume.   The portraits are on average four pages long, so they contain a fair amount of detail, though more information on specific
compositions would have been welcome.   Arrangement is approximately by date of birth, the youngest composer included being born
in 1880.   Among those represented are William Bradbury, George
F. Root, Philip P. Bliss, Fanny Crosby, Robert Lowry, T. F.
Seward, W. J. Kirkpatrick and George C. Stebbins.   There is no
index but a contents list of the individual biographies.

73.   KNIPPERS, Ottis J.   Who's who among Southern singers and
        composers.   Lawrenceburg, Tenn.:   James D. Vaughan,
        1937.   168p.   illus.
      A biographical dictionary of 145 white gospel singers and com-
posers, with portraits of almost all of them.   Many, but not all of
the sketches, mention specific compositions; 135 are listed in the
song title index.   There is also a name index.

74.   SANKEY, Ira D.   Sankey's story of the gospel hymns, and of

      Sacred songs and solos; with an introduction by Theodore L.
Cuyler.   Philadelphia: Sunday School Times, 1906.   272p.
illus.

      _____ . My life and sacred songs; with an introduction by
Theodore L. Cuyler.   London: Hodder and Stoughton, 1906.
306p. illus.

      _____ . _____ . Philadelphia: Ziegler, 1907. 410p.
illus.

     The name of Ira D. Sankey (1840-1908) is coupled in perpetuity
with that of the celebrated urban evangelist, Dwight L. Moody (1837-
1899), for whom he acted as singer, organist, music leader and partner in a 30-year alliance, the effects of which on America and Great
Britain are still felt. A number of his gospel hymns are perennial
favorites (e. g. , the tunes to "Beneath the Cross of Jesus" and "There
were Ninety and Nine that Safely Lay") and no amount of ecclesias-
tical or musicological snobbery will alter that fact. The volumes
listed above are basically the same; each contains Sankey's own account of his life, written in blindness towards its close, and not without a gentle humor. The major part of each is devoted to giving
background information on individual hymns in his important collections, Sacred Songs and Solos, 1873 etc. , and Gospel Hymns, 1874
etc. (with Philip P. Bliss and others). There is little about the
music; the comments are generally anecdotal, and concern events
connected with the writing or the singing of each hymn. There are
slight variations between volumes in the hymns remarked upon. In
connection with this part of his book Sankey tells how he had for
years collected historical incidents connected with gospel hymns,
but had lost them all in a fire and had to rewrite from memory.
Index.

75.   STEBBINS, George C. Reminiscences and gospel hymn stories;
      with an introduction by Charles H. Gabriel. New York:
      George H. Doran, 1924. (Repr. New York: AMS Press,
      1971). 327p. illus.

     Stebbins was associated from 1876 with the evangelical campaigns
of Moody and Sankey. He was himself a singer and composer of
hymns, many of which were published in Sankey's collections, and
his descriptions of the numerous campaigns in which he was involved suggest something of the significance of music in the movement, as
well as relating anecdotes associated with many of the hymns. He
was widely acquainted with other hymn writers and singers, and devotes a portion of his autobiography to portraits of 18 of them, with
descriptions of their work. They include George F. Root, Philip P.
Bliss, Sankey, Robert Lowry, James McGranahan, and others.
There are examples of 16 hymns (texts, and tunes with harmony).

76.   WEISBERGER, Bernard A. They gathered at the river: the
      story of the great revivalists and their impact upon religion
      in America. Boston: Little, Brown, 1958. (Repr. Chicago:
      Quadrangle Books, 1966). 345p. illus. , bibliog. notes.

     This informally told story of the itinerant revivalists, from
camp meetings in 1800 to Sankey and Moody, Billy Sunday and Homer
Rodeheaver, provides an illuminating background to the study of re-

ligious music in 19th century America, particularly as it depicts the
role of emotion in revivalism. Though not directly concerned with
music, the author is conscious of its great importance in the movement.

77. WHITTLE, D. W., ed. Memoirs of Philip P. Bliss; contributions by E. P. Goodwin, Ira D. Sankey and Geo. F. Root;
introduction by D. L. Moody. New York: Barnes, 1877.
367p. illus.

These memoirs form an enduring testimony to the deep affection in which evangelist and gospel hymn writer Philip P. Bliss
(1838-1876, compiler with Sankey of Gospel Hymns, author of words
and music to "Whosoever Will May Come," and "I Am So Glad,"
among many others) was held by his colleagues and friends. Apol-
ogizing for any "literary crudeness," Whittle declares his aim is "to
truthfully narrate what could be recalled from memory, and gathered
from all reliable sources, of the life of Mr. Bliss" (preface). A
biographical account of Bliss occupies the first eleven chapters, and
is followed by a compendium of writings by and about him. Most
interesting among his own prose and verse are the extracts from his
correspondence to family and friends, which reveal a delightful sense
of humor, a love of strange spellings, a boundless zest and energy,
and a view of Christianity as essentially joyful--in other words, the
spirit of his gospel hymns is seen to be mirrored in their creator.
Other material includes letters to or about him and a selection of
tributes; but contrasting darkly with Bliss's own writings are the
stark eye-witness and newspaper accounts, reproduced in full, of
his tragic death on Dec. 29, 1876, in a railway accident at Ashta-
bula, Ohio, when a wooden bridge broke and the train it was carry-
ing plunged into the river.

d. Moravians and German Pietists

78. DAVID, Hans T. Musical life in the Pennsylvania settlements
of the Unitas Fratrum; with a foreward by Donald M. Mc-
Corkle. Winston-Salem: Moravian Music Foundation, 1959.
(Publications, No. 6) 44p. bibliog. notes.

David's pioneer paper appeared originally in the Transactions
of the Moravian Historical Society, 1942. McCorkle describes it as
"the basic scholarly study of Moravian music in Pennsylvania."
David sketches the religious, political and musical background, surveys the beginnings of musical life, and describes the music of
several individual composers (Jeremiah Dencke, Immanuel Nitsch-
mann, Simon and Johann Friedrich Peter, Johannes Herbst and
David Moritz Michael, as well as other lesser figures). It is not
entirely a story of individuals, however, for as he remarks: "In
the development of music ... the people themselves provided and
even created the music they needed or wanted ... The Moravian
settlements ... accomplished a wonderful union of religion and art,
and the perfect saturation of daily life with music" (p. 42).

79. GOMBOSI, Marilyn. Catalog of the Johannes Herbst Collection.

Chapel Hill: University of North Carolina Press, 1970.
255p. illus.

From the large quantity of music manuscript material in Moravian archives in America the Herbst Collection, housed in Winston-Salem, N. C., was selected for cataloging because it contained much music of significance in the development of Moravian musical practices. Johannes Herbst (1735-1812), Moravian minster, born in Swabia, was a prolific composer, and his personal library of 464 mss. contained scores of approximately 1,000 anthems and arias for use in worship, scores and parts of forty-five extended vocal works, and some miscellanea. All are copies made by Herbst himself in Europe and America. The catalog itself lists them all, with the following information: composer, adapter or compiler, title, musical incipit, description (performance medium, key, tempo, duration, sources of text and tune, etc.). The most prominently featured composers are Johann Christian Geisler, Christian Gregor and Herbst himself. There are indexes of composers and titles.

80. GRIDER, Rufus A. Historical notes on music in Bethlehem, Pennsylvania, from 1741 to 1871. Philadelphia: Printed by John L. Pile for J. Hill Martin, 1873. (Repr. Winston-Salem: Moravian Music Foundation, 1951). (Publications, No. 4) 41p.

Grider's is the only first-hand account of Moravian music in Bethlehem in the mid-19th century, although he relied on others older than he (he was born in 1817) for recollections of an earlier, more flourishing age, 1780-1820. His notes describe the many aspects of musical life--the first orchestra, music instruction, church music, observance of festivals, societies, the Philharmonic Society --and also provide a record of the names of individuals involved with music, arranged by date of birth (1696-1855).

81. McCORKLE, Donald M. The "Collegium Musicum Salem": its music, musicians and importance. Winston-Salem: Moravian Music Foundation, 1956. (Publications, No. 2) pp. 483-498. illus., bibliog. notes.

(Reprinted from the North Carolina Historical Review, October 1956). While 18th century New England musicians were mainly concerned with psalms and fuging tunes, in the Moravian settlements quite elaborate sacred and secular music was being composed and performed. The principal medium for secular performance was the "Collegium Musicum," based on the amateur societies of Germany. McCorkle describes the history of the third oldest (founded 1786)-- the musicians connected with it, the music performed, and changes in taste and emphasis--up to 1835.

82. McCORKLE, Donald M. John Antes, "American dilettante." Winston-Salem: Moravian Music Foundation, 1956. pp. 486-499. illus., bibliog. notes.

(Reprinted from the Musical Quarterly, October 1956). McCorkle here describes the life and work of the Moravian composer of possibly the earliest chamber music by a native American, and "one of the finest early American composers of sacred music"

(p. 497). In his 71 years he not only made instruments, wrote chamber music, anthems and hymns; he also experienced an eventful period as a missionary in Egypt, and probably knew Haydn in England, where he died, at Bristol, in 1811. McCorkle discusses his music in general terms, and provides a list of works.

83. McCORKLE, Donald M. The Moravian contribution to American music. Winston-Salem: Moravian Music Foundation, 1956. (Publications, No. 1) 10p. bibliog. notes.

Originally published in the Music Library Association's Notes in September 1956--at a comparatively early stage in research on the subject--this brief article summarizes the known features of Moravian music (in particular the trombone choir and the "Collegium Musicum"), the musical instruments used, and the music performed.

84. RAU, Albert G., and DAVID, Hans T., comps. A catalogue of music by American Moravians 1742-1842, from the Archives of the Moravian Church at Bethlehem, Pa. Bethlehem, Pa.: Moravian Seminary and College for Women, 1938. (Repr. New York: AMS Press, 1970). 118p. illus.

The Moravian settlement at Bethlehem was founded in 1742, and music was always an important element in worship; but only with the coming of Jeremiah Dencke in 1761 was the type of music--solo and chorus anthems--introduced that is the subject of this scholarly catalog. The first music manuscript the compilers record dates from 1766. The subsequent steady succession of music for all religious seasons was composed for various congregations, but copies of almost all of it are located in the Bethlehem Archive. The catalog lists music composed in America by eleven main composers, including Dencke, J. F. Peter and Johannes Herbst (whose works composed in Europe are also given), with notes on six lesser figures and their compositions. Biographies of the composer in question precede each section, and the detailed catalog entries include extensive notes. There are also 24 facsimiles of "selected compositions and interesting pages from original manuscripts." (Rau wrote an article on Peter in Musical Quarterly, 23:3, 1937.)

85. SACHSE, Julius Friedrich. The German Pietists of Provincial Pennsylvania, 1694-1708. Philadelphia: Printed for the author, 1895. (Repr. New York: AMS Press, 1970). 504p. illus., bibliog. notes.

The first part of Sachse's history of German sects in Pennsylvania includes information on Johann Kelpius (1673-1708), whose musical manuscript, "Die klaglige Stimme der verborgenen Liebe" ("The lamenting voice of the hidden love"), containing ten hymns and melodies, is described, with full hymn titles, a brief description of each, and facsimiles of the music. The early date of this compilation, 1705, gives it a special significance in the development of music in the colony. Sachse's work also includes a chapter on Justus Falkner (1672-1723), author of many hymns.

86. SACHSE, Julius Friedrich. The German sectarians of Pennsylvania, 1708-1800: a critical and legendary history of the

Ephrata Cloister and the Dunkers. Philadelphia: Printed for the author, 1899-1900. (Repr. New York: AMS Press, 1971). 2v. illus., bibliog. notes.

In the continuation of his monumental history Sachse includes a chapter specifically on music (Vol. 2, Chapter 6), in which he describes the development of music in the Ephrata Cloister, (a celibate community founded by Conrad Beissel in 1732), Beissel's musical methods and ideas and the reactions of other members to his regime. His brief history culminates in the hymn book Turtel Taube (1747), whose contents he describes, together with a translation of Beissel's prefatory material on voice and harmony. The text also includes eleven facsimiles of music manuscripts, three of which are also given in modern notation, done "by a gentleman of Philadelphia." From Sachse's own remarks in his Music of the Ephrata Cloister (no. 87), it seems criticism was leveled at him following this chapter; certainly in that book another attempt is made to translate Beissel, and the contribution of the aforementioned citizen of Philadelphia is disowned.

87. SACHSE, Julius Friedrich. The music of the Ephrata Cloister; also Conrad Beissel's treatise on music as set forth in a preface to the "Turtel Taube" of 1747, amplified with facsimile reproductions of parts of the text and some original Ephrata music ... Lancaster, Pa.: Printed for the author, 1903. (Repr. New York: AMS Press, 1971). 108p. illus.

The community Beissel founded on the Cocalico River in 1732, in present-day Lancaster County, was particularly notable for the importance attached to music in worship, and for the use of original music, created in the community. Sachse outlines the features of Ephrata music, the ideas of Beissel, and the development of the community's hymns up to the compilation known as Turtel Taube (1747), the printed version of which--containing 277 hymns, mainly by Beissel himself--is described. Beissel's writings on music--a series of rhetorical questions called Apology for sacred song, and the theories on voice instruction and harmony that preface Turtel Taube--are given in English translation (that for the dissertation on harmony being translated, no English version being known, by a Rev. J. F. Ohl. Carl Engel, in Musical Quarterly, XIV:2, April 1928, criticizes this translation). Sachse's book is illustrated with some examples of Ephrata music, in facsimiles of the original manuscripts, and modern notation. (For further information on Beissel and his music, see Stevenson (no. 63), and a 1959 thesis at the University of Southern California by Carl T. Holmes, "A Study of the Music in the 1747 Edition of Conrad Beissel's 'Das Gesang der einsamen und verlassenen Turtel-Taube'.")

7. Musical Life

a. General Works

Note: For works on the musical life of particular periods, see B. 5, C. 4, and D. 2. d

88. ATHERTON, Lewis. Main street on the middle border.
Bloomington: Indiana University Press, 1954. 423p. illus.,
bibliog. notes.

This detailed account of country town life in the Mid-West from
the Civil War to 1950 contains interesting information about the cultural as well as the social and economic life. The cult of utili-
tarianism and the high regard for all practical achievement made
artistic flowering in the small towns negligible; anyone with artistic
ambition moved to the cities. But of all the arts, music was the
most popular. The various kinds of music to be found in the years
after the war originated both outside and inside the communities
themselves. Minstrel and medicine shows, Negro jubilee choirs singing spirituals, circus bands, and the music of the "opera house"--
originally a euphemism for theatre, but later the scene of light opera
--all came from outside. But within the towns and villages singing
societies were popular, as was the local band. Band concerts continued to be popular, when the small towns became more like small
cities in the 20th century.

89. BUREAU OF MUSICAL RESEARCH, INC. Music and dance in
California and the West; Richard Drake Saunders, editor.
Hollywood: Bureau of Musical Research, 1948. 309p.
illus.
————. Music and dance in Texas, Oklahoma and the South-
west; edited by E. Clyde Whitlock and Richard Drake Saunders. Hollywood: Bureau of Musical Research, 1950. 256p.
illus.
————. Music and dance in the central states; edited by
Richard Drake Saunders. Hollywood: Bureau of Musical
Research, 1952. 173p. illus.
————. Music and dance in the Southeastern states, including Florida, Georgia, Maryland, North and South Carolina,
Virginia and the District of Columbia; Sigmund Spaeth, editor-in-chief ... William J. Perlman, director and managing
editor. New York: Bureau of Musical Research, 1952.
331p. illus.
————. Music and dance in New York State; Sigmund Spaeth,
editor-in-chief ... New York: Bureau of Musical Research,
1952. 435p. illus.
————. Music and dance in the New England states; includ-
ing Maine, New Hampshire, Vermont, Massachusetts, Rhode
Island and Connecticut; Sigmund Spaeth, editor-in-chief ...
New York: Bureau of Musical Research, 1953. 347p.
illus.
————. Music and dance in Pennsylvania, New Jersey and
Delaware; Sigmund Spaeth, editor-in-chief ... New York:
Bureau of Musical Research, 1954. 339p. illus.

(The California volume was first published in 1933 as Who's
Who in Music and Dance in Southern California, edited by B. D.
Ussher, with a second edition, Music and Dance in California, edited
by Jose Rodriguez, in 1940.) Taken together these seven volumes
constitute a good source of biographical information on mid-20th century musicians in almost all parts of the United States. The driving

force behind the series was William Perlman (died Nov. 1954), playwright, humorist, theatrical producer. He it was, evidently, who obtained the raw material for the various volumes, leaving it to the editors to organize it. With slight variations each volume follows the same pattern. There is a collection of short articles (sometimes as many as 100) on music and, more especially, on the musical life of each area, by local experts on their subjects, with occasional contributions from more famous figures (e.g., the California volume includes pieces by Schoenberg, Stravinsky, Antheil and Still). These are followed by a (more valuable) biographical directory of local music and dance personalities, with many photographs. The biographies are strictly factual, data for each being supplied by the individuals themselves.

90. CAMPBELL, John C. The Southern highlander and his homeland. New York: Russell Sage Foundation, 1921. 405p. illus., bibliog.
  _____. _____; with a new foreword by Rupert B. Vance, and an introduction by Henry D. Shapiro. Lexington: University Press of Kentucky, 1969. 405p. illus., bibliog.
  Under the auspices of the Russell Sage Foundation, Campbell spent four years in the 1910s on a survey of the Southern Appalachian way of life. His intimate knowledge of, and love for, the area, the people and their culture radiates from his classic, posthumously published study. He was acutely conscious of the importance of traditional culture, and saw it as a central pillar in a revitalized society. His survey describes the early pioneers and their ancestry, and discusses at length the individualism, home and religious life, living conditions and education of the contemporary highlander. It was during her travels with her husband that Olive Dame Campbell first began a collection of folk songs that subsequently attracted the interest of Cecil Sharp (no. 469). The role of secular and sacred music in the life of people is described, chiefly in chapters on ancestry, on the highlander at home (ballads, instruments, funeral music, folk songs, with some music examples), and on religious life, in which texts and tunes of several hymns are given (p. 176ff.). There are almost a hundred photographs.

91. EATON, Quaintance, ed. Musical U.S.A. New York: Allen, Towne & Heath, 1949. 206p. illus.
  Expanded from articles written for Musical America (from whose files the numerous illustrations also come) these are 13 concise historical outlines of the development in musical life in major American cities. The cities covered are: Philadelphia, Chicago, Baltimore, New York, Boston, Cincinnati, Minneapolis, St. Louis, New Orleans, major Texas cities, San Francisco, Los Angeles and Seattle. Among the contributors are Robert Gerson, Cecil Smith, George Kent Bellows, and Herbert Peyser.

92. FISHER, William Arms. Music festivals in the United States: an historical sketch. Boston: American Choral and Festival Alliance, 1934. 86p.
  Intended chiefly as a "stimulus to greater endeavor," this short

history surveys the development of festivals in Boston, New York,
Philadelphia, Chicago and San Francisco, briefly describes fifteen
major festivals and fifteen minor ones from Maine to Kansas, and
lists American choral works given first performances at festivals
between 1873 and 1932.

93. GOLDIN, Milton. The music merchants. New York: Macmil-
    lan, 1969. 242p. illus., bibliog.
    An informal chronicle of "the business of music in America"
(preface), describing the background to the growth in musical life in
opera house and concert hall in the 19th and 20th centuries. Goldin
focuses his attention on three groups of individuals responsible for
the business side of this growth: the impresarios (P. T. Barnum
in the 1840s; later the Steinways, the Chickerings, James Henry
Mapleson, Maurice Grau); the patrons (notably Henry Lee Higginson
and Otto H. Kahn); and the organizers (a mainly 20th group whose
gradually changing function is noted). His account is concluded with
the creation of the Lincoln Center in New York.

94. LANG, Paul Henry, ed. One hundred years of music in Amer-
    ica. New York: Schirmer, 1961. 322p.
    A Festschrift for the firm of Schirmer, containing sixteen es-
says by established writers on a variety of aspects of American musical life from the year of the firm's foundation, 1861. The first
section, on music making, contains essays on the composer (by
Nathan Broder), the orchestra (Helen M. Thompson), opera (Philip
L. Miller), church music (Robert Stevenson), concert life (Nicolas
Slonimsky), band music (Richard Franko Goldman) and popular music
(Arnold Shaw). The business of music--publishing, recording and
music literature--is considered by Richard F. French, Roland Gelatt
and R. D. Darrell. Other essays are devoted to "music as a field
of knowledge" (education, criticism, and music libraries) and to the
relationship of music to government and the effects of copyright.
There is no index.

95. SCHAUFFLER, Robert Haven, and SPAETH, Sigmund. Music
    as a social force in America and the science of practice.
    New York: Caxton Institute, 1927. (Fundamentals of Mu-
    sical Art, Vol. 19) 118p.
    Two accounts, very different in approach, of the social value
of music. Schauffler takes a light-hearted, slightly facetious look
at the part played by music in the transformation of "trackless
wilderness" into modern community, as seen in a fictional town
("Main Street"), embodying those features known as "typical," among
a fictional family called Robinson, blessed with the same virtue of
conformity. Spaeth, more serious, looks at music-making in social,
economic and educational groups; his ignorance of folk traditions (he describes America as "poor in folk music") makes it a rather ill-
balanced description of the social influence of music.

b. Regional Studies (excluding opera)

New England

BOSTON

96. HANDEL AND HAYDN SOCIETY, Boston. History of the Han-
del and Haydn Society of Boston, Massachusetts. Vol. 1.
From the foundation of the Society through its seventy-fifth
season: 1815-1890. Boston: Mudge, 1883-1893. 518p.
_____. _____. Vol. 2. Nos. 1-2. From May 26, 1890
to May 25, 1903. Cambridge, Mass.: Caustic-Claflin Co.,
Printers, 1911-1913. 185p. illus.
_____. _____. Vol. 2. No. 3. From May 25, 1903 to
May 1, 1933. Boston: Anchor Linotype Printing Co., 1934.
163p. illus.

The second oldest and the most illustrious of the 19th century
choral and instrumental societies, formed to perform music of the
European masters and very significant in the development of American concert life, the Handel and Haydn Society was founded in 1815
by Gottlieb Graupner (1767-1836). This set is an extremely detailed record of the Society's activities, especially in Vol. 1, which
describes and comments on performances. All volumes report public reactions, Vol. 2 being rich in quotations of press reports and
reviews. Charles C. Perkins compiled chapters 1-3 of Vol. 1, and
John S. Dwight chapters 4-15. The first two parts of Vol. 2 are
the work of William F. Bradbury, and Vol. 2 No. 3 that of Courtenay
Guild.

96a. HOWE, M. A. De Wolfe. The Boston Symphony Orchestra:
an historical sketch. Boston: Houghton Mifflin, 1914.
279p. illus.
_____. The Boston Symphony Orchestra, 1881-1931; semi-
centennial edition, revised and extended in collaboration with
John N. Burk. Boston: Houghton Mifflin, 1931. 272p.
illus.

The 1st edition of Howe's history covers, in seven chapters,
the development of the orchestra from its foundation in 1881 to the
outbreak of hostilities in Europe in 1914 (a situation full of fore-
boding for the orchestra because of its German conductor, Karl
Muck). In his account of the beginnings under Georg Henschel, the
establishing process under Wilhelm Gericke and the eras of Arthur
Nikisch, Emil Paur, Karl Muck and Max Fiedler, Howe makes extensive use of contemporary documents, especially local newspapers.
His emphasis is on behind-the-scenes activity, and the principal
figure is undoubtedly the founder and patron, Henry Lee Higginson
(1834-1919). The 1931 edition adds an "interlude" by Howe, covering the war years, and two chapters--on Henri Rabaud and Pierre
Monteux, 1918-1924, and on Serge Koussevitzsky ("new fires from
Russia")--which are largely the work of John N. Burk. In the appendices to this edition are the text of an address by Bliss Perry
on Higginson, a listing of the orchestra's repertoire, 1881-1931, a
roster of personnel, and a catalog of the orchestra's Casadesus
collection of old instruments. There is also an index.

97.   JOHNSON, H. Earle. Hallelujah, Amen! the story of the
      Handel and Haydn Society of Boston. Boston: Bruce Hum-
      phries, 1965. 256p. illus., bibliog. notes.
      This "anecdotal history" was written at the Society's behest
for its 150th anniversary. Lighter in tone and less reverential than
Perkins-Dwight (no. 96), it is an enjoyable chronicle that is fully
aware of the Society's achievement since its first concert in 1815,
and manages to convey a good impression of methods and styles of
performance, as well as providing details of repertoire and taste.
The 20th century is more sketchily covered than the 19th. Included
in an appendix is a list of works associated with the Society, with
some dates of first performances by other American groups for comparison. Index.

98.   JOHNSON, H. Earle. Musical interludes in Boston, 1795-
      1830. New York: Columbia University Press, 1943. (Repr.
      New York: AMS Press, 1967). 366p. illus., bibliog.
      notes.
      One of the great merits of Johnson's detailed account of the
musical life of Boston in the early 19th century is the author's ability to organize and pass on a mass of information (mainly gleaned
from contemporary newspapers) and maintain a lively interest in his
subject. After first setting the cultural scene in Part 1, with particular attention to the theater, he describes the city's concert
life in Part II, devoting a separate chapter to the Philharmonic Society. The dominating personalities, the pivots around whom the
entire musical scene revolved, are described in detail in Part III:
first, the Von Hagens--Peter the father (1750-1803) and son (1781-
1837), teachers, publishers and performers; second, the Graupners-
Gottlieb (1767-1836), a German immigrant, and his English wife
Catherine (1769-1821), a noted singer (Graupner's list of enterprising activities included publishing, conducting, teaching, and assisting
in the foundation of the Handel and Haydn Society); third, the organist and composer George K. Jackson (a list of whose works is included). Part IV deals with associated activities--publishing (not
only Von Hagen and Graupner, but also such enterprises as John R.
Parker's "Euterpeiad"), musical businesses and music teaching.
The appendices give catalogs of the publications issued by Von Hagen,
Graupner, and lesser publishers, and a list of works granted copyright in Boston between 1791 and 1827. There is also an index.
Bibliographical information is confined to footnotes.

99.   JOHNSON, H. Earle. Symphony Hall, Boston; with a list of
      works performed by the Boston Symphony Orchestra compiled
      by members of the staff of Symphony Hall. Boston: Little,
      Brown, 1950. 431p. illus.
      The story of Symphony Hall is also principally the story of
the Boston Symphony Orchestra (though the latter started life in 1881
under Wilhelm Gericke--Johnson begins here). The book describes
the history of both--the course taken by the orchestra, particularly
in the Koussevitzky era (1923-1948), the features of the hall, and
the development of its concert life. The appendices contain not only
a list of works performed between 1881 and 1949, with performance

dates, but also lists of permanent and guest conductors, and soloists, with dates of performances and number of appearances.

100.   WINSOR, Justin, ed.   The memorial history of Boston, including Suffolk County, Massachusetts, 1630-1880.   Vol. IV.   The last hundred years.   Part II.   Special topics. Boston: Osgood, 1881.   713p.   illus.

Chapter 7 of this volume (pp. 415-464) is devoted to "The History of Music in Boston," by John Sullivan Dwight, whose approach is clearly established on his first page when he says, "Before the year 1800, all that bore the name of music in New England may be summed up in the various modifications of the one monotonous and barren type, the Puritan Psalmody ... Music, for us, had to be imported from an older and a richer soil." (Take that, Bill Billings, Sam Holyoke!) So the growth in musical activity in Boston, which Dwight divides into four periods covering 1810-1881, is measured in terms of the Bostonians' increasing success in performing European music in concert hall, theater and church, and in the development of associations to cultivate a European taste, school curricula to teach it, and a musical press to applaud it.

HARTFORD

101.   JOHNSON, Frances Hall.   Musical memories of Hartford; drawn from records public and private.   Hartford: Witkower's, 1931.   (Repr. New York: AMS Press, 1970). 313p.   illus.

A collection of miscellaneous reminiscences rather than an organized history, this account of musical activity in a part of Connecticut in the late 19th and early 20th centuries includes a series of portraits of musical sons of the city (among them Dudley Buck, Waldo Selden Pratt and Richmond Peck Paine), a description of the origin and development of the Hartford Philharmonic Orchestra (including numerous concert programs), and an account of visiting celebrities (Jenny Lind, Theodore Thomas, Paderewski).   No index.

MAINE

102.   EDWARDS, George Thornton.   Music and musicians of Maine: being a history of the progress of music in the territory which has come to be known as the State of Maine, from 1904-1928.   Portland, Me.: Southworth Press, 1928. (Repr. New York: AMS Press, 1970).   542p.   illus.

A meticulously prepared regional history, beginning with the Indians of Maine and the missionary records from the earliest colonial settlements.   The main text is a detailed chronological survey in which one chapter is devoted to the colonial era, another to the post-Revolutionary years to 1819, three to sections of the 19th century, and a final one to the early 20th century.   A biographical dictionary of living musicians of Maine concludes the book.

NEW HAMPSHIRE

103.   PICHIERRI, Louis. Music in New Hampshire, 1623-1800.
        New York: Columbia University Press, 1960. 297p.
        bibliog.

Responding to Sonneck's call for "correct and abundant literature of city and state musical histories" (Suum Cuique, no. 42),
Pichierri provides a scholarly study of 200 years of musical life
(especially music instruction) that relates the particular area of study
to other New England states and to Europe. His coverage includes
instruments, religious and secular music performed, music for public occasions, opera before and after the Revolution, concert life,
and education. He examines in particular the lives and works of
John Hubbard (1759-1810), Benjamin Dearborn (1754-1838) and Samuel
Holyoke (1762-1820), all three teachers (Holyoke was also a composer, and a compiler of sacred music). The tunebook Village Harmony (5th ed., Exeter, N.H., 1800) is also discussed. In the appendices are teachers' advertisements and selected opera programs.
The bibliography lists both published and unpublished material and
there is an index.

RHODE ISLAND

104.   MANGLER, Joyce Ellen. Rhode Island music and musicians,
        1733-1850. Detroit: Information Service, 1965. (Detroit
        Studies in Music Bibliography, No. 7) 90p. bibliog.

An alphabetical directory of Rhode Island musicians, with
dates and brief biographical data. Sources of information for each
entry are also given. There are professional indexes (church music, concert life, music education and trade), and the personal
names are grouped into five periods for a chronological list. The
bibliography lists books, articles, directories, periodicals and manuscript sources.

New York

(See also nos. 377-383)

105.   ALDRICH, Richard. Concert life in New York, 1902-1923.
        New York: Putnam, 1941. 795p. illus.

Richard Aldrich's music criticism for the New York Times,
a large selection of which is reproduced here, was catholic in taste,
generous in temper and stylish in execution. The volume comprises
a collection of concert reviews, chronologically arranged, that provide a reliable guide to concert life in New York City in the first
decades of the 20th century. The index, by Harold E. Johnson, is
to concert artists and organizations that performed in New York in
the period covered by the book; references are not to pages of the
book, but are given in the form of dates on which a notice or review
appeared in the New York Times. There is also a list of Aldrich's
Sunday articles, only a few of which are included in the book.

106.   DOWNES, Olin. Olin Downes on music: a selection from his
                writings during the half-century 1906 to 1955; edited by
                Irene Downes, with a preface by Howard Taubman.   New
                York: Simon and Schuster, 1957.   473p.   illus.
        One of the most widely-read music journalists of the first
half of the 20th century, Downes was critic for the Boston Post from
1906 to 1924, and the New York Times--where he succeeded Aldrich--
from 1924 till his death in 1955.   This chronologically arranged selection of his criticism, almost all written to meet a deadline, presents a good cross-section of New York concert life in particular.
Specifically American music reviewed includes Gershwin's "Rhapsody
in Blue" and "Porgy and Bess," Thomson's "Four Saints in Three
Acts," and Deems Taylor's "Through the Looking Glass."   There are
also pieces on Ives, Carpenter, MacDowell, Menotti, Blitzstein,
Bernstein and Copland.   Index.

107.   KLEIN, Hermann. Unmusical New York: a brief criticism
                of triumphs, failures, and abuses.   London: John Lane,
                The Bodley Head; New York: John Lane, 1910.   144p.
                illus.
        Critical attacks, whether ill-founded or not, are always a
valuable tonic when the air grows heavy with deference--though when
they are mounted by foreigners there is automatically suspicion of
the motive.   Klein, an English journalist who visited the U.S. for
an eight-year period, 1901-1909, as teacher, critic and concert performer, professes only the purest of motives, hoping his criticism
may be taken constructively.   Describing the various sides of musical life in New York--audiences, individual performers, opera,
orchestras, churches, education, music criticism--he finds a lack
of taste and judgment, a yearning for the sensational (hence the "star"
system), and a neglect of native talent, to name but a few.   His
criticism, though sometimes a little smug, is generally considered
and realistic.

108.   KREHBIEL, H. E. Notes on the cultivation of choral music
                and the Oratorio Society of New York.   New York: Schu-
                berth, 1884.   (Repr. New York: AMS Press, 1970).   106p.
        Krehbiel's outline of the development of singing societies in
New York considers the European background, the early amateur
societies, and the first eleven years of the Oratorio Society (in which
Leopold Damrosch is prominent), founded in 1873.   The programs
for these eleven seasons are given in an appendix, together with the
Society's officers.

109.   PEYSER, Ethel. The house that music built: Carnegie Hall.
                New York: McBride, 1936.   371p.   illus., bibliog.
        A history of a central pillar in New York's musical life in
the 20th century, describing the situation in the city prior to the construction of the Hall, giving a portrait of Andrew Carnegie, telling
the story of the planning and construction of the building and of the
opening festival of 1891, and describing something of the subsequent
pageant of musical activity it witnessed.   Some physical aspects of
the Hall, and developments in acoustics, etc., are also discussed.

There is a list of first performances given at the Hall, and an index.

110.   REDWAY, Virginia Larkin.   Music directory of early New
       York City: a file of musicians, music publishers and mu-
       sical instrument-makers listed in New York directories
       from 1786 through 1835, together with the most important
       New York music publishers from 1836 through 1875.   New
       York: New York Public Library, 1941.   102p.
       The main object of this directory is to assist those interested
in music in 18th and 19th century New York to date music imprints
having no copyright date.   There are four alphabetical lists: of musicians, professors and teachers; of publishers, printers, lithograph-
ers and dealers; of instrument-makers and dealers; and of dancers
and dancing teachers.   Each name is followed by field of activity,
addresses and dates.   In the appendices are a chronological list of
all firms and individuals, 1786-1811, and a list of musical societies,
1789-1799.

111.   WILSON, James Grant, ed.   The memorial history of the city
       of New York: from its first settlement to the year 1892.
       Vol. 4.   New York: New York History Co., 1893.   650p.
       John D. Champlin contributes a relatively brief account of mu-
sical activity in New York covering "nearly two centuries" in Chapter
5 (pp. 165-187).   Beginning around 1700, he recounts the early musical developments at Trinity Church, the English ballad opera, the
formation and growth of musical societies, the invasion of Italian
opera and subsequent operatic activity, concluding with brief reference to lighter works for the musical stage.

NEW YORK PHILHARMONIC SOCIETY

112.   ERSKINE, John.   The Philharmonic-Symphony Society of New
       York: its first hundred years; with programs of subscrip-
       tion concerts 1917-1942.   New York: Macmillan, 1943.
       168p.   illus.
       Erskine summarizes the early history of the Society covered
by Krehbiel (no. 114) and Huneker (no. 113), giving some new information, before going on to outline the developments in the period
1917 to 1942.   The concert programs from the period occupy half
the book, which lacks any index.

113.   HUNEKER, James Gibbons.   The Philharmonic Society of New
       York and its seventh-fifth anniversary: a retrospect.   (New
       York: The Society, 1917).   130p.   illus.
       Carrying on from Krehbiel (no. 112), but lamenting the "mea-
gre documentary evidence" that obliged him to secure most of his
information "by haphazard hearsay" (p. 1), the one-time brewer of
"foaming paragraphs" presents here an unambitious, rather sketchy
survey of the intervening years, 1892-1917.   Despite his lack of very
great enthusiasm Huneker raises himself to declare that "the history
of the Philharmonic Orchestra is the history of music in America.
Let there be no ambiguity in this statement."   There are six por-

traits, and a list of the compositions performed by the orchestra, season by season, 1892-1917, in New York and on tour.

114.   KREHBIEL, Henry Edward. The Philharmonic Society of New York: a memorial. New York, London: Novello, Ewer, 1892. 183p.
This first history of the New York Philharmonic covers the Society's initial 50-year period, 1832-1892. Krehbiel had access to numerous documents--programs, announcements, reports, letters --from which he quotes freely in his outline of the significant facts and the relationship of developments in New York to the broader question of orchestral music in urban America. Appendices, occupying half the book, list the full programs for the period, and give details of the Society's finances. Krehbiel acknowledges help he received from Richard Aldrich.

115.   SHANET, Howard. Philharmonic: a history of New York's orchestra. New York: Doubleday, 1975. 788p. illus., bibliog.
Shanet's extensively researched history of the Philharmonic Orchestra from its beginnings to the early 1970s occupies 400 pages --the rest consists of notes to the text, bibliography and several massive appendices--and makes all previous histories rather perfunctory. With one of his predecessor's (Huneker's) view that the history of the Philharmonic equals the history of orchestral music in America Shanet fundamentally disagrees; to him it is a cultural mirror, and one of the fascinating aspects of his book is the portrait of the interaction between New York society and the orchestra throughout its history. Particularly interesting are the accounts of the birth and early life of the orchestra, and the eras of Theodore Thomas, Anton Seidl, Gustav Mahler and Arturo Toscanini. Included in the appendices are a list of first subscribers, a critical summary of the first season, and a complete record of the works performed and artists involved in the seasons 1942-1971. Index.

Pennsylvania, Maryland, Virginia

116.   DRUMMOND, Robert Rutherford. Early German music in Philadelphia. New York: Appleton, 1910. (Repr. New York: AMS Press, 1972). 88p. bibliog. notes.
A concise study of musical life in Philadelphia in the 18th century, and of the growth of public taste for secular German music. Drummond divides the century into three: pre-1750, when church music still dominated, but a musical culture outside the church was developing; 1750-1783, when music teachers and dealers greatly influenced the progress of musical taste, and a concert tradition began; and 1783-1800, in which the major contribution to musical life was made by Alexander Reinagle (1765-1809), seconded by Philip Roth and Philip Phile. A number of previously unpublished concert programs are given, and there is also a list of Reinagle's compositions.

117. GERSON, Robert A. Music in Philadelphia: a history of Philadelphia music, a summary of its current state, and a comprehensive index-directory. Philadelphia: Presser, 1940. (Repr. Westport: Greenwood Press, 1970). 422p. illus., bibliog.

Conscious of the large amount of purely historical data assembled in his account (which was originally a thesis), Gerson remarks in his preface that, although he had attempted to make the book a pleasant narrative, it had become "reference material for the most part." As a history its chief merit is thus not in overall perspectives but in the detail on musical life and on minor figures. One chapter is devoted to the Colonial period (including music of the Swedes and Germans, early secular and sacred music), one to the years immediately following the Revolution (featuring Hopkinson and Reinagle), and two to the 19th century as a whole. Part 2 looks in detail at the musical life of the first 40 years of the 20th century: instrumental groups and orchestras, opera, singing societies, music in education, church music, and publishers. As an appendix Gerson provides a not-too-successful hybrid he calls an "index-dictionary," which, besides serving as an index, includes also very brief items of reference information, particularly on individuals, omitted from the text itself.

118. KEEFER, Lubov. Baltimore's music: the haven of the American composer. Baltimore: Printed by J. H. Furst, 1962. 343p. bibliog.

The 19th century musical life of Baltimore is exhaustively chronicled in this history, while the Colonial era is less thoroughly treated. Constantly relating music to social life, the author conveys a mass of information (with most of the necessary scholarly documentation) without ever abandoning an apparent sense of pleasure and enjoyment. The scene covered extends to include church, opera stage and concert hall, and though no personalities are dominant, those of Asger Hamerik, Sidney Lanier and George Peabody emerge as the most significant, Hamerik's period as director of the Peabody Institute (1871-1898) being particularly carefully outlined. There is an index and a 14-page bibliography.

119. KUPFERBERG, Herbert. Those fabulous Philadelphians: the life and times of a great orchestra. New York: Scribner, 1969; London: Allen, 1970. 257p. illus., discog.

An enjoyable account of the history of the Philadelphia Orchestra, covering the genesis and first dozen years rather briefly (these are dealt with in greater detail in Wister, no. 124), and concentrating on the eras dominated by the two great conductors: Leopold Stokowski, who was principal conductor from 1912, and Eugene Ormandy, who succeeded him officially in 1938 (though they overlapped for a number of years). There is also a portrait of the life of the orchestra. The author obtained information from the scrapbooks, and from the personal recollections of orchestra members. He incorporates this into a detailed, readable narrative that declines to encumber itself with references and similar impediments. In the appendices are lists

of the orchestra (with dates), and a list of currently available LPs.
There is also an index.

120.   NATIONAL SOCIETY OF THE COLONIAL DAMES OF AMER-
         ICA, Pennsylvania. Church music and musical life in
         Pennsylvania in the eighteenth century; prepared by the
         Committee on Historical Research. Philadelphia: The So-
         ciety, 1926-47. (Publications of the Pennsylvania Society
         of the Colonial Dames of America, IV) 3v. in 4. illus.,
         bibliogs.
         An impressive collection of material on the wide range of
musical activities in 18th century Pennsylvania. Mrs. Alvin A.
Parker, Chairman of the Committee and driving force behind the
project (she died in 1931), announces the series as "the first attempt to collect, illustrate and bring together the music of the early
settlers of Pennsylvania" (foreword). The set is not a formal history, but a series of (often substantial) essays on individuals and aspects of musical life in which each author (they are not acknowledged,
save in Vol. 3, part 2) assembles available data from existing
sources, not attempting to explore new directions ("in this sense the
work is a compilation"). Subjects examined include: Vol. 1--Jo-
hannes Kelpius (with a facsimile of his ms. hymnal and of Christopher Witt's translation), Justus Falkner, Swedish church music,
American Indian music; Vol. 2--Francis Daniel Pastorius, the Men-
nonites and Dunkers, Schwenkfelder hymnology, the Moravian contribution; Vol. 3, part 1--the background to English musical life,
the lyric stage (notably "The Beggar's Opera," and a facsimile of
"The Fool's Opera" libretto by Anthony Aston); Vol. 3, part 2--
music of the Episcopal, Lutheran and Roman Catholic churches,
Jewish music, Welsh music, Francis Hopkinson, Benjamin Franklin,
and songs of freemasonry. Each volume has a good bibliography
and an index.

121.   ROHRER, Gertrude Martin. Music and musicians of Pennsyl-
         vania; compiled under the auspices of The Pennsylvania
         Federation of Music Clubs. Philadelphia: Presser, 1940.
         (Repr. Port Washington: Kennikat Press, 1970). 121p.
         illus.
         Included in this compendium of musical activity in Pennsyl-
vania are short accounts of Pennsylvania Indians and their music,
by the compiler; of folk music, by Marian E. Ottoson; of the development of music in the public schools, by M. Claude Rosenberry; and
of the Pennsylvania Federation of Music Clubs, by Mrs. William C.
Dierks. There follows a 45-page historical survey of music in
Pennsylvania by Harvey Gaul, and a biographical dictionary, containing brief entries for about 230 composers, teachers, performers,
and writers, including Stephen Foster, Ethelbert Nevin, Marian Anderson, C. W. Cadman, Ira D. Sankey and Philip P. Bliss.

122.   STOUTAMIRE, Albert. Music of the Old South: Colony to
         Confederacy. Rutherford: Fairleigh Dickinson University
         Press, 1972. 349p. illus., bibliog.
         A scholarly historical survey of musical activity in the South

up to 1865, as illustrated by a detailed study of two Virginian centers: Richmond and, to a lesser extent, Williamsburg. Following an examination of music in colonial Virginia, centering on Williamsburg (where the English influence predominated), the scene shifts to Richmond, whose musical life from 1780 to 1865 is divided into four sections of 20-25 years. Within each period the author describes the music on social and public occasions, musical merchantry and instruction (omitted for the final period), the theater, concerts, and the music of the church. In his conclusion he notes the extent of European influence, the growth in a tendency to view musical events in terms of social status, and the lack of leading creative musicians. The appendices list public buildings in Richmond used for music performances, and selected programs representative of concerts in the city, 1797-1865. Index.

123. WALTERS, Raymond. The Bethlehem Bach Choir: an historical and interpretative sketch. Boston: Houghton Mifflin, 1918. (Repr. New York: AMS Press, 1971). 289p. illus.

An account of the origins and early history of the choir formed in 1900 by Dr. J. Fred Wolle to continue the tradition of Bach singing begun with the Bethlehem Choral Union (1882-1892). Appendices list the singers, programs, soloists, orchestra and officers, and there is an index.

124. WISTER, Frances Anne. Twenty-five years of the Philadelphia Orchestra, 1900-1925. Philadelphia: privately printed, 1925. (Repr. Freeport: Books for Libraries Press, 1970). 253p.

From its foundation in 1900 three figures dominated the early history of the Philadelphia Orchestra: the first conductor, Fritz Scheel; his successor, Carl Pohlig; and Leopold Stokowski, who took over in 1912. The author of this account draws a portrait of each era, and describes the development and activities of the orchestra with much use of quotations from contemporary press accounts, concert announcements and circular letters. Included in the appendices are a list of officers and directors, a summary of concerts played in the period, the names of conductors and personnel, biographies of the principal orchestral players, and the first season's programs. No index.

Chicago

125. FFRENCH, Florence, comp. Music and musicians in Chicago: the city's leading artists, organizations and art buildings; progress and development... Chicago: the author, 1899. 236p. illus.

A document of turn-of-the-century musical life in Chicago, comprising biographical sketches of approximately 160 individual musicians, from the famous to the insignificant, and a number of short historical accounts of specific musical aspects or events. These concise surveys cover such topics as early concerts, music in the Civil War, music after the Great Fire, music at the 1893 World's Fair, concert life in the 1880s and 1890s, and the German musical societies. The biographies, most of which include a photographic portrait, tend to be short on facts and long on complimentary phrases. There are also some historical sketches of various Chicago musical institutions. Index.

126.   OTIS, Philo Adams. The Chicago Symphony Orchestra: its organization, growth and development, 1891-1924. Chicago: Summy, 1924. (Repr. Freeport: Books for Libraries Press, 1972). 466p. illus.

Otis served for many years on the Board of Trustees of the orchestra, including a term as its secretary, and the main part of his book is a very meticulous chronicle, season by season, of the orchestra's programs, with information on public reaction, and on the contribution of significant individuals. The stage is dominated by Theodore Thomas (whom Otis defends vigorously against charges of bribery made by the Bureau of Music at the World's Columbian Exposition in 1893). The book begins with an outline of the musical conditions in Chicago before the organizing of the orchestra, and concludes with an appendix listing in full its officers and orchestral players for the period, and an index.

127.   UPTON, George P. Musical memories: my recollections of celebrities of the half century 1850-1900. Chicago: McClurg, 1908. 345p. illus.

George Putnam Upton (1834-1919) was a journalist on the Chicago Daily Tribune from 1862 to his death, during which time he had a lengthy spell as music critic. Not musically trained, he was nevertheless knowledgeable and enthusiastic, and under the pen-name of "Peregrine Pickle" was a generally kind and gentle critic. The window he opens on Chicago's musical life reveals a rich variety of activity in concert hall, opera house and music society. While European visitors dominate the earlier years, American musicians play increasingly important roles as the century progresses. Outstanding among these are Theodore Thomas (whom Upton championed, often in virtual isolation) and Patrick Gilmore. Index.

The West and Southwest

128.   HAAS, Oscar. A chronological history of the singers of German songs in Texas. New Braunfels, Tex.: the author, 1948. 73p.

A year-by-year record of the song festivals and other singing activities of the various German singing leagues in Texas from 1845, when the first festival was organized, to 1948.

129.   ROUSSEL, Hubert. The Houston Symphony Orchestra, 1913-1971. Austin: University of Texas Press, 1972. 247p. illus.

This history by a Houston music critic of 30 years' standing focuses chiefly on the background to the music--the organization and

administration of the orchestra, the appointment of conductors, etc.
--and says little about the music played, or the public taste. Roussel relates the orchestra's development closely to other aspects of
the city's life. The most notable individual figure is Miss Ima Hogg,
the orchestra's founder and guiding hand, while among the conductors
Ernst Hoffmann, Leopold Stokowski and Sir John Barbirolli are prominent. The personnel of the 1913 and 1971 orchestras are given, and
there is an index.

130. SMITH, Carolina Estes. The Philharmonic Orchestra of Los
Angeles: "the first decade," 1919-1929. (Los Angeles:
Press of United Printing Co., 1930). 283p. illus.
An unexceptionable, somewhat prosaic chronicle, written from
close quarters (the author is described as the "personal representative" of founder William Andrews Clark, Jr.) and strictly confined
to the doings of the orchestra. There are portraits of Clark and of
Walter Henry Rothwell, the first conductor, and details of the genesis of the orchestra and its first concert. A season-by-season diary,
lists of members, etc., and excerpts from press reviews form the
substance of the work, which includes in the appendices a list of
premiere performances by the orchestra that numbers 33 American
works, and complete lists of the repertoire performed and of the
orchestral personnel. The numerous illustrations include photographs
of individuals, of the orchestra, and of auditoriums, and there is an
index.

131. SPELL, Lota M. Music in Texas: a survey of one aspect of
cultural progress. Austin: privately printed, 1936. 157p.
The history of music in Texas is mainly a story of the introduction and assimilation of music from outside the state. This account describes this progress, from a "period of dissemination,"
which encompasses Indian and mission music, Spanish-Mexican folk
music, the Anglo-American tradition and the early German contribution, through a "period of absorption from a wider field" (lasting
from the Mexican War to World War I), to a "period of amalgama-
tion," in which are included accounts of English and German singing
societies (which began in the 19th century), opera and concert life,
and developments in music education. The ensuing survey of music
created within the state--including Negro and cowboy songs and the
music of Texas composers--is quite short. In the course of the
book the text is illustrated with 29 examples of Texas songs, Spanish-American, Anglo-American and Germanic. A Texas concert
calendar for 1920-21 appears in the appendix, and there is an index.

132. SWAN, Howard. Music in the Southwest, 1825-1950. San
Marino: Huntington Library, 1952. 316p. illus., bibliog.
A scholarly history that examines the development of musical
life in the Southwest in relation to evolving social and cultural patterns, from the westward migration of the early 19th century to the
variety of activity in post-war Los Angeles (but excluding any study
of Indian music). The first manifestations of music that are examined concern its place among the Mormons (in particular their
devotion to music during exile and persecution), the mining camps

of Arizona and Nevada in the 1860s, and in Spanish-American California ("mission, rancho and pueblo"). The growth of concert life and professional musicianship in Southern California, especially Los Angeles, is spread over two detailed chapters, beginning with the unpromising situation in the early 1860s, marking the cultural transformation that took place in the next 30 years, and describing the deeds of the "unusual and indefatigable" impresario Lyndon Ellsworth Behymer from 1886 to the Depression (he died in 1947). The bibliography lists books, periodicals, unpublished manuscripts and newspapers, and there is an index.

133. UNITED STATES. Works Projects Administration. California. History of music in San Francisco series. San Francisco, 1939-1942. (Repr. New York: AMS Press, 1972). 7v. illus.

This lasting monument to the arts relief work of the WPA (the national, government-funded program for providing employment in the Depression and post-Depression years) is a fascinating record of aspects of musical activity in one city over a hundred-year period. Written by a team of writers under Cornel Lengyel the series of mimeographed volumes, each fully documented and with massive appendices, is presented in a clear, readable, entertaining style. San Francisco became a mecca for musicians at the time of the Gold Rush, and remained a vital center ("more music was performed," says the editor, "and more murders committed in San Francisco during this decade than in any other city in America" [vol. 1]). The set contains biographical information a-plenty as well as details of musical life and collections of music. The volumes are:

(1) Music of the Gold Rush era. 1939. 212p.
(2) A San Francisco songster. 1939. 208p.
(3) The letters of Miska Hauser, 1853. 1939. 185p.
(4) Celebrities in El Dorado, 1856-1906. 1940. 266p.
(5) Fifty local prodigies. 1940. 203p.
(6) Early master teachers. 1940. 149p.
(7) An anthology of music criticism. 1942. 473p.

Vol. 3 contains the specially translated letters of the Hungarian violinist. Vol. 5 covers the period 1900-1940, and Vol. 7, 1850-1940. Most of the volumes are illustrated with photographs of musicians, each one separately pasted in.

Other Centers

134. KMEN, Henry A. Music in New Orleans: the formative years, 1791-1841. Baton Rouge: Louisiana State University Press, 1966. 314p. illus., bibliog.

A well-documented scholarly history of the rich musical life in a unique musical melting pot, centered primarily on the French opera. Kmen begins with an account of the dancing in the city--the white and quadroon balls--and proceeds to chronicle in detail the development of the opera. There are also sections on the brass bands, the concerts, and on the various kinds of Negro musical activity. An appendix lists compositions played at New Orleans concerts, 1806-

1841. The bibliography gives primary and secondary sources, and there is an index.

135.   KROHN, Ernst C. <u>A century of Missouri music.</u> Saint Louis: privately printed, 1924. 134p.
_____. <u>Missouri music.</u> New York: Da Capo, 1971. 380p. bibliog. notes.

Unlike most regional American histories this one emphasizes creative composition in the state rather than interpretative activity, although Krohn's short chapters on the 19th and early 20th century composers in Missouri are not much more than straightforward lists. Missouri's contribution to music criticism is also considered (Rupert Hughes being the most notable figure). The extensive index incorporates biographical sketches for composers and writers mentioned in the text. The Da Capo edition contains a reprint of the 1924 text, a new introduction, a supplementary list of composers, musicians and musicologists, a bibliography of Krohn's writings, and nine essays on Missouri music by him, written since 1924.

136.   MARSH, Robert C. <u>The Cleveland Orchestra;</u> foreword by George Szell. Cleveland: World, 1967. 205p. illus.

This is a clear, interesting historical account--a "sort of verbal and pictorial fanfare," Marsh calls it--of one of America's most celebrated orchestras, describing events, trends, personalities and attitudes from the orchestra's first concerts in 1917, through the periods under Nikolai Sokoloff (the formative years to 1932) and Arthur Rodzinski, and the war years under Erich Leinsdorf, culminating in the arrival of George Szell, whose illustrious career with the orchestra began in 1946. Ancillary material includes selected personnel lists, 1918-1967, and a repertory of subscription seasons nos. 1-49 by Harvey Sachs. No index.

137.   OSBURN, Mary Hubbell. <u>Ohio composers and musical authors.</u> Columbus, O.: F. J. Heer Printing Co., 1942. 238p. bibliog.

A thorough, painstaking work, presenting information collected from individuals by letter and interview, and from printed sources, over a number of years. A historical sketch of music in Ohio precedes a biographical dictionary of about 500 native and adopted composers and musical authors of Ohio, including those working "in a lighter vein." The entries are mostly very full, and many include a complete list of works, with publishers. There are supplementary lists of composers with incomplete data, of temporary Ohio residents, of Ohio-born concert artists, and of Ohio songs; there is also a composer index.

138.   SHERMAN, John K. <u>Music and maestros: the story of the Minneapolis Symphony Orchestra.</u> Minneapolis: University of Minnesota Press, 1952. 357p. illus., discog.

A cheerful chronicle of the growth and development of a famous orchestra from humble origins, and of the musical life of which it became the focus. After a short account of the last quarter of the 19th century, when the first attempts to form an orchestra were made in the city, Sherman organizes his history from 1900-1950 around the careers of the orchestra's successive conductors: Emil Oberhoffer (conductor 1900-1922), Henri Verbrugghen (1922-1931), Eugene Ormandy (1931-1937), Dimitri Mitropoulos (1937-1949), and Antal Dorati (1949-   ).   Ancillary material includes lists of personnel, of out-of-town engagements, and of repertoire for the period 1903-1952.   Index.

c.   Operatic Life

   (i)   General Works

139.   GRAF, Herbert.   The opera and its future in America.   New
         York: Norton, 1941.   (Repr. Port Washington: Kennikat
         Press, 1973).   305p.   illus., bibliog.
         Much of this work by the Austrian-born stage director who
came to the U.S. in 1934 is an attempt to show how, in its origins
and historical development, opera has reflected changing society.
Part 3 relates this to America, with a historical sketch and an outline of the contemporary situation.   Part 4 confidently predicts the
development of a native American operatic form ("we may expect
that the next chapter in the history of opera will be written in America and that its title will be 'Opera of the People,'" p. 290).

140.   GRAF, Herbert.   Opera for the people.   Minneapolis: Uni-
         versity of Minnesota Press; London: Geoffrey Cumberlege,
         Oxford University Press, 1951.   289p.   illus., bibliog.
         notes.
         Here Graf elaborates on some ideas first suggested in no.
139, offering, on the basis of 25 years' experience in opera (many
of these as stage director at the Metropolitan), "facts and suggestions
to stimulate further thinking about the production of opera in America" (preface).   First he discusses some practical aspects of operatic production, with special reference to problems confronting the
growth of opera in America, as they concern language, sponsorship,
rehearsal and the training of artists.   His examples and illustrations
are drawn mainly from the European repertoire, but as he turns to
consider "American opera in the making"--operatic production in
the community, in schools, in the cinema, and on television--he
gives some attention to the works of Gershwin, Thomson, Blitzstein,
Weill, Menotti and Gruenberg.   His final offering is a "blueprint for
the future," in which he suggests ways that a "people's opera"--
opera that is "important to the people because it takes meaning from
and gives meaning to their lives" (p. 237)--might be born.   Index.

141.   HOUSEMAN, John.   Run-through: a memoir.   New York:
         Simon and Schuster, 1972.   507p.   illus.
         In this totally absorbing account of his life to the early 1940s
the celebrated producer and director recreates, with considerable
feats of memory and a flair for telling anecdote and astute characterization, the excitement surrounding the theatrical productions--
particularly the Mercury Theatre--radio shows and films with which

he was involved. Dominating the book is the awesome, enigmatic figure of Orson Welles. For our purposes there are fascinating accounts of two important musical premières: of Virgil Thomson's "Four Saints in Three Acts" (1934), and of Marc Blitzstein's "The Cradle Will Rock" (1937), the account of the latter being a particularly gripping piece of theatrical history. Also featured from time to time are Lehman Engel and Bernard Herrmann (who not only wrote the score for "Citizen Kane," but also provided music for the "Mercury Theatre of the Air").

142. LAHEE, Henry C. Grand opera in America. Boston: L. C. Page, 1902. (Repr. New York: AMS Press, 1973). 348p. illus.
   A chronicle of the development of opera in America from the second half of the 18th century to the turn of the 19th, with particular attention to individuals--almost entirely European--who sang, conducted or organized it, especially in New York. The account begins with ballad opera in the 1770s, followed by the period of opera in English, 1819-1847. William Henry Fry's "Leonora" (1845) is briefly discussed. The bulk of the book deals with the succession of artists singing Italian opera, the dominating fashion of the 19th century. The progress of German opera in the second half of the century and the tireless advocacy of Theodore Thomas are also described. In conclusion there is an account of the short-lived efforts to organize American opera companies singing in English (including the American Opera Company, 1886-1888, and the Metropolitan Grand English Opera Company, 1900-1901); brief portraits are given of some of the American singers involved. Index.

143. MATTFELD, Julius. A handbook of American operatic premières, 1731-1962. Detroit: Information Service, 1963. (Detroit Studies in Music Bibliography, No. 5) 142p.
   A title listing of some 2,000 opera premières, including operas by native and naturalized American composers, a selection of light operas and musicals (European and American), dramatic stage presentations with significant incidental music, and oratorios and cantatas in scenic presentations. Each entry gives composer, number of acts, original language, location and date of American première. There is a composer index.

144. SONNECK, O. G. Early opera in America. New York: Schirmer, 1915. (Repr. New York: Blom, 1963). 230p. illus.
   Sonneck's meticulously researched chronicle of opera in 18th century America had an odd publishing history. In his preface he tells us that it was originally written for serial publication in New Music Review, where a part of it appeared in 1907-8. The exigencies of this form meant considerable condensation of his material, resulting in the "tabular form of dry but indispensable statistics of performances," but also, as he admits, in a "lighter touch" than is found in his other books. Publishers were evidently reluctant to publish the entire work until 1914, by which time it was "almost cast aside by me as 'hopeless'," and Sonneck lacked the time or the enthusiasm to revise it. Nevertheless his searches among contempor-

ary sources had revealed much information about operatic activity. He proceeds chronologically, examining first the course of opera in pre-Revolutionary America (especially the activities of David Douglass). In Part 2 the historical survey is continued to 1792, centering on Lewis Hallam's Old American Company, after which date he focuses attention on the major areas in turn: New York; Philadelphia; Boston and New England; Baltimore, Charleston and the South. The numerous charts and tables give full details of operatic productions. A final chapter concerns French opera; this was however, "a mere episode and entirely subordinate to English opera," which, as Sonneck's book shows, "was cultivated in America to a very considerable extent, interpreted skilfully and enjoyed intelligently" (p. 218). Index.

145. THOMPSON, Oscar. The American singer: a hundred years of success in opera. New York: Dial Press, 1937. 426p. illus.

A chronicle of the lives and careers of outstanding opera singers (mostly female), including native Americans and those foreign-born persons who came to the U.S.A. at an early age and were Americans by adoption. Beginning with the first notable singers in the 1830s--Julia Wheatley and Charlotte Cushman--the story progresses through the 19th and early 20th centuries to the heyday of Geraldine Farrar and Mary Garden, and some subsequent stars. Over 400 singers are featured. The compiler declares (p. 396): "honesty compels him to confess his inability to verify all dates, places, names, titles and roles." In the appendices are lists of Metropolitan Opera debuts, and of Americans in the Chicago Opera, 1910-1936. Index.

(ii) New York

146. BRIGGS, John. Requiem for a yellow brick brewery: a history of the Metropolitan Opera. Boston: Little, Brown, 1969. 359p. illus.

An informal, flesh-and-blood history of the New York opera house from its opening in 1883 to its closure, prior to the transfer to the Lincoln Center, in 1966. From the opening of Josiah Cady's building, through the regimes of Maurice Grau, Heinrich Conried, Giulio Gatti-Casazza, Edward Johnson and Rudolf Bing as managers, the narrative focuses on the personalities of the artists and the administrators, giving anecdotes, behind-the-scenes stories, and general background history and information, and only brief descriptions of significant performances and receptions. Chapter 15 relates the "Search for the great American opera," from Converse's "Pipe of Desire" in 1910 to Barber's "Vanessa" in 1958. There is a chronology (p. xix) and an index.

147. DA PONTE, Lorenzo. The memoirs...; translated into English by some of my Italian pupils. New York: Printed by Gray & Bunce, 1829. 2v. in 1.
_____. Memoirs of Lorenzo Da Ponte, Mozart's librettist;

translated, with an introduction and notes, by L. A. Sheppard. Boston: Houghton, Mifflin; London: Routledge, 1929. 387p. illus.

_____. Memoirs; translated by Elizabeth Abbott; edited and annotated by Arthur Livingston. Philadelphia: Lippincott, 1929. (Repr. New York: Dover Publications, 1967). 512p. illus.

The protean existence of the author of "Don Giovanni" and "The Marriage of Figaro" (1749-1838) took a turn even he hardly anticipated in 1805, when, having fled London and his creditors for Philadelphia, he found himself in New York plying the trade of a grocer. ("Anyone with a little imagination may think how I laughed at myself every time my poetic hand was obliged to weigh out two ounces of tea..."--p. 310, 1929 Boston ed.) Parts 4 and 5 of his memoirs (originally published in Italian in New York, 1823-1826) describe his life in America, where he seems to have been regularly swindled, but where music was not greatly in evidence until 1825, when Manuel Vincente Garcia ("New York's musical Columbus," according to Champlin in no. 111), whom Da Ponte had known in Europe, introduced Italian opera to New York with "The Barber of Seville," and soon afterwards produced "my Don Giovanni."

148. EATON, Quaintance. Opera caravan: adventures of the Metropolitan on tour, 1883-1956; with a foreword by Rudolf Bing. New York: Farrar, Strauss and Cudahy; London: Calder, 1957. 400p. illus.

A chronicle of the extensive touring which has been a regular feature of the Metropolitan's program from its first season under Henry E. Abbey. Over half the book is given over to a chronological list of operas performed each season, grouped by city, with dates, conductor and full cast. Index.

149. GATTI-CASAZZA, Giulio. Memories of the opera. New York: Scribner, 1941. (Repr. New York: Vienna House, 1973). 326p. illus.

Manager of the Metropolitan for 27 years, from 1908 to 1935, Gatti-Casazza (1869-1940) is generally credited with having brought a period of artistic and financial prosperity to the institution. His memoirs, mostly written in 1933, dwell at some length on this period of his life, and reveal a confident business man. He gives his versions of various incidents and relationships (e.g., the difficulties between Andreas Dippel and himself), but is reticent about himself ("I am a man who never talks a great deal and I never discuss my affairs"--p. 169). There is some discussion of the mechanics of opera production.

150. KOLODIN, Irving. The Metropolitan Opera, 1883-1935. New York: Oxford University Press, 1936.

_____. The Metropolitan Opera, 1883-1939. New York: Oxford University Press, 1940.

_____. The story of the Metropolitan Opera, 1883-1950. New York: Knopf, 1953.

_____. The Metropolitan Opera, 1883-1966: a candid

history. New York: Knopf, 1967. 762p. illus.
Many millions of New Yorkers may never have been more
than marginally aware of the Metropolitan, but to a very large number it was the focal point of musical life. Kolodin's history (the
4th ed. covers the story of the opera house from foundation to demo-
lition) gives a painstakingly detailed portrait of the productions and
artists New Yorkers saw over the years. The writer had long personal experience of opera-going at the Metropolitan, and this is apparent in the accuracy and insight of his history. He first traces
the course of private patronage and of the general financial affairs
of the opera house, examines the history of the structure, particularly
with relation to the prestigious boxes, and, in the main part of the
work, assembles a multitude of facts and opinions into a chronological account of the various succeeding opera companies and their
productions, which he arranges in three main sections--1883-1908,
1908-1932, and 1932-1966, with subdivisions. Details of productions,
the quality and character of individual performances, and public reaction are all duly chronicled. There is a useful listing of the
repertory, by Gerald Fitzgerald, and an index.

151.   KREHBIEL, Henry Edward. Chapters of opera; being histor-
       ical and critical observations and records concerning the
       lyric drama in New York from its earliest days down to
       the present time. New York: Holt, 1908. 435p. illus.
       _____ . 3rd ed. New York: Holt, 1911.
       460p. illus.
       As music critic for the New York Tribune Krehbiel witnessed
the whole of the first 25 years (1883-1908) of the Metropolitan Opera
House, and this is his detailed chronicle of the vicissitudes of the
quarter-century, including the seven-year German regime (1884-
1891), overthrown--"in obedience to the command of fashion"--in
favor of Italian opera, the return of German opera to popularity, and
the managerial eras of Maurice Grau (1898-1903) and Heinrich Conried (1903-1908). Preceding this central portion of the book are
seven chapters describing the early history of opera in New York
from English ballad opera in the mid-18th century to the managerial
careers at the Academy of Music of Max Maretzek and Col. James
H. Mapleson (the latter overlaps with the early years of the Met).
Particular attention is also given, at the end of the book, to the
first two seasons of Oscar Hammerstein's Manhattan Opera House.

152.   KREHBIEL, Henry Edward. More chapters of opera; being
       historical and critical observations and records concerning
       the lyric drama in New York from 1908 to 1918. New
       York: Holt, 1919. 474p. illus.
       Krehbiel opens his continuation of the saga of opera in New
York by remarking, "the artistic sins of commission and omission
of the first twenty-five years are petty peccadillos compared with the
follies and scandals which marked the beginning of the lustrum which
followed" (p. 3, a reference to the Gatti-Casazza-Andreas Dippel difficulties at the Metropolitan). His reporting, refashioned for the
book from the pages of the New York Tribune, is forthright, and his
chronicle of the various rivalries and success stories is accompanied

by keen critical comment on features of the operas themselves and their productions (including an account of Parker's "Mona"). In the appendix are the records of the Metropolitan's ten seasons and the Manhattan's two in the period covered. Index.

153. MARETZEK, Max. Crotchets and quavers; or, Revelations of an opera manager in America. New York: French, 1855. 346p.

_____. Sharps and flats; a sequel to "Crotchets and quavers." New York: American Musician Publishing Co., 1890. 87p. illus. (Repr. as: Revelations of an opera manager in 19th-century America: Crotchets and Quavers & Sharps and Flats; (two volumes bound as one) with a new introduction by Charles Haywood. New York: Dover Publications, 1968. 346p, 94p.)

Born in Brno, Maretzek (1821-1897) came to New York via Paris and London in 1848 to manage the Astor Place Opera House and its Italian Opera Company, staying to become, at the Astor Place and later at the Academy of Music, the major opera impresario of the latter half of the 19th century. His importance in the development of an operatic tradition in America was never doubted by Maretzek himself, but has been little examined. His highly picturesque memoirs are a colorful account of musical and theatrical life. The first volume is written in the form of letters to European musical luminaries (among them Berlioz) in which Maretzek describes his first seven years in America. H. E. Krehbiel, who knew the impresario much later, considered the book to have been written "most obviously with the help of some literary hack, who, I imagine, got the thoughts from Maretzek, but supplied the literary dress for them. A good many old scores are paid off in the book, and a good many grudges fed fat; but there are not many instances of bad humor. There is a sugar coating even to his malice" (no. 151, p. 55). The second volume, written when Maretzek was further removed in time from the period, fills in some details of the first, but mainly continues the tale into the 1860s, sketching portraits of numerous musical and theatrical figures en route. Maretzek himself calls it a "serio-comic history ... with reminiscences and anecdotes, of artists, maestros, impresarios, journalists, patrons, stockholders and other deadheads" (p. 2). The reprint contains a new, combined index.

154. MATTFELD, Julius. A hundred years of grand opera in New York, 1825-1925: a record of performances. New York: New York Public Library, 1927. 107p. bibliog.

Originally issued in the Bulletin of the New York Public Library for October, November and December 1925, this commemoration of the introduction of Italian opera to New York in 1825 includes a bibliography of over 60 books and articles, a brief historical survey of the establishment of grand opera, an alphabetical record of operatic productions (excluding light opera), arranged by title, with details of composer, librettist, first ever performance, first New York performance, plus notes on other American performances, and a chronology.

155.   SELTSAM, William H., comp.   Metropolitan Opera annals:
       a chronicle of artists and performances; with an introduc-
       tion by Edward Johnson.   N.Y.: Wilson, 1947.   751p. illus.
       _____.   First Supplement: 1947-1957; with a fore-
       word by Rudolf Bing.   New York: Wilson, 1957.   115p. illus.
       _____.   Second supplement: 1957-1966; with a
       foreword by Francis Robinson.   New York: Wilson, 1968.
       126p. illus.
           Seltsam's massive compilation of data is not only a factual
       chronicle of all performances at the Metropolitan Opera in New York
       by the resident company, but also a record of changing public taste
       and artistic method.   The compiler proceeds season-by-season, list-
       ing each season's personnel, and providing a diary of each opera
       production, with details of conductor and cast, and selected excerpts
       from reviews.   There are two illustrations for each season.   The
       main volume has an index to operas and artists, with composers
       listed in a separate, supplementary leaflet (with the errata).   The
       two supplements themselves each have a comprehensive index.   Sup-
       plement 2 concludes with the April 16th, 1966 Gala performance.
       It also includes a list of artistic debuts, 1883-1966, by Gerald Fitz-
       gerald and John W. Freeman.

OSCAR HAMMERSTEIN I

156.   CONE, John Frederick.   Oscar Hammerstein's Manhattan
       Opera Company.   Norman: University of Oklahoma Press,
       1966.   399p. illus., bibliog.
           The brief lifespan of the Manhattan Opera Company, 1906-
       1910, is the most eventful period in American operatic history, and
       is very thoroughly and absorbingly covered in this scholarly account.
       Aiming consciously to create a greater appetite for opera among
       Americans and to demonstrate its vitality free from wealth and social
       elitism, Hammerstein (1847-1919) declared war on the Metropolitan
       --a conflict terminated when, under financial pressure, he sold out
       to his rivals for over $1 million and a contract to refrain from
       operatic productions in New York for ten years--and forced that in-
       stitution to re-examine its standards.   Cone's meticulous narrative
       relates the rise and fall of this remarkable enterprise, examining
       the status of opera in New York and Philadelphia (where Hammer-
       stein opened a second opera house in 1908) at the turn of the century,
       exploring the background to the venture in Hammerstein's own career,
       chronicling the productions, evaluating contemporary reaction as it
       appeared in the press, exploring the Manhattan-Metropolitan relation-
       ship, and assessing the Manhattan's significance in American operatic
       history (Hammerstein not only enlarged the repertoire, increased the
       number of performances and made the stage generally visible, he
       also greatly encouraged native American singers).   Leading roles
       are taken by conductor Cleofonte Campanini, sopranos Nellie Melba
       and Mary Garden, and tenor Charles Dalmorès.   (Mary Garden gave
       her own account in Mary Garden's Story, New York, Simon & Schus-
       ter, 1951.   Geraldine Farrar, who made her debut at the Manhattan
       in 1906, also wrote an autobiography, Such Sweet Compulsion, New
       York, Greystone Press, 1938.)   Appendices include complete casts
       for the New York and Philadelphia seasons.   Index.

157.   SHEEAN, Vincent.   Oscar Hammerstein I: the life and ex-
ploits of an impresario; with a preface by Oscar Hammerstein II.   New York: Simon & Schuster, 1956.   363p.
illus.

_____.   The amazing Oscar Hammerstein: the life and ex-
ploits of an impresario ...   London: Weidenfeld & Nicolson, 1956.   363p.   illus.

This biography of the flamboyant, indomitable genius, whose
single-minded dedication to opera revolutionized operatic standards in
America in the first decade of the 20th century, is a fascinating tale
of musical and theatrical enterprise.   Sheean sees him as having a
personality "to which the people intuitively respond whenever and
wherever it appears" (p. 5), and his biography, with its accounts of
Hammerstein's successive enterprises, his fortunes that changed
dramatically almost as often as the wind ("he dealt in millions but
he borrowed from newsboys"--p. 8), and his brilliance as an impresario at his Manhattan Opera House, makes abundantly plain
why he was so well-known a figure in New York.   Yet, for all his
notoriety, as the author admits, "nobody claims to have known him,"
and Sheean stops short of penetrating too deeply himself.   Hammerstein's whole life is covered, from his birth in Germany and his arrival in America in 1862--a "classic" immigrant: penniless and
hopeful--to the buying out of his opera company in 1910, his London
opera house's failure, and his death in 1919.   Special attention, as
one would expect, is given to the era of the Manhattan Opera Company, in which Hammerstein realized his greatest dream.   Index.

(iii)   Other Regions

158.   ARMSTRONG, W. G.   A record of the opera in Philadelphia.
Philadelphia: Porter & Coates, 1884.   274p.

These annals of the "lyrical presentations" staged in Philadelphia from 1825 to 1883 demonstrate the vigorous nature of the city's
operatic life.   Armstrong proceeds chronologically, giving precise
date, opera title, performers, and frequent notes and comments
(e.g., "Shrival, the tenor, was so wretched that the performance
left no impression on me").   The dominating influence of Italian
opera is clearly apparent, though the first performance of "Leonora,"
in 1845, is duly noted.   There is an index of artists and operas,
and an appendix lists performances by various musical societies in
Philadelphia from 1833 to 1878.

159.   DAVIS, Ronald L.   A history of opera in the American West.
Englewood Cliffs: Prentice-Hall, 1965.   178p.   illus.,
bibliog.   notes.

Davis' object is to demonstrate that "while the Metropolitan
may still be the recognized guardian of the nation's operatic treasury,
its western siblings possess a freshness and artistic dynamism which
has become increasingly apparent" (p. 154).   He admits his definition of the West is "unconventional ... covering everything west of
and including Chicago and New Orleans" (p. vii), though within this
vast slice of territory he covers only the major companies.   Two

chapters are devoted to New Orleans (from the end of the 18th century to the mid-20th), two to Chicago (1850-1950), two to San Francisco (from 1851), one to Dallas, one to Central City, Colorado, and Santa Fe, and a concluding chapter to San Antonio. The tone is kept light, though there is considerable detail. Index.

d. Musical Instruments

160.　BOWERS, Q. David. Put another nickel in: a history of coin-operated pianos and orchestrions. New York: Vestal Press, 1966. 248p. illus.
　　　This history focuses particular attention on the business and commercial side of mechanical instruments in the U.S. Following a short account of the instruments in Europe in the 18th and 19th centuries, the author recounts the story of the development of particular instruments in America from the late 19th century to about 1930, and of the business ventures involved. The Wurlitzer firm and its various instruments are described in detail. The book is extensively illustrated with photographs and reproductions of advertisements, and concludes with a photo collection of the various instruments that survive in public and private collections. Bowers is also the compiler of Encyclopedia of Automatic Instruments (New York: Vestal Press, 1972), and A Guidebook of Automatic Musical Instruments (New York: Vestal Press, 1967).

161.　LOESSER, Arthur. Men, women and pianos: a social history. New York: Simon & Schuster, 1954; London: Gollancz, 1955. 654p. bibliog.
　　　Loesser's thoroughly readable history relates the growth in the use of the piano in particular countries to the musical life of the country as a whole, and to contemporary historical and social events. Section 6 is devoted to the United States, an account of some 140 pages covering the piano in America to the end of the 19th century. Particular attention is paid to the growth in the domestic manufacture of pianos, culminating in the success of both the Steinway and Chickering firms at the Paris Exposition of 1867. The author also relates such stories as that of the businesslike Joseph P. Hall, who made pianos that more people could afford, and the technical innovations with a two-tier keyboard of Hungarian Paul von Janko, an idea converted into practice by the firm of Decker Bros., but which failed to take a hold. Developments in piano repertoire and the achievements and influence of pianists such as Gottschalk are also discussed.

162.　OCHSE, Orpha. The history of the organ in the United States. Bloomington: Indiana University Press, 1975. 512p. bibliog.
　　　A scholarly history, in which technical development of the organ in America is set against a lively picture of the social and musical background. Various questions relating to the design and construction of modern instruments are discussed in the latter part of the book. Index.

163.   SPILLANE, Daniel. History of the American pianoforte: its technical development and the trade. New York: the author, 1890. 369p. illus.

———————. —————— ; new introduction by Rita Benton. New York: Da Capo. 383p. illus.

Irish-born Spillane describes his history as the first to treat the piano in America "from the technical, historical, industrial, national and personal standpoints" (p. ix); the impressive, painstakingly accumulated data came from "city directories, patent offices, contemporary newspapers, journals, and diaries, proceedings of early scholarly societies ... and ... miscellaneous documents stored in historical societies dating from the colonial and early Federal periods" (p. xii)--though he omits a list of sources. The early chapters survey the origin of the instrument, its first importation into America, and the first piano made in the colonies (by John Behrent of Philadelphia). From this point, as musical independence grew, Spillane proceeds mainly city-by-city, describing developments in instrument-making in Boston, New York, Philadelphia, Charleston, Baltimore and Albany as well as in other cities to a lesser extent; he also considers the influence of the music press on piano manufacturers. An appendix lists chronologically the important patents, 1796-1890. The reprint edition adds an index.

e.   Publishing

164.   AYARS, Christine Merrick. Contributions to the art of music in America by the music industries of Boston, 1640 to 1936. New York: Wilson, 1937. (Repr. New York: Johnson, 1969). 326p. bibliog.

A historical and contemporary survey of Boston's music publishers, engravers, printers and instrument makers, full of details about lesser-known figures in the musical life of the North East. Based on published information, on correspondence, and on interviews, the book chronicles first the development of publishing in Boston from the Bay Psalm Book and other early ventures, through the busy 19th century to the 1930s, giving brief accounts of the history of numerous enterprises, dividing the contemporary scene into general, educational and specializing publishers, and providing a list of music journals with descriptions. The short section on engraving and printing describes the development of techniques and lists the various firms, with details. Historical and contemporary information is also given in Part 3, which divides instrument makers into groups by instrument: piano; organ; bells; band, orchestra, fretted and miscellaneous. Appendices are devoted to supplementary information on instrument manufacturers, and to a catalog of interesting instruments and where they may be seen. The extensive bibliography is mainly devoted to material on instruments. There is a general index and an index of publications mentioned.

165.   BOARD OF MUSIC TRADE OF THE UNITED STATES OF AMERICA. Complete catalogue of sheet music and musical works published by the Board of Music Trade. (New York,

1870) (Repr. New York: Da Capo, 1973). 573p.

Publishers' catalogs can be a valuable source of information on the quality of life of a given period, and so it is with this one, a joint effort representing 20 music publishers, and reflecting something of the variety of musical life, particularly in the home, in the second half of the 19th century. It is a huge title list arranged in classified groups, with large sections of, for example, guitar and piano music; the list of solo songs in English occupies 150 double-column pages. (Quite incidentally, the whole thing is a monument to good business sense and cooperation; even without any composer listing it stands as a lesson and reproach to contemporary music publishing.)

166. EPSTEIN, Dena J. Music publishing in Chicago before 1871: the firm of Root and Cady, 1858-1871. Detroit: Information Coordinators, 1969. (Detroit Studies in Music Bibliography, No. 14) 243p. bibliog.

At once a historical study and a reference work, this book focuses on a firm that played a significant part in the developing musical life of the Mid-West. The historical part of the study comprises a survey of Chicago publishers other than Root and Cady, biographical portraits of composer/educator George Frederick Root (1826-1895), brother Ebenezer Towner Root (1822-1896), and partner Chauncey Marvin Cady (1824-1889), and an account of the firm from 1858, through the Civil War--the era of its biggest expansion--to bankruptcy following the Chicago fire. Reference material covers four appendices: a checklist of the firm's plate numbers, and a list of copyrighted works without plate numbers; a composer index to the plate numbers of sheet music (in which the firm specialized, and among which a large number of American songwriters are represented); a subject index (e.g., Civil War, Reconstruction); a directory of the music trade in Chicago (names, addresses, dates) before 1871. Index.

167. FISHER, William Arms. Notes on music in old Boston. Boston: Ditson, 1918. 96p. illus.
. One hundred and fifty years of music publishing in the United States: an historical sketch with special reference to the pioneer publisher, Oliver Ditson Company, Inc., 1783-1933. Boston: Ditson, 1933. (Repr. Grosse Pointe: Scholarly Press, 1971). 146p. illus.

The second of these books is "a revision and extension of the earlier work, broadening its scope and excluding many pages no longer relevant" (footnote to preface). Coverage is widened beyond the confines of Boston to encompass the development of music publishing elsewhere in America, and to set the Boston story in the context of that development. Thus a survey of the first music shops and publishers in Philadelphia, Baltimore and New York precedes the central account of publishing activity in Boston from the 18th century, through the foundation of the Ditson firm in 1835 to its purchase by Presser in 1931. Further developments in other cities (including Cincinnati and Chicago) in the 19th century are also chronicled. The many portraits add to the value of a most informative book.

168.   HARWELL, Richard B. Confederate music. Chapel Hill: University of North Carolina Press, 1950. 184p. illus., bibliogs.

The immense amount of songwriting and publishing that took place within the borders of the Confederacy is a particularly interesting facet of its cultural history. Harwell's historical and bibliographical record centers on the activities of the music publishers, of whom he has extensive knowledge. A bibliography of sheet music provides full bibliographical information for approximately 650 titles; from this the author is able to recreate the musical world of the Confederacy as shown, for example, in Dan Emmett's "Dixie" (and the question marks surrounding its authorship), the careers of Harry B. MaCarthy and James Ryder Randall, the songs describing a soldier's life in the war, and the stories behind numerous songs that became popular.

169.   KROHN, Ernst C. Music publishing in the Middle Western states before the Civil War. Detroit: Information Coordinators, 1972. (Detroit Studies in Music Bibliography, No. 23) 44p. bibliog. notes.

A preliminary survey of sheet music publishing in St. Louis, Cincinnati, Louisville, Detroit, Cleveland, and Chicago. The author notes that the chief obstacle to further research is the lack of indexes of publishers, dates and cities in the various library collections.

f.   Education

170.   BIRGE, Edward Bailey. History of public school music in the United States. Boston: Ditson, 1928. 296p. illus. _____. _____; new and augmented ed. Philadelphia: Ditson, 1937. 323p. illus., bibliog.

Birge declares that this history "endeavors to describe merely the main trend of the evolution of public school music, and to account as far as possible for the direction this evolution has taken" (preface). Beginning with the development of the singing school in the 18th century he follows this evolution through the establishment of music education in the Boston schools (and the part played by Lowell Mason), a period of "pioneering" (1838-1861) in which Boston's pattern of progress was reproduced elsewhere, a rise in the standard of teaching (1861-1885), a period of attention to problems of music reading (1885-1905), to the 20th century, marked by the many-sided nature of public school music, and the development of teachers' associations (particularly the work of the Music Supervisors' National Conference). Index.

171.   IVEY, William. A dose of reality therapy: university musicianship in a commercial world. (Nashville: Country Music Foundation, 1973?) 20p.

In an address originally published in the National Association of Schools of Music Proceedings for 1972 the Director of the Country Music Foundation in Nashville makes out a case for the usefulness of commercial music--music performed for profit--in university music education. He bases this on a view of commercial music as an eclectic art form, selecting and continuing, from a wide variety of styles, "musical trademarks which are culturally meaningful." He also urges music education to re-style music programs in recognition of the commercial world of professional music.

172. RIKER, Charles. The Eastman School of Music: its first quarter century, 1921-1946. Rochester: University of Rochester Press, 1946. 99p. illus.
A short history of the distinguished music school, its various departments and activities. The appendices include honors and awards, and faculty publications.

173. SEWARD, Theodore F. The educational work of Dr. Lowell Mason. Published works of Dr. Mason. Lowell Mason, by A. W. Thayer. n.p. (1878?) 32p.
Pupil, collaborator and friend, Seward summarizes Mason's achievement in music education, describing how he "educated the American people out of a false and into a true style of sacred music" with his various collections, his pioneering of systematic music instruction for children, and his part in creating the music convention. (Not all would agree; c.f., Lucas, no. 216.) Thayer's eight-page appreciation is reprinted from Dwight's Journal of Music.

174. SOLLINGER, Charles. String class publications in the United States, 1851-1951. Detroit: Information Co-ordinators, 1974. (Detroit Studies in Music Bibliography, No. 30) 71p.
Sollinger's bibliography opens the door to an interesting approach to the study of music education in America. In a historical introduction he describes the origins of instrumental class teaching, the work of Lewis A. Benjamin in the second half of the 19th century, and the development of class teaching in the conservatories and the public schools. The bibliography itself--which aims to be comprehensive for string class methods, and selective in areas showing the influence of the system and in published solutions to problems teachers encountered--is divided into sections: class methods for beginners on stringed instruments; string class methods with a special purpose; music for string class instruction and performance; music for instruction and performance suitable for string class instruction; books for teachers concerning string class teaching techniques, 1891-1951; string class methods and materials published in other countries. Entries include notes, which are often quotations from the publications themselves.

g. Phonograph

175. ASSOCIATION OF RECORDED SOUND COLLECTIONS. Program Committee. A preliminary directory of sound recordings collections in the United States and Canada. New York: New York Public Library, 1967. 157p.
A listing of private individuals and institutions alphabetically

under states. Where complete information was made available to the compiler the entry gives addresses, curator's name (for institutions), scope of the collection, special subjects, type of recordings, size of collections, note on cataloging, indication of willingness to exchange, references to articles on the collections, and additional notes. Many of the collections have an American bias of some kind, but there is no subject index to help in locating them.

176.   CHEW, V. K.   Talking machines, 1887-1914: some aspects of the early history of the gramophone.   London: H. M. S. O., 1967.   (A Science Museum Book) 80p.   illus., bibliog.
A short history of the technical development of the gramophone, including its invention and exploitation in the U.S. up to 1902, and the subsequent dealings in Europe of American companies, as far as 1914.   There are numerous illustrations of instruments and people closely connected with its history.

177.   CONVENTION OF LOCAL PHONOGRAPH COMPANIES OF THE UNITED STATES, 1890.   Proceedings.   Milwaukee, 1890. (Repr. Nashville: Country Music Foundation Press, 1974). 210p.
A glimpse into the early history of the phonograph, when the recording industry still had little idea of the direction it was to take. Much of the discussion at this convention was taken up by the role of the cylinder phonograph in business and by aspects of its production. Demonstrating the value of their product, the delegates had their proceedings recorded on cylinders, from which the transcript was compiled.   The reprint has an introduction by Raymond R. Wile, and an essay by Oliver Read and Walter Welch.

178.   GELATT, Roland.   The fabulous phonograph: from tin foil to high fidelity.   Philadelphia: Lippincott, 1955.   320p. illus.
_____.   : the story of the gramophone from tin foil to high fidelity.   London: Cassell, 1956.   250p.   illus.
_____.   : from Edison to stereo.   Rev. ed.   New York: Appleton-Century, 1965.   336p.   illus.
The standard work and an engrossing narrative, tracing the development of sound recording from its beginnings in the U.S. and France along three main lines: the scientific, business and musical aspects.   The first two appear first, being joined by the third about the turn of the century.   Each technical and commercial development is chronicled in a non-technical style.   The author is not concerned in any detail with social aspects and implications.   The revised edition contains a supplementary chapter on the decade 1955-1965, dealing with tape-recording and stereo.

179.   READ, Oliver, and WELCH, Walter L.   From tin foil to stereo: evolution of the phonograph.   Indianapolis: Howard W. Sams, 1959.   524p.   illus., bibliog.
An immensely detailed history of the development of sound recording from pre-Edison days to hi-fi, with particular attention to technical aspects, and to the growth of the phonograph and record-

ing industries. The large number of illustrations include many pictures of early machines as well as reproductions of advertisements, and photographs of recording sessions and of pioneers in the field. The bibliography lists technical books, texts and articles from a musician's viewpoint, articles and reports. Index.

B.   THE MUSICAL TRADITION TO 1800

(See also nos. 38, 41.)

1.   General Works on Psalmody and the Puritans

180.   BROOKS, Henry M.   Olden-time music: a compilation from newspapers and books; with an introduction by Edward S. Morse.   Boston: Ticknor, 1888.   (Repr. New York: AMS Press, 1973).   283p.   illus.
An interesting attempt to illuminate the musical life of a period with contemporary documents.   Brooks himself makes no historical interpretations, but groups extracts from the books, journals, newspapers, announcements and advertisements to describe aspects of sacred and secular music-making in New England (especially Boston and Salem) from the Puritans to 1830.   There are accounts of singing schools, societies, concerts and choirs; a chapter is devoted to Billings, and there is considerable attention to early keyboard instruments.   A reliance on Ritter's history (no. 20) is evident in Brooks' own linking narrative.   Index.

181.   HOOD, George.   A history of music in New England; with biographical sketches of Reformers and Psalmists.   Boston: Wilkins, Carter, 1846.   (Repr. New York: Johnson, 1970).   250p.
Though subsequent historians of New England psalmody have held views at variance with Hood (1807-1882), who was a staunch supporter of the movement to reform church music associated with Mason, Hastings, and others, he pointed the way by discovering and examining original sources, and by including generous portions of contemporary texts (especially regarding regular singing) in his book. (Scholes, cross about the inaccuracy of the title, remarks: "in the case of this oft-quoted work silence is more eloquent than words" [no. 184, p. 7], but Hood does state in his preface that his work "pretends only to be a history of psalmody.")
There are four sections.   The first is a historical outline of New England psalmody to 1745, with much attention to John Cotton, and to the reforming zeal of John Tufts, Thomas Walter, etc., and an emphasis on the need to connect developments in psalmody with the history of the church.   The second section continues the history by listing chronologically and commenting upon important books of the period 1741-1799.   This is followed by an account of the origins of choirs, including a résumé of the lining-out controversies.   The

concluding part is devoted to the biographical sketches, with data collected partly from books and partly from correspondence. Here Hood makes plain his view that progress in sacred music is evidence of a divine scheme to establish in America a purer church. (Johannes Riedel contributes an interesting preface to the reprint edition.)

182.   MacDOUGALL, Hamilton C. Early New England psalmody: an
        historical appreciation, 1620-1820. Brattleboro: Daye,
        1940. (Repr. New York: Da Capo, 1969). 177p. illus.,
        bibliog. notes.
        A study of the music of the New England Pilgrims and Puritans, tracing its sources in European Protestantism and psalters, its arrival and development in the colonies, from the first independent textual compilation employing European music to the evolution of an independent musical tradition with William Billings and others, and the eventual decline of this tradition with the arrival of a number of European musicians at the dawn of the 19th century. MacDougall identifies and describes the work of numerous individuals, from John Tufts to Andrew Law, but avoids both biographical information and musical analysis. His principal concern is with musical practice, standards and values, which he attempts to judge "by twentieth century taste" (preface). Included in his coverage are such topics as the singing school and notational experiments. Music examples appear in one of the several appendices, and there is also an index.

183.   METCALF, Frank J. American psalmody; or, Titles of books
        containing tunes printed in America from 1721 to 1820.
        New York: Charles F. Heartman, 1917. (Repr. New
        York: Da Capo, 1968). 54p. illus.
        Not a full bibliography, but a useful aid to identification of 18th century sacred music from John Tufts on, excluding German books originating in or around Ephrata. Metcalf's list, which he based on Warrington (no. 185), is arranged in one alphabetical sequence by composer (or title for collections). The brief information given includes place and date of publication, location of copies if known (or mention in Evans), and occasional notes. Dates of some composers are also given.

184.   SCHOLES, Percy A. The Puritans and music in England and
        New England: a contribution to the cultural history of two
        nations. Oxford: Clarendon Press, 1934. 428p. illus.,
        bibliog.
        An interesting and lively study that states and systematically refutes the charge that the Puritans in England and America were basically anti-musical, except where music aided worship. Scholes' description of the richness of musical life on both sides of the Atlantic makes convincing reading, but his objectivity in handling his evidence has been doubted (Haraszti, no. 191, p. 63). Eleven appendices give further details of various aspects of this musical activity, and there is also a glossary of terms used by writers of the period, an index of works cited, a subject index in 14 sections, an index of persons and another of places. (For a challenge to Scholes'

thesis, see Cyclone Covey, "Puritanism and Music in Colonial America," William and Mary Quarterly, 3rd Series, 9/1, January 1952.)

185. WARRINGTON, James. Short titles of books relating to or illustrating the history and practice of psalmody in the United States, 1620-1820. Philadelphia: privately printed, 1898. (Repr. New York: Franklin, 1972). 96p.
      This modest booklet contains a list which was to have formed the basis of a historical study of American psalmody up to the era of the ascendancy of Thomas Hastings and Lowell Mason. The compiler states that he made the list public in order to induce interested persons to report omissions. Chronologically arranged by date of publication (from 1538 to 1898), the abbreviated bibliography lists psalters, tune books, hymnals, books, pamphlets and, occasionally, articles, giving short titles, with place and date of publication. All editions are listed under the year of the first. Coverage includes numerous background books on Puritan history. There are no indexes. Metcalf (no. 183) based his listing on Warrington.

2. 17th Century Psalmody

186. AINSWORTH, Henry. The book of Psalmes: Englished both in prose and metre; with annotations, opening the words and sentences, by conference with other scriptures. Amsterdam: Giles Thorp, 1612. 342p.
      The psalter was brought over by the Pilgrims in 1620, and used at Plymouth until the end of the century, when it was superseded by the Bay Psalm Book, in use at Massachusetts Bay from 1640. Described by Chase (no. 25) as "a document fully worthy to be the cornerstone of America's music," it was compiled in Holland for the English Separatists, and contains prose translations of the Psalms, with notes and metrical arrangements. It also includes 39 tunes, a majority of which are French in origin. Later editions were published in 1617, 1626, 1639, 1644 and 1690.

187. PRATT, Waldo Selden. The music of the Pilgrims: a description of the Psalm-book brought to Plymouth in 1620. Boston: Ditson, 1921. (Repr. New York: Russell & Russell, 1971). 80p. bibliog.
      Pratt's brief study of the Ainsworth Psalter describes its history and contents, some literary aspects, and the characteristics of its music, which he sees as vivacity and variety of rhythm and meter, demonstrating strong links with folk song style. The significance of this is that the psalter preserves "the naive freshness of song that was characteristic of Protestantism at its youthful stage." Unfortunately, its influence was restricted and its prestige overshadowed by the Bay Psalm Book (of less "intrinsic importance"), which severely limited the variety of meter, and by an attendant growth in the importance of homiletics over corporate worship, bringing about a debilitation of congregational song. The study also gives

the 39 tunes from the psalter, with a single stanza of regularly used text, and some notes.

BAY PSALM BOOK

188. THE WHOLE BOOKE OF PSALMES faithfully translated into English metre. Whereunto is prefixed a discourse declaring not only the lawfullnes, but also the necessity of the heavenly ordinance of singing scripture psalmes in the churches of God. (Cambridge): Imprinted (by Stephen Daye), 1640. (Repr. Chicago: University of Chicago Press, 1956). 148p.
THE PSALMS HYMNS AND SPIRITUAL SONGS OF THE OLD AND NEW TESTAMENT, faithfully translated into English metre, for the use, edification, and comfort, of the Saints, in publick, & private. Especially in New-England. Cambridge: Printed by Samuel Green, 1651. 314p. [3rd. ed.
THE PSALMS HYMNS AND SPIRITUAL SONGS ... Boston: Printed by B. Green, and J. Allen, 1698. 420p. [9th. ed
This, the first book printed in the English colonies of North America--though it contained not a note of music until later editions --exercised a considerable influence on music in New England. The psalter had its origins in Puritan dissatisfaction with the translations of the psalms in the Sternhold and Hopkins version then in common use. The new translations were prepared by a committee of 30, and the resulting volume was immediately adopted in the Massachusetts Bay Colony (hence its popular name, the Bay Psalm Book). The seventeen meters used in Sternhold and Hopkins were reduced to six, three of which--common (8686), long (8888) and short (6686)--predominated; this development "had the practical result of pronouncing the death sentence in New England upon almost all the old Genevan tunes" (Lowens, no. 38, p. 29). In place of music there was an "admonition," instructing the reader to use, for common meter psalms, tunes in Thomas Ravenscroft's Whole Booke of Psalmes (London, 1621), and, for others, tunes in Sternhold and Hopkins (referred to as "our english psalm books"). The 3rd edition for which the title was changed, was the basis of all subsequent editions for over a century (Lowens, p. 32). It further increased the number of common meter texts. With the 9th edition music is included for the first time--thirteen tunes in two-part arrangements, derived from John Playford's A Brief Introduction to the Skill of Musicke (London, 1654, and later eds.). They are given in fasola notation (from Playford's 1672 ed.). Lowens (pp. 36-7) suspects the unknown compiler of not being a New Englander at all, and postulates an English edition with tunes of about 1689.

189. APPEL, Richard G. The music of the Bay Psalm Book, 9th edition (1698). Brooklyn: Institute for Studies in American Music, 1975. (I.S.A.M. Monographs, No. 5) 43p. bibliog.
This small volume performs a valuable service in providing facsimiles of the tune supplement to the first known edition of the Bay Psalm Book to contain music, and of the prefatory remarks,

with clear edited transcriptions on the facing pages. There is also a concise discussion of the music of the Bay Psalm Book, with a facsimile of the "admonition" concerning tunes to use that appeared in the first edition of 1640.

190. FOOTE, Henry Wilder. An account of the Bay Psalm Book. New York: Hymn Society of America, 1940. (Papers of the Hymn Society, No. 7) 18p.
A booklet containing a short history of the psalter, an appreciation of the text, and a brief consideration of the music associated with it and of Puritan musical practice.

191. HARASZTI, Zoltan. The enigma of the Bay Psalm Book. Chicago: University of Chicago Press, 1956. 143p. bibliog. notes.
Written to accompany the facsimile reprint (no. 188), this scholarly study is mainly concerned with the text of the psalter. It describes the situation which led up to the new translation, and examines the question of authorship by means of a textual analysis. There is a chapter on the psalm singing of the Puritans which describes their approach to music, other types of music in the colonies, and the use of music with the first and subsequent editions of the Bay Psalm Book.

JOHN COTTON

192. COTTON, John. Singing of Psalms, a gospel ordinance. Or, a Treatise wherein are handled these foure particulars. 1. Touching the duty itselfe. 2. Touching the matter to be sung. 3. Touching the singers. 4. Touching the manner of singing. London: Printed by M. S. for Hannah Allen at the Crowne in Pope's Head Alley..., 1647. 72p.
The author of this important document for the Puritan attitude to music in New England was a "Puritan scholastic steeped in medieval habits of thought" (Haraszti, no. 191, p. 20), who left England in 1633. "Cast out into a wilderness," as he himself put it, Cotton (1584-1652) was closely involved in the genesis of the Bay Psalm Book, and, as Haraszti shows, was the author of its Preface. His tract is concerned with four aspects of music in worship in the wake of the new psalter, and with the potential conflict between aesthetic and devotional ("ceremoniall" and "morall") claims of the art. The first question is whether music should be used at all. Citing scriptural authority (his basic procedure), Cotton demonstrates that "singing of Psalmes with a lively voyce, is an holy Duty of Gods worship" (p. 2). Concerning the second topic given in his title Cotton rejects the notion that "such spiritual Songs, as shall be endited by the personnall (but ordinary) gifts of any ordinary officer or member of the Church" may be used in worship; only scriptural songs have a place. (In an interesting passage on music outside worship, Cotton allows that "any private Christian, who hath a gift to frame a spirituall Song, may both frame it, and sing it privately, for his own private comfort" [p. 15], adding, "Nor doe we forbid the private use of an Instrument of Musick therewithall; so that attention to the

Instrument doe not divert the heart from attention to the matter of the song.") Turning to who shall sing, Cotton declares the whole church should participate, women included. On the manner of singing, Cotton defends the use of English metrical tunes, and of contemporary melodies ("such grave and melodious tunes, as doe well befit both the holinesse and the gravitie of the matter" [p. 54]). He also--reluctantly--concedes that the practice of lining-out should continue, "that so they who want either booke or skill to reade, may know what it is to be sung, and joyne with the rest in the dutie of singing" (p. 62). Throughout the book Cotton uses the objection-and-answer method to dispose of opposing arguments (most of which propose far more restrictions than he does), and his final section answers objections brought from the ancient practice of the "Primitive Churches."

3. Regular Singing*

193.   (SYMMES, Thomas). The reasonableness of, regular singing, or, singing by note; in an essay, to revive the true and ancient mode of singing psalm-tunes, according to the pattern in our New-England psalm-books; the knowledge and practice of which is greatly decay'd in most congregations. Writ by a minister of the gospel. Perused by several ministers in the town and country; and published with the approbation of all who have read it. Boston: Printed by B. Green for Samuel Gerrish, 1720. 22p.

During the first decades of the 18th century in New England there had grown up among clergymen a strong desire to see improvement in congregational singing. The number of tunes in general use had declined; no one could read music, hence the ubiquitous practice of "lining-out" (in which the congregation repeats each line as it is sung by a leading singer), which encouraged great liberties to be taken with each tune (or so it seemed to the clergymen, who saw no virtue in any of these improvisations). The campaign for musical reform combined the objectives of teaching strict adherence to music as notated ("regular singing") and of musical literacy (for the sacred individuality of each note could only be learned when the note itself could be recognized). Rev. Thomas Symmes (1678-1725), of Bradford, Massachusetts, became with this pamphlet one of the leading voices in the reform movement (and one of the most readable of its writers). He defines "singing by note" (which, he maintains, is the original New England practice--"Your usual way of singing is but of yesterday, an upstart novelty"), and while maintaining a critical attitude to the contemporary singing style, gives an account of its development in the 18th century, and describes its characteristics. As Gilbert Chase points out, he does even more than this: "Rev. Thomas Symmes is truly invaluable; what he tells us is interesting,

*This section is basically chronological

but what he reveals between the lines is priceless" (no. 25, p. 29); this revelation is precisely how the early folk tradition of New England was formed. (Biographical data on Symmes appears in a contemporary account, A Particular Plain and Brief Memorative Account of the Reverend Thomas Symmes, Boston, S. Gerrish, 1726.)

194. MATHER, Cotton. The accomplished singer. Instructions first, how the piety of singing with a true devotion, may be obtained and expressed; the glorious God after an uncommon manner glorified in it, and his people edified. Intended for the assistance of all that would sing psalms with grace in their hearts; but more particularly to accompany the laudable endeavours of those who are learning to sing by rule, and seeking to preserve a regular singing in the assemblies of the faithful. With an attestation from Dr. Increase Mather. Boston: Printed by B. Green for S. Gerrish, 1721. 24p.

With this small tract the famous Puritan clergyman Cotton Mather (1663-1728) lent his considerable influence to the cause of regular singing. In general he is more concerned with historical and theological aspects of the subject than with practical instructions, leaving those to his nephew Thomas Walter (no. 197), and to John Tufts (no. 196). His criticism of congregational singing, while unmistakable, is not so condemnatory as that of his contemporaries; he speaks of singing as having "degenerated into an odd noise."

195. JONES, Matt B. Some bibliographical notes on Cotton Mather's "The accomplished singer." Boston, 1933. 9p. illus., bibliog. notes.

An extract from the Publications of the Colonial Society of Massachusetts, Vol. XXVIII, describing briefly the conditions of psalmody in New England in 1720, the bibliographical features of Mather's work and its relation to Thomas Walter's tunebook (no. 197).

196. TUFTS, John. An introduction to the singing of psalm-tunes, in a plain and easy method. With a collection of tunes in three parts. 5th ed. Boston: Printed for S. Gerrish, 1726. (Repr. Philadelphia: Musical Americana [Harry Dichter], 1954.) 9, 12p.

In all the concern among the New England Puritans in the early 18th century over the state of congregational singing and the lack of musical knowledge, Rev. John Tufts (1689-1750) of Newbury, Mass. was the first to make a practical effort to improve matters by providing some rudimentary instructions in reading music, and a sample of unharmonized tunes. Of his little book, the first book of music instruction published in America, Irving Lowens remarked: "If one were to choose any single event to mark the beginning of organized music education in America, it would be the publication of this modest work" (no. 38, p. 39). (In his foreword to the 1954 facsimile Lowens describes the work as "the foundation stone of the singing school movement....") The date of the first edition has been long disputed (the earliest suggested date being 1710) and remains uncertain. The weight of opinion favors 1721. This edition apparently contained 20 psalm tunes. By the 5th edition, the earliest extant, that number had increased to 37, given in three-part harmony and in letteral notation. It is likely that Tufts' book also contains the first piece of music composed and published in the American colonies-- a psalm tune (100 Psalm Tune New) possibly by Tufts himself. (For an informed discussion of the history and significance of Tufts' work and an analysis of its contents, see Chapter 3 in Lowens book. For biographical information, see Metcalf, no. 62.)

197.   WALTER, Thomas. The grounds and rules of musick explained; or, An introduction to the art of singing by note. Fitted to the meanest capacities. Recommended by several ministers. Boston: Printed by J. Franklin for S. Gerrish, 1721. 25p, 16ℓ.

This, the second tunebook published in America (Tufts being the first), has the distinction of having been the first music book printed in the colonies to have bar lines. Whereas Tufts used letteral notation, Walter used diamond-shaped notes, and presented the tunes in three-part harmony from the outset. Thomas Walter (1695-1725), a nephew of Cotton Mather, was pastor of Roxbury, Massachusetts, a popular, sharp-witted young preacher who died of tuberculosis at the age of 29. With his book of instructions on singing "by note" (i.e., exactly as notated, with no liberties taken) and collection of 24 English psalm and hymn tunes he joined his famous uncle and other New England clergymen in the campaign for musical literacy and against the prevalent style of congregational singing. His command of rhetoric is obvious: "many Men, without any other Tutor, may be able to strike upon a few notes tolerably; yet this bears no more Proportion to a Tune composed and sung by the Rules of Art than the vulgar Hedge Notes of every Rustic does to the Harp of David. Witness the modern Performance both in the Theatres and the Temple" (p. 1-2). (A line of argument, based upon a particular interpretation of what constitutes "art," that occurs again and again, in different contexts, in America's musical history.) Larger than Tufts, Walter's book was also more widely used, remaining popular for 40 years, during which time it went to six editions (described in Jones, no. 198). By the 5th (1760) the number of tunes had increased to 40. (A pamphlet by Walter entitled The Sweet Psalmist of Israel, Boston, J. Franklin for S. Gerrish, 1722, contains the text of a sermon in which he declares the three-part harmony used in his tunebook to have been the type used in biblical days.)

198.   JONES, Matt B. Bibliographical notes on Thomas Walter's "Grounds and rules of musick explained." Worcester, Mass.: American Antiquarian Society, 1933. 14p.

A biographical sketch of Walter is followed by a detailed description of each of the six editions of his tunebook. Locations are given of known copies. (Reprinted from the Proceedings of the American Antiquarian Society for October, 1932.)

199.   SYMMES, Thomas. Utile dulci, Or, a joco-serious dialogue, concerning regular singing: calculated for a particular

town (where it was publickly had, on Friday Oct. 12 1722.)
but may serve some other places in the same climate.
Boston: Printed by B. Green for Samuel Gerrish, 1723.
59p.

Symmes' highly entertaining follow-up to his first pamphlet
gives an excellent idea of the controversy aroused by the movement
to reform singing. It takes the form of an imagined conversation
between a clergyman advocating regular singing (himself) and a neighbor opposing it. Though the neighbor comes off decidedly the worse
for Symmes' powers of argument and ridicule, each of his objections
being demolished with great fervor, his words provide some insight
into the feelings of ordinary people. Among other things, he objects
to regular singing because it is not so melodious and pleasant as
the usual way, has too many tunes, causes people "to behave themselves indecently and disorderly," is "Quakerish and Popish and in-
troductive of instrumental musick," gives names to the notes that
are "bawdy and blasphemous" ("as the fool thinketh, so the bell
clinketh," replies Symmes), is sung by young people anywhere, including the "Plow and Cart" ("they make nothing to sing part of a
psalm tune and then, cry, "St'r up Darby"--nay, they'll sing Fa,
Sol, La in the Tavern"). By the time the battered neighbor retires
from the fray, converted by some over-the-garden-wall oratory that
would make most 20th century neighbors move house, Symmes has
also told a good deal about what the regular singing movement was
accomplishing.

200.   CHAUNCEY, Nathaniel. Regular singing defended, and proved
       to be the only true way of singing the songs of the Lord;
       by arguments both from reason and scripture: having been
       heard and approved of, by the General Association at Hart-
       ford, May the 12th 1727 with their recommendation of it
       to the publick. New London: Printed and sold by T.
       Green, 1728. 54p.

Of the various campaigners for the reform of congregational
music, Rev. Chauncey (1681-1756) is the most outspoken critic of
the "country way of singing." The situation for him is sharply defined in black and white; to admit shades of grey would be heresy.
His polemical little pamphlet, highly serious in tone and somewhat
turgid in style, puts foreward 16 arguments for the absolute correct-
ness of regular singing (strict adherence to the music as written),
arguments which rest substantially on his having correctly interpreted
the mind of the Almighty on the subject, for it is as a divine rule
to guide in the performance of duty that he advocates this singing
method ("one certain rule" is a favorite phrase): worship is a discipline, and singing, as part of worship ("the command to sing")
should be a discipline too. Five typical objections are dealt with at
the end; these, at least, reveal something of the opposition's opinions
(we have no written record from the pens of the country singers).
Three objections are: the country way of singing is more solemn
and becoming; young people fall in with the new way, so it's unlikely
to be the right one; so much bitterness has been aroused, it were
as well the new method had never been heard of.

4. Individual 18th Century Composers

WILLIAM BILLINGS

201.   BARBOUR, James Murray.   The church music of William
            Billings.   East Lansing: Michigan State University Press,
            1960.   167p.   bibliog.
        An analysis of the musical and textual aspects of Billings'
anthems and psalm tunes.   The author examines Billings' choice of
texts, and proceeds, with a wealth of music examples, to analyze
rhythm and metre, melody, counterpoint and harmony, modality and
tonality, concluding with texture and form.   There are six appendices:
an index of psalm tunes, first lines indexes of psalm tunes and anthems, indexes of tunes not by Billings, and sources of secular
examples.   The extensive bibliography includes books and articles,
collections of music, and modern editions.   General index.

202.   McKAY, David, and CRAWFORD, Richard.   William Billings
            of Boston, eighteenth-century composer.   Princeton:
            Princeton University Press, 1975.   303p.   illus., bibliog.
        With this outstanding biographical study we are at last able to
see Billings the man, musician and writer clearly and in remarkable
detail in the context of his time.   The authors' stated aim is "at
every point to describe Billings' life and musical career from the
perspective of the musical tradition in which he worked" (prefatory
note), and in this they are richly successful.   In the manner pioneered
by Sonneck, contemporary materials--public records, private journals,
correspondence, press items, Billings' own and other tunebooks, etc.
--are used, whenever they will shed light on a period or episode in
his life, to establish the cultural context necessary for a balanced
view.   The book opens with a prologue in which the scene is set
with an account of the New England tradition of sacred music which
Billings inherited.   In the biography itself the previously rather scant
information is considerably amplified by numerous discoveries among
contemporary records (made mainly by McKay during over ten years'
research).   One particularly interesting revelation--namely, that
Billings edited the first issue of Boston Magazine (Oct. 1783), before
being ousted--is an interesting instance of the incipient tug-of-war
between the American vernacular and arbiters of cultivated taste
(though the authors admit this was one of Billings' less noteworthy
endeavors).   The pivotal elements in the narrative are Billings' tunebooks, each of which, from New-England Psalm-Singer (1770) to
Continental Harmony (1794) is described and discussed in detail from
historical, bibliographical, textual and stylistic angles.   Analysis of
Billings' music is not attempted, but considerable attention is given
to him as a writer of prose and verse.   The main text concludes
with an account of Billings' changing reputation from his death to
the present.   Supplementary material includes discussions of Billings
and copyright, and of the performance of Billings' music, a bibliography of Billings' works, and of other material in manuscript,
newspaper and book form, and an index.

FRANCIS HOPKINSON, JAMES LYON

203. HASTINGS, George Everett. The life and works of Francis
      Hopkinson. Chicago: University of Chicago Press, 1926.
      516p. illus., bibliog.
      The name of Francis Hopkinson of Philadelphia (1737-1791)--
lawyer, politician, judge of admiralty, signatory of the Declaration
of Independence, designer (according to Hastings) of the U.S. flag,
poet, pamphleteer, satirist, painter, and amateur musician/com-
poser--deserves, at the very least, to be remembered as synony-
mous with 18th century versatility; that this versatility, in his artistic life, was little more than dilettantism, does not detract from
his position (which he claimed for himself) as the first native American composer, and if the gentle arts were, at any rate at the peak
of his professional life, mainly a personal therapy (versatility being,
as Hastings indicates, a clue to his serenity), that is a good indication of the role of secular music in 18th century America. Hasting's lucid, well-documented and objective (but generous) biography
chronicles the course of this busy life, from uncertain beginnings to
a climax during the Revolutionary War, and subsequent private and
professional activities. Hopkinson's various musical efforts are
placed in their biographical context (including what may have been the
first secular American song--"My days have been so wondrous free"),
and questions of authenticity are discussed. Hasting's debt to Sonneck (no. 204) is acknowledged. The texts of various songs and ballads are quoted, with general comment, but there is no attempt at
musical description or analysis. The bibliography lists Hopkinson's
writings in manuscript and published forms, and secondary literature,
and there is a general index.

204. SONNECK, Oscar G. T. Francis Hopkinson, the first Amer-
      ican poet-composer (1737-1791), and James Lyon, patriot,
      preacher, psalmodist (1735-1794): two studies in early
      American music. Washington: Printed by H. L. McQueen,
      1905. (Repr. New York: Da Capo, 1966). 213p. illus.
      These are two excellent monographs in one, on the life, ca-
reer and music of the first two native American composers. Sonneck describes musical life in Philadelphia (Hopkinson's birthplace),
his musical education, his concerts, and his theories on the organ
and harpsichord, concluding with an assessment of his compositions.
What little is known of Lyon's life and career is told, but the author
focuses attention on his publications, especially Urania, the pioneer
tunebook, examining its bibliographical history, describing its contents and investigating its sources. He also traces its influence on
later collections. An appendix contains the music of five pieces by
Hopkinson and two by Lyon, and there is an index. The Da Capo
edition contains a new introduction by Richard Crawford.

ANDREW LAW

205. LAW, Andrew. Essays on music. Philadelphia: Printed for
      the author (by Robert and William Carr), 1814. 24p.
      _____. Essays on music. Hartford: Bowles and Francis,

1821. pp. 25-36.

Singing school teacher, compiler of tunebooks of sacred music from 1779 to 1819, indifferent composer, self-appointed arbiter of musical taste, advocate of the superiority of European over American music, one of the first Americans to be granted copyright protection, and one of the initiators of shape-notation, Andrew Law (1749-1821) occupies a significant position in the musical life of the new Republic. These two short volumes, consecutively paged, contain expressions of his views on music (which he normally proclaimed in the prefaces to his tunebooks). There are four main "numbers" --an examination of the function of music, connecting it with moral feeling; an attack on an unnamed tunebook (identified by Crawford [no. 207] as Eli Roberts' Hartford Collection); a revelation of his own preferences and dislikes in music; and a piece on musical expression. In two short concluding pieces Law responds to criticism of his shape-note system.

206. LAW, Andrew. The musical primer; containing the rules of psalmody, newly revised and improved: together, with a number of practical lessons and plain tunes, designed expressly for the use of learners. Cheshire, Ct.: William Law, 1793. 32p.

This small collection of fourteen simple tunes (probably all Law's own), is significant for its thirteen-page introduction, in which Law introduces the belief that a teacher of music should aim to improve taste as well as instructing people in reading music (a course he subsequently followed closely himself). In a series of short articles he describes how beginners should start, discusses the simplified methods of notation used, expresses his conviction that music should be well performed to achieve its moral and spiritual objectives, and, using voice production as a peg, attacks American singing, and, through that, American music. The primer had several successive editions--1794, 1803 (in shape-notation, and much expanded), 1810 (abbreviated again) and 1817, with a supplement in 1811. (For a detailed discussion, see Crawford, no. 207, Chapter 4.)

207. CRAWFORD, Richard A. Andrew Law, American psalmodist. Evanston: Northwestern University Press, 1968. (Pi Kappa Lambda Studies in American Music, No. 2) 124p. bibliogs.

A particularly fine, scholarly study of Law's life and work. Though modern thought may repudiate his "genteel orientation" and his musical taste, Crawford views Law as a memorable figure, whose hard life, industriously, if self-righteously lived, showed in its dogged persistence with schemes to which his beliefs committed him a unity of thought and action. In this career--"an illustration of some of the forces which shaped American cultural life in the eighteenth and early nineteenth century" (epilogue)--Crawford sees four major turning-points, and, with the help of the Law Papers at the University of Michigan, he reconstructs Law's life around these. The first was Law's decision to abandon a ministerial career in favor of one teaching in singing schools and compiling tunebooks.

(The account of the period of the early tunebooks, 1778-1783, is dominated by a detailed examination of the Select Harmony [1779]). Law moved to Philadelphia in 1783, and made his second significant direction change, not only becoming an itinerant teacher, but also making an (unsuccessful) attempt to secure national distribution for his tunebook. Then, back in Connecticut in 1793, he redirected his energies to the reformation of musical taste, based on European hymnody, with his Musical Primer (1793) and Art of Singing (1794). Prosperity and wide acceptance eluded him then, and continued to do so after his final shift in direction, which came with the publication of the Art of Singing in 1803 in staffless shape-notation. His life from then on is seen as a struggle to gain acceptance for this system; that he did not succeed, as did Little and Smith (no. 523), to whom, ironically, the system was not as important as the music (American), is ascribed to his continued rejection of the staff. (The history of Law's involvement with shape-notation is clearly examined.) The extensive supplementary material includes an examination of the musical style of the tunebooks, a detailed bibliography of Law's publications, an investigation of the sources of the tunes in his books, and a 50-page index to these tunes.

5. Secular Musical Life in the 18th Century

(See also nos. 2, 116, 120, 144.)

208. CRIPE, Helen. Thomas Jefferson and music. Charlottesville: University of Virginia Press, 1974. 157p. illus., bibliog.

A lesser-known aspect of the amazingly versatile Jefferson-- his love of music and the musical life of his household--is revealed in this study, which includes an introductory summary of secular music in the American Colonies, a chronicle of the place of music (his "delightful recreation") in Jefferson's life, and accounts of the musical education of his daughters and granddaughter, of his musical instruments, of his interest in mechanical aspects of music, and of his family's music collection at Monticello (a full catalog of which appears in Appendix 2). The author draws extensively on contemporary sources, especially the letters of friends and family, and Jefferson's correspondence and account books. Her text is accompanied by abundant footnotes, and the extensive bibliography lists primary and secondary material. From these fragments of material she pieces together a portrait that shows the high place Jefferson accorded his musical activities. His idealistic thoughts about improving his countrymen's musical taste, however (expressed in a letter quoted on p. 92) were not translated into any achievement; music remained a "delightful recreation." Index.

209. HOWARD, John Tasker. The music of George Washington's time; preface by Sol Bloom. Washington: United States George Washington Bicentennial Commission, 1931. 96p.

An account of musical life in early America (concerts, popular songs, dances, instruments and bands) is followed by descriptions of various musical pieces associated with national historic events from pre-Revolutionary days to Washington's death. The tunes of many of these are included. There are three supplementary listings: of authentic 18th century music in modern editions; of modern music commemorating Washington or otherwise appropriate for the bicentennial celebrations of his birth; and of suggested programs. (A 15-piece collection made by William Arms Fisher, The Music that Washington Knew, Boston, Ditson, 1931, includes a 19-page introduction in which the compiler sketches the background to each piece --among them works by Hopkinson and Billings--surveys other music Washington heard or knew, and briefly describes dance music of the time.)

210. SONNECK, O. G. Early concert-life in America (1731-1800). Leipzig: Brietkopf & Härtel, 1907. (Repr. New York: Musurgia, 1949; Wiesbaden: Sändig, 1969). 338p. bibliog. notes.

Sonneck's superlative study was based on his Bibliography of Early American Secular Music (no. 2), and on an examination of 18th century newspapers, which he showed to be indispensable to a proper understanding of period. The text takes the form of chronicle of concert activity in four areas--Charleston and the South (with accounts of Baltimore and Richmond), Philadelphia, New York, Boston and New England (Salem, Providence, Hartford). Each area is separately treated. The result, which Sonneck describes as a "mosaic," is an immensely detailed demonstration of just how extensive were performances of secular music. Among the outstanding individual participants are Francis Hopkinson, James Bremner, Alexander Reinagle, Andrew Adgate, James Hewitt, William Tuckey, Josiah Flagg and James Juhan. Index.

6. 19th Century Revival of Psalmody

211. KEMP, Robert. Father Kemp and his Old Folks: a history of the Old Folks' concerts, comprising an autobiography of the author, and sketches of many humorous scenes and incidents, which have transpired in a concert-giving experience of twelve years in America and England. Boston: the author, 1868. 254p. illus.

In a reaction against the European-influenced hymnody of Lowell Mason and others in the mid-19th century there appeared a popular form of entertainment, the Old Folks Concert, whose object was to perform, in a suitable historical style and in suitable period costume, the music of the New England singing schools of the 18th century. As leader of the most celebrated of the Old Folks Concerts Robert Kemp takes most of the credit for the success of this new type of entertainment, which, despite its extremely jovial tone, responded sincerely to a deeply-felt nostalgia among the ordinary

people of New England (and fell foul of Mason in the process). Kemp
implies in his autobiography that the original idea was his; he describes how it occurred to him to "revive old memories by singing
some of the tunes which strengthened the religious faith of our grand-
fathers ...," and scoured the country round about for tunebooks.
But Judith Steinberg ("Old Folks Concerts and the Revival of New
England Psalmody," Musical Quarterly, LIX, 4, Oct. 1973) casts
doubt upon this, suggesting he capitalized on a trend but did not
inaugurate it.   There is no doubting his extreme proficiency as an
entertainer, however, as is clearly seen in his book, with its humor
and its endless supply of anecdotal stories.   His account is especially
interesting for the information it contains on how the concerts were
performed, on popular reaction, and on the successful tours undertaken by his troupe.   In 1860 Kemp published a collection of the music performed (Father Kemp's Old Folks Concert Music: a Collection of the Most Favorite Tunes of Billings, Swan, Holden, Read,
Kimball, Ingalls and Others ... Boston: Ditson, 1860, 71p.) The
contents of this, with comments on later editions, are described in
Judith Steinberg's article.

C. THE CULTIVATED TRADITION
IN THE 19TH CENTURY

1. Arbiters of Taste

J. S. DWIGHT

212.   COOKE, George Willis. John Sullivan Dwight, Brook-farmer, editor, and critic of music: a biography. Boston: Small, Maynard, 1898. 297p. illus.
_____. (New ed.) Hartford: Transcendental Books, 1973. 84p. illus.

Modern taste may be out of sympathy with the musical snobbishness that likens Stephen Foster's songs to "a morbid irritation of the skin" ("Journal," 1853, quoted in Howard, no. 24) but the breadth of influence of Dwight (1813-1893) as high priest of the cultivated musical palate and leading music critic of the second half of the 19th century is undeniable. Cooke, faithful chronicler of the New England Transcendentalists, devotes the central portion of his book to an account and assessment of Dwight's musical achievements--the foundation of "Dwight's Journal" in 1852, his study abroad in 1860, and subsequent work for music in Boston. Extensive use is made of Dwight's correspondence, and of extracts from the "Journal." Cooke is aware of his subject's shortcomings--he calls him "autocrat of music," "musical dictator"; more than that, he sees as Dwight's greatest weakness his inability to rise above personal preference; on the positive side his "power lay in what he approved."

THOMAS HASTINGS

213.   HASTINGS, Thomas. Dissertation on musical taste; or, General principles of taste applied to the art of music. Albany: Printed by Webster and Skinner, 1822. (Repr. New York: Da Capo, 1974). 228p.
_____. New York: Mason, 1853. (Repr. New York: Johnson, 1968). 296p.

Six hundred hymns and about one thousand hymn tunes are said by Metcalf (no. 62, p. 195) to stand to the credit of Thomas Hastings (1784-1872), not to mention the fifty or so volumes of music he compiled, and his numerous writings. Of the latter the Dissertation is the best known, and the most influential. With his colleague Lowell Mason, Hastings labored to reform church music in accordance with his interpretation of European taste, as outlined here. The main aims of the book as given in the preface are "to invite the publick attention to a neglected science, and to contribute towards the revival of church musick in our American congregations." Among the subjects covered are the principles of style in singing; vocal and instrumental music united, and related to church musick; composition; harmony; melody; and design. In the preface to the 1853 edition Hastings remarks that in the thirty years since the first edition "the musical art in this country has advanced, to say the least, quite to the level of the Dissertation."

JOHN HUBBARD

214.   HUBBARD, John. An essay on music. Pronounced before the Middlesex Musical Society, Sept. 9, A.D. 1807, at Dunstable, (Mass.). Boston: Manning & Loring, 1808. 19p.

Hubbard (1759-1810), a professor at Dartmouth College and a scholar with a great love for European sacred music, wrote this influential essay in praise of his heroes (especially Handel), with whom he contrasts unfavorably the offerings of New England composers. The fuging tune comes in for a particularly harsh offensive. (For fuller information on Hubbard, see Gould, no. 58, p. 65, and Pichierri, no. 103, ch. 11. For a discussion of the significance of Hubbard's views in the move against native American psalmody in the 19th century, see McKay & Crawford, no. 202.)

LOWELL MASON

215.   MASON, Lowell. Musical letters from abroad; including detailed accounts of the Birmingham, Norwich, and Dusseldorf musical festivals of 1852. New York: Mason, 1854. (Repr. New York: Da Capo, 1967). 312p.

Gilbert Chase remarked of Mason (1792-1872)--whose various accomplishments and interests appear in several places in this bibliography (see Index)--"of all musicians active in the United States during the nineteenth century, Lowell Mason has left the strongest, the widest, and the most lasting impress on our musical culture. This not a tribute of praise: it is merely an objective statement of fact" (no. 25, p. 151). One of the marks of his influence was the transportation of European standards of taste in music, and in these impressions of his second visit to Europe, 1852-1853, one may see Mason reacting to European culture at first-hand, and contrasting what he sees with the situation in America.

216.   LUCAS, G. W. Remarks on the Musical Conventions in Boston, &c. Northampton, Mass.: Printed for the author, 1844. 27p.

The image of Lowell Mason as a stern, moral, hymn-writing patriarch surrounded by happily singing children is badly tarnished by his one-time friend. Lucas' outspoken, aggressive little pamphlet reveals the underbelly of this virtuous 19th century world, showing how the Musical Conventions, one of Mason's and George Root's major achievements, were shot through with jealousies, intrigues and political wheeler-dealing. Whether or not his anti-Mason polemics were justified (he speaks of Mason's "bare-faced duplicity," his "selfishness and illiberality"), Lucas' account of the conventions of 1838-1844 (especially the last) is riveting reading. Not only Mason is attacked, but the whole body of his allies in the arguments over the form of the conventions is mercilessly pilloried. Lucas speaks of "the arrogance of those who could endure nothing but the glorification of their idol, and who formed the curtain behind which he concealed his plots" (p. 5). Root is also criticized, but Thomas Hastings, who addressed the 1844 Convention, is lauded; George Hood's portrait of Billings is faulted on several points (no. 181).

217. MASON, Henry Lowell. Lowell Mason: an appreciation of his life and work. New York: Hymn Society of America, 1941. (Papers of the Hymn Society, No. 8) 12p. illus.
A short biographical sketch by one of Mason's grandsons (and brother of Daniel Gregory Mason), in which his character is highly spoken of and his ideas briefly outlined.

218. RICH, Arthur Lowndes. Lowell Mason: "the father of singing among the children." Chapel Hill: University of North Carolina Press, 1946. 224p. illus., bibliog.
Lowell Mason left an indelible mark upon American musical life, particularly through his outstanding contributions in the field of music education. Rich's book is a scholarly historical account of the extent of these contributions. He begins by relating Mason's pioneer work in music instruction for school children (he believed strongly that all average children could and should be taught to sing), and his time as music superintendent in Boston schools, during which music was introduced into the regular curriculum. His dominant role in the Boston Academy of Music is described, followed by an account of the solid foundations he laid for the training of music teachers through conventions, teachers' institutes, music normal institutes, etc. Placing him in the context of the history of education, Rich outlines Mason's educational theory, his belief in the moral influence of music, and his methods of teaching (which were based on Pestalozzi), and compares his views with those of significant precursors and contemporaries, such as M. T. Pfeiffer, H. G. Nägeli and William C. Woodbridge. He also examines later developments in music education, relating them to Mason's approach, and summarizes his contribution. The extensive bibliography contains a full list of Mason's own published writings and related sources. Index.

2. History and Collected Biography

(See also no. 36.)

219. HUGHES, Rupert. Contemporary American composers, being a study of the music of this country, its present conditions and its future, with critical estimates and biographies of

the principal living composers ... Boston: Page, 1900. 456p. illus.

_____. American composers: a study of the music of this country, and of its future, with biographies of the leading composers of the present time; being a new revised edition of Contemporary American Composers; with additional chapters by Arthur Elson. Boston: Page, 1914. 582p. illus.

Inveighing in his foreword against "the active policy of those who despise everything contemporary or native, and substitute sciolism for catholicity, contempt for analysis," novelist and critic Hughes declares his own belief, "lo, these many years! that some of the best music in the world is being written here at home, and that it only needs the light to win its meed of praise." These informative biographical and critical studies of numerous late 19th century composers are intended to go some way towards shedding this light. The 1900 edition is entirely the result of his own research, in obtaining biographical data from composers, and in seeking out and studying their music in published and manuscript form. His subjects are grouped in collective categories: "the innovators" (detailed studies of MacDowell, Edgar Stillman Kelley, Harvey Worthington Loomis, Ethelbert Nevin, Sousa, Henry Schoenefeld, and also including Maurice Arnold and N. Clifford Page); "the academics" (Paine, Buck, Parker, Frank van der Stucken, W. W. Gilchrist, G. W. Chadwick, Arthur Foote, Henry K. Hadley, Adolph M. Foester, Charles C. Converse and L. A. Coerne); "the colonists" (less detailed descriptions of minor figures from New York, Boston, Chicago, Cleveland and St. Louis); and women composers (Mrs. H. H. A. Beach and Margaret Ruthven Lang). Elson's chapters in the 1914 edition provide further information on several of these examined by Hughes, plus studies of Frederick S. Converse, Victor Herbert, Charles Wakefield Cadman and others. He also gives brief information on a host of "recent names" writing both orchestral and non-orchestral music. In all there are 48 musical illustrations and 32 photographic portraits. Index.

220. MATHEWS, W. S. B., ed. A hundred years of music in America: an account of musical effort in America during the past century.... Chicago: Howe, 1889. (Reprinted New York: AMS Press, 1970). 715p. illus.

Combining the objectives of an historical account of individuals, organizations and influences in American music (beginning with William Billings), a portrait of the state of music at the time of writing, and a forecast of future development, this work of unnamed collaborators, who did much of their research by questionnaire, is a source of considerable biographical information about 19th century individuals in music--composers, performers, teachers, instrument makers and journalists. Biographical sketches of over 400 persons (240 of whom are represented by plates) are grouped in chapters devoted to genres, instruments, and other subjects (such as education and festivals). Whole chapters are devoted to Billings and to Lowell Mason, and there is a supplementary directory of a further 300 or so musicians, with brief biographical information. The lack of a complete index to the book is a drawback to its use.

221. MUSSULMAN, Joseph A. Music in the Cultured Generation: a social history of music in America, 1870-1900. Evanston: Northwestern University Press, 1971. (Pi Kappa Lambda Studies in American Music) 298p. illus., bibliog.

Scholarly in method, but making also a conscious appeal to the layman, this is a stimulating investigation of the musical philosophy of a small clan of people--the intellectual, rational, sometimes superior minority--and of their attempt to direct musical activity in the concert halls, theaters, homes and churches of late 19th century America. A cultured life, which to this group was the be-all and end-all, was embodied for them in the industrious writers on music for four literary periodicals--Atlantic, Harper's, Century and Scribner's--particularly W. P. Apthorp, J. S. Dwight and C. W. Curtis. The author describes the character of the journals and their readership; the place of music in the prevailing philosophies (the pervading influence of Darwin, and the relation of music to emotions and the intellect); the links between music and morality (attitudes to personal conduct and eccentricity); faith in the progress of musical taste and accomplishment, influenced by the great musical development that followed German immigration; belief in the cultivating agency of music, and the gradual embodiment of this in education; the search for a national musical identity (including feelings about indigenous folk and popular material); contrasting reaction to opera, and the performances, challenge and influence of Wagner; attitudes to amateur music, the vitality of the choral tradition, and the debate about church music. In conclusion he pinpoints subsequent changes in thinking about music and areas where the influenced of the Cultured Generation persists. Appendices give listings of the articles on music in the four journals, and there is an index.

3. Individual Composers of the 19th Century

ARTHUR BIRD

222. LORING, William C. The music of Arthur Bird: an explanation of American composers of the Eighties and Nineties for Bicentennial Americana programming. Washington: the author, 1974. 68p.

Loring's interest in the figure of Arthur Bird (1856-1923) goes back at least to 1943, when he wrote a biographical article for Musical Quarterly (Vol. 29, January 1943). This later monograph is concerned to make known the kind of music Bird wrote, and to offer practical suggestions as to its performance. For the author, Bird "is to be remembered in American music as our first compose of ballets, of excellent chamber music for woodwinds and horns, and of an 'electrifying' representation of a Mardi Gras Carnival scene" (p. 2). In his account of many of the pieces Loring incorporates a good deal of historical information including contemporary reaction; an enthusiastic advocate, he also offers sound practical advice for potential performers, remarking that "it is necessary to winnow out ... the commonplace chaff" (p. 53). Interesting parallels are drawn with Luminist painters. A complete classified catalog of Bird's works is included. (Most of the music is obtainable on hire from the Fleisher Collection of the Free Library of Philadelphia.)

ARTHUR FOOTE

223. FOOTE, Arthur. Arthur Foote, 1853-1937: an autobiography. Norwood, Mass.: Plimpton Press, 1946. 135p. illus.
One of the group of composers known as the "Boston Classicists" which included Parker and Chadwick (and was termed by Hitchcock in no. 30 the "Second New England School"), Foote was a prolific composer of sacred and secular music who, after education at Harvard, was for 32 years the organist at the First Unitarian Church in Boston. His autobiography makes clear the struggle he had, in later life, to come to terms with new musical trends, which seemed "to fly in the face of all that one has cared for." The book also contains a tribute by Moses Smith (pp. 115-130) and a homage by Frederick Jacobi (pp. 131-135, reprinted from Modern Music, 1947).

WILLIAM HENRY FRY

224. UPTON, William Treat. William Henry Fry, American journalist and composer-critic. New York: Crowell, 1954. 346p. illus.
Irving Lowens wrote of Fry (1813-1864): "his lasting monument is ... his eloquence in behalf of American music" (no. 38, p. 222). One of the first champions of the American composer, a man of proverbial sincerity and critical independence, he was also "probably the most quarreled with musician of his time" (Lowens, p. 221). Though his campaigns left more mark than his music he was the composer of the first significant American opera, the Italian-influenced "Leonora" (1846). Upton's study describes and examines three phases of Fry's life: his first 33 years, spent in Philadelphia; his time in Paris, 1846-1852, as correspondent of the New York Tribune; his subsequent occupation of the music critic's chair at the Tribune in New York, a position he held until his death. These biographical sections are followed by a critical examination of Fry's music, with examples, and by a selection of his music criticism from 1862 to 1864. In an appendix Upton provides a full catalog of Fry's works in the Library Company of Philadelphia.

LOUIS MOREAU GOTTSCHALK

225. GOTTSCHALK, Louis Moreau. Notes of a pianist ...; preceded by a short biographical sketch with contemporaneous criticisms; edited by his sister Clara Gottschalk; translated from the French by Robert E. Peterson. Philadelphia: Lippincott, 1881. 480p. illus.
_____. _____; edited, with a prelude, a postlude, and explanatory notes, by Jeanne Behrend. New York: Knopf,

1964. 420p. illus., bibliog.

Gottschalk (1829-1869), the child prodigy who had been dispatched from his New Orleans home to Paris in 1842, at the age of 13, and had taken that capital by storm, returned a virtuoso to America in 1853, to spend three hectic years demonstrating his prowess as pianist and composer (and becoming a popular idol at the same time), before departing for the West Indies, where he spent almost six contented years, soaking up all the Caribbean had to offer. Hereabouts he began the journal that is the basis of this book, which describes this period in Cuba and other islands, before concertizing began again in earnest in 1862, and took him on increasingly gruelling tours of the U.S., Panama, Mexico and South America between 1862 and 1868 (he died in Rio de Janeiro). In his journal he notes impressions, gives vent to feelings and opinions, relates occurrences, laments the continuous pressure of his way of life and describes the public's reaction in an evocative, picturesque style. Beneath the flamboyant exterior there was, we see, a sensitive creative artist, who, in Irving Lowens' words, "sacrificed himself on the altar of the gods of sentimentality" (no. 38, p. 233). The 1964 edition contains a note on Gottschalk's music, a bibliography of books and articles, and an index.

226. ARPIN, P. Biographie de L. M. Gottschalk, pianiste américain. New York: Imprimerie du Courrier des Etats-Unis, 1853. 64p.
_____. Life of Louis Moreau Gottschalk, from the French of P. Arpin by Henry C. Watson. New York? 1853? 14p. illus.

A contemporary account of Gottschalk's early career, giving an idea of the impression he created in Europe during his time, from 12 to 24 years old, in France, Switzerland and Spain.

227. FORS, Luis Ricardo. Gottschalk. Habana: La Propaganda Literaria, 1880. 444p. illus., bibliog.

Described by its Cuban author as "a homage to the memory of the great composer, wonderful pianist and loyal friend," this Spanish volume of biography and criticism makes great use of contemporary documents by Gottschalk and others. The composer's own correspondence and writings feature prominently in the biographical part of the book, which is followed by "fragments and anecdotes" relating, among other things, to the circumstances of composition of some of his music. The critical study of Gottschalk "as pianist, as composer, as critic and as a man of encyclopedia knowledge" is mainly a survey of contemporary critical opinions of him, and of his views of others. There is also a catalog of his works.

228. HENSEL, Octavia. Life and letters of Louis Moreau Gottschalk. Boston: Ditson, 1870. 213p.

Written shortly after Gottschalk's death in 1869, this was the first biography to give an account of his entire life. Octavia Hensel (a pseudonym for Mary Alice Seymour) was a pupil of Gottschalk's, and drew on her own reminiscences, and on those of the Gottschalk sisters, Clara and Celestine. Her idealized portrait is heavily overladen with exaggerated emotion and the excesses of late Romantic expression--well beyond the requirements for even so overblown a persona as Gottschalk. (A small sample, re the infant LMG: "if ever his baby-voice was lifted in fretful wail, the soft music of his young mother's slumber song stilled in an instant the sorrow and pain, and wove into his soul loving melodies that were to thrill into beauteous expression throughout his glorious young life.") The biographical account is also studded with recollected master-pupil conversation (pupil usually weeps). There are, however, a number of letters of Gottschalk's to various friends and acquaintances, and extracts from his articles.

229. LANGE, Francisco Curt. "Vida y muerte de Louis Moreau Gottschalk en Rio de Janeiro (1869): el ambiento musical en la mitad del segundo Imperio." Mendoza: Universidad Nacional de Cuyo, 1951. (Revista de Estudios Musicales, Ano 11, Num. 4, 5/6, Agosto 1950 & Diciembre 1950/ Abril, 1951). pp. 43-147; 97-350. illus., bibliog. notes.
　　　　Although as a publication in a periodical it falls outside the scope of this bibliography, this work is included here for three reasons: it is a book-length study; it is a primary source for information on the last month of Gottschalk's life in Brazil, and on his death; it is a particularly thorough piece of work that should be translated into English.

230. LOGGINS, Vernon. Where the word ends: the life of Louis Moreau Gottschalk. Baton Rouge: Louisiana State University Press, 1958. 273p. illus., bibliog. notes.
　　　　An informal, somewhat effusive biography of the pianist/composer, describing his early life in New Orleans, his experience as a child prodigy, his studies, travels and success in Europe, his return to the U.S. and subsequent, almost endless, but very successful traveling in North and South America for a period of some 17 years. The account evokes Gottschalk's colorful personality, but does not attempt to examine his unique musical position and influence. A list of his published works is included in an appendix. Several sources of material are referred to in a note, but no references are quoted in the text.

231. OFFERGELD, Robert. The centennial catalogue of the published and unpublished compositions of Louis Moreau Gottschalk; prepared for Stereo Review. New York: Ziff-Davis, 1970. 34p. illus.
　　　　A catalog of 298 entries, many of which are for works the manuscripts of which are wanting. Much information was gained from a previously unknown pamphlet of 1863, "Life of Louis Moreau Gottschalk," which includes a list of published and unpublished works. The pamphlet and other questions relating to Gottschalk's music in published and manuscript form are discussed in the introduction. The catalog is arranged alphabetically by work title, with details of instruments and date, comments by an unknown annotator of the pamphlet, notes on the manuscript, and publication details where relevant. There is also a chronology of composition dates.

ANTHONY PHILIP HEINRICH

232.   UPTON, William Treat. Anthony Philip Heinrich: a nineteenth-century composer in America. New York: Columbia University Press, 1939. (Columbia University Studies
in Musicology, 4) (Repr. New York: AMS Press, 1967).
337p. illus., bibliog.

The major source of biographical information about "Father
Heinrich," "the Beethoven of America," the self-taught composer,
who was one of the first in the 19th century to attempt to compose
a music distinctly American in character. His long and varied life
(1781-1861) took him from birth into a wealthy Bohemian family--
whose riches he lost--to America (first in 1810, then to settle in
1816), where he attempted to make a living as music director of a
theater, then as violin teacher, and--beginning only in his late thir-
ties--as a composer. Constantly having to promote his own music
in a perpetual struggle for existence he lived variously in Philadelphia, Pittsburgh, Boston, London, Boston again, returning from a
final European sojourn to die in New York. Upton recounts the details of this "weird and fantastic career" (Sonneck) and also attempts
to draw a picture of the broader cultural life of the age. He follows his narrative with a summary of the man and the musician,
examining in particular "The War of the Elements" and "To the
Spirit of Beethoven." Appendices include the texts of press announcements, a list of works and a list of compositions in manuscript
and printed form in the Library of Congress (with descriptive notes).
There are musical illustrations in the text, which also includes reproductions of programs and other documentary material. (Upton
also quotes from one particular published source--F. A. Mussik:
Skizzen aus dem Leben des sich in Amerika befindenden deutschen
Tondichters Anton Philipp Heinrich, nach authentischen Quellen bear-
beitet, Prag, 1843).

SIDNEY LANIER

233.   LANIER, Sidney. Music and poetry: essays upon some aspects and inter-relations of the two arts. New York:
Scribner, 1898. (Repr. New York: AMS Press, 1969).
248p.

This collection of 13 essays on the two arts that Lanier
(1842-1881) himself practiced includes six on specifically musical
topics: from the nature, role and physics of music, and the contemporary orchestra, to interpretations of contemporary works, a
report of the Maryland Festival of 1878, and a letter to the New
York Tribune concerning his Centennial Cantata. This last piece
in particular links the two themes of the book.

234.   MIMS, Edwin. Sidney Lanier. Boston: Houghton Mifflin,
1908. (Repr. Port Washington: Kennikat Press, 1968).
386p.

A biography of the poet and musician from Georgia, who was,
in Gilbert Chase's words, "a stifled genius, perhaps the most magnificent and tragic failure in the annals of American music" (no. 25,

p. 341). It describes his early life and exceptional musical proficiency, especially on the flute, his time as a Confederate soldier,
his settling in Baltimore, the attempts there to lead a life wedding
music and poetry, and his death from consumption. Though his musical compositions were few--his death prevented the full flowering
of his talent--they were of a high standard, and his flute playing was
exceptional (chap. 6). (Another portrait of Lanier, Sidney Lanier:
a Biographical and Critical Study, by Aubrey Starke [Chapel Hill:
University of North Carolina Press, 1933] is principally concerned
with Lanier the poet.)

EDWARD MacDOWELL

235. MacDOWELL, Edward. Critical and historical essays: lec-
      tures delivered at Columbia University; edited by W. J.
      Baltzell. Boston: Schmidt, 1912. (Repr. New York:
      Da Capo, 1969). 282p.
   The first American composer to achieve wide fame and recognition in his lifetime, MacDowell (1861-1908) became Head of the Music Dept. at Columbia in 1896. These essays, first published four
years after his death, are the lectures he gave for his general music courses up until his resignation in 1904. Their subject is principally the early history of music (from the Greeks to the troubadours), and apart from occasional parenthetical observations there
is nothing about American music. (In a passage omitted by Baltzell
but quoted by Gilman, no. 236, MacDowell rejects a national school
based on folk music, and hopes to see in American music "the youthful optimistic vitality and the undaunted tenacity of spirit that characterizes the American man.") The essays are interesting, nevertheless, for what they tell us about MacDowell's thought, though--as
Irving Lowens' introduction to the reprint shows--the accuracy of
the picture is in some doubt by reason of Baltzell's editing, and the
fact that these were basically lecture notes.

236. GILMAN, Lawrence. Edward MacDowell: a study. London,
      New York: Lane, 1908. (Repr. New York: Da Capo,
      1969). 190p. illus.
   A sympathetic account of MacDowell, beginning with a 50-
page record of his life. Gilman (1878-1939), who went on to enjoy
a successful career in the footsteps of H. E. Krehbiel as critic
for the New York Tribune, was, when the book was written, music
critic and assistant editor of Harper's Weekly. He had known Mac-
Dowell, and follows the biography with an appreciation of his character and attitudes and with an 80-page study of his music, assessing general characteristics and describing (without examples) the development of his work, with chapters on the sonatas and on the songs.
There is a list of MacDowell's compositions, but no index. The Da
Capo edition contains a new introduction by Margaret L. Morgan.
(For a detailed biography of MacDowell, see also Irving Lowens,
"Edward MacDowell," in Hi Fi/Stereo Review, 19/12, December
1967, pp. 61-72.)

237. MacDOWELL, Marian. Random notes on Edward MacDowell

and his music. Boston: Schmidt; London: Elkin, 1950.
36p. illus.

The composer's widow resisted attempts to persuade her to
write a biography of her husband, but she did provide these informal
notes on some of his piano music, the circumstances of their composition and something of their inspiration. There is a biographical
note by Una L. Allen.

238.   PAGE, Elizabeth Fry.   Edward MacDowell: his work and
       ideals; with poetical interpretations by the author.   New
       York: Dodge, 1910. 85p. illus.

Of slight value as biography or critical appreciation, this
work may indicate something of the kind of sentiment MacDowell inspired.   The poetical interpretations are twelve rather undistinguished
poems on some of MacDowell's piano pieces.

239.   PORTE, J. F.   Edward MacDowell: a great American tone
       poet, his life and music.   London: Kegan, Paul, Trench,
       Trübner, 1922. 180p. illus.

A short biographical sketch precedes an assessment of Mac-
Dowell's achievement as a composer, a character study, and a description of the MacDowell Colony for creative artists at Peterboro,
New Hampshire.   The major part of the book is devoted to the music in the form of analytical and descriptive notes to each work, in
opus number order.   Publication details are given for each item,
and there are some music examples.   An index to the works follows, grouped by category.

240.   SONNECK, O. G.   Catalogue of first editions of Edward Mac-
       Dowell (1861-1980).   Washington: Library of Congress,
       1917. (Repr. New York: Arno; Da Capo, 1971).   89p.

With his customary bibliographic precision Sonneck provides a
five-part catalog, based on Library of Congress collections (with
some outside assistance).   The sections are: compositions with opus
number; without opus number; compositions under pseudonyms; part-
songs and orchestral music edited by MacDowell; piano music edited
by MacDowell.   Each title page is transcribed, with details of date,
pagination and size, and detailed descriptive notes.   There is a
classified index, and other indexes of titles, first lines, authors
and translators, composers edited, and publishers.

ETHELBERT NEVIN

241.   HOWARD, John Tasker.   Ethelbert Nevin.   New York:
       Crowell, 1935. 423p. illus., bibliog.

From an apparent wealth of source material available to him,
Howard produced a very detailed biography of the 38 years of Ethelbert Nevin (1862-1901), who excelled in miniatures--songs like "The
Rosary," and many short piano pieces--which were amongst the
most popular of their day, but who, when he died, had virtually ex-
hausted his limited talent.   From this account of his life, from his
early years in Pittsburgh to his death in New Haven (and including
two spells in Europe, 1884-86 and 1891-97), he emerges as a likable

but highly nervous man with a tendency to morbid introspection. Howard's portrait makes little attempt to examine his music in detail. Supplementary material includes a chronology from Nevin's father's birth up to 1935, a list of published works, a bibliography of books, magazines and newspaper articles, and an index.

HORATIO PARKER

242. CHADWICK, George W. Horatio Parker. New Haven: Yale University Press, 1921. 26p.
   Fellow-composer, teacher and life-long friend of Parker, Chadwick delivered the text of this generous tribute to the American Academy of Arts and Letters on July 25, 1920, seven months after Parker's death. In it he recollects Parker as a pupil, surveys his subsequent career, and dwells on aspects of his personality and musicianship. Concluding, he remarks, "it was perhaps inevitable that he should be classed as an ecclesiastic composer ... but ... his real place is among the romanticists, and it is a high one." The text is the same as in Chadwick's Commemorative Tribute to Horatio Parker (New York: American Academy of Arts and Letters, 1922).

243. SEMLER, Isabel Parker. Horatio Parker: a memoir for his grandchildren, compiled from letters and papers; in collaboration with Pierson Underwood. New York: Putnam, 1942. (Repr. New York: Da Capo, 1973). 330p. illus.
   Parker's daughter gives us a loving, unpretentious portrait of her father (1863-1919), allowing him to speak for himself as often as possible through letters; the narrative, based on the recollections of Parker's wife, press clippings, and the author's own memory of her father, is intended as "a thread on which to string the letters themselves" (foreword). The story moves from New England childhood and student days in Germany, through early professional struggles, the beginning of a long connection with Yale University in 1894, and a spell in England (1899-1902), to his two prize-winning operas, "Mona" and "Fairyland" (1912 and 1913). A portrait of the Parker family life shows him as an affectionate parent, a man of integrity, devoutly religious, but with a strong sense of humor and a love of outdoor life. A catalog of his works, by W. Oliver Strunk, appears in an index.

4. Musical Life in the 19th Century

(See also no. 220.)

244. HOFFMAN, Richard. Some musical recollections of fifty years; with a biographical sketch by his wife. New York: Scribner, 1910. 168p. illus.
   Born in Manchester, England, Hoffman (1831-1909) came to the U.S. in 1847, and had a distinguished career as pianist, teacher

and composer. His wife's biography of him occupies one third of
the book; in the remainder Hoffman describes some particular sections of his life--his youth in England, his first American concerts,
the state of American concert life in the mid-century--and relates
some specific recollections (e.g., accompanying Jenny Lind, and
playing duets with Gottschalk).

245. MASON, William. Memories of a musical life. New York:
         Century Co., 1901. (Repr. New York: AMS Press; New
         York: Da Capo, 1970). 306p. illus.
     Third son of the redoubtable Lowell, William Mason (1829-
1908) was highly influential as a piano teacher, developing standards
for performances in America paralleling those achieved by Theodore
Thomas for orchestra (both are referred to from time to time as
"musical missionaries"). His autobiography, though it begins with
his early days in New England, and contains portraits of his father
and of the Boston of the early 1840s, is much concerned with his
time of study in Europe (1849-1853), during which he met many of
the leading composers and was taught by Liszt. Part 4, describing
him "at work in America," sees him turn from the career of a virtuoso concert pianist to a life centered on teaching. Reflecting in
Part 5 on music in America at the turn of the century, he sees no
more need for fledgling pianists to study abroad, such has been the
advance in America in the latter half of the 19th century.

246. RUSSELL, Charles Edward. The American orchestra and
         Theodore Thomas. Garden City: Doubleday, 1927. (Repr.
         Westport: Greenwood Press, 1971). 344p. illus.
     A fine biographical study and appreciation of the life and ca-
reer of Theodore Thomas, rich in understanding of the cultural context in which he arose, of the man himself, and of the nature of his
attempt to educate America in symphonic music. The book traces
his life from his birth in Germany in 1835, his parents' migration
to America ten years later, his early musical life (he was an itinerant violinist at 15), his first conducting experience in 1860, his
subsequent vocation to cultivate musical taste in America with his
own orchestra, and his long single-handed struggle to achieve this.
(He died in Chicago in 1905.) Thomas emerges as a figure of heroic
proportions, battling continually against the odds, a combination of
"dreamer and executive, visionary and relentless performer, con-
ceiver and doer." Included in the appendices are a list of American
grand orchestras to 1927 and a reprint from Thomas's autobiography
of the list of works he introduced into America. There is also a
good general index.

247. THOMAS, Rose Fay. Memoirs of Theodore Thomas. New
         York: Moffat, Yard, 1911. (Repr. Freeport: Books for
         Libraries Press, 1971). 569p. illus.
     This biography by Thomas's second wife is full of detailed in-
formation and the fruits of diligent research. Basically a straightforward, objective chronicle of his career it uses letters, programs
and articles to give a full picture, quoting periodically from various
sources to provide some assessment and evaluation.

248.   THOMAS, Theodore.   A musical autobiography; edited by
        George P. Upton.   Chicago: McClurg, 1905.   (Repr.
        Grosse Pointe: Scholarly Press, 1974?).   2v.   illus.
        _____ .   _____ ; with a new introduction by Leon Stein.
        New York: Da Capo, 1964.   378p.   illus.
            Conductor and impresario, Thomas made possibly the single
        largest contribution to the development of American concert life in
        the second half of the 19th century, creating standards of orchestral
        performance among musicians and a gradual taste for symphonic mu-
        sic among listeners, the influence of which is still felt.   He was
        not, however, of the fraternity that excel in--even enjoy--talking
        about themselves.   His own recollections, which occupy the first
        hundred pages of the first volume, are reluctant and diffident.   Upton
        attempts to fill in some details in his "reminiscences and apprecia-
        tion," and to give some idea of Thomas's character.   Volume 1 in-
        cludes in an appendix Thomas's paper of 1881 on "Musical Possibil-
        ities in America," and a selection of tributes to him by an assort-
        ment of people.   Volume 2, much the more valuable, is devoted to
        the details of a large selection of Thomas's concert programs from
        1855 to 1905 (his own collection approached 10,000), arranged in
        groups corresponding to concert series in New York, Boston, Cin-
        cinnati, Philadelphia, Chicago, etc.   These illustrate Thomas's sys-
        tem of program construction--usually meaty European masterworks
        as the main course, preceded and succeeded by the hors d'oeuvres
        and whipped cream of the orchestral repertoire--which had much to
        do with his success.   A long list of the works Thomas introduced
        into America confirms John Tasker Howard's description of him as
        a "musical missionary."

249.   WEICHLEIN, William J.   A checklist of American periodicals,
        1850-1900.   Detroit: Information Coordinators, 1970.   (De-
        troit Studies in Music Bibliography, No. 16) 103p.   bibliog.
            An alphabetical title-listing of 19th century American music
        periodicals.   Each entry gives main title, subtitle (except for en-
        tries under a later name), place and date of publication, numbers
        issued, publisher, frequency, editors, notes and library location.
        There is also a chronological register of titles by decade, a table
        of their geographical distribution, an index of editors and publishers,
        and a short bibliography.

D. THE CULTIVATED TRADITION
IN THE 20TH CENTURY

1. 20th Century Music in General
(with particular reference to America)

a. Reference Works

250. BASART, Ann Phillips. Serial music: a classified bibli-
        ography of writings on twelve-tone and electronic music.
        Berkeley: University of California Press, 1961. 151p.
      International in sources and coverage, this bibliography is
arranged in four sections; twelve-tone music, electronic music, the
Viennese school, other composers. The first two sections list material on philosophy, history, analysis and theory and include numerous articles by American composers. The fourth section includes
coverage of Milton Babbitt and John Cage. Arrangement is chronological under each topic, with frequent brief annotations, and there
are author and subject indexes.

251. BULL, Storm. Index to biographies of contemporary com-
        posers. New York: Scarecrow Press, 1964. 405p. bib-
        liog.
      _____. _____. Vol. 2. Metuchen: Scarecrow Press,
      1974. 567p. bibliog.
      The first of these volumes indexes biographies of almost
6,000 20th century composers in 69 reference sources. In Vol. 2
these numbers are increased to 8,000 composers in 108 sources, almost all of which appeared between 1964 and 1973. Of these 8,000,
half were also included in Vol. 1; their appearance in Vol. 2 indicates the location of further information (not a revision of the earlier
entry). The criteria for both volumes are that a composer was
either born in this century, and/or was alive at the time each volume was compiled, or died in 1950 or later. Each volume is arranged alphabetically by composer, and each entry contains the composer's dates, country of birth (or country with which he is identified),
and citations of reference sources; these are listed fully and described at the front of each volume, and include books, pamphlets,
brochures, journal issues and record sleeves. In many cases they
contain discographical and bibliographical data, as well as biographies. Vol. 2 includes upwards of 1,500 U.S. composers--so as a
striking-out point in the quest for information on these Bull's work
is well-nigh indispensable.

252. CARLSON, Effie B. A bio-bibliographical dictionary of
      twelve-tone and serial composers. Metuchen: Scarecrow
      Press, 1970. 233p. bibliogs.
      Fifteen American composers are represented in the part of
this guide--the central section--that is devoted to biographical and
bibliographical information on 80 composers of serial piano music
since the Schoenberg school. Each individual entry provides date
and place of birth, address (or date of death), a brief biographical
sketch, a description of the characteristics of the composer's approach to twelve-tone technique, a list of piano scores and their
publishers, and a bibliography of secondary sources. Other sections are devoted to a study of the emergence of serialism, a comparative geographical survey and a general bibliography. The 15
Americans are: Milton Babbitt, Earle Brown, Aaron Copland, Ellis
Kohs, Ernst Krenek, Donald Lybbert, Donald Martino, Barbara
Pentland, George Perle, Roger Reynolds, Wallingford Riegger,
George Rochberg, Ben Weber, Adolph Weiss and Stefan Wolpe.

253. COHN, Arthur. The collector's twentieth-century music in
      the Western hemisphere. Philadelphia: Lippincott, 1961.
      256p.
      Intended primarily as a handbook for record buying and listen-
ing in the early 1960s, this is a collection of information and comment on the recorded music of 27 contemporary composers (23 of
whom are American). A general summary of each composer is followed by concise summaries of each piece by that composer that
had been recorded up to May 1960, with comments on the recorded
performances. Given the lack of published discographical information on 20th century American music the data and comment on the
recordings are useful, while the many "capsule surveys" of individual
pieces, particularly less well-known ones, provide some valuable insights.

254. EWEN, David. Composers of tomorrow's music: a non-
      technical introduction to the musical avant-garde move-
      ment. New York: Dodd, Mead, 1971. 176p. illus.
      Of the ten composers selected for this introductory work, in
which "avant-garde" is given a broad historical scope, four are native Americans--Ives, Babbitt, Cage, Partch--and one, Varèse, is
American by adoption. Ewen provides basic biographical information,
and outlines something of the development of each composer's ideas
and approach, with reference to particular works. It all seems a
little unexciting--as conveyor belt music criticism must inevitably
become.

255. EWEN, David. The world of 20th century music. Engle-
      wood Cliffs: Prentice-Hall, 1968; London: Hale, 1969.
      989p. bibliog.
      This bulky reference book could be recommended as a vade
mecum, but only kangaroos would have pockets big enough. It re-
places Ewen's Complete Book of 20th Century Music (Prentice-Hall,
1955, etc.), only one-tenth of the text of which is said to be retained. "The attempt has always been," says the preface, "to be

sufficiently informative to make this book of interest to the trained musician and sufficiently non-technical to make it useful for the layman. " Ewen treads his familiar tightrope with confidence, giving biographical and critical information on almost 150 composers, of whom over 40 are American. Each composer has a separate section, which begins with general critical appraisal, followed by biographical information and analysis of the main--and, sometimes, the lesser--works in chronological order. The Americans included range from Foote and Gilbert to Cage and Foss.

256. FOREMAN, Lewis. Discographies: a bibliography of catalogues of recordings, mainly relating to specific musical subjects, composers and performers. London: Triad Press, (1974). 65p.

The practice of discography in relation to American art music composers and performers would seem, from the relatively few entries in this book, to leave a lot to be desired. Foreman confines himself to concert music, dividing his bibliography into four sections: separately published discographies (including two of Americans, Sousa and, in the appendix, Ives); series and books of multiple discographical interest (including Cohn's Collector's 20th Century Music, no. 253); discographies in book-length studies (including general American, Bernstein, Copland, Gershwin and Previn); and discographies in periodicals (including general American music, Copland, Gershwin, Ives, Persichetti, Cole Porter, Riegger, and Varèse). Index. (See also No. A3 in the Appendix.)

257. SLONIMSKY, Nicolas. Lexicon of musical invective: critical assaults on composers since Beethoven's time. New York: Coleman-Ross, 1953. 296p.
_____. _____. 2nd ed. New York: Coleman-Ross, Seattle: University of Washington Press, 1965. 325p.

Included among the targets in this entertaining anthology of prejudiced, ill-informed and ill-considered criticism of composers are six who come right within our compass: Copland, Cowell, Gershwin, Harris, Ruggles and Varèse (no Ives, strangely enough). The criterion for inclusion seems to be that the composer's place in history shows such judgments to be singularly lacking in foresight. (As a bonus for our amusement Slonimsky provides an "Invecticon" --an alphabetical list of abusive terms, such as "coal scuttles, upsetting of, " and "tonal piggery. ")

258. THOMPSON, Kenneth. A dictionary of twentieth-century composers (1911-1971). London: Faber & Faber, 1973. 666p. bibliog.

Of the 32 twentieth-century composers covered in this reference work, whose scope includes only composers dead at the time of compilation, two are of interest here: Ives and Varèse. The entries for each contain a biographical sketch, a catalog of works (the main item, arranged in chronological order, with dates of composition and publication, and, for extended works, details of movements and of first performances, and orchestral instrumentation where relevant), and a selective bibliography of primary and secondary literature.

Bibliographic entries for criticisms of individual works are given following the relevant entry in the works catalog. The Ives catalog is far from complete--186 items are listed--and no criteria for omission are given (c.f. nos. 328 / 330). The Ives bibliography lists 100 items. Secondary literature on Ives may not compare with that on, say, Debussy, but it is rather more extensive than that. The Varèse bibliography lists 57 items.

259. VINTON, John, ed. Dictionary of contemporary music. New York: Dutton, 1974. 834p. bibliogs.
_____. Dictionary of twentieth-century music. London: Thames & Hudson, 1974. 834p. bibliogs.

The principal raison d'être for this impressive reference work is the provision of biographical, bibliographical and, in many instances, critical information on composers of the Western concert tradition born, for the most part, after 1880, and/or alive after 1930. Composers of the United States fare very well, both in terms of numerical representation and depth of study. In numerous cases articles depart from the purely biographical to include some critical assessment, description of stylistic phases and characteristics, and to note influences. In addition to the individual entries there are articles on technical subjects, emphasizing the distinctively contemporary, on national characteristics and movements of the music of individual countries (including the U.S.A.), and on genres. The last category includes jazz (ragtime and blues), popular music and the musical. The general articles are concise, well-informed, and often illustrated with music examples. All articles have bibliographies, and many are followed by subject cross references. The entries on individuals are exclusively concerned with composers, many of whom contributed the information on which their entry is based. Longer, signed articles are the work of individual experts, drawn from an international field.

b. Composers' Writings

260. HINES, Robert Stephan, ed. The composer's point of view: essays on 20th century music by those who wrote it. Norman: University of Oklahoma Press, 1963. 342p. bibliog.

Included in these essays is a section devoted to United States composers, in which Lukas Foss, Howard Hanson, Ernst Krenek, Peter Mennin, Vincent Persichetti, Bernard Rogers and Leo Sowerby each discuss one of their own compositions and the principles on which they worked. The music examples they refer to are collected at the end book, where there is also a catalog of the composers' choral works and an index.

261. HINES, R. S., ed. The orchestral composer's point of view: essays on twentieth-century music by those who wrote it. Norman: University of Oklahoma Press, 1970. 254p. bibliog.

Five of the twelve contributors to this collection were born in the U.S.--Milton Babbitt, Elliott Carter, Ross Lee Finney, Vincent Persichetti and Gunther Schuller; one, Ernst Krensk, is a naturalized American. They discuss their own orchestral music, and the present state and future development of composition for orchestra. Several lament the lack of the right conditions for the creation of modern orchestral music. There are frequent music examples, and there is a catalog of the orchestral works of the twelve composers.

262.   LANG, Paul Henry, ed. Problems of modern music: the Princeton Seminar in Advanced Musical Studies. New York: Norton, 1962. 121p.
These seven papers include three by native American composers: Roger Sessions on the problems and issues facing the composer today, Elliott Carter's shop talk (also in no. 263), and a technical essay by Milton Babbitt on twelve tone invariants as compositional determinants. Ernst Krenek also writes on serial techniques.

263.   SCHWARTZ, Elliott, and CHILDS, Barney, eds. Contemporary composers on contemporary music. New York: Holt, Rinehart & Winston, 1967. 375p.
These essays by and interviews with 33 20th-century composers are collected together in an attempt to make accessible musical attitudes and philosophies of those most able to articulate them. There are two sections--on pre-1945 European music, and on experimental music and recent American developments. Among the contributors to the second part (in pieces reprinted, in the main, from other sources) are Copland, Harris, Sessions, Varèse, Partch, Babbitt, Carter, Foss, with interviews with Cage, Feldman and Wuorinen. Subjects discussed include aspects of composition in general and their own works in particular. Music examples in the text.

c.   Histories

264.   AUSTIN, William W. Music in the 20th century, from Debussy through Stravinsky. New York: Norton; London: Dent, 1966. 708p. illus., bibliog.
One of the most thorough, well-balanced books on 20th century music, and one of the few general histories to give prominence to a sympathetic account of the emergence and development of jazz (a place it shares with Stravinsky, Schoenberg and Bartok). All major modern American composers born before 1910 are considered, but the author deliberately avoids direct evaluation of those born later. The chapters devoted to the emergence and the mainstream and modern developments in jazz include music analysis and examples. Morton, Armstrong, Ellington and Parker in particular are closely studied, and there is a roster of outstanding musicians, divided by date of birth, and instrument, and covering 1885-1932. The immense annotated bibliography is divided into international surveys, surveys of particular areas, a long listing of writings about individual musicians, a section on jazz in general and a miscellany. Index of persons, titles and subjects.

265. NEW OXFORD HISTORY OF MUSIC. Vol. X. The modern
    age, 1890-1960; edited by Martin Cooper. London: Ox-
    ford University Press, 1974. 764p. illus., bibliog.
    Richard Franko Goldman contributes to this volume a 65-
page chapter on American art music from 1918-1960, in which he
surveys the styles of outstanding individual composers--in particular
Ives, Gershwin, Copland, Cowell, Thomson, Riegger, Sessions, Piston, Harris and Carter--and relates them to developing trends.
There is a generous number of music examples (sixteen in all),
some in full score. Goldman does not consider jazz or popular music in their own right, nor are they examined elsewhere in the book.

266. SALZMAN, Eric. Twentieth-century music: an introduction.
    Englewood Cliffs: Prentice-Hall, 1967. 196p. illus.,
    bibliog. notes.
    _____. 2nd ed. Englewood Cliffs: Prentice-
    Hall, 1974. 242p. illus., bibliog. notes.
    A concise and perceptive survey of developing musical ideas
in the "serious" music tradition in the 20th century. American music is discussed in relation to international stylistic development
from the point of view of national style, and the continuity of twelve-
tone ideas. (Hitchcock's book, no. 30, is intended to complement
this one for the study of American music.) Ives is discussed as
the first great original. The final chapters (much expanded in the
2nd. edition) are concerned with contemporary trends, and American
composers predominate. Analytical comment is deliberately minimal
but usually illuminating (it is relegated to an appendix in the 2nd. edition with the music examples). Bibliographical notes follow each chapter and there is an index.

267. STERNFELD, F. W., ed. Music in the modern age. New
    York: Praeger; London: Weidenfeld & Nicolson, 1973.
    (A History of Western Music, Vol. 5) 515p. bibliog.,
    discog.
    Under the national approach adopted by this volume we are
given a separate 42-page chapter on North America, in which Wayne
D. Shirley provides a summary of individuals and trends in concert
and popular music in the 20th century, followed by a short analysis
of experimentalism by R. T. Beck, and an essay on jazz improvisation by Jon Newsom. Shirley proceeds mainly by groups sharing
common characteristics, from those attempting to break from the
European tradition, through Impressionists, popular composers,
symphonists, independents, early experimentalists, immigrants, with
special mention of Ives, and of Kirchner and Carter, to serialists,
choral and electronic music, and the "new" popular music. This
enormous canvas is painted, of necessity, with a wide brush, but
with occasional precise detail, usually achieved by music example.
Newsom's contribution is a fine, closely argued musical analysis--
again, with music examples--of the increasing rhythmic and harmonic complexity in the improvisations of Lester Young, Charlie
Parker and Lennie Tristano. The LP discography and the bibliography of books and articles each have a companion section to the American chapter, and there are indexes of persons and places, and of
subjects.

268.   YATES, Peter. Twentieth century music: its evolution from
       the end of the harmonic era into the present era of sound.
       New York: Pantheon Books, 1967; New York: Minerva
       Press; London: Allen & Unwin, 1968. 367p. bibliog.
       notes.
       A study of the evolution of serious musical composition in
the last hundred years, directed at the lay reader (but not over-
simplified on his account) and aiming to "assemble an aesthetic
which will serve the listener to break through the confusion caused
by those who do not understand, by those who do not wish to understand, and by those who deny what has been happening in music" (introduction).   Yates discusses the developments in the American musical tradition (there are references in the index) and pays particular attention to the Gertrude Stein-Virgil Thomson partnership, to
Copland, Ives and Cage, with two chapters on the "American experimental tradition" (Seeger, Cowell, Varèse, McPhee, Hovhaness,
Brant and others).   One appendix contains extracts from Harry
Partch's description of his "Delusion of the Fury." No music examples; index.

d.   Critical Works

269.   COPE, David. New directions in music. Dubuque: Brown,
       1971. 140p. illus., bibliog., discog. notes.
       A study for music students of avant-garde music to 1970,
examining philosophies, materials, techniques, composers and works,
with particular emphasis on the "relation of these to significant and
realistic directions of style and thought." The extensive influence
and contribution of American composers, noted by Bertram Turet-
zky in the preface, is apparent in each part of the study, which
first explores the divergence of ideals of music as thought (control)
and music as sound (freedom), and follows this by various aspects
of modern music: sound mass, instrument exploration, electronic
music, multimedia, improvisation, indeterminacy, and anti-music.
The text includes many diagrams and music examples.   Recommendations for further reading and listening conclude each chapter.   A
glossary and a collection of biographical sketches are included in
appendices, and there is an index.

270.   COPLAND, Aaron. Our new music: leading composers in
       Europe and America. New York: Whittlesey House, 1941.
       305p. discog.
              . The new music, 1900-1960. Rev. ed. New York:
       Norton; London: Macdonald, 1968. 194p.
       The revised version of this collection contains articles cover-
ing 1927-1967, divided equally into sections on European and American composers of the 20th century, with a short concluding section
on the music of the 1950s and electronic music.   The American section includes assessment of the works of Ives, Harris, Sessions,
Piston, Thomson, Blitzstein and the Mexican Chavez.   There is
also an autobiographical chapter.   Though he does not analyze the
music closely, Copland has many perceptive and persuasive things

to say. He describes his attitude to contemporary music as "permissive." There are various references to the role of jazz in the work of some of the composers discussed.

271. EWEN, David. David Ewen introduces modern music; a history and appreciation; from Wagner to Webern. Philadelphia: Chilton, 1962. 303p. illus.

_____. _____; from Wagner to the avant-garde. Rev. ed. New York: Chilton, 1969. 323p.

An undemanding work in which Ewen divides 20th century composers into categories (e.g., Wagnerites, the Eccentrics, the Nationalists, etc.) and within these takes the principal figures individually and briefly discusses their major works and the main features of their music. American composers discussed range from Ives through Cage. There are no bibliographical references or music examples.

272. KOSTELANETZ, Richard, ed. The new American arts. New York: Horizon, 1965. 270p. discog.

_____. _____. New York: Collier Books; London: Collier-Macmillan, 1967. 270p. discog.

Includes an essay by Eric Salzman, "The New Music," which defines the creative possibilities in contemporary American music, and describes the salient features of the work of Babbitt, Varèse, Brown, Foss, Wolpe, Wuorinen, Cage and others. There is a six-page LP discography.

273. KOSTELANETZ, Richard. The theatre of mixed means: an introduction to happenings, kinetic environments, and other mixed-means performances. New York: Dial Press, 1968. 311p. illus., bibliog.

This series of conversations with outstanding contributors to the new theatrical movement, which Kostelanetz calls "mixed means" --to distinguish it from "traditional, predominantly literary monomean practice" (foreword)--includes two with individuals known principally for their work in music: John Cage and La Monte Young. By the nature of this theater the others interviewed have all had associations with music. They are: Ann Halprin, Robert Rauschenberg, Allan Kaprow, Claes Oldenberg, Ken Dewey, Robert Whitman, and members of the USCO community. The Cage interview is reproduced in part in Kostelanetz's book on the composer, no. 310.

274. MACHLIS, Joseph. Introduction to contemporary music. New York: Norton, 1961; London: Dent, 1963. 714p. illus., bibliog., discog.

A valuable general survey which places emphasis on contemporary American music, devoting 200 pages to the subject, from Ives to Varèse and other experimental composers. There are sections outlining the life and work of over 30 individuals, and many more are mentioned more briefly. A section on music theater includes Gershwin, Weill, Blitzstein, Menotti and Bernstein. There are music examples, and included in the appendices are a description of basic musical concepts, a set of texts and translations of vocal works, and a chronology. Index.

275. NYMAN, Michael. Experimental music: Cage and beyond.
London: Studio Vista, 1974; New York: Schirmer, 1975.
154p. illus., bibliog.

Nyman's sympathetic study begins by isolating and defining the
characteristics that distinguish experimental music of the 1950s and
1960s from other music of the avant-garde, taking Cage's "4'33'"
as a point of reference. From here he proceeds in a broadly chronological way, examining first the backgrounds to experimental music in the light of Cage's approach to historical influence (present
practice influences the way we see the past, rather than vice versa),
and outlining the work of composers of the 1950s (Feldman, Brown,
Wolff, Cage), George Brecht and the Fluxus School in the 1960s,
experimental uses of electronic systems, the indeterminacy of Christian Wolff and others, and the "minimal music, determinacy and the
new tonality" of Terry Riley, La Monte Young and Steve Reich.
Numerous British composers are also considered. There are several music illustrations, the useful bibliography of books and articles
is arranged by chapters, and there is also an index of names and
titles.

276. ROSENFELD, Paul. Discoveries of a music critic. New
York: Harcourt, Brace, 1936. (Repr. New York: Vienna
House, 1972). 402p.

In his day a controversial critic, principally because of his
avoidance of the tools of music analysis and his eloquent but over-
mannered style, Rosenfeld (1890-1946) was an ardent advocate of
new music. Roger Sessions, in his Reflections (no. 370), wrote
that "it is impossible to overestimate Rosenfeld's contribution as a
writer and as an enthusiastic propagandist for the contemporary music of his period, and for the development of the music of this country" (p. 130). A sequence of chapters in this collection of Rosenfeld's critical articles is concerned with American music. Here he
turns his uncompromising but unanalytical gaze on a series of individual composers and works: Varèse's "Ionisation," Gershwin,
Cowell, recent operas by Taylor, Gruenberg, Thomson, Hanson,
Antheil and Bennett (with some recollections of Parker's "Mona,"
which for Rosenfeld remains "the great American opera"), Ives,
Harris, Copland and Riegger. A biographical appendix provides
sketches of Varèse, Gershwin, Cowell, Ives, Harris, Copland and
Riegger, and there is an index. (Several of these pieces reappear
in Musical Impressions, no. 278.)

277. ROSENFELD, Paul. An hour with American music. Philadelphia: Lippincott, 1929. 179p.

In this book Rosenfeld first writes dismissively of jazz ("the
best of Jazz stands inert") and of folk music, neither of which fills
his bill of an original American music. Beginning then with Edward MacDowell he continues his search for originality in a series
of examinations, conducted with considerable critical acumen, of a
number of composers: Charles Loeffler, Leo Ornstein, Dane Rudhyar, Roger Sessions, Adolph Weiss, Virgil Thomson, Carl Ruggles, Horatio Parker, Deems Taylor, Roy Harris, Aaron Copland,
the Mexican Carlos Chavez, and finally Edgard Varèse, who alone

seems to Rosenfeld to "orientate us to a kind of world to which America is closer than Europe is," the others showing, to a greater or lesser degree, eclectic and/or derivative tendencies.

278. ROSENFELD, Paul. Musical impressions: selections from Paul Rosenfeld's criticism; edited and with an introduction by Herbert A. Leibowitz. New York: Hill & Wang, 1969; London: Allen & Unwin, 1970. 302p. bibliog.
    A wide-ranging collection of Rosenfeld's essays on contemporary musical topics, including a section of nine on aspects of American music, among which are several reprinted from An Hour with American Music (no. 277: those on jazz, MacDowell, Copland, Sessions, Varèse and Ruggles). The three other pieces are on Ives, Gershwin, and Varèse's "Ionisation" (Rosenfeld was among the first to champion both Ives and Varèse). The introduction is an excellent appreciation of Rosenfeld by the editor. Index.

c. Electronic Music

> Note: Much of the growing body of literature on electronic music is international in scope and/or technical in nature. The following books are chiefly reference works, plus one or two illustrating problems faced by American composers.

279. CROSS, Lowell M., comp. A bibliography of electronic music. Toronto: University of Toronto Press, 1967. 126p.
    International in scope, this alphabetical list of books and articles contains 1,562 items. The compiler aims at "as extensive a bibliography as possible for 'musique concrète,' 'elektronische Musik,' 'tape music,' 'computer music' and closely related fields in experimental music." The index contains references to American studies, to Babbitt, Cage, Tudor, Varèse and Wuorinen, to general topics (history, aesthetics), to computers and to instruments.

280. DAVIES, Hugh, comp. Répertoire international des musiques electroacoustiques. International electronic music catalog. Paris: Le Groupe de Recherches Musicales; Trumansburg, N.Y.: Independent Electronic Music Center, 1968. 330p.
    In his impressive catalog, useful to both planner and student, the compiler lists every known electronic composition from the earliest attempts in the medium up to early 1967. He groups his material by country, providing an opportunity for the examination of national characteristics. The U.S.A. listing occupies 65 pages, and is sub-arranged by state and by town. Each studio is listed by title or owner's name, with a designation (permanent or improvised). Compositions are given chronologically, with details of composer, title, function (concert, theater, radio, etc.), date, duration, tracks, recordings, other aspects (jazz, painting, poetry) and notes. There are separate cumulative lists of commerical records and tapes, arranged by company, and there is also a composer index.

281. HILLER, Lejaren, and ISAACSON, Leonard M. Experimental
      music: composition with an electronic computer. New
      York: McGraw-Hill, 1959. 197p. bibliog. notes.
      Detailed discussion of a series of pioneer experiments under-
taken on an Illiac computer at the University of Illinois, and of the
various problems--aesthetic and technical--involved. A definition
of experimental music is attempted, and technical and artistic
achievements in the field in Europe and America are described.
The "Illiac Suite" for string quartet, which was the main result of
the experiments, is described, and its score is given in the appendix.

282. LINCOLN, Harry B. , ed. The computer and music. Ithaca:
      Cornell University Press, 1970. 354p. bibliog. notes.
      Twenty-one articles by American contributors examine the
use of computers in composition and musical analysis, and illustrate
the possibilities for developing their use in both areas. There are
two articles on the use of computers for music information retrieval.

283. SCHWARTZ, Elliott. Electronic music: a listener's guide.
      New York: Praeger; London: Secker & Warburg, 1973.
      306p. illus., bibliog., discog.
      Schwartz's lucid, relaxed outline of the past, present and fu-
ture of electronic music draws heavily for its examples on developments in America and on American compositions. His aim is "to
make the basic facts of electronic music as clear as possible for
the typical listener" (p. ix), showing that these can be grasped without a sophisticated knowledge of technology. Part I, on the period
from 1906 (the date of Thaddeus Cahill's electric keyboard that so
fired Busoni's imagination) to 1960, examines and explains musical
and technical precedents, outlining changing musical vocabulary and
instruments, and pointing to significant compositions. Part II, on
the 1960s, discusses the synthesizer, computer-generated sound, and
the live performance of music using electronic material (the latter
being illustrated by an all-American cast that includes Cage, Hiller,
Foss, Reich, Pauline Oliveros and others). Following a pause to
suggest further listening and reading, Schwartz moves on to some
considerations for the future, on the nature of performance, the interactions between "serious" music, jazz, rock and pop, and on new
approaches to music teaching. At this point he hands over to a bevy
of composers (23 in all, mostly American) and their observations
(specially elicited) on electronic music. The bibliography and discography, though both selective, are quite extensive, and there is an
index.

2. 20th Century American Art Music

a. Reference and Collected Biography

284. EDMUNDS, John, and BOELZNER, Gordon. Some twentieth

century American composers: a selective bibliography.
Vol. 1. With an introductory essay by Peter Yates. New
York: New York Public Library, 1959. 57p. illus.
_____. _____. Vol. 2. With an introductory essay by
Nicolas Slonimsky. New York: New York Public Library,
1960. 55p. illus.

Thirty-two composers are represented in this very useful
compilation. They are: (Vol. 1) Brant, Cage, Carter, Copland,
Cowell, Harris, Harrison, Hovhaness, Ives, Partch, Riegger, Ruggles, Sessions, Thomson and Varèse; (Vol. 2) Barber, Bernstein,
Blitzstein, Creston, Dello Joio, Diamond, Foss, Glanville-Hicks,
Hanson, Kirchner, Moore, Piston, Porter, Schuman, Thompson and
Weber. Under each there are lists of the composer's writings in
article and book form, writings about him in general, articles about
individual compositions, and references to relevant entries in reference works. There are numerous photographic portraits. Vol. 2
contains appendices devoted to lists of composers whose names appear in reference works, and of composers not listed in the same
works. Both volumes have a name index.

285.   EWEN, David, ed. American composers today: a biograph-
       ical and critical guide. New York: Wilson, 1949. 265p.
       illus., bibliogs., discogs.
       Ewen describes this 20th century biographical dictionary as
a "guide to creative figures in serious music who have been function-
ing in this country and in Latin America between 1900 and the present day, and whose work has found acceptance in the concert hall,
opera house, over the radio, or on phonograph records." Approximately 180 composers are represented, including numerous Europeans who emigrated in the 1930s, regardless of whether they became American citizens (hence we have Schoenberg, Stravinsky,
Hindemith, Martinu, etc.). Ewen claims that for most of the
sketches "the composers themselves provided the factual data and
have carefully checked them"; a number contain a paragraph or two
on general outlook, likes and dislikes, by the composer himself,
while one or two are almost entirely in the composer's own words.
In general the biographical information is quite detailed, and the
critical assessment rather generalized. Almost every entry (average length one and a half pages) has a photograph and all are followed by a list of principal works, with occasional discographies.
(In five instances--Chadwick, Gilbert, Griffes, Herbert and Parker
--the compiler refers the reader to his Composers of Yesterday,
New York, Wilson, 1937, which also contains biographies of Billings,
De Koven, Foster, Hopkinson and Paine.)

286.   GOSS, Madeleine. Modern music-makers: contemporary
       American composers. New York: Dutton, 1952. (Repr.
       Westport: Greenwood Press, 1968). 499p. illus., bib-
       liog.
       Thirty-seven composers born between 1874 and 1922 (from
Ives to Foss) are each given a section in this very useful chronologically arranged work. Each section contains an account of the composer's life and work, a chart listing main events and works chron-

ologically, a classified facsimile of a portion of a manuscript. With
the exception of Ives the compiler talked personally with each composer.

287. HOWARD, John Tasker. Our contemporary composers: Amer-
      ican music in the twentieth century; with the assistance of
      Arthur Mendel. New York: Crowell, 1941. 447p. illus. ,
      bibliog. , discog.
      Howard's enviable capacity for obtaining, organizing and lu-
cidly communicating vast quantities of information on American music (while maintaining his enthusiasm) remains unimpaired in this
assembly of concise biographical and critical portraits of 20th century American composers. Designed as a supplement and companion
to his Our American Music (no. 24), this volume takes individuals
in turn within broad groups (Howard admits they are somewhat ar-
bitrary) with titles such as "Safe and Sound," "Unfamiliar Idioms,"
"Newcomers" and "Experimenters." The portraits normally include
a general description, biographical summary, mention of a number
of compositions, and quotes from contemporary reviews. (Howard
declares his view that his own opinions "should be supplemented by,
and even subordinate to, the best critical attitudes of the present
day" [p. viii].) Much information was apparently obtained from
questionnaires. Of his content Howard says, "an earnest attempt
has been made to render it as comprehensive as possible, to include
all those who have made themselves known for works in the larger
forms." Though the major part of the book is devoted to concert
music, there are sections for Broadway composers and a select
number of jazz musicians. When the names included are grouped
for an appendix under their home states they total 207. Among the
13 other appendices is a discography by Florence Strauss giving
composer, title of work, performers and recording company. The
14 full-page photographic portraits are particularly fine. Index.

288. JACOBI, Hugh Wm. , comp. Contemporary American com-
      posers based at American colleges and universities; edi-
      torial consultant, Margaret De Voss. Paradise, Ca. :
      Paradise Arts, 1975. 240p.
      An alphabetical biographical directory of 749 composers--a
large total, which bears witness to what Milton Babbitt in his brief
foreword calls "the intellectual reorientation of musical creation in
this country." The information in the entries normally consists of
date and places of birth, education, awards, major compositions,
membership of associations, guilds and other organizations, present
appointment, and address. They are written in the crisp staccato
style of a "Who's Who," without comment of any kind. The compiler attempts to add a little zip to the book by periodically inserting
groups of quotations on the composer in academe (with attributions
where known, but no sources).

289. MACHLIS, Joseph. American composers of our time. New
      York: Crowell, 1963. 237p. bibliog.
      A non-technical introduction to the life and work of 16 Amer-
ican composers. Biographical information is combined with descrip-

tion of each composer's stylistic development, and each chapter contains an outline of a typical work. There is a glossary of terms, a guide to further reading, and an index. Apart from MacDowell, all are 20th century figures: Ives, Griffes, Moore, Piston, Hanson, Thomson, Harris, Gershwin, Copland, Barber, Schuman, Menotti, Dello Joio, Bernstein and Foss.

290.   PAN AMERICAN UNION. Composers of the Americas: biographical data and catalogs of their works. Washington: Organization of American States, 1955- .
This most useful on-going series of annual publications includes in its first eighteen fascicules (to 1972) catalogs of 102 United States composers of the 20th century (out of a total of around 300). The pattern of each composer section is the same: photograph, short biography, facsimile of a page of music manuscript, and a classified chronological catalog of compositions (date, title, instrumentation, duration, publisher and notes on first performances). Each volume contains an index to previous issues.

291.   REIS, Claire R. Composers in America: biographical sketches of living composers with a record of their works, 1912-1937. New York: Macmillan, 1938. 270p.
_____. _____: biographical sketches of contemporary composers with a record of their works. Rev. and enlarged ed. New York: Macmillan, 1947. 399p.
The first edition of this work gives biographical sketches and lists of works for composers, American-born or American citizens, who were alive at the time of compilation. For the second edition the policy was changed to include music written between 1915 and 1945, regardless of the nationality of the composer in question, and his temporal or eternal state. In addition, certain pre-1915 works of a "prophetic" nature are included. The second edition, more extensive than the first, lists over 300 composers, all of whom had received at least one major performance. Composers best known for operetta or musical comedy are excluded, but film music is listed. The biographies of each composer include details of awards, commissions and broadcasts. The lists of compositions are arranged in groups, with details of duration, publisher and date.

b.   Critical Works   (See also no. 364.)

292.   BORETZ, Benjamin, and CONE, Edward T., eds. Perspectives on American composers. New York: Norton, 1971. 268p. bibliog. notes.
A "representative selection" of 21 articles from Perspectives of New Music, 1962-1968, by composers about composers. The subjects are all 20th century figures, including Ives, Varèse, Sessions, Copland, Piston, Wolpe, Steuermann, Carter, Berger and Finney. The articles are examinations of their music, not of their lives or personalities. Varèse, Sessions, Krenek, Schuller and Carter are among the 20 authors. Many of the articles have music examples and bibliographic references. No index.

293.   COWELL, Henry, ed. American composers on American music: a symposium. Stanford: Stanford University Press, 1933. 226p.

_____. ; with a new introduction. New York: Ungar, 1962. 226p.

Cowell's purpose in this symposium of 31 essays (some originally published elsewhere, but most commissioned for this volume) was "to present the composer's own point of view concerning creative music in America" (preface). In this Cowell felt his book was "an experiment unprecedented in musical history." The composers were asked to contribute articles on one another's music, or on a more general musical topic, expressing their opinions "seriously, fearlessly and in detail." Among the contributing composers are Charles Seeger, Riegger, Weiss, Hanson, Copland, Slonimsky, Harris, Still, Gershwin, Becker, Rudhyar and Ives. All these save Still, Gershwin and Rudhyar are also individually examined, as are Ruggles, Varèse, Sessions, Brant, Ruth Crawford Seeger and Walter Piston, among others. More general topics covered include oriental influences (Rudhyar), an Afro-American viewpoint (Still), the relation of jazz to American music (Gershwin), and the future of music (Ives). (Paul Rosenfeld, though a staunch supporter of Cowell, felt that his anthology showed "an obsession with the means of music and a neglect of its substance"--Discoveries of a Music Critic, no. 276, p. 280.)

294.   HANSON, Howard. Music in contemporary American civilization. Lincoln: University of Nebraska, 1951. (Montgomery Lectures on Contemporary Civilization) 50p.

Composer and teacher, with a wide experience of conducting American music, Howard Hanson surveys trends and individuals in American music from the late 19th century in three lectures. In the first he discusses the problems of evaluating contemporary music, and makes a case for "the progress of historical judgement" with an evaluative survey of American symphonists from the 1880s (Paine, Chadwick) to 1920 (Leo Sowerby), in which many individuals are briefly discussed. His second lecture, covering 1920-1950, demonstrates the progress made in creating a helpful environment for young composers--notably the Eastman School's "American Composers' Concerts"--and summarizes the work of a number of composers. In the third lecture he discusses obstacles to progress in music education, the need for America to give an international cultural lead, and some problems of the connection between music and private enterprise.

295.   HOWARD, John Tasker. Studies of contemporary American composers. New York: Fischer, 1925-1940. 10v. illus.

A series of pamphlet studies on nine composers: Alexander Russell, Eastwood Lane, James P. Dunn, A. Walter Kramer, Deems Taylor (two editions, the second being issued in 1940 with additional material), Emerson Whithorne, Bainbridge Crist, Charles Sanford Skilton and Cecil Burleigh. Each study combines a brief biography with a critical description of the music, involving quite frequent use of music examples. Each also contains a list of works.

296.   REIS, Claire R.   Composers, conductors and critics.   New
       York: Oxford University Press, 1955.   264p.   illus.,
       bibliog. notes.

       _____.   ; with a new introduction by the author;
       new preface by Aaron Copland; foreword by Darius Mil-
       haud.   Detroit: Detroit Reprints in Music, 1974.   264p.
       illus., bibliog. notes.

Of the two important bodies encouraging contemporary music
in 20th century America by arranging performances and commission-
ing compositions--the International Composers' Guild and the League
of Composers--Aaron Copland wrote, "To these two societies a new
generation of American composers turned for support ... What our
fate would have been without their help is difficult to visualize" (no.
270, p. 103).   When she wrote this personal account of the activities
of the League Mrs. Reis had been its Director for 25 years, from
which position she had an excellent view of the changing musical
scene, in particular of developments in the position of the composer.
Her informal chronicle is, in her own words, "a kaleidoscope record of the times in contemporary music" (p. xi).   It includes an account of how the League developed as a breakaway group of Varèse's
Guild in 1923, and how Modern Music, the League's famous journal,
was launched the following year.   The appendix includes a list of
25th anniversary commissions.   Index.

297.   STEARNS, Harold E., ed.   Civilization in the United States:
       an enquiry by thirty Americans.   New York: Harcourt,
       Brace; London: Cape, 1922.   (Repr. St. Clair Shores:
       Scholarly Press, 1970; Westport: Greenwood Press, 1971).
       577p.   bibliog. notes.

Stearns calls this symposium an "adventure in intellectual cooperation" (p. xiii), stressing the heterogeneous nature of 20th century America and what he sees as emotional and aesthetic starvation,
and spiritual poverty.   Deems Taylor, made responsible for the musical side of the enquiry into contemporary America, takes a very
gloomy view both of the achievements of the American composer and
of the attitude towards music of the typical American.   The composer he accuses of a lack of taste, of technical equipment and of
staying power; worse still, "the American composer's most complete
failure is intellectual" (p. 202).   The average American male is
criticized for viewing music in terms of potential amusement, instruction or edification, never for its own sake, and for holding it
as basically un-masculine (hence the responsibility for cultivating
music has passed to women).

298.   THOMSON, Virgil.   American music since 1910; with an in-
       troduction by Nicolas Nabokov.   London: Weidenfeld &
       Nicolson; New York: Holt, Rinehart & Winston, 1971.
       (Twentieth-Century Composers, Vol. 1)   204p.   illus.,
       bibliog.

Although the title seems to imply a historical survey this is
an anthology of essays on selected aspects of modern American music and America's arrival at a "musical maturity," all very readable
and containing many insights, but markedly personal in approach.

The main text covers 90 pages, and includes essays on Ives, Ruggles, Varèse, Copland, Cage and, briefly, a crowded gallery of other contemporary figures. (Thomson's view of Ives is basically a dissenting one; he castigates Ives for not giving all to his art, and thinks "MacDowell may well survive him"--p. 30.) There are also chapters on Thomson's operas, by Victor Fell Yellin, and on Latin American music, by Gilbert Chase. Following the text there is a biographical directory of 106 composers, with lists of their principal works, and dates. This section does seem disproportionate in length to the main text.

c. Individual Composers

DAVID AMRAM

299. AMRAM, David. Vibrations: the adventures and musical times of David Amram. New York: Macmillan, 1968. 352p. illus.
_____. _____. New York: Viking Press, 1971. 469p. illus.
A somewhat diffuse but enjoyable autobiographical account of Amram's "first 37 years" (he was born in 1930), in which his widely varying activities (including composition, conducting jazz and rock) come clearly across, as does his achievement in reaching the position of successful composer through considerable hard work and dedication (with lots of fun along the way). There are perhaps rather many episodes of little significance (his memory is remarkable), but we encounter an enormous number of musicians, and get an idea of the wide variety of experience available to a man of so many parts and such boundless energy.

GEORGE ANTHEIL

300. ANTHEIL, George. Bad boy of music. Garden City: Doubleday, 1945. 378p.
_____. _____. London: Hurst & Blackett, 1947. 295p.
Autobiographical account of the composer's life from 1922 to 1945, covering the period in Europe--Berlin, Paris and Vienna, and including the first performance of his best known work, "Ballet Mécanique"--his return to New York in 1933 and subsequent period in Hollywood, where he wrote for films and ballet in particular. Many literary and musical personalities are encountered, and there are stories of the performance and reception of his works, with little comment on their creation. (Antheil was born in New Jersey in 1900, and died in 1959 in New York.)

301. POUND, Ezra. Antheil and the Treatise on harmony. Paris: Three Mountains Press, 1924. 106p.
_____. _____. Chicago: P. Covici, 1927. (Repr. New York: Da Capo, 1968). 150p.
Pound's idiosyncratic pronouncements on music presented here

are perhaps more of interest to students of their author than of
their subject, though some of his thoughts on sound are a herald of
contemporary approaches. The apotheosis of Antheil and his musical
innovations forms the main part of the book. The treatise under-
lines Pound's fascination with sound. His writings on music of the
"New Age" under the pseudonym of William Atheling are collected
together, with marginal notes by Antheil, who is prominent again in
the section of varia that concludes the book. Ned Rorem's introduction to the reprint almost annihilates Pound the music critic, but
allows him to survive by virtue of certain passages of insight.

SAMUEL BARBER

302.   BRODER, Nathan. Samuel Barber. New York: Schirmer.
         1954. 110p. illus., bibliog., discog.
         A concise biographical portrait of Barber (b. 1910) in the
first part of this study is followed by an analytical examination of
his music in the second part. Revising and extending an article
that originally appeared in Musical Quarterly, July 1948, Broder
proceeds from a description of general stylistic features of Barber's
music to a short analysis, with numerous music examples, of his
work in particular categories (choral, piano, chamber, etc.). The
appendix gives a list of Barber's published compositions in chronological order (1927-1953), with notes on first performances. The
discography includes performers, year of release and catalogue number for each record. Index.

LEONARD BERNSTEIN

303.   BRIGGS, John. Leonard Bernstein: the man, his work and
         his world. Cleveland: World, 1961. 274p. illus., dis-
         cog.
         Aimed at a wide audience, this biographical account of Bern-
stein's musical development and career from his birth in 1918 to
1959 traces the awakening of his passion for music at the age of
ten, his early tuition, his academic career at Harvard and the Curtis
Institute, his apprenticeship as a conductor, his early compositions,
his friendship with Serge Koussevitzky, his first faltering steps as a
professional musician, followed by his rapid rise to fame as assistant conductor of the New York Philharmonic, and his subsequent career as a world-famous virtuoso. Fortune often seemed to attend
him in his progress to the peaks of achievement, but Briggs emphasizes Bernstein's readiness when opportunity arose, and his great
assurance in seizing it. The genesis, general character, and reception of his major compositions are described in their context, but
without any attempt at analysis.

304.   GRUEN, John, and HEYMAN, Ken. The private world of
         Leonard Bernstein; text by John Gruen, photographs by Ken
         Heyman. New York: Viking Press; London: Weidenfeld
         and Nicolson, 1968. 191p. illus.
         An attempt to capture, in words and pictures, something of
the essence of Leonard Bernstein, private individual and family man,

and Leonard Bernstein, artist, reflecting on his life and art. Gruen spent several weeks with the Bernsteins as they vacationed in Italy in the summer of 1967; in his relaxed text he describes Bernstein in a domestic context, observes and converses with members of the family, and relates his own frequent attempts to draw the maestro into self-examination and revelation. Though in a somewhat depressed state, Bernstein radiates energy, and talks articulately about his life, influences upon him, his conducting career (including the 1943 Philharmonic debut), and, in a concluding conversation, the functions of music in a world in crisis. The large number of photographs support the text with informal illustrations of the family in Italy and of Bernstein conducting in New York.

JOHN CAGE

305.   CAGE, John. M: writings '67-'72. Middletown: Wesleyan University Press; London: Calder & Boyars, 1973. 217p.
        This third collection of Cage's writings (mostly previously published elsewhere) includes four more sections of his "Diary: how to improve the world," in which epigrammatic comments on life and society, anecdotes (some funny, some with no apparent significance), rhetorical questions and other items flow into each other (with the aid of typography) yet remain unconnected. The influence of Buckminster Fuller, Norman O. Brown, and Mao Tse-Tung, spoken of by Cage in his preamble, are apparent. Other material includes "mesostics" (acrostics in which the base word runs down the center, not the edge) in various stages of removal from syntactical English. There is also a piece, "Mureau," in which Thoreau's thoughts on music are subjected to I Ching chance operations; justification for the results of this (the original is still more interesting) is given by Cage as "the twentieth-century way Thoreau listened."

306.   CAGE, John. Notations. New York: Something Else Press, 1969. unpaged.
        Described by Cage as a large aquarium, this book contains reproductions of excerpts from music manuscripts of 269 contemporary composers, including many Americans, arranged in alphabetical order of composer, without explanatory comment. Chosen from a collection made to raise money for the Foundation of Contemporary Arts, the manuscripts illustrate the individual approach and style of each composer and the multitude of notational methods in use. Some are accompanied by texts written by the composers, or chosen or written by Cage and Alison Knowles, with the typography and number of words determined by I-Ching operations.

307.   CAGE, John. Silence: lectures and writings. Middletown: Wesleyan University Press, 1961; London: Calder & Boyars, 1968. 276p.
        For the way it reflects his main preoccupations, this selection of Cage's writings and lectures on musical aesthetics covering the period from 1939 to 1961 stands as the major and most influential source for his views and approach. Among the topics covered are: experimental music, composition processes, Satie, Varèse,

dance, and indeterminacy. There is also a "Lecture on Nothing" and a "Lecture on Something. "

308. CAGE, John. A year from Monday. Middletown: Wesleyan University Press, 1967; London: Calder & Boyars, 1968. 167p.

The period covered by this second collection of his writings sees Cage "less and less interested in music," finding all other sounds "more useful aesthetically. " The wide range of subjects touched on does include musical ones, however, in particular Ives, and Schoenberg's letters. Marcel Duchamp, Miro, Zen and mushrooms also feature. Each piece has a prefatory note including description of the method employed to determine lay-out on the page and typography. Cage's diary, called "How to improve the world (you will only make matters worse)," makes its first appearance here.

309. CARDEW, Cornelius. Stockhausen serves imperialism, and other articles; with commentary and notes. London: Latimer, 1974. 125p.

Arguing from a Marxist viewpoint, Cardew (English composer, and founder of the Scratch Orchestra) makes a strong attack on both Stockhausen and Cage, whom he regards as "leading figures of the bourgeois musical avantgarde. " In an essay, "John Cage, Ghost or Monster," he describes Cage's music as irrelevant to the struggles of the working people. An introduction by John Tilbury to Cage's "Music of Changes"--which he sees as resembling capitalist society, in which apparent freedom and spontaneity are achieved by laws of supply and demand--discusses the links between a composition and its creator's ideology.

310. KOSTELANETZ, Richard, ed. John Cage. New York: Praeger, 1970; London: Allen Lane, 1971. 237p. illus. , bibliog. , discog.

Cage himself is the leading contributor to this collection of readings recording his various activities, but which is mainly concerned with his music and musical ideas. Critics represented include Henry Cowell, Virgil Thomson, Eric Salzman, Dick Higgins, Olin Downes and the editor. A transcript of a conversation between Cage and the editor opens the book. The various pieces that follow are arranged chronologically, covering 1927-1970. The many illustrations include pages of some scores, and there is a catalog of Cage's compositions. (Cage is also discussed in Calvin Tomkins, The Bride and the Bachelors: the Heretical Courtship in Modern Art [New York: Viking Press; London: Weidenfeld & Nicholson, 1965].)

311. WADDINGTON, C. H. , ed. Biology and the history of the future: an IUBS/UNESCO symposium, with John Cage, Carl-Goeran Heden, Margaret Mead, John Papaionnou, John Platt, Ruth Sagar, and Gunther Stent. Edinburgh: Edinburgh University Press, 1972. 72p. bibliog. notes.

Cage's contributions to the discussions in this small volume, which focuses on the theme of the contribution of biological sciences in providing a philosophical framework for man's future, throw an interesting light on his views on society and the nature of modern man.

ELLIOTT CARTER

312.　EDWARDS, Allen.　Flawed words and stubborn sounds: a conversation with Elliott Carter.　New York: Norton, 1971.　128p.　bibliog.

Condensed from a series of interviews with the composer between 1968 and 1970, this work is arranged in three parts.　In the first, more general, section there is discussion of the relative state of support for and interest in music in Europe and America, and Carter outlines the way his concept of his own music has evolved in relation to his practical and social situation.　The second part is concerned with his personal musical development and the major influences upon him, European and American.　The final section is devoted to technical and aesthetic aspects of his work and of contemporary music in general.　The bibliography lists articles by and about Carter, and there is an index.

313.　NEW YORK PUBLIC LIBRARY.　Elliott Carter: sketches and scores in manuscript; a selection of manuscripts and other pertinent material from the Americana Collection of the Music Division, The New York Public Library, on exhibition December 1973 through February 1974....　New York: New York Public Library, 1973.　64p.　illus., bibliog., discog.

An exhibition catalog that also serves as a useful reference tool, for in addition to short descriptions of the 118 items, biographical notes, photographs, and reproductions of manuscript excerpts, it also contains an alphabetical list of Carter's compositions, with details of date, publisher and first performance, a selective bibliography listing Carter's own writings, general writings about him and criticism of specific works, and a discography with full details of performers, record label and number, and year of release.　The catalog was prepared by Richard Jackson, assisted by Pamela S. Berlin and John Shepard.

AARON COPLAND

314.　COPLAND, Aaron.　Copland on music.　Garden City: Doubleday, 1960; London: Deutsch, 1961; New York: Norton, 1963.　280p.

Copland's approach to music, his knowledge, preferences and critical acumen are illustrated in this selection of pieces, mostly articles, written over a 30-year period.　He discusses the art of music, and some favorite practitioners, describes the scene in the 1920s and 1930s, and considers the younger American composers (plus some from South America).　There are also eight reviews, including ones of works by Stefan Wolpe, William Schuman and Virgil Thomson.　Aspects of contemporary music are examined in the final section.　No index.

315. COPLAND, Aaron. Music and imagination. Cambridge, Mass.: Harvard University Press, 1952. 116p. bibliog. notes.

These are six talks given by Copland as Charles Eliot Norton Professor for 1951-52--a native-born composer in the chair of poetry. The first three consider music and the imaginative mind--questions of listening, of sound, and of interpretation; and the second three, musical imagination and the contemporary scene. The fifth talk relates this theme specifically to the Americas, while the sixth considers the role of the composer in American industrial society.

316. BERGER, Arthur. Aaron Copland. New York: Oxford University Press, 1953. (Repr. Westport: Greenwood Press, 1971). 120p. illus., bibliog., discog.

Berger divides his short study of Copland (b. 1900) into two parts. The first is a portrait of the man, outlining especially "the stages of his musical evolution and his relation to the American musical scene as a whole" (p. vi). The second is devoted to an analysis, with frequent music examples, of particular features of Copland's music, such as economy of means, jazz influences, declamatory style. The Piano Variations and Third Symphony are singled out for special attention, and there are also sections on the film music, and on Copland's Americanism and influence. In the appendix there is a complete catalog of Copland's works up to the Piano Quartet (1950), with first performances and publishers. The bibliography includes books and articles by and about Copland, and there is an index.

317. DOBRIN, Arnold. Aaron Copland: his life and times. New York: Crowell, 1967. 211p. illus., bibliogs.

An informal biography aimed chiefly at younger readers, in which the author outlines Copland's life and career, and relates something of his musical development and the influence upon him. The circumstances of the composition of his most important works, their principal features and their critical reception are described. There is a classified list of his compositions with dates, a list of pocket scores, of scores for young people and of Copland's own books. Index.

318. SMITH, Julia. Aaron Copland: his work and contribution to American music. New York: Dutton, 1955. 336p. illus., bibliog., discog.

A workmanlike study of Copland's life and music to 1955, linking biographical detail and musical development in the one narrative, with a pronounced emphasis on study of his music. Following the early chapters, which describe Copland's childhood and youth in Brooklyn and his period of study in Paris, biographical information is confined to facts of the composer's outer (not very eventful) life--his movements, his commissions, etc.--and is used as a simple framework for detailed study of the music. The author sees three main periods in Copland's musical development: (i) "French-Jazz," subdivided into "Jazz Idiom" and "Experimental and Recapitulation"; (ii) "Abstract," coinciding with the Depression, culminating in the

Piano Variations; and (iii) "American Folksong," in which Copland's musical language is seen to simplify, and he makes great use of folk materials. The music of the third period, which the author describes as basically functional in character, is further divided into "Gebrauchsmusik American Style" (including theater and film music) and "Patriotic and Absolute Works." A great many works are examined in detail--their genesis, structure, character and reception --with frequent use of musical example. A final chapter is devoted to an examination of Copland critical writings. In the appendices are a detailed list of musical works, a list of recordings on 78 and LP, with performers, release numbers, and a chronological list of critical writings in books and articles. There is also an index.

HENRY COWELL

319.   COWELL, Henry. New musical resources. New York: Knopf, 1930. 143p.
　　　　　　　. ; with a preface and notes by Joscelyn Godwin. New York: Something Else Press, 1969. 158p.
One of the primary innovators of the first half of the 20th century, and a tireless promoter of modern music, Cowell (1897-1965) wrote most of this technical work on the potential of harmony and rhythm for a new approach to music between 1917 and 1919, with the encouragement of Samuel Seward and Charles Seeger. It is in three parts--tone combinations, rhythm, and chord-formation (including tone clusters)--and constitutes, in Joscelyn Godwin's words the "earliest comprehensive statement of intent by a "modernistic" American composer" (p. xiii).

ARTHUR FARWELL

320.   FARWELL, Brice, ed. A guide to the music of Arthur Farwell and to the microfilm collection of his work; prepared by his children ... Briarcliff Manor, N.Y.: Brice Farwell, 1972. 138p. illus., bibliog.
Only one-fifth of the music of Arthur Farwell (1872-1952) was ever published in his lifetime, and at the time this valuable guide and catalog was compiled most of that was out of print. In order to provide access to this neglected body of music, his entire output, in published or manuscript form, was microfilmed and is available through Brice Farwell at 5 Deer Trail, Briarcliff Manor. One hundred sixty-eight items appear in the catalog part of this volume, listed chronologically, each with a descriptive note and information on year of composition, publication status, location of manuscript (and of published editions where appropriate), and microfilm reel number. For those planning to perform some of Farwell's music the compiler includes the composer's own program notes for certain of his pieces, and a classified list of works. Preceding the catalog is a short biography, pointing to Farwell's efforts on behalf of the status of the American composer, his interest in the use of native American materials in art music, his Wa-Wan Press enterprise for publishing American music (launched in 1901), his community singing movement during and after World War I, and his "mystical reverence for the

creative process. " Other material includes a reprint of Gilbert
Chase's introduction to the reprint of the Wa-Wan Press's publications (New York: Arno Press, 1907. 5 vols.), some examples of
Farwell's writings (including excerpts from an unpublished book on
the intuitive process of the mind), facsimiles of several manuscripts,
a bibliography of writings about Farwell, the music of four later
pieces, an index of works, and a general index. (Further material
on Farwell may be found in Edgar Lee Kirk's 1959 Eastman School
dissertation, "Toward American Music: a Study of the Life and
Music of Arthur Farwell. ")

CHARLES TOMLINSON GRIFFES

321. MAISEL, Edward M. Charles T. Griffes: the life of an
American composer. New York: Knopf, 1943. (Repr.
New York: Da Capo, 1972). 347p. illus.
As the single most important source for information on
Griffes (1884-1920) Maisel's biography suffers from an unfortunate
lack of documentation; that said, however, it must be admitted that
it is hard to avoid feeling involved in the narrative, which conveys
a mass of information (some fairly peripheral) in a thoroughly readable way. If a major aim of a biography is to stimulate the reader to pursue further investigations himself, Maisel succeeds well.
The primary sources available to him were widely scattered, and
it took much patience to reassemble them. He evidently took pains
to be accurate, having, in his introduction, castigated other writers
for their inaccuracies (including J. T. Howard, whose 26-page
Charles Tomlinson Griffes, New York, Schirmer, 1923, is described
as a "not very usable monograph"). Griffes' homosexuality is a re-
current theme, receiving "unwarranted overemphasis" in the view of
Donna K. Anderson in her preface to the reprint edition. Maisel
deliberately excludes musical analysis of Griffes' works with the exception of the Piano Sonata (1918), an interpretation of which occupies Chapter XVII. Index. (A bibliography of Griffes' compositions
was compiled by Donna K. Anderson in 1966: "The Works of
Charles T. Griffes," Ph.D. dissertation, University of Indiana.)

LOU HARRISON

322. HARRISON, Lou. Music primer: various items about music
to 1970. New York: Peters, 1971. 50p.
The 50 or so individual "items" in this little volume are arranged in an apparently random order, and consist of reflections on
the art of composition, ranging from brief, epigrammatic sentences
to explanations of technical features of composition and advice to
composers. Harrison's own interests (especially Asian music) and
the influences upon him (e.g., Cowell, Partch) are prominent, and
there are various references to aspects of his own music. The entire text is written in calligraphy by Ron Pendergraft.

DICK HIGGINS

323. HIGGINS, Dick. Postface. New York: Something Else Press,

1964. 90p. illus., bibliog. notes.

(Published back-to-back with his "Jefferson's Birthday.") A discussion of the contemporary situation in the arts, including a chapter "Towards Musical Activity" in which Higgins (b. 1938) describes and criticizes what he calls "international stylism," the dominating group of composers whose approach and methods may be different, but whose end products are very similar. He also describes his time as a pupil of Cage and his subsequent activity in America and Europe.

CHARLES IVES

324.   IVES, Charles.   Essays before a sonata.   New York: Knickerbocker Press, 1920. 124p.
     .   Essays before a sonata, and other writings; edited by Howard Boatwright.   New York: Norton, 1962; London: Calder & Boyars, 1969.   258p.
     .   New York: Norton, 1964.   (Norton Library edition)   148p.

Ives' own description of his book should have pride of place: "The following pages were written primarily as a preface or reason for the (writer's) second pianoforte sonata--'Concord, Mass., 1845' --a group of four pieces, called a sonata for want of a more exact name, as the form, perhaps substance, does not justify it. The music and preface were intended to be published together, but as it was found that this would make a cumbersome volume, they are separate. The whole is an attempt to present (one person's) impression of the spirit of transcendentalism that is associated in the minds of many with Concord, Mass., of over a half century ago" (preface). The subjects of the essays--as of the sonata's four movements--are Emerson, Hawthorne, the Alcotts, and Thoreau. To these Ives adds a prologue and epilogue. Both thematically and stylistically the essays form the clearest expression of his approach to music and to life. They do not directly describe the music, but, in Cowell's words, "demonstrate the mind that made it." Among the other writings included are "Some Quarter-tone Impressions," the "Postface to 114 Songs," and a draft of a letter to a newspaper about the availability of the song volume. Ives' political awareness is demonstrated in several documents: "Stand by the President and the People" (on the occasion of America's entry into World War I), the long essay "The Majority," the suggested 20th amendment, and a piece, "A People's World Nation." All these show Ives' concern with the will of the people and its expression. The text of Ives' article for insurance agents, "The Amount to Carry," is also included. (The Norton Library edition contains only the first two of these various writings.)

325.   IVES, Charles.   Memos; edited by John Kirkpatrick.   New York: Norton, 1972; London: Calder & Boyars, 1973.   355p.   illus.

This collection of Ives' previously unpublished memos represents an impressive piece of patient scholarship, and is an important source book for information on his life and music. The latter is what Ives intended the memos to be. He wrote some in manuscript form, but mostly they were dictated, as a "partly improvised reminiscence." The editor indicates the source of each memo with a symbol in the margin. He has arranged the body of material in three sections to provide some continuity for the reader. The first, "Pretext," is concerned with Ives' aims, approach to music and to music criticism. The second, "Scrapbook," discusses his own music, and the third, "Memories," presents some autobiographical recollections. The editor also provides copious footnotes. There are 21 appendices, devoted to lists, other writings of Ives, clarification of his relations with people who influenced him, and two works he considered for possible operas. There is also a chronological index of dates, an index of his music and writings, and a name index.

326. BERNLEF, J., and LEEUW, Reinbert de. Charles Ives.
       Amsterdam: De Bezige Bij, 1969. 272p. illus., bibliog.
       Well in advance of the outburst of American interest in Ives, this Dutch volume includes a short biography by Bernlef, a translation of the "Essays" and other prose, selected song texts (in English, with Dutch translations at the rear of the book), the opinions on Ives of Stravinsky, Schoenberg and Cage, a discussion of the music by De Leeuw, and a list of works, based on Kirkpatrick (no. 330).

327. COWELL, Henry, and COWELL, Sidney. Charles Ives and
       his music. New York: Oxford University Press, 1955.
       245p. illus., bibliog.
       _____. _____. (Rev. ed.) London, New York: Oxford University Press, 1969. 253p. illus., bibliog.,
       discog.
       This was the first fully developed biography and critical study of Ives (1874-1954), and it remained the only one for almost 20 years. Subsequent research has shown how much relevant information on Ives' life and music was unavailable to the Cowells, but their book is still, and will always be, of value for two main reasons: the authors knew Ives personally, and Henry Cowell's insight into Ives' music is that of a fellow-composer who, like Ives, had experience of straining against the conventional leash. The book is in two parts: biography, by Mrs. Cowell, and criticism by Cowell, who examines Ives' use of music materials and studies three works in particular--"Paracelsus," the "Concord" sonata, and the "Universe" symphony. The 1969 edition has a new postscript and discography, and a revised list of compositions.

328. DE LERMA, Dominique-René. Charles Edward Ives, 1874-
       1954: a bibliography of his music. Kent, O.: Kent
       State University Press, 1970. 212p.
       This handy quick-reference work lists each work of Ives alphabetically by uniform title, with information under each entry on medium, literary source, date, opus number (from Kirkpatrick's catalog), duration (when easily ascertainable), contents, publication and recordings. The extensive cross-references are helpful (though the inclusion under the main entry of alternative titles from which

reference has been made seems over-zealous). Each piece is identified by a Cutter number, the advantages of which over more traditional systems using ordinal numbers are dubious for this particular
purpose. Indexes include publishers, medium, compositions arranged chronologically, arrangers, poets, recordings (by label), and
performers.

329. ELKUS, Jonathan. Charles Ives and the American band tradition: a centennial tribute. Exeter: University of Exeter,
American Arts Documentation Centre, 1974. (American
Arts Pamphlet No. 4) 32p. bibliog.
    Just how closely Ives knew and identified with the traditions
and outlook of the New England bandsmen, how he absorbed their
techniques, shared their sense of musical estrangement and loved
their music is shown by Jonathan Elkus in his short monograph.
Not only is Ives' own band and theater music seen to be clearly a
part of this tradition, Elkus also demonstrates how tellingly Ives,
in his later masterworks, used the various techniques he had become acquainted with in his youth, and, in this way, created high
art from democratic materials. There are music examples in the
text, and the bibliography includes a checklist of Ives' published
works for band (original and arranged).

330. KIRKPATRICK, John, comp. A temporary mimeographed
catalogue of the music manuscripts and related materials
of Charles Edward Ives, 1875-1954, given by Mrs. Ives
to the Library of the Yale School of Music, September 1955;
compiled by John Kirkpatrick in 1954-60. New Haven:
Library of the Yale School of Music, 1960. (Repr. without alteration, 1973). 279p.
    Kirkpatrick's remarkable, highly valued catalog, originally
issued in a limited edition of 114 copies, is a painstakingly thorough,
devoted work that continues to perform a great service to all who
are interested in Ives' music and in his way of working. In his
preface the compiler describes the lengthy operation, undertaken by
himself and others, of creating order out of the confused state of
Ives' manuscripts at his death in 1954. Seven major groups are
defined: orchestra music, chamber music, keyboard music, music
for the stage, choral music, solo songs, exercises and miscellanea.
The table of contents, itself a useful short catalog, lists each work
in these groups, with dates of composition and titles of movements
where appropriate, and also (of great importance with Ives) indicates
what other piece or pieces of his music each was derived from and/
or developed into. These indications reappear in the body of the
catalog proper, where one also finds, wherever relevant, lists of
quoted tunes (also of vital significance in Ives' work). Kirkpatrick's
achievement in spotting all these quotations was considerable, but
even he is driven on various occasions to remark: "what else?"
The very full bibliographical description of each manuscript includes
format of paper, number of measures, presence of marginalia and
numbers of the negative copies (Ives himself began to have his mss.
photographed; the job was finished after his death). The exhaustive
indexes are as follows: titles and incipits; song-texts and hymn-

texts; dedications; music paper; negative numbers in numerical order; tunes quoted; Ives' whereabouts (residences, business, vacations, etc.) with dates; copies by other hands but his; publishers; names.

331.   PERLIS, Vivian.   Charles Ives remembered: an oral history.
       New Haven: Yale University Press, 1974.   237p.   illus.
       This fascinating compilation is made up of 58 edited interviews with friends, associates, composers, musicians and members of the Ives family, carried out by Mrs. Perlis between 1968 and 1972 as a funded oral history project, the first of its kind for an American composer, and triumphantly successful in conveying a many-sided portrait of Ives.   The interviews are grouped in four sections: youth and Yale years; insurance; family, friends and neighbors; music.   Mrs. Perlis provides a linking narrative and introduces each interviewee.   Among the composers and musicians interviewed are Elliott Carter, Nicolas Slonimsky, Bernard Herrmann, Lehman Engel, Jerome Moross, Carl Ruggles, Lou Harrison and John Kirkpatrick, who concludes his reminiscences by remarking that "Ives is like a reminder of values that are eternal."   The book contains over 80 illustrations, many of them photographs previously unpublished, and there is an index.

332.   PERRY, Rosalie Sandra.   Charles Ives and the American
       mind.   Kent, O.:   Kent State University Press, 1974.
       137p.   bibliog.
       Dr. Perry's comparative cultural study sets out, with Ives as a test case, "to explore the social psychology of music"--to see how much a composer's creativity is fashioned by prevailing intellectual traditions.   Examining the features of successive, closely related trends from Transcendentalism to Pragmatism, and seeing these reflected in Ives' music and thought, she attempts to show Ives as basically the product of the 19th century intellectual stream, to draw attention to his dependence rather than his isolation (save for an examination of the influence of Horatio Parker in her chapter on Ives' life, she does not attempt to study Ives vis-à-vis the musical tradition).   Consideration of Transcendentalists' views of life and attitudes to music, and of the occurrence of similar preoccupations in Ives, leads to an outline of the doctrine of the subconscious, and an examination of Ives' methods of presenting the stream-of-consciousness in his music (free association of tunes and memories, montage, non-metrical melody, etc.).   In a similar way the reflections in Ives of Realism, Social Christianity and Pragmatism are also analyzed.   The author's strong grasp of intellectual and psychological concepts, and her relation of these to Ives, illuminate many aspects of his music, though one is bound to doubt if he can be so pigeon-holed, tied down, accounted for.   The bibliography includes material on the intellectual movements and books, articles and theses on Ives himself.

333.   ROSSITER, Frank R.   Charles Ives and his America.   New
       York: Liveright, 1975.   420p.   illus., bibliog.
       In this thoughtful, well-documented and impressive study of Ives the man and the artist, Rossiter seeks to reinterpret the para-

doxes of his life and art--the radical political views, the successful
business career, the innovative compositional technique and the nostalgia for 19th century folkways and their musical equivalents--
through examination of the reason for, and results of, his extreme
artistic isolation. The key to this Rossiter sees as Ives' inward
acceptance of the traditional American approach to all art as "some-
how unmanly, undemocratic, and un-American," which "made it difficult for him even to reach the point where he could accept himself
as an artist" (preface). In Part 1, "Development, 1874-1921," the
sources of these Ivesian paradoxes and their effects in his active
creative life are explored, together with the general evolution of
his attitudes, in study of his childhood and early manhood, and in
chapters on the composer, the businessman, the political thinker,
and the "self-conscious artist in isolation." Part 2, " Recognition,
1921-1974," charts and interprets the progress of his reputation
among both the avant-garde and the general musical public, and of
Ives' own attitudes towards this progress. A concluding chapter
offers an overall interpretation in which Rossiter suggests a parallel
between the inward pressure exerted on Ives by his inheritance--
and acceptance--of an "extramusical ideology that reflected the dominant values of American society" (p. 318), and the external pressure
that the Soviet Union exerts on its composers, in line with an ideology formulated to resist anything it regards as decadent.

334. VINAY, Gianfranco. L'America musicale di Charles Ives.
          Turin: Einaudi, 1974. 178p. bibliog. notes.
     This study seeks to isolate some recurrent structural and
thematic features in Ives' artistic experience, and on these to base
an interpretation of his work. The two threads of American musical culture explored by H. Wiley Hitchcock--the cultivated and the
vernacular--are demonstrated in Ives' early life (the vernacular in
Danbury, the cultivated at Yale), and are seen to be united in the
Transcendentalist philosophy the author regards as the principal
motivating force in Ives' life. The influence of European composers
is also examined. An analysis of the outstanding features of Ives'
musical syntax deals in detail with his use of superimposition and
quotation, and his interpretation of sonata form. A catalog of Ives'
compositions, based on Kirkpatrick with some data from De Lerma,
is included, and there is an index of works referred to.

335. WARREN, Richard. Charles E. Ives: discography. New
          Haven: Historical Sound Recordings, Yale University Li-
          brary, 1972. (The Historical Sound Recordings Publica-
          tion Series, 1) 124p.
     This discography is a listing of commercially issued record-
ings of Ives' works (copies of most of which are in Yale University
Library's Charles E. Ives collection), and of tape copies of performances (also in the collection?). The total number of musical
performances listed is 603. They are arranged alphabetically by
title of work (based on Kirkpatrick, no. 330). Each entry has the
Kirkpatrick catalog number and, when appropriate, the source of the
text. These items are followed by a chronological list of recordings, giving in most instances performers, location, date, and, for

some tapes, the recordist; for commercial issues there are also details of country (if not U.S.), year of issue, label name and number, indication of mono or stereo, and matrix number, if different from the release number. Each recording is numbered, and entries in the performer index refer to these. There are cross references from alternate titles and first lines. There are also lists of the Library's collection of broadcasts on Ives and of people interviewed about Ives, mostly in connection with Vivian Perlis's oral history project, begun in 1968.

336. WOOLDRIDGE, David. From the steeples and mountains: a study of Charles Ives. New York: Knopf, 1974. 342p. illus., discog.

_____. Charles Ives: a portrait. London: Faber, 1975. 342p. illus., discog.

There are very few books on musicians that seek so deliberately and successfully to disturb the reader's post-prandial equanimity as does this biography. This, whatever its faults (and Wooldridge's handling of his biographical data in particular has been criticized), is the book's great triumph, for it achieves what Ives himself--the brusquely masculine side of him at least--set out to achieve. As his music stretches our ears, Wooldridge's presentation extends our literary senses (those accustomed to musical biography, at any rate; rated as literature Wooldridge's style is distinctly sub-Olson-- and sub-Ives, too) and is to be judged, not only for the great vitality he pours into his portrait, but for the way he attempts to prepare us for, and lead us into, the Ivesian world by his adopted style, tone, lay-out, even punctuation. There are--inevitably, in so unusual a book--many irritations: good detective work can be followed by totally unfounded speculation that at once reflects upon the original interpretation of the evidence; and Wooldridge's own pet dislikes (e.g., Horatio Parker) intrude a lot. But there is a wealth of biographical detail, and of insight into Ives as a man, as a composer (Wooldridge is an English composer and conductor who has resided for some years in America), and as a cultural figure.

DANIEL GREGORY MASON

337. MASON, Daniel Gregory. Music in my time, and other reminiscences. New York: Macmillan, 1938. (Repr. Freeport: Books for Libraries Press; Westport: Greenwood Press, 1970). 409p. illus.

The most significant published source for information on Mason's life as a composer, educator and writer (though he is somewhat reluctant to describe his teaching experience in any detail), this autobiography, composed partly of reprinted articles, also provides a view of his opinions on music. An urbane, polished writer, not without humor, he devotes much of his account of his life to portraits of others. Among the musicians who are prominent are Edward Burlingame Hill (a long-time friend), Daniel Gregory's uncle, William Mason and his New York circle, Arthur Whiting, John Powell and Ossip Gabrilowitsch. Index.

338. KLEIN, Mary Justina. The contribution of Daniel Gregory Mason to American music. Washington: Catholic University of America Press, 1957. 154p. bibliog.

Reproduced from a thesis, this is a (rather unexciting) study of the man and his music. In Part 1 the author gives a biographical sketch and accounts of Mason's accomplishments as educator, author (18 of his 19 books are briefly examined) and composer. In Part II she analyzes Mason's music from the points of view of form and style (including use of melody and rhythm, texture, and orchestration), concluding that his best work was done in the field of chamber music. Appendices provide a Mason family tree, and lists of mss. in public institutions, and of the contents of the Mason Collection at Columbia University.

GIAN CARLO MENOTTI

339. GRIEB, Lyndal. The operas of Gian Carlo Menotti, 1937-1972: a selective bibliography. Metuchen: Scarecrow Press, 1974. 193p. bibliog.

An annotated bibliography of primary and secondary material arranged in seven sections: works by Menotti (separate lists of operas, scores, librettos, recordings, opera selections and book adaptations); monographs on Menotti (two dissertations and one book); general reference works containing information about him; periodical articles on specific operas; general periodical articles on the composer; newspaper articles and reviews relevant to specific operas; general newspaper articles. Many of the annotations are quite detailed. There is also a biographical sketch of the composer, a "bibliographical essay" on Menotti literature, and a name index.

340. TRICOIRE, Robert. Gian Carlo Menotti: l'homme et son oeuvre. Paris: Seghers, 1966. (Musiciens de Tous les Temps) 186p. illus., bibliog., discog.

An introduction to Menotti and his work in two parts: an account of his life and career from his birth in Italy in 1911 up to 1965 (he came to the U.S. in 1928); and a description and examination of his work--operas, ballets, concertos and miscellaneous works. The bibliography is a chronological catalog of Menotti's compositions, with publisher and date. The discography is limited to title, conductor and recording company. Although in Tricoire's view Menotti has never ceased to be an Italian, he sees him as having drawn considerable inspiration from America, and as occupying a significant position in American musical life.

HARRY PARTCH

341. PARTCH, Harry. Genesis of a music; monophony: the relation of its music to historic and contemporary trends; its philosophy, concepts, and principles ...; with a foreword by Otto Luening. Madison: University of Wisconsin Press, 1949. 362p. illus.

_____. Genesis of a music: an account of a creative work, its roots and its fulfillments. 2nd ed., enlarged.

New York: Da Capo, 1974. 517p. illus., bibliog., discog.

One of the truly original figures in 20th century American music, Partch (1901-1974) here expounds his approach to music, his theories, and the instruments he developed. In the preface to the 2nd edition he tells us that by the age of 20 he had "tentatively rejected both the intonational system of modern Europe and its concert system." The first draft of the book was written in 1927, the seventh (which became the 1st edition) in 1947. The cornerstone of Partch's approach is a belief in the Corporeal rather than the Abstract (Corporeal being monophonic verbal and vocal music, "harmonized spoken words"), along with which goes a dedication to the theater. In place of tonality Partch developed a 43-microtone scale, and, to realize this music, a set of instruments (which caused him to describe himself, in a celebrated remark, as "a philosophic music-man seduced into carpentry"). The main additions to the 2nd edition are chapters on construction and tuning of his string and percussion instruments, and on the background to six of his works. Among the appendices are a list of major performances, a bibliography of writings about Partch and a chronology of his instruments. There is also an index.

STEVE REICH

342. REICH, Steve. Writings about music. Halifax, N.S.: Nova Scotia College of Art and Design, 1974. 78p. illus., bibliog., discog.

In the short introduction to his collection Reich (b. 1936) makes his view of music clear: "... although there is always a system working itself out in my music, there would be no interest in the music if it were merely systematic ... musical intuition is at the rock bottom level of everything I've ever done." His writings include some pieces on aspects of music in general, and an account of Ewe drum patterns, which he studied in Ghana; but for the most part they are concerned with describing his own music in predominantly non-technical terms. The appendix includes lists of works--title, instrumentation, date, and details of important performances--and of recordings.

NED ROREM

343. ROREM, Ned. The Paris diary; with a portrait of the diarist by Robert Phelps. New York: Braziller; London: Barrie & Rockliff, 1966. 240p. illus.
_____. Music from inside out. New York: Braziller, 1967. 144p.
_____. The New York diary. New York: Braziller, 1967. 218p. illus.
_____. Music and people. New York: Braziller, 1968. 250p.
_____. Critical affairs: a composer's journal. New York: Braziller, 1970. 216p.
_____. Pure contraption: a composer's essays. New

York: Holt, Rinehart & Winston, 1974. 149p.
_____. The final diary. New York: Holt, Rinehart &
Winston, 1974. 439p.
America's leading art-song composer, Rorem (b. 1923) probably has more words without music to his credit than any of his
fellow composers. Much of what has appeared in books takes the
form of a diary, beginning in France and North Africa in 1951-1955.
As a diarist Rorem is a keen observer, with a good memory for
bons mots; but it is chiefly his own frank self-analysis, and the
change in his attitudes to himself, that give these journal confidences
their appeal. His other writings listed above--some of which contain journal extracts--range widely across the field of the arts in
20th century society. Sometimes polemical, they are also often subjective. They include pieces on individuals (e. g. , in Music and
People, Foss and Pound) and reviews.

CARL RUGGLES

344. HARRISON, Lou. About Carl Ruggles: Section Four of a
book on Ruggles; with a note by Henry Cowell. Yonkers:
Oscar Baradinsky at the Alicat Bookshop, 1946. 19p.
illus.
In total commitment to Ruggles (1876-1971) and his music,
Harrison offers some suggestions and aids to understanding. In
particular he draws attention to Ruggles' use of polyphony, seeing
in him the continuing perfecting of a tradition that faded with Bach
and Handel, when contrapuntal techniques languished, and the restoration of the devout and reflective purpose of music. "Evoca-
tions" is examined, and related to Schoenberg's "Three Piano Pieces,"
op. 11.

WILLIAM SCHUMAN

345. SCHREIBER, Flora Rheta, and PERSICHETTI, Vincent.
William Schuman. New York: Schirmer, 1954. 139p.
illus. , bibliog. , discog.
In two sections: a biography (rather lightweight) of Schuman
(b. 1910) by Schreiber, and an analysis of his style and of five particular works by fellow-composer Persichetti. The five works are:
"American Festival Overture," "Symphony no. 3," "Symphony for
Strings," "Undertow" (ballet), and "Judith" (choreographic poem).
There are numerous music examples in the second part, and there
is also a complete list of Schuman's works with dates of first performances, and an index. (One caveat: Schirmer also publishes
most of Schuman's music.)

ROGER SESSIONS

346. SESSIONS, Roger. The musical experience of composer,
performer and listener. Princeton: Princeton University
Press, 1950. 127p.
_____. _____. New York: Atheneum, 1962. 121p.
A short work on musical aesthetics, consisting of six lectures

given in 1949 in New York. An interesting example of one composer's view. (Sessions was born in 1896.)

WILLIAM GRANT STILL

347. ARVEY, Verna. William Grant Still; with an introduction by
John Tasker Howard. New York: Fischer, 1939. (Studies of Contemporary American Composers) 48p. illus.,
bibliog.

A concise biographical and critical study of Still (b. 1895) by
his second wife (they married in 1939), in which she recounts his
life up to the time (circa 1925) of his decision to adopt a Negroid
idiom in composition, and describes in turn each of the subsequent
works, up to "Lenox Avenue" (published 1938). His early career,
especially his professional apprenticeship in New York vaudeville
and revue, is particularly notable for the varying influences at work
upon him (he was taught by Varèse at the same time as he was
writing arrangements for Sophie Tucker and others). The discussion of his music contains several music examples, and there are
lists of publications and first performances.

348. HAAS, Robert Bartlett, ed. William Grant Still and the
fusion of cultures in American music; by Robert Bartlett
Haas (editor), and Paul Harold Slattery, Verna Arvey,
William Grant Still, Louis and Annette Kaufman, with introductions by Howard Hanson and Frederick Hall. Los
Angeles: Black Sparrow Press, 1972. 201p. illus.,
bibliog., discog.

Haas attempts to construct a portrait of Still, "Dean of American Negro Composers" and citizen of the universe, out of a mixed
bag of original and reprinted material, beginning with some excerpts
from a thesis by Slattery--a biographical sketch, and detailed analyses, with charts and music examples, of the Afro-American Symphony and Symphony no. 4. These are followed by shorter reviews,
without examples, of Still's vocal music by his wife, Verna Arvey,
and of his violin music by the Kaufmans. A section, "The Stills
on Still," contains ten reprinted articles, from 1933 to 1970, by
Still and Verna Arvey, on aspects of his life and work, and on his
attitudes to composition. Verna Arvey also provides a very full catalog of Still's works, chronologically arranged, with details of medium,
first performance and duration, background information and descriptive notes. In addition to the 78 and LP discography and the bibliography of general works, Still's own writings, and articles about
him, there are ten suggested concert programs, complete with notes.

VIRGIL THOMSON

349. THOMSON, Virgil. Virgil Thomson. New York: Knopf,
1966. 424p. illus.

Thomson's productive pen turns to his own life (he was born
in 1896), which he describes with the same lucidity, perception and
candor that he brings to musical appreciation. His eminently readable memoirs, which begin with his childhood in Missouri and his

education at Harvard, are especially valuable for the accounts of the circumstances of composition of a number of his works for concert hall, stage and screen, and for the descriptions of the artistic circles, in France particularly, in the period 1920 to 1950. Copland and Antheil make several appearances in the narrative, and there are illuminating comments on some younger composers. There is a name index, and an index to Thomson's compositions mentioned in the text.

350. HOOVER, Kathleen, and CAGE, John. Virgil Thomson: his life and music. New York, London: Yoseloff, 1959. (Repr. Freeport: Books for Libraries Press, 1970). 288p. illus.
The biographical section, by Kathleen Hoover, traces Thomson's life from school days to the 1950s, setting the works in their context. Cage, in the musical section, examines the works chronologically, studying Thomson's technique in detail, and providing an evaluation of the music itself and of Thomson's place in 20th century music. There is a chronological list of works, and there are several music examples.

EDGARD VARESE

351. CHARBONNIER, Georges. Entretiens avec Edgard Varèse, suivis d'une étude de l'oeuvre par Harry Halbreich. Paris: Belfond, 1970. 169p. discog.
Charbonnier and Varèse (1883-1965) recorded these conversations in French for O.R.T.F. in 1955. There is some biographical material but mainly they are concerned with Varèse's views on music: the listener, the role and significance of percussion, the creative artist, music and physics, etc. There are also French translations of two speeches made by Varèse in 1939 at Princeton, and the University of Southern California. Halbreich's study takes each of Varèse's works, gives details of composition, instrumentation, editions and recordings, and briefly analyzes the piece, with music examples.

352. KLAREN, J. H. Edgar Varèse: pioneer of new music in America. Boston: Birchard, (1928?). 24p. illus.
A brief outline of Varèse's ideas is followed by a selection of 18 excerpts from reviews of his music, taken from various American journals, 1923-1927, by critics such as Lawrence Gilman, Paul Rosenfeld, Olin Downes and Richard Stokes.

353. OUELLETTE, Fernand. Edgard Varèse. Paris: Seghers, 1966. 287p. illus., bibliog.
_____. ; translated from the French by Derek Coltman. New York: Orion Press, 1968; London: Calder & Boyars, 1973. 271p. illus., bibliog.
Written with the active assistance of Varèse, this biography is described by its Canadian author as "a first document, which attempts to encompass the elements constituting the life of the composer ... " (foreword). It follows his life and career from early

life and studies in France, through his various struggles for acceptance in his adopted country, the U.S., his acquaintances and contacts in the world of the arts, up to his eventual recognition, and his death in 1965. The works are approached by a "passionate music lover" rather than a musicologist, and are placed in the context of the composer's development. Besides a list of works there is also a list of Varèse's articles, 1915-1965, an extensive bibliography of books and articles about him, a discography and an index.

354. VARESE, Louise. Varèse: a looking-glass diary. Vol. 1.
      1883-1928. New York: Norton, 1972; London: David-
      Poynter, 1973. 290p. illus.
      A personal memoir by the composer's American wife, covering the years from Varèse's birth in Paris, his studies and early musical career, up to his embarkation for America in 1915 and the first attempts to establish a reputation there. It contains a great deal of biographical information, but no musical comment, though the circumstances of composition, and the reception of several of his works form part of the narrative. A clear view of the character, outlook and behavior of the young Varèse comes across.

355. VIVIER, Odile. Varèse. Paris: Editions du Seuil, 1973.
      (Solfèges, 34) 189p. illus., bibliog., discog.
      Within a biographical framework the author makes a probing examination of each of Varèse's works from "Amériques" (1921) to "Nocturnal" (1961), with frequent music examples. Varèse's letters to her over a number of years provide her with a valuable source of material for his attitudes and theories, which she relates--using also information in the other published book on the composer--to each work in its context. Notes taken from conversations with Varèse are also put to good effect. The French text is liberally illustrated, and there is a chronology, but no index. The bibliography does not include any articles.

LA MONTE YOUNG

356. YOUNG, La Monte, and ZAZEELA, Marian. Selected writ-
      ings. Munich: Heiner Friedrich, 1969. unpaged.
      The main item in this collection is an interview with the experimental composer (b. 1935) by Richard Kostelanetz (also in no. 273). Other pieces include line patterns by Young's wife, Marian Zazeela, some notes on the realization of a work combining sound, light projection and design (part of his "The Tortoise"), his program notes for "The Dream House," and a lecture in 1960.

d. 20th Century Musical Life

357. BACON, Ernst. Notes on the piano. Syracuse: Syracuse
      University Press, 1963; Seattle: University of Washington
      Press, 1967. 167p.
      In this collection of observations by the Chicago-born composer and pianist one chapter is devoted chiefly to the way America

organizes its musical life; it remarks critically on patronage, centralization, and the over-cultivation of non-native music.

358. BARZUN, Jacques. Music in American life; with a foreword by Edward N. Waters. Garden City: Doubleday, 1956; Bloomington: Indiana University Press, 1962. 126p. bibliog.

Various aspects of the increasing prevalence of and interest in music on educational, professional, industrial and amateur levels are examined in a stimulating and entertaining essay. Barzun is concerned mainly with the way these aspects strike him personally. He describes the general scene and picks out the main trends, considers the music trade and music education, the effects of and opportunities offered by musical machinery, particularly in disseminating music, and the advantages and difficulties facing modern composers. Index.

359. BAUMOL, William J., and BOWEN, William G. Performing arts: the economic dilemma; a study of problems common to theater, opera, music and drama. New York: Twentieth Century Fund, 1966. 582p. bibliog.

A somber survey by two economics professors of the monetary problems besetting the performing arts in America in the 1960s. The authors describe and explain the current position, analyze apparent trends and explore the sources of financial support. Composing and performing musicians, and musical ventures in general are included, though chiefly in the serious music bracket. There is a summary of future prospects, which broadly sees the professional performance as surviving only at considerable cost, while amateur activity may flourish.

360. CARPENTER, Paul S. Music: an art and a business. Norman: University of Oklahoma Press, 1950. 245p. bibliog.

A critical, often outspoken examination of the American musical world at the end of the 1940s. The author explores aspects of the conflict implicit in the two words "music business" as illustrated by radio, motion pictures, the recording industry, the concert hall and the opera house, the booking and licencing agencies, the music unions (especially the figure of Petrillo), music education, and the problems of a composer's livelihood. Among the many recommendations are ones for public recognition of American composers, and better standards of music teaching. Index.

361. CHASINS, Abram. Music at the crossroads. New York: Macmillan; London: Collier-Macmillan, 1972. 240p.

A trenchant critique of the contemporary music scene in America, in which composer, teacher and pianist Chasin's aggression and the force of his arguments are somewhat tempered by the chatty style he adopts. The art music world--including such questions as music as profession, music in the universities, competitions the concert manager--is the focus of his attention, and its representatives bear the brunt of his criticism for their failure to recognize changes that have taken place in the 20th century as a result of the influence of jazz, rock and other styles. Chasins sees confusion and lack of direction, and suggests fundamental re-examination for "the poor and pathetic" revolutionaries "of the sterile classical avant garde; the performers and their diminishing audiences; the officials of the cultural centers, whose supertheaters are becoming mildewed ..." (p. 175). The worlds of jazz and rock and roll do not escape either. Chasins is disappointed at the increasing commercialism of rock and skeptical about the syntheses with other musical styles that were hoped for by many.

362.   CLARK, Kenneth S. <u>Music in industry: a presentation of facts brought forth by a survey, made by the National Bureau for the Advancement of Music, on musical activities among industrial and commercial workers.</u> New York: National Bureau, 1929. 383p. illus.

Presented in a bright tone probably unfamiliar to perusers of modern socio-economic reports these are the results of a survey into the extent of musical activities, both in and out of work time, among the nation's work force in the late 1920s, and into the practical value of such activities for both employer and employee. Whether in leisure time or in breaks granted by indulgent employers, the music-making surveyed was all connected in some way with place of work. Among the groups whose musical activities are described and evaluated are railroad workers, personnel in department stores, in manufacturing and public utility industries, and business office staff. The author's findings in general convince him of the social value of music in improving morale, counteracting monotony, even raising production levels. The responses of the various companies and organizations to his survey are summarized state-by-state and organization-by-organization, giving an idea of the extent of the bands, barber's shop groups, and so on. The majority respond to questions on the value of musical activity in the affirmative.

363.   DAMROSCH, Walter. <u>My musical life.</u> New York: Scribner, 1923; London: <u>Allen & Unwin,</u> 1924. (Repr. Westport: Greenwood Press, 1972). 376p. illus.
_____. _____. New York: Scribner, 1930. 390p. illus.

Born in Breslau in 1862, Walter Damrosch came to the U.S. in 1871 in the wake of his father Leopold (1832-1885) who had been invited to conduct the Arion Society. Damrosch père stayed to found the New York Symphony Society and organize the German Opera Company (who gave the first Wagner performances in America). Walter (who lived until 1950) gives his own recollections of his father and his contribution to American musical life, before recounting his own busy, distinguished life as conductor, teacher and composer. Taking over from his father at the Metropolitan, he conducted German opera there from 1885 to 1891, formed the Damrosch Opera Co. in 1894, conducted the New York Philharmonic for one season, 1902-1903, and the New York Symphony Society from 1903 to 1927. These and other activities he describes. Index.

364.   LEICHTENRITT, Hugo. <u>Serge Koussevitzky, the Boston Sym-</u>

phony Orchestra and the new American music.   Cambridge,
Mass.: Harvard University Press, 1946.   199p.   illus.
A measure of the debt owed by 20th century American composers to Koussevitzky is that, between his appointment as conductor of the Boston Symphony Orchestra in 1924 and the 1944 season,
66 new American compositions received their premières in Boston,
and over 150 American works appeared in the programs.   This book
surveys the symphonic music Koussevitzky performed, describing
the individual works, some in general terms and others quite closely.   The survey begins with composers of older generations (Foote,
Loeffler, Chadwick, MacDowell, Gilbert and others) and continues
through the symphonic writing of Randall Thompson and Howard Hanson, the Impressionism of Griffes, the "local color" of Gershwin,
the program music of Charles Converse, John Alden Carpenter and
Deems Taylor, the influence of Neo-Classicism on Sessions and Piston, to the "new Americanism" of Copland, Harris (whose debt to
Koussevitzky was particularly marked), Schuman, Barber, Creston,
Diamond and Bernstein.   (Koussevitzky cared little for Ives, Ruggles, Cowell or Varèse.)   There are profiles of Koussevitzky himself as a conductor and as an educator, and there is an index.

365.   LEITER, Robert D.   The musicians and Petrillo.   New York:
Bookman Associates, 1953.   202p.   illus., bibliog.
This study of the involvement of music with trade unionism
in America describes and examines the growth of the American Federation of Musicians as an economic force from the first attempts
to unionize musicians up to the early 1950s, considering the economic effects of the union's actions in that period and the personalities of its leading lights.   The central figure is James Caesar Petrillo (born 1892), the Chicago-bred union leader, first elected
president of the Chicago local in 1922, whose tough, aggressive
methods took him to the presidency of the AFM in 1940.   His most
notorious action--the imposing of a recording ban that lasted from
June 1942 to November 1944, in an attempt to end the production of
musical records and transcriptions--is described in Chapter 8.
There is an index, and a bibliography of books, documents and articles.

366.   LEVANT, Oscar.   A smattering of ignorance.   Garden City:
Doubleday, 1959.   189p.
Turning his considerable powers of contumely upon himself,
Levant (1906-1972) describes his book as "wholly undramatic" adventures "of the Kaffeeklatsch type."   But as pianist, conductor,
composer (Broadway and concert hall), actor, noted wit and hard-
bitten realist, he was widely acquainted with people from a cross-
section of musicmaking.   Here, with an unending supply of anecdotes, he draws five highly entertaining pictures of the American
musical scene, especially in the 1930s: a down-to-earth inside
view of the relationship between orchestra (mainly the New York
Philharmonic) and conductor; a portrait of musical evenings in Hollywood chez Harpo Marx; a biting account of attitudes to music for
films characteristic of Hollywood producers, and of the position of
the composer ("cog in a machine"); a deeply affectionate, unsenti-

mental view of George Gershwin; and a survey of contemporary American composers (especially Copland). Levant wrote two subsequent volumes: The Memoirs of an Amnesiac (New York: Putnam, 1965) and The Unimportance of Being Oscar (New York: Putnam, 1968).

367. McDONALD, William F. Federal relief administration and the arts: the origins and administrative history of the arts projects of the Works Progress Administration. Columbus: Ohio State University Press, 1969. 869p. bibliog. notes.

The WPA's concern for the arts during the 1930s, its belief that the arts, no less than any other human institution, merit support in times of crisis, was a unique event in civilized history. McDonald chronicles in detail the origins of this concern, and examines each of the fine arts projects in turn. In three chapters on music he describes the origins of the Federal Music Project (the position of musicians in the Depression, etc.), its organization and operation (in particular the contribution and results of the Directorship of Nikolai Sokoloff), and its program as it concerned orchestras, opera companies, composers, teachers, folk musicians.

368. MUELLER, John H. The American symphony orchestra: a social history of musical taste. Bloomington: Indiana University Press, 1951; London: Calder, 1958. 437p. illus., bibliog. notes.

Mueller devotes the central part of his history to profiles of the development of 17 major American orchestras from the New York Philharmonic to the National Symphony Orchestra of Washington. With this as a base he proceeds to outline a kind of composers' popularity stakes, devising six categories, from the pre-eminently popular to those luckless ones the fickle world forgets to remember, fitting several dozen composers into those groups, and describing how each has fared in the American repertoire. Four Americans only are included: Copland and Ives in the "ascending" group, MacDowell and Harris in a group with "full cycles." From here Mueller considers the social function of the orchestra, and such practical affairs as orchestral seating plans, union/management relations, and concert-goers' habits. With all these historical and social considerations behind him he offers in conclusion a discussion of "the elusive problems of aesthetic taste." Index.

369. PAVLAKIS, Christopher. The American music handbook. New York: Free Press; London: Collier Macmillan, 1974. 836p.

The aim of this Herculean achievement is "to bring together information on all areas of organized musical activity in the United States within the limits of a single volume." Coverage is heavily slanted towards concert music ("America's most telling music," Pavlakis comments, "appears not to need a book of this kind yet"), and includes over 5,000 entries, the information for which was obtained principally by questionnaire, backed up by additional research. The material is presented as in a directory, and is arranged in fourteen parts: 1) <u>organizations</u> serving music directly or indirectly, from educational bodies and foundations to trade unions and amateur groups; 2) <u>instrumental ensembles</u> (symphony orchestras, conductors, concertmasters, chamber ensembles and bands); 3) <u>vocal ensembles</u> (academic and independent); 4) <u>music and the stage</u> (state-by-state listing of academic and independent opera-producing groups, dance companies, music tents and summer theaters); 5) <u>performers</u> (brief biographical sketches arranged by instrument and voice); 6) <u>composers</u> (biographical directory of about 200 living composers); 7) <u>music festivals</u>; 8) <u>contests, grants, fellowships</u>; 9) <u>music and education</u> (including 863 universities and colleges offering music instruction, and 83 public and academic libraries of research standard, with details of holdings); 10) <u>radio and television</u>; 11) <u>music industries</u>; 12) <u>music periodicals</u>; 13) <u>concert managers</u>; and 14) <u>foreign supplement</u>. Information in all sections is given in very considerable detail, and the value of the work is enhanced by the 80-page comprehensive index. Although a proportion of the information is inevitably soon out-of-date, no praise can be too high for this one-man accomplishment.

370. SESSIONS, Roger. <u>Reflections on the music life in the United States</u>. New York: Merlin Press, (1956). 184p.

A clear exposition of what Sessions sees as the causes and distinctive characteristics of the "tremendous musical development of the United States during the past thirty-five years" (i.e., since World War I). Identifying first some salient features of American cultural life affecting musical attitudes, he summarizes the development of musical life to 1900, then examines in turn the concert system (especially the business mentality and its effects), opera, radio and sound recording, education (in some detail), and music criticism. His final chapter points to some aspects of the music itself, notably to various manifestations of nationalism, including folk and jazz elements, and concludes with his own ideas on attitudes and objectives ("what the public really wants from music ... is neither the mirrored image of itself nor fare chosen for easy digestibility, but vital and relevant experience"--p. 176).

371. STODDARD, Hope. <u>Symphony conductors of the U.S.A.</u> New York: Crowell, 1957. 405p.

Thirty-two 20th century conductors whose careers have influenced American orchestral life are portrayed here; only a few are American-born. There are also thumbnail sketches of over 400 others. Index.

372. SWOBODA, Henry, ed. <u>The American symphony orchestra</u>. Washington: Voice of America, 1967. (Forum Lectures) 218p. illus.

_____. New York: Basic Books, 1967. 208p.

These 17 interviews and lectures, originally broadcast as a series on the Forum program of the Voice of America, provide, in the editor's words, "a selective overview of achievements, shortcomings, and trends, as well as cultural and financial aspects of our symphonic life." The topics covered include Americanism in

American symphonic music, the composer as conductor, the orchestral musician and the community, the university symphony orchestra, music on radio and television, and the financial evolution of the orchestra; there are also discussions of individual orchestras (Boston, San Francisco and Utah). Participants include composers Piston, Copland, Hanson, Kirchner and Schuman, conductors Slonimsky, Abravanel, Krips, Leinsdorf, Rudolf and Stokowski, plus teachers, broadcasters and writers. Index.

373. ZANZIG, Augustus Delafield. Music in American life, present and future; prepared for the National Recreation Association; with a foreword by Daniel Gregory Mason. London, New York: Oxford University Press, 1932. (Repr. Washington: McGrath, 1972). 560p. illus., bibliog.
    Based on a two-year national survey undertaken in 1928-1930, this is a report on amateur music-making among white Americans at home, in the school, church and community, at a time when radio and the phonograph were playing ever-increasing parts in people's lives. Zanzig's model is clearly the type of economic report that speaks in terms of resources and the wealth that stands to be derived from their development.

e. Outstanding Critics

374. HUNEKER, James Gibbons. Steeplejack. New York: Scribner, 1920. 2v.
    "Jack of the Seven Arts, master of none" was one of Huneker's descriptions of himself, while his autobiography recounted his "adventures among mediocrities" (p. 6). So great was his facility with the pen that he wrote these 600-plus pages in 15 weeks. Among many other things this well-heeled "professional egoist" was an influential figure in music journalism in New York from the start of his association with the Musical Courier in 1887 to his wartime tenure of Aldrich's chair at the New York Times. He was also a native of Philadelphia and gives some account of music in that city. (For further, more objective information on the life of Huneker (1860-1921), consult Arnold T. Schwab, James Gibbons Huneker [Stanford: Stanford University Press, 1963]; Huneker's published correspondence, Letters of James Gibbons Huneker; collected and edited by Josephine Huneker [New York: Scribner, 1922], contains letters to Aldrich, Mencken, Krehbiel, Gilman and Hughes.)

375. MASON, Daniel Gregory. The dilemma of American music, and other essays. New York: Macmillan, 1928. (Repr. New York: Greenwood Press, 1969). 306p.
    A composer of the Second New England School, and an advocate of moderation and propriety, Mason (1873-1953) contributed stylish essays to various journals. The selection contained in this volume begins with a discussion of the dilemma of the title--the multiplicity of traditions and influences apparent on the American musical scene in the early 20th century. Mason examines the features of musical nationalism (especially English), finds folk elements

too limited "emotionally and intellectually," and recommends eclec-
ticism. Various essays are concerned with aspects of contemporary
music, including orchestral policies and the position of American
music in the repertory. A piece called "Stravinsky as a Symptom"
makes a disdainful, elitist attack on jazz and Stravinsky's use of
jazz elements. (The remaining essays are partly on general topics,
partly on Beethoven.)

376. MASON, Daniel Gregory. Tune in, America: a study of our
     coming musical independence. New York: Knopf, 1931.
        (Repr. Freeport: Books for Libraries Press, 1969). 205p.
     This further collection of reprinted articles and essays cen-
ters on the "immediate conditions and problems of musical development as they press upon us" (p. 170). Among the subjects discussed are the extent of the performance of American music in concert halls (with lists showing the variations from progressive Chicago to reactionary New York); conductors and their programs (with
particular attention to a New York Philharmonic season under Toscanini); audiences; radio and the phonograph; and the aesthetic qualities American music needs. An appendix lists American works performed in other cities (including Cincinnati, Detroit and Los Angeles).
Mason maintains his total prejudice against jazz on the one hand,
while on the other what Cowell calls his "ultra-conservative attitude"
will not recognize "any composer who has the slightest inkling of
indigenous American style" (no. 293, p. vi). Anti-semitic opinions
on the "Jewish menace to our artistic integrity" (p. 160) were re-
tracted in his Music in My Time (no. 337).

377. ROSENFELD, Paul. Musical chronicle, 1917-1923. New
     York: Harcourt Brace, 1923. (Repr. New York: Blom,
     1972). 314p.
     These thirty-five essays, which appeared originally in a vari-
ety of journals, give a highly articulate account of American, particularly New York, concert life after the first World War. Rosenfeld
remains in general unimpressed by the musical scene around him
("the concert room in America is the classic wasting-place of energies. It is the spot where the river of life is arrested by means
of the misuse of the living substance enclosed in musical literature,"
p. 62). American composers are represented by Horatio Parker,
John Alden Carpenter and Leo Ornstein. There is no index. (See
also nos. 276-278.)

378. MELLQUIST, Jerome, and WIESE, Lucie, eds. Paul Rosen-
     feld, voyager in the arts. New York: Creative Age Press,
     1948. 284p. illus., bibliog.
     This "mosaic of critiques" is a testimony to the pervasive in-
fluence of critic Paul Rosenfeld (1896-1946), whose versatile, in-
quisitive spirit touched the minds of countless other Americans in
literary and musical life in the early 20th century. Mellquist calls
the volume "a work in which the criticized turn back to criticize the
original critic" (preface), but the 49 contributors--musicians and
authors--do little criticizing in their generous tributes. The longest
pieces are a biography by Mellquist, recollections by Edmund Wilson,

Alyse Gregory, Alfred Kreymbourg, Marianne Moore and Lewis Mumford, and a portrait of Rosenfeld the listener by Waldo Frank. Other reminiscences and testimonies on particular aspects of Rosenfeld's character and achievement come from Elliott Carter, Charles Ives, Aaron Copland, Ernest Bloch, Edgard Varèse, Roy Harris Lehman Engel, William Carlos Williams, Robert Penn Warren and Wallace Stevens among others. The bibliography lists Rosenfeld's works.

379. THOMSON, Virgil. The state of music. New York: Morrow, 1939. 250p.
_____. _____. 2nd ed. New York: Random House, 1962. 226p.
This study is mainly concerned with aspects of music, especially composition, as a profession in the U.S. and Europe in the 1930s. Questions of status, economics, politics, administration and censorship are among those examined with Thomson's unique blend of wit and wrath. The revision of the 1939 version consists of some parenthetical paragraphs, pointing out what has changed and what has not, and the addition of a preface and a postlude. No index.

380. THOMSON, Virgil. The musical scene. New York: Knopf, 1945. (Repr. New York: Greenwood Press, 1968). 301p.
A selection of essays and reviews by the noted composer, covering a variety of aspects of music in general, and American musical life in particular, with New York the chief focus of attention. They were first published from 1940 to 1944 in the New York Herald Tribune, where Thomson showed his mettle as a journalist in a provocative and very readable column. Many of the pieces here are on European musical subjects, but some concern creative American musicians; there is a section on a variety of American orchestras, and a good picture of musical activity emerges from the large selection of concert reviews. Index.

381. THOMSON, Virgil. The art of judging music. New York: Knopf, 1948. (Repr. New York: Greenwood Press, 1969). 318p.
This second volume of Thomson's criticism for the New York Herald Tribune covers mainly 1944-1947, with the addition of the lecture that gives the book its title, which was given at Harvard in 1947 and published in Atlantic Monthly. Besides revealing much about the musical life of New York, it also shows Thomson's approach to musical judgment, and the standard of his own criticism. Among the rich variety of subjects are performers, opera, composers, provincial music, and music overseas. Index.

382. THOMSON, Virgil. Music, right and left. New York: Holt, 1951. (Repr. New York: Greenwood Press, 1969). 214p.
A further sample of Thomson's writing for the New York Herald Tribune, this collection of reviews and articles represents the period from 1947 to 1950.

383.   THOMSON, Virgil. Music reviewed, 1940-1954. New York:
        Vintage Books, 1967. 422p.
        The 183 reviews and articles reprinted here are selected
from the whole of Thomson's period as music critic for the New
York Herald Tribune. Most of the pieces up to 1950 appear in his
three other collections (nos. 380-382); those from 1951-54 appear
here in reprint for the first time. Unlike the other collections,
this one is chronologically arranged. The whole collection is interesting for its light on wartime and post-war musical practice in
America, as a landmark in music journalism, and as a reflection
of the composer's own approach and attitudes.

E. THE MUSIC OF THE AMERICAN INDIANS

1. Reference Works

(See also nos. 429, 431)

384. BONNERJEA, Biren. Index to Bulletins 1-100 of the Bureau
of American Ethnology; with index to Contributions to North
American Ethnology, introductions and miscellaneous publications. Washington: Smithsonian Institution, 1963.
(Bureau of American Ethnology, Bulletin No. 178) 726p.
 The great wealth of information on the North American Indian
contained in the bulletins is made considerably more accessible by
this reference work, which contains (particularly in the main index,
but also in the indexes of illustrations and of the Contributions)
many references to music, songs, and dancing.

385. HODGE, Frederick Webb, ed. Handbook of American Indians
north of Mexico. Washington: Smithsonian Institution,
1907-1910. (Bureau of American Ethnology, Bulletin No.
30) (Repr. Grosse Pointe: Scholarly Press, 1968; Westport: Greenwood Press, 1969; Totowa: Rowman and Lit-
tlefield, 1971). 2v. illus., bibliogs.
 A dictionary-style reference book of over 2,000 pages containing a whole treasure-store of information on the North American
Indian, anthropological, cultural, ethnographical and historical. The
illustrated article in the first volume on music and musical instruments is by Alice C. Fletcher. There are also articles on dance
(by J. N. B. Hewitt), on ceremony (by G. A. Dorsey), and on religion (by Franz Boas).

386. MURDOCK, George Peter. Ethnographic bibliography of
North America. 3rd ed. New Haven: Human Relations
Area Files, 1960 (repr. 1972). 393p.
 This monumental bibliography of over 17,000 items (the 1st
ed. in 1941 contained 9,400), indispensable to anthropologists, is
also a valuable reference work for the study of Indian music, not
only because of the large number of references to cultural studies,
but also by reason of the many specifically musical items included.
Because the work is arranged geographically (into 15 broad areas,
subdivided into 253 tribal groups, with general works listed in an
appendix) and there is no subject index (the construction of one for
such a vast collection would clearly be an enormous undertaking),

any approach from the point of view of music must be geographically based. Under each tribe heading there are not only monographs and articles directly relevant to the tribe, but also references to sections of more general works. The book also contains a model introduction, several maps and an index of tribal names.

2. General Studies

387. AUSTIN, Mary. The American rhythm: studies and reexpressions of Amerindian songs. New York: Harcourt, Brace, 1923. 155p. illus.

_____. _____. New and enlarged ed. Boston: Houghton Mifflin, 1930. (Repr. New York: Cooper Square, 1970). 174p.

Mrs. Austin (1868-1934), poet and novelist with long personal experience of the West and a leaning to mysticism, sees American Indian song as a response to the rhythmic form of nature, "singing in tune with the beloved environment," and advocates a similar response, with associated freedom and sense of communality--"happy states of reconciliation with the Allness"--as a basis for a new American verse. Her own "reexpressions" are free treatments of the verses of Indian songs from a variety of tribes.

388. BAKER, Theodor. Über die Musik der nordamerikanischen Wilden: eine Abhandlung zur Erlangung der Doctorwürde an der Universität Leipzig. Leipzig: Breitkopf und Härtel, 1882. (Repr. New York: AMS Press, 1973). 82p. illus., bibliog. notes.

Baker's work for his dissertation represented the first attempt at a serious examination of North American Indian music. He stayed among the Seneca in New York State in the summer of 1880, and visited the Indian School at Carlisle, Pennsylvania. His study discusses the poetry of the songs he heard, and such musical aspects as vocalization, tonality, melody, rhythm and instruments. He also includes transcriptions of 43 songs (32 of which he noted himself).

389. COLLAER, Paul. Music of the Americas: an illustrated music ethnology of the Eskimo and American Indian peoples; with contributions by Willard Rhodes, Samuel Marti, Vicente T. Mendoza, Eva Lips and Rolf Krusche. New York: Praeger, 1973. 207p. illus. (some col.), bibliog.

(Originally published with German text in Leipzig in 1968.) A beautifully produced book in which, with the aid of 97 major illustrations, Collaer and his colleagues outline the musical practices of the American Indian from the North of Canada to Tierra del Fuego, indicating stylistic differences, and demonstrating the significance of music in the Indians' lives. The introduction gives an anthropological and cultural account of pre-Columbian America, followed by a discussion of general characteristics of the music of the Eskimos, the North American Indians, the Mexican Indians, and the

Indians of South America. Music examples are used as illustrations. The main part of the book is devoted to illustrations with descriptions. These follow a broad geographical arrangement from North to South, the first 53 being devoted to Canada and the U.S.A. There are drawings, paintings and photographs of instruments and ceremonies, and the accompanying text describes the picture and relates its significance. A detailed bibliography, divided into geographical areas, and numbering 901 items, is followed by an index.

390. CURTIS, Edward S. The North American Indian; being a series of volumes picturing and describing the Indians of the United States, the Dominion of Canada and Alaska; edited by Frederick Webb Hodge; foreword by Theodore Roosevelt; field research conducted under the patronage of J. Pierpont Morgan. Cambridge, Mass.: Harvard University Press (Vols. 1-5); Norwood, Mass.: Plimpton Press, 1907-1930. 20v. + 20 portfolios of illustrations.

This superb, comprehensive survey of all the important Indian tribes includes a great deal of information about the role of music. Taking each tribe in turn in a geographic sequence Curtis records details of their homeland, social customs, religious beliefs, mythologies, ceremonies, arts and language. Each volume contains references to the types and uses of music--in ceremony, medicine, war and daily life--and to musical instruments. Vols. 3-12 and 19 contain musical transcriptions, chiefly by the composer Henry F. Gilbert (1868-1928), often both in the main text and the appendices. There are two notes on the music--in Vol. 3, by Curtis himself, and in Vol. 6, by Gilbert. The song transcriptions give the melody, metronome markings, sometimes drum accompaniment, and are in standard notation, transcribed as exactly as possible from cylinders made by Curtis. (Gilbert notes the difficulties and drawbacks of this system.) Among the multitude of unique photographs comprising the magnificent portfolios and illustrating the volumes there are many depicting musicians and their instruments. (According to "Henry F. Gilbert: His Life and Works," Ph.D. dissertation by Katherine M. E. Longyear, Eastman School of Music, 1968, Curtis commissioned Gilbert to compose pieces using the melodies to accompany showings of the photographs at lectures, and also engaged Gilbert to conduct the small orchestra which accompanied Curtis on his tours, [p. 26].)

391. CURTIS, Natalie, ed. The Indians' book: an offering by the American Indians of Indian lore, musical and narrative, to form a record of the songs and legends of their race.... New York: Harper, 1907. 572p. illus.
_____. _____. New York: Harper, 1923. (Repr. New York: Dover Publications, 1968). 584p. illus.

This beautiful book contains 149 songs collected from 18 tribes, with description of their functions and with stories and legends, as told by the Indians themselves. No harmonization has been added to the original melodies, which were recorded by hand and are given in standard notation, with time signatures and metronome markings. Indian and English texts are given for a large number of the songs. When Miss Curtis (1875-1921, later Mrs. Burlin) began collecting, native Indian music was prohibited in government schools; she appealed successfully to President Roosevelt to have this changed.

392. DENSMORE, Frances. The American Indians and their music. New York: The Womans Press, 1926. (Repr. New York: Johnson, 1970). 143p. illus., bibliog.

This is a useful overall picture by the third of the lady pioneers in the study of Indian music, using material presented in her many works for the Bureau of American Ethnology (no. 403). The initial chapters describe social aspects--tribal organization, home life, language, arts, dances, ceremonies. The chapters specifically on music examine the role of songs, their texts, song types, and the various kinds of wind and percussion instruments. Two chapters survey developments in the study of Indian music, and there is consideration of certain characteristics including scale. The book concludes with a survey of adaptations. There are music examples in the text. No index.

393. DENSMORE, Frances. The study of Indian music. Seattle: Shorey Book Store, 1966. (Repr. from Smithsonian Institution Annual Report, 1941). pp. 527-550. illus.

A paper tracing the outline of the author's work in the field from the 1890s, and dealing in particular with her methods of recording the music, and the variety of equipment used.

394. DRIVER, Harold E. Indians of North America. Chicago: University of Chicago Press, 1961. 667p. illus., bibliog. _____. _____. 2nd ed. Chicago: University of Chicago Press, 1969. 632p. illus., bibliog.

Included in this survey of Indian cultures, which covers economic, social and artistic aspects, is a chapter on music by Wilhelmine Driver outlining the main features and functions of music in Indian life, and dividing it stylistically into geographical areas, with similar information for each area. The bibliography includes references to sources on music.

395. FLETCHER, Alice C. Indian games and dances with native songs; arranged from American Indian ceremonials and sports. Boston: Birchard, 1915. (Repr. New York: AMS Press, 1970). 139p. illus.

Miss Fletcher's chief aim in describing these dances and games is to give directions to enable schoolchildren to perform them. The words and melodies of 30 songs are included to help convey a sense of the Indian's view of, and intimate relation with, the natural world. Twenty of these melodies are associated with dances, eight with games, and two with naming ceremonies.

396. FLETCHER, Alice Cunningham. Indian story and song from North America. Boston: Small, Maynard, 1900. (Repr. New York: AMS Press, 1970). 126p.

This collection of stories, legends and songs, many published here for the first time, represents one of the first conscious attempts

to present the subject of Indian music in a popular form. Miss
Fletcher (1845-1923), one of the pioneers in the field, gives the
words and melodies of over 20 songs, the music for which is transcribed from phonograph recordings. The harmonizations, mostly
by J. C. Fillmore, are based on the theory he elaborates in no.
406, namely that the Indian possesses a subconscious harmonic sense,
in the European manner. (Contrast this with the approach of Benjamin Ives Gilman, in no. 407.)

397.   HOFMANN, Charles. American Indians sing; drawings by
       Nicholas Amorosi. New York: John Day, 1967. 96p.
       illus., bibliog., discog.
       An introduction for the younger reader, explaining in general
terms the role of music in Indian life, their instruments, some
characteristics of poetry and dance, and describing the origin, purpose and principal features of eleven specific ceremonies from various tribes. Beside the drawings there are also some photographs
and short music examples. A 7"-record contains seven examples
of music.

398.   HOFMANN, Charles, ed. Frances Densmore and American
       Indian music: a memorial volume, compiled and edited by
       Charles Hofmann. New York: Museum of the American
       Indian, Heye Foundation, 1968. (Contributions from the
       Museum of the American Indian, Heye Foundation, Vol.
       XXIII) 127p. illus., bibliog., discog.
       Highly respected as a pioneer and leading authority in the
study of American Indian music--she began her work in 1893--
Frances Densmore died in 1957, aged 90. This volume commemorates the centenary of her birth. So prolific a writer was she that
the editor is able to compile the volume, describing her life and
work, largely from her own writings. Autobiographical pages, diary
entries, reports, lectures, papers, these are arranged first to describe her early years up to 1907, including her first experiences
of collecting and studying Indian music. Extracts from Bureau of
American Ethnology Annual Reports from 1907 to 1946 tell the story
of her continuing research, and are followed by a selection of letters, and by seven representative articles on subjects including the
use of music in the treatment of the sick, the connection between
song and the supernatural in the Indian mind, and the poetry of Indian songs. There is also, in conclusion, a general article on the
study of Indian music, originally published in the Smithsonian Annual
Report for 1941. The bibliography gives a fine idea of the extent
of her writing, and includes the Library of Congress LPs made
from her recordings.

399.   NETTL, Bruno. North American Indian musical styles.
       Philadelphia: American Folklore Society, 1954. (Memoirs,
       No. 45) 51p.
       A brief survey of past studies of North American Indian mu-
sic prefaces the main part of this slim volume, which examines
stylistic features of the music in six geographical areas, each of
which possesses individual characteristics, and assesses the extent

to which some features are common to all. Other subjects covered include the lack of coincidence between culture areas and those of language and of music. An appendix contains music examples.

400.   ROBERTS, Helen H.   Musical areas in aboriginal North America.   New Haven: Yale University Press, 1936. (Yale University Publications in Anthropology, No. 12) 41p.   bibliog.
An attempt to provide an overall, comparative picture of North American Indian musical characteristics.   Miss Roberts discusses first some popular generalizations regarding technical and aesthetic aspects of Indian music, drawing examples from different areas.   She then examines, with the aid of maps, the various Indian musical instruments--strings, winds and percussion--their geographical distribution, and the characteristic instruments of each area; following this she investigates vocal musical areas and their characteristics.   Her conclusions are that instrumental and vocal areas are much alike in geographical extent, and that musically defined areas tend to coincide with ones definable by other cultural traits.   (For comments on this study, see Nettl, no. 399, pp. vii, 3.)

3.   Music of Particular Tribes

401.   BOAS, Franz.   The social organization and the secret societies of the Kwakiutl Indians.   Washington: Government Printing Office, 1897.   (Annual Report of the Board of Regents of the Smithsonian Institution, 1895) pp. 311-738.
This important anthropological study of Indians of the North West Pacific coast contains much information on song and dance in Kwakiutl ceremonial (particularly the winter ceremonial), and the texts and tunes of 46 songs (mostly in the appendix) transcribed from phonograph records by Boas and J. C. Fillmore.

402.   BURTON, Frederick.   American primitive music, with especial attention to the songs of the Ojibways.   New York: Moffat, Yard, 1909.   (Repr. Port Washington: Kennikat Press, 1969).   357p.   illus.
A detailed study by an American composer, examining Ojibway music from technical, social, literary and artistic points of view, and setting it in context in the general field of American Indian music.   Burton (1861-1909) obtained much of his information at first hand, and regards Ojibway song as superior technically and aesthetically to all other American Indian music.   In the final chapter the transcribed melodies of the collected songs are given, with Ojibway words, translations, and comment on the story of each song. In addition 28 songs are given in harmonized versions, with Ojibway and English texts.

403.   DENSMORE, Frances.   Chippewa music.   Washington: Government Printing Office, 1910-1913.   (Smithsonian Institu-

tion, Bureau of American Ethnology. Bulletin Nos. 45, 53) 2v. illus.

———. Choctaw music ... 1943. (Bureau of American Ethnology. Anthropological Paper, No. 28; from Bulletin No. 136). pp. 101-188, illus.

———. Mandan and Hidatsa music ... 1923 (... Bulletin No. 80), 192p. illus., bibliog.

———. Menominee music ... 1932 (... Bulletin No. 102) 230p. illus., bibliog.

———. Music of the Acoma, Isleta, Cochiti, and Zuni Pueblos ... 1957 (... Bulletin No. 165) 117p. illus.

———. Nootka and Quileute music ... 1939. (... Bulletin No. 124) 358p. illus., bibliog.

———. Northern Ute music ... 1922 (... Bulletin No. 75) 213p. illus.

———. Papago music ... 1929 (... Bulletin No. 90) 229p. illus.

———. Pawnee music ... 1929 (... Bulletin No. 93) bibliog.

———. Seminole music ... 1956 (... Bulletin No. 161) 223p. illus., bibliog.

———. Teton Sioux music ... 1918 (... Bulletin No. 61) 561p. illus.

———. Yuman and Yaqui music ... 1932 (... Bulletin No. 110) 216p. illus., bibliog.

(All vols. repr. New York: Da Capo, 1972. Chippewa vol. also repr. New York: Johnson, 1970; Minneapolis: Ross & Haines, 1973.)

Taken together, these monographs, the fruit of over 50 years' work by the tireless Miss Densmore (1867-1959), represent the most outstanding contribution by a single individual scholar in the field of American Indian music. Miss Densmore herself recorded much Indian music, transcriptions of which appear in these volumes in conventional notation, together with analytical commentary. The Chippewa volumes, the first of the series, also contain the highest number of transcribed items, 340 in all. Miss Densmore does not, however, study and present the music of these tribes as an isolated phenomenon. She also describes in detail the cultural and religious life of which it is a part, and frequently comments on ceremonial and mythological features of individual songs. The physical aspect-- how the music is performed--is also considered, with many descriptions of instruments and individual singers, and numerous photographs. One criticism of Miss Densmore's method--raised, for example, by Bruno Nettl, no. 399, p. vii--is that her transcriptions rely too heavily on European standards. Nettl goes on to say, however, that Miss Densmore's "monumental achievements ... must be recognized as a prime and unique contribution." (For two further volumes by Densmore of the same type, see Appendix.)

404. FENTON, William N., and GULICK, John, eds. Symposium on Cherokee and Iroquois culture. Washington: Smithsonian Institution, 1961. (Bureau of American Ethnology, Bulletin No. 180) 292p. bibliogs.

Includes a contribution by Gertrude P. Kurath, "Effects of environment on Cherokee-Iroquois ceremonialism, music, and dance," and a comment on this paper by William C. Sturtevant. There is also a concluding evaluation, "Iroquoian culture history," by William N. Fenton.

405. FERGUSSON, Erna. Dancing gods: Indian ceremonials of New Mexico and Arizona. New York: Knopf, 1931. 276p. illus.

Based on the author's own observation, the descriptions given here of the principal ceremonial dances of the Southwestern Indians (who include Rio Grande Pueblo, Hopi, Navajo and Apache) include occasional passages on the particular role of the musicians.

406. FLETCHER, Alice C. A study of Omaha Indian music; aided by Francis La Flesche, with a report on the structural peculiarities of the music by John Comfort Fillmore. Cambridge, Mass.: Peabody Museum of American Archaeology and Ethnology, 1893. (Archaeological and Ethnological Papers of the Peabody Museum, Vol. 1, No. 5) 152p.

Miss Fletcher began her study of the Omaha in 1883, making a large collection of phonograph recordings with the assistance of Francis La Flesche, a son of the chief. The book--which marks the start, according to Frances Densmore, of popular interest in Amer-indian music--includes transcriptions of 92 of the songs she collected, harmonized by Prof. Fillmore. Miss Fletcher herself discusses the relationship of music to the life of the Plains Indians, grouping the songs into three categories: "class" (sung by the initiated), "social" (sung by groups) and "individual," and examining the characteristics of each group. Prof. Fillmore, a devotee of the European Romantic tradition, investigates various technical aspects of the music as he sees it: scales, implied harmonies, tonality, rhythms, etc. He sees relationships between Indian modulations and those practiced by Romantic composers. His approach is based on a belief in the Indians' having a "natural harmonic sense" (a view he expanded in an article in the American Anthropologist, n.s., 1899, pp. 297-318, called "The Harmonic Structure of Indian Music").

407. GILMAN, Benjamin Ives. Hopi songs. Boston: Houghton Mifflin, 1908. (A Journal of American Ethnology and Archaeology, Vol. 5) 235p. illus.

This particularly interesting early work on Indian music was one of the fruits of the Hemenway Southwestern Expedition, financed by Mrs. Mary Hemenway between the 1880s and her death in 1894, and which resulted in the five-volume set of which this is the final part. The groundwork for Gilman's study was done by J. Walter Fewkes, who made recordings using a phonograph, first in Maine, then among the Zuni Indians in 1890, and finally among the Hopi in 1891. The recordings of the Zuni resulted in a short account by Gilman, "Zuni Melodies," in Vol. 1 of the Journal, pp. 65-91. Those made of the Hopi at the Pueblo Walpi form the basis for the larger work, which begins with a technical discussion in which Gilman elaborates on his thesis that Indian music is "music without scale" (an attitude contrasting markedly with that of J. C. Fillmore, harmonizer of Alice C. Fletcher's melodies in no. 406). The volume also contains transcriptions and analysis of 17 songs, given in conventional and in "phonographic" notation. The latter is an early attempt to devise a system to indicate minute differences in intervals between tones by employing an expanded musical staff accommodating up to 1/14th of a single tone. Gilman's endeavors in this field represent one of first scientific uses of the phonograph in ethnomusicology.

408. KILPATRICK, Jack Frederick, and KILPATRICK, Anna Gritts. Muskogean charm songs among the Oklahoma Cherokees. Washington: Smithsonian Press, 1967. (Smithsonian Contributions to Anthropology, Vol. 2, No. 3) 40p. bibliog.
These are ten songs used for medico-magical purposes, originating in the Muskogean enclaves among the Cherokees. Tunes are given for each, in regular notation, with texts in Sequoyah syllabary and Cherokee captions. There are also English explanations and short commentaries.

409. KLAH, Hasteen. Navajo creation myth: the story of the Emergence; recorded by Mary C. Wheelwright. Santa Fe: Museum of Navajo Ceremonial Art, 1942. 237p. illus. (some col.).
Klah was a Navajo medicine man, and this volume includes translations of the texts of 30 ceremonial songs based on the creation myth. Klah himself sang the songs, which were recorded and translated by Harry Hoijer and edited by George Herzog.

410. KLUCKHOHN, Clyde, and WYMAN, Leland C. An introduction to Navaho chant practice, with an account of the behaviors observed in four chants. Menasha: American Anthropological Association, 1940. (Memoirs of the American Anthropological Association, 53) 204p. illus., bibliog.
A follow-up to the same authors' classification of song ceremonials (no. 419), indicating the general pattern of Navaho chant practice (combination of song ceremonies), and illustrating this with descriptions of four chants. In Part I the authors show how Navaho chant is a framework into which units of ceremonies are fitted. They define and describe ceremonial equipment and medicines, show how these are used in various acts and procedures, give an account of how chant is normally started, and, with particular reference to the Holy Way chants, describe the component ceremonies making up the chants, and give examples of the way they are combined. In Parts II-V four chants are described: the Navaho Wind Way, the Chiricahua Wind Way, the Female Shooting Way, and the Hand Trembling Evil Way. Appendices are devoted to addenda to no. 419, a glossary of ceremonial terms, and a concordance of plant names. There are also 26 plates of equipment and paintings.

411. KURATH, Gertrude P. Iroquois music and dance: ceremonial arts of the two Seneca longhouses. Washington: Government Printing Office, 1964. (Smithsonian Institution, Bur-

eau of American Ethnology, Bulletin No. 187) 268p. illus. bibliog. , discog.

A detailed description and analysis of the music and dance of the Iroquois of the Coldspring and Tonawanda Reservations in New York State, with a collection of the songs and texts, transcribed from recordings by two other collectors made between 1933 and 1951. The songs are accompanied by choreographic symbols. Translations of the texts precede the songs themselves, which are arranged in seven groups for each longhouse (e. g. rituals addressed to the Creator, social dances). Index.

412. KURATH, Gertrude Prokosch. Music and dance of the Tewa Pueblos; with the aid of Antonio Garcia. Santa Fe: Museum of New Mexico Press, 1970. (Research Records, No. 8) 309p. illus. , bibliog.

The problems involved in adequately translating the patterns of Indian art ceremonials onto paper are solved in this description and analysis of the rituals of the Tewa Pueblos of New Mexico by a system of "choreo-musical displays," in which standard musical notation (with the addition of diacritics for glide, pulsation, etc.) is combined with a series of glyphs and other devices denoting participants, dance movements, quality (tension, relaxation) and so on. The resulting scores, given in Part 3, are graphic recreations of particular ceremonies, allowing the author to analyze them in an attempt to reach a "deeper esthetic and cultural understanding of the Tewa people" (p. 1). Prior to this she describes, in Part 1, the relation of Tewa ceremony to the people's life and environment; and in Part 2 analyzes choreographic and tonal patterns with the aid of ground plans as well as glyphs and music scores. In all, the book contains over 150 figures. Texts are included for many of the songs, though they do not affect dance patterns (the correlation of speech and melody "needs further exploration"). The method used for integrating the factors involved in ceremonial drama, the author feels, may prove a stepping stone for similar studies.

413. McALLESTER, David P. Enemy way music: a study of social and esthetic values as seen in Navaho music. Cambridge, Mass. : Peabody Museum, 1954. (Reports of the Rimrock Project, Value Series No. 3. Papers of the Peabody Museum, Vol. 41, No. 3) 96p. bibliog.

A highly regarded study, the significance of which lies in McAllester's relating--for the first time in ethnomusicology--the fields of music and cultural values, as well as in the large number of music examples given. Basing his study on field work done in 1950, from which he obtained interview material and answers to a questionnaire, McAllester demonstrates how Navaho cultural values are expressed in music, in particular in the music associated with the Enemy Way ceremonial, a war ceremonial protecting the Navaho from the ghosts of alien peoples. Supporting and illuminating the discussion are transcriptions and analyses of 75 Enemy Way songs.

414. McALLESTER, David P. Indian music in the Southwest. Colorado Springs: Taylor Museum of the Colorado Springs

Fine Arts Center, 1961. 15p.

A pamphlet on the music of the Pueblo, Apache and Navajo tribes, outlining outstanding characteristics.

415. McALLESTER, David P. Peyote music. New York: Viking Fund, 1949. (Viking Fund Publications in Anthropology, No. 13) (Repr. New York: Johnson, 1971). 104p. bibliog.

The peyote cult combines Christian and pagan elements, and involves in its rituals the consumption of the peyote cactus. In this musicological and cultural study of the music associated with the cult among the Comanche Indians McAllester sketches the spread of the cult, quotes the Comanche's own story of its origin and their description of the ritual, before going on to discuss, separately and comparatively, the music and texts of their songs, as illustrated by the 84 songs he includes. The influences of Ghost Dance are examined in a conclusion.

416. MERRIAM, Alan P. Ethnomusicology of the Flathead Indians. Chicago: Aldine, 1967. (Viking Fund Publications in Anthropology, No. 44) 403p. illus., bibliog.

Based on field work carried out in 1950 and 1958, chiefly among older members of the Flathead people of Western Montana, this is a scholarly study in two sections. Part 1 describes the Flathead concept of the spiritual origin of music, their musicianship, the uses of music, and the musical instruments. Part 2 analyzes a sample of songs and dances, categorizing them according to function, and concluding that Flathead music is a series of sub-styles, and is a part of the Plains culture. There is a large number of music examples and photographs of the Flathead, their instruments and dances, as well as extensive bibliographic information and an index.

416a. PAIGE, Harry W. Songs of the Teton Sioux. Los Angeles: Westernlore Press, 1970. 201p. illus., bibliog.

A revised doctoral dissertation on the song texts of the Teton Sioux, in which the author (who visited the Sioux in South Dakota in 1964 and 1965) studies the "characteristic features of the primitive imagination" (p. xii) and the purpose and nature of primitive song, examining types of Sioux song (individual, ceremonial, secular, sacred) in their traditional contexts. The bias of the study is clearly literary and cultural, with some attention to historical background. There is no musical discussion, and the book's unsure handling of anthropological approaches was remarked on by one critic (Thomas M. Kiefer, American Anthopologist, 1971, p. 1364), who declared: "All the dead horses of primitive mentality are alive and well in this book."

417. ROBERTS, Helen H. Form in primitive music: an analytical and comparative study of the melodic form of some ancient Southern California Indian songs. New York: Norton, 1933. (American Library of Musicology, Contemporary Series, Vol. 2.) 180p. bibliog.

An examination of structural features of 25 ceremonial songs

in the Luiseño, Gabrielino and Catalineño languages, collected by
the author at Pala, California. The songs themselves are given, arranged in language groups, with an additional group of songs forming a deer-hunting cycle. The melodies are presented in European
notation, with Indian words and English translations. Each song has
an introductory note on its context and its place in ritual. The music is accompanied by a system of symbols indicating structural features. These are used in the subsequent tabular analyses of each
song, which the author presents with comments on the structural
and stylistic features each table reveals. General features of the
songs are examined in the following chapter, and there are also examinations of tonal material, and of Luiseño musical instruments.

418. WEINMAN, Paul L. A bibliography of the Iroquoian literature; partially annotated. Albany: University of the State
of New York, 1969. (New York State Museum and Science
Service, Bulletin No. 411) 254p.
This bibliography of approximately 3,000 items, including
books and articles, is divided into subject areas (archaeology, biography, folklore, language, etc.). References to music occur in
the section "Ceremonialism and religion."

419. WYMAN, Leland C., and KLUCKHOHN, Clyde. Navaho classification of their song ceremonials. Menasha: American
Anthropological Association, 1938. (Memoirs of the American Anthropological Association, No. 30) 38p. bibliog.
notes.
A summary classification table shows six main categories in
which the Navaho group their song ceremonials (complexes of ceremonies): Blessing Way, Holy Way, Life Way, Evil Way, War ceremonials, and Game Way. Each group is sub-divided, giving a total
of 58 ceremonials (reduced, after duplication is removed, to 35). An
appendix discusses sub-rituals, phases and etiological factors of the
Holy Way group. In the supplementary notes the authors provide
documentation on the uses and circumstances of performance of each
category. Corrigenda and addenda appear in the same authors' Introduction to Navaho Chant Practice (no. 410).

F. FOLK MUSIC

Note: This section is primarily, though not exclusively, concerned with the folk music of white
Americans. Works specifically devoted to black
folk music will be found in Section G.

1. General Works on Folk Music

420. BOATRIGHT, Mody C., et al., eds. A good tale and a bon-
nie tune; edited by Mody C. Boatright, Wilson M. Hudson
and Allen Maxwell. Dallas: Southern Methodist University
Press, 1964. (Publications of the Texas Folklore Society,
32) 274p.
Of these 16 contributions on various aspects of folklore and
folk song a number are specifically concerned with America. A section of five essays, with introductory remarks by Roger D. Abrahams, is devoted to "folksong and folksong scholarship: changing
approaches and attitudes." Four of these were given at a Texas
symposium in 1961. These are: Tristram Coffin on the literary
approach to the ballad; John Greenway on the anthropological approach
to folk song; W. Edson Richmond on the comparative approach; and
D. K. Wilgus on the rationalistic approach. The fifth essay is by
George Foss, and examines the question of folk music transcription
and analysis. Index.

421. FINKELSTEIN, Sidney. Composer and nation: the folk heritage of music. New York: International Publishers; London: Lawrence & Wishart, 1960. 333p. bibliog. notes.
A historical study of national character in music and of the
place and influences of folk music. The author examines figures
from the art music tradition from the Baroque to the mid-20th century, to demonstrate the various forms in which the questions of
national expression in music have been raised. In this framework
he discusses Ives (pp. 237-243) and concludes with a chapter on
jazz--the interplay of folk and art elements in its development, and
its influence on musical theater and concert hall composers.

422. GILLIS, Frank, and MERRIAM, Alan P., eds. Ethnomusicology and folk music: an international bibliography of
dissertations and theses. Middletown: Wesleyan University
Press, 1966. (Special Series in Ethnomusicology, No. 1)
148p.

A partially annotated alphabetical list of 873 theses and dissertations from 170 institutions in the U.S. and Europe. Coverage includes folk music, jazz, sociological and psychological aspects, and computer usage in musical research. Entries give author, title, institution, degree granted, date, collation and publication details where relevant. There is also a subject index.

423. HOOD, Mantle. The ethnomusicologist. New York: McGraw-Hill, 1971. 386p. illus., bibliog. notes.

A thorough exposition of the practice of ethnomusicology, illustrated principally with examples and recordings from Indonesia and West Africa, but providing relevant background to the developing study of music in America in relation to its cultural context. All the tools and methods used are described, from the degree of musical literacy required, to field and laboratory methods. Three EP recordings are included in a pocket.

424. KENNEDY, Peter, ed. Films on traditional music and dance: a first international catalogue; compiled by the International Folk Music Council, London. Paris: Unesco, 1970. 261p.

A catalog of 381 films "showing performances by traditional exponents of authentic folk dance, song and instrumental music ... " arranged in alphabetical order of countries. Twelve films are listed under United States. Their subjects include Negro folk music and blues, jazz, white country and folk music, and Indian music. The information given for each film includes title, location, type (documentary, etc.), duration, characteristics (16mm, etc.), production, distribution and synopsis. All the films were available at the time of compilation for hire, purchase or exchange. There are title and subject indexes.

425. LOMAX, Alan. Folk song style and culture; with contributions by the Cantometrics staff and with the editorial assistance of Edwin E. Erickson. Washington: American Association for the Advancement of Science, 1968. (Publication No. 88) 363p. bibliog.

An important book, describing the work of the Cantometrics Project at Columbia University. Based on extensive world sociological data and folk song collections, a system was evolved to describe and assess stylistic aspects of folk song in relation to social structure. The Coding Book, containing 37 musical criteria for measuring a song precisely, is described. Three bodies of American song are included: Indian, Afro-American, and the Western European tradition in the U.S. The main conclusions proposed in this volume are that the song style map traces the main paths of human migration, and that folk song style crystalizes a people's cultural behavior patterns: a society's soul is reflected in its songs. In addition to the bibliography there are lists of sources of texts and films.

426. NETTL, Bruno. Folk and traditional music of the Western continents. Englewood Cliffs: Prentice-Hall, 1965. 213p.

illus., bibliogs., discogs.

_____. _____; with chapters on Latin America by
Gérard Béhague. 2nd ed. Englewood Cliffs: Prentice-
Hall, 1973. 258p. illus., bibliogs., discogs.
A survey of styles and uses of folk music in Europe, Africa
south of the Sahara, and the Americas, with introductory material
on general aspects of the cultural role and the structure of vernacular music. A chapter on Germanic folk music discusses characteristics of the Child ballads and other English folk song groups. Both
general and regional features of African sub-Saharan music are considered. The folk music of the Americas is divided into three
groups: Indians, Negroes, and the descendants of Europeans. The
discussion of Indian music covers its uses, its place in Indian
thought and culture, as well as instruments, regional styles and
texts, while that on Afro-Americans considers questions of the origins and principal characteristics of their folk music and their instruments. The chapter on white folk music includes both rural and
urban traditions. There are music examples in the text, bibliographies and discographies follow each chapter, and there is an index.
The book is part of the same series as Hitchcock's history (no. 30).
Hitchcock purposely omits all areas covered by Nettl.

427. NETTL, Bruno. Reference materials in ethnomusicology: a
bibliographic essay. Detroit: Information Service, 1961.
(Studies in Music Bibliography, No. 1) 46p.
_____. _____. 2nd ed. Detroit: Information Co-
ordinators, 1967. (...) 40p.
A short guide to information sources, describing various aspects of the subject--surveys, research techniques, musical elements,
instruments--and citing, describing and evaluating the relevant publications; 129 books and articles are mentioned. Folk music is included when it appears as a branch of ethnomusicology, which is
concerned with the music of non-literate or primitive cultures, and
of oriental high culture. Some 20 publications dealing with American
music--particularly that of the Indians--are included. African music is also represented.

2.   Folk Music in the United States

a.   Reference Works

428. CLEVELAND PUBLIC LIBRARY. John G. White Dept. Catalog of folklore and folk songs. Boston: G. K. Hall, 1964.
2v.
The John G. White Collection of Folklore, Orientalia and Chess
is a vast library which contained over 110,000 volumes in 1964. The
25,000 or so in this catalog include a considerable amount of American folk music material, both collections and critical works. The
items are arranged by subject, the major groups for American music being "Ballads and Songs--American" and "Folk-Songs--American."
Very little American Negro material is included.

429. HAYWOOD, Charles. Bibliography of North American folk-lore and folksong. New York: Greenberg, 1951. 1292p. discogs.

————. ————. 2nd ed. New York: Dover Publications, 1961. 2v. discogs.

A vast, indispensable compilation of books and articles (including song collections) in two parts (corresponding to the two volumes in the Dover edition): the American people north of Mexico, and the American Indians. In both parts the sequence folklore-folk song is followed. Book 1 is divided into General, Regional (Northeast, Midwest, etc.), Ethnic (Negroes, and non-English-speaking groups), Occupational (cowboy, lumberjack, railroader, etc.) and Miscellaneous. The section on the Negro includes spirituals, work songs, blues and jazz, and minstrelsy. In Book 2 the tribes are grouped in ten cultural areas and material on the myths, customs, music and dance of each tribe is arranged alphabetically by tribe within each area. Both parts contain occasional annotations, and discographies follow each section wherever applicable, with a particularly detailed one for blues and jazz. There is a combined index to both parts. The 2nd edition contains no new material, merely revisions of the original text.

430. HENRY, Mellinger Edward. A bibliography for the study of American folksongs, with many titles of folk-songs (and titles that have to do with folk-songs) from other lands. London: Mitre Press, (1936). 142p.

Useful in its day, but superseded by Haywood (no. 429), this checklist of some 3,000 references to books, articles and parts of books is arranged in one alphabetical sequence of authors or titles, with no indexes to allow for the subject approach. Quite a lot of the references are to popular music items, and there is a considerable amount of material in the "other lands" category. Bibliographical detail is sometimes scant.

431. HERZOG, George. Research in primitive and folk music in the United States: a survey. Washington: American Council of Learned Societies, 1936. (Bulletin No. 24) 97p.

A lucid survey of the state of research into primitive (most notably, American Indian) and folk music in America in 1936, imbued with a sense of urgency, lest the primary materials disappear before the necessary professional collecting is done. Herzog divides his examination into two parts, scrutinizing the primitive and the folk field in turn under broadly similar heads: a brief history of the study done so far; present interests; the various possible approaches to the subject (e.g., music and the psychological setting, interrelation of music and text) and techniques to record, study and present it; the currently available facilities for research in the form of courses and collections; bibliographies; and summary of objectives and guidelines for future progress. In the folk music section the author concentrates on study of the music, rather than of the texts, and excludes from his coverage early hymnbooks and commercially recorded folk music. The usefulness of his work is not merely historical; the breakdown of the various possible approaches to each subject is valuable, and one particularly helpful feature of the folk music bibliographies is that the number of musical items in each collection or study is indicated.

432. LAWLESS, Ray M. Folksingers and folksongs in America: a handbook, biography, bibliography and discography; illustrated from paintings by Thomas Hart Benton and others, and from designs in Steuben glass. New York: Duell, Sloan & Pearce, 1960. 662p. illus., bibliogs., discogs.
_____. _____. New ed. with special supplement. New York: Meredith, 1965. 750p. illus., bibliogs., discogs.

A versatile reference work, combining in one volume the functions of biographical directory, bibliography and discography. The biographical part contains some 200 biographies, written in a narrative style, with frequent--usually generous--comment on an artist's style, character, etc. The annotated, evaluative bibliography begins with the works of the major collectors, and works through some 300 titles, including categories for minor compilations and background books. The compiler's decision not to group collections by region, occupation, etc. is in many ways regrettable, as is his method of arranging items in title order, so that--major figures excepted--an individual compiler's works are scattered. Book 3 contains a check-list of 844 folk song titles and sources in collections, and a discography of 700 LPs. There are indexes to names, subjects, LP and book titles. Each section contains an introductory chapter, and there are also short essays on instruments, societies and festivals. The supplement in the 1965 edition updates the work, which is otherwise unchanged for this edition. The tacking-on of the supplement to follow the major indexes makes easy location and use of these indexes unnecessarily difficult.

433. LIBRARY OF CONGRESS. Music Division. Archive of American Folk Song. Check-list of recorded songs in the English language in the Library of Congress Archive of American Folk Song to July, 1940; alphabetical list with geographical index. Washington, 1942. 3v. (Repr. in one volume, New York: Arno Press, 1971).

The 10,000 or so recordings in this list were made between 1933 and 1940. Although numerous collectors made contributions the bulk of the actual collecting was done by John A. Lomax and Alan Lomax, who covered virtually the entire country on field trips. "Fiddlers, evangelists, cotton pickers, housewives, convicts, school children, miners, hoboes, lumber-jacks, old-timers--a cross section of America sang into our field microphone" (Alan Lomax--Introduction). The main part of the checklist consists of an alphabetical title index, in which each title is followed by the singer's name, the location, the name of the collector, the year, and the call number. This is followed by a geographical index in which the titles are listed under state and county where they were recorded.

434. LOMAX, Alan and COWELL, Sidney Robertson. American folk song and folk lore: a regional bibliography. New

York: Progressive Education Association, (1942). 59p.

Aimed at a popular rather than an academic audience, this extensive, briefly annotated bibliography of about 400 monographs and collections is still useful. It is arranged in 13 sections, including general, regional and occupational groups, with sections for the Negro South, white spirituals and Spanish-Americans.

435. MATTFELD, Julius. The folk music of the Western hemisphere: a list of references in the New York Public Library. New York: New York Public Library, 1925. 74p.

An early attempt to provide references for the study of the folk music of both North and South America, largely superseded for North American material by Haywood (no. 429). Over 1,000 references are arranged in eleven sections: Canadian, cowboy, Creole, Eskimo, Indian (North American), Indian (Central and South American), Latin American, Negro (North American), Negro (Central and South American), U.S. general and regional, and musical instruments. Books, song collections and articles are included. Notes give the number of tunes in a collection (something Haywood does only rarely), and references to reviews. Index.

b. General Studies

436. AMES, Russell. The story of American folk song; foreword by Thomas K. Scherman. New York: Grosset & Dunlap, 1960. 276p.

A handy survey of folk song from colonial times to the present, concentrating on the influence of the British tradition. Song forms are seen in their historical context, and the influence of contemporary events and traditions is indicated. There are chapters on the songs of specific periods (Revolutionary War, Gold Rush, etc.), and on songs grouped by type (broadside ballads), ethnic group (Negro spirituals) and occupations (cowboys, miners). There are no music examples; Ames' interest is mainly textual, and he illustrates his discussion freely with quotations from the texts of songs.

437. BARRY, Phillips. Folk music in America; introductory essay by George Herzog. New York: National Service Bureau, 1939. (U.S. Works Progress Administration, New York. Federal Theatre Project) 113p.

A collection of fifteen essays, reprinted from various journals, and including the texts and tunes of numerous folk songs. There is also a bibliography of Barry's work (he died in 1937). Wilgus (no. 472), who devotes considerable space to discussing the theories of this important figure, says of him, "He combined the experience of the field collector with the erudition, if not always the equanimity, of the academic scholar" (p. 68).

438. BLUESTEIN, Gene. The voice of the folk: folklore and American literary theory. Amherst: University of Massachusetts Press, 1972. 170p. bibliog. notes.

Bluestein's stimulating cross-disciplinary study is concerned with the attitudes of a succession of mainly literary figures (Johann Gottfried Herder in Germany, Emerson, Whitman, Constance Rourke, John A. and Alan Lomax, William Faulkner and Ralph Ellison in America) towards folk culture, in particular their belief in the high cultural value of material from the folk tradition.   In the case of the Lomaxes and of Faulkner and Ellison he relates his study to American folk music.   The development of the thought and attitudes of the Lomaxes is examined and assessed in the context of previous ballad scholarship.   Bluestein sees in their conception of folksong "a democratic affirmation which also underscores their affinity with the Emerson-Whitman tradition" (p. 108-9), this beginning at a time when traditional scholarship "denied the existence (or the value) of an American folksong tradition outside the confines of Child variants" (p. 98).   In his discussion of Faulkner and Ellison, Bluestein examines the use of jazz and blues as literary themes.   An epilogue on the poetry of rock music points out what the author sees as Herder's and Emerson's influence as well as that of black musical styles.   Appendix is devoted to the five-string banjo.   Index.

439.   COFFIN, Tristram, ed.   American folklore.   Washington: Voice of America, 1968.   (Forum Lectures, 1968) 325p. illus.

_____.   Our living traditions: an introduction to American folklore.   New York: Basic Books, 1968.   301p.

Of the 25 lectures included here (both volumes have the same text), a number have specifically musical themes, including those on ballads (G. Malcolm Laws), the lyric tradition (W. Edson Richmond), spirituals (Bruce Jackson), the musical characteristics of the American folk song (Bruno Nettl), hillbilly music (D. K. Wilgus), and Negro music (John Szwed).   The contributors are all noted authorities, but their lectures are aimed at a wide (the editor considers, often misguided) rather than a specialist audience.   Some of the other talks are also relevant to folk music.

440.   DORSON, Richard M.   American folklore.   Chicago: University of Chicago Press, 1959.   329p.   bibliog.

Clearly and deliberately set against a background of American history, this is a chronological survey of true American folklore and of its study from colonial days to the 20th century, relating it to the uniquely American combination of social and cultural elements involved in colonization, slavery, immigration, westward migration, etc.   Folk song appears in several contexts, especially in the chapter on Negroes.   The bibliographical references are arranged by chapters, and there is an index.

441.   GLASSIE, Henry, et al.   Folksongs and their makers, by Henry Glassie, Edward D. Ives, John F. Szwed.   Bowling Green: Bowling Green University Popular Press, (1970). 170p.   illus., bibliog. notes.

The authors of the three essays in this volume share the view of folksong expressed by Ray B. Browne in his introduction: "the creative act of a single individual and the recreative acts of many persons."   Each essay (two long, one short) is an investigation into the creative acts of one individual whose works have entered tradition. Glassie's subject is Dorrance Weir of New York State, whose song "Take the Night Train to Selma," a modern song about prejudice, is examined in detail. Ives explores the work of Joe Scott from New Brunswick (he worked in Maine), in particular the relation between tradition and invention, and between the poet's personality and his work. Szwed's shorter piece is a study of Paul E. Hall of Newfoundland.

442.   GORDON, Robert Winslow. Folk-songs of America. New York: National Service Bureau, 1938. (Publication No. 73-S) 110p.
        These fifteen essays by the first curator of the Library of Congress's Archive of American Folk Song were originally published in the New York Times Sunday Magazine, 1927-1928. Their publication in book form was a project sponsored by the Joint Committee on Folk Arts of the W.P.A. The essays describe Gordon's extended field trip, stretching from the South East to Minnesota, which he undertook with Harvard sponsorship, after first collecting the names of likely sources of material through a column in Adventure Magazine (the resulting cylinders were among the first items in the Archive). The various types of song described include Negro folk songs, cowboy songs and songs of the lumberjack, as well as fiddle and banjo tunes. In his approach to the origins of folk-song, Gordon acknowledges individual authorship, but at the same time belittles it.

443.   IVES, Burl. Wayfaring stranger. New York: Whittlesey House, 1948. 253p.
        A lively autobiography of the singer and actor (b. 1909) who popularized a great number of folk songs. This account covers the period from his birth to 1945, and includes his background and early life, his training in singing, the importance of song in the lives of people he knew, the two years spent on the road adding to his repertoire, his arrival in New York and eventual success.

444.   IVES, Edward D. Larry Gorman, the man who made the songs. Bloomington: Indiana University Press, 1964. 225p. bibliog.
        Gorman (1846-1917) was a lumberman who lived in North-East Canada (Prince Edward Island) and Maine; he was also the author of numerous satirical songs that found their way into local tradition. Ives' important study is an attempt to examine the songs in the context of Gorman's life, to see how far this might cast light on the creation of folk songs, and on the relation of the songwriter to his tradition. It is also a portrait of a powerful, dominating personality, who became almost legendary in his own locality. Numerous tunes and texts are included in the course of the study.

445.   LAWS, G. Malcolm. Native American balladry: a descriptive study and bibliographical syllabus. Philadelphia: American Folklore Society, 1950. (Publications of the American Folklore Society, Bibliographical Series, Vol. 1) 276p. bibliog.

_____ . _____ . Rev. ed. Philadelphia: American
Folklore Society, 1964. (...) 298p. bibliog.

Defining a ballad as "a narrative folksong which dramatizes a
memorable event" (p. 2), Law's scholarly study examines the ballads written in America from various angles: ballad types, ballads
as dramatic narratives, origin and distribution, ballads as a record
of fact, forms and variants, the Negro contribution, the British
tradition, and the ballad as an expression of the spirit of the American people. These chapters are followed by four appendices, in
the first of which 248 ballads are classified into nine groups (war,
cowboys, lumberjacks, sailors, criminals, murder, tragedies, various, and Negroes). The usual title of each ballad is given, followed by a summary of the story, a sample stanza, and a list of
printed texts. The other appendices list native ballads of doubtful
currency in tradition, ballad-like pieces, and imported ballads and
folk songs. Title index.

446. LOMAX, John A. Adventures of a ballad hunter; sketches by
      Ken Chamberlain. New York: Macmillan, 1947. 302p.
      Though his editorial methods have been criticized, John A.
Lomax's reputation rests securely on his achievements as a collector. His autobiography is particularly interesting for the information
on his collecting methods and experiences, first in the preparation
of Cowboy Songs (no. 561), then in the field trips undertaken in the
1930s (particularly among Negroes in Southern penitentiaries), which
led to further collections and, more importantly perhaps, to the en-
richment of the Archive of American Folk Song at the Library of
Congress. They also led to his encountering numerous unforgettable
individuals, and some of these he describes. The story of this
sometime academic, sometime business man, who, having collected
fitfully and been a keen amateur, became in his sixties one of the
great folk song collectors, is an interesting one on a personal level
too: the country boyhood in Texas, eventual education at Austin and
Harvard (where he met George L. Kittredge and others), the hunt
for cowboy songs, the long interim, spent alternately in academic and
business communities, broken by the Wall St. crash, serious illness
and family tragedy--a triple disaster which led to his resuming his
collecting career--and the 1933-35 field trip with Alan Lomax, during which they covered 16,000 miles. As befits a great popularizer,
Lomax tells it all in an easy, anecdotal style, through which his
fascination with "the intimate poetic and musical expression of un-
lettered people" is clear.

447. NETTL, Bruno. An introduction to folk music in the United
      States. Detroit: Wayne State University Press, 1960.
      122p.

_____ . _____ . Rev. ed. Detroit: Wayne State University Press, 1962. 126p.

A good overall survey of the various strands making up
American folk music. Nettl begins by defining folk music and outlining its general characteristics, and then examines the music traditions of various ethnic groups: Indians, British, European, African. He also discusses urban folk song, the professional singer,

and some aspects of the collecting and studying of folk music. The
emphasis is on the music rather than the texts; 32 music examples
are given at the end of the main text. There is also a bibliographical guide by chapters, and an index.

c. General Collections

448.   BOTKIN, B. A.   The American play-party song.   Lincoln,
           Neb.: University of Nebraska Press, 1937. (Repr. New
           York: Ungar, 1963). 400p. bibliog.
       A study and collection of a unique American genre of folk
entertainment that mingled game, song and dance, and flourished in
the 19th and early 20th centuries. Botkin examines its origins and
background, the elements of game, song and dance, and the language
and style of the texts. In Part 2 the texts of 128 songs from Oklahoma are given, with variants and 62 tunes. They are arranged
alphabetically by title, with notes on informants, probable origins,
possible sources, printed versions, journal references, similarities
in phrase, line, stanza and tune between songs, and directions for
playing the games, where available. An appendix contains interviews with Oklahoma residents. The bibliography lists books and
articles, and there are indexes to both parts of the book.

449.   BOTKIN, B. A., ed.   Sidewalks of America: folklore,
           legends, sagas, traditions, customs, songs, stories and
           sayings of city folk.   Indianapolis: Bobbs-Merrill, 1954.
           605p.
       A collection of folk material illustrating the impact of the city
on folk imagination. It includes a chapter on songs, giving a description of various types of city songs (including street cries) and a selection of texts with 15 tunes and a number of fragments. Index.

450.   BOTKIN, B. A., ed.   A treasury of American folklore:
           stories, ballads, and traditions of the people; with a fore-
           word by Carl Sandburg.   New York: Crown, 1944. 932p.
           bibliog. notes.
       This cornucopia of American folk material in English contains
one section (Part 6) specifically devoted to songs and rhymes. This
includes the texts and tunes of over 60 ballads and songs (occupational songs of sailor, cowboy, hobo, etc., plus mountain and Negro
songs) with footnotes giving the source of each item, and occasional
commentaries. Also in the section are texts and tunes of several
songs used in singing and play-party games. The other sections of
the book consist mainly of prose items, but here and there among
the tales of "Heroes and Boasters," "Jesters," animals, ghosts,
etc. one may find the occasional song. There are two very extensive indexes: of authors, titles and first lines of songs, and of subjects and names.

451.   CARMER, Carl, ed.   Songs of the rivers of America; music
           arranged by Albert Sirmay.   New York: Farrar & Rine-
           hart, 1942. 196p.

Part folk, part popular song, this attractive collection of 98 songs (tunes and piano accompaniment) is arranged in three geographical groups (East, South and West), sub-arranged by river. Four general types of song are included: songs of nostalgic yearning, songs of historical content, folk songs and minstrel songs. There are indexes of titles and first lines.

452.   COFFIN, Tristram P., and COHEN, Hennig, eds. Folklore in America: tales, songs, superstitions, proverbs, riddles, games, folk drama and folk festivals. New York: Doubleday, 1970. 256p. bibliog. notes.
A selection from the Journal of American Folklore, including a section devoted to a modest selection of folk songs. This contains the texts of 24 songs, with the tunes of 15, chosen to illustrate the large variety of American folk song: Anglo-American, Sioux Indian, Dutch-American, Spanish-American, Negro, etc. Some of the songs have introductory remarks.

453.   DORSON, Richard M., ed. Buying the wind: regional folklore in the United States. Chicago: University of Chicago Press, 1964. 573p. bibliog.
Intended as a supplement to Dorson's American Folklore (no. 440), this is a collection of folk tales, sayings and beliefs, folk songs and articles. Sections are devoted to the people of seven areas: Maine, Pennsylvania Dutch, Southern Mountaineers, Louisiana Cajuns, Illinois Egyptians, Southwest Mexicans and Utah Mormons. The texts of a large number of songs and ballads from these areas are included, eleven of them with tunes. The songs are mostly chosen to illustrate historical themes. Details of the informant, place, date and collector are given. An interesting piece by Harry Oster is included, on acculturation in Cajun music, adapted from an article published in 1958. The extensive bibliography is followed by five indexes.

454.   DOWNES, Olin, and SIEGMEISTER, Elie. A treasury of American song. New York: Howell, Soskin, 1940. 351p.
_____. _____. 2nd ed., rev. and enlarged. New York: Knopf, 1943. 408p.
A wide-ranging anthology of 142 folk and popular songs (193 in the 2nd ed.), each with a piano accompaniment by Elie Siegmeister, who notes, "I have tried to compose settings that would fit the special environment in which each song arose." The songs are arranged in a broadly historical sequence (from the pre-Revolutionary days to the early 20th century) in 16 subject groups, such as: songs of the sea, of frontier life, emancipation and Civil War songs, spirituals, Anglo-American folk songs, minstrel songs, cowboy songs, railroad songs, blues. Each group has an informal introduction and each song a brief preamble. Olin Downes' introduction discusses in particular the need for art and popular music to meet and mingle more. Index of titles.

455.   LOMAX, Alan, ed. The folk songs of North America in the English language; melodies and guitar chords transcribed

by Peggy Seeger, with one hundred piano arrangements by Matyas Seiber and Don Banks.... Garden City: Doubleday; London: Cassell, 1960. 623p. illus., bibliog., discog.

This is a fine general collection of 317 songs, in which Lomax succeeds in combining the scholarly and the popular approach. The songs are arranged in four broad groups: North, Southern mountains, West, Negroes. Within each group there are subdivisions by type of song, singer, subject, etc. Each of these smaller sections is preceded by an introduction and a commentary on each song. Sources are quoted with the songs themselves, for which tunes and texts are given (with piano accompaniments for 100). There is a 15-page general introduction. The bibliography gives full details of the sources, and a selection of collections and studies. There is also a guitar guide, and an index of titles and of first lines.

456. LOMAX, Alan, ed. The Penguin book of American folk songs; piano arrangements by Elizabeth Poston. Harmondsworth: Penguin Books, 1964. 272p. discog.
———. ———. Baltimore: Penguin Books, 1966. 159p. discog.

A well-presented anthology containing 111 English-language songs--words, tunes, piano accompaniments and guitar chords--arranged in six groups: Yankee songs, Southern mountain songs, lullabies and reels, spirituals and work songs, Western songs, and songs of modern times. An introduction by Lomax describes the characteristics of each song type, and there are notes on the theme of each song. (Sources are given in the acknowledgments.) Appendices are devoted to American folk guitar style, and to a short discography of American and British releases. There are indexes of titles and first lines.

457. LOMAX, John, and LOMAX, Alan, eds. American ballads and folk songs; with a foreword by George Lyman Kittredge. New York: Macmillan, 1934. 625p. bibliog.

This wide-ranging anthology, containing examples of all the major types of American folk song, appeared at a time when Americans were turning more to their native culture. The words of some 270 songs are given, chosen from a huge mass of material available to the Lomaxes following their collecting trips, with the tunes for an impressive number of these. Music of both white and black Americans is included, and the songs are arranged by type, subject or singer's occupation into 25 sections, including railroad and chaingang songs, blues, white and Negro spirituals, play party songs, songs of bad men, of drink and drugs, of war, cowboy and miners' songs, etc. Many of the texts are composite versions. If there is a linking thread it is that these songs are mostly the expression of what average society considers to be its fringes, but which the Lomaxes show to be the heart of native culture. John Lomax provides an especially valuable introduction, the bibliography is by Harold W. Thompson, and there is a title index.

458. LOMAX, John A., and LOMAX, Alan, comps. Our singing country: a second volume of American ballads and folk

songs; Ruth Crawford Seeger, music editor. New York: Macmillan, 1949. 416p. bibliog.

The Lomaxes' second collection was published when the Library of Congress's Archive of American Folk Song (for which they had obtained material from all over the country, but especially the South) had amassed over 4,000 discs, with over 12,000 English songs. With this volume "earlier apologies for the dearth or inferiority of American songs were replaced by a full-throated declaration of musical independence" (Bluestein, no. 438, p. 106). In their preface father and son say of the songs: "They are often repetitious; they are frequently trite and sententious; but, taken all together, they reflect the (American) life with more honest observation, with more penetrating wit and humor, with more genuine sentiment, with more true, energetic passion than other forms of American art, cultivated or subsidized." The tunes to the 204 songs were transcribed by Ruth Crawford Seeger from duplicates of the Lomaxes' field recordings; making clear the conscious appeal of the book to a popular audience, she expresses her wish "to include as many characteristics of singing-style as is possible, yet to keep most of the notations simple enough to be sight-read by the average amateur" (p. xix). The songs themselves are arranged in six broad groups by type, subject or function (religious songs, social songs, men at work, outlaws, hollers and blues, Negro gang songs) with further subdivisions. Each has a headnote giving pitch of the final tone, LC Archive disc number, singer's name, location, date, and reference to other printed sources. The headnote is frequently followed by informal comments and, in numerous instances, by quotes from singers' own explanations. There are indexes of song titles and first lines.

459. LOMAX, John Avery, and LOMAX, Alan, eds. Folk song: U.S.A.; the 111 best American ballads; Charles Seeger and Ruth Crawford Seeger, music editors. New York: Duell, Sloan & Pearce; New York: Meredith Press, 1947. 407p. bibliog., discog.
_____. Best loved American folk songs (Folk song: U.S.A.); music arrangements by Charles Seeger and Ruth Crawford Seeger. New York: Grosset & Dunlap, 1947. 407p. bibliog., discog.

With this influential collection the Lomaxes' combined efforts in the field of American folk song reached their climax. It is a well-presented popular anthology, intended for performance, of the editors' own favorite songs from their years of collecting. Limited to English-language material home-grown in America, and omitting children's songs and game songs, the collection of 111 items is divided into seven broad thematic groups, with entertaining and informative introductory material on each song, sources being given in an appendix. (To Wilgus, no. 472, p. 220, this means that for the editors, documentation is "considered more a legal necessity or a polite gesture than a scholarly responsibility.") The excellent arrangements include piano accompaniment and guitar chords. The annotated bibliography lists 126 items, and the selective discography 58 LPs. Indexes of explanatory material, titles, and first lines complete the book.

460. OKUN, Milton, ed. Something to sing about: the personal choices of America's folk singers. New York: Macmillan, 1968. 241p. illus.

A popular songbook containing 76 songs in arrangements for piano or guitar accompaniment, chosen by well-known singers from a wide range of folk song styles (including Muddy Waters and Simon and Garfunkel). The editor includes a biographical sketch and a photograph of each artist, but nothing about the songs themselves, which are mainly American traditional (though some are relatively recent in origin).

461. POUND, Louise, ed. American ballads and songs. New York: Scribner, 1922. (The Modern Student's Library) 266p.

One of the first academic collections, this volume groups the texts of 120 Anglo-American ballads and folksongs from various parts of America in seven distinct groups: English and Scottish ballads in America; other imported ballads and songs; native ballads and songs; ballads of criminals and outlaws; western ballads and songs; miscellaneous; dialogue, nursery and game songs. Although she states that music keeps ballads and folk songs alive, Miss Pound includes no melodies. There are notes, giving the informant of each item and its provenance (many come from Nebraska), and an index. In her introduction Miss Pound gives a clear account of the characteristics and diffusion of ballads and songs. (An outspoken opponent of the communal theory of ballad origins, she made her views clear in her Poetic Origins and the Ballad, New York, 1921.)

462. SANDBURG, Carl. The American songbag. New York: Harcourt, Brace, 1927. 495p. illus.

Poet, biographer, itinerant lecturer and singer, Sandburg (1878-1967) describes his collection as "a ragbag of strips, stripes, and streaks of color from nearly all ends of the earth" (introduction). It is an immensely varied anthology of "singable songs," 280 of them in all--words, melodies and piano accompaniment. They include popular and folk items from the repertoire of both whites and blacks, and 100, according to Sandburg, are folk items never before published. There are 24 loose divisions, mostly corresponding to topics or occupations. Each song has a prefatory note on the theme and the source of the version given. These notes frequently provide Sandburg with an opportunity to exercise the wings of his poetic fancy, as this description of "Turkey in the Straw" (p. 94), which "smells of hay mows up over barn dance floors, skips around like an apple-faced farmhand, has the whiff of a river breeze when the catfish are biting, and rolls like a good wagon slicked up with her axlegrease on all four wheels." Fifteen musicians, among them Ruth Crawford Seeger, Charles Edson, Arthur Farwell, R. Emmet Kennedy and Leo Sowerby, are listed as being responsible for the musical arrangements, and there is an index.

3. Anglo-American Folk Song Studies and Collections

463. ABRAHAMS, Roger D. , and FOSS, George. Anglo-American folksong style. Englewood Cliffs: Prentice-Hall, 1968. 242p. bibliog. , discog.

An examination of the characteristic features of white American folk song descended from the British tradition. The authors describe what constitutes art in folk song, and outline the oral transmission cycle as exemplified in the Anglo-American style. Literary and textual aspects are discussed--ballad and lyric forms, style, thematic content--and metrical features of both verse and music are examined. Two chapters explore various specific musical features. The text is illustrated with examples of song texts with tunes, drawn mainly from the Southern Appalachians and the Ozark Plateau. Appendices are devoted to collecting procedures, transcribing, analyzing and classifying. Index.

464. BRONSON, Bertrand Harris, ed. The traditional tunes of the Child ballads with their texts, according to the extant records of Great Britain and America. Princeton: Princeton University Press, 1959-1971. 4v. bibliog.

A monumental work of scholarship on the Anglo-American ballad tradition, which, through the editor's belief in the importance of the "fruitful marriage" of ballad and tune, their interaction and interdependence, completes rather than merely complements Child's original work (no. 465). An introduction describes the significance of the "marriage," the editor's position vis-à-vis the Child authenticity canon, the basis and scope of the collection, and editorial procedure. Texts are given as well as tunes to facilitate the study of mutual influences. Almost all of Child's 305 texts are represented, mainly by tunes collected in the 20th century; many have large numbers of variants, included in order to study patterns of the frequency of mode, cadence, etc. The ballads are presented in Child order. For each there is an introduction on its musical history and recorded tradition, followed by a summary list of variants. The full tunes and texts follow, grouped according to shared melodic features. Under each variant title there are references to sources, informant and place. The tunes are headed by initials representing the mode. They are usually transposed, with the pitch of the original, and any change in time signature is indicated. Child's text follows.

465. CHILD, Francis James, ed. The English and Scottish popular ballads. Boston: Houghton Mifflin, 1882-1898. (Repr. New York: Folklore Press, 1956; New York: Dover Publications, 1965). 5v. illus. , bibliog.

This fundamental, pioneer collection of English and Scottish ballads acted as a great stimulus to ballad collecting in Great Britain and America, and became the basic source book for Anglo-American ballad scholarship. There are 305 ballads, with an enormous number of variants. Each ballad has introductory notes containing references to copies, parallels in other languages, information on the story, etc. At the head of each variant there is a note on the printed or ms. source and the informant. The aim of the collection was to present every obtainable version of all known ballads. There is no introduction (Child died in 1896), but there is a biography of the great American scholar by G. L. Kittredge. The final volume includes a list of published airs, with an appendix of 55 airs from manuscript. The work concludes with a glossary, lists of sources, of books of ballads, a vast supplementary bibliography completed after Child's death, and indexes of titles and of matters and literature.

466.   COFFIN, Tristram P.   The British traditional ballad in
        North America.   Philadelphia: American Folklore Society,
        1950.   (Publications of the American Folklore Society,
        Bibliographical Series, Vol. 2) 188p. bibliog.
        _____ . _____ . Rev. ed.   Philadelphia: American
        Folklore Society, 1963. (Publications..., Vol. 11) 186p.
        bibliog.
        A guide for the scholar to story variation in the Child ballads
in America.   There are two essays on specific questions--variation
in American traditional ballads, and the traditional ballad as an art
form--but the main body of the text consists of a bibliographical
guide to story variation, which takes around 150 Child ballads and gives
references to their appearances in collections, story types and critical discussion of the texts.   There is also a general bibliography
listing the references in this section, and a title index.

467.   LAWS, G. Malcolm.   American balladry from British broad-
        sides: a guide for students and collectors of traditional
        song.   Philadelphia: American Folklore Society, 1957.
        (Publications of the American Folklore Society.   Biblio-
        graphical and Special Series, 8) 315p. bibliog., discog.
        A lucid historical, analytical and bibliographic guide to tradi-
tional broadside ballads imported into America from the British
Isles, excluding Child ballads.   The ballads are first described by
type in eight groups: war, sea, crime, family opposition to lovers,
lovers' disguises, faithful lovers, unfaithful lovers, humorous and
miscellaneous.   There follows an account of the origin of the ballads
in Britain and of their distribution in America, and an examination
of the broadside vis-à-vis the Child ballads, and Child's attitude towards them.   The critical text concludes with a discussion of broadside ballad forms and variants, in which valuable guidance is given
for handling the problems of identification and classification, and in
particular of ballad recomposition.   The bibliographical syllabus in
Appendix 1 groups about 300 British broadside ballads recorded from
tradition in the U.S. and Canada into the categories defined earlier
(with symbols following on from those used in Native American Balladry, no. 445).   Under each ballad number and title there is a
summary of the story, a sample stanza, and a list of printed texts.
Further appendices list 19th century British ballad printers and some
American recordings.   Title index.

468.   SCARBOROUGH, Dorothy.   A song catcher in the Southern

mountains: American folk songs of British ancestry. New
York: Columbia University Press, 1937. (Repr. New
York: AMS Press, 1966). 476p. illus.
    Miss Scarborough, tireless teacher, novelist and collector,
spent the summer of 1930 in the mountains of Virginia and North
Carolina, where she gathered a large amount of material with her
special dictaphone. From this she selected for this volume only the
importations from the British Isles. (She died in 1935, before this
volume reached the press, and the indigenous material was never
published.) Following an introductory portrait of the areas she visited, and accounts of some of her experiences, the 220 or so variants of 89 song texts are presented in two groups: ballads and songs.
Arrangement in each follows what she terms a "mountain 'hit-or-
miss' quilt-pattern," texts being linked by an informal commentary
which seeks to give the necessary information on song and singer
without resorting to somewhat duller notes and lists. One hundred
twenty-one tunes are given in an appendix. There are three indexes: first lines, music (titles and first lines), and general.

CECIL SHARP

469.   CAMPBELL, Olive Dame, and SHARP, Cecil J., eds. Eng-
        lish folk songs from the Southern Appalachians; comprising
        122 songs and ballads and 323 tunes; with an introduction
        and notes. New York, London: Putnam, 1917. 341p.
        SHARP, Cecil J., comp. English folk songs from the South-
        ern Appalachians; comprising two hundred and seventy-four
        songs and ballads with nine hundred and sixty-eight tunes,
        including thirty-nine tunes contributed by Olive Dame Camp-
        bell; edited by Maud Karpeles. London: Oxford University
        Press, 1932. 2v. bibliogs.
        Monuments of Anglo-American folk song collecting, the influ-
ential volumes of the noted English collector Cecil James Sharp
(1854-1924), for all his aesthetic bias and his exclusion of various
types of material, remain an outstandingly rich and varied corpus
of ballads and folk songs that is of particular musical interest because of Sharp's emphasis on tunes. The 1st edition was published
less than halfway through the period, in 1916-1918, during which
Sharp and Miss Karpeles made three hugely energetic and profitable
trips to Appalachia (mainly Carolina, Kentucky and Virginia). In
this they were following Mrs. Campbell (see also no. 90), who had
first called Sharp's attention to this body of song, and had collected
many items herself. Her material is included in the 1917 edition
together with the fruits of Sharp's first nine weeks. In all, these
historic trips resulted in a massive total of some 1,600 tunes, all
noted by Sharp (while Miss Karpeles took down the words). Miss
Karpeles' edition of 1932 draws freely on this huge body of material
to provide a collection rich in variants, and with an amount of music unsurpassed in any other collection. There are six groups of
material: ballads, songs, hymns (only five of these; George Pullen
Jackson claimed Sharp missed a great opportunity here, preferring
to collect love songs), minstrelsy songs, jigs and play party games.
They are presented with brief details of singer, location, and date,

and with a note placing each tune in a modal system of classification. An introduction (reprinted from the 1917 ed.) describes the region, its music and the method of collecting. Notes on other versions of each item are given at the back. Each volume contains a full title index to both volumes.

470. KARPELES, Maud. Cecil Sharp: his life and work. Chicago: University of Chicago Press, 1967. 288p. illus., bibliog.
    A revision of the biography by A. H. Fox-Strangways and Miss Karpeles (London: Oxford University Press, 1933; 2nd ed., 1955), largely rewritten and including new material. Chapters 11-13 describe Sharp's American visits, in particular his collecting expeditions to the Southern Appalachians in 1916-1918, on which Miss Karpeles accompanied him. The bibliography is a list of Sharp's publications: arrangements, books and articles. Fox-Strangways' summary from the first edition of his biography is included in an appendix.

471. WELLS, Evelyn Kendrick. The ballad tree: a study of British and American ballads, their folklore, verse and music; together with sixty traditional ballads and their tunes. London: Methuen; New York: Ronald Press, 1950. 370p. illus., bibliog.
    A combined study and collection of the ballad on both sides of the Atlantic, in which the author groups the ballads by type and theme (e.g., Robin Hood ballads, supernatural and Christian elements, minstrel and broadside ballads) and examines their history and development, aspects of style and language, and narrative qualities. She also discusses the question of origin. Chapters are devoted to the work of Child and Sharp, to the characteristics of folk tunes (with examples), to American folk song and folk singers, and to the literary ballad. Many of the chapters conclude with the texts and tunes of a selection of relevant ballads, with sources. An appendix contains examples of the texts of literary ballads, and there are title and first line indexes.

472. WILGUS, D. K. Anglo-American folksong scholarship since 1898. New Brunswick: Rutgers University Press, 1959. 466p. bibliog., discog.
    Expanded from a thesis, this is an illuminating critical discussion of the work of 20th century scholars. Wilgus examines the controversy over the origin of ballads between communalists and "neo-Emersonians," describes the work of the great folk song collectors in Britain and the U.S. and evaluates their collections, and discusses in detail the scholarship that has been founded on them (with reference to a great many collections of greater and lesser significance). In an appendix he explores the question of the origin of the Negro spiritual, with particular reference to its hybrid nature, which he finds fundamental to all American folk music. The selected discography lists 138 LPs, and the extensive bibliography includes collections, book-length studies and articles. Index.

4. Spanish-American Folk Song

473. HAGUE, Eleanor, comp. Spanish-American folk songs...
Lancaster, Pa.: American Folk-lore Society, 1917. 115p.
bibliog.

These 95 songs were collected by phonograph or dictation in
California, Arizona, Mexico, Costa Rica, Cuba, Central America and
as far south as Chile. There are tunes for each, and texts in Span-
nish and English. Very brief headnotes give information on the provenance of each song, and a 15-page introduction discusses the background of music in Spanish America. Another volume by the same
compiler (Early Spanish-Californian Folk-Songs; harmonized and set
for voice and piano by Gertrude Ross, New York, Fischer, 1922.
23p.) presents the Californian items from the first collection in a
version for singing. Ten songs (tunes and piano accompaniment)
appear in William J. McCoy's Folk Songs of the Spanish Californians
(San Francisco: Sherman, Clay, 1926. 31p.).

474. LUMMIS, Charles F., comp. Spanish songs of old California;
collected and translated by Charles F. Lummis; pianoforte
accompaniments by Arthur Farwell. Los Angeles: Chas.
F. Lummis; New York: Schirmer, 1923. 31p.

Intended to be sung among Farwell's community song movement, these 14 assorted folk songs in Spanish and English are but
a small sample of Lummis's collection, amassed over 38 years.
Farwell notes "a characteristic wit, quaintness, charm of phrase,
peculiarity of construction, not to be found elsewhere."

5. Regional Studies and Collections

a) The North and Mid-West

NEW ENGLAND

475. FLANDERS, Helen Hartness, ed. Ancient ballads, tradition-
ally sung in New England; from the Helen Hartness Flanders Ballad Collection, Middlebury College, Middlebury,
Vermont; correlated with the numbered Francis James
Child collection; critical analyses by Tristram P. Coffin;
music annotations by Bruno Nettl. Philadelphia: University of Pennsylvania Press, 1960-1965. 4v. bibliog.

The material in these scholarly volumes represents New
England variants of 92 Child ballads, slightly over half from Vermont. Thirty-one have one tune each, eight have two tunes, 17
have three to seven tunes, 14 have eight or more, and one (Child
286--"The Sweet Trinity," or "The Golden Vanity") has 19. There
are some 400 variants of ballad texts. The section for each ballad
begins with an introductory commentary; variants are grouped by
plot family, and for each there are notes on informant, published

versions and collector. Each tune given is preceded by a musical analysis noting structure, rhythm and scales, and any melodic relationship to other tunes. Each volume has a title and a geographical index.

476. FLANDERS, Helen Hartness, and OLNEY, Marguerite, comps. Ballads migrant in New England; with an introduction by Robert Frost. New York: Farrar, Straus and Young, 1953. 248p.

A further selection of material from Mrs. Flanders' large collection, this loosely organized anthology contains the texts and tunes of 97 ballads (51 of which are Child ballads) from Rhode Island, New Hampshire, Maine, Massachusetts, Connecticut, but principally from Mrs. Flanders' main collecting area--Vermont. Headnotes give the singer's name, plus occasional snippets of informal background information. Introductions to the various short sections mingle personal experiences and impressions with factual information. The tune transcriptions are the work of Marguerite Olney. Of the importance of ballad tunes Frost remarks in his introduction: "The voice and ear are left at a loss what to do with the ballad until supplied with the tune it was written to go with" (p. xiii). Index of titles.

MAINE

477. BARRY, Phillips, et al. British ballads from Maine: the development of popular songs with texts and airs, by Phillips Barry, Fannie Hardy Eckstorm, Mary Winslow Smyth. Versions of ballads included in Professor F. J. Child's collection. New Haven: Yale University Press; London: Oxford University Press, 1929. 535p. illus., bibliog.

The collectors of the material presented here--all Child ballads--set out to provide a handbook for field collectors, and also to demonstrate the richness of the New England ballad tradition. Their belief in the organic unity of text and music in the life of a ballad results in a high number of tunes (almost all of which were recorded and notated by George Herzog on a special, flying visit to the State). Variants of 56 Child ballads are given (up to 15 for one ballad) with about 80 tunes in all, followed by texts of eight secondary ballads, also with tunes, and 30 fragments. The collection is arranged in Child order, and each variant has a headnote, giving date, informant, location and, in the case of a tune, who recorded it. The texts are interspersed with critical notes and, occasionally, longer commentary. There are indexes of titles, melodies and subjects.

478. BARRY, Phillips, ed. The Maine woods songster. Cambridge, Mass.: Powell Publishing Co., 1939. 102p. illus.

A collection of the tunes and texts of 50 songs of Maine lumbermen and river-drivers. Notes in the rear of the book give sources for texts and tunes, comment on aspects of the texts, and refer the reader to other critical discussions.

VERMONT

479.   FLANDERS, Helen H., comp. Country songs of Vermont;
with piano accompaniment by Helen Norfleet. New York:
Schirmer, 1937. (American Folk-Song Series, No. 19)
50p.

──────. Garland of Green Mountain song; piano settings
by Helen Norfleet. Boston: Worley, 1934. (Green
Mountain Pamphlets No. 1) 86p.
Two modest collections emanating from the Vermont Archive
of Folk Song (as the collection of material made by the Vermont
Commission on Country Life became). Each volume contains 24
songs in arrangements for singing, each with a headnote.

480.   FLANDERS, Helen Hartness, et al., eds. The new Green
Mountain songster: traditional folk songs of Vermont col-
lected, transcribed and edited by Helen Hartness Flanders,
Elizabeth Flanders Ballard, George Brown and Phillips
Barry. New Haven: Yale University Press; London: Oxford University Press, 1939. (Repr. Hatboro: Folklore
Associates, 1966). 278p. bibliog.
An anthology of the words and tunes of 100 songs from the
Vermont Archive of Folk Songs, aiming to perform the same function as the original Green Mountain songster (compiled by the "Unknown Soldier of Sandgate" in 1823): to please people who are fond
of singing. The arrangement follows the basic pattern: Child ballads, other British ballads, local American songs and ballads. The
tunes were transcribed from dictaphone recordings. Each song is
accompanied by Barry's notes on the theme and other versions, and
information is also supplied on the informant, the recorder and the
transcriber. There is also a checklist of the writings of Phillips
Barry and an index of titles.

481.   FLANDERS, Helen Hartness, and BROWN, George, eds.
Vermont folk-songs and ballads. Brattleboro: Stephen
Daye Press, 1931. 256p.
A committee of the Vermont Commission on Country Life began collecting Vermont folk songs and ballads in 1930; this collection of 102 items represents the first fruits of the enterprise. Sixty-
two tunes are given, and the songs are arranged in one unbroken sequence, with 24 Child ballads grouped together at the end. Headnotes give details of who collected each item, the singer and the location, with some notes and comments. References to other printed
versions are given at the end. There are no indexes.

PENNSYLVANIA

482.   KORSON, George, ed. Pennsylvania songs and legends.
Philadelphia: University of Pennsylvania Press, 1949.
(Repr. Baltimore: Johns Hopkins, 1960). 474p. illus.
A representative collection of writings by various authors on
folk song and folklore from all parts of Pennsylvania. Seven chap-
ters contain both study of folk song and examples presented in sing-

able form. These are chapters on the British folk tradition in the state (with 24 tunes and texts), Pennsylvania German songs (28), Amish hymns as folk music (8), Conestoga wagoners (5), lumber-jacks and raftmen (7 texts and 2 tunes), coal miners (20), Pitts-burgh (20). Sources are given for all the songs, and there are title and general indexes.

483. LEACH, MacEdward, and GLASSIE, Henry. A guide for col-lectors of oral traditions and folk material in Pennsylvania. Harrisburg: Pennsylvania Historical and Museum Commis-sion, 1968. 70p. illus., bibliog.
Suggestions on the collection of Pennsylvania folk materials, including songs and dances, make up the first part of this guide. The second part contains examples of English, Pennsylvania German and Dutch, and Slovakian song texts, with a linking commentary and one tune.

484. SHOEMAKER, Henry W., comp. North Pennsylvania min-strelsy, as sung in the backwood settlements, hunting cabins and lumber camps in Northern Pennsylvania, 1840-1910. Altoona, Pa.: Altoona Tribune Co., 1919. 158p. illus.
_____. 2nd ed. Altoona, Pa.: Times Tribune Co., 1923. illus.
_____. Mountain minstrelsy of Pennsylvania; being a third ed. ... Philadelphia: McGirr, 1931. 319p.
The area covered by this collection of texts (no tunes) is the "Black Forest" region in the Pennsylvania mountains. Shoemaker regrets the lack of interest in this area by collectors, and intends his collection to act as a stimulus. The collection grew from 104 texts in 1919 to 140, plus 80 fragments, in 1931. They are given in a single sequence, with collector's name (frequently John C. French) where known, and some informal notes and comments which show a good deal of local knowledge, and sometimes also a cheerful disregard for the more solemn side of folk song collecting (e.g., "Tale of 'Our Wandering Boy Tonight' (as told by one of them)").

MICHIGAN

485. GARDNER, Emelyn Elizabeth, and CHICKERING, Geraldine Jencks, eds. Ballads and songs of Southern Michigan. Ann Arbor: University of Michigan Press; London: Ox-ford University Press, 1939. 501p. illus., bibliog.
An academic collection containing the texts of 201 ballads and songs, with 126 variants, and the tunes for 117. They are arranged in nine groups: unhappy love, happy love, war, occupations, disas-ters, crimes, religion, humor, nursery. Twenty-nine Childs ballads are distributed among these categories. Each ballad or song has a headnote giving references to other printed versions, and for each variant the name of the informant is given. (Biographical sketches of informants who contributed three or more items are given fol-lowing the appendix of additional song titles.) Miss Gardner's intro-duction recounts the development of the collection (made during the

1930s), discusses theories of origin and transmission, and describes the editorial methods used. The bibliography lists books and articles, and there are indexes of tunes and song titles.

OHIO

486.   EDDY, Mary O. , comp. Ballads and songs from Ohio, collected and arranged by Mary O. Eddy; introduction by James Holly Hanford. New York: Augustin, 1939. 330p. illus. , bibliog.

Notable features of Mary O. Eddy's collection are that it was the product of "a very intensive search in a comparatively small area" and that she was collecting in an area she knew very well--Perrysville, her home town--from people who were either friends or relatives. The representative selection of material included in the collection is arranged in Child/non-Child sections, Child ballads accounting for 25 of the total of 153 items (258 including variants). There are 150 melodies, some of which are alternatives. The informant of each version is given, together with notes and comments, and references to other versions. There are indexes of contributors, titles and first lines.

INDIANA

487.   BREWSTER, Paul G. , comp. Ballads and songs of Indiana; collected and edited by Paul G. Brewster. Bloomington: Indiana University Press, 1940. (Indiana University Publications, Folklore Series, No. 1) 376p. bibliog.

Brewster's collection originated in an assignment he gave a group of his high school students in 1935. Their initial investigations demonstrated that Indiana was rather more fertile ground for folk song collecting than had been anticipated. The material collected over the next few years came mainly from Southern Indiana, and fell into six groups: Child ballads, later British and American ballads, game-songs, folk-lyrics, Hoosier songs, and carols. The published collection presents the texts of 100 songs and ballads, 27 Child ballads being given first. Including variants there are 261 texts in all, but the percentage of tunes collected (only 36) is fairly small. The texts are given with full scholarly headnotes, which include references to other printed versions, and details of each contributor. There are indexes of titles, first lines and tunes.

b.   The South

488.   COMBS, Josiah H. Folk-songs du Midi des Etats-Unis. Paris: Presses Universitaires de France, 1925. 230p. bibliogs.
_____ . Folk-songs of the Southern United States, (Folk-songs du Midi des Etats-Unis); edited by D. K. Wilgus. Austin: University of Texas Press, 1967. (American Folklore Society, Bibliographical and Special Series, No. 19) 254p. bibliog.

The French text (which was relatively unknown in America for many years) was that of Combs' doctoral dissertation at the University of Paris. The 1967 edition incorporates his own manuscript in English, with additional translation by the editor. The book first surveys the topography of the region and the ancestry of the people, and then examines the question of folk song authorship, deciding in favor of individual authorship with subsequent individual remaking. Characteristics of the songs of both British and American origin are discussed. Part 2 of the book consists of the texts of 26 British and 34 American songs, all previously unpublished. They came mainly from Kentucky, the Virginias and Tennessee; many were contributed by Combs' own family (he was one of the few early collectors who combined a folk background with an academic training). Index of titles and first lines.

489.   RICHARDSON, Ethel Park, comp. American mountain songs; edited and arranged by Sigmund Spaeth. New York: Greenberg, 1927. 120p.

These 61 examples of mountain folk music all come from very isolated communities in Tennessee, the Carolinas, North Georgia, Kentucky, Virginia and Missouri. Of the compiler, herself a native of the mountain regions, Spaeth says, "(she is) a sentimentalist, for actually it requires a sentimentalist to appreciate the full impact of such primitive folk-lore" (foreword). The melodies, with simple piano accompaniment, are given in four groups: ballads Americanized and American, lonesome and love tunes, spirituals (i.e., white spirituals), and nonsense songs. The compiler's introduction speaks of the mountain dweller's life, describes his speech and discusses characteristics of his songs. Her notes to each song are general comments on themes and background details, with no pretense at folklore scholarship. Though most are anonymous, some of the songs are ascribed to individuals (one being by Gid Tanner, leader of the Skillet Lickers).

490.   RITCHIE, Jean. Folk songs of the Southern Appalachians as sung by Jean Ritchie: 77 traditional songs, tunes and ballads from the singing of Jean Ritchie and the Ritchie family, with guitar chords and notes on the songs; foreword by Alan Lomax. New York: Oak Publications, 1965. 96p. illus., discog.

An informal collection of words and melodies, with guitar chords. Miss Ritchie's notes, which preface each song, comment personally on its origin and its place in her family's heritage (the Ritchies from Kentucky are described by Lawless, no. 432, p. 190ff). Many of the songs are family variants of well-known songs, while others are less well-known. Title index.

ALABAMA

491.   ARNOLD, Byrom, ed. Folksongs of Alabama. University, Ala.: University of Alabama Press, 1950. 193p. illus., bibliog.

Intended to be both a historical survey and a songbook, this

collection contains the words and tunes of 153 songs taken down by
the editor. No variants are included. The arrangement is, unusually, under the name of the singer, which has the advantage of making
the variety of an individual's repertoire apparent. There are short
biographies of a substantial number of the 45 singers. A section is
also devoted to spirituals obtained from black singers. A short bibliography listing regional sources is followed by indexes of titles and
first lines, and of the Old English ballads, Negro folk songs and
play party songs in each collection.

FLORIDA

492. MORRIS, Alton C., comp. Folksongs of Florida; musical
    transcriptions by Leonhard Deutsch. Gainesville: Univer-
    sity of Florida Press, 1950. 464p. illus., bibliog.
       The cosmopolitanism of Florida, remarked on by the compiler
in his introduction to this particularly good collection, is reflected
in the large variety of songs. Commenting on "the land, the people,
the songs," Morris stresses his view of the collection as a social
commentary on Florida and the people. The bulk of the 300 or so
song texts (with over 150 tunes--a high proportion) came from
agrarian communities. Over 150 individuals made contributions, but
80 songs were collected from one lady, the septuagenarian Mrs.
G. A. Griffin. The songs are arranged in two main groups--songs
of the New World and Songs of the Old World (i.e., Child ballads
second, not first)--subdivided by subject (war, love, etc.) and type
(work songs, children's songs, and so forth). A headnote to each
gives the informant's name; there are also references to other
printed versions and knowledgeable comments on background and
thematic content. Index of titles and first lines.

KENTUCKY

493. THOMAS, Jean. Ballad makin' in the mountains of Kentucky;
    with music arranged by Walter Kob. New York: Holt,
    1939. 270p. illus.
    _____. _____. New York: Oak Publications, 1964.
       268p. illus.
       Jean Thomas came from the mountain regions, and in her
collection of the songs of the "mountain minstrels" the words and
tunes are framed in the homely narrative of her travels and encounters, in which she recreates her experiences and shows her
great familiarity with the ways of the people. Piano arrangements
are provided for the 23 of the 90 songs for which the tunes are
given. The narrative centers round a succession of themes important in the folk heritage of the people: feuds, chanteys, war, flood
and fire, the railroad, liquor, murder, laments, hymns and, finally,
progress. There is an index of titles. Jean Thomas's autobiographical account, The Sun Shines Bright (New York: Prentice-Hall, 1940)
includes more reminiscences.

494. THOMAS, Jean, and LEEDER, Joseph A. The singin' gather-
    in': tunes from the Southern Appalachians. New York:

Silver Burdett, 1939. 113p. illus.

The "singin' gatherin'" was an annual festival of folk singing held in the Kentucky mountains every Sunday in June. The 32 songs in the collection come from these festivals. They include play songs, work songs, love songs, and instrumental items for fiddle, dulcimer and other mountain instruments, and are given with basic piano accompaniment, notes on the informant, mode and distinctive features. Jean Thomas' introduction describes her involvement with the "gatherins'" and there is also a play script for the festival, incorporating the music.

LOUISIANA

495.   WHITFIELD, Irène Thérèse, ed. Louisiana French folk
        songs. University, La.: Louisiana State University Press,
        1939. 159p. bibliog.
                  . _____ . 2nd ed., with a new appendix of additional
        songs. New York: Dover, 1969. 171p. bibliog.

The standard anthology of Louisiana French songs, 103 of which are included in the original edition, and 114 (with 113 tunes) in the Dover edition. All were collected by the compiler, and she describes her experiences in an introductory chapter. The songs come from three groups: Louisiana-French, Cajun and Negro Creole. Under each of these heads the songs are arranged in subject groups (e.g., songs of love and marriage, songs of animals). The texts are given phonetically as well as in standard spelling, alternative versions are included, and in addition the Cajun and Creole dialect texts are given in French translation. Each song is followed by explanatory notes and details of the singer's background. Title index.

MISSISSIPPI

496.   HUDSON, Arthur Palmer. Folksongs of Mississippi and their
        background. Chapel Hill: University of North Carolina
        Press, 1936. 321p. bibliog.

A leading folklorist, Hudson had the misfortune to see the manuscript of his book, ready for publication in 1930, fall foul of the Depression. When it was eventually published many variants and all 27 tunes were omitted. The volume itself contains 157 songs, collected in the 1920s in many different parts of Mississippi. All the items had an existence independent of print, and had retained their vitality through a fair period. Hudson describes his editorial principle as being "to respect the integrity of the text" (p. vii). The songs are given in three main groups: imported, of American origin (including songs of the West, outlaws, criminals and vagrants), and "folk fancies from far and near." Headnotes supply information on informant and collector, noteworthy facts about the singer or the song, and references to other printed versions. Forty-two pages of introductory material describe in full the social background in which the songs were current. There are indexes of titles and first lines. (See also no. 497.)

497. HUDSON, Arthur Palmer. <u>Folk tunes from Mississippi;</u>
        edited by George Herzog. New York: National Play Bur-
        eau, 1937. (Federal Theatre Project, National Service
        Bureau Publications, No. 25) 45p.
    A mimeographed volume of 45 tunes (including ones omitted
from Hudson's 1936 collection of texts) with texts. A number of the
texts do not appear in the 1936 book. Headnotes identify the tran-
scribers, and there is a melodic index.

MISSOURI

498. BELDEN, H. M., ed. <u>Ballads and songs collected by the</u>
        <u>Missouri Folk-Lore Society.</u> Columbia: University of
        Missouri Press, 1940. (University of Missouri Studies,
        Vol. 15, No. 1) 530p. illus., bibliog.
        _____. _____. 2nd ed. Columbia: University of
        Missouri Press, 1955. (...) 532p. illus., bibliog.
    This scholarly collection contains the texts of 287 ballads
and songs, and the tunes for over 60, collected in all parts of the
state between 1903 and 1940 by some 100 collectors. The arrangement begins with Child ballads, and continues with romantic ballads
and songs, and humorous pieces of mainly British origin. These
are followed by childhood songs, Irish songs, songs of American
history, later ballads, satires, religious pieces, folk-lyric songs,
children's games and some French songs. The editor's detailed
prefatory notes to each text list other versions and give the contributor of the Missouri version. The melodies are included in the
main text. Index of titles, contributors and Missouri counties.

499. RANDOLPH, Vance, comp. <u>Ozark folksongs;</u> edited for the
        State Historical Society of Missouri by Floyd C. Shoemaker
        and Frances G. Emberson. Columbia, Mo.: The State
        Historical Society of Missouri, 1946-1950. 4v. illus.,
        bibliog.
    One of the outstanding achievements in the collecting of Amer-
ica's folk songs, this set by an amateur collector and resident of
the Ozark region contains 883 songs (some 1,600 texts when variants
are included), with tunes for over 800. In his introduction Randolph
describes the problems of collecting among the hill people, and recounts the diverse, often amusing methods devised to overcome them.
His main interest lies in the texts, but the melodies were recorded
as accurately as possible, at first by assistants noting them directly,
and later (1938) on acetate discs, subsequently deposited in the Library of Congress. Vol. 1 contains 41 traditional Child ballads and
89 later importations. Vol. 2 consists of songs of the South and
West in five groups: songs about murderers and outlaws, Western
songs and ballads, Civil War songs, Negro and pseudo-Negro songs,
and songs of temperance. Vol. 3 is devoted to humorous and play-
party songs, and Vol. 4 to religious songs and other items. Each
chapter has its introduction, and each song had a headnote with informant, date and reference. The twelve-page bibliography in Vol. 1
lists monographs, collections and articles, and there are indexes of
titles, first lines, contributors and towns in Vol. 4.

500. RIDDLE, Almeda. A singer and her songs: Almeda Riddle's
      book of ballads; edited by Roger D. Abrahams; music
      editor, George Foss. Baton Rouge: Louisiana State Uni-
      versity Press, 1970. 191p. illus., bibliog.
      Roger D. Abrahams recorded a series of interviews with
traditional Ozark folksinger Granny Riddle in 1964-67, and from
these created this unusual "folk-autobiography" (his phrase) in which
she describes in her own words her life, her environment and her
music. She herself had been unhappy at first at the emphasis on
her own experiences--she had wanted a songbook--until Abrahams
convinced her that a portrait of a folk artist within a small community was as valuable as the songs themselves. A compromise
was agreed to in which songs were incorporated into the text.
What emerges as Granny Riddle recounts the story of a life filled
with song is a picture of how the folk singer functioned in rural
America. Melodies and verses to 50 songs are interwoven, and
there is a musical analysis by George Foss in which each scale is
described and classified.

NORTH CAROLINA

501. DUKE UNIVERSITY. Library. Frank C. Brown Collection.
      The Frank C. Brown Collection of North Carolina Folk-
      lore: the folklore of North Carolina collected by Dr.
      Frank C. Brown during the years 1912 to 1943 ... Gen-
      eral editor: Newman Ivey White ... wood engravings by
      Clare Leighton. Durham, N.C.: Duke University Press,
      1952-64. 7v.
      The volumes in the vast collection most relevant to our sub-
ject are 2-5, containing the texts and music of the ballads and folk
songs. The 900 or so items were collected from white and black
people of N. Carolina by Frank C. Brown, friends and associates.
The majority are "survivals or modifications of ballads and songs
imported from the Old World," a number originated in the U.S. outside N. Carolina, and a relatively small number originated in N.
Carolina itself.

_____. Vol. 2. Folk ballads from North Carolina; edited
      by Henry M. Belden and Arthur Palmer Hudson. 1952.
      747p. illus., bibliog.
      This volume contains the texts of 314 ballads in three se-
quences: older, mainly British ballads, native American ballads,
and N. Carolina ballads. Each text is prefaced by a note including
comment on the character or theme of the ballad and reference to
other printed versions. The informant of each version is also given
with date and place. Index of titles.

_____. Vol. 3. Folk songs from North Carolina, edited
      by Henry M. Belden and Arthur Palmer Hudson. 1952.
      709p. illus., bibliog.
      The texts of 58 folk songs in thirteen categories: courting;
drinking and gambling; homiletic; play-party and dance; lullabies and
nursery rhymes; jingles about animals; work songs; folk-lyric; satir-

ical; prisoners and tramps; martial, political and patriotic; blackface minstrel and Negro secular; religious. The editorial method is the same as in Vol. 2. Title index.

_____. Vol. 4. The music of the ballads; edited by Jan Philip Schinhan. 1957. 420p. illus., bibliog.
All available melodies to the texts in Vol. 2 are given, transcribed from discs, onto which the original wax cylinders had been transferred by Library of Congress staff. In addition, there are 36 new ballads not received by the editors of Vol. 2. Each melody is preceded by a note giving singer, place and date of recording, and indicating melodic relationships with other versions. Following each melody is an analysis of scale or mode, tonal center and structure (these are all discussed in the editor's introduction). Appendices give tables of musical analysis and scales, and there are indexes of singers, titles and first lines.

_____. Vol. 5. The music of the folk songs; edited by Jan Philip Schinhan. 1962. 639p. illus., bibliog.
Here are the melodies to the texts in Vol. 3. In addition to the 658 songs there are 128 additional items and 66 children's game songs. The editorial method of headnotes and comments follows the same pattern as Vol. 4. In his introduction the editor admits that many folk songs display extremes of gross sentimentality. Appendices and indexes are given as in Vol. 4. The bibliography in this and the other volumes is an extensive list of collections and monographs referred to in the text.

SOUTH CAROLINA

502. JOYNER, Charles W. Folk song in South Carolina. Columbia, S.C.: University of South Carolina Press, 1971. (Tricentennial Booklet, No. 9) 112p. bibliog.
A selection of 45 ballads, religious songs and secular items of white and black provenance, almost all with tunes. Most were transcribed from recorded sources (Library of Congress and commercially released recordings). Headnotes give the singer's name, location, recording information and transcriber's name. Each of the three sections (ballads, religious, secular) has an introductory text, commenting on features of the songs with reference to particular items, and giving some historical information. An introduction discusses the "importance of folk music."

VIRGINIA

503. DAVIS, Arthur Kyle. Folk-songs of Virginia: a descriptive index and classification of material collected under the auspices of the Virginia Folklore Society. Durham, N.C.: Duke University Press, 1949. (Repr. New York: AMS Press, 1965). 389p. discog.
Designed to convey an idea of the rich variety of material collected by the Society in Virginia, this index groups almost a thousand song titles into 18 categories, beginning with Child ballads

and including also other narrative and lyrical songs, humorous and nonsense songs, songs of married and single life, children's and play party songs, songs of the sea, of history, of crime, the West, the railroads, white religious songs, Negro songs and literary ballads. The local title of each song is given, plus the first line, the name and address of both singer and collector, place, date, and number of stanzas. The presence of music with the text is also noted. A list of recordings is arranged under singer, and there is an index of titles and first lines.

504. DAVIS, Arthur Kyle, ed. Traditional ballads of Virginia; collected under the auspices of the Virginia Folk-Lore Society. Cambridge, Mass.: Harvard U.P., 1929. (Repr. Charlottesville: University Press of Virginia, 1969). 634p. illus., bibliog.

Founded in 1913 by C. Alphonso Smith, the Virginia Folk-Lore Society's primary aim was to collect "all the old English and Scottish survivals in the state. Its success was phenomenal ... " (p. 11). Fifty-one of Child's 305 ballads were found between 1913 and 1924, and these, with large numbers of variants and a fair proportion of tunes, are presented here. In all, 390 variant texts are given, plus a listing of a further 203 (collector, informant, location, date, number of stanzas) in an appendix. The 148 tunes are given separately, with the words of the first stanza. In the part of his lengthy introduction devoted to the music the editor speaks of "a certain amount of regret" at the separation; he also describes the music as having presented "one of the most difficult problems of the volume," the original notations having "varied all the way from the impeccable copy of Mr. Cecil J. Sharp to the musical monstrosities of less gifted contributors" (p. 16). Each Child ballad has a detailed introductory note, including references to other printed versions, and each variant has a headnote with names of collector and informant, location and date, and an indication of whether the tune was noted. Each tune has a headnote also. The introduction contains a detailed account of the history of the ballad movement in Virginia. Though very clearly aimed at the ballad scholar, the collection attempts to keep the interest of the general reader by "preserving some of the human factors of ballad collecting" (p. 13). Davis himself shows a very human side in his preface, speaking of the often tedious work of editing, and his own "astonished contemplation of his stoic achievement" (p. x) at the finish. Title index.

505. ROSENBERG, Bruce A. The folksongs of Virginia: a checklist of the WPA holdings, Alderman Library, University of Virginia. Charlottesville: University Press of Virginia, 1969. 145p. bibliog.

The Alderman Library possesses a collection of 1,604 folk songs (2,700 with variants) of both white and black Americans, collected in Virginia by the Federal Writers Project between 1939 and 1942. This catalog lists them alphabetically by title (first lines being given where no accepted title exists), with bibliographic references to printed collections, number of verses, name and address of informant, date of collection and collector's initials. Variants are all listed, and there are occasional notes (e. g. , "art song," "composed by informant").

506.   SHELLANS, Herbert, ed. Folk songs of the Blue Ridge
          Mountains: 50 traditional songs as sung by the people of
          the Blue Ridge Mountains country... New York: Oak
          Publications, 1968. 96p. illus.
    A selection from material collected in the mountains of Virginia in the late 1950s from people living in communities that were still relatively isolated. Descendants of English, Scots and Irish pioneers, their songs are arranged in thematic groups--love, marriage, work, play, etc. Tunes and words are given, and each song has a headnote giving the singer's name and commenting on the theme and history of the song. There are many evocative photographs of the people and the area.

WEST VIRGINIA

507.   COX, John Harrington, ed. Folk songs of the South; collected
          under the auspices of the West Virginia Folk-Lore Society.
          Cambridge, Mass.: Harvard University Press, 1925.
          (Repr. New York: Dover Publications, 1967). 545p.
          illus.
    Illustrating the immense variety of Appalachian folk song, this collection of the words and variant versions of 185 ballads and songs is the result of work done in West Virginia mostly between 1915 and 1918. The melodies of 26 of the songs are included at the rear of the book, each with one verse of text (this section is edited by Lydia I. Hinkel). The main text begins with 33 Child ballads and continues with indigenous songs arranged broadly by theme. Notes on the text precede each song with information on related songs, the event described, the contributor and the date. Indexes of titles and first lines.

c.   The West

    See also F. 8. a

508.   FIFE, Austin E. , and FIFE, Alta S. , eds.   Cowboy
          and Western songs: a comprehensive anthology; music
          editor, Mary Jo Schwab; with illustrations by J. K. Ralston. New York: Potter, 1969. 372p. illus.
    Contrasting their approach with that of previous collectors, whose books were "based on relatively small and fragmentary field resources" (p. x), the Fifes give as their sources "all the previously published collections, plus some forty volumes of notes and transcriptions of field recordings made by the authors and their colleagues in a dozen western states. " The 128 songs are arranged in subject groups, beginning with the West before the cowboy, and progressing in a broad chronological pattern through westward migration, aspects of frontier life, the encounter with the Indian, up to the passing of the frontier. The words and tunes of each song are

given, with guitar chords and symbols, and short, informative notes
on theme and source. There is a lexicon of western words, an index of titles and first lines, and a general index.

509.   FINGER, Charles J.   Frontier ballads, heard and gathered
            by Charles J. Finger; woodcuts by Paul Honoré.   Garden
            City: Doubleday, 1927.   181p.   illus. (some col.)
            _____.   Frontier ballads: songs from lawless lands,
            heard and gathered by Charles J. Finger.   London: Heine-
            mann, 1927.   181p.   illus.
        The compiler, a prolific author on a variety of subjects, and
apparently an inveterate rover, gathered his texts and tunes from a
motley variety of characters--gold hunters, smugglers, bartenders,
etc.--in North and South America, and presents them in a spirited
descriptive narrative, frequently punctuated by yarns and frontier
lore.   There are texts for over sixty songs, and tunes for a good
proportion of these (a number of them shanties); Finger claims that
many are making their first appearance in print.   He arranges his
material in four sections: "outlaws, hard-cases ...," "New Mexico
troubadours" (gathered when prospecting), "a night in a barroom,"
and "Patagonia."   Index of first lines.

510.   GREENWAY, John, ed.   Folklore of the Great West: selec-
            tions from eighty-three years of the "Journal of American
            Folklore."   Palo Alto: American West Publishing Co.,
            1969.   453p.   illus.
        Included in this anthology of articles are several specifically
on music.   Part 5 is devoted to cowboy songs, and includes pieces
by John I. White, W. Prescott Webb, J. Frank Dobie, and an essay
by John Lomax on the decline of the cowboy ballad.   Part 6 contains
articles on "Songs of the Old Country, Songs of the New," including
a Missouri dance call, the songs of Kentucky migrants in Wisconsin,
Mormon songs (by Levette J. Davidson), Jimmie Rodgers and Woody
Guthrie (these last two by the editor).   Part 7 includes an essay by
Archie Green on the Wobbly folklorist John Neuhaus, and in Part
10 there is a piece by Mrs. L. D. Ames on play party songs.
There are frequent textual quotations, but no music examples.   Index.

511.   LINGENFELTER, Richard E., et al., eds.   Songs of the
            American West; compiled and edited by Richard E. Lingen-
            felter, Richard A. Dwyer and David Cohen; drawings by
            Steven M. Johnson.   Berkeley: University of California
            Press, 1968.   595p.   illus., bibliog.
        A fascinating compendium, containing the texts of 283 songs,
folk songs and ballads (with tunes and guitar chords for the majority) "selected from many times that number to be found in manuscript archives, melodion company and political campaign songsters,
broadside sheets, and old newspaper clippings" (introduction) as well
as published volumes.   The songs are grouped in 30 occupational
categories, arranged in a chronological order corresponding to the
development of the West: from stage drivers, railroad men, miners
and soldiers to the Wobblies, and ending with the old settlers' rem-

iniscences. Each group has an introductory commentary on the background and themes of the songs; under each song the author of the text is given if known, and there are references to published sources and variants. While many sets of words and tunes are established units a large number of melodies are selected and adapted from different sources, not exclusively Western. Composer credits are given where applicable. There is a bibliography of references, a chord chart, and a first line and title index.

512. SILBER, Irwin, ed. Songs of the great American West; music annotated, edited, and arranged by Earl Robinson. New York: Macmillan, 1967. 334p. illus., bibliog., discog.

An informative songbook, containing the words and music of 92 traditional and popular songs, presented whenever possible in their original versions and covering a period from 1840 to 1920. Silber states his aim as "to provide, through song, a representative picture of the main historical experiences which contributed to the winning of the West" (p. xvi). There are eight sections: westward migration, Mexican War, Gold Rush, the post-Civil War peak for cattle raising and cowboys, the plains farmers of the 1860s and 1870s, the outlaws, and the early 20th century West of industrialization and the Wobblies. Each section has a historical introduction, and there are notes on the origin and immediate sources of the versions included. Guitar chords are provided, with piano accompaniment for 30, and a minimum of editorial alteration of the melodies. Indexes of subjects, titles, and first lines.

CALIFORNIA

513. DWYER, Richard A., and LINGENFELTER, Richard E., eds. The songs of the gold rush; music edited with guitar arrangements by David Cohen. Berkeley: University of California Press, 1964. 200p. bibliog.

These 88 "original songs of the gold rush ... written and sung in the mining camps of California in the first decade following the discovery of gold" were collected by the editors mainly from song books published in San Francisco between 1852 and 1861. They are almost entirely ephemeral items, in which popular and minstrel melodies of the Foster and Emmett type are adapted to words describing various subjects and moods connected with gold mining. Only a few entered tradition. Tunes are given for almost all the song texts, with guitar chords. The scholarly introduction includes an account of the most prolific author of mining songs, John A. Stone, "Old Put." Each song group has a brief preamble, and a note to each song gives its source.

OKLAHOMA

514. MOORE, Ethel, and MOORE, Chauncey D., eds. Ballads and folksongs of the Southwest; more than 600 titles, melodies and texts collected in Oklahoma. Norman: University of Oklahoma Press, 1964. 414p. illus., bibliog.

A scholarly collection, made over a period of 25 years, of material gathered from an urban population, principally in Tulsa. There are 194 titles, 204 texts and 213 tunes. These are arranged in three groups: Child ballads, British folk songs, and American folk songs. Editorial headnotes on the song and the singer, with references to any of 50 British and American collections, precede each song. The book is illustrated with photographs of the singers, and there are three indexes--title, first line, and general.

TEXAS

515. OWENS, William A. , comp. Texas folk songs; musical arrangements by Willa Mae Kelly Koehn. Austin: Texas Folklore Society, 1950. (Publications of the Texas Folklore Society, No. 23) 302p. bibliog.

The 118 songs in this anthology were collected by the compiler himself, mostly east of Trinity River in Texas. A native of the area, he describes the Texan heritage in his introduction. The songs (texts, tunes and piano accompaniment) are arranged in a Child/non-Child division, the second category containing such groups as love songs, comic songs, children's songs, Civil War songs. Headnotes give informally presented historical information supported by personal recollection and experience. References to other printed versions are given at the back of the book, which ends with a title index.

UTAH

516. HUBBARD, Lester A. , ed. Ballads and songs from Utah; music transcription by Kenly W. Whitelock. Salt Lake City: University of Utah Press, 1961. 475p. illus., bibliog.

A collection of texts of 250 songs and ballads of the Mormons, with the tunes of a substantial number. The songs are grouped in ten sections: versions of Child ballads, songs of love and courtship, of youth and childhood, of domestic relationships, of crime and war, of the West, miscellaneous and nursery songs, and songs about Utah and the Mormons. Each text is preceded by references to other versions, and a note on the singer. The bibliography lists both song collections and critical literature, and there are title and first line indexes.

6. Instrumental Folk Music

517. BAYARD, Samuel Preston, comp. Hill country tunes: instrumental folk music of Southwestern Pennsylvania; collected and edited by Samuel Preston Bayard. Philadelphia: American Folklore Society, 1944. (Memoirs of the American Folklore Society, Vol. 39) unpaged, illus., bibliog.

The major collection of instrumental folk tunes--94 in all

(plus four variants), collected from nine inhabitants of Southwestern Pennsylvania by Bayard himself, who noted the melodies by ear. In his introduction he remarks on the tradition of instrumental folk music, as seen from Pennsylvania, on fiddle techniques, and on the origins and characteristics of the repertoire of music. He also laments the dearth of information on which to base theories. Notes on the players precede the tunes. Each tune is followed by commentary and by references to manuscript and printed sources (which, in addition to Ford [no. 519], also refer to E. F. Adams: Old Time Fiddlers' Favourite Barn Dance Tunes, St. Louis, Hunleth, 1938, and to popular dance collections). The tunes themselves are notated with special devices to show slurs, sharpening of the pitch, etc. Title index.

518.   BURMAN, Linda C.   The technique of variation in an American fiddle tune. Los Angeles: John Edwards Memorial Foundation, (1968?). (Reprinted from Ethnomusicology, 12, 1968). (Reprint No. 12) pp. 49-71. bibliog., discog.
     A brief, unusual study in which techniques of art-music analysis are applied to a particular item from the folk tradition: a recording of "Sail Away Lady" made for Columbia Records by Uncle Bunt Stephens from Tennessee in 1926. Music examples are included, and there is a complete transcription of the recording.

519.   FORD, Ira W.   Traditional music of America.   New York: Dutton, 1940.   480p.
     _____ .   _____ ; introduction by Judith H. McCulloh. Hatboro: Folklore Associates, 1965. 480p. bibliog. notes.
     Ford's collection is principally, though not uniquely, of instrumental folk music, and is more extensive though less thoroughly documented than Bayard's (no. 517). The bulk of the book consists of old-time fiddle tunes, mainly from Missouri-square dances, tunes with the violin "discorded," and round dances. (There is a separate section of verses for these tunes.) These are followed by an account of traditions associated with special tunes, square dance calls, and a description of round dances. The part of the book devoted to folk song includes texts and melodies for play-party songs, children's play songs, old-time ballads and songs of entertainment. No details of informants are given. The reprint contains a biographical sketch of Ford (1878-1960) in the introduction.

520.   THEDE, Marion.   The fiddle book: the comprehensive book on American folk music fiddling and fiddle styles, including more than 150 traditional fiddle tunes, compiled from country fiddlers.   New York: Oak Publications, 1967. 160p.   illus.
     The 160 tune transcriptions in this volume, representing material collecting over many years from 1928 on, are accompanied by informal commentary that combines historical information, personal anecdotes, and technical comment. The name of each informant is given (most of the material comes from Oklahoma), and there are texts for all the sung items. Index of tune titles.

7. The Religious Folk Song Tradition
of White Americans

a. Tunebooks*

521. HOLYOKE, Samuel. The Christian harmonist: containing a
set of tunes adapted to all the metres ... Designed for the
use of the Baptist churches in the United States. Salem,
Mass.: Joshua Cushing, 1804. 198p.
According to Irving Lowens (no. 38, p. 141) the first tunebook to include folk-hymns was probably not Ingalls' (no. 522), but
this one of singing-master Holyoke (1762-1820), which includes
numerous tunes not in any previous collection; these tunes appear to
be partly the result of Holyoke's attempt to compose in a folk idiom,
and partly recorded from oral tradition among the Baptists.

522. INGALLS, Jeremiah. The Christian harmony; or, Songster's
companion. Exeter, N.H.: Printed by Henry Ranlet, for
the compiler, 1805. 198p.
Ingalls (1764-1828), a native of Andover, Mass., who removed to Newbury, Vermont in his mid-twenties, describes his tunebook in an advertisement as "a pleasing variety of hymns and spiritual songs, with music appropriate; some being wholly, and some
in part, the original composition of the author, and others selected
from various authors, (which are credited where they are known)."
The significance of the collection in three- and four-part harmony
lies in its being (according to George Pullen Jackson in his Story of
the Sacred Harp, no. 531) the first tunebook to contain printed
versions of the old Baptist tunes that were usually lined out for congregational singing. It was also one of very few examples of a
compilation including religious folk songs to emanate from New England. Apart from the fuging tunes of Billings, Swan, Read and
others (including Ingalls himself, whose "Northfield" remains popular), the collection includes a good deal of lively music, probably
of Anglo-Celtic popular origin. It appears that the idea of a songbook incorporating their favorite tunes did not greatly appeal to the
New England country singers. It took the invention of shape notes,
and a change of scene to the rural South for the inclusion of folk
material to become an intrinsic part of these collections. (Biographical information on Ingalls is given in Metcalf, no. 62, p.
121ff.)

523. LITTLE, William, and SMITH, William. The easy instructor, or A new method of teaching sacred harmony. Containing the rudiments of music on an improved plan, wherein the naming and timing the notes are familiarized to the
weakest capacity. With a choice collection of psalm tunes
and anthems from the most celebrated authors, with a number composed in Europe and America, entirely new ...

---

*This section is basically chronological.

Published for the use of singing Societies in general, but
more particularly for those who have not the advantage of
an instructor. (Philadelphia, 1801) 105p.
_____. _____. (New York: G. & R. Waite, 1802).
105p.
_____. _____. Albany: Charles R. and George Web-
ster, and Daniel Steele, 1805. 108p.
_____. _____. Rev. and enlarged edition. Albany:
Websters & Skinners and Daniel Steele, (1817). 127p.
_____. _____. Albany ... 1831. 135p.
The system of four solmization syllables (fa, sol, la, mi)
was introduced into the American colonies by early English settlers,
and although during the 18th century it was gradually pushed aside by
reformers in favor of the more recent European fashion of do-re-
mi, it survived in rural areas. It not only survived, it flourished
(and does to this day in areas of the South and West), its endura-
bility largely the result of its having been teamed up with the device
of shape notation, a method for teaching the reading of music at
sight in which each of the four syllables is represented by a different shaped note. The credit for this sytem goes to the compilers of
this, the first shape-note tunebook (the system of the other con-
tender, Andrew Law, abandoned staff lines and was not widely
adopted), who introduce their scheme with the declaration, in an-
advertisement on the title-page, "we know of no objection to this
plan, unless that it is not in use; which is no objection at all."
(For informed discussion of the various problems of bibliography
and authorship associated with this highly significant publication see
Irving Lowens' chapter, "The First Shape-note Tune-book" and also
his Appendix B in no. 38; Lowens' conclusions are followed here.
See also Frank Metcalf's article, "The Easy Instructor: a Bibliographical Study," Musical Quarterly, 23, 1937, pp. 89-97). Very
little is known of the compilers, but it appears that Little may have
invented the system, while Smith ("one of the most tantalizingly
mysterious figures in the history of American music"--Lowens, p.
124) gave the work its markedly American flavor. A title-page deposited for copyright in 1798 (belonging to an edition probably never
published) bears the names of Little and Edward Stammers, and
describes a work of predominantly European content. The first
known edition, however, under the names of Little and Smith, contains only five European compositions, while 41 of the 105 items
were claimed as "never before published." In all, 34 editions were
published: the last, in 1831, contained 153 tunes, but by then 126
of them were European compositions.

524. WYETH, John. Repository of sacred music. Part Second.
       Original and selected from the most eminent and approved
       authors in that science. For the use of Christian churches,
       singing-schools & private societies ... Harrisburg: John
       Wyeth, 1813. 132p.
_____. _____. 2nd ed. Harrisburg: John Wyeth,
1820. (Repr. New York: Da Capo, 1964). 132p.
       The religious folk song, whether a sacred text to a secular
folk tune, an original tune in a folk idiom, or a tune made up of

fragments already in existence (cf. Horn, no. 546, p. 18), had existed in America for a considerable part of the 18th century, but had rarely appeared in print (Ingalls [no. 522] and Holyoke [no. 521] being exceptions), mainly because the people with whom the songs were popular could not read the music. With the invention of shape-notes, however, that situation was changed, and the 19th century saw a flowering in print of America's folk hymnody. Wyeth's book stands at the very beginning of this era, and is hence a very significant volume. Wyeth (1770-1858) was a New Englander who had established a publishing business in Harrisburg, Pennsylvania. His first Repository of Sacred Music, which he published in 1810, was modeled on Little and Smith's Easy Instructor; it is in shape-notes, and contains a similar body of music, chosen mainly from 18th century New England composers. Apart from the shape-notes, "Part Second" is very different. Wyeth seems to have recognized a new potential market, and although there are, in this volume also, pieces by New Englanders and Europeans, the kernel of the collection is the large number of songs from oral tradition (44 out of a total of 149, in the estimate of Irving Lowens, in his introduction to the reprint edition). Wyeth's audience was the Methodist and Baptist revival meetings (although the collection includes no revival spirituals, but only folk hymns and ballads). The musical brain behind the book appears to have been Rev. Elkanah Kelsay Dare (1782-1826), who is credited with thirteen tunes and probably notated those that are not attributed to any individual. Harrisburg stood on a migration route to the South, and it would be only natural for copies of Wyeth's book to be distributed widely in rural Southern areas. It certainly appears to have influenced Ananias Davisson (no. 525), who borrowed a number of tunes, and who himself was much copied. The tunes themselves are given in Wyeth in two-, three- and four-part harmony, and there is a title index.

525.   DAVISSON, Ananias. Kentucky Harmony. Or, A choice collection of psalm tunes, hymns and anthems, in three parts. Taken from the most eminent authors, and well adapted to Christian churches, singing schools, or private societies. (Harrisonburg, Va.: the author?) 1816. 140p.

_____. _____. 4th ed. Harrisburg, Va.: the author, 1821. 158p.

_____. _____. A supplement to the Kentucky Harmony. Harrisonburg, Va.: the author, 1820. 103p.

As the shape-note system established itself in the South and West in the early 19th century, shape-note songbooks began to appear in these areas, their authors continuing the tradition of New England singing school masters and compilers of tunebooks on the rural frontier. Davisson (1780-1857), of North West Virginia, was apparently a singing teacher and his collection seems to have been the first to emanate from the South. The 144 tunes are given in four-part harmony. In his introduction the compiler explains the arrangement of the parts, in which the melody is assigned to the higher male voice. The songs themselves are drawn mainly from existing collections (Billings, Wyeth, Little and Smith, etc.) and consist very largely of fuging tunes. Over 50 composers are listed, including Davisson himself, who claims 15 tunes (plus 11 in the Supplement)--though, as Chase remarks (no. 25, p. 191), "The whole question of individual authorship is not of prime importance.... These self-taught rural musicians were not composers in any academic sense of the term.... They were craftsmen rather than creators. The tradition was more important than the individual." A number of subsequent shape-note books drew heavily on Davisson, among them William Moore's Columbian Harmony (Cincinnati: Morgan, Lodge & Fisher, 1825), and William Caldwell's The Union Harmony (Maryville, Tenn.: A. Parkam, 1837). (For further details on Davisson, consult Rachel A. Harley: "Ananias Davisson, Southern Tune-book Compiler." Ph.D. thesis, University of Michigan, 1972.)

526.   MASON, Lowell, and MASON, Timothy B.   The sacred harp; or Eclectic harmony, consisting of a great variety of psalm and hymn tunes, anthems, &c., original and selected; including many new and beautiful subjects from the works of the most eminent composers, harmonized and arranged expressly for this work by Lowell Mason and by Timothy B. Mason. Cincinnati: Truman, 1834. 232p.
Sometimes called the "Ohio Sacred Harp," this collection, which appeared in the middle of the period during which the compilation of shape-note songbooks using four notes was a flourishing activity (1801-1855), is a microcosm of the conflicting practice of singing methods and instructions that revolved around four-note solmization. Timothy Mason (1801-1861), in Ohio in the early 1830s, found the people singing the music of the 18th century singing schools from shape-note hymnals. Having no sympathy with either the music or the manner of its communication he prepared this volume of music and instruction. Bigger battalions were called up in the form of brother Lowell and together they wrote a 20-page introduction attacking the four-note system and advocating the seven-note, do-re-mi, solution. So far so good, but the publishers, while not averse to textual arguments, clearly viewed with alarm the prospect of a reduced market for a volume in different notation, so produced the volume in the traditional four shapes. The Masons counseled disregard of the notation, and later editions, while using both forms-- shape and round-note--contained the publishers' admission that the "patent" notes were "contrary to the wishes of the authors."

527.   WALKER, William.   The Southern harmony, and musical companion: containing a choice collection of tunes, hymns, psalms, odes and anthems; selected from the most eminent authors in the United States: together with nearly one hundred new tunes, which have never before been published ... New Haven: Nathan Whiting, 1835. 216p.
_____.   _____. New ed., improved and enlarged. Philadelphia: E. W. Miller, 1847. 304p.
_____.   _____. New ed., thoroughly revised and much enlarged. Philadelphia: Miller, 1854. 336p.
_____.   The Southern harmony songbook ... reproduced, with an introduction by the Federal Writers' Project of

Kentucky Works Progress Administration... New York: Hastings House, 1939. 336p.

___. The Southern harmony; edited by Glenn C. Wilcox; first line index by Charles L. Atkins. Los Angeles: Pro Musicamericana, 1966. 336p.

The popularity in the South of Singing Billy Walker's four-shape songbook was only exceeded by that of his brother-in-law B. F. White's Sacred Harp (no. 528). Walker (1809-1875), a popular music teacher of Welsh descent from Spartanburg, South Carolina, claimed in 1866 that 600,000 copies of the various editions of his Southern Harmony had been sold. Among the many fasola collections Walker's and White's were richest in the folk material of their areas. Altogether, according to Jackson's reckoning (White and Negro Spirituals, no. 548, p. 74), "Walker put into notes no less than seventy-four folk melodies from the southern and western oral tradition, that is, tunes which had not appeared ... in any other printed collection." The first edition contained 209 pieces in three- and four-part harmony, of which Walker himself claimed 25 (40 by 1854). The remaining songs came from a variety of American sources, and included Yankee fuging tunes, songs from Baptist and Methodist collections, and even tunes by Lowell Mason. According to White's biographer, Joe S. James, Walker and White collaborated on this songbook. Walker took the manuscript north to get it printed, and brought it out under his name only, for which nefarious trick his brother-in-law never spoke to him again. In 1932 G. P. Jackson, though he thought use of Walker's four-note volume had died out, discovered it in service in Benton, Kentucky, where a Southern Harmony singing had been held each May since 1884. The 1939 WPA reprint--a facsimile of the 1854 edition--includes an account of the use of the volume at Benton. The 1966 reprint is also a facsimile of the 1854 edition. (Walker also compiled a small volume of revival spirituals, Southern and Western Pocket Harmonist, Philadelphia, 1845.)

528. WHITE, B. F., and KING, E. J. The sacred harp, a collection of psalm and hymn tunes, odes, and anthems, selected from the most eminent authors: together with nearly one hundred pieces never before published... Philadelphia: T. K. Collins, 1844. 262p.

___. to which is added an appendix, containing a variety of standard and favourite tunes not comprised in the body of the work, composed by a committee approved by the Southern Musical Convention. Philadelphia: T. K. Collins, 1850. 366p.

___. (Rev. & enl. ed.) Philadelphia: S. C. Collins, 1869. 478p.

The most popular of all the four-shape songbooks, White's and King's collection not only lived on into the 20th century, it flourishes in it (see nos. 529-30). Singing teacher Benjamin Franklin White (1800-1879), like Walker a native of Spartanburg, South Carolina, moved to Georgia around 1840, where he founded the Southern Musical Convention in 1847. His co-author King is an obscure figure, who is thought to have died about the time of the first edition. Like Walker, White drew on existing collections, and also included a lot of tunes from local oral tradition, of the kind that, in Robert Stevenson's description (no. 63, p. 91), sound as if they "should have been collected by Cecil J. Sharp and edited by Maud Karpeles." White's volume also contains a number of revival spirituals, the rather livelier offspring of the camp meeting, in use since the beginning of the century, but only now recorded. The tunes are given in three- and four-part harmony. By the 1869 edition, three years after Walker succumbed to seven notes, White was still holding out strongly, advising his readers to "ask for the old paths and walk therein."

529.   WHITE, B. F., and KING, E. J. The sacred harp, revised and improved by W. M. Cooper... Dothan, Ala.: (W. M. Cooper?), 1902. (577p?)
      _____ . _____ . Panama City, Fla.: R. D. Blackshear, 1909. 577p.
      _____ . The B. F. White sacred harp was revised and improved by W. M. Cooper and others; the selections are from the old Sacred Harp, remodeled and revised... Troy, Ala.: Sacred Harp Book Co., 1960. 577p. illus.

Following the 1869 edition The Sacred Harp apparently suffered a temporary decline in popularity; its revival seems to have been due, not to anyone from Georgia, its home state, but to Alabamian Cooper, whose revision, though not so extensively used as The Original Sacred Harp, continues to reappear. The 1960 edition, described inside as the 12th, retains the old habit of including a section of "rudiments." The songs in this edition, in four-part harmony with the melody in the tenor, include several from 18th century New England, a number by White, King and others from the peak of the fasola era, a quite substantial contribution by Cooper himself, and a still considerable proportion of unknown authorship. There are indexes of titles.

530.   WHITE, B. F., and KING, E. J. The original sacred harp; containing a superior collection of standard melodies, of odes, anthems, and church music, and hymns of high repute... (Atlanta), 1911. 550p. illus.
      _____ . The "original sacred harp" (Denson revision); the best collection of sacred songs, hymns, odes and anthems, ever offered the singing public for general use. Haleyville, Ala.: Sacred Harp Publishing Co., 1936. 460p. illus.

The most widely used of the four-shape songbooks still in active service. The 1911 edition was made under the chairmanship of Joe S. James, the major revision work being carried out by S. M. Denson. This consisted of composing 327 alto parts to make almost all 609 tunes consistent in having four-part harmony. Of these 609, 71 were songs that had been included in the earliest editions of the 1840s and 1850s, but dropped from the 1869 edition, which is otherwise the basis for this revision. The Denson revision of 1936, according to Jackson's Story of the Sacred Harp (no. 531), discarded 176 from the 1911 edition, and added 41.

531.   JACKSON, George Pullen. The story of the Sacred Harp,
        1844-1944: a book of religious folk song as an American
        institution. Nashville: Vanderbilt University Press, 1944.
        46p. illus.
    Jackson's centennial study of B. F. White's and E. J. King's
Sacred Harp (no. 528), the four-shape songbook with the wonderful
powers of survival, begins with an investigation of the origins of the
type of music it contains. In particular he describes how country
Baptist preachers, in the late 18th century, collected hymn texts;
these, at first unwritten, were "spiritualized" versions of Anglo-
Celtic folk melodies. From the first, Old Baptist music books also
contained fuging tunes, and the process whereby this occurred is
also explained. From there Jackson goes on to describe the origin
and early editions of the Sacred Harp itself, with details of the life
of White, to discuss the music "from the casual listener's point of
view," and to give an account of the body of singers that has grown
up around the book. Both for this book and for his earlier discussion of the Sacred Harp in his White Spirituals in the Southern Uplands Jackson drew on a book by Joe S. James, A Brief History of
the Sacred Harp (Douglasville, Ga.: New South Book and Job Print,
1904, 159p.).

532.   AIKIN, J. B. The Christian minstrel: a new system of mu-
        sical notation; with a collection of psalm tunes, anthems,
        and chants, selected from the most popular works in
        Europe and America. Designed for the use of churches,
        singing-schools and societies. Philadelphia: T. K. Col-
        lins, 1846. 352p.
    The four-note fasola system had, by the early 19th century,
become so closely identified with rural areas as to be regarded as
indigenously American, despite its European origin. Perhaps because of this very association with traditional practices it was im-
periled by new influences, in the form of the European seven-note
do-re-mi system, for it could not hope to remain an exception
"among a people which has habitually discarded its own homespun
cultural goods for 'store-bought' ones, its domestic civilization stuff
for foreign fabrics" (G. P. Jackson, White Spirituals in the Southern
Uplands, no. 547, p. 319). As a compromise there appeared songbooks employing seven shapes instead of four. The first was Jesse
B. Aikin's book. In his preface the compiler is hopeful that musical taste in the South and West, that held "unscientific and trashy
publications" in high esteem, would improve as a result of his book.
Although its popularity in the South is not proved the idea was much
copied, and Aikin's own book went to no less than 171 editions by
1873 (Jackson, p. 320). Its notation is standard in 20th century
seven-note compilations. The songs themselves are a very varied
collection, including English, German and American, Lowell Mason,
one of the leading advocates of the do-re-mi system, being represented by 18. (For an account of legal action threatened by Aikin
in 1877 against the printers, in Singer's Glen, Va., of Joseph
Funk's Christian Harp for using Aikin's shapes at a different angle,
see Jackson, no. 547, p. 353ff.)

533.   HAUSER, William. The Hesperian harp... (Philadelphia,
       1848), 552p.
       Reputedly the largest of the shape-note songbooks employing
the four shapes, this volume contains, in addition to a wide selection of European and American tunes from other sources and some
compositions of Hauser's own, a number of melodies noted by the
compiler from the singing of individuals. Hauser himself (1812-
1880), from North Carolina, was a truly versatile man--preacher,
doctor, professor, editor, composer and compiler--who spent most
of his days in Georgia. He also compiled The Olive Leaf (Wadley,
Ga. , 1878), a collection using the seven-shape system that also
shows the growing influence of the gospel hymn, and was the last
to include revival spirituals. (The only extant copy of The Hesperian Harp in a library appears to be the one in George Pullen
Jackson's Collection in the University of California at Los Angeles.)

534.   McCURRY, John G. The social harp: a collection of tunes,
       odes, anthems, and set pieces... Philadelphia: T. K.
       Collins, 1855. 254p.
       _____ . The social harp; edited by Daniel W. Patterson
       and John F. Garst. Athens: University of Georgia Press,
       1973. 254p.
       One of the less well-known and copied of the rural Southern
shape-note hymnals, but one of the richest in native, frontier revival hymns and spirituals of the 19th century, and one notable also
for its choral settings. Although McCurry (1821-1886) leaned heavily
on The Sacred Harp and included several pieces by New England
singing school composers, half of his 222 pieces appeared in The
Social Harp for the first time. These were mainly by McCurry himself or other Georgian musicians of his acquaintance, and were the
product of the camp meeting tradition. There are also six secular
pieces. In his introduction McCurry explains the rudiments of music and of the shape-note system. Most of the settings are in
three parts, the melody being carried by the middle voice. The
1973 edition is a facsimile based on the 1855 edition, with corrected
indexes (alphabetical and metrical) and a new one devoted to arrangers and composers. The editors' introduction sketches the background of McCurry and other contributors, discusses his objectives
and achievement, and the causes for the little attention the work has
received. In addition to its rich content McCurry's work has the
distinction of having been the last original four-shape book to be
published. All subsequent fasola compilations were either reissues
or revisions. That McCurry's was never reissued was doubtless
due partly to the Civil War, and partly to the advent of the seven-
shape system.

535.   WALKER, William. The Christian harmony: in the seven-
       syllable character note system of music ... containing the
       choicest collection of hymn and psalm tunes, odes and an-
       thems, selected from the best authors in Europe and
       America... Philadelphia: Miller's Bible and Publishing
       House, 1866. 361p.
       _____ . _____ . Revised 1958, by John Deason and

O. A. Parris. n.p., Christian Harmony Publishing Co.,
1958. 381p.
Although he claimed in 1854 that the system based on the
four shape-notes was entirely adequate for his teaching purposes,
by 1866 Walker had changed his mind, and this collection appeared
in seven-shape notation. It was not Jesse Aikin's system, however;
Walker--apparently at William Hauser's instigation--attempted to ob-
tain permission to use Aikin's shapes, but failed; so he invented
seven more of his own, defending his change of heart by declaring,
"Would any parent having seven children, ever think of calling them
by only four names?" As in his Southern Harmony, Walker included
here a number of melodies from oral tradition, but also included
European music, as well as drawing on the collections of Hauser,
White and others, and contributing 43 songs of his own. The 1958
edition removed 179 of the originals, and added 182 new ones.

536. HILLMAN, Joseph. The revivalist: a collection of choice
revival hymns and tunes, original and selected. Rev. L.
Hartsough, musical editor. Troy, N.Y.: J. Hillman,
1868. 240p.

_____. _____. Rev. and enl. ed. Troy, N.Y.: J.
Hillman, 1869. 264p.

_____. _____. Harmonized and rev. ed. Troy, N.Y.:
J. Hillman, 1872. 350p.

There had been several small collections of Northeastern revival spirituals in the 1840s, all emanating from Boston; one, Joshua
Himes' Millenial Harp was associated with William Miller and his
predictions of the world's impending end. The type of song these
volumes included had been in circulation for 40 years, but very little of the music had appeared in print. Hillman (1833-1890), following on after the Civil War, produced a collection of almost 500
hymns that summarized the history of revival hymnody in the North
East. According to G. P. Jackson (White and Negro Spirituals, no.
548, p. 122) the collection included "21 religious ballads, 93 hymns
of praise and 99 revival spirituals, all of the folk type." Finding
little influence of southern compilations, Jackson brackets Hillman
with Walker, White and McCurry as recorders of the local oral tradition of religious song.

b. Later Collections

537. ASBURY, Samuel E., and MEYER, Henry E. Old-time white
camp-meeting spirituals. Austin: Texas Folk-Lore Society, 1932. (Publications, X) 17p.
A small collection of camp meeting spirituals in arrangements
by Meyer, with a text by Asbury in which he describes camp meeting
singing as he heard it in South Carolina in the 1880s. (Asbury also
furnished George Pullen Jackson with some songs of the same type
for his Spiritual Folk-Songs, no. 540.)

538. BUCHANAN, Annabel Morris, comp. Folk hymns of America;
collected and arranged by Annabel Morris Buchanan. New

York: Fischer, 1938. 94p. bibliog.

A both practical and scholarly selection of 50 hymns, many of which come from the compiler's family tradition. In her introduction she traces the history of folk hymns in America, and gives a classification of the hymns included. Notes to each hymn are collected together and precede the music; they give titles, commentary (including mode and structure), source, and versions for comparison. The hymns themselves are arranged in four-part harmony. The extensive bibliography includes both closely relevant and more broadly related publications.

539. BUFFINGTON, Albert F., comp. Dutchified German spirituals. Lancaster, Pa.: Franklin and Marshall College, Fackenthal Library, 1965. (Pennsylvania German Society, Vol. 62) 232p.

A collection of "religious folksongs sung at camp meetings, revival meetings and prayer meetings of the German revivalistic churches in Pennsylvania during the second half of the 19th and the first half of the present century" (preface); 104 songs are included, with variants. There are tunes for each song, and the texts are given in both the "dutchified" German (which is neither Pennsylvania German nor standard German) and English translation. A specially devised system of orthography (the "Buffington-Barba" system) is used and described. The introduction discusses the source of texts and tunes, the language and the singers (who are named in notes at the end). No index.

540. JACKSON, George Pullen, comp. Spiritual folk songs of early America: two hundred and fifty tunes and texts, with an introduction and notes. New York: Augustin, 1937. (Repr. New York: Dover Publications, 1964). 254p. illus., bibliog.

This collection complements the historical and critical survey Jackson undertook in no. 547, providing a selection of the music and texts of the shape-note and other hymnals in a scholarly edition. The material is divided into religious ballads (51), folk hymns (98), and revival spirituals (101). For each Jackson gives source (mainly the 19th century country singing books--shape-note compilations, Southern Baptist and Methodist hymnals), headnote on the mode, and commentary. In his introduction he states that upward of 60 of the songs "have been found to be the legitimate tune-and-words forbears of the same number of Negro spirituals" (p. 9).

541. JACKSON, George Pullen, comp. Down-East spirituals and others: three hundred songs supplementary to the author's "Spiritual folk-songs of early America"; collected and edited by George Pullen Jackson. Locust Valley: Augustin, 1939. 296p. illus., bibliog.

The second of Jackson's three major collections of religious folk songs contains the balance of his collection from the Southeast, plus about a hundred songs from a Northeastern area including eastern New York and New England. His sources were old song books and rural group singings. In his introduction he revises his view

of probable British sources to make the Baptists the group chiefly
responsible for the introduction and first dissemination of folk hymn-
singing in America. The songs are presented in three groups: 60
religious ballads (suited to singing by individuals), 152 folk hymns
(songs of praise for group singing), and 88 revival spirituals, which
he describes as "sung-to-pieces hymns," which are subsequently
"patched together with the help of repetitions, refrains and choruses."
Tunes and texts are given, the latter more fully reproduced than in
the earlier volume, and with more source data. Modes are indicated and each song is accompanied by a commentary or brief note.
There are indexes of titles and first lines.

542.　JACKSON, George Pullen, comp.　Another sheaf of white
　　　　spirituals; collected, edited, and illustrated by George
　　　　Pullen Jackson.　Gainesville: University of Florida Press,
　　　　1952.　233p.　illus., bibliog.
　　　　The third and last of Jackson's collections of rural white religious folk songs contains 363 tunes and texts, arranged in nine
groups and obtained from living singers, printed sources and unpublished collections. Each song has a note on the source and on particular features (much information on tune histories coming from
Samuel P. Bayard). Jackson's introduction summarizes the growth
of the rural tradition of religious song, provides a map to illustrate
the shift in the singing of the songs away from the North to the
South and West between 1750 and 1950, and reflects upon tune families. This volume contains a comprehensive index to all Jackson's
books on white and Negro spirituals--titles, first lines, refrains
and choruses.

543.　McDOWELL, L. L., comp.　Songs of the Old Camp Ground:
　　　　genuine religious folk songs of the Tennessee Hill Country.
　　　　Ann Arbor: Edwards Brothers, 1937.　85p.　illus.
　　　　To say simply that this is a collection of the melodies and
words of 44 white religious folk songs from a remote area of Tennessee is a pale, inadequate description, for the book breathes the
air of the turn-of-the-century hill country and is imbued with the
compiler's intimate knowledge of the region and of its revival music.
All the songs are given as recollected from the memories of Mc-
Dowell and his friends, printed sources being searched for additional
information--often fruitlessly--only after each song had been written
out. They are presented in three groups: traditional rote songs,
traditional song refrains, and old hymns. Informal notes and comments accompany each one, and there is an index of first lines.
The compiler has no doubt that the material is part of the folk tradition, "with the possible exception of the longer hymns" (p. 82).

544.　POWELL, John, ed.　Twelve folk hymns from the old shape
　　　　note hymnals and from oral tradition; the harmonizations
　　　　by John Powell, Annabel Morris Buchanan and Hilton Rufty.
　　　　New York: Fischer, 1934.　23p.
　　　　Virginian composer John Powell (1882-1963) was a lifelong
enthusiast for Anglo-American folk music. This little collection is
designed to introduce a few selected items from the Southern shape-

note tradition into the 20th century church repertoire. Eight of the tunes come from hymnals (Original Sacred Harp, Union Harmony and Southern Harmony), and four are from the collection of Annabel Buchanan. All are given in four-part harmony, with the air in the soprano. The mode of each hymn is indicated, and there are brief notes by Powell.

c. Studies

545. GREEN, Archie. Hear these beautiful sacred selections. Los Angeles: John Edwards Memorial Foundation, 1972. (Reprinted from 1970 Yearbook of the International Folk Music Council). (Reprint No. 26) pp. 28-50. bibliog. notes, discog.

In this paper the author discusses George Pullen Jackson's ambivalent view of and limited response to sound recordings in his work on white religious folk song, and himself examines this body of commercially recorded sacred folk music, in particular the recordings made on the Okeh label in the 1920s. As a first step towards a fuller discography he lists the old-time sacred items in Okeh's popular 40000 series. (Another paper by Green, "Hillbilly Music: Source and Symbol," Journal of American Folklore, 78, July 1965, is an excellent general survey of early country music which also discusses the Okeh label.)

546. HORN, Dorothy. Sing to me of heaven: a study of folk and early American materials in three Old Harp books. Gainesville: University of Florida Press, 1970. 212p. bibliog.

Continuing George Pullen Jackson's work on white religious song, the author examines in detail the New Harp of Columbia, Southern Harmony and Sacred Harp, analyzing them musically, describing the musical life of which they were a part, and assessing the extent of American awareness of the music. Her main interest lies in the folk hymns and in the early American compositions in the books. These, especially, the first group, she analyzes in great detail, with many examples. Appendices are devoted to lists of folk hymns. The bibliography includes books, articles and hymnals, and there is a tune and a general index.

547. JACKSON, George Pullen. White spirituals in the Southern Uplands: the story of the fasola folk, their songs, singings, and "buckwheat notes." Chapel Hill: University of North Carolina Press, 1933. (Repr. New York: Dover Publications, 1965). 444p. illus., bibliog.

With this seminal study of Southern white religious folk song in the shape-note tradition Jackson (1874-1953), a professor of German at Vanderbilt University, opened the eyes of American musical scholarship to a body of vernacular material that, with all the attention given to secular Appalachian folk material, etc., had been all but ignored; a body, moreover, still living and breathing when it was thought dead and buried in the Southern mountains. "It has been my good fortune, and good fun," says Jackson in his foreword, "to have uncovered a goodly batch of the aged handbooks of spiritual folk-song which seem to have completely escaped all other collectors and all other diggers into American institutions. How and where I found them, what strange sorts of songs they contained, whence the unique notation ... who made, collected, and sang them, how, when, and where they came into being, and how and where their singing persists at present--these are a few of the problems which have claimed my interest for a number of years..." and are the subjects of this book.

Part 1 narrates the history of the shape-note tradition, following the trail of successive tunebooks South and West. It was in the Southern Uplands that Jackson discovered the Sacred Harp still in use, and realized that this was a creative folk-song tradition. Besides the explanations he offers for the shape-note system, and the information on the various compilations, Jackson also examines the songs themselves, classifying them, discussing their origins, and suggesting that Negro spirituals were borrowed and adapted from white revival songs. Part 2 explores the genesis and spread of the seven-note shape system. The text includes music examples of the 80 most popular tunes.

548. JACKSON, George Pullen. White and Negro spirituals: their life span and kinship. Locust Valley: Augustin, 1943. 349p.

This, the most controversial of Jackson's volumes, presents the results of his continued research into the origins of white and black spiritual folk songs. Part 1 offers a "review and reinterpretation of the nineteenth-century heyday and decline of religious folk song among the white people" (p. 3), from the Great Awakening on. Part 2 begins with a brief survey of the body of published Negro spirituals, and follows this with a "tune comparative list," in which 116 white spiritual melodies (on the one side of the page) are paired with the same number of "Negro-sung variants" (on the other side), demonstrating the huge percentage of close melodic relationships. These juxtapositions are sufficient proof for Jackson that the Negro spiritual is an adaptation of the white spiritual. The ensuing chapters discuss folksinging style, rhythm and texts, and any notion of African sources for any of these elements is discarded. To forestall those who argue that the black version might have been the first, Jackson attempts to show that these tunes come originally from Britain. The final chapter, somewhat provocatively entitled "Farewell to Africa," does not deny that there might be African "hang-overs": "I would merely like to state that I haven't found any yet." Jackson has been accused of racial bias, but it is only fair to point out that he does not deny the Negro made the spiritual into "something expressive of his own soul" (Yoder, no. 551, p. 18).

549. JOHNSON, Charles A. The frontier camp meeting: religion's harvest time. Dallas: Southern Methodist University Press, 1955. 325p. illus., bibliog.

A scholarly study of the camp meeting in the trans-Allegheny West (especially Kentucky) between 1800 and 1840, containing much that is relevant to the religious folk music of both whites and blacks. In addition to describing the development of this form of worship Johnson gives a detailed portrait of the characteristics of frontier revivalism in which references to singing are common, but one chapter in particular (10) is devoted to camp meeting hymns. In addition, Appendix 3 gives examples of songs, and Negro participation in meetings, and the manner of their singing (particularly with reference to the distinctive Negro revival-spiritual) is described in Chapter 6. Hymnals are included in the bibliography.

550. REVITT, Paul J., comp. The George Pullen Jackson Collection of Southern Hymnody: (a bibliography); with an introduction. Los Angeles: University of California Library, 1964. (Occasional Papers, No. 13) 26p.

Sold to UCLA in 1945, the 112 books listed here served Prof. Jackson in his pioneer work on the hymnody of the rural South and form a unique collection of source material on the subject. Hymnals, mostly in shape-notes, constitute the largest body of material. There are also collections of Negro spirituals and various monographs on religious practices of whites and blacks, and on Negro folk song. Brief notes following each entry give call number, pagination and occasional comments. In the introduction the compiler describes in detail Jackson's incipit index to the tunes, a photostat of which is also in UCLA Library. There is a title index to the bibliography.

551. YODER, Don. Pennsylvania spirituals. Lancaster, Pa.: Pennsylvania Folklife Society, 1961. 528p. illus., bibliog.

A study of the Pennsylvania Dutch revivalist folk hymn, with a collection of 150 songs (with tunes). Yoder examines first the origins of the American spiritual, summarizing also the question of the provenance of the Negro spiritual and its relation to the broader topic. He then describes and analyzes sociologically the Methodist camp meeting revivalism out of which the Pennsylvania spiritual was born, tracing the spiritual tradition in the state up to the 1960s. The songs have Pennsylvania Dutch words with English translations and notes on sources. Subsequent chapters examine the history of the songs, their dissemination outside the state, and their outstanding themes. The bibliography is extensive, including hymnals and songsters, and there are two indexes.

d. Shakers

552. ANDREWS, Edward D. The gift to be simple: songs, dances and rituals of the American Shakers. New York: Augustin, 1940. (Repr. New York: Dover Publications, 1962). 170p. illus., bibliog.

An examination and collection of the music of the remarkable religious sect, an experiment in primitive Christianity and the "oldest and most consistently pure communism in the new world" (p. 7). An introduction traces the history of the movement and outlines the place of music. The author then discusses the texts of the songs and the accompanying rituals, illustrating this with a collection of song texts divided into ten types. From this he proceeds to a description of Shaker music theory and practice, giving 79 tunes, with texts and introductory notes. The final chapter examines the different dances. Indexes of first lines and of tunes and songs.

553. COOK, Harold E. Shaker music: a manifestation of American folk culture. Lewisburg: Bucknell University Press, 1973. 302p. illus., bibliog.

A fine scholarly study of the historical and, more especially, technical aspects of the development of Shaker music in the context of 19th century American religious song, based largely on research into the large collection of Shaker manuscript materials (music, letters, diaries) at Western Reserve Historical Society, Cleveland, Ohio. An account of the social and historical background sets the scene for an examination of the emergence of characteristic Shaker hymn tunes and words from the body of common folk hymnody, with particular attention to the phenomenon of the "gift" of song (songs received in dreams and visions, and linked with "speaking in tongues"). Known Shaker musicians are listed, with dates. Shaker notation (round notes, shape-notes and lettered notation) is discussed, and the theories of Isaac N. Youngs and Russell Haskell related to non-Shaker tunebook theory. Aspects of musical practice and characteristics of performance (emotional fervor and sincerity, use of rhythm and pitch, etc.) are described. All technical discussions are profusely illustrated with musical examples. A group of 71 songs, illustrating the functions music performed for the Shakers, is presented, with identification and classification of modes, and commentary. A collation of manuscript hymnals at Western Reserve and elsewhere, a list of printed hymnals, a bibliography of secondary printed and manuscript material, and an index conclude the volume.

554. (EVANS, Frederick William, comp.) Shaker music: inspirational hymns and melodies illustrative of the resurrection life and testimony of the Shakers. Albany, N.Y.: Weed, Parsons, 1875. (Repr. New York: AMS Press, 1974). 67p.

Seventy-seven Shaker hymns, printed for the Mount Lebanon Shakers. This was the first Shaker hymnal to be printed in conventional round notation, instead of the traditional letter notation, and the first to include songs in four-part harmony. Harold E. Cook, in his Shaker Music (no. 553), ascribes these changes to the coming, beginning in 1870, of misguided Boston music teachers, who "in five short years ... through lack of appreciation for the peculiar pattern of an expression unique with the Shakers, imposed upon them a foreign musical idiom" (p. 163). The reprint contains no additional information of any kind, (e.g., on Evans, English-born reformer and Shaker elder, who joined the Mount Lebanon community in 1830).

555. PATTERSON, Daniel W. Nine Shaker spirituals; with a brief account of early Shaker song. Old Chatham, N.J.: Shaker Museum Foundation, 1964. 34p. illus.

Selected from a body of song numbering several thousand items the small sample of nine Shaker melodies and texts presented here are given in modern notation, with sources and dates. They are followed by a description of the beginnings of this unique American religious song, its characteristics, the methods of notation and instruction, and the effect on musical practice of Shaker doctrine (e.g., unison singing resulting from the goal of spiritual union). Some groups of song, and some of the characteristics of Shaker texts are also briefly described.

556. A sacred repository of anthems and hymns for devotional worship and praise. Canterbury, N.H., 1852.
The first appearance of music in a printed Shaker hymnal. The tunes are given without harmony, using a form of small letteral notation on three lines. (17 printed hymnals, covering 1813-1908, are listed by Harold E. Cook, no. 553.)

e. Mormons

See also no. 516.

557. CHENEY, Thomas E., ed. Mormon songs from the Rocky Mountains: a compilation of Mormon folksong. Austin: University of Texas Press, 1968. bibliog.
This collection of 100 songs "only from oral tradition or from manuscript journals" is drawn from material in the compiler's own collection as well as in those of the Fifes, Olive W. Burt and others. The songs are arranged in five groups: Mormon history, locale, customs and teachings, satire and sin. Tunes are given for most of them. Headnotes provide information on informant and source, but there is no attempt to provide lists of other printed sources for comparative study. A 20-page introduction discusses general aspects of Mormon folk song, and each group has a preamble.

8. Occupational Folk Song

a. Cowboys

558. ALLEN, Jules Verne. Cowboy lore. San Antonio: Naylor, 1933, 1950. 165p. illus.
_____. _____. San Antonio: Naylor, 1971. 174p. illus.
"The farther Americans became removed from the cowboy past," wrote Bill C. Malone, "the more intense became their interest in cowboy songs and lore" (no. 606). Jimmie Rodgers was the most influential figure in this vogue, which took a great hold in the 1930s, but singers such as Carl T. Sprague and Jules Verne Allen, both of whom made their first recordings in the 1920s, were also instrumental in creating this interest. Both were also far more

familiar with the cowboy's life. Allen (1883-1945) was born in Texas,
spent some time as a cowboy and as a rodeo rider in the 1890s, and
acquired a generally authentic repertoire of songs, a selection of
which he gives here. In the first part of his book he describes,
with an emphasis on Texas, the cowboy's life and his manner of
speech. In the second part he tells the stories behind various cattle brands, and in the third he gives the meanings of many cowboy
words and phrases. The 37 songs in Part 4 were taken down from
his own singing and harmonized by Mrs. G. Embry Eitt. Complete
texts are given.

559. FIFE, Austin, and FIFE, Alta, comps. Heaven on horse-
        back: revivalist songs and verse in the cowboy idiom.
        Logan: Utah State University Press, 1970. (Western
        Texts Society Series, Vol. 1, No. 1) 114p. bibliog. notes.
    The Fifes' collection aims to show how sacred and secular
song reacted to and influenced one another in frontier culture, and
how Anglo-American revival songs created a new idiom in the West,
in which the image of heaven was seen as an extension of the Western experience--how, in effect, eternity was remodeled to conform
to the cowboy's terrestrial environment. The collection of 49 songs
focuses on texts rather than music, in line with the compilers' interest in the cowboy's expression of religious ideas in his verse,
but 31 melodies are included (some of which are alternatives for one
song). There are seven sections: coexistence of ruggedness and
the Christian ethic; Nature; a witness to religion; death on the range;
hymns-parodies of cowboy songs; cowboy hymns; prayers and homiletic songs and verse; decline of the genre. The songs were taken
from varied sources: oral tradition, the press, 78 rpm records,
etc. There is an index of titles and first lines.

560. LARKIN, Margaret, comp. Singing cowboy: a book of West-
        ern songs; arranged for the piano by Helen Black. New
        York: Knopf, 1931. 196p. illus.
    Gathered, the compiler states, "with my voice and my guitar,"
these 42 representative cowboy songs include "work songs, love
songs, dance tunes, dirges, sentimental ditties, hymns, and narratives of daring deeds" (introduction). Each song is preceded by an
informal background note, and there are a number of evocative illustrations, taken from Joseph G. McCoy's Historic Sketches of the
Cattle Trade in the West and Southwest, 1874. The compiler's introduction discusses characteristics of the cowboy song, and compares the cowboy milieu with other settings and occupations that have
been a breeding ground of folk songs. Glossary and index.

561. LOMAX, John A., comp. Cowboy songs and other frontier
        ballads; with an introduction by Barrett Wendell. New
        York: Sturgis and Walton, 1910. 326p.
        LOMAX, John A., and LOMAX, Alan, comps. Cowboy songs
        and other frontier ballads; revised and enlarged. New
        York: Macmillan, 1938. 431p.
    John A. Lomax himself describes the genesis of this pioneer
collection in his Adventures of a Ballad Hunter (no. 446)--the en-

dorsement of his first efforts by Harvard professors Wendell and Kittredge, and his two-year hunt for material (1908-1910). The first edition contained texts of 112 songs, a great many in print for the first time. Only 18 tunes were included, all with piano accompaniment. The revised edition was enlarged to include 207 songs with unaccompanied melodies to about half. The songs in this edition are arranged in groups depicting aspects of the cowboy's life: "up the trail," "the round-up," "Dodge City," "campfire and bunkhouse," "off guard" (leisure, liquor and love), "son of a gun" and "way out West." The texts are generally allowed to speak for themselves, though some have prefatory comments, and there are some footnotes on sources of both texts and tunes. Both editions contain an interesting note on collecting cowboy songs by the elder Lomax. Title index in revised edition.

562. LOMAX, John A., comp. Songs of the cattle trail and cow camp; with a foreword by William Lyon Phelps. New York: Macmillan, 1919. 189p.
_____. Songs of the cattle trail and cow camp. London: T. Fisher Unwin, 1920. 111p.
_____. Songs of the cattle trail and cow camp; illustrated with 78 drawings and sketches by famous Western artists. New York: Duell, Sloan and Pearce, 1950. 189p. illus.
A by-product of Lomax's first collection, Cowboy Songs (no. 561), this is a selection of cowboy verse, collected from oral and printed sources. No music is included, though Lomax states that "many of these have claim to be called songs; they have been set to music by the cowboys, who, in their isolation and loneliness, have found solace in narrative or descriptive verse devoted to cattle scenes." The American editions contain about 70 songs, the English edition only 50 or so.

563. OHRLIN, Glenn. The hell-bound train: a cowboy songbook; with a biblio-discography by Harlan Daniel. Urbana: University of Illinois Press, 1973. 290p. illus., bibliog., discog.
That the cowboy song tradition is alive is amply indicated by this anthology of the texts of 100 songs, with melodies of 73. Continuing the tradition of Jack Thorp (no. 564), for he is a working cowboy, Ohrlin presents a section of his own repertory--some items with a long tradition and others which he learned quite recently. Each song has a detailed headnote, describing Ohrlin's personal associations with it (and showing how big a part the rodeo circuit, of which Ohrlin is a member, has in continuing the tradition). The impressive, 40-page biblio-discography gives printed and recorded versions for each song (separating academic listings from the informality of the songbook itself), dividing information into six categories: basic reference works, selected songsters and folios, additional bibliographic references, 78rpm records, LPs and electrical transcriptions. The book has an index, a foreword by Archie Green, and the tunes were transcribed from tape by Judith McCulloh. There is an accompanying 7" disc with six items performed by Ohrlin.

564. THORP, N. Howard. Songs of the cowboys. Estancia, N. M. :
      News Print Shop, 1908. 50p.
      _____. _____; with an introduction by Alice Corbin
      Henderson. (2nd ed.) Boston: Houghton Mifflin, 1921.
      184p.
      _____. _____; variants, commentary, notes and lexi-
      con by Austin E. and Alta S. Fife; music editor, Naunie
      Gardner. New York: Bramhall House, 1966. 346p.
      bibliogs.
      "Jack" Thorp, who spent 50 years riding the ranges and
raising cattle, was, according to the Fifes, the "first person who
recognized in cowboy and western songs a creativity capable of
serving as a nucleus around which a new culture might identify itself" (p. 4). The 1908 edition, reproduced in facsimile in the 1966
version, represents the first attempt to record cowboy songs. It
contains the words of 23 songs without melodies. The 1921 edition
expands the total to 101. The excellent 1966 edition begins with an
article by Thorp on the singing of the cowboys, followed by an extensive editorial commentary on each of the songs in the first edition, with Thorp's text, one or more tunes (obtained from various
printed, MS. , and recorded sources), other versions, and a bibliography of references to printed versions, commercial recordings,
manuscripts and field recordings, and critical discussions. There
is also an extensive general bibliography, and a lexicon of cowboy
terms. Title, first line, and general indexes.

565. WHITE, John I. "Great Grandma, " and A ballad in search
      of its author. Los Angeles: John Edwards Memorial
      Foundation, (1969?). (Reprint No. 13) pp. 27-32, 58-62.
      bibliog. notes.
      Two short articles on cowboy songs. The first, reprinted
from Western Folklore, Vol. 27, 1968, concerns the writer's own
authorship of a song sometimes thought to be traditional. The second, reprinted from Western American Literature, Vol. 2, 1967,
is about Joseph Mills Hanson and his authorship of the ballad known
as "Railroad Corral. "

b. Lumberjacks

    See also no. 574.

566. BECK, Earl Clifton, comp. Songs of the Michigan lumber-
      jacks. Ann Arbor: University of Michigan Press, 1941.
      296p. illus. , bibliog.
      _____. Lore of the lumber camps. Ann Arbor: Univer-
      sity of Michigan Press, 1948. 348p. illus. , bibliog.
      The second of these collections of occupational songs is a
revised and enlarged version of the first. The 1941 edition contains
104 songs (with variants) and 16 tunes, arranged in eleven groups
with an introduction supplying background information, and headnotes.
The 1948 edition rearranges the songs into six groups, adding 14
and increasing the number of tunes to 23. In both editions the group

are descriptive of parts of the "Shantyman's" life: "lumberjack and lumberjill," bunkhouse ballads, song of work, of death, dialect songs, and so on. For the second version the introduction is re-written and the headnotes are revised. Both versions have an index.

567. BECK, Earl Clifton. They all knew Paul Bunyan; illustrated by Anita Eneroth. Ann Arbor: University of Michigan Press, 1956. 255p. illus.
Beck's third volume of lumberjack songs in fifteen years testifies to his enduring enthusiasm for his subject and his zealous collecting. This anthology of 67 songs, mainly from Michigan, in-cludes a number that appear in identical versions in his two previ-ous volumes. Few tunes are included.

c. Miners

568. GREEN, Archie. Only a miner: studies in recorded coal-mining songs. Urbana: University of Illinois Press, 1972. 504p. illus., bibliog., discog.
Based on the author's own field work, this splendidly thorough study of mining songs recorded between 1925 and 1970 examines the songs as a portrait of mining life and of miners' values, and as a documentation of the changes caused by increasing mechanization. Through this Green outlines the significance of the change from folk to mass and popular culture. Following an introduction in which he defines terms and assesses previous collectors (especially George Korson), and an examination of the role of the recording industry, Green embarks on case studies of eleven pre-1950 recorded songs, including "Only a Miner," "Coal Creek Troubles," and "Nine Pound Hammer." Drawing on ballad scholarship, labor history and popu-lar culture studies he sets each song in its context, studying both theme and content, and relating it to other items with a similar basis. The words and tunes of each of the main songs are given, with the words of many of the related items. Each case study is followed by textual references and a checklist of recordings referred to. The author also surveys the continuing tradition of the 1950s and 1960s, and concludes with an impressive bibliography of books and articles, lists of interviews and illustrations, and an index.

569. KORSON, George. Coal dust on the fiddle: songs and stories of the bituminous industry. Philadelphia: Univer-sity of Pennsylvania Press, 1943. (Repr. Hatboro: Folk-lore Associates, 1965). 460p. illus., bibliogs.
Complementing no. 570, and organized on similar lines, with editorial study preceding and linking texts of songs, stories and some melodies, this collection was made mainly in Pennsylvania, Ohio, Illinois, Indiana, Virginia, W. Virginia, Kentucky, Tennessee and Alabama between 1938 and 1943. Korson divides the material into 19 chapters in three main sections: "Minstrelsy in the Coal Camps," "Folklore of the Coal Mines," and "The Union in Story and Song." For each item recorded by Korson the date and place of the recording are given, and the name of the informant. Sources

of all other items are also given. There are transcriptions of 13 tunes, made by Ruth Crawford Seeger. An appendix is devoted to individual bands and minstrels, and the bibliography lists books, government publications and articles. Index. John Greenway contributes a foreword to the reprint edition.

570. KORSON, George. Minstrels of the mine patch: songs and stories of the anthracite industry. Philadelphia: University of Pennsylvania Press, 1938. (Repr. Hatboro: Folklore Associates, 1964). 332p. illus., bibliog.

A pioneer collection of industrial folklore begun in 1924, dealing mainly with native and Anglo-Celtic lore from N. E. Pennsylvania from the period 1865-1902, the industry's peak time. The material is arranged in nine chapters ("the mine patch," "miners in good humor," "boy colliers," etc.). Each chapter contains a substantial amount of editorial study based on personal observation, interviews and existing local history sources. In addition to the verses of a large number of songs and ballads, and numerous stories, there are tunes to a dozen of the songs. There are also biographical sketches, and the book concludes with a glossary, a bibliography of books and articles, and an index. The reprint contains a new foreword by Archie Green.

d. Railroad Men

571. COHEN, Norman. Railroad folksongs on record: a survey. Los Angeles: John Edwards Memorial Foundation, 1970. (Reprinted from New York Folklore Quarterly, June 1970). (Reprint No. 15) pp. 91-113. bibliog. and discog. notes.

In this paper a survey of the recording history of hillbilly and race records, with particular attention to railroad songs, is followed by a description of the various types of railroad song (e.g., the train-wreck ballad, railroad construction, the railroad as a symbol of both freedom and death). The appended discography presents sample listings of five railroad songs (including 78 rpm, 45 rpm and LP discs and Library of Congress recordings).

572. SHERWIN, Sterling, and McCLINTOCK, Harry K., comps. Railroad songs of yesterday ... foreword by William M. Jeffers. New York: Shapiro, Bernstein, 1943. 47p. illus.

As an arena for the production of songs the railroads of America were particularly fruitful. This colorful little collection, with its old photographs and humorous comments, is a very modest sample--20 songs with piano accompaniment, mostly adaptations of the words or music of traditional ballads. Both compilers were songwriters. Sherwin (real name John Milton Hagen) also compiled several small collections of Western songs. McClintock, known popularly as Haywire Mac, also made a number of recordings of railroad and cowboy songs.

e. Sailors

573. COLCORD, Joanna C., comp. Roll and go: songs of American sailormen; with an introduction by Lincoln Colcord. Indianapolis: Bobbs-Merrill, 1924. 118p. illus.
_____. Songs of American sailormen; with an introduction by Lincoln Colcord; enlarged and revised edition. New York: Norton, 1938. 212p. illus., bibliog.
The daughter of a sea-captain who voyaged with her father to China Sea ports, the compiler speaks not only with first-hand experience of sailors' songs, but also with a deep love of her subject. After first discussing the origins and development of the shanty she presents and describes 108 songs (in the revised version) in four distinct groups: short-drag shanties (the earliest forms, used to accompany short pulls on the ropes), halliard shanties (for longer, heavier tasks), windlass or capstan shanties (for continuous processes), and forecastle songs (for leisure). Texts, melodies and linking commentary are combined in one readable narrative, in which uses, features and history of the various songs are all discussed. There is also an index.

574. DOERFLINGER, William Main, comp. Shantymen and shantyboys: songs of the sailor and lumberman. New York: Macmillan, 1951. 374p. illus., bibliog.
The two occupations represented in this well and knowledgeably presented collection (the main title may be misleading: shantymen are sailors, shantyboys are loggers) are connected by region. Doerflinger collected for 20 years in the Northeastern U.S.A. and Canada, where sea and lumber songs were equally closely identified with the area. Of the 156 songs included (over 200 including variants), 97 are sea songs, 31 are lumber songs, 28 are common to both groups. The sea songs--sung by the merchantmen who manned the square-riggers of the 19th century--are divided into six groups: three types of work songs (short-haul shanties, etc.), deep-water songs, ballads of the fishing banks, and forecastle songs. In the midst of these there is an informative essay on the rise of shantying. The logger songs are in two groups (songs and ballads of lumber-woods life, and satirical ballads), and the three groups of shared material are divided by subject (adventure, murder, love). The tunes (transcribed from recordings by Samuel P. Bayard, Hally Wood and Joseph Wood) and texts are presented with informal linking commentary that aims "to set the songs against their natural backgrounds ... and to explore their interesting history." Scholarly notes, identifying informants and referring to printed versions, are grouped at the end of the book, which thus achieves a remarkable success in catering for popular and scholarly needs. Short biographical notes on the singers precede a bibliography of collections and secondary material and a title index.

575. HUGILL, Stan, comp. Shanties from the Seven Seas: shipboard work-songs and songs used as work-songs from the great days of sail. London: Routledge & Kegan Paul; New York: Dutton, 1961. 609p. illus., bibliog.

A fine international collection, in which the compiler turns his long experience at sea and extensive knowledge, particularly of the Liverpool versions of many songs, to good scholarly advantage. Tunes and texts are given for approximately 450 items (plus variants), with generous amounts of discussion on their use and their historical background, and frequent comparative study. Both piano and guitar accompaniment are provided for. An excellent introduction explores questions of the origin of shanties, including discussion of Anglo-American work songs, and of white American folk songs. There is also a glossary and an index of titles.

576. SHAY, Frank. Iron men and wooden ships: deep sea chanties; decorations and woodcuts by Edw. A. Wilson; introduction by William McFee. Garden City: Doubleday, Page, 1924. 154p. illus. (some col.)
_____. American sea songs and chanteys from the days of iron men and wooden ships; illustrated by Edward A. Wilson; musical arrangements by Christopher Thomas. New York: Norton, 1948. 217p. illus. (some col.)

The second of these two collections, an expanded version of the first, is the only one to contain tunes. It has 78 songs, with melodies for a good many of them. They include chanteys, fore-castle songs, wardroom ballads, and a miscellany. Many, but by no means all, are accompanied by informative explanatory comments. Wilson's full-page color illustrations are a delightful addition.

f. Others

577. FONER, Philip S., ed. American labor songs of the 19th century. Urbana: Univ. of Illinois Press, 1975. 600p. illus., bibliog.
An impressive collection of the words of 550 labor songs, grouped by subject with introductions to each section.

578. MILBURN, George, comp. The hobo's hornbook: a reper-tory for a gutter jongleur; collected and annotated by George Milburn; decorations by William Siegel. New York: Ives Washburn, 1930. 295p.
This highly unusual and diverting collection of "the songs and poems originated by American vagrants and current among them" was made in Chicago and on the road in 1926-1927. "Not in the Tennessee hills," Milburn declares, "or among the Sea Island Ne-groes, or in any other such arrested community is there a more vigorous balladry than that which has been flourishing for the past fifty years in America's peripatetic underworld" (introduction). This virile oral tradition, centering round the feats and adventures of the vagrant life, was doomed for extinction, as Milburn saw it; his collection preserves a part. The 86 texts are arranged in eight broad groups: monika (nickname) songs, a Leigh Valley sequence, parody and burlesque, Wobbly songs, homeguard versions, hobo classics, "packing the banner," and songs of the road. Prefatory notes to each song give the poet's name if known, and explain spe-

cific details; like the songs these comments are vibrant, incisive, down-to-earth. Only 17 tunes are included; many of the songs were sung to well-known melodies (the reader may supply his own). Index.

9. Protest and Social Song Movements

a. General Studies and Collections

579. BRAND, Oscar. The ballad mongers: the rise of modern folk song. New York: Funk & Wagnalls, 1962. 240p. bibliog.

An informal and subjective account by a noted and versatile folksinger (b. 1920) of some reasons for, and memorable episodes in, the growth of interest in American folk song up to the 1960s. Brand considers the varied sources of American folk song, recounts the pioneering deeds of the first collectors and progenitors, describes the singing of groups committed to particular social outlooks (the Weavers and their successors in particular), and the reactions of government in terms of censorship, blacklisting and general political interference in folk singing. His interest is mainly social and economic. Numerous song texts are quoted, but no music. Index.

580. DENISOFF, R. Serge. American protest songs of war and peace: a selected bibliography and discography. Los Angeles: California State College Center for the Study of Armament and Disarmament, 1970. (Bibliography Series, No. 1) 15p.

    . Songs of protest, war and peace: a bibliography and discography. (Rev. ed.) Santa Barbara: ABC-Clio, 1973. 70p.

The first edition of this reference work lists books, periodical articles, songbooks containing American Left-wing propaganda songs, selected propaganda songs in Communist Party Publications, literature on the Radical Right's attack on protest songs, and material relating to modern social protest; there is also a short LP discography. Besides expanding and updating these, the revised version adds details of protest songs in Sing Out and Broadside, a list of country and western patriotic songs, and a discography of these on singles.

581. DENISOFF, R. Serge. Great day coming: folk music and the American Left. Urbana: University of Illinois Press, 1971. 219p. illus., bibliog., discog.

A study of the use of folk music by the American Left for specific socio-political ends. The author first examines the growth of folk consciousness, its roots in the rural South, its urban growth in the 1930s, and some outstanding individuals (Will Geer, Woody Guthrie, Earl Robinson), proceeding from this to describe the first

organized attempt to put this consciousness into practice--the Almanac Singers--, the fate of People's Songs, Inc., and the mobiliz-
ing efforts in the 1940s. Turning to the folk entrepreneurs (Pete
Seeger, Guthrie, etc.), Denisoff describes how, in spite of social
and ideological isolation, the Cold War era saw the appearance of
the folk singer before the Congressional Committee for Un-American Activities. The final chapters discuss the 1960s: the relationship with the Radical Right, and the protest song revival (with particular attention to Bob Dylan). There is a selected LP discography,
a list of books and articles, and an index.

582. DENISOFF, R. Serge. Sing a song of social significance.
        Bowling Green: Bowling Green University Popular Press,
        1972. 229p. illus., bibliog. notes.
        Based largely on articles by the author for a variety of jour-
nals between 1966 and 1970, this is the most stimulating study of
protest song since Greenway (no. 587). While it is primarily a
sociologist's book (Denisoff's critical vocabulary is, as yet, alien
to musicology), and the author's mentors are mainly sociologists, it
is generally approachable by the non-specialist. The book's compass
is wide, including the protest song of the 1930s and 1940s, and paying considerable attention to rock. Denisoff first defines what constitutes a protest song, and establishes who are the "folk entrepreneurs" who sing them, proceeding then to discuss the exploitation
of the genre by religious movements and left-wing (particularly Communist) organizations. Moving into the 1960s, he examines folk-
rock, the presence of protest songs in the hit parade and their effect, the social aspects of rock in the light of Karl Mannheim's
ideas on "generational units in conflict," and the relation of rock to
the political and social upheavals of the 1960s. Index.

583. DENISOFF, R. Serge, and PETERSON, Richard A., eds.
        The sounds of social change: studies in popular culture.
        Chicago: Rand McNally, 1972. 332p. bibliogs.
        An anthology of articles and essays, mainly reprinted from
other publications, collected with a view to directing attention to the
uses of music "as an opiate, weapon and/or harbinger of social change."
The 25 pieces are grouped in five sections plus epilogue: music as
protest (protest song, avant-garde jazz, country jazz music); music
in social movements (IWW, Nazis and music, country, soul, folk
music and the left); rock; changing taste (popular song, popular and
rock and roll protest song); musicians and the music industry. Many
of the pieces have lists of references or bibliographical footnotes,
and there is an index.

584. DOWDEY, Landon Gerald, ed. Journey to freedom: a case-
        book with music. Chicago: Swallow Press, 1969. 106p.
        illus., bibliog.
        An anthology of poems, songs and short prose extracts, main-
ly 20th century American, grouped to illustrate general characteristics of the urge to find freedom from tyranny in any form. The
song texts are accompanied by guitar chords, and the tunes are collected together in an appendix. The book is designed to be read and
sung aloud by any gathering of people.

585. DUNSON, Josh. Freedom in the air: song movements of
the sixties. New York: International Publishers, 1965.
127p. bibliog. and discog. notes.
    Two parallel streams of songs of social significance that cap-
tured attention in the 1960s are examined in this short study: the
Northern topical songs and the songs of the Southern freedom movement. The line of development of the topical song is traced from
ballads, union songs and people's songs through the revival of interest in the songs of Woody Guthrie, the influence of Pete Seeger, and
the foundation of Broadside magazine, to the emergence of the central figure in 1960s topical song--the singer-songwriter (Dylan,
Ochs, Paxton, etc.). Parallel to this, but avoiding most of the opportunities for a comparative study, the author describes the developing role of the freedom song in the Civil Rights movement,
noting particularly the importance of Guy Carawan as the one who
focused the leaders' and demonstrators' minds on the need for song,
the significance of the Albany Movement and the Freedom Singers,
and of the Atlanta "Sing for Freedom" meeting in 1964 at which,
finally, North and South met. There is a suggested reading and
listening list.

586. FOWKE, Edith, and GLAZER, Joe, comps. Songs of work
and freedom; music arrangements, Kenneth Bray; art work,
Hope Taylor. Chicago: Labor Education Division, Roosevelt University, 1960. (Repr. as Songs of Work and Protest. New York: Dover Publications, 1973). 209p. bibliog., discog.
    A collection of the words and music (melodies, piano accom-
paniment and guitar chords) of 100 songs--mainly American labor
songs--designed to provide trade unions with a songbook, and to
demonstrate the important role of song in "mankind's struggle for a
better life." The songs are arranged in eleven groups: general
union songs, songs of specific occupations--railway, textile and steel
workers, miners, farmers and a posse of cowboys, sailors and lum-
berjacks--, travel songs, comments on the economic system, freedom songs (including slave songs), and a clutch of more forward-
looking songs focussing on hope. Each song is accompanied by a
detailed historical note on its origins and the context of its use.
While many are traditional items a number of songs are individual
creations of recent origin (e.g., the songs of Merle Travis, Woody
Guthrie, Joe Glazer himself) and still more are formed by setting
new words to familiar tunes (e.g., the songs of Joe Hill, Ralph
Chaplin). Index of titles and first lines.

587. GREENWAY, John. American folksongs of protest. Philadelphia: University of Pennsylvania Press, 1953. (Repr.
New York: Octagon Books, 1970). 348p. illus., bibliog.,
discog.
    A classic survey, published at the end of the McCarthy era,
of the use of song by the American working classes to protest against
economic and social injustice in the 19th and 20th centuries. Beginning with a study of the way songs have sprung up to illustrate and
comment on various aspects of U.S. history, Greenway examines the

occupational songs of the textile workers, the miners, the migratory workers and the Wobblies, the farmers, and a variety of industrial laborers, ending with protest songwriters such as Aunt Molly Jackson and Woody Guthrie. Each section contains examples of song texts and music, and the author relates the songs of each group closely to their conditions of work, to social developments, and to historical events. The discography is arranged by title, and the bibliography lists books, articles and song collections. There are indexes of composers, titles, and general matters. (For a brief, but illuminating discussion of Greenway's approach, see R. S. Denisoff, "Urban Folk Music 'Movement' Research: Value Free?", Western Folklore, 28, July 1969; repr. in no. 582.)

588. LOMAX, Alan, ed. Hard hitting songs for hard-hit people; notes on the songs by Woody Guthrie; music transcribed and edited by Pete Seeger. New York: Oak Publications, 1967. 368p. illus.
      This collection of the words and music of 180 songs of the Depression and New Deal eras was originally compiled at the end of the 1930s, based on songs in the Library of Congress Folk Song Archive, but was too controversial for a publisher to handle at the time. Copies of the manuscript were dismembered, but one was discovered whole in 1961. It lacked music, but 90% of the tunes were recalled. Evocative photographs were added, and the result is an impressive and moving document of the times. The songs are arranged in 13 categories by subject or group of people, and each has a characteristically picturesque introductory comment by Guthrie (some of whose own songs are included, as are songs by other folk and blues artists, such as Leadbelly and Aunt Molly Jackson). Many songs consist of anonymous words to well-known tunes. Pete Seeger's transcriptions give guitar chords for each tune. All original sources are indicated were known, and there is a song index.

589. ROSEN, David M. Protest songs in America; foreword by David Manning White. Westlake Village, Ca.: Aware Press, 1972. 159p. bibliog., discog.
      The author divides the period covered by his book (1765-1968) into three: (i) 1765-1915, an era of anti-British, anti-slavery, industrial and agrarian protest, common features of which were "individualism, ruralism, innocence and naivete"; (ii) 1915-1960, a period of racial labor protest (IWW, etc.), of the Depression, of opposition to discrimination and to war, characterized by "class-consciousness, urbanism and increased sophistication"; (iii) the 1960s, a decade notable for social consciousness beyond the lines of class, a diversity of topics in protest song, and of the popularity of the form among the young. The large number of textual examples offered for each period make the book more a running commentary than a fully developed study.

590. SEEGER, Pete. The incompleat folksinger; edited by Jo Metcalf Schwartz. New York: Simon & Schuster, 1972. 596p illus., bibliogs., discogs.
      Neither an autobiography, nor a history or tutor--though all

these forms are represented--this is above all a book to browse in, a potpourri of Seeger's writing, old (mainly for Sing Out and similar magazines, plus liner notes) and new--"just a bramble patch you must wade through in hopes of plucking some sweet berries" (p. 6). Whether he is recollecting his early involvement with folk song, portraying such outstanding singers as Leadbelly or Woody Guthrie, describing and quoting examples of labor and protest songs (this in Part 1), chronicling the folksong revival, 1954-1969, in the pages of Sing Out (Part 2), giving detailed practical advice on the making of homemade music (Part 3), or reflecting on social issues as they have affected him (e. g. , his subpoena by the Committee on Un-American Activities in 1955), the most striking things about his anthology are its richly human qualities, and his ability to communicate something of his fascination with folk songs (or "amateur music," as he likes to think of it) of many types. A generous number of song melodies and texts are included. There is an index and a general discography, and several sections of the book have their own short bibliography and discography.

b. The Wobblies

591. HILL, Joe. Songs of Joe Hill; edited by Barrie Stavis and
        Frank Harmon. New York: People's Artists, 1955. (Repr.
        New York: Oak Publications, 1960). 46p.
        Song played an immensely important role in the strategy of
the militant labor organization, the Industrial Workers of the World
(or Wobblies); as Joyce Kornbluh remarks, "IWW songs were sung
on picket lines, in hobo jungles, at mass meetings, during free
speech demonstrations--wherever members gathered to agitate for a
new world built 'from the ashes of the old'" (introduction to Smith,
no. 594). The leading Wobbly songwriter was the Swedish-born Joe
Hill (1879-1915), whose view was: "A pamphlet, no matter how good,
is never read more than once, but a song is learned by heart and
repeated over and over" (Letter, quoted in Smith, p. 19). Many of
Hill's songs appeared in the so-called Little Red Song Book, the
Wobblies' anthology of song texts "to fan the flames of discontent,"
which was first issued in Spokane in 1909 (and had gone to 31 editions by 1964). Twenty-three of Hill's songs are included in this
volume; most are set to popular tunes (for a large part of Hill's
effectiveness was his ability to parody the words of a well-known
song or hymn), but some to original melodies. Guitar chords are
provided.

592. FONER, Philip S. The case of Joe Hill. New York: Inter-
        national Publishers, 1965. 127p. illus. , bibliog. notes.
        In January, 1914, Hill was arrested in Salt Lake City following a shooting incident. Foner's book is a detailed examination of
Hill's arrest, trial and subsequent execution, concluding that various
interested parties (church and industry) conspired to ensure his
death. (Foner's The Industrial Workers of the World, 1905-1917,
New York, 1965, is the basic historical work.)

593. KORNBLUH, Joyce L., ed. Rebel voices: an I.W.W. anthology. Ann Arbor: University of Michigan Press, 1964.
419p. illus., bibliog.

A collection of material relating to the Wobblies, written by
themselves in the first decades of the 20th century. It includes
numerous examples of protest songs, most of which appeared originally in the IWW songbook. The material is grouped according to
subject or a particular group of workers, with one section devoted
to Joe Hill, including the texts of many of his songs. There is also
a glossary of the language of hobo, lumberjack and miner, but no
index.

594. SMITH, Gibbs M. Joe Hill. Salt Lake City: University of
Utah Press, 1969. 286p. illus., bibliog.

This study of the life and influence of Joe Hill begins with a
chapter on his songs, in which the author describes something of
their background, and discusses their meaning and their significance
for the IWW. One of the appendices contains a chronological checklist of Hill's songs by Archie Green, with the complete texts as they
appear in the many editions of the Little Red Song Book. (Smith
also makes a lengthy examination of Hill's arrest and trial.)

c. Woody Guthrie

595. GUTHRIE, Woody. American folksong. New York: Asch,
1947. 48p.
_____. ; edited by Moses Asch. New York:
Oak Publications, 1961. 54p. illus., bibliog.

A short account of his life by Guthrie, and of his acquaintance
with Leadbelly, precedes a selection of the words of 30 of his songs,
accompanied by pencil sketches, occasional notes and comments, and
the tunes (with guitar chords) for 18 of them.

596. GUTHRIE, Woody. Born to win; edited by Robert Shelton.
New York: Macmillan, 1965; New York: Collier Books,
1967. 250p. illus.

A collection of prose, poems, songs, letters and drawings,
mainly from the second half of the 1940s, and written in New York.
No music.

597. GUTHRIE, Woody. Bound for glory. New York: Dutton,
1943. 428p. illus.
_____. . Garden City: Doubleday, 1953. 353p.
illus.
_____. . New York: Dutton, 1968; London:
Dent, 1969. 430p. illus.
_____. . New York: New American Library,
1970. 320p. illus.

Woody Guthrie's own phrase, "a lifebound novel, real and un-
real," perhaps best describes this highly individual autobiography,
the chronicle of a personal odyssey, the first edition of which was a
much edited version of a mammoth second draft. The whole spirit

of Guthrie's life and songs is captured in the picturesque recreation of events from his childhood in Okemah, Oklahoma, his hoboing to California and early years there. His portrait of himself as just another man, no more, no less--albeit one with a great gift of song --and his very effective colloquial prose style lend a cheerful air to a fundamentally tragic story, tragic both in the personal sense (of family, especially) and, more generally, in his portrait of the after-effects of the oil boom, the dust storms, the hobos, and the California migrants. The text is illustrated with some of his sketches.

598. GUTHRIE, Woody. California to the New York Island; being a pocketfull of brags, blues, bad-men ballads, love songs, Okie laments and children's catcalls... New York: Guthrie Children's Trust Fund, 1960. 48p. illus., discog.
    The words and music of 29 of Guthrie's songs are linked by a narrative by Millard Lampell, based on Woody's own writings, to form a script for a concert illustrating the man and his music. There are brief staging directions, and Pete Seeger contributes an introductory note.

599. REUSS, Richard A., ed. A Woody Guthrie bibliography, 1912-1967. New York: Guthrie Children's Trust Fund, 1968. 94p.
    A listing of every known item (as of January, 1968) in print by or about Guthrie. It is divided into two sections: Woody's own published writings, 1937-1967, and published writings about him, 1929-1968, including obituaries. Both sections are arranged chronologically, and in both each item is annotated. The compiler regrets, in his foreword, the low standard of much of the writing in the second part.

600. YURCHENCO, Henrietta. A mighty hard road: the Woody Guthrie story; assisted by Marjorie Guthrie; introduction by Arlo Guthrie. New York: McGraw-Hill, 1970. 159p. illus., discog.
    A biography, mainly for younger readers, using information left by Guthrie in both published and unpublished forms. From Oklahoma in 1912 to a Long Island hospital where he died, following a long illness, in 1967, the story of his life is clearly and simply told, illustrated with excerpts from his prose and verse, and from accounts by Marjorie Guthrie, his second wife. The narrative describes, but does not attempt to analyze, his unique contribution to socially meaningful song or his political involvement; but his way of life and something of his attitude to his music are apparent. The last, sad years are unsentimentally described.

10. Folk Song Revival

601. BAEZ, Joan. Daybreak. New York: Dial Press, 1968.

159p.

———— . ————— . New York: Avon Books, 1969. 191p.
———— . ————— . London: MacGibbon & Kee, 1970.
164p.
———— . ————— . London: Panther, 1971. 141p.

The autobiography of the folk singer and leading figure in the folk song revival of the 1960s, written in the form of a pastiche of recollections, largely from her childhood and youth, and with poetic interludes. There is little about music, but it is a revealing self-portrait.

602. COON, O. Wayne. Some problems with musical public-domain materials under United States copyright law as illustrated mainly by the recent folk-song revival. Los Angeles: John Edwards Memorial Foundation, 1973. (Reprinted from Copyright Law Symposium No. 19, 1971). (Reprint No. 27) pp. 189-218. bibliog. notes.

In this useful exposition of copyright problems raised by folk song material, and of some suggested solutions, the author defines "public-domain" and "folk song," explores the apparent need, felt by the media, for a copyright owner, and examines the claims of government, private folk foundation, informant, collector and popularizer to own the copyright. He also draws attention to lessons which are relevant to musical public-domain materials generally, and offers his own suggestions in conclusion.

603. DE TURK, David A., and POULIN, A., eds. The American folk scene: dimensions of the folksong revival. New York: Dell, 1967. 334p. bibliog. notes.

A collection of 32 essays, mostly reprinted from journals, on social, commercial and artistic aspects of the folk song revival in the U.S. in the 1960s. The text is in four parts. The first is concerned with definitions, the traditional-modern controversy, and questions of interpretation, cultural interaction and future developments. In the second part specific aspects of protest song are discussed. Part 3 is devoted to Woody Guthrie, Pete Seeger, Joan Baez and Bob Dylan, and in Part 4 contributors examine commercialization, and the relation of folk music to folk-rock. There are also biographical sketches of the contributors, who include B. A. Botkin, John Greenway, Irwin Silber and Josh Dunson, and introductory editorial comments on each article, but there is no index.

11. The Commercial Idiom:
Hillbilly and Country Music

a. General Reference Works and Histories

604. COUNTRY MUSIC WHO'S WHO. Edited by Thurston Moore. Cincinnati: Cardinal Enterprises, 1960. [Subsequent, not quite annual, volumes published Denver: Heather Publica-

tions, and New York: Record World.]

Though primarily intended for the music trade this series of volumes contains much interesting information in the shape of articles on individuals in the industry, scholarly features on early stars (mostly emanating from JEMF publications), and plentiful pictures (including a several part series called "Pictorial History of Country Music"). Other features include (in the 1970 edition) a classified directory of artists, publishers, disc jockeys, etc., and a year-by-year diary of country music news items.

605. GENTRY, Linnell, ed. A history and encyclopedia of country, western and gospel music. Nashville: McQuiddy Press, 1961. 380p.

_____. _____. 2nd ed. Nashville: Clairmont, 1969. 598p.

Like some other reference books in country music this one claims more in its title than it delivers, but within its limits it is a useful guide. There are two sections. In the 2nd edition Part 1 contains a collection of 76 articles, ranging from the popular to the scholarly and written between 1908 and 1968. They are chosen from magazines, brochures and newspapers, and examine various aspects and personalities of gospel and country music. Part 2 is devoted to concise, factual biographies of over 600 singers, musicians, comedians and comediennes. These give date and place of birth for each artist, information on family, education and career, and details of recordings made and television appearances. Gentry is remiss in not making clear that the gospel music he is concerned with is the white kind.

606. MALONE, Bill C. Country music U.S.A.: a fifty-year history. Austin: University of Texas Press, 1968. (Publications of the American Folklore Society, Memoir Series 54) 422p. illus., bibliog.

A fine, scholarly survey of the rise and development of white commercial country music, from small beginnings in the 1920s to big business. Chronologically arranged, it describes the folk background, the first commercialization and the first individual star (Jimmie Rodgers), the expansion through Depression and World War 2, and the even greater post-war boom. The author examines the development of particular styles--the Nashville sound, bluegrass-- and analyzes their influence on American popular music. The careers and styles of prominent individuals are outlined, and the development of the music related to the changing social and economic environment, particularly in the South. The extensive bibliography includes primary and secondary sources of published and unpublished material, and lists albums cited in the text. Index.

607. PRICE, Steven D. Take me home: the rise of country and western music. New York: Praeger, 1974. 184p. illus., bibliog., discog.

A general introduction to the evolution of country music from European and African antecedents, concentrating on song themes and the relation of these to social and cultural history. Price describes first the changes in the ways of expressing the theme of love in the transfer of the ballad tradition from Britain to rural America, with brief attention also to the treatment of the theme in the blues. The black musical tradition is the focal point of a discussion of occupational song, which includes consideration of the role of the railroads and the cattle ranges. Chapter 3 relates the theme of adventure to increased mobility, and the fusion of aspects of white and black rural styles to produce country and western music, the appeal and influence of which is the subject of the final chapter. Many song texts are quoted as illustrations and identified in notes at the back. The author's often-generalized comments on such things as musical practice are, however, presented without documentation. Few individuals are featured (a roster at the end gives very brief sketches of a select band of outstanding performers), and there is little attention to musical features of individual singers' styles or songs. Indexes of names and titles.

608.　SHELTON, Robert.　The country music story: a picture history of country and western music; photos by Burt Goldblatt.　New Rochelle: Arlington House, 1966.　256p. illus., discog.

The first full-length publication devoted to country music, this useful, liberally illustrated history traces the development of the music and its associated industry, describing the personalities who have contributed to its forty-year rise to widespread popularity, from the first recordings in the 1920s.　The life and music of Jimmie Rodgers, and the contributions of other influential figures--the Carter Family, Roy Acuff, Woody Guthrie, Hank Williams, Johnny Cash--are described.　The history and significance of the Grande Ole Opry radio show are also told.　Sections are devoted to two specific styles, bluegrass and western, and to the careers of their exponents, to the themes of the songs, the songwriters, and an account of the industry based on Nashville.　The selective LP discography includes labels and numbers, there is a list of the sources of the photographs, and an index.

609.　SHESTACK, Melvin.　The country music encyclopedia.　New York: Crowell, 1974.　410p.　illus., discog.

One should not be misled by the title.　An encyclopedia of a subject is properly concerned with all branches of that subject, but this book falls considerably short of meeting that description (more so than Gentry, no. 605, or Stambler, no. 610), being a collection of biographical portraits of country music recording stars, chosen by reference to Billboard charts.　These portraits are highly personalized, inclined to be chatty, and rather thin on detailed information--though essential career data is given.　As a substitute for detail, and for critical appreciation, many excerpts from other printed sources--usually fulsome articles--are quoted.　Because of the Billboard criterion early country music is covered only sketchily.　There are some articles on distinctive forms of country music--e.g., bluegrass--but producers, songwriters, etc. are included only in reference to the recording stars.　The discography is a representative selection of available LPs by each artist.　Other material includes a list of country music radio stations, with call letters and frequencies, and the words and music of eight sample songs.

610. STAMBLER, Irwin, and LANDON, Grelun. Encyclopedia of folk, country and western music. New York: St. Martin's Press, 1969. 396p. illus., bibliog., discog.

A broadly-based reference work, containing about 500 entries and 100 photographs from the fields of American folk and country music, covering in one sequence artists, songwriters, instruments, collectors, institutions, festivals. There is a bias towards country music, but folk artists are well represented and include in their number Negro blues singers (Leadbelly, Lightnin' Hopkins) and folk-rock artists (Dylan). Entries for individuals give basic biographical information and career history, obtained from interviews whenever possible. They are written in an informal narrative style, uncritical and undemanding. The book also includes three essays on folk and country music. The appendices provide a representative LP discography, a list of performers, and a selected bibliography of books and articles.

b. Early Country Music

611. CARSON, Gerald. The roguish world of Doctor Brinkley. New York: Rinehart, 1960. 280p. illus., bibliog.

This biography tells the strange story of one of the greatest medical quacks of all time, who, first in Kansas and later in Mexico, made much use of hillbilly musicians on his radio stations, which existed mainly to promote his goat gland operation for men (which made him a millionaire), and to further his political ends. The "X" stations of the Mexican border area--of which Brinkley owned the first at Villa Acuna--were particularly significant in the spread of hillbilly and country music outside the South. The Carter Family made a series of broadcasts over Brinkley's XERA and others, beginning in 1938.

612. COHEN, Norm. Robert W. Gordon and the second wreck of "Old 97." Los Angeles: John Edwards Memorial Foundation, 1974. (Reprinted from Journal of American Folklore, 87, Jan.-March 1974). pp. 12-38. discog.

In 1924 the Victor Talking Machine Co. released a record by Vernon Dalhart (his first hillbilly record) called "Wreck of Old 97" --a song about a rail crash in Virginia in 1903 that had entered oral tradition--and was subsequently accused of infringing copyright by one David Graves George, who claimed authorship of the song. This paper is a reconstruction of the history of the ballad--Cohen shows its early origins to be in "a complex of nineteenth-century folk and popular ballads"--and of the progress of the lawsuit, which ended after ten years in Victor's favor. To aid the company Victor enlisted Robert W. Gordon, noted folklorist, and it is Gordon's investigations that are principally described and assessed, not only for the light they shed on an interesting instance of the involvement of copyright law with folk material, but also as an early example of a folklorist appreciating the significance of phonograph records.

613.   EDWARDS, John. The published works of the late John Ed-
        wards. Kingswinford, Staffs: Society for the Preserva-
        tion and Promotion of Traditional Country Music, 1973.
        75p. discogs.
        John Edwards, pioneer Australian enthusiast of early country
music ("old time," "hillbilly," "traditional," etc.) was killed in an
automobile accident in 1960, aged 28. His collection formed the
core of the John Edwards Memorial Foundation, which American
friends set up in his memory at UCLA in 1962, to provide an archive and to further research in early, commercially recorded folk
music. The articles reprinted here--originally written for New
Zealand's Country and Western Spotlight between 1955 and 1958 (plus
two for Folk Style in 1957 and 1959)--are a testament to his zeal in
tracing, assembling and disseminating biographical and discographical information on artists whose names had all but faded into ob-
scurity in the U.S.A., and were unknown--in all probability--to all
but him in Australia. Written from a clear passion for the music,
and a detestation of all modern country and popular music, the
articles that are of greatest interest are the biographical portraits
of old-time singers (Frank Crumit, Cliff Carlisle, Vernon Dalhart,
Lester McFarland and Robert Gardner, the Delmore Brothers, Jimmie Davis, Red Foley, Carson Robinson, Wade Mainer, Frank
Luther, Goebel Reeves, the Sons of the Pioneers, Gene Autry, Tex
Ritter, Jimmie Rodgers and Buell Kazee). The discographical information refers to Australian issues. The booklet was originally
issued as a special issue of Spotlight in 1962, with various tributes;
these are kept in this reissue, by two British devotees, which also
has a preface describing JEMF by Archie Green.

614.   KAHN, Ed. Hillbilly music: source and resource. Los
        Angeles: John Edwards Memorial Foundation, (1966?).
        (Reprinted from Journal of American Folklore, July-Sept.
        1965). (Reprint No. 7) pp. 256-266. bibliog.
        Writing in the infancy of the JEMF (and before the ex-
istence of the Country Music Foundation), Kahn regrets the lack of
interest taken by folklorists in phonograph records of country music,
and surveys the existing literature on the subject--which, at the
time, was somewhat meager (approximately 60 references are given
in the bibliography).

615.   McCULLOH, Judith. Hillbilly records and tune transcriptions.
        Los Angeles: John Edwards Memorial Foundation, (1968?).
        (Reprinted from Western Folklore, Vol. 26, 1967). (Re-
        print No. 9) pp. 225-244. bibliog. & discog. notes.
        A paper outlining in brief the history of published transcrip-
tions of commercially recorded early white country music, from
those made of Fiddlin' John Carson in 1923 to the 1940s, with a
discussion of the (rather limited) attention given to this body of material by folklorists, and the work achieved in terms of published
transcriptions by the Lomaxes and others.

616.   McCULLOH, Judith. Some Child ballads on hillbilly records.
        Los Angeles: John Edwards Memorial Foundation, (1967?).

(Reprinted from Folklore and Society: essays in honor of Benjamin A. Botkin, 1966). (Reprint No. 10) pp. 107-129.

Transcriptions of the tunes and texts of eight hillbilly versions of Child ballads recorded between 1927 and 1938, with biographical notes on performers and analytical comment on the songs. The Child ballads are 68, 85, 200, 274 (3 versions), 278 and 289. The performers are Cliff Carlisle, Dick Justice, Kenny Harrell, Bill Cox and Cliff Hobbs, "Pop" Stoneman, Earl Johnson, Frank Rice and Ernest Stokes, and a Cajun group, the Jolly Boys of Lafayette.

617. NEW LOST CITY RAMBLERS. The New Lost City Ramblers song book; edited by John Cohen and Mike Seeger; musical transcriptions by Hally Wood. New York: Oak Publications, 1964. 256p. illus., discog.

Cohen and Seeger were two of the three original members of this folk singing group when it formed in 1958. The 125 songs in the collection date from the 1920s and 1930s, and are white old-time, early country songs by the Carter family, Uncle Dave Macon, Charlie Poole, Fiddlin' John Carson, Blind Alfred Reed and many others. Following an introduction on styles in old-time music by Cohen, some thoughts by Seeger and a musical note, the collection itself is arranged in twelve sections by subjects (love, "Bible tales," "wild men and murder") or type (lonesome blues, etc.). Each song has a note on the original singer, with references to recordings and printed sources, and a comment on the music. Tunes and texts are given, and guitar chords indicated. There is a title index, and a Rambler album discography with listing of individual track titles. The book is illustrated with contemporary photographs, some of them of the original singers.

618. WESTERN folklore, XXX. 3, July, 1971. Commercially disseminated folk music: sources and resources; (a symposium). Los Angeles: California Folklore Society, 1971. (Repr. Los Angeles: John Edwards Memorial Foundation, 1971). (Repr. Nos. 17-25) pp. 171-246. bibliog. & discog. notes.

Something of the character and value of the contribution to the study of commercially recorded folk music made by the John Edwards Memorial Foundation may be judged from this JEMF issue (reissued as a monograph), all the contributors to which were or are associated with the Foundation's work. Eugene W. Earle's introduction to the genesis and objectives of the JEMF is followed by an account by Norm Cohen of the computerized hillbilly discography pilot project (work on which was subsequently held up for want of cash). Archie Green describes the long search for information about a group of hillbilly musicians (principally Asa Martin and Doc Roberts), Joseph C. Hickerson discusses the significance of song folios in hillbilly research, and Guthrie T. Meade illustrates with examples the value of song material deposited for copyright registration at the Library of Congress as a source of information on the repertoire of the country musician. The importance of studying radio and personal appearances in connection with the commercialization of folk

culture is underlined by Bill C. Malone, and D. K. Wilgus studies
one song: "Billy the Kid." Finally, Cohen reviews selected LP reissues of material from the period 1922-1942.

619. WILGUS, D. K. Country-western music and the urban hillbilly.
Los Angeles: John Edwards Memorial Foundation, 1970.
(Reprinted from Journal of American Folklore, April-June
1970). (Reprint No. 16) pp. 157-179. bibliog. & discog.
notes.

An excellent short account of the development of country music from a folk tradition in a rural culture to a vastly successful
urban commercial enterprise (with a historical consciousness). The
author views country music as a "laboratory for the study ... of
the urbanization of rural folkways," as a mirror of cultural feeling,
particularly among that section of the population that feels a strong
dichotomy between city and country, and sees country music as a
bridge between the two.

c.   Grand Ole Opry

620. HAY, George D. A story of the Grand Ole Opry. Nashville:
the author, 1953. 62p. illus.

Called "the Solemn Old Judge" in country music circles, Hay
was responsible for popularizing country music on the radio. In
these reminiscences he describes how, as a newspaper reporter, he
visited a country dance in the Ozarks and later drew on this experience when, as station director for the newly-formed WSM in Nashville, he began the first hillbilly radio show in November 1926 (with
two performers--one an octogenarian fiddler called Uncle Jimmy
Thompson).   The enormous popularity of this show "presaged country music's coming commercial success" (Malone, no. 606, p. 78).
Hay also tells the now famous story of how the name "Grand Ole
Opry" came about, as a downhome jest at the expense of Walter
Damrosch's classical music program, which Hay's Barn Dance followed on the air, and with whose grand opera Hay contrasted his
"opry."

621. McDANIEL, William R., and SELIGMAN, Harold. Grand Ole
Opry. New York: Greenberg, 1952. 69p. illus.

A concise account of the development of the Grand Ole Opry
radio show and of its significance in the country music story. The
authors sketch the history of folk music in America and of the origins of country music, tell the story of George D. Hay and the
early radio shows, and discuss reasons for their popular appeal.
Some common characteristics of country singers are described--
background, clothes, singing style, types of song--and there are
portraits of 24 outstanding country artists and groups. Some song
titles, with publishers, are given in an appendix.

622. WOLFE, Charles K. The Grand Ole Opry: the early years,
1925-35. London: Old Time Music, 1975. 128p. illus.,
bibliog. notes, discogs.

Although, as the author of this fine study declares in his preface, "the history of the Grand Ole Opry is an excellent case of how history becomes transformed into mythology," his concern is strictly with factual data. Aware that country music literature is "long on generalization and short on evidence," he sets out to provide a solid foundation of facts as a basis for future, fuller interpretation. His first subject is the genesis of the Opry (with special attention, naturally, to George D. Hay). This account is followed by an attempt to place the show in the context of music in Nashville in 1926-30. Much of the remainder is devoted to information on the musicians themselves, particularly such outstanding figures as Dr. Humphrey Bate, Uncle Jimmy Thompson, Uncle Dave Macon, and the first black country star, Deford Bailey, plus many others. The book is illustrated with many contemporary photographs and contains numerous facsimiles of newspaper reports. It is an excellent achievement, and a triumph of Anglo-American cooperation (Wolfe is from Tennessee; his English publisher also produces a quarterly journal of the same name, edited by Tony Russell).

d. Bluegrass

623. ARTIS, Bob. Bluegrass. New York: Hawthorn Books, 1975.
        182p. illus., bibliog., discog.
    Aimed at a wide audience, this is a knowledgeable historical survey of bluegrass, which concentrates on the careers and stylistic characteristics of a selection of outstanding individuals or partnerships--Bill Monroe, the Stanley Brothers, Lester Flatt and Earl Scruggs, Don Reno and Red Smiley, etc. Other chapters consider the bluegrass festivals and the future of the music, while appendices are devoted to a rather incomplete discography, and lists of radio programs and magazines. Index.

624. HAGLUND, Urban, and OHLSSON, Lillies. A listing of bluegrass LP's. Vasteras, Sweden: Kountry Korral, 1971. 71p.
    With one or two exceptions all the U.S. and international LP's listed here feature a five-string banjo and contain at least one bluegrass-style song. Arrangement is by artist or band, with LP's listed (release no. and titles only--no contents) alphabetically by record label. No dates are given, except in the separate listing of bluegrass records released in Japan (apparently a goldmine for collectors).

625. MARSHALL, Howard Wight. "Keep on the sunny side of life": pattern and religious expression in bluegrass gospel music. Los Angeles: John Edwards Memorial Foundation, 1974. (Repr. from New York Folklore Quarterly, 30/1, March 1974). (Reprint No. 31) 43p. bibliog. notes.
    This scholarly paper examines the historical climate and cultural environment of bluegrass gospel music, discusses its musical and cultural nature, constructs a pattern of common themes from a study of five familiar song texts (given in an appendix), and views bluegrass as a whole in the light of Ralph Linton's theories of "na-

tivistic movements." (These are described in William Lessa and Evan Vogt, Reader in Comparative Religion, New York, 1958; a "nativistic movement" is "any conscious, organized attempt on the part of a society's members to revive or perpetuate selected aspects of its culture"--p. 449.) Other appendices contain a selected list of religious songs in the bluegrass repertoire, and a selected concordance of scriptural references.

626.   PRICE, Steven D. Old as the hills: the story of bluegrass
        music. New York: Viking Press, 1975. 110p. illus.,
        discog.
        A brief, modest introduction to bluegrass music. Like any thoroughbred with Kentucky connections it has to have a pedigree, and Price establishes one by first tracing the development of rural musical styles from Anglo-Celtic folk music in Appalachia, noting the influence of black folk styles, of minstrelsy and of church music, and describing the first commercial country musicians and their recordings and broadcasts. So much for the mare; now to the sire. None other, of course, than Bill Monroe (b. 1911), whose Kentucky background exposed him to white and black rural music, and who shaped the sound of the string band to a personal style, with a mandolin leading, that came to be known after the name of his band--the Blue Grass Boys. The uncles, brothers and cousins of the new offspring follow--a parade of bloodstock that includes Lester Flatt, Earl Scruggs, the Stanley Brothers, Reno and Smiley and numerous others.

627.   ROONEY, James. Bossmen: Bill Monroe and Muddy Waters.
        New York: Dial Press, 1971. 159p. illus., discogs.
        A juxtaposition of the careers of two outstanding exponents of post-war popular music, one from the field of white bluegrass music, the other from black urban blues. The book takes the form of two separate accounts, in which excerpts from interviews are linked by a narrative commentary. Each account follows the subject's career, noting early acquaintance with music, influences, aspects of the gradual development of their individual styles, their approach to music and to music-making. Some similarities between the two are noted in the introduction: both are regarded by the author as individuals deeply rooted in an inherited culture, aware of its value, professionally committed to making the best possible music from it, and to developing a self-contained style. Other similarities and contrasts are by implication only, as no direct lines of comparison are drawn in the text. There are two selective LP discographies and numerous photographs.

628.   ROSENBERG, Neil V. Bill Monroe and his Blue Grass Boys:
        an illustrated discography; compiled, with an introduction
        and commentaries, by Neil V. Rosenberg. Nashville:
        Country Music Foundation Press, 1974. 120p. illus.,
        bibliog. notes.
        This excellent achievement in the field of single artist discographies outclasses many of the same family on jazz artists by its inclusion of well-informed and balanced commentaries on histor-

ical and stylistic aspects of Monroe's recordings. These render
help to the reader and support the discography without in any way
overshadowing it. The discography itself lists all known commercial
recordings in three sections by record company: Victor (1940-1941),
Columbia (1945-1949) and Decca (1950-1973). Ninety-five sessions
are listed, 87 of them for Decca. For each session the information
given is: location, date, matrix numbers, titles, copyright credits,
and American release numbers on 78 rpm, 45 rpm, and LP. Beneath each title those taking the vocal parts are identified and there
is a complete personnel list, with instruments, at the end of each
session. Each session listing is preceded by a discussion "intended
to help the reader interpret the relationships between the information in the discography and the sound on record" (introduction), and
each is followed by a numerical list of singles, EPs and LPs. Other material includes a biographical sketch, a short discussion of
the role of recordings in Monroe's career, and a song title index.

629. ROSENBERG, Neil V. From sound to style: the emergence
        of bluegrass. Los Angeles: John Edwards Memorial
        Foundation, (1967). (Repr. from Journal of American
        Folklore, Vol. 80, No. 316). (Reprint No. 11) pp. 143-
        150. bibliog. notes.
        An excellent short essay describing and analyzing the emer-
gence of bluegrass music as a distinctive type of commercial country music in the recording and performing careers of Bill Monroe,
Lester Flatt, Earl Scruggs and the Stanley Brothers, and noting how
this development illustrates the tensions between tradition and economics, and between imitation and innovation that characterize a
folk art in a commercial environment.

e. Contemporary Country Music

630. BART, Teddy. Inside Music City, U.S.A. Nashville: Au-
        rora Publishers, 1970. 164p. illus. , bibliog.
        A series of rather insubstantial interviews with nine Nashville
songwriters, aimed at providing a "guide to writing songs the Nashville way" (preface). The nine are described as "a unique breed of
craftsmen working in a unique setting," which is fine. It is not the
author's fault if so much about this setting, even the re-naming of
the city, has a self-congratulatory ring.

631. HEMPHILL, Paul. The Nashville sound: bright lights and
        country music. New York: Simon & Schuster, 1970.
        289p.
        An informal portrait of the people inhabiting the country mu-
sic scene in 1968-1969. The author's popular approach, recreating
conversations, captures something of the atmosphere in which the
very successful business, centered on Nashville, operates. Index.

632. WHITBURN, Joel, comp. Top country and western records,
        1949-1971. Menomonee Falls, Wis.: Record Research,
        1972. 152p. illus.

Based, like other Whitburn compilations (nos. 890, 1340), on Billboard charts, this volume contains details of over 4,000 country music hit singles. The main sequence is an artist listing, with details of the date each of his/her records entered the chart, the highest position it reached, how many weeks it remained in the chart, its label name and release number. There is also an index of song titles.

f. Individuals and Groups
    (excluding Bluegrass)

ROY ACUFF

633. DUNKLEBERGER, A. C. King of country music: the life
       story of Roy Acuff. Nashville: Williams, 1971. 137p.
       illus.
Popular, somewhat fulsome biography in animated journalese, describing Acuff's Tennessean ancestors and upbringing (a turning-point in which was the vicious attack of sunstroke that confined him to the house for two years, and led to his taking up the violin), his early musical career, first breakthrough on WSM in 1937, and the foundation of the Smoky Mountain Boys in the same year. Chronology gives way hereabouts to a collage of short sketches illustrating aspects of his subsequent, enormously successful, career, his attitudes, character and way of life. Much material was apparently obtained from interviews with Acuff himself.

CARTER FAMILY

634. ATKINS, John, et al. The Carter Family, by John Atkins,
       Bob Coltman, Alec Davidson, Kip Lornell. London: Old
       Time Music, 1973. 62p. illus., bibliog., discog.
This nicely produced booklet, devoted to the outstandingly influential exponents of 19th century sentimentality in early country music, contains five features; John Atkins's biography of the Carters; an appreciation of A. P. Carter by Bob Coltman; a brief account by Kip Lornell of blues singer Leslie Riddles's relationship with A. P., with whom he went on collecting trips; a 26-page computer-produced discography by Alec Davidson, arranged chronologically (1927-1968), with full discographical details, including LP reissues, and vocal and instrumental descriptions (e.g. "guitar and autoharp, Sara and A. P."); and, finally, a bibliography of folios and articles. The booklet is well illustrated with contemporary photographs and reproductions of advertisements.

635. JOHN EDWARDS MEMORIAL FOUNDATION. The Carter fam-
       ily on border radio. Los Angeles: J. E. M. F., (1972).
       58p. illus., bibliog., discogs.
This booklet accompanies the Foundation's long-playing record of the same title, but is such a fine example of country music research as to be worthy of inclusion in its own right. The twenty-one recordings on the record were selected from electrical transcrip-

tion discs made from the Carter Family's broadcasts over Dr. Brinkley's XERA radio station at Villa Acuna, Mexico. The booklet consists of a brief history of the Carter Family, texts and tune transcriptions of each song, with detailed background information and references to other versions on record and in print, a selected Carter Family bibliography, and LP discography. Contributors are William H. Koon, Norman and David Cohen, and Archie Green.

JOHNNY CASH

636. DANKER, Frederick E. The repertory and style of a country singer: Johnny Cash. Los Angeles: John Edwards Memorial Foundation, 1973. (Reprinted from Journal of American Folklore, Vol. 85, no. 338, Oct.-Dec. 1972). (Reprint No. 28) pp. 309-329. bibliog. and discog. notes.
The author examines Cash's repertory in some detail, dividing it into traditional songs, ballads, heartsongs/blues songs (by "heartsong" is meant the country love song), folk and folk-country lyrics (including railroad, sharecropper, prison, mining and cowboy songs), religious songs, and a miscellany. In this examination, and the look at aspects of Cash's performance style that follows, Cash's position, and that of country music--both straddling lines of traditional and popular culture--are briefly scrutinized.

637. WREN, Christopher S. Winners got scars too: the life and legend of Johnny Cash. New York: Dial Press, 1971. 229p. illus.
———. Johnny Cash: winners got scars too. London: Allen, 1973. 229p. illus.
This illuminating popular biography divides naturally into three parts. In the first Wren draws a clear picture of Cash's Arkansas background and upbringing, noting his first exposure to country music through radio. His uncertain early manhood leads into the second, longest part, which describes his first records for "Sun," rise to stardom and consequent lifestyle, in which the decline from rumbustious high jinks to destructiveness, domestic disruption and drug addiction is chronicled in detail--a task the author is happy enough to undertake, as he knows his story will go on to tell how drug addiction was overcome, and contentment came in the shape of June Carter. The final chapters are given over to a contemporary portrait. Wren draws extensively on material from close associates of Cash, particularly Marshall Grant. There is little attention to music, other than some brief references to Cash's performing style, and occasional attempts to relate song lyrics to experience.

UNCLE DAVE MACON

638. RINZLER, Ralph, and COHEN, Norm. Uncle Dave Macon: a bio-discography. Los Angeles: John Edwards Memorial Foundation, 1970. (Special Series, No. 3) 50p. illus., bibliog., discog.
Combining documentation with some appreciation this booklet commemorates the 100th anniversary of the birth of one of the out-

standing figures in early country music, the "first featured star of the Grand Ole Opry," whose dry wit, integrity and musicianship endeared him to thousands. Ralph Rinzler's biographical sketch of Uncle Dave (and, briefly, of his musical associates), is followed by an essay on his songs by Norm Cohen, and a list of songs sung (but not recorded) by Uncle Dave. The discography, chronologically arranged, gives full discographical details (locations, dates, personnel, master numbers, titles, composer credits, release labels and numbers) and also provides a cross reference list of release and master numbers. The bibliography of 58 items is also chronologically arranged, and contains brief annotations. Reminiscences by Smoky Mountain Glenn conclude the booklet.

CHARLIE POOLE

639.　RORRER, Clifford Kinney. Charlie Poole and the North Carolina Ramblers. Reidsville, N.C.: Reidsville Printing Co., 1968 (reprinted 1974). 22p. illus., discog.
　　　The repertory and techniques of such an outstanding old-time music group as the North Carolina Ramblers would merit detailed investigation. This modest booklet provides some brief but useful information on the backgrounds of the two principal figures in the band--Poole and the fiddle player Posey Rorer (Poole's brother-in-law, and the author's grandfather)--and on their performing and recording careers up to and beyond their split in 1928. (Poole continued to record with the Ramblers until his death in 1931.) The discography lists the Ramblers' recordings from 1925 to 1930, with dates, personnel and matrix numbers. There is also a list of reissues on the "County" label. (The booklet is available from the author at Java Star Route, Box 22A, Chatham, Va.)

JIMMIE RODGERS

640.　RODGERS, Mrs. Jimmie. My husband, Jimmie Rodgers. San Antonio: Southern Literary Institute, 1935. (Repr. Nashville: Country Music Foundation Press, 1975). 264p. illus.
　　　The "Singing Brakeman," as Rodgers was known, occupies a place of primary importance in country music history for the legacy of his songs, for his mingling of elements from white and black traditions, and as the first commercially successful star. "One would be hard pressed," writes Bill C. Malone, "to find a performer in the whole broad field of 'pop' music ... who has exerted a more profound and recognizable influence on later generations of entertainers ... Rodgers singlehandedly originated a new tradition in country music" (no. 606, pp. 91-2). This biography of Rodgers (1897-1933) by his wife Carrie, whom he married in 1920, has its sentimental side, but in general avoids the maudlin, and, coming from the closest possible source to Rodgers himself, is valuable. There is plenty of fond recollection of their courtship and married life, as one would expect, but there are also interesting accounts of Rodgers' childhood in Mississippi, including his contact with black singers, and of his early work on the railroads, his experiences on the vaude-

ville circuit, and his work as a detective. The success that followed his first records for Ralph Peer in 1927 was tempered by an endless struggle with the T. B. that killed him. The account of his death in New York, and of the return of his body to his home town of Meriden (the train engineer blew a long, mournful whistle) is something of a dramatic tour de force, the fragmented prose giving an idea of a world breaking up. (For a balanced, perceptive account of Rodgers' career and achievement, containing biographical detail not in Mrs. Rodgers' book, Malone's Chapter 3 in no. 606 is first-rate.)

SONS OF THE PIONEERS

641.   GRIFFIS, Ken. Hear my song: the story of the celebrated
        Sons of the Pioneers. Los Angeles: John Edwards Mem-
        orial Foundation, 1974. (Special Series, No. 5) 148p.
        illus., bibliog., discog.
   The Sons of the Pioneers, as Norm Cohen points out in his preface, created a new style of Western country music from a blending of elements from different areas of the country. Griffis, pioneering in his turn, provides a history of the group from its formation in 1933 by Roy Rogers, Tim Spencer and Bob Nolan, through the various changes of personnel to 1974. This is followed by detailed biographies of the 15 members who stayed for four years or more (Lloyd Perryman having the longest tenure--from 1936 on). The immense discography gives full details for all commercial recordings (grouped by company), and also lists other material such as standard radio transcriptions and orthacoustic transcriptions. Supporting these catalogs are a title list with composer credits and dates, and lists of LP albums with contents, of the compositions of Bob Nolan and of Tim and Glenn Spencer, of the motion pictures in which the group appeared, and of song books.

POP STONEMAN

642.   JOHN EDWARDS MEMORIAL FOUNDATION. The early re-
        cording career of Ernest V. "Pop" Stoneman: a bio-
        discography. Los Angeles: John Edwards Memorial Foun-
        dation, 1968. (Special Series, No. 1) 20p. illus.
   The short biographical sketch of pioneer hillbilly artist "Pop" Stoneman (1893-1968) covers his career up to 1934, and is based on an interview by Eugene W. Earle. The chronological discography, using initial research by John Edwards, covers the same period, giving full discographical details and some notes. (Stoneman recorded again in the 1950s and 1960s.)

HANK WILLIAMS

643.   MOORE, Thurston, ed. Hank Williams: the legend. Den-
        ver: Heather Enterprises, 1972. 63p. illus., bibliog.,
        discog.
   A nicely illustrated album of writings about the legendary country singer (1923-1953), including a brief critical appreciation by

Bill C. Malone, a personal reminiscence by Williams' sister Irene, numerous other recollections, liner notes and newspaper reports. The most substantial piece, by John Stephen Doherty, is a candid biographical portrait of Williams' personal and professional life, and his tragic degeneration.

644.   RIVERS, Jerry. Hank Williams: from life to legend; edited
        by Thurston Moore. Denver: Heather Enterprises, 1967.
        39p. illus. , bibliog. , discog.
        Rivers played the fiddle in Williams' band, the Drifting Cowboys, during the final four years of the country star's career--from his arrival in Nashville from Alabama in 1949 to his death--and his personal recollections, informally told, are interesting as a firsthand account of the type of life led by a leading country band at this time. He is a little diffident about approaching Williams too closely, as man or artist. The bibliography (song folios, books and articles) and discography (78s, 45s, LPs--but no dates) are almost identical with those in Moore, no. 643.

645.   WILLIAMS, Roger. Sing a sad song: the life of Hank Wil-
        liams. New York: Ballantine Books, 1973. 276p. illus. ,
        discog.
        A considerable mythology has grown up around Hank Williams' name, but Roger Williams' level-headed biography shows how, though enigmatic, the real Hank was a pale, ordinary, rather shy country boy, who came to life only when making or composing music. Despite stardom his life was fundamentally tragic, destroyed, as the author sees it, by paradox: emotional immaturity and a depth of sensitivity, which were the wellsprings of his songs, providing the psychological basis for the alcoholism that undermined him. With much use of interview material from family and associates, the author interweaves the private and professional threads of his story well. In the first half he describes Williams' upbringing in Alabama, with his mother's overriding influence, his early musical apprenticeship (especially at the hands of a black street singer), through his embarkation on a musical career in the dance halls around Montgomery, to his breakthrough as a songwriter, as a recording artist, and, finally, as a star of the Opry. The rapid rise was followed by a rapid degeneration, marked by increasing drunkenness and falling reputation, culminating in his death in the car on a trip to Canton, Ohio, New Year's Day, 1953. In the course of his account of these events, particularly at the high point of Williams' career, the author examines the character and appeal of his songs, their spread into the popular market, the life of a country star, and the qualities and style of a typical Hank Williams performance.

12. Cajun Music

(See also no. 495.)

646.   AMERICAN folk music occasional, (No. 2). Compiled and

edited by Chris Strachwitz and Pete Welding. New York:
Oak Publications, 1970. 80p. illus., bibliogs., discogs.
The principal feature in this collection of original articles is
a group of pieces by Paul Tate, Harry Oster and Chris Strachwitz,
on Cajun music, including an LP survey. Blues also figure prominently, with an interview with Muddy Waters by Pete Welding, reminiscences of Robert Johnson by Johnny Shines, a portrait of Sonny
Boy Williamson No. 2 (Willie "Rice" Miller) by Paul Oliver, and a
brief account of his career as a recording director, especially of
blues, by Lester Melrose. Other subjects include string band festivals (Bob Baldwin), Hank Williams' death (Eli Waldron), Rev. F. W.
McGee and early gospel song (Don Kent), folk song texts, hill country recording pseudonyms (an index by Harlan Daniel) and Texas
polka music (Chris Strachwitz).

647. DAIGLE, Pierre V. Tears, love and laughter: the story of
      the Acadians. Church Point, La.: Acadian Publishing
      Enterprise, 1972. 135p. illus.
      Written mainly for children, to increase knowledge and pride
in the Acadian (Cajun) heritage, and the place of music. A short,
subjective history of the Acadian people--the French colonization of
Acadia (Nova Scotia), the Acadians' expulsion at the hands of the
British in 1755, and their settling in Louisiana--is followed by two
collections, with portraits, of short biographies of Cajun musicians,
the first of 24 dead or retired, and the second of 28 active individuals
or groups. There are tunes and texts of six traditional songs.

648. LEADBITTER, Mike. French Cajun music. Bexhill-on-Sea:
      Blues Unlimited, 1968. (Collectors Classics, 12) 15p.
      illus.
      A catalog of the recordings of French Cajun music of Louisi-
ana available at the time of compilation. There are sections devoted
to record producers, with names and addresses, 45 rpm singles, arranged under label names, with artist, title, catalog number, and
LP issues, a short section similarly arranged.

649. LEADBITTER, Mike, and SHULER, Eddie. From the bayou:
      (the story of Goldband Records). Bexhill-on-Sea: Blues
      Unlimited, 1969. 62p. illus.
      A booklet outlining the beginnings and development of a small
company in Lake Charles, Louisiana, which has been producing records mainly of Cajun music since 1948. Shuler, the founder, and
Leadbitter tell the story as a duologue, with Leadbitter filling in
background to Shuler's personal recollections. The current Gold-
band catalog is included.

G. BLACK MUSIC

Note: As mentioned in the Preface, literature on the Social and Cultural Background of Black Music is relevant to the study of Black Music, but constitutes such a huge body of writing that an entirely separate book would be required to deal with it adequately. Section G. 1 indicates some guides to this literature, while Sections G. 2. a. and G. 2. b. list some of the more important background books that make music an integral part of their area of study.

1. Guides to the Social and Cultural Background

650. BRIGNANO, Russell C. Black Americans in autobiography: an annotated bibliography of autobiographies and autobiographical books written since the Civil War. Durham, N. C.: Duke University Press, 1974. 118p.

Given the importance as source material of first-hand accounts, both in the field of black music and in related areas, this is a useful preliminary guide. The two principal sections--autobiographies, and other autobiographical works such as diaries and narratives covering short periods in a person's life--contain 60 items relevant in some way to music and dance (out of a total of 417 books covering everything from preaching to baseball). All books in these sections were published after 1865. A further section lists 41 books written before 1865 that have recently been reprinted. The main sections have four- or five-line annotations that concentrate on brief biographical information and make no attempt to evaluate, assess the level, or describe the character or style of the books. The third section has no annotations. All the annotated books are accompanied by locations in U.S. libraries. There are three indexes: of experiences, occupations and professions; of geographical locations and educational institutions; and of titles.

651. McPHERSON, James M., et al. Blacks in America: bibliographical essays by James M. McPherson, Laurence B. Holland, James M. Banner, Nancy J. Weiss, Michael D. Bell. Garden City: Doubleday, 1971. 430p.

The literature on the history and culture of black Americans is very extensive, and much of it, while not specifically discussing black music, provides relevant background information to its study.

This interdisciplinary bibliographical guide, which maps out the various categories and discusses briefly the most important books, is a most useful work, and one which can be used as a supporting text to the present bibliography. Music itself is covered in various places, but particularly in Part 2, Section 4 ("African Cultural Survivals among Black Americans"), and Part 8 ("Blacks in American Culture, 1900-1970"). There is a combined name and subject index.

652.　MAJOR, Clarence.　Black slang: a dictionary of Afro-American talk.　New York: International Publishers, 1970; London: Routledge and Kegan Paul, 1971.　127p.　bibliog.

In his introduction to this listing of about 2,000 words in use by black Americans, the compiler emphasises the socio-cultural roots of black slang, and sees it as motivated by needs of self-defence and the will to survive unhappiness; the central figure in the imagery is the "sinner-man--black musician." In the dictionary itself dates indicating the period a word or phrase was in use are included where it was possible to establish them. A brief comparison with some jazz glossaries suggests there are numerous omissions-- and a study of blues lyrics would probably have increased the number of words given.

653.　PORTER, Dorothy B., ed.　The Negro in the United States: a selected bibliography.　Washington: Library of Congress, 1970.　313p.

This useful bibliography is a good adjunct to black music study by virtue of its wide coverage of historical, social and artistic aspects of black experience in the U.S. Based on Library of Congress collections it includes 1,781 books, arranged in an alphabetical order of subjects. These include art, biography, civil rights, education, folklore, history, music, and religion. The emphasis is on more recent monographs, and there are occasional annotations. The music section itself is short, listing 37 items, but musical figures appear also in the section for biography.

654.　SMITH, Dwight L., ed.　Afro-American history: a bibliography; introduction by Benjamin Quarles.　Santa Barbara: ABC-Clio, 1974.　856p.

A bibliography of almost 3,000 abstracts of periodical articles from over 300 periodicals from the period 1954 to 1972. The abstracts originally appeared in the journal America: History and Life. Six main sections--a general one on Afro-American cultural traditions, and five historical ones from colonial to contemporary America --are subdivided along subject lines. For the historical, sociological and cultural background to black music in America this is a valuable guide to scholarly information and comment. Specifically musical articles are few in number, however--14 in a section on contributions to American culture (p. 55ff.) and 18 elsewhere. The only musical journal abstracted is Ethnomusicology. No doubt it was awareness of such a paucity of scholarly material on black music that led to the foundation of The Black Perspective in Music in 1973. To note the contrast between the number of music articles abstracted in this volume and the mass of information and criticism, on jazz and blues especially, in less scholarly American and European journals, is sufficient comment on past attitudes and a clear indication of where our gratitude should be directed.

655. UNIVERSITY OF UTAH. Marriott Library. Black bibliography. Salt Lake City: University of Utah, 1974. (Bibliographic Series, Vol. 2) 825p.

Within its limits (library holdings of post-1954 material only) a valuable reference tool for black studies that includes musicians in its section of individual bibliographies, and has a separate section for more general books on black music. Inevitably, because the lists are confined to the contents of one library, there are gaps; thus, although the section on individuals includes material on Louis Armstrong, Count Basie and Duke Ellington it omits anything on Billie Holiday or Bessie Smith. The more general section lists 86 books (collections and monographs) and 37 articles. Name index.

656. WORK, Monroe N., comp. A bibliography of the Negro in Africa and America. New York: Wilson, 1928. (Repr. New York: Octagon Books, 1965). 698p.

Though very limited in black music material because of its date, this huge bibliography of books, pamphlets and articles is still a useful source of references, particularly for 19th century materials. Music and folklore items are included in the first section, on the Negro in Africa. Three sections of Part 2 are particularly relevant to music: Section 23, on Negro folk music, lists collections of sacred and secular songs, and critical works; Section 24, on the Negro and modern music lists both music and criticism in the area of concert music, and also criticism on jazz; Section 35, on the Negro and the stage, includes material on both minstrelsy and musical comedy. Some entries have annotations.

2. Black Music in Books on Black Culture and Society

a. Histories and Studies

657. ABRAHAMS, Roger D. Deep down in the jungle: Negro narrative folklore from the streets of Philadelphia. Hatboro: Folklore Associates, 1964. 387p. illus., bibliog.
_____. _____. Rev. ed. Chicago: Aldine, 1970. 278p. bibliog.

A study and collection of Negro jokes and "toasts" (theatrically presented narrative poems) made by the author while living in a Negro area of Philadelphia, Camingerly. In the first part of the book Abrahams shows how, for young Negro males, "family life ... created ... emotional ambivalence that had great effect on the traditional modes of expression." He explores the social milieu of these young Negroes in Camingerly, and examines the relationship of their storytelling to the rest of their lives. In the second part he presents

and discusses the stories themselves, and studies aspects of style
and performance. The first edition is revealingly commented upon
by Charles Keil in Urban Blues (no. 860). The revised edition
places less emphasis on the matrifocal family. It has a glossary,
a bibliography of 120 or so items, and an index.

658. ABRAHAMS, Roger D. Positively black. Englewood Cliffs:
      Prentice-Hall, 1970. 177p. bibliog.
      Written from a sense of concern about the lack of understand-
ing of lower-class black life, this study seeks, by analyzing forms
of Negro expressive culture--particularly stories and songs--to break
down the stereotype of the American Negro. With examples from
stories, toasts and songs the author examines first how blacks consider conflict and aggression as normal, and how themes of distrust
and adversity are converted into creative form. He also shows how
the stereotyped pictures white people have are used by blacks in
their own expression, and how black folklore displays its own stereotypes. Attitudes of black men and women to each other are explored,
with illustrations from songs and blues, showing a "low affect level"
in interpersonal relationships. The final chapter explores the soul
movement, its birth in the musical tradition and its place in that
tradition, contrasting the communal emotion and group involvement
of soul music with the alienation of the individual in the blues. Index.

659. BENNETT, Lerone. Before the Mayflower: a history of the
      Negro in America, 1919-1962. Chicago: Johnson, 1962.
      404p. illus., bibliog.
      _____. , 1919-1964. Rev. ed. Chicago: Johnson,
      1964. 435p. illus., bibliog.
      _____. , 1919-1964. Rev. ed. Baltimore: Penguin,
      1966. 435p. illus., bibliog.
      _____. , 1919-1966. 3rd ed. Chicago: Johnson,
      1969. 449p. illus., bibliog.
      A detailed and readable history, beginning with the African
past, in particular the Sudan and Nile valley empires, and tracing
the history of Negro Americans from the first Jamestown slave
landing through the Revolution, the age of slavery, the Civil War
and Reconstruction, on through the tempestuous years of the 20th
century to Martin Luther King and the 1960s. Music is examined
in three main places: in the African context (pp. 26-7), the slaves'
secular and sacred music and dance (p. 79f), and the birth of jazz
in the Jim Crow era (p. 239f). There is a useful list of dates, a
full bibliography and an index.

660. BONTEMPS, Arna, and CONROY, Jack. They seek a city.
      Garden City: Doubleday, 1945. 266p. illus., bibliog.
      notes.
      _____. Anyplace but here. New York: Hill & Wang,
      1966. 372p. bibliog.
      This account of Negro migration within America and the re-
ception Negro migrants received in Northern and Western cities is
told mainly through accounts of the lives and experiences of various

individuals who played significant parts. The importance of migrating musicians, and something of the effect on black music of the impulse to migrate, are described in chapters on W. C. Handy and Scott Joplin (8) and on Jelly Roll Morton (15). The latter also describes the different backgrounds of jazz musicians in New Orleans.

661.   BRAWLEY, Benjamin. The Negro genius: a new appraisal
        of the achievement of the American Negro in literature and
        the fine arts. New York: Dodd, Mead, 1937. (Repr.
        New York: Biblo & Tannen, 1966). 366p. illus., bibliog.
    In this account of the black artistic accomplishment Brawley includes three chapters on music (5, 7, and 11), and refers also to musicians in the ante-bellum period in Chapter 3. Chapter 5 considers music and art, 1865-1895, including the Jubilee Singers, opera singers Marie Selika, Flora Batson and Sissieretta Jones. Chapter 7 takes this subject to 1920, and includes Harry T. Burleigh, Will Marion Cook, and J. Rosamond Johnson. In Chapter 11, R. Nathaniel Dett, William Grant Still, Roland Hayes and Marian Anderson are included among others. There is little attention to jazz, blues or ragtime. Index.

662.   BUTCHER, Margaret Just. The Negro in American culture;
        based on materials left by Alain Locke. New York: Knopf,
        1956. 294p.
        _____. _____. 2nd ed. New York: Knopf, 1972.
        313p.
    This penetrating study of the black contribution to American culture includes two chapters of particular musical interest: on the "early folk gifts" of music, dance and folklore, and on Negro music and dance. The first discusses the phenomenon of the influence of slave music on white Southern society; this is an extension of the argument in the previous, very interesting chapter concerning the extent of the black contribution in general through folk qualities and their manifestations. The second of these chapters examines the thread of folk song in the various black musical styles of spiritual, blues, ragtime, jazz and concert music. The legacy of Alain Locke may be discerned when the author says, "Eventually the art music and folk music of this country must be fused into a vital, superior form" (p. 91).

663.   FRAZIER, E. Franklin. The Negro church in America.
        New York: Schocken Books; Liverpool: Liverpool University Press, 1964. (Studies in Sociology) 90p. bibliog.
        notes.
    This brief but basic historical and social survey by the noted black historian, which relates changes in black religious life to the "social organization and social disorganization" of black life in general in the U.S., refers specifically to music on several occasions, notably on pp. 12-16, where he discusses the spirituals (in particular their religious sentiment and otherworldly outlook), and on pp. 72-75, where gospel singers are examined as symbols of the accommodation between traditional Negro religion and a newer, more secular outlook. (Frazier's attitude towards African survivals, expressed

more fully elsewhere in his writings, is that--with the possible exception of dance--the African in North America was stripped of his
social and cultural heritage.)

664. GAINES, Francis Pendleton. The Southern plantation: a
    study in the development and accuracy of a tradition. New
    York: Columbia University Press, 1924. (Repr. Glou-
    cester, Mass. : Smith, 1962). 243p. bibliog.
    A study of the evolution of the concept of the plantation and
of slavery in literature, the arts and the popular mind, and a comparison of the concept and the reality, as Gaines sees it. One chapter (5) discusses the role played by minstrelsy, and another (6) that
of popular song (Foster, Henry Clay Work, spirituals as popularized
by the Jubilee Singers) in this development. The minstrel show
Gaines views as having moved, by the mid-19th century, far away
from a position where it could be said to reflect any reality; popular song, however (including minstrel song), became, for the popular
mind, the most powerful means of evoking plantation life.

665. HANNERZ, Ulf. Soulside: inquiries into ghetto culture and
    community. New York: Columbia University Press, 1969.
    236p. bibliog.
    An anthropological study, based on field work in Washington,
D. C. , and containing references to the role and significance of music in various contexts of ghetto society--life-style, male-female
relations, streetcorner men, the collective idea of manliness, areas
of unrest, ghetto culture. (These may be traced through the index.)

666. HERSKOVITS, Melville J. The myth of the Negro past.
    New York: Harper, 1941. 374p. bibliogs.
    _____. _____. Boston: Beacon Press, 1958. (Repr.
    Gloucester, Mass. : Smith, 1970). 368p. bibliogs.
    In his epoch-making study of African culture and of its sur-
vival in the New World, Herskovits presents evidence for the origins
of African tribes and examines their cultural heritage, proceeding
from this to an analysis and discussion of acculturation in America,
in which he attempts to destroy the myth that the American Negro
is a man without a past. For music, Chapter 8, on language and
the arts, is important. Suggesting that scholarship has been too
rigid in its choice of likely sources of information, Herskovitz traces
changing viewpoints on the origins of black music, and appeals for
more musicological study of folk song.

667. HUGGINS, Nathan Irvin. Harlem Renaissance. New York:
    Oxford University Press, 1971. 343p. illus. , bibliog.
    notes.
    The black intellectuals of the Harlem Renaissance of the 1910s
and 1920s aspired in general to the creation of high art, and, in
Huggins' view, regarded ragtime, jazz and blues only as sources for
this superior culture-to-be. Only Langston Hughes took a deep interest in the forms and performers for their own sake. The promo-
tion of spirituals (discussed on pp. 75-78), motivated in the main by
a desire to preserve a rich heritage, is also seen as having cultural

elitist overtones. Most of the book is devoted to literary and social aspects of the Renaissance, but in his last chapter the author turns to the Negro in the musical theater, particularly minstrelsy, in order to explore the white-black interdependency characteristic of the history of American race relations. In the development of the minstrel show he sees the creation, by white Americans imbued with the achievement ethic, of a deliberately contrasted ethnic type, to give themselves greater cultural confidence. As Negroes became themselves involved in minstrelsy the form reflected the duality of life that was in any case typical for many. In the Negro musical revue Huggins sees a perpetuation of the "darky" tradition; although there was, from "The Octoroons" (1895) to "Shuffle Along" (1921), a desire for innovation and modest change, "Negro shows ... mainly continued to exploit a corrupt tradition" (p. 291).

668. OTTLEY, Roi, and WEATHERBY, William J. , eds. The Negro in New York: an informal social history. New York: New York Public Library, 1967. 328p. illus., bibliog.
Based on material in the Schomburg Collection, this regional history from 1626 to the 1930s gives a many-sided portrait of Negro life in New York, and though music is by no means prominent (there are short accounts on minstrelsy and the Black Swan recording company, and descriptions of house rent parties and clubs, but few mentions of musicians by name) the social and entertainment context in which it developed is clear enough.

669. QUARLES, Benjamin. The Negro in the making of America. New York: Collier, 1964. 288p. bibliog.
————————. ————————. Rev. ed. New York: Collier, 1969. 318p. bibliog.
In this description of the importance of the black contribution to America from the earliest colonial times to (in the rev. ed.) the Nixon era (an area the author feels has been neglected by many historians), Quarles discusses African survivals as illustrated by Negro songs, includes spirituals in his chapter on slavery, and briefly surveys the role of black music and musicians in contemporary society.

670. SCHOENER, Allon, ed. Harlem on my mind: cultural capital of black America, 1900-1968; preface by Thomas F. Hoving; introduction by Candice Van Ellison. New York: Random House, 1968. 255p. illus.
The 1968 Metropolitan Museum of Art exhibition on Harlem (of which this book is an extension) "documented the struggle to establish an urban black culture" in the 20th century American society. This is achieved in book form by a "cluster of documentary newspaper stories and photographs assembled as units interpreting the character of each decade" (foreword). The superb collection of photos includes numerous ones of musical interest (especially jazz) for each decade, while among the short press features may be found pieces on the Negro's contribution to music in America (1913), Ellington (1930), Basie (1938), bop (1948) and others, revealing a little of the cultural context of black music in New York.

671. STAMPP, Kenneth M. The peculiar institution: slavery in the American South. New York: Knopf, 1956; New York: Vintage Books, 1964. 435p. bibliog. notes.
_____. _____: Negro slavery in the American South. London: Eyre & Spottiswoode, 1964. 431p. bibliog. notes.
Chapter 8 of this standard history of slavery, "Between Two Cultures," is particularly relevant to music. In it Stampp examines the social structure and pattern of Negro plantation life, characterized in particular by family instability, and looks at the way folklore and--especially--music (as the Negro's "most splendid vehicle for self-expression" [p. 349]) reflect the slave's life and attitudes, and the extent to which these elements represent a fragment of retained African culture.

b. Anthologies of Criticism

672. BROWN, Sterling A., et al., eds. The Negro caravan: writings by American Negroes; selected and edited by Sterling A. Brown, Arthur P. Davis and Ulysses Lee. New York: Dryden Press, 1941. (Repr. New York: Arno Press, 1969). 1082p.
A vast anthology of the writings of black Americans, with one section on folk literature. This contains a 21-page introduction by Brown on the spirituals, secular slave songs, ballads, work songs, protest songs and blues, as well as folk tales and sermons, followed by an anthology of 60 or so examples of texts of each type. A further section of cultural essays includes pieces by James Weldon Johnson on early Negro shows, and E. Simms Campbell on "Early Jam." There is also a useful chronology, 1607-1941, and an index.

673. CHAMETZKY, Jules, and KAPLAN, Sidney, eds. Black and white in American culture: an anthology from "The Massachusetts Review." Amherst: University of Massachusetts Press, 1969. 478p. illus.
The coverage of this anthology of prose, verse and illustrations that appeared originally between 1959 and 1969 includes cultural, social and historical matters affecting black life in America, among which are several pieces on musical topics: Sterling Stuckey on spirituals (see also no. 790); Max Margulis on the irreconcilable elements of creativity and self-caricature in early jazz; impressions of a Duke Ellington concert, by John Mackay; and the blues as a literary theme, by Gene Bluestein (see also no. 438).

674. CUNARD, Nancy, ed. Negro anthology, made by Nancy Cunard, 1931-1933. London: Published by Nancy Cunard at Wishart & Co., 1934. 854p. illus.
_____. Negro: an anthology; edited and abridged, with an introduction, by Hugh Ford. New York: Ungar, 1970. 464p.
This legendary volume is described by Ford in his introduction as "the first comprehensive documentation that supported the black man's claim and demands for equal treatment." Ford's selec-

tion contains over 100 of the original 250 pieces. Of the sections
devoted to specific subjects, one, on Negro stars, includes articles
on jazz orchestras by the French critic Robert Goffin, on Armstrong
by Ernst Moerman (another Frenchman), and on Florence Mills by
U.S. Thompson. One section is concerned specifically with music.
It is sub-divided: America, Creole, West Indies, and Africa, and
contributors include George Antheil ("The Negro on the Spiral"), Edward G. Perry ("Negro Creative Musicians"), Zora Neale Hurston
("Spirituals and Neo-spirituals"), Lawrence Gellert ("Negro Songs
of Protest"), Goffin again ("Hott Jazz"), and Maud Cuney-Hare
("Folk Music of the Creoles," and "Negro Music in Porto Rico").

675. DAVIS, John P., ed. The American Negro reference book.
       Englewood Cliffs: Prentice-Hall, 1966. 969p. bibliog.
       notes.
       Of the 25 chapters in this compilation two cover music. One,
by Zelma George, on Negro music in American life, considers folk
and gospel music, black and white art music composers who have
used Negro thematic material, and the future of Negro music. There
are copious bibliographical footnotes to this chapter. The second,
by LeRoi Jones, "Blues, Jazz and the Negro," is a concise summary
of the origins and development of these styles. A chapter by Langston Hughes, "The Negro in American Entertainment," includes
minstrelsy and musicals. Very full index.

676. EBONY. The Negro handbook; compiled and edited by the
       editors of Ebony. Chicago: Johnson, 1966. 535p.
              . The Ebony handbook, by the editors of Ebony;
       editor, Doris E. Saunders. Chicago: Johnson, 1974.
       553p.
       This reference work includes in the section "Creative Arts"
a chapter by Phyl Garland on the Negro in music, covering briefly
art music, jazz and popular music, and concluding with a list of
"Grammy" awards made to black musicians. Various individuals in
black music appear in the biographical dictionary at the end of the
book. Index.

677. GAYLE, Addison, ed. The black aesthetic. New York:
       Doubleday, 1971. 432p.
              . _____. New York: Anchor Books, 1972.
       409p.
       The editor of this collection of powerful, passionately com-
mitted writing sets the book's direction and tone in his introduction
when he speaks of the contemporary black artist as "engaged in a
war with this nation that will determine the future of black art."
He conceives the black aesthetic as "a means of helping black people
out of the polluted mainstream of Americanism." There are seven
essays on music, three of which are very close to this spirit. Jimmy Stewart demonstrates the inadequacies of "cultural paternalism"
in white historiography, and sees a coherent theory of the aesthetic
value of black music as being based on a reappraisal of the relationship of music to its social place and function--a relationship which
has changed dramatically in the 1960s. For Ron Wellburn the black

aesthetic is a mystical one (unlike that of rock culture) in which music, as the "foremost expressive quality of our being," is vitally
important; describing the activities of black jazz musicians since the
late 1950s, he tries to show how music has been in the forefront of
the search for the "expression of true black sensibility." Ortiz
Walton compares African and Western European musical values,
tracing antiphony and polyphony to African sources. The other
pieces are: Du Bois' essay on the sorrow songs from his Souls of
Black Folk; a chapter from LeRoi Jones' Black Music (no. 1052) on
rhythm and blues and the new jazz; a (late 1920s?) piece by a Ja-
maican, J. A. Rogers, on the past and possible future of jazz; and
some reflections on the evolution of post-war jazz by Leslie B. Rout,
reprinted from Negro Digest, 1969.

678. INTERNATIONAL CONGRESS OF AMERICANISTS, 29th, New
York, 1949. Selected papers; edited by Sol Tax. Vol. 2.
Acculturation in the Americas; with an introduction by Melville J. Herskovits. Chicago: University of Chicago Press,
1952. (Repr. New York: Cooper Square, 1967). 339p.
illus., bibliog.
The central concern of this volume is the mixing of American Indian, European and African cultures in America, and in this
context it turns its attention to music twice. The first occasion is
a paper by Willard Rhodes, on acculturation in Indian music, in
which he outlines some of the principal factors and problems involved,
and concludes that acculturation in this field is relatively small, and
mostly one-way. The second paper, on African influence on the music of the Americas by Richard Alan Waterman, is an important
study that begins by challenging theories of the absence of harmony
in African music, and shows that its presence made Euro-African
musical syncretism--the union of diverse practices--easy and widespread. It also outlines some features of African music not found
in Europe, but which occur in America--the dominance of percussion,
polymeter, etc.

679. SZWED, John F., ed. Black Americans. Washington:
Voice of America, 1970. (Forum Lectures) 321p. illus.,
bibliog. notes.
_____. Black America. New York: Basic Books, 1970.
303p. bibliog. notes.
One section in this collection of talks is given over to "Black
Culture" and contains two discussions of musical subjects. The
first, "Background of the Blues" by Harry Oster, explores the sources,
development and recording history of country blues, with examples
of blues texts. The second, "Black Music and White America" by
Don Heckman, examines the way music has been a motivating factor
in cultural and social change for the Negro, how a cycle of black
creativity/white fascination/white exploitation has evolved, and finally how, with rhythm and blues and rock music this cycle seems to
have broken and a synthesis emerged.

680. WHITTEN, Norman E., and SZWED, John F., eds. Afro-
American anthropology: contemporary perspectives; fore-

word by Sidney W. Mintz. New York: Free Press; London: Collier-Macmillan, 1970. 468p. illus., bibliog.

A significant collection of essays, containing four of particular relevance to black music: 1) Alan Lomax explains, with charts and tables, how Cantometric analysis (the systematic rating of the presence or absence of pre-defined song characteristics, applied to the body of world song styles) shows Africa to be a homogeneous musical region, and Afro-American music to be a sub-system of the African tradition. (Although the Cantometric system shows up marked European influences on Afro-American music, the weight of evidence represents a formidable challenge to the theories of George Pullen Jackson.) 2) John F. Szwed demonstrates, in a study of the dichotomy between sacred music and the blues in black America (in particular the way characteristics of each relate to patterns of social behavior) that song forms and performances represent alternative strategies of adaptation within a single society to human and natural environments; he also shows how changing stylistic modes, from spirituals to soul, symbolize and reinforce social behavioral changes. 3) Robert Blauner attacks the view of the Negro as having no ethnic culture, and in the course of his re-examination of the theory repudiates Bennett Berger's views--of "soul" ideology especially--as expressed in his review of Keil's Urban Blues (no. 860). This leads to 4) Michael Haralombos' examination of the significance of soul music and blues for Northern black ghettoes, in which he illustrates and explains the decline of interest in the blues and the rise in popularity of soul.

3. Black Music--General Works

a. Histories, Reference Works, Critical Studies

See also Section I, 11.b, c.

681. COURLANDER, Harold. Haiti singing. Chapel Hill: University of North Carolina Press, 1939. (Repr. New York: Cooper Square, 1973). 273p. illus., bibliog.

The West Indies are particularly interesting, from the viewpoint of Afro-American music history, in that they display, in forms much clearer and less open to doubt than in the U.S., the survival of African musical culture and its development in contact with traditions from Europe. Though the mixing of cultures in New Orleans was more complex, there were at one time, no doubt, strong similarities in African acculturation between there and Haiti; in both places, for one thing, the European influences were predominantly French and Spanish. Courlander shows how in Haiti, where Dahomean tribes exerted most influence, music and dance played and play a central part in Negro life. The role of music and dance in religion (vodoun) and in secular activities is described and dances and songs are grouped under seven headings, with descriptions. (These include various Congo dances, and the Juba.) There is also music for 126 songs.

682.   CUNEY-HARE, Maud.   Negro musicians and their music.
       Washington: Associated Publishers, 1936.   439p.   illus. ,
       bibliog.
       Following more than fifty years after Trotter (no. 700), this
book kept in existence the frail line of succession of works on the
whole of black music that culminated in Eileen Southern's monumental history (no. 697).   The historical account of Negro vernacular
music with which it opens discusses African music, African influences, types and features of Negro sacred and secular folk songs,
the origin of the spirituals (contra-Jackson), ragtime, jazz, blues
and the musical.   Turning to the, one imagines, safer ground of
cultivated music the author presents a gallery of pioneer Negro musicians of the 19th century, with information on their lives and careers.   Valuable biographical detail is also contained in her survey
of contemporary "torch bearers, " among whom are composers Harry Burleigh, Clarence Cameron White, William Grant Still, R. Nathaniel Dett, and artists Roland Hayes, Marian Anderson, Jules
Bledsoe and Paul Robeson.   Index.

683.   DE LERMA, Dominique-René, ed.   Black music in our cul-
       ture: curricular ideas on the subjects, materials and
       problems.   Kent, O. : Kent State University Press, 1970.
       263p. bibliogs. , discogs.
       Based on the first seminar organized by the Black Music Cen-
ter of Indiana University in June, 1969, this collection of papers and
discussions takes in a wide range of black music in an overall educational context.   The objectives and work of the Center as of 1970
are described at the start of the book.   Four papers are devoted to
particular aspects of black music: in church and school (Lena Mc-
Lin), jazz (an autobiographical account of his role in recording jazz,
with reference to Billie Holiday, by John Hammond), dance (Verna
Arvey), and art music (William Grant Still), with a discussion
among T. J. Anderson, Hale Smith and Olly Wilson on black composers and the avant-garde.   There are four discussions on materials and problems from the points of view of publishing and recording, faculty and students, and administration.   The appendices include selective lists of scores, recordings, out-of-print recordings,
an annotated film list, a selective bibliography of books and articles,
and sample curricular syllabi.   Index.

684.   DE LERMA, Dominique-René.   A discography of concert mu-
       sic by black composers.   Minneapolis: AAMOA Press,
       1973.   (AAMOA Resource Papers, No. 1) 29p.
       A provisional listing, arranged by label name and number, of
approximately 200 records, both on 78 rpm and LP, representing
36 composers.   Dates of issue are given where known.   Each entry
includes composer, dates, work title (uniform titles), and performers.
There is an index of composers' names, with references to the label
numbers.   Black European and American composers are included--
Coleridge-Taylor being, in fact, the most strongly represented of
all.   It is intended that the list should assist librarians and private
collectors to survey their holdings.

685. DE LERMA, Dominique-René, ed. Reflections on Afro-American music. Kent, O. : Kent State University Press, 1973. 271p. bibliogs.

The edited proceedings of the second and third seminars organized by the Black Music Center (1971 and 1972) range broadly, and at varying levels, over black art and vernacular music, without any central theme, but with a particular interest in educational aspects in the American context. The curricular position of black music in general, and of jazz in particular is discussed. Other topics include the black composer in relation to society, the social role of jazz, 19th century black art music, soul, gospel, journalism, black dance, and information sources. David Baker provides some guidelines for a general view of black music history, and there are two papers on African music: on foreign versus traditional culture in Nigeria, and on field work among the Venda tribe. Contributors include Richard Abrams, Cannonball Adderley, Thomas A. Dorsey (once the blues singer Georgia Tom), T. J. Anderson, Phyl Garland, Geneva Southall, Undine S. Moore and John Blacking.

686. EMERY, Lynne Fauley. Black dance in the United States from 1619 to 1970; with a foreword by Katherine Dunham. Palo Alto: National Press Books, 1972. 370p. illus., bibliog.

This pioneer study aims to provide a "documented, historically accurate account of the dance performed by Afro-Americans in the United States," and at the same time to serve as a basic reference source for in-depth research (preface). Proceeding chronologically, the author commences with the slave-trade and the accounts of dancing left by the traders themselves, pauses to consider at length the history of black dance in the Caribbean, 1518-1900, and begins her account of America with the dancing on the plantation, in the Northern cities, on the levee and in New Orleans in the period before the Civil War. (The folkdances of the plantation are described in detail--buck and wing, juba, ring-shout, etc.--with due regard for social function, instruments used, movements and patterns.) From here we move to the theater, following the development of black dance from the early imitations by whites ("Daddy" Rice), and the authentic black dancing of William Henry Lane ("Master Juba"), on through minstrelsy, revue, and musical comedy. Among those featured are Bill Robinson, Williams and Walker, and Florence Mills. In conclusion a chapter is devoted to the black concert dance of Katherine Dunham, Alvin Ailey and others. The extensive bibliography lists books, periodicals, newspaper articles, and unpublished material, and there is a good index.

687. HOWARD UNIVERSITY, Washington D.C. Library. Dictionary catalog of the Arthur B. Spingarn Collection of Negro Authors. Boston: G. K. Hall, 1970. 2v.

The noted Spingarn Collection contains a substantial amount of concert and popular music by Negro composers--scores, sets of parts and sheet music--all of which is listed in a special section in Vol. 2 of this catalog. There are approximately 2,500 items in all, with a particularly large amount of early 20th century popular song.

(The Moreland Collection at Howard University is the location for the
master-file of a bibliography by Zelma George containing 9,592
titles of "published Negro folk music, music by Negro composers,
music by non-Negroes using Negro thematic material, and history
and criticism of Negro music. ")

688.   JOHNSON, James Weldon. Black Manhattan. New York:
        Knopf, 1930. (Repr. New York: Atheneum, 1968). 284p.
        illus.
        One of the best-known black leaders and writers of the 1920s,
Johnson (1871-1938) was personally involved in much black musical
activity through his brother, the composer J. Rosamond Johnson,
and as a lyricist in his own right. His history of black New York,
particularly his portrait of Harlem in the 1920s, while it may be a
"period piece" (as Allen H. Spear describes it in his preface to the
reprint edition), is a rich source of first-hand information on black
musical activity from the late 19th century to the end of the 1920s.
Among the topics covered are minstrelsy (chap. 8), black concert
singers, and Will Marion Cook's "Clorindy" (1898) (chap. 9), Williams and Walker, Bob Cole and J. Rosamond Johnson (chap. 10),
early jazz and James Reese Europe (chap. 11), Sissle and Blake's
"Shuffle Along," other black musicals, and Florence Mills (chap. 16),
the revues of the late 1920s, and the blues (chap. 17). Index. (For
a good biography of Johnson, including his musical activities, see
Eugene Levy, James Weldon Johnson: Black Leader, Black Voice,
Chicago: University of Chicago Press, 1973.)

689.   JONES, LeRoi. Blues people: Negro music in white Amer-
        ica. New York: Morrow, 1963; London: MacGibbon &
        Kee, 1965. 244p. bibliog. notes.
        A very challenging examination of the Negro's progress in
America from "slave to citizen"--and of his awakening to consciousness of being a Negro and an American--as seen through his music,
especially blues and jazz. Basing his work on the principle that the
Negro's most expressive music at any time must portray the Negro
himself at that time, Jones makes a social and anthropological study
of the basic nature of black life in America. He proceeds historically, examining the implications of uprooting and of slavery, dwelling
on cultural survival and on the distinctive cultural creations resulting
from this process. He makes a penetrating and extensive examination of the development of blues and jazz forms up to the end of the
1960s, seeing blues as a starting point for the emergence of the
American Negro, and adds a particularly incisive chapter on the
Negro middle class. Having analyzed the Negro's progress through
his music, Jones concludes by asking whether the values the American Negro is asked to defend are valid. Index.

690.   LANDECK, Beatrice. Echoes of Africa in the folksongs of
        the Americas; instrumental arrangements by Mitta Kaye ...
        New York: McKay, 1961. 184p. illus., bibliog., discog.
        _____.   . 2nd ed. New York: McKay, 1969.
        184p. illus., bibliog., discog.
        A collection of some 100 songs chosen to illustrate the con-

tinuity of the African musical tradition in the music of the Americas.
There are four sections: "From Africa to the New World"; the
Caribbean; South and Central America; and "Song Roots of Jazz in
the U.S." The editor provides a note on instruments, general comments on each area and style, and notes on each song. Scoring is
for voice, piano, guitar and drum (or bongo, etc.), and the texts
are in English.

691. LOCKE, Alain Leroy. The Negro and his music. Washing-
        ton: Associates in Negro Folk Education, 1936. (Repr.
        Port Washington: Kennikat Press, 1968; (with his Negro
        art, New York: Arno Press, 1969). 142p. bibliogs.
        Locke (1886-1954), a leading black educator and central figure
in the Harlem Renaissance, was profoundly interested in the nature
and extent of the black contribution to American culture, and in this
book, aimed largely at black students (with suggestions for discussion
after each chapter), he turns his attention to the types and influence
of black music. His emphasis is on the folk (spirituals, blues,
work songs) and popular styles (minstrelsy, ragtime, musical comedy,
jazz, and the influence of jazz on classical music), though he also
considers outstanding black concert musicians. Locke's knowledge
and understanding of black folk and popular styles are accompanied
by an inability--characteristic of his time--to appreciate them for
their own sakes and on their own terms. His description of the
black musical achievement--"creditable and interesting" (p. 6)--is
less than enthusiastic, and he continues to look for its maturing in
a great "classical tradition." (It is interesting to note here the influence of white artistic standards, based on "progress" towards
masterpieces.)

692. PATTERSON, Lindsay, ed. The Negro in music and art.
        New York: Publishers Co., 1967. 304p. illus., bibliog.
        .   . 2nd ed. New York: Publishers Co.,
        1969. 304p. illus., bibliog.
        An anthology of readings on aspects of Negro music and art
in America, comprising reprints of articles and excerpts from books,
the earliest published in 1903, the latest in 1967. There are 16
subject sections, eleven of which are devoted to music. These range
from spirituals, minstrels and ragtime, through blues, gospel, jazz
and rock and roll to popular composers, famous singers (Bessie
Smith, Billie Holiday, Marian Anderson, Leontyne Price) and black
music in the classical tradition. Contributors include W. E. B.
Du Bois, Zora Neale Hurston, Alain Locke, James Weldon Johnson,
Sterling A. Brown, Arna Bontemps, William Russell, Ralph Gleason,
Jack Yellen, George Hoefer and Maud Cuney-Hare. Index.

693. RIEDEL, Johannes. Soul music black and white: the influence of
        black music on the churches. Minneapolis: Augsburg,
        1975. 159p. bibliog., discog.
        This is a confusing, elusive book. Although it is short and
can only be introductory, it is nowhere made clear just what it is an
introduction to. The subject suggested by the subtitle sounds interesting, but only occupies the last four chapters, where such topics

as the black elements in contemporary religious music, the new folk hymn, and criteria for evaluating new church music are cursorily discussed (and actual black church music is mysteriously absent). Before this the text ranges far and wide over African origins, the transfer to the Americas (with more attention to South than North), "soul" elements in black and white music, and the influence of black music on popular music in general. The object of these pages would seem to be to help identify the origin and nature of the elements of "soul" common to all black music; the trouble is, when Riedel discusses what "soul" means (Chapter 4) it takes on such all-embracing significance, culturally speaking, that an attempt to discuss it in so few pages is at once preposterous, and leads nowhere. Does it help to have a book on the "nature of black music," as the cover puts it, that can give more space to Pennsylvania Pietists than to black gospel music?

694.   ROACH, Hildred. Black American music: past and present.
        Boston: Crescendo, 1973. 199p. illus. , bibliog. , discog.
        This is a short book for such a big subject. Its bias is toward composers and musical forms rather than performers, which will make strange reading to those who are accustomed to thinking of jazz as basically a performer's art. The writer's declared intention, however, is to supplement standard historical works by stressing aspects they omit. The text is in three historical segments: 1619-1870s (African heritage, early folk music, spirituals), 1870s-1950s (minstrelsy and the musical stage, jazz, art music), and 1950s-1970s (contemporary jazz and art music, and younger African composers). Within the compass of jazz somewhat cursory treatment is given to ragtime, blues, boogie-woogie, gospel and rock. Many of the chapters consist almost entirely of potted biographical sketches with general music comment (and some music examples). Those on the younger art music composers are useful to have, but in spite of what the author thinks standard histories omit, it is possible to find out more about the two dozen jazz composers elsewhere--which inclines one to think art music (occupying 60 of the text's 170 pages) is where her interest lies. The picture of black music that emerges is a strangely unbalanced one, because the author's chosen bias excludes consideration of so many musicians who made an outstanding contribution to the black musical heritage--e.g. , Art Tatum, Lester Young, Robert Johnson. The combined bibliography and discography includes some background books as well as some inaccuracies and some strange omissions. Index.

695.   ROBERTS, John Storm. Black music of two worlds. New
        York: Praeger, 1972; London: Allen, 1973. 286p. illus. ,
        bibliog. , discog.
        A wide-ranging study of the transfer of African musical traditions to the New World, the extent of their survival, the blending process with elements of European music, and the distinctive results in different areas of the Americas. Roberts first identifies "neo-Africanisms" in instruments, singing styles, etc. , and gives a broad outline of the points of contact with white musical traditions, seeking the fundamental causes for the processes in functional aspects

of the music. He then relates this outline to the music of South and Central America, and the Caribbean; turning to the U.S. he discusses African characteristics as they appear in work songs and field hollers, spirituals, blues and jazz. In conclusion he describes what has taken place in postcolonial urban African musical styles. A lucid and interesting account, which would command authority if Roberts had shown more evidence of returning to primary materials (there are no music examples) and less reliance on the views of other historians as principal sources of information (contrast Eileen Southern's exemplary procedure in no. 697). The total absence of references (frequently not even the title of the quoted source is given) is unfortunate also. Both bibliography and discography are divided geographically, and there is an index.

696. SIDRAN, Ben. Black talk. New York: Holt, Rinehart & Winston, 1971. 201p. bibliog.
    The premise behind this stimulating examination of the historical and cultural basis of black music in America is that black culture is oral culture, and that black music is "part and perpetrator of that orality" (introduction, p. xi). The book itself is a chronological exploration of the way music fulfills its social function within this oral culture, from the early history of black American music to the 1960s. As the book progresses black music becomes almost synonymous with jazz, and it is increasingly apparent that the author is more interested in what the music stands for than what it sounds like and why. It is possible, as Richard Middleton showed (no. 863), to make a cultural study by first examining the music. Sidran's basic source material consists of sociological and cultural studies, in which he is well versed, and from which he makes a framework that will admit music as one of its constituents. If, as he says, "music is potentially a basis for social structure" in black society (p. xiii), a study of how this operates must examine the music, but as the book stands, musical insight--perhaps even familiarity with the music--is absent. All of which detracts from some very thought-provoking writing, which, as we have it, is based on a thesis for a doctorate at the University of Sussex (though Sidran is American).

697. SOUTHERN, Eileen. The music of black Americans: a history. New York: Norton, 1971. 552p. illus., bibliog.
    The first truly comprehensive history of its kind, this masterly work, with its fine sense of historical development, covers the period from the first slave ships to the present. Mrs. Southern's determination to consult and use original source material, no matter how fragmentary, and her scholarly handling of it should serve as a model to future black music historians. She divides her account into four chronological sections, and follows the musical currents-- popular, folk, religious, theatrical, concert--in each. Part 1 is concerned with the African heritage and the extent and significance of black music in the American colonies. In Part 2 the author explores the character of music in ante-bellum rural and urban Negro life, and discusses the spiritual. In the period from emancipation to 1919 (Part 3) the parallel and intertwining developments of min-

strelsy, black nationalist composition, ragtime and blues, and band
music are described. The final part follows the course of jazz and
art music to date, with much information on individuals, and consideration also of rhythm and blues and gospel music. Each chapter is usefully subdivided, and there are many music examples and
textual quotes. The bibliographic guide includes discographical information. Index.

698. SOUTHERN, Eileen, ed. Readings in black American music.
      New York: Norton, 1971. 302p.
      A companion volume to no. 697, this collection of 37 signifi-
cant readings is designed as a documentary history of black music
in America, covering the years 1623-1969. Arrangement is chronological under eight group headings (African heritage, music on the
plantation, music of a free people, etc.). Many of the documents
that played a central role in the author's history are reproduced,
e. g., Jobson, Park and Bowdich on Africa, Rev. Samuel Davies
on black singers in colonial America, Richard Allen's hymnal, John
F. Watson's Methodist Error, and slave narratives. The final section, on the 20th century, is devoted entirely to black writers, many
of them musicians (Will Marion Cook, James Reese Europe, LeRoi
Jones, etc.). All sources are indicated, and there is an editorial
preface to each piece and an index.

699. STANDIFER, James A., and REEDER, Barbara. Source
      book of African and Afro-American materials for music
      educators. Washington: Contemporary Music Project,
      1972. 147p. bibliogs., discogs.
      The impulse to compile this introductory reference work (com-
prising bibliographical, discographical and practical educational information) was a recognition of the need to widen the music curriculum, particularly in urban America. Choosing material principally
for accuracy, usefulness in reading, and availability, the compilers
aim to provide a partly annotated source book to black music not
only for students and teachers, but also for librarians. The first
of the two sections--on African music--lists background books, books
and articles on music, instruments, dance and art, and includes a
discography. Part 2, on Afro-American music, includes 56 background books, 36 biographies (mainly jazz), 87 books on music
(covering all fields, and including some song collections), 55 articles,
books on poetry, and lists of dissertations; there is also a discography, divided by genre. Each section includes a set of "classroom
experiences," in which the compilers offer suggestions for incorporating the source materials. A small percentage only of the bibliographical items is annotated (the compilers have not examined all
the material listed), and numerous significant works pass without
comment, while several items of lesser significance--particularly
articles--receive disproportionate treatment. The criteria employed
for selection in the Afro-American section leave some significant
works unmentioned (e. g., various discographies), and the selection
of 55 articles from the vast corpus available is bound to be an extremely personal exercise. An appendix gives useful lists of black
musicians' names, arranged into categories. There is no index.

700. TROTTER, James M. Music and some highly musical peo-
         ple ... (with) sketches of the lives of remarkable musicians
         of the colored race; with portraits, and an appendix con-
         taining copies of music composed by colored men. Boston:
         Lee & Shepard, 1878. (Repr. New York: Johnson, 1968;
         Chicago: Afro-Am Press, 1969). 353, 152p. illus.

This first historical account of black American music, and
the best source of information on black musicians of the 19th century, was, according to Eileen Southern, "a landmark ... not
matched by a similar study for more than fifty years" (no. 697, p.
308). Maud Cuney-Hare, in 1936, relied heavily on Trotter's work
(no. 682). Trotter disaffirms any suggestion of racial motives, but
asserts that "the haze of complexional prejudice has so obscured the
vision of so many persons that they cannot see ... that musical
faculties ... are not in the exclusive possession of the fairer-skinned
race" (p. 4). His book spells out the accomplishments of Negro
musicians in sacred and secular music in a series of biographical
accounts of the careers of individuals, families and groups. Part 1
deals with the more famous, including Elizabeth Taylor Greenfield,
the Luca family, Thomas Greene Bethune, the Colored American
Opera Company, the Jubilee Singers and the Georgia Minstrels.
Part 2 is devoted to less well-known artists. Particularly in the
first part Trotter draws frequently for his material on contemporary
press notices. There are twelve illustrations, reproductions of programs, and, in the appendix, thirteen pieces of vocal and instrumental music. No index, unfortunately. (See also Robert Stevenson,
"America's First Black Music Historian," Journal of the American
Musicological Society, XXVI, 3, pp. 382-404.)

701. WALTON, Ortiz. Music: black, white and blue; a socio-
         logical survey of the use and misuse of Afro-American
         music. New York: Morrow, 1972. 180p. bibliog. notes.

A provocative study whose central themes are the close relationship between Afro-American music ("a derivation of African music tempered by the American experience") and the social and cultural matrix in which it has been created, and the effects for black
musicians of working in an industry dominated by "ethnic groups
other than Afro-Americans" (preface). Walton writes from a committed viewpoint and is at times outspokenly critical of the way musical life is ordered in America. Part of his text is a socio-historical survey of black music from Africa (where aspects of African music are discussed and compared with features of the European
tradition) through slave songs, blues and ragtime to jazz--his central preoccupation--which he discusses at some length from New Orleans to the contemporary period. A chapter is devoted to Duke
Ellington, as the supreme example of an outstanding black musician
confronted by cultural exploitation. In some ways the most interesting portions of the book are the final chapters, one dealing with
alleged racial discrimination by symphony orchestras (as evidenced
by the case of Arthur Davis and the New York Philharmonic), and
others with the need for Afro-American musical training programs,
and the steps necessary to create an Afro-American music industry.

b.   Collected Biography

See also A. 4.

702.   ADAMS, Russell L.   Great Negroes past and present; illus-
        trations by Eugene Winslow; David P. Ross, editor.   Chi-
        cago: Afro-Am Pub. Co. , 1963.   182p.   illus. , bibliog.
   This collection of biographical portraits of outstanding black
individuals was compiled to provide a "popular rendering of histor-
ical source material. " The section devoted to music includes James
A. Bland, Harry T. Burleigh, R. Nathaniel Dett, W. C. Handy,
William Grant Still, William L. Dawson, Paul Robeson, Roland
Hayes, Dean Dixon, Louis Armstrong, Duke Ellington and Marian
Anderson.   Elsewhere in the book we find James Monroe Trotter,
Richard Allen, Daniel Payne, Alain Locke, James Weldon Johnson,
Bert Williams and Gustavus Vassa.   The unambitious biographies
cover the central facts in an easily assimilated presentation.

703.   HANDY, W. C.   Negro authors and composers of the United
        States.   New York: Handy Brothers (1938?).   24p.   bib-
        liog.
   A publicity venture for black composers in general and Handy's
publishing firm in particular, this booklet lists in classified order
those pieces by black composers in the concert, stage and popular
fields published by the company, with very short biographical notes.
Other lists supply the names and best known works of song writers
and composers not published by Handy (e. g. , those in Clarence
Williams' catalog of blues and popular song).

704.   HUGHES, Langston.   Famous Negro music makers.   New
        York: Dodd, Mead, 1955.   179p.   illus.
   This series of portraits, intended primarily for younger readers, illustrates the Negro's contribution to music from the Jubilee
Singers on by describing 16 personalities from jazz, gospel music,
the concert hall and the operatic stage.   The concluding chapter is
devoted to some "Famous Jazz Musicians, 1800-1955. " Index.

705.   LOVINGOOD, Penman.   Famous modern Negro musicians.
        Brooklyn: Press Forum Company, 1921.   68p.   illus.
   It would be simple to mock the earnest effusions of praise
that mark these 19 biographies (too many rhetorical questions eventually provoke rude answers), but that would be to overlook the fact
that this little-known book follows on from Trotter (no. 700) in presenting, on a much smaller scale, portraits of contemporary black
musicians, with the aim of furthering both their recognition and the
practice of music among the black population.   ("A book of eulogy
it is, never-the-less, one of fact, with the ultimate racial evolution
in Art as the foremost consideration"--preface.) The 19 composers
and performers are Coleridge-Taylor, Burleigh, Dett, J. Rosamund
Johnson, Will Marion Cook, Carl R. Diton, Roland Hayes, Florence
Cole-Talbot, Cleota J. Collins, Marian Anderson, William H. Richardson, Joseph H. Douglas, Clarence Cameron White, Kemper Har-
reld, Eugene Mars Martin, Augustus Lawson, Helen Hagan, Melville
Charlton and Azalia Hackley.

4. Concert Performers

MARIAN ANDERSON

706. ANDERSON, Marian. My Lord, what a morning: an auto-
     biography. New York: Viking Press, 1956. 312p. illus.
                      . New York: Avon Books, 1964. 222p.
     The celebrated black contralto (b. 1902) describes her child-
hood and early life in Philadelphia, her training, the unfolding of
her musical career in Europe and America, and her rise to fame
as one of the country's outstanding singers, both of spirituals and
of operatic and concert music. The culmination of her professional
life was being the first black singer to perform at the Metropolitan
Opera. Some less agreeable experiences relating to color are also
described, in particular an encounter with the D.A.R. on Easter
Sunday, 1939, over a performance in Constitution Hall, Washington.

707. VEHANEN, Kosti. Marian Anderson: a portrait. New
     York: McGraw-Hill, 1941. (Repr. Westport: Greenwood
     Press, 1970). 270p. illus.
     Her Swedish accompanist gives a personal, rhapsodic account
of Marian Anderson's concerts in Europe (particularly Scandinavia),
South America and the United States from 1931 to 1941. The book
was written "with the collaboration of George J. Barnett."

ROLAND HAYES

708. HELM, MacKinley. Angel Mo' and her son, Roland Hayes.
     Boston: Little, Brown, 1944. 289p. illus.
     The inspiring achievement of Roland Hayes, to rise, largely
by his own resourcefulness, from the poverty in which he was born
in 1887 to become the first black singer to achieve world-wide recognition as a concert artist, blazed a trail for others to follow. Helm's
decision to write this biography in the first person, as if the words
were all Hayes' own, certainly allows the narrative to move freely,
whatever its implications for the reliability of the text; there is no
denying that what is by any standards a great story is told movingly
and well. Beginning with Hayes' boyhood in Georgia and after the
death of his part-Cherokee father in 1898, in Chattanooga (where
Hayes worked in a foundry), it describes how an Oberlin student,
hearing Hayes at a church concert, opened the 16-year-old's eyes
to his talent. There followed study at Fisk, where Hayes helped to
pay his way by working as a butler, and from whose portals he was
dismissed after four years. His experience with the Jubilee Singers,
however, led to his joining them in Boston, where he subsequently
made his home. After several years' study his patience was re-
warded when a concert at Symphony Hall, promoted by himself, was
a success. Hayes left for England in 1920 and, after near disaster,
established an outstanding reputation, performing before King George
V. White America was conquered in 1923--though both in the U.S.
and Europe prejudice was frequently encountered. (By this time his
mother, an ex-slave whose personality and approach to life profoundly

influenced Hayes, had died.) Although he admits to having neglected them in his early days, as a celebrity Hayes regularly included spirituals in his programs, as the account of his subsequent career makes clear. Helm's techniques do not permit any assessment of what was probably the single largest contribution to the establishment of solo spiritual singing as concert music.

PAUL ROBESON

709. HOYT, Edwin P. Paul Robeson, the American Othello.
　　　　Cleveland: World, 1967. 228p.
　　　　＿＿＿＿＿. Paul Robeson. London: Cassell, 1968. 228p.
　　　　Though an interesting biography Hoyt's book contains very little about Robeson's outstanding musical career and ability, other than mentioning some of the occasions when he sang spirituals in support of particular causes, and duly chronicling his successful appearance in Kern's "Show Boat," first in London and later in New York. His chief concern is to trace how the life and thought of this versatile man (actor, singer, lawyer, footballer), 1898-1976, became increasingly involved in social and political issues. (Robeson's own book, Here I Stand, New York, 1958, is a credo of his personal concern for black rights. Hoyt suspects that Robeson's wife's contribution to its making might have been considerable.)

710. SETON, Marie. Paul Robeson; with a foreword by Sir Arthur
　　　　Bryant. London: Dobson, 1958. 254p. illus.
　　　　A biography by an English film critic of Robeson's career as actor and singer, of the development of his social and political views, and the reaction of America. The book includes an article by Robeson written in 1936, on the need for Negroes not to abandon their roots and adopt the approach to life of Western intellectuals.

711. WOOLLCOTT, Alexander. While Rome burns. New York:
　　　　Viking Press, 1934. 328p.
　　　　＿＿＿＿＿. ＿＿＿＿＿. London: Barker, 1934. 280p.
　　　　As a drama critic, author and radio commentator, Alexander Woollcott (1887-1943) had many enemies. One, equally gifted in wit and venom, Oscar Levant, called him "the agent-provocateur of dross" (no. 366). As a writer he is often a pleasure to read, with an urbane wit and considerable command of language, and he was as equally capable of generosity and loyalty as of malice. The portrait of Paul Robeson in these reminiscences (pp. 91-101) is an affectionate tribute to an "old friend and neighbor," of whom he says, "of the countless people I have known ... he is one of the few of whom I would say that they have greatness" (pp. 92-3).

5.　The African Heritage

a.　Eye-Witness Accounts

712. BOWDICH, Thomas Edward. Mission from Cape Coast

Castle to Ashantee; with a statistical account of that kingdom ... London: Murray, 1819. 512p. illus.
Bowdich was a member of a commercial mission from London in 1817, during which he noted down numerous African songs,
reproducing them in his account of the mission with comments.

713. CANOT, Theodore. Captain Canot; or, Twenty years an
African slaver; being a true account of his career and adventures ... written out and edited from the Captain's journals, memoranda and conversations by Brantz Mayer. London: Routledge; New York: Appleton, 1854. (Repr. New
York: Dover Publications, 1969). 448p. illus.
This first-hand account of the slave trade in the first half of
the 19th century contains some information on the music making of
the Africans (Chapters 21, 22). Chapter 11 refers briefly to the
singing of the slaves.

714. DONNAN, Elizabeth, ed. Documents illustrative of the slave
trade to America. Washington: Carnegie Institution, 1930-
1935. (Repr. New York: Octagon Books, 1965). 4v.
bibliog. notes.
This definitive work, covering the slave trade from 1441 to
1808 through the eyes of governments, merchants and voyagers, is
mainly concerned with matters economic, and the compiler herself
admits that the records "shed little light upon the manner of the
people enslaved, their origins and the differences among them"
(preface). Nevertheless there are one or two references in the indexes to music and dancing, particularly in Vol. 2.

715. EQUIANO, Olaudah. The interesting narrative of the life of
Olaudah Equiano, or Gustavus Vassa the African... London: Printed for the author, 1789. (Repr. London:
Dawsons, 1969); New York: Printed by W. Durrell, 1791.
2v.
_____. _____. Boston: Knapp, 1837. (Repr. New
York: Negro Universities Press, 1969). 294p.
Equiano's story of his early life in Africa, his capture, en-
slavement, freedom and subsequent life includes in its early pages
some observations about music and instruments in what is now Nigeria.

716. JOBSON, Richard. The golden trade; or, A discovery of the
River Gambra, and the golden trade of the Aethiopians...
London: Printed by N. Okes, 1623. 166p.
This account by an English sea-captain of his travels in West
Africa to assess its commercial potential includes one of the earli-
est known descriptions, albeit a brief one, of African musical prac-
tices (pp. 105-107; quoted in Southern, no. 698).

717. PARK, Mungo. Travels in the interior districts of Africa,
performed under the direction and patronage of the African Association, in the years 1795, 1796 and 1797...
London, 1799; Philadelphia: Printed by James Humphreys,

1800. 484p. illus.

The dauntless Scottish explorer Mungo Park (1771-1806) was the first European to attempt to follow the course of the Niger River. His remarkable journals, which have been republished many times, include several references to music.

b. Studies and Reference Works

718. BLACKING, John. Venda children's songs: a study in ethno-musicological analysis. Johannesburg: Witwatersrand University Press, 1967. 210p. illus., bibliog.
Northern Transvaal, the home of the Bantu-speaking Venda, was not an area from which Africans were taken to be slaves on the North American continent, but this fine study, in which the author analyzes 56 songs and shows "how musical structures grew out of the cultural pattern of which they are a part" (p. 191), could serve as an example of what might be achieved by applying tools of ethnomusicological and functional analysis to black music and culture.

719. BRANDEL, Rose. The music of Central Africa: an ethno-musicological study; former French Equatorial Africa, the former Belgian Congo, Ruanda-Urundi, Uganda, Tanganyika. The Hague: Nijhoff, 1961. 272p. illus., bibliog.
Transcriptions of 52 songs made from recordings are preceded by a scholarly study that describes the functions of musical expression in these regions of Africa--ceremony, work song, entertainment, dance--and analyzes, with music examples, the technical features of the music itself, such as melody types, rhythm and polyphony. Singing styles are also discussed. In conclusion the author remarks that "non-literacy and the most simple music are neither logically nor actually concomitant" (p. 101). Both symmetry and asymmetry are present, leading to abstraction on the one hand, and realism and emotionalism on the other.

720. GASKIN, L. J. P. A select bibliography of music in Africa, compiled at the International African Institute under the direction of K. P. Wachsmann. London: International African Institute, 1965. (Repr. with additions, Boston: Crescendo, 1971). (Africa Bibliography Series B) 83p.
International in coverage, this listing of books and articles by scholars and travellers contains 3,040 items, arranged in six sections: general; Africa (general); African music geographically arranged; musical instruments; dance; catalogs, bibliographies and periodicals. There are author and geographic/ethnic indexes.

721. GORER, Geoffrey. Africa dances: a book about West African Negroes. London: Faber, 1935. 363p. illus.
_____. _____. New York: Knopf, 1935. 237p. illus.
_____. _____. London: Lehmann, 1949. 254p. illus.
_____. _____. New York: Norton, 1962. 254p. illus.
A widely-read classic of African travel literature, this account of a visit to West Africa in 1934, that turned an aesthetic

young Englishman into a social anthropologist, contains many descriptions of West African music and dance. Gorer went to Africa to accompany the Negro dancer Feral Benga on an expedition to study dance, and in his description of the culture and customs dance holds pride of place. One chapter is devoted to accounts of five different dance types. Gorer observes that music and other arts have evolved to supplement dance. Index.

722. JONES, A. M. Studies in African music. London, New York: Oxford University Press, 1959. 2v. illus., bibliog. notes.
The most exhaustive and most frequently referred to work on African music, this is also a valuable source of reference for comparative studies. In addition to the text in the first volume, which discusses various songs and dances, mainly from Ghana, arranged in order of complexity, the second volume contains 238 pages of transcription in full score. Discussion of particular musical features in Vol. 1 is normally related to these transcriptions. The emphasis in the discussion is on drumming and dancing, and on polyrhythmic combinations. There are also chapters on musical homogeneity, tone and tune, and the neo-folk music.

723. KUBIK, Gerhard. Mehrstimmigkeit und Tonsysteme in Zentral- und Ostafrika: Bemerkungen zu den eigenen, im Programmarchiv der Osterreichischen Akademie der Wissenschaften archivierten Expeditionsaufnahmen. Vienna: Böhlau, 1968. 65p. illus., bibliog.
A study of the extent of certain types of polyphony and of systems based on particular modes and scales in Central and East African music, and of parallels between them, with special reference to organum singing in parallel thirds, fourths and fifths. The author tabulates the modes and the types of polyphony found in 86 tribes, and finds a correlation between heptatonic and hexatonic styles and singing in parallel thirds, and also between use of the pentatonic mode and unison singing. A detailed structural examination of parallelism in tribes using pentatonic and heptatonic systems follows.

724. NKETIA, J. H. Kwabena. African music in Ghana. Accra: Longmans; Evanston: Northwestern University Press, 1963. 148p. illus., bibliog.
An examination of traditional folk music, principally devoted to technical aspects of harmony, melody, rhythm and instruments. General African characteristics and specific Ghanaian developments are outlined. There are music examples, and a set of 18 songs is included.

725. NKETIA, J. H. Kwabena. Drumming in Akan communities of Ghana. Edinburgh: Nelson, 1963. 212p. illus., bibliog., discog.
A study of the techniques, uses and significance of the drumming of the Akan of Southern Ghana.

726. NKETIA, J. H. Kwabena. Music in African cultures: a review of the meaning and significance of traditional African

music. Legon: University of Ghana, Institute of African
Studies, 1966. 62p. bibliog. notes.

A short examination of what traditional African music means
to those who make it. Musical styles are discussed, together with
some of the social and artistic aspects of the heritage.

727. NKETIA, J. H. Kwabena. The music of Africa. New York:
Norton, 1974; London: Gollancz, 1975. 278p. illus.,
bibliog., discog.

A lucid introduction for the general reader and college student
to the diverse musical traditions of Africa, "with respect to their
historical, social and cultural backgrounds, as well as ... musical
organization, musical practice, and significant aspects of style"
(preface). Section 1 examines the social and cultural background
(music in community life, the recruitment and training of musicians),
while Section 2 outlines the instrumental resources and the uses to
which instruments are put. In Section 3 Nketia turns to structures
in African music, describing, with music examples, the organization
and technical features of instrumental and vocal music. Section 4
broadens the frame of the study to examine music's relation with
speech, dance and dance drama. Supplementary material includes
maps, a list of locations of ethnic groups mentioned, a glossary of
African terms and an index.

728. WARREN, Fred. The music of Africa; with Lee Warren.
Englewood Cliffs: Prentice-Hall, 1970. 87p. illus.,
bibliog., discog.

A short, lucid introduction, describing the vital role of music in black African life, the characteristics of its melody, rhythm
and form, the various instruments, and the kind of music being
made today. Points of comparison with black American music are
indicated. The author is critical of the narrow view of music that
confines itself to the European tradition, and stresses the importance
of adopting different criteria to judge the music of Africa. There
are music examples, and the text is illustrated with line drawings
and some photographs.

6. Black Musical Life in the Slave Era

729. ALLEN, Richard. A collection of hymns and spiritual songs
... Philadelphia: Printed by John Ormrod, 1801. 72p.
_____. _____. Philadelphia: Printed by T. L. Plow-
man, 1801. 88p.

Though it contains no music, this hymnal by the founder of
the African Methodist Episcopal Church is of considerable significance,
for it shows in its texts (as is demonstrated by Eileen Southern, nos.
697 & 698, to whom we are indebted for pointing out the importance
of the collection) a partiality for hymns of the stanza and chorus
type so beloved of the revival and gospel song traditions, but which
are apparently not found in print in white Protestant hymnody at

this date. It also appears that these 54 texts (64 in the Plowman edition) may have served as sources for the Negro spirituals. Because Allen (1760-1831) compiled the book soon after organizing the Bethel Church in Philadelphia it follows that it is a reflection of the type of song his congregation liked--but which was not adequately provided by existing hymnals. No tunes are indicated, and it is probable that tunes of his congregation's own inventing were among those used (cf. Watson, no. 741), as well as folk tunes. (Allen himself wrote an autobiography, The Life, Experience and Gospel Labours of the Right Reverend Richard Allen, Philadelphia, 1887. Two books containing information about him are Charles H. Wesley, Richard Allen, Apostle of Freedom, Washington, 1935; and Howard D. Gregg, Richard Allen and Present Day Social Problems, Nashville, n. d.)

730. BOTKIN, B. A. , ed. Lay my burden down: a folk history of slavery. Chicago: University of Chicago Press, 1945. 297p. illus.
This large selection from the narratives of former slaves, collected for the Federal Writers Project in the 1930s, contains several specific references to music, especially to black fiddlers and to dancing (which can be reached via the index). A list of informants is included.

731. BREMER, Fredrika. The homes of the New World: impressions of America; translated by Mary Howitt... New York: Harper, 1853. 2v.
_____ . _____ . London: A. Hall, Virtue, 1853. 3v.
Swedish novelist Fredrika Bremer (1801-1865) visited the U.S.A. in 1849-1850, and her account includes numerous descriptions of the songs and the singing of blacks in both religious and secular contexts, and among both the slaves and the free. There are accounts of black singing and dancing at camp meetings--the most important point of contact between black and white--and in their own services, both in the South and the North. (Excerpts are provided in Southern, no. 698.)

732. BROWN, William Wells. The anti-slavery harp: a collection of songs for anti-slavery meetings. Boston: Bela Marsh, 1848. (Repr. New York: Kraus, 1971). 47p.
This is an early collection by a former slave of the texts of 48 abolitionist songs, most of which were contemporary, and had not previously been published. Tunes are suggested for most songs (e. g. , "Auld Lang Syne," "Sweet Afton"), and the authors of the verses are given in the index. Many of the songs take the form of abstract exhortations or laments, while a few are ballad-like.

733. BROWN, William Wells. Narrative of William Wells Brown, a fugitive slave, written by himself. Boston: Anti-Slavery Office, 1847. (Repr. New York: Johnson, 1970). 110p. illus.
NORTHUP, Solomon. Twelve years a slave: the thrilling story of a free colored man, kidnapped in Washington...

Auburn, N. Y.: Derby & Miller, 1853. (Repr. Baton
Rouge: Louisiana State University Press, 1968; New York:
Dover Publications, 1970). 336p. illus.
After Douglass' autobiography these are two of the best known
slave narratives, and both have things to say about the music of the
slaves. Brown (1816-1884), an active abolitionist like Douglass, includes the texts of some of the slave songs. Northup (1808-1863),
who was born a free man but became a slave when he was kidnapped
in 1841, was a musician himself--a fiddler to be exact--and his book
is interesting for its accounts of black music in both North and
South. Both texts are reproduced in Gilbert Osofsky, Puttin' on Ole
Massa (New York: Harper & Row, 1969). Brown also mentions
black music in My Southern Home (Boston: Brown, 1880).

734.　COFFIN, Levi. Reminiscences of Levi Coffin, the reputed
President of the Underground Railroad.... Cincinnati: Western Tract Society, 1876. (Repr. New York: AMS Press,
1971). 712p. illus.
This account of a lifetime's abolitionist activity, besides providing useful information on the Underground Railroad, which, on
one level at least, may have significance for the texts of many
spirituals, refers very briefly to singing in a Sunday School organized
for black children in 1821 by the author (pp. 70-71). The way that
black music scholarship handles such snippets of information is illustrated in an important article (which quotes Coffin among other
accounts of greater significance) by Dena J. Epstein, "Slave Music
in the United States before 1860: a Survey of Sources" (Music Library Association Notes, 2nd Ser., XX, 1963).

735.　DOUGLASS, Frederick. Narrative of the life of Frederick
Douglass, an American slave, written by himself. Boston:
Anti-Slavery Office, 1845. 125p. illus.
_____. My bondage and my freedom; with an introduction
by James McCune Smith. New York: Miller, Orton &
Mulligan, 1855. 464p. illus.
_____. Life and times of Frederick Douglass, written by
himself...; with an introduction by George L. Ruffin.
Hartford: Park, 1881. 516p. illus.
_____. _____. New rev. ed. Boston: De Wolfe,
Fiske, 1892. 752p. illus.
The autobiography, gradually enlarged over the years, of the
outstanding black abolitionist and orator (1817-1895), who was born
into slavery in Maryland, includes several descriptions of and comments
on the music of the slaves. Among the aspects he touches on are
the double meanings in many of the spirituals, the circumstances of
their use, and the mental state of the singers. (The various 20th
century editions, abridgments and reprints of the autobiographies
are too many to be listed here.)

736.　FORTEN, Charlotte L. Journal; with an introduction and
notes by Ray Allen Billington. New York: Dryden Press,
1953. 248p.
_____. The journal of Charlotte L. Forten: a free Negro

in the slave era; edited, with an introduction and notes, by Ray Allen Billington. New York: Collier Books, 1961. 286p.

The illuminating journal of a Philadelphia-born black girl who became a teacher and abolitionist, and, during the Civil War, participated in a teaching experiment with freed slaves in Port Royal, South Carolina. The journal describes various instances of singing among the ex-slaves, and includes the words of two "singular" hymns (pp. 158-9, 1961 ed.) and of "one of the most beautiful hymns I have ever heard" (p. 193).

737. FOSTER, G. G. New York by gas-light; with here and there a streak of sunshine. New York: Dewitt & Davenport, 1850. 127p.

George Foster's picture of the "unploughed sod of metropolitan life" in New York, in which he attempts "to penetrate beneath the thick veil of night and lay bare the fearful mysteries of darkness in the metropolis," includes a description of a dance hall with a predominantly black clientele and black musicians. This is Pete Williams', or Dickens' Place (after the English novelist who visited it in 1842 and described it in Notes on America), and it is the center of attention in Chapter 9, p. 72 ff. The Saturday night band consists of a fiddler, a trumpeter, and a bass drummer, and Foster speaks of the "red-hot knitting needles spirted out by that red-faced trumpeter, who looks precisely as if he were blowing glass," while the drummer "sweats and deals his blows on every side, in all violation of the laws of rhythm." There is also, in Chapter 10, brief description of theater orchestras, and of Maretzek's Astor Place Opera House; and, in Chapter 11, of dances at the houses of notorious courtesans.

738. KEMBLE, Frances Anne. Journal of a residence on a Georgian plantation, 1838-1839. London: Longman, Green, 1863. 434p.
_____. _____; edited, with an introduction, by John A. Scott. New York: Knopf, 1961. 415p. illus., bibliog.

This picture of slavery on a plantation near the Sea Islands, as recorded by an English actress (1809-1893) who married a Georgia plantation owner in 1834 (and was also, in later years, the grandmother of Owen Wister), provides us with some of the earliest extant comment on the musical customs of the slaves and their manner of singing. The author's attitude to the songs changes from one which considers them based solely on white popular songs when she hears some that are "wild and unaccountable." In the 1961 edition, pp. 162-164 and 259-264 are of particular interest.

739. OLMSTED, Frederick Law. The cotton kingdom: a traveller's observations on cotton and slavery in the American slave states; based upon three volumes of journals and investigations. New York: Mason, 1861. 2v.
_____. _____; edited with an introduction by Arthur M. Schlesinger. New York: Knopf; London: Routledge, 1953.

626p. bibliog.

Olmsted (1822-1903) was a New Englander whose three books recording in detail his impressions of the South in the 1850s (A Journey in the Seaboard Slave States, 1856; A Journey through Texas, 1857; and A Journey in the Back Country, 1860) were regarded at the time as giving an accurate picture. The 1861 edition was a condensation of this material, and it includes references to the slaves' fondness for music and dancing (pp. 349-350, 467).

740.   PAYNE, Daniel Alexander.   Recollections of seventy years; with an introduction by F. J. Grimke; compiled and arranged by Sarah C. Bierce Scarborough; edited by C. S. Smith.   Nashville: A. M. E. Sunday School Union, 1888. (Repr. New York: Arno Press, 1968). 335p. illus.

An influential figure in 19th century black church life and education, Bishop Payne (1811-1893) was largely responsible for introducing choral singing and instrumental music into the African Methodist Episcopal Church.   His autobiography devotes a chapter (no. 24) specifically to "music and literature in the church."   This valuable source of information describes the struggle to bring choirs into church services (Bethel, Philadelphia, 1841-2, and elsewhere), and similar battles over instrumental music (Bethel, Baltimore, 1848-9).   Looking back, Payne is proud of the great progress since 1850, and reflects "two things are necessary to make choral singing always profitable to a Church--that the congregation shall always join in singing with the choir, and that they shall always sing with the spirit and the understanding" (p. 237).

741.   (WATSON, John F.)   Methodist error; or, Friendly, Christian advice, to those Methodists, who indulge in extravagant emotion and bodily exercises.   By a Wesleyan Methodist. Trenton: D & E. Fenton, 1819. 180p.

In the wake of revivalism that sprang up around 1800 in the rowdy, frenzied atmosphere of the camp meeting clergymen of a more staid frame of mind were highly critical of what they saw as excessive, undignified behavior.   One such was John F. Watson, whose account of what he saw in Philadelphia unwittingly provides us with our first known account of the singing and dancing of the blacks, both in their own church (Richard Allen's A. M. E. Church in Philadelphia) and at the camp meetings.   In the space of four pages (29-31) he first speaks of the growing practice of singing "merry airs ... often miserable as poetry, and senseless as matter, and most frequently composed and first sung by the illiterate blacks of the society"; then of the blacks' quarter at the camp meetings, where the songs were "lengthened out with long repetitious choruses," and where a dance took place which Eileen Southern (no. 697, p. 98-9) identifies as the ring-shout.   He also remarks on the influence of all this on the whites, and on their all-night sessions spent singing "tune after tune ... scarce one of which were in our hymn books."   With this picture Watson provides vital clues in the study of the growth of black and white religious folk song in the 19th century.

7. Folk Song

a. Collections

742. CARAWAN, Guy, and CARAWAN, Candie, eds. Ain't you
        got a right to the tree of life? the people of John's Is-
        land, South Carolina--their faces, their words and their
        songs; photographed by Robert Yellin; music transcribed
        by Ethel Raim; with a preface by Alan Lomax. New
        York: Simon & Schuster, 1966. 190p. illus., bibliog.

A well-illustrated collection of recollections, opinions and
observations of the inhabitants of one of the Sea Islands off South
Carolina, including transcriptions of the words and melodies of
over 20 songs. Because of their remoteness the islanders have
preserved folk traditions, and in Lomax's words one may "hear
this American music still growing at its roots" (p. 7).

743. CARAWAN, Guy, and CARAWAN, Candie, eds. Freedom is
        a constant struggle: songs of the Freedom Movement;
        with documentary photographs; music transcriptions by
        Ethel Raim. New York: Oak Publications, 1968. 224p.
        illus.

This collection of about 60 black songs sung on demonstrations, marches and protests in the period 1963-1968 is divided into
five groups: the campaigns in Birmingham, St. Augustine, etc.; the
1964 Mississippi project; the blues, spirituals and work songs that
form the base of the music (illustrating growing awareness of the
roots of black music and experience); Selma, Ala., in 1965; and the
Northern ghettoes. Some of the songs are traditional, others are
adaptations, but most are the creations of the particular time and
place. Words and tunes are given, with guitar chords, and the
songs are interspersed with quotations describing conditions and
events.

744. CARAWAN, Guy, and CARAWAN, Candie, eds. We shall
        overcome: songs of the Southern Freedom Movement;
        compiled by Guy and Candie Carawan for the Student Non-
        Violent Coordinating Committee. New York: Oak Publi-
        cations, 1963. 112p. illus.

A collection of the words and tunes, with guitar chords, of
46 songs, intended to contribute to the documentation of the Freedom
Movement of the 1960s, and to convey something of its spirit. The
majority are adaptations of traditional songs (mainly spirituals and
hymns), with the addition of some contemporary items and some importations. The five sections in which the book is arranged are:
sit-ins and demonstrations, the Freedom Riots of 1961, songs of
the Albany Movement in Georgia, songs from the drive to register
voters, and songs that grew out of the demonstrations in Greenwood
and Birmingham.

745. COURLANDER, Harold, comp. Negro songs from Alabama;
        music transcribed by John Benson Brooks. New York:

Published with the assistance of the Wenner-Gren Foundation for Anthropological Research, 1960. 76p.
These 45 songs, selected from those gathered by the compiler on a 1950 field trip, include work songs, play songs, religious songs, field calls, one blues, and one ballad. A booklet accompanying the six record set of vocal and instrumental music collected in 1950 (Negro Folk Music of Alabama..., New York, Folkways Records, 1956) includes some comment on West African elements, and notes on performers--in particular Rich Amerson, from whom Courlander obtained a large amount of material.

746. GELLERT, Lawrence, comp. Negro songs of protest; arranged for voice and piano by Elie Siegmeister; foreword by Wallingford Riegger; illustration by Hugo Gellert. New York: American Music League, 1936. 47p. illus.
_____. (Vol. 2) "Me and my captain" (chain gangs): Negro songs of protest from the collection of Lawrence Gellert; arranged for voice and piano by Lan Adomian. New York: Hours Press, 1939. 31p.
Gellert, born in Hungary in 1898, grew up in New York and later lived in Tryon, North Carolina for twelve years, during that time haunting the Negro Quarters "with impunity" (preface), and painstakingly cultivating trust and friendship there and all over the black belt. Armed with primitive recording equipment and a profound interest in the Negro's songs primarily as social documents, he gathered, between 1933 and 1937, over 300 "songs that reveal for the first time the full heroic stature of the Negro, dwarfing for all time the traditional mean estimate of him." These two volumes contain a small sample--24 songs in the first, 23 in the second-- of this folk material (including work songs and blues) collected from the "hapless Negro in the clutches of Southern justice." The piano accompaniment to the songs is added to supply background to any who feel a background to be necessary. (18 recordings made by Gellert appear on Rounder Records 4004.)

747. HURSTON, Zora Neale. Mules and men; with an introduction by Frank Boas. Philadelphia: Lippincott, 1035. (Repr. New York: Negro Universities Press, 1969), 342p. illus.
_____. _____. New York: Harper & Row, 1970. 342p. illus.
A collection of Negro folktales from Florida and Louisiana, compiled by a black novelist and folklorist. An appendix gives the words and tunes, with harmony, of nine folk songs. A section of the book itself, 30 tales in all, is devoted to the theme of voodoo.

748. JACKSON, Bruce, ed. Wake up dead men: Afro-American worksongs from Texas prisons. Cambridge, Mass.: Harvard University Press, 1972. 326p. illus., bibliog., discog.
A rich and moving collection, made in 1964-1966, of the words and tunes of 65 work songs (with some variants) used by Negro prisoners in Texas "to make it through Hell." Following the introduction, in which the compiler states his reasons for making

the collection, his overall approach, and the importance of an understanding of the context for an appreciation of these "fleurs du mal," there is a chapter in which the prisoners, in taped comments, describe this context in their own words--the work, the conditions, the other prisoners--and also indicate the role and significance of the songs. In a further chapter the compiler describes the functions of the songs, the system of song leading, and the content. The songs themselves are arranged in groups by the work they accompany (e.g., axe songs, flatweeding songs); notes provide variant titles, informant of each version (used and not used), the work being done during the song, the location and the date. Each song has a commentary, noting special points of interest, and giving bibliographical and discographical references where relevant. The tunes and words of the songs are transcriptions from recordings. Appendices are devoted to nicknames and to responsorial patterns. There is a glossary, a song and a name index, the bibliography includes book and articles, and the LP discography lists American release numbers.

749. JOHNSON, J. Rosamond, ed. Rolling along in song: a chronological survey of American Negro music with eighty-seven arrangements of Negro songs ... edited and arranged by J. Rosamond Johnson. New York: Viking Press, 1937. 224p.

Brother of James Weldon Johnson and composer of numerous musical shows (and the song "Life Every Voice and Sing," amongst many others), J. R. Johnson (1873-1954) was one of the first black composers, in Eileen Southern's words, "to assimilate the characteristic idioms of Negro folksong into a body of composed music" (no. 697, p. 302). This collection provides the words and piano accompaniment for 87 ring shouts, spirituals, jubilees, plantation ballads, plantation and levee pastimes, minstrel songs, work-songs, street cries, blues and chain songs.

750. JONES, Bessie, and HAWES, Bess Lomax. Step it down: games, plays, songs, and stories from the Afro-American heritage. New York: Harper & Row, 1972. 233p. bibliog., discog.

This book of black children's games and associated songs came out of a meeting between Bessie Jones from Georgia and Bess Lomax Hawes at a California educational workshop. The material is all home-made entertainment as Mrs. Jones recollected it, and it is presented so that other groups of children can copy and enjoy it. There are nine categories, including clapping plays, ring plays and outdoor games. Each section has a general introduction, and each game or play has an explanatory note, comments from Mrs. Jones (from taped interviews), and the melody and text of the accompanying song. The music is given simplified transcription, omitting slides, scoops, etc. In essence, each play or game is a dramatization of a small part of life. Index.

751. PARRISH, Lydia. Slave songs of the Georgia Sea Islands; music transcribed by Creighton Churchill and Robert Mac-Gimsey; introduction by Olin Downes. New York: Creative

Age Press, 1942. (Repr. Hatboro: Folklore Associates, 1965). 256p. illus., bibliog.

A field collection of unique material gathered in the anachronistic community of the Sea Islands by an amateur enthusiast over a 25-year period from 1912. There are 60 songs in all, representing something of a link between Africa and ante-bellum America. They are divided into five sections: African survivals, shout-songs, ring-games, religious songs and work songs. Mrs. Parrish provides notes and comments on the songs of a not-too-scholarly type, and more general descriptions of the various types of song and the role of music in the lives of the people. The reprint edition has a foreword by Bruce Jackson.

752.   TALLEY, Thomas W.   Negro folk rhymes, wise and otherwise: with a study.   New York: Macmillan, 1922.   (Repr. Port Washington: Kennikat Press, 1968).   347p.

This anthology by a professor at Fisk University contains the texts of over 300 American folk rhymes, with a small section of rhymes from Africa and elsewhere. A few isolated examples of the tunes are included. In the study which follows Talley somewhat diffidently surveys the origins, structure, and uses of rhymes, and divides them for a comparative study index into twelve categories, including love songs, dance songs, nursery songs, play songs, etc. These he studies in three groups, based on a division between instinct and conscious thought. He also examines rhyming technique and Africanisms.

753.   WHITE, Newman Ivey.   American Negro folk-songs.   Cambridge, Mass.: Harvard University Press, 1928.   (Repr. Hatboro: Folklore Associates, 1965).   501p. illus., bibliog.

In the wake of scholarly interest in black folk music that followed Krehbiel's book (no. 761) there was much discussion of his arguments on the origin and character of the music. The virtue of White's volume was that it brought the scholarly resources and methods of folklore scholarship to bear, firstly to assemble a collection of texts, then to draw conclusions based on that data. An introduction examines the origins question in general, concluding that "the American Negro song was not at first original with the Negro. It originated in an imitation frustrated by imperfect comprehension and memory, and by a fundamentally different idea of music" (p. 25). But, "the songs of the Negro to-day are beyond question the Negro's songs, not the white man's ... They have become thoroughly naturalized as vehicles of the Negro's imagination." The texts that follow--over 800 in all, a collection begun in 1915 and carried out mainly by students--are divided into 13 groups, including religious, social and work songs, songs about animals, women, recent events, the "seamier side" and blues. There are introductions to each group and headnotes to each text. There also 15 specimen tunes, but relegated to an appendix. Indexes of titles and first lines.

b. Studies

754. AMERICAN folk music occasional, No. 1. Chris Strachwitz,
editor. Berkeley: American Folk Music Occasional, 1964.
99p. illus., discog.

The first in an irregular series, intended to act as a forum
for writers on folk music. The collection of articles covers a range
of topics, with some emphasis on music of the Negro folk tradition.
The three most substantial pieces are by Mack McCormick on censorship of folk songs, by Chris Strachwitz on J. E. Mainer's Mountaineers (with a discography), and by Roger D. Abrahams on the
"dozens" (the Negro practice of insult-dialogue that also features in
the blues). Two pieces feature gospel music: an interview with the
Staples Family, and an article on Mahalia Jackson by Leonard Feather. Blues are considered in a piece by Samuel Charters, a set of
photographs by Chris Strachwitz, a humorous view of the less rosy
side of blues field trips by Paul Oliver, and a portrait of Mance
Lipscomb by Mack McCormick. Other pieces cover ballad writer
Carson J. Robinson (a 1929 article by H. Leamy), Okie songs (a
1940 article by Charles Todd and Robert Sondkin), and bluegrass
(by Toni Brown).

755. CHAPPELL, Louis W. John Henry: a folk-lore study. Jena:
Frommann, 1933. 144p. bibliog.

Chappell began research into the John Henry tradition before
Johnson (no. 760), and has some acrimonious and scornful things to
say about the latter's investigation--not only his failure to give
Chappell's work any acknowledgment, but also his method of approach,
his handling of the data, and several of his conclusions. Chappell's
work--folklorists' quarrel aside--is thorough, authoritative, and more
positive than Johnson's, though many of their conclusions tally. It
is in three main parts. First, he presents and comments on various
popular (hearsay) accounts of the John Henry story. Second, pinning
the tradition down to the Big Bend Tunnel, W. Va., he examines the
history of drilling on the railroad, confirms the possibility of a contest between hand drilling and machinery, and, presenting authoritative personal testimonies of the tunnel, has no doubt the contest occurred, but admits the lack of documentary evidence for the con-
junction of the events that form the nucleus of the tradition. Third,
he explores the various possible sequences of events following the
contest; in view of the immense dangers to life involved in tunneling
he favors the theory that John Henry succumbed, not to exhaustion
from the contest, but to one of the tunnel's many mortal perils. In
a fine conclusion he portrays the genesis of the ballad in among the
Negro tunnel gangs. An appendix provides 11 texts of John Henry
hammer songs, 45 John Henry ballads, and 20 John Hardy ballads,
with details of informants. Index.

756. COURLANDER, Harold. Negro folk music, U.S.A. New
York: Columbia University Press, 1963. 324p. illus.,
bibliog., discog.

A valuable, scholarly survey of the whole range of black country folk music, describing its importance as part of a large, inte-

grated cultural framework, and discussing it stylistically, historically and sociologically. The first chapters recognize the influence of
African music, in the light of the greater degree of knowledge about
African practices than was available to earlier detractors of this
approach (especially as they concentrated on the narrower field of
spirituals). They also examine specific characteristics of black folk
music closely. The following chapters examine different types of
song: anthems and spirituals, cries, work songs, blues, ring games,
Creole songs, and ballads, concluding with a discussion of dances
and instruments. There are music examples in the text, and the
words and tunes of 43 songs in an appendix. Index.

757. JACKSON, Bruce, ed. The Negro and his folk-lore in 19th
      century periodicals. Austin: University of Texas Press,
      1967. (Publications of the American Folklore Society.
      Bibliographical & Special Series, Vol. 18) 374p. bibliog.
      A collection of 35 articles from Dwight's Journal of Music,
Lippincott's Magazine, Atlantic Monthly and others, arranged chrono-
logically and covering the period 1838-1900. About half are on mu-
sical subjects, including minstrelsy (Y. S. Nathanson), Negro songs
(J. M. McKim), spirituals (T. W. Higginson), slave songs (John
Mason Brown), plantation music (Joel Chandler Harris), Creole slave
songs and Congo Square, New Orleans (G. W. Cable), music in
America (Antonin Dvorak), and African musical survivals (Jeanette
Robinson Murphy). There is also a review of Allen et al., Slave
Songs of the United States (no. 768). Jackson provides an editorial
prefaces to each piece. There are indexes of authors and titles, of
articles and periodicals, and of songs.

758. JACKSON, Clyde Owen. The songs of our years: a study of
      Negro folk music. New York: Exposition Press, 1968.
      54p. bibliog.
      Taking as his pivotal point Dvorak's remarks that American
composers should turn to Negro melodies for their raw material for
a great and noble school of music (1895), Jackson traces the study
and use of black folk music in the 19th and 20th centuries. In the
first period he discusses the pioneer collection of Allen et al. (no.
768) and the popularizing efforts of the Jubilee Singers. His discussion of post-1895 developments takes in Krehbiel's analysis (no.
761), various performers, the use of Negro music in concert works,
and brings the story rather sketchily to 1950 with the conclusion that
the students and performers of the music had more influence than
did Dvorak.

759. JOHNSON, Guy B. Folk culture on St. Helena Island, South
      Carolina. Chapel Hill: University of North Carolina Press,
      1930. 183p. bibliog.
                        .   ; foreword by Don Yoder. Hatboro:
      Folklore Associates, 1968. 183p. bibliog.
      Johnson's study of black culture in an isolated area of the
South is a significant one in the debate over the originality of American black folk music and the extent of African retentions. In the
second of the three sections that make up the book he approaches

the question of the origins of the Negro spiritual, outlining the principal features of St. Helena Island spirituals as he found them, describing the white revivalist folk hymn, and investigating parallels between these and the Negro spiritual. This investigation examines, with examples, similarities in words (subject matter, specific lines, and forms or patterns), tunes (modes, scales, modulations, etc.), rhythm and tempo, and also provides specific instances of "kinship" (by which is meant borrowing by blacks from whites). Johnson's conclusion is that "the general pattern and many of the particulars of the music developed in slavery were borrowed from white folk music" (p. 128). In his search for parallels he anticipated the painstaking research of George Pullen Jackson (no. 548). It should be noted, however, that no comparisons are attempted between the spiritual and African or West Indian music, nor is any consideration given to the possibility of whites borrowing from blacks. The first section of the book, on Gullah dialect, reaches similar conclusions, finding few Africanisms and many examples of 17th century English dialects. Index.

760.   JOHNSON, Guy B. John Henry: tracking down a Negro legend. Chapel Hill: University of North Carolina Press, 1929. (Social Study Series) 155p. bibliog.
An interesting piece of detective investigation (though one of rather spurious integrity, according to Chappell, no. 755) into the folk-hero of Negro work song and ballad--the "steel-drivin' man" who defeated the steam drill. Johnson's researches obtained for him many variations of the story regarding the kind of work John Henry did, where the event took place, how he died, etc.; weighing them up, despite what he considers the inconclusive nature of the evidence (and changing his mind from 1926, when in Negro Workaday Songs (no. 764) he believed John Henry to be a myth), he concludes that John Henry did exist, that he worked on the Big Bend Tunnel of the Chesapeake & Ohio Railroad in West Virginia, competed with a steam drill in a test of practicality of the device, and died soon after, probably of fever. (Chappell called Johnson's rather half-hearted conclusions about John Henry the man "damning his reality with faint praise.") Comparing the legends of John Henry and John Hardy, Johnson concludes they were two different men and their ballads are separate entities (John Henry coming first). The valuable collection of words and tunes contains eleven texts and four tunes of John Henry work songs--the first to evolve--plus 30 texts and fourteen tunes of ballads (some white). Though he discusses the hold of the story on the Negro imagination the author does not seem in great sympathy with the tradition, and seems unaware of some of the symbolism in the text.

761.   KREHBIEL, Henry Edward. Afro-American folksongs: a study in racial and national music. New York: Schirmer, 1914. (Repr. New York: Ungar, 1962). 176p.
This epoch-making book was the first attempt at a musical analysis of black folk music (especially spirituals), and the earliest fully-developed argument in favor of solely black origins of the music. Krehbiel, by profession a music journalist, with several books on musical life in New York to his credit, claims that African tradi-

tion and the emotional effects of plantation life on the slaves alone created this body of song, which he calls the only true American folk song--the necessary climate not having existed for the white tradition. (In this last respect he was clearly wrong, as George Pullen Jackson, who described Krehbiel as a "Negro song apologist," demonstrated.) In a detailed analysis of the music Krehbiel describes many of the characteristics of the songs, and relates them to the African tradition (little explored though this was at the time). In the opinion of John Lovell (no. 794, p. 105), "Many writers have complained about Krehbiel ... No one, however, has destroyed his fundamental arguments with respect either to melody or words." There are numerous music examples, an appendix of ten songs, and an index.

762. METFESSEL, Milton. Phonophotography in folk music: American Negro songs in new notation; with an introduction by Carl E. Seashore. Chapel Hill: University of North Carolina Press, 1928. (Social Study Series) 181p. illus., bibliog.

The phonophotographic method of recording singing by a sound wave photograph, avoiding the phonograph and the normal method of notation, was developed at the University of Iowa as a much more accurate system than conventional notation for reproducing fully the many features of human singing. The experiments reported here use Negro folk song as an example, not to prove any thesis, but because it is a suitable body of material with which to demonstrate the techniques involved. The methods of study are fully described in Part II. They involve the use of a portable sound photography camera, from which a sound wave photograph is obtained; the frequency of vibration changes in the sound wave are graphed on a half-step musical staff ("pattern notation"). Part III describes in detail, with graphs for each item, the results of applying the method to 33 songs of five types (workaday religious songs, spirituals, work songs, blues, and general songs). In Part IV Metfessel analyzes the results in terms of technical features such as ornaments and vibrato, and in conclusion speculates on the potential usefulness of the technique in evaluating the distinctive originality or otherwise of American Negro folk music (conventional notation, he feels, will never provide an adequate answer to this question).

763. ODUM, Howard W., and JOHNSON, Guy B. The Negro and his songs: a study of typical Negro songs in the South. Chapel Hill: University of North Carolina Press, 1925. (Repr. Hatboro: Folklore Associates, 1964; New York: Negro Universities Press, 1968). 306p. bibliog.

This, the first of two volumes by these authors examining black folk song from a sociological standpoint, concentrates on what the various types of song can tell us about the people who sing them. The authors are not basically concerned--as Roger D. Abrahams says in his foreword to the 1964 reprint--"to preserve the songs either for their own sake or for the sake of the old order. The purpose here ... was to reveal the character and quality of the Negro's way of thinking and self-expression." Dividing the songs (which

were collected mainly in Mississippi and Georgia) into three groups
--religious, social, and work songs--the authors study the variety
among the songs of each type, their themes, and the relation of the
singer to his song.   They also present a collection of examples of
each kind (some 200 in all), with commentary, but without sources
or music.   Contrasting Odum and Johnson's approach with that of
Newman I.   White, Bruce Jackson remarks (in his preface to the reprint of White, no. 753) that the sociological approach to folk song
dates the most quickly, because sociological theories change so fast.
The final chapter, however, also shows the authors' concern for literary features--imagery, style, poetic effect.   The selected bibliography in the original edition remains unaltered in the reprints.
Title index.

764.   ODUM, Howard W. , and JOHNSON, Guy B.   Negro workaday
        songs.   Chapel Hill: University of North Carolina Press;
        London: Oxford University Press, 1926.   (Repr. New
        York: Negro Universities Press, 1969).   278p.   bibliog.
          As in their earlier book (no. 763), the authors' emphasis
here "is primarily social, although this indicates no lack of appreciation of the inherent literary and artistic values of the specimens
presented" (preface).   Included are the texts of some 250 songs collected in 1924-1925 from black singers in North and South Carolina,
Tennessee and Georgia.   The authors begin with a survey of the
blues, one of the earliest on this subject (and one that shows more
understanding than does White, no. 753, whose collection was only
slightly later); the central theme of the discussion is a comparison
between textual features of folk music and the more formal recorded
blues.   Subsequent chapters examine songs by theme (bad men, jail,
John Henry, etc.), and occupation (chain gang songs, other work
songs).   One chapter is devoted to specifically musical features,
and includes 14 tunes.   There is also an account of Metfessel's
phonophotographic methods (see no. 762) of sound wave analysis.
Again, the reprint leaves the old, 1926 bibliography untouched.   Index of songs.

765.   RAMSEY, Frederic.   Been here and gone.   New Brunswick:
        Rutgers University Press, 1960.   177p.   illus.
          A record of an "imagined" journey through part of the Deep
South (compressed from five field trips through the 1950s), portraying
Negro life, mostly in rural areas, but also including uptown New
Orleans.   Ramsey documents the continuing musical activity and records, often in the people's own words, how music sprang from
their way of life and is an expression of it.   The account includes
the words of several songs, woven into the narrative.   The text is
illustrated with numerous evocative photographs.   Ramsey's sense
of urgency, that an accurate picture of the people and their music
should be established before such survivals of an earlier culture are
finally lost, gives his book an added poignancy.

766.   RAMSEY, Frederic.   Where the music started: a photograph-
        ic essay.   New Brunswick: Rutgers University Institute of
        Jazz Studies, 1970.   34p.   illus.

A catalog of an exhibition devoted to photographs of the people of the Deep South and their music, taken between 1951 and 1960. There are notes and commentary to 31 photographs, 15 of which are reproduced in the booklet. They are divided into 15 sections of musical activity, such as church, work, children's play, etc.

767.   SCARBOROUGH, Dorothy.   On the trail of Negro folk-songs; assisted by Ola Lee Gulledge.   Cambridge, Mass.: Harvard University Press, 1925.   289p.

_____.   _____; foreword by Roger D. Abrahams.   Hatboro: Folklore Associates, 1963.   295p.

Aiming to be at once a study and a collection of Negro folk songs this volume does neither terribly well, though it has its place in the development of interest in black secular musical material. Nine of the ten chapters are devoted to specific types of song (traditional English and Scottish songs and ballads as preserved by Negroes, native Negro ballads, dance-songs, game-songs, lullabies, songs about animals, work songs, railroad songs and blues); in each the songs quoted (there are 108 tunes and many more texts) are the servants of author's own text, which is a not-too-enlightening amalgam of personal experiences while collecting, names of collectors, general descriptive comments and flights of fancy (Miss Scarborough is tirelessly enthusiastic, but never rids herself of a tendency to find all manner of things amusing).   Access to the songs, independent of the comment, is unfortunately severely restricted by the total absence of an index.   A large number of the songs were sent to the author by other amateur collectors, many of whom are quoted as having noted down the item; others, however, are recalling items known in childhood.   For the chapter on the blues the two compilers sought out and interviewed W. C. Handy.

8.   Spirituals and Religious Music
of the 19th Century

a.   Collections

768.   ALLEN, William Francis, et al., eds.   Slave songs of the United States; (edited by) William Francis Allen, Charles Pickard Ware, Lucy McKim Garrison.   New York: Simpson, 1867.   (Repr. New York: Smith, 1929; New York: Books for Libraries Press, 1971).   115p.

This highly significant volume, the first collection of slave songs in book form, was the result of an awakening of interest in this music following contact with ex-slaves during the Civil War. The songs were taken down by the editors (with the addition of some material from other collectors, e.g., T. W. Higginson) from black singers in South Carolina and Virginia.   Of the 136 songs most are religious in theme, but these are interspersed with some secular items.   The tunes are given without accompaniment, and are grouped in three broad geographical areas.   A 38-page introduction by Allen

(1830-1899) describes the difficulties of notating the music and the characteristics of Negro singing, concluding that the music is genuinely original, and commenting on the great musical capacity of the Negroes, "which has been long enough associated with the more cultivated race to have become imbued with the mode and spirit of European music--often, nevertheless, retaining a distinct tinge of their native Africa" (p. viii). He also dwells on the "shout," and the question of dialect.

769. ARMSTRONG, Mrs. M. F., and LUDLOW, Helen W. Hampton and its students, by two of its teachers; with fifty cabin and plantation songs, arranged by Thomas P. Fenner. New York: Putnam, 1874. (Repr. Freeport: Books for Libraries Press, 1971). 255p. illus.

Following the example of the Fisk Jubilee Singers a touring group was organized at the Hampton Institute in 1872 (also to raise money), and enjoyed a considerable success with its rendering of spirituals (as is indicated by the numerous editions and reissues of music director Fenner's "Hampton" collection--see no. 774). The activities of the Hampton Singers are described in the text, which is followed by the first appearance of Fenner's collection. The 50 songs are given with accompaniment for piano. Fenner claims that, with three exceptions, the melodies are published here for the first time. Title index. (A sidelight on the Hampton and the Fisk volumes is provided by folk song collector Lawrence Gellert, who remarked: "The songs were taken down from students who were freshly arrived from folk-lore productive areas. However, with endowments from white corporations and individuals their main revenue ... it is understandable that the songs were carefully chosen and edited..." [sleeve-note to "Negro Songs of Protest," Rounder Records].)

770. BALLANTA, Nicholas George Julius. Saint Helena Island spirituals; recorded and transcribed at Penn Normal, Industrial and Agricultural School, St. Helena Island, Beaufort County, South Carolina. New York: Schirmer, 1925. 93p.

Ballanta (or Ballanta-Taylor, as he is sometimes known) was a native of Sierra Leone who made a special study of connections between American Negro spirituals and West African melodies, and his knowledge of Africa gives an authority to his introduction not common at this time. There are 115 spirituals in his collection, in four-part harmony.

771. BARTON, William E. Old plantation hymns: a collection of hitherto unpublished melodies of the slave and the freedman, with historical and descriptive notes. Boston: Lamson, Wolffe, 1899. (Repr. New York: AMS Press, 1972). 45p.

Another important 19th century source for Negro religious folk songs of before and after the Civil War, Barton's book is a descriptive collection, giving the melodies and texts of 67 songs, with running commentary on song types, themes, images, musical features, spiritual aspects, and circumstances of collection. Barton lived in the South from 1880 to 1887, and took down all the songs himself. He claims that some appear here for the first time, and that many others are given in different versions from those already in print. His book first appeared in three articles in the New England Magazine, Dec. 1898-Feb. 1899. The three sections are: old plantation hymns (27); hymns of slave and freedman (27, some showing effects of war and emancipation); and recent Negro melodies (13, mainly railroad songs with religious content, sung by construction groups).

772. CHAMBERS, H. A. , ed. The treasury of Negro spirituals. New York: Emerson Books, 1963. 125p. illus.
      A modest collection of the words and melodies of 35 traditional spirituals plus seven compositions of the 1940s and 1950s, with piano accompaniment. The foreword is by Marian Anderson.

773. DETT, R. Nathaniel, ed. Religious folk-songs of the Negro, as sung at Hampton Institute. Hampton, Va. : Hampton Institute Press, 1927. 236, 13p.
      The piano music of black composer Robert Nathaniel Dett (1882-1943) is his lasting memorial, but he was also very active as an arranger of spirituals. As music director at Hampton Institute he carried on the work of Thomas P. Fenner, expanding, reorganizing and re-directing the material from the earlier Hampton collections to give it greater impact. His approach is more aggressive, less diffident; the collection becomes a weapon in a crusade for recognition, and for the restoration of the songs among black people. In his substantial introduction he makes his own position on the origin of the spirituals clear when he says they "express moods born of (the Negro's) own peculiar experience and ... are quite original with him" (p. xiii). The 1909 Hampton collection is increased by 23 extra songs, making a total of 165. They are arranged in 26 categories relating to Christian life (Admonition, Penitence, Tribulation, etc.). Arrangements are for unaccompanied chorus, save for some from Dett's own collection that are given unharmonized. In 1936 a four-volume anthology was published under the (slightly unfortunate!) title of The Dett Collection of Negro spirituals (Chicago: Hall & McCreary, 1936).

774. FENNER, Thomas P. , ed. Cabin and plantation songs as sung by the Hampton students; arranged by Thomas P. Fenner and Frederic G. Rathbun ... Enlarged ed. New York: Putnam, 1891. 127p.
      _____ .   ; arranged by Thomas P. Fenner, Frederic G. Rathbun and Miss Bessie Cleaveland ... 3rd ed. , enlarged by the addition of forty-four songs ... New York: Putnam, 1901. 166p.
      _____ . Religious folk songs of the Negro as sung on the plantations; arranged by the musical directors of The Hampton Normal and Agricultural Institute from the original edition of Thomas P. Fenner. (New ed.) Hampton, Va. : Hampton Institute Press, 1909. 178p.
      These successive editions of Fenner's collection of spirituals

build on and re-arrange his material in Armstrong and Ludlow (no. 769), gradually increasing the number of songs included from the 50 in the 1874 edition to 142 in the 1909 version. Index of titles.

775.   GRISSOM, Mary Allen, ed. The Negro sings a new heaven.
         Chapel Hill: University of North Carolina Press, 1930.
         (Repr. New York: Dover Publications, 1969). 101p.
The words and melodies of 45 spirituals are included in this collection, which contains traditional and relatively new songs in transcriptions as close as possible to the original. They were collected in churches near Louisville and in Adair Co. , Kentucky, and are arranged in six groups: death, heaven, Bible stories, songs of exhortation, of service and experience, shouting songs and songs of triumph.

776.   HALLOWELL, Emily, comp. Calhoun plantation songs; collected and edited by Emily Hallowell. Boston: C. W. Thompson, 1901. 61p.
         _____. _____. 2nd ed. Boston: C. W. Thompson,
         1907. 74p.
The second edition gives 69 spirituals in four-part harmony, and incorporates the songs included in a 1905 supplement. In her preface the compiler states, "the songs in this volume are those sung by the students at the Calhoun Colored School and are all well known throughout the Black Belt of Alabama. I have tried to write them just as they are sung, retaining all the peculiarities of rhythm, melody, harmony and text. . . . "

777.   JOHNSON, James Weldon, ed. The book of American Negro spirituals; edited with an introduction by James Weldon Johnson; musical arrangements by J. Rosamond Johnson; additional numbers by Lawrence Brown. New York: Viking Press, 1925. 187p.
         _____. The second book of Negro spirituals ... New
         York: Viking Press, 1926. 189p.
         _____. The books of American Negro spirituals, including The book of American Negro spirituals and The second book of Negro spirituals ... New York: Viking Press, 1940. (Repr. 1969). 2v. in 1.
This was and remains the outstanding collection of Negro spirituals for performance, made so not only by the generous number of items (120, in arrangements for voice and piano) but by the distinguished hands and mind that compiled it. In the first of his two valuable prefaces James Weldon Johnson claims the spirituals are a purely Negro creation. He discusses their origin (describing their genesis as a "miracle" which it is easier to believe "than some of the explanations of it that are offered"--p. 13), examines their characteristic form, rhythm and harmony, and analyzes some aspects of the poetry. In the second preface he explores some more general questions, the variety of the spirituals, their role and their influence. (For an interesting account of Johnson's approach, see Wendell P. Whalum, "James Weldon Johnson's Theories of Performance Practices of Afro-American Folksong," Phylon, 32/4, 1971.)

778. KENNEDY, R. Emmet. Mellows: a chronicle of unknown
singers; decorations by Simmons Persons. New York:
Boni, 1925. 183p.

A "mellow," or melody, is used by the Southern Louisiana
Negroes who are the subject of this book to denote a devotional song.
Kennedy, a Southerner from New Orleans, makes his deep affection
for the region and his familiarity with its black population clear in
his preamble, in which he dwells also on the various qualities of
the spiritual. The main part of the text takes the form of a collection of harmonized spirituals. The amount of music included is
fairly small--27 harmonized songs (23 spirituals and four folk songs)
plus 21 sketches and fragments of spirituals, street cries and work
songs. The book's raison d'être lies in its composite picture of
Negro life and music in Louisiana at the turn of the century; this
emerges from the balance of songs and textual description. In More
Mellows (no. 779) Kennedy says "the descriptive matter accompanying these songs is in no way intended as an explanatory analysis; it
is nothing more than a sincere endeavour to give a simple picture
of the truth and beauty of a racial life which has not yet completely
'suffered a sea-change' ..." (p. 60). This "simple picture" is
made up of evocative portraits of the circumstances in which Kennedy
heard and noted each song, of the singer, and of the singer's environment. To these, and to his recollection of childhood episodes
involving black singers in and around New Orleans, Kennedy responds
emotionally, and invites the reader to share this response. Among
the songs are; "Rock Mount Sinai," "Louisiana Valley," and "Go
down, Death."

779. KENNEDY, R. Emmet. More mellows. New York: Dodd,
Mead, 1931. 178p.

In his follow-up to no. 778 Kennedy includes less music and
more description and discussion. Twelve harmonized spirituals and
two harmonized folk songs only are included, with quotations from
seven unharmonized spirituals, and the texts of 16 "ballets" (a kind
of hymn). The lengthy introduction includes further discussion of
the role of song in Southern Negro life, detailed description of a
typical Negro church service, and accounts of the compiler's experiences. The songs include "Wasn't that Hard Trials" and "Li'l Boy
named David."

780. McILHENNY, E. A., comp. Befo' de war spirituals: words
and melodies collected by E. A. McIlhenny. Boston:
Christopher, 1933. 255p.

The compiler's principal source for the 120 songs in this collection were two elderly black ladies, Becky Ilsey and Alberta Bradford, who had grown up on or near his family's sugar plantation in
southern Louisiana. The songs are presented in four-part harmony
by Henri Wehrmann, who "has written the notes exactly as they were
sung or as near exact as the harmonic or rhythmic tones of the Negro voice can be represented by written notes." The words are
given in dialect. In a lengthy introduction the compiler describes
plantation life before the Civil War, his own early recollections of
Negro singing after the war, and the collecting of his material. A

degree of condescension unfortunately mars this interesting first-hand account.

781.　WORK, John W., ed.　American Negro songs and spirituals:
　　　　a comprehensive collection of 230 folk songs, religious and
　　　　secular; with a foreword.　New York: Howell, Soskin,
　　　　1940.　(Repr. New York: Bonanza Books, n. d.).　256p.
　　　　bibliog.

Most of the songs in this collection are spirituals and are
given in harmony.　There are also some secular folk songs, for
which melodies and words alone are given.　Five introductory chapters explore the question of origins, and look in turn at spirituals,
blues, work songs and social and miscellaneous songs.　Work's view
of black religious folk song is that it is a re-assembling, based on
the African heritage, of white gospel song, and not at all a simple
imitation.　(The editor is the son of the author of no. 798.)

b.　Jubilee Singers

782.　MARSH, J. B. T.　The story of the Jubilee Singers, with
　　　　their songs.　London: Hodder and Stoughton, 1875.　227p.
　　　　illus.
　　　　　　　　.　　　　　　　.　Rev. ed.　Boston: Houghton Mifflin,
　　　　1880.　248p.　illus.
　　　　　　　.　The story of the Jubilee Singers, including their
　　　　songs; with supplement, containing an account of their six
　　　　years' tour around the world, and many new songs, by
　　　　F. J. Loudin.　Cleveland: Cleveland Printing & Publish-
　　　　ing Co., 1892; London: Hodder & Stoughton, 1898.　311p.
　　　　illus.

Marsh's account of the Jubilee Singers is in part an abridgment and re-writing (in more concise and readable form) of Pike's
two volumes.　It describes the germination of the idea of a fund-
raising singing group, the first American tour, the many encounters
with prejudice, and the second, triumphant campaign; the successful
visits to Europe (marked by an apparent absence of racial antagon-
ism) are included also.　The revised edition extends the story to
cover the eight-month visit to Germany in 1877, and gives fuller
personal histories of the singers.　The supplement to the 1892 version (by the black manager of the company) describes the long tour
of 1884-1890.　Each successive edition (the main ones only are
given above) included a larger number of spirituals.　The 1892 version gives 139, in four-part harmony.

783.　PIKE, Gustavus D.　The Jubilee Singers and their campaign
　　　　for twenty thousand dollars.　Boston: Lee and Shepard,
　　　　1873; London: Hodder and Stoughton, 1874.　(Repr. New
　　　　York: AMS Press, 1974).　219p.　illus.

We owe much of our familiarity with Negro spirituals to the
touring groups of Negro singers, of whom the Jubilee Singers of
Fisk University were the first and the most famous.　This group
(originally nine, all but one freed slaves), with their white teacher

George L. White, embarked on a tour in 1871 to raise money for
Fisk, and achieved not only their financial target, but also considerable renown.   Rev. Pike, a secretary in Connecticut of the American Missionary Association (founders of Fisk), who joined the campaign around December, 1871 as concert manager, gives, in his
pious, discursive way, a detailed account of this first tour (October
1871-April 1872), from early discouragements to eventual success,
with background information on Fisk, the genesis of the group, personal histories of the singers.   The presentation, as a series of
addresses, detracts from the impact somewhat.   Sixty-one Jubilee
songs are included in four-part harmony, compiled by Theo F.
Seward (see no. 784).   A further book by Pike, The Singing Campaign for Ten Thousand Pounds; or, The Jubilee Singers in Great
Britain; with an appendix containing Slave songs, compiled and arranged by Theodore F. Seward, (London: Hodder & Stoughton, 1874;
New York: American Missionary Association, 1875) describes the
triumphant British tour of 1873-1874, with 71 songs.

784.   (SEWARD, Theodore F.), comp.   Jubilee songs: as sung by
        the Jubilee Singers, of Fisk University, (Nashville, Tenn.)
        under the auspices of the American Missionary Association.
        New York: Biglow & Main, 1872.   28p.
        During the first national tour of the Jubilee Singers in 1871-2
Seward (1835-1902), who was identified with the educational ideas
and practices of Lowell Mason, compiled this modest collection of
24 songs, distributing the first copies for 24¢ at the New York Steinway Hall concert in March, 1872.   In his preface he assures the
public that the printed versions of the songs are authentic, having
been "taken down from the singing of the band, during repeated interviews held for the purpose."   The collection, in four-part harmony, marks the first appearance in print of such world-famous
spirituals as "Swing Low, Sweet Chariot," and "Steal Away."   The
subsequent historical volumes by Pike and Marsh (nos. 782 & 783)
contain collections of Jubilee songs which are expanded versions of
Seward's initial collection (up to 139 songs in Marsh-Loudin), and
often include part of his preface.   The collection itself made another
appearance in 1872, in 64 pages, and again, further expanded, in
1884, when compilation is credited to Seward and to George L.
White, whose inspiration and leadership lay behind the Singers' success.

c.   Studies and Reference Works

785.   CLEVELAND PUBLIC LIBRARY.   Index to Negro spirituals.
        Cleveland: Cleveland Public Library, 1937.   149p.
        This useful little volume is a great help in locating a printed
source for the words and music of particular spirituals.   A title index, listing alphabetically the individual spirituals contained in 30
published collections, refers the reader to the appropriate collection,
and also provides a system of cross references for variants and for
spirituals with similar titles.   The collections analyzed are listed
before the main index.

786.   CONE, James H. The spirituals and the blues: an interpretation. New York: Seabury Press, 1972. 152p. bibliog. notes.

This is a provocative study by a black theologian and critic of the theological and sociological implications of the spirituals and blues ("secular spirituals"), in which he quotes many textual examples to demonstrate his case that these black forms of expression can be totally understood as a response to, and a battle to resist, white oppression. Whatever validity his various arguments have, he ruins his case in several ways. Firstly, he begins by stating his conviction that "it is not possible to render an authentic interpretation of black music without having shared and participated in the experience that created it. Black music must be lived before it can be understood" (p. 4), a curiously misjudged statement that, for instance, would invalidate all attempts to comprehend Biblical psalms. Secondly, he gives no evidence of having approached his source material--the texts of spirituals and blues--with any degree of impartiality; indeed, there seems no doubt that he selects his examples to suit his preconceived ideas. Thirdly, he takes no account of the fact that these are texts to be sung. This is particularly noticeable in his chapter on blues, in which his discussion of features of blues texts abounds in such massive generalizations as: "the blues tell us about a people who refused to accept the absurbity of white society" (p. 117)--which one might believe if only there was any evidence that he realized these were songs sung by mendicant street-corner singers, or tent-show entertainers, whose recorded songs we possess because commercial enterprise made money out of them, and sought to maintain those profits through changing fashions. Fourthly, he is given to some extraordinary racial polemicism; e.g., "White people obviously cannot understand the love that black people have for each other.... Only those who have been hurt can appreciate the warmth of love that proceeds when people touch, feel and embrace each other" (p. 132). Such a total collapse of the critical faculties and of the ability to understand something of the web of human relationships among and between races puts all his saner pronouncements in doubt.

787.   DIXON, Christa. Wesen und Wandel geistlicher Volkslieder: Negro spirituals. Wuppertal: Jugenddienst-Verlag, 1967. 333p. bibliog.

Originally a dissertation, this is a thorough study of the textual content of spirituals, in particular of the relationship of the spirituals to the Bible. Following a preliminary discussion of origins, forms and style the author presents a detailed exploration of Negro adaptation and appropriation of biblical themes, images and stylistic features. The margins of this section are filled with references to the relevant places in the second part of the book, which consists of texts of several hundred spirituals (in English), arranged in 57 groups corresponding to Old and New Testament stories and parables (e.g., Adam and Eve, Jacob's ladder, a house built on a rock, Jesus' trial and crucifixion). In the margins here are references to the appropriate Biblical passage. A bibliography of references lists 184 books and 43 articles, and there are two indexes: of books of the Bible (giving chapter, verse and relevant spiritual), and of first lines of the spirituals themselves.

788.   DU BOIS, W. E. Burghardt. The souls of black folk: es-
        says and sketches. Chicago: McClurg, 1903; London:
        Constable, 1905. (Repr. New York: Johnson, 1968).
        264p.
        This justly famous collection of pieces by the outstanding
black leader (1868-1963), evoking the spirit of Negro life and culture,
includes as its final chapter an eloquent description of the Negro
spiritual, "Of the Sorrow Songs." The depth of his personal feeling
for the songs is clear but it is, above all, for their significance as
a Negro gift to an "ill-harmonized and unmelodious land" that he
values them, as the articulate message of a despised people to
the world, telling of their sorrow, and also of their faith in ultimate
justice. Several texts and tunes are quoted, including one described
as having been sung by his great-great grandmother. A line of mu-
sic--"some echo of haunting melody from the only American music
which welled up from black souls in the dark past"--is placed at
the head of each of the book's chapters. (In addition to the many
editions of this work that have been published, the chapter on the
sorrow songs appears in Katz, no. 792; Southern, no. 698; and Patterson, no. 692.)

789.   FISHER, Miles Mark. Negro slave songs in the United
        States; with a foreword by Ray Allen Billington. Ithaca:
        Cornell University Press; New York: Citadel Press, 1963.
        (Repr. New York: Russell & Russell, 1969). 223p. bib-
        liog.
        This study seeks to interpret the spirituals as historical docu-
ments, in which the slaves recorded the events they lived through
and their reactions to them. In attempting in this way to use the
spirituals to depict the slave life, Fisher pointed out that there were
other channels of investigation open, besides those of origins, musical features and textual analysis. Following an introduction in
which he outlines the role music played in African society as a recitation of the African's history, and the existence of this function in
the New World the author examines a number of songs, interprets
them historically, and discusses their significance. The songs are
grouped in a chronological sequence from 1740-1867, and usually
center on a particular theme (return to Africa, secret meetings,
etc.). Critical opinion of Fisher's approach has varied, but many
would agree with Lawrence W. Levine in his article, "Slave Songs
and Slave Consciousness" (in T. K. Hareven, Anonymous Americans,
Englewood Cliffs, Prentice-Hall, 1971): "Fisher's rich insights are
too often marred by his rather loose scholarly standards" (p. 100).

790.   FRAZIER, Thomas R., ed. The underside of American his-
        tory: other readings. Vol. 1. To 1877. New York:
        Harcourt, Brace, Jovanovich, 1971. 307p. bibliog.
        A selection of essays on some neglected aspects of American
history, including an excellent survey by Sterling Stuckey: "Through
the Prism of Folklore: the Black Ethos in Slavery," reprinted from
the Massachusetts Review, 9, 1968. In this the author examines the
Negro spirituals for insights into the life-style of the slaves, through
which, in his view, they were able to avoid total dehumanization.

Accepting the premise that the slaves borrowed many songs and greatly improved many others, he uses examples of the words of the songs and contemporary accounts to illustrate his claim that the slaves were aware that, in the aesthetic realm at any rate, they were superior.

791.   HIGGINSON, Thomas Wentworth. Army life in a black regiment. Boston: Fields, Osgood, 1870. (Repr. Williamstown: Corner House Publishers, 1971). 296p.
_____. _____. New ed., with notes ... Boston: Houghton Mifflin, 1900. 413p. illus.
Unitarian minister, abolitionist, friend of the poet Emily Dickinson, Higginson (1823-1911) commanded the First South Carolina Volunteers--a regiment of former slaves--in the Civil War, an experience which afforded him the opportunity to study at first hand the songs of the slaves; as he put it, to "gather on their own soil these strange plants, which I had before seen as in museums alone" (p. 197). An article on Negro spirituals appeared in The Atlantic Monthly, XIX, June, 1867, and was subsequently included in Higginson's account of his wartime experiences as Chapter 9. It was-- and remains--by far the most detailed and most revealing of the first-hand accounts of the music of the slaves. Higginson includes the words of 36 songs, with comments and explanatory notes, and descriptions of how the songs were sung. In conclusion he remarks: "These songs are but the vocal expression of the simplicity of their faith and the sublimity of their long resignation" (p. 222). (The chapter is reproduced in Jackson, no. 757; Katz, no. 792; and Southern, no. 698.)

792.   KATZ, Bernard, ed. The social implications of early Negro music in the United States; with over 150 of the songs, many of them with their music. New York: Arno Press, 1969. 146p. illus., bibliog.
A convenient anthology of reprinted articles and prefaces, drawn from the 19th century in the main. Included are the prefaces to their collections of W. F. Allen, James Weldon Johnson, R. Nathaniel Dett, and pieces by W. E. B. Du Bois, T. W. Higginson, John Lovell, William E. Barton, G. W. Cable and Lucy McKim Garrison. The major subject is religious folk music--spirituals, camp meeting melodies and plantation hymns. Each piece is prefaced by a short editorial note, and there is an introduction.

793.   LEHMANN, Theo. Negro Spirituals: Geschichte und Theologie. Berlin: Eckhart, 1965. 414p. bibliog.
A comprehensive and scholarly study of the background, historical development and theological aspects of the Negro spiritual. The author traces the development and nature of slavery in America and the significant results of the Negro's encounter with Christianity, which released the emotions slavery had concealed and gave the sense of common feeling which led to the formation of the all-black churches. In examining the evolution of the spiritual itself Lehmann explores its relationship with white gospel song, delves deeply into the question of originality in the Negro creation (emphasizing the im-

portance of cultural intermingling), and assesses the literary aspects of the genre. In Part 2 he approaches the spiritual as an expression of religious belief and examines it eschatologically. A concluding section discusses its unity and its relation to jazz and blues. Name and subject indexes.

794. LOVELL, John. Black song: the forge and the flame; the story of how the Afro-American spiritual was hammered out. New York: Macmillan, 1972. 686p. illus., bibliog.
Judged by size alone this historical and critical study, the result of a lifelong fascination with the subject, promises much, but turns out to be a very cumbersome volume which, despite many insights, does not generally fulfill that promise. It is in three parts. In the first Lovell presents a lengthy account of the origin of the spiritual (the "forge"), in the course of which he assesses the extent of the transfer from Africa, discusses the role of religion, dismisses the claims of G. P. Jackson and others that the white spiritual was a primary influence in the genesis of the black genre, and ardently champions the view that the Afro-American spiritual is "an independent folk song, born of the union of African tradition and American socioreligious elements," whose creators were religious "in the broad sense of the African," using Christianity because it was the nearest available system within which to express their "concepts of freedom, justice, right and aspiration" (p. 111). The second part establishes that the spiritual is a folk song, before moving on (in the most rewarding part of the book) to identify and analyze themes, objectives and devices, interpreting the spiritual as philosophy and as literature. Part 3, the spiritual as "world phenomenon" (the "flame"), charts the worldwide reception of the spiritual, its influence and its continued popularity.

There is much of interest in the book's innumerable nooks and crannies, but as a whole it contains many disappointments. Of these one might mention the absence of detailed musical discussion (an unfortunate omission, if the writer hopes to unseat G. P. Jackson), the lack of a sense of chronology in the history of Afro-America, a regrettable tendency to talk dismissively of opinions running counter to the writer's own, and an associated weakness for generalization about large subjects (especially Protestantism). To these should be added a reservation about Lovell's handling of his source material. It is soon apparent that, having read extensively, he is determined that every word that accords with his opinions should be made to work for him. The result is that many passages become strings of references (without footnotes--sources are listed in a very awkward bibliography at the back) without the assimilation one expects. Many of the terms used ("evidence," "detectives," "investigation") suggest a court of law, and clearly Lovell views his authorities as an attorney does his witnesses, looking to the case to be proved by sheer weight of numbers. It is, however, doubtful if the spiritual's obscure history is susceptible to the same methods of exposure as acts of felony. In works of critical analysis one expects greater discrimination in the use of source material; one anticipates that such material will have been subjected to the mill of critical scrutiny and become the grist to feed the author's insights. In

Lovell's case this is not so. He is at his best when, free from the crippling impedimenta of his reading, he sets off on an investigative trail all his own.

795. MAYS, Benjamin E. The Negro's God as reflected in his literature. Boston: Chapman & Grimes, 1938. (Repr. New York: Negro Universities Press, 1969). 269p. illus., bibliog.

Chapter 2 of this study, "Ideas of God in the Literature of the Negro Masses," includes a consideration of spirituals in which Mays summarizes their theological ideas, which he describes as adhering to the "traditional, compensatory pattern" (p. 23).

796. SOCIETY FOR THE PRESERVATION OF SPIRITUALS. The Carolina low-country, by Augustine T. Smythe ... (et al.) New York: Macmillan, 1932. 326p. illus. (some col.)

The all-white Society was formed in Charleston in the 1920s to collect and perform spirituals. The published collection they intended was changed into a book expressing "the feelings of members of the Society, and of all others of similar heritage, towards the songs themselves, and the black people who sing them, and towards the region in which they live, its natural aspects, its history...." In the event, the number of songs included was fairly small--48 texts (in dialect) and melodies--and most of the book was devoted to a portrait of the low-country in prose and verse (including a chapter, "The Negro in the Low-Country" by DuBose Heyward). One chapter, by Robert W. Gordon, is devoted specifically to the spiritual. This is a concise account of spirituals in Negro life, their origins, the influences upon them, the extent of borrowing and assimilation both in structure and in subject matter, aspects of the poetry and music, and rhythmic characteristics (the complexity and variety of which are one of the spiritual's outstanding features). The book is illustrated with color plates of paintings, and with pen and ink drawings and etchings.

797. THURMAN, Howard. Deep river: an interpretation of Negro spirituals. Mills College, Ca.: Eucalyptus Press, 1945. 39p.
        . Deep river: reflections on the religious insight of certain of the Negro spirituals. New York: Harper, 1955. (Repr. Port Washington: Kennikat Press, 1969). 93p. illus.

This illuminating little book looks first at the sources of religious inspiration in the texts of the spirituals--the Bible, Nature, and religious experience--and examines six spirituals: "The Blind Man," "Heaven, Heaven!," "Balm in Gilead," "Deep River," "Jacob's Ladder," and "Wade in the Water, Children," looking at the texts, the treatment of the theme and its significance.

798. WORK, John Wesley. Folk song of the American Negro. Nashville: Press of Fisk University, 1915. (Repr. New York: Negro Universities Press, 1969). 131p. illus.

A study, by a Fisk University professor, of the development

and characteristic features of the Negro's spiritual folk songs. Tracing the transition from Africa to the New World, Work declares, "the conclusion is irresistible that the music which expresses the characteristic of the Negro's soul alone, was produced by the Negro alone" (p. 32). He then describes the musical expression of these characteristics and groups the songs in eleven categories, with a selection of texts. He also examines the original inspiration and subsequent evolution of a number of songs, and discusses agencies of preservation and development. The final chapters describe the original tour of the Jubilee Singers and the significance of the spirituals for the Negro. Each chapter concludes with the words and music (with harmony) of a spiritual (nine in all).

9. Ragtime

799. BLESH, Rudi, and JANIS, Harriet. They all played ragtime: the true story of an American music. New York: Knopf, 1950; London: Sidgwick & Jackson, 1958. 338p. illus., bibliog., discog.

_____. _____. Rev. ed. New York: Grove Press, 1959. 345p. illus., bibliog., discog.

_____. _____. Rev., and with new additional material, including complete scores to 13 never before published ragtime compositions. New York: Oak Publications, 1966. 347p. illus., bibliog., discog.

_____. _____. (4th ed.). New York: Oak Publications, 1971. 347p. illus., bibliog., discog.
    The standard history of ragtime, thoroughly researched and readable, and sympathetic in its treatment. The authors describe the rise, development and decline of the idiom through the lives, careers and compositions of its exponents, especially Scott Joplin, the dominating figure in the book. The characteristics of the music and its lines of evolution are outlined, but the authors' main interest lies in providing a rich source of information on the people involved. There is a chronology, and a list of compositions with publishers, arranged in sections under composer and titles. There are also select lists of records, of cylinders and piano rolls. Index.

800. GAMMOND, Peter. Scott Joplin and the ragtime era. London: Angus & Robertson; London: Sphere Books; New York: St. Martin's Press, 1975. 223p. illus., bibliog., discog.
    Finding that existing studies of ragtime, for all their merits, make no concessions to the beginner, British critic Peter Gammond contributes a "fairly straightforward, unbiased account" for popular consumption, one not too cluttered by facts and names, but which fills in the background for the interested amateur. The central thread is provided by the life of Scott Joplin, the account of which is interspersed with various kinds of background and foreground material, from the popular music of his youth to the other leading

"classic" ragtime composers, so that his work and his achievement are seen in context. A chapter specifically of Joplin's music takes each piece in turn in chronological sequence, commenting on salient musical features. In the appendices are bibliographies of books, and of published editions and anthologies, and an extensive list of ragtime on LP (reissues of piano rolls and early discs, plus "revivals").

801.   JASEN, David A. Recorded ragtime, 1897-1958. Hamden: Archon Books, 1973. 155p. bibliog.
A discography of commercial 78rpm recordings from the beginning of ragtime recording to the last of the 78rpm issues. All reissues and dubs are excluded, and the compiler lists only those pieces meeting his definition of ragtime (as given in his introduction): "the syncopation of an entire melodic strain combined with a continuously even rhythm." Also in his introduction, he identifies eight styles (cakewalks, folk rags, St. Louis rags, Tin Pan Alley rags, Midwestern rags, Jelly Roll rags, Stride rags, and novelty rags) and briefly chronicles ragtime's recording history. The main part of the discography is an alphabetical title listing, in which each title is followed by the composer's name, with a list of performers, the record company and number, and the date of recording (or, sometimes, of release). There is also a composer listing (giving dates of birth and death, and an alphabetical table of compositions, with copyright dates) and a performers index.

802.   JOPLIN, Scott. The collected works; edited by Vera Brodsky Lawrence; editorial consultant Richard Jackson. New York: New York Public Library, 1971. 2v. illus.
Of the various enterprises resulting from the belated discovery, in the 1970s, that Scott Joplin (1868-1917), the greatest exponent of ragtime, deserves to rank among America's musical immortals, none is more likely to assure of him permanent interest and respect than this fine edition. For our purposes it contains an extensive (about 17,000 words) biographical and interpretative essay by Rudi Blesh--printed in both volumes--and a historical and critical note on Joplin's opera "Treemonisha" by Carman Moore.

803.   SCHAFER, William J., and RIEDEL, Johannes. The art of ragtime; form and meaning of an original black American art; with assistance from Michael Polad and Richard Thompson. Baton Rouge: Louisiana State University Press, 1973. 249p. illus., bibliog.
An important historical and musicological analysis that sets out to study the form and structure of piano ragtime, its "aesthetic and musical contribution to black and white musical culture," and to encourage study and performance. The authors propose a stylistic definition of ragtime as an art form born out of an impulse to create music for dancing, that took black folk and white minstrel materials and organized them in patterns based on black folk dance and white parlor dance, with a basic two-step rhythm. The result possessed the expressive qualities of a decorous music and some of the showmanship of minstrelsy. The music that arose in a context of racism in the prevailing entertainment grew to have deep effects on

the music industry, on the image of the black composer, and on contacts between blacks and whites, and to create legions of hostile and friendly critics (some of whom are quoted). Structural features of classic ragtime, and the characteristics of the ragtime of three outstanding exponents (Joplin, Scott and Lamb) are analyzed, with music examples. Considerations of ragtime as a popular song vehicle (particularly of so-called "Indian intermezzos") and of ragtime ensemble music (brass bands, country string bands, hokum bands, jazz bands) are followed by an essay on how ragtime should be played. There are appendices on cover illustrations, on distinctions between ragtime and jazz piano styles, and on Joplin's opera "Treemonisha." The bibliography lists books, music collections, articles and liner notes, and there is an index.

804.   WALKER, Edward S., and WALKER, Steven, eds. English ragtime: a discography. Mastin Moor, Derbyshire: Walker, 1971. unpaged. illus.
        Covering the period from 1898 to 1920 approximately, this listing of recorded performances of ragtime in England bears witness to the wave of enthusiasm which ragtime generated, and which was led principally, for countries like England, by New York publishers and touring bands. Arrangement is alphabetical by artists with full discographical information. American ragtime musicians who recorded in England are included. No supplementary indexes.

10.   Blues

a.   Reference Works

805.   BOGAERT, Karel. Blues lexicon: blues, cajun, boogie woogie, gospel. Antwerp: Standaard Uitgeverij, (1972). 480p. illus., bibliog., discogs.
        A most useful biographical dictionary, in Flemish, of blues and related fields. Each entry gives dates, summary of career, and short LP discography. There are also entries for a selection of subjects (styles, places). Information was obtained by personal interview and correspondence with artists and record companies. John Godrich, in his English introduction, remarks on the need for an English translation. Index.

806.   DIXON, R. M. W., and GODRICH, John, eds. Blues and gospel records 1902-1942. Kenton, Middx.: Steve Lane, 1964. 765p.
        GODRICH, John, and DIXON, R. M. W., eds.   .
        Rev. ed. London: Storyville Publications, 1969. 912p.
        This invaluable compilation attempts to list "every distinctively Negroid folk music record" made up to the end of 1942 (breaking off at the same point in time as Rust, no. 930), excluding music deriving from and copying white styles. The introduction includes lists of field trips made by companies putting out race labels, and some

information on the companies themselves. The main section is an
alphabetical listing by artists and groups of artists. Their records
are listed chronologically with full details of personnel and instrumentation, date, place, matrix, take and issue number. Microgroove reissues are indicated, and there is a microgroove appendix.
There is a good network of cross references, and an index of ac-
companists. Notes on the identity of the artist, or explaining the
exclusion of certain types of recording by an artist, etc. are included immediately following the artist's name. Additions and corrections have appeared regularly in Storyville magazine since 1969.

807. FERRIS, William R. Mississippi black folklore: a research
bibliography. Hattiesburg: University and College Press
of Mississippi, 1971. 61p. illus.
A useful compilation for the student of rural black culture,
particularly the blues, in Mississippi. The listing is divided into
general, social and historical background, Negro life in Mississippi,
the blues, folk songs (including collections), prose narrative, literature and field techniques. There are no annotations. The discography section lists microgroove issues in four categories, with label
names and catalog numbers: Library of Congress, surveys containing traditional singers, traditional blues singers, and urban blues
and pop singers. A separate section is devoted to records by gospel
singers, and there is also a film list.

808. LEADBITTER, Mike, and SLAVEN, Neil, eds. Blues records, January 1943-December 1966. London: Hanover
Books, 1968; New York: Oak Publications, 1969. 381p.
This discography continues the Godrich and Dixon compilation
(no. 806), including only blues recordings made after 1942 and subsequent reissues of these recordings (i. e., omitting gospel music).
The main alphabetical sequence of artists and their recordings includes some biographical information. Records are listed chronologically, with personnel and instrumentation, all known matrix numbers, locations and dates of recordings, and release numbers. Alternative names and joint performances are cross-referenced, but
there are no supplementary indexes. A revised and expanded edition is being prepared by Neil Slaven, following Mike Leadbitter's
untimely death in 1974.

809. MAHONY, Dan. The Columbia 13/14000-D series: a numerical listing. Stanhope, N. J.: Walter C. Allen, 1961.
(Record Handbook No. 1) 80p. illus.
_____. _____. 2nd ed. Stanhope, N. J.: Walter C.
Allen, 1966. (...) 80p. illus.
A listing of the race label which spanned almost ten years
(September 1923-April 1933) and included 689 numbers. The series
comprised predominately blues and vaudeville songs (including a substantial number of female artists), but also instrumental groups, and
popular and religious items. Arrangement is under catalog number,
with information on release and supplement date, and figures for the
manufacturing order, artist credits with instrument and accompaniment, matrix and take numbers, recording location and date, tune

title, composer credit, tempo, publisher and copyright dates. Four plates illustrate the label used. There are indexes of tune titles, primary and supporting artists.

810. STEENSON, Martin, comp. Blues Unlimited 1-50: an index. London: the author, 1971. 76p.

The British magazine Blues Unlimited, begun in May 1963, was the first regular English-language blues journal, and has been consistently diligent in the unearthing of biographical information in particular. This index covers 1963-1968, and is useful above all in helping to locate information on individuals. (Other index entries are a little unsystematic, and consist mainly of record and book titles. No generic subjects are indexed.) References are to issue and page numbers (without any table to convert these to dates), and cover feature articles, discographies, obituaries, record and book reviews.

811. VREEDE, Max E. Paramount 12000/13000 series. London: Storyville Publications, 1971. unpaged. illus.

A long-researched and finely produced discography, listing in Paramount catalog number order the blues and jazz records that appeared on the famous race label in the 1920s and 1930s. Information given includes titles, composer credits, principal and secondary artist credits, performance description (e.g., vocal blues), label, wax and take numbers. There are notes on the label types, wax colors, take combinations, month of release, and date of first advertisement. All nine label types are illustrated in color, and almost every page of the listing is accompanied on the opposite page by a reproduction of an advertisement for a new Paramount release, reproduced from the Chicago Defender. There is also an artist and title index.

b. Mainly Historical

812. BEALE STREET, U.S.A.: where the blues began. Bexhill-on-Sea: Blues Unlimited, n.d. 12 unnumbered pages. illus., bibliog.

A reissue of a booklet produced by the City of Memphis Housing Authority. It gives an accurate picture of Beale Street at the turn of the century, confining itself in the main to the buildings and their occupiers.

813. DIXON, Robert M. W. and GODRICH, John. Recording the blues. London: Studio Vista, 1970. 109p. illus., bibliog.

An account of the recording of blues and gospel singers in the various so-called race series, 1920-1945, complementing the same authors' discography (no. 806). They begin by describing the beginnings of race records, and continue with the classic singers, 1923-26; the peak period for recording, 1926-1930; the decline, 1931-34; the success of urban blues recordings, 1934-40; and the last years for the race labels, 1941-45. In these sections the methods

of discovering singers, recording them, and marketing the records
are all examined. The illustrations consist mainly of record labels,
and advertisements in company catalogs. There is also a graph
showing the number of issues per year, 1919-42, with significant
events marked in, and an index.

814. GROOM, Bob. The blues revival. London: Studio Vista,
     1971. 112p. illus., bibliog.
     An introduction to the growth of white interest in the blues,
and the results of this increase in popularity. The author describes
the European visits of Leadbelly and Big Bill Broonzy, and examines
the influence of blues on the popular music of the 1950s, and the
surge of interest when this influence was discovered. The field
trips, the reissues, the growth of blues research and literature, especially in journals, the blues festivals--all these are described and
illustrated.

815. JOHNSON, Charles S. Shadow of the plantation. Chicago:
     University of Chicago Press, 1934. 214p. illus.
     This sociological and cultural study of the life of a rural
black community in Macon, Georgia after the end of slavery, while
it contains only a handful of references to music, is important for
an understanding of the early history of the blues. Johnson examines
the family and economic life, with attention to education, religion,
leisure, and concludes that it was the plantation system, rather than
slavery itself, which shaped black habits, and that any cultural back-
wardness can be blamed on social relations that evolved under the
system. Plantation communities are likely to be areas of cultural
isolation.

816. LEE, George W. Beale Street: where the blues began;
     foreword by W. C. Handy. New York: Ballou, 1934.
     (Repr. College Park: McGrath, 1969). 296p. illus.
     This history of the "Main Street of Negro America," written
by a black army lieutenant, describes many of the incidents, personalities and activities, from respectable business to underworld
night-life, that were connected with the Memphis Street from the
1860s to the 1930s. Chapters 5 and 6, on the dope and gambling
rings and the saloons, introduce the world where the music was
made. Chapter 8 describes the bands and their leaders from the
end of the Civil War, and Chapter 9 is devoted to W. C. Handy,
and includes information on the sources of some of his songs.

817. OLIVER, Paul. Savannah syncopators: African retentions in
     the blues. London: Studio Vista, 1970. 112p. illus.,
     bibliog. notes, discog.
     An outline of the problems involved in questions of the trans-
mission of the African musical tradition to America, with suggestions
for further research. The author describes the various conceptions
and misconceptions of jazz historians, and relates these to the blues.
Examining the characteristics of West African music and musical
instruments, particularly the singing style of the Savannah regions,
and relating this, with information on the provenance of the slaves,

to the development of the blues, he suggests that while the music of
the West African rain forests has little to do with American Negro
folk music, the music of the Savannah regions "would have accorded
with Scots and English folk forms...." There is a glossary of African musical instruments, and an index.

818.   OLIVER, Paul. The story of the blues. London: Barrie &
       Rockliff; Philadelphia: Chilton, 1969; Harmondsworth:
       Penguin Books, 1973. 176p. illus., bibliog., discog.
       For a lucid, knowledgeable outline of the origin and develop-
ment of the blues, of the evolution and distinctive features of particular blues styles, of the relation of the idiom to black society and
the way it changed as society changed; for basic information on how
the blues singers themselves, great and small, fitted into and influenced the course followed by the music up to and including rhythm
and blues--this is the one basic text. Its unusual genesis (it grew
out of a photographic exhibition Oliver mounted in London in 1964,
using his own large collection, with supplements from other specialists and enthusiasts) give it a head start over most illustrated histories, in that the illustrations--of which there is a huge number--
are an integral part of the historical text, not an afterthought. The
book pursues a chronological course, beginning with the slave trade,
and following the blues from its rural beginnings through the "city"
and "urban" idioms, switching to and fro to indicate the concurrence
of these idioms, and devoting chapters to all their manifestations--
string bands, boogie woogie, tent shows, etc. Within this framework there is basic information on the place and style of a very
large number of individual artists (the index lists upwards of 700).
In conclusion, Oliver suggests that the blues today "shows every
sign of cultural decline" (p. 168), but that black Americans may one
day regard their creation with pride. References are made in the
text to music examples, and these are given, with notes, at the
end of the book.

819.   RUSSELL, Tony. Blacks, whites and blues. London: Studio
       Vista, 1970. 112p. illus., bibliog., discog.
       A revealing examination of the extent of the interaction be-
tween the folk music of black and white Americans up to the late
1930s. After considering minstrelsy the author explores the folk
song repertoire common to white and black, describing styles and
differences of approach. He then discusses the extent of musical
exchange in the blues, with particular attention to the blues yodel of
Jimmie Rodgers and its influence. In his concluding chapter he examines the way the interplay continued in Western and Eastern states,
with the urbanization of the blues and the changes in country music.
The text makes frequent use of titles by individual artists as examples, and many of these appear in the illustrations. The bibliography
lists books and articles; the discography refers the reader to the
text, and is divided into artists and anthologies. There is also an
artist index.

c. Regional Studies

820. BASTIN, Bruce. Crying for the Carolines. London: Studio
        Vista, 1971. 112p. illus., bibliog., discog.
        A study of "Piedmont blues"--blues singers from North and
South Carolina, Northern Georgia, and part of Virginia--based on
field work, and illustrating the distinctive features of the blues of
this region. One chapter is devoted to Blind Boy Fuller, with many
quotations from the verses of his songs. The author then embarks
on a tour of important centers: Durham, Atlanta, Greenville, Spartanburg, Charlotte; blues activities in these cities are described, and
blues verses quoted. He concludes with a chapter following singers
who moved North (including Brownie McGhee, and Sonny Terry). The
text is well illustrated with many photographs. There is a brief
bibliography, a selected LP discography and an index.

821. FERRIS, William. Blues from the Delta. London: Studio
        Vista, 1970. 111p. illus., bibliog., discog.
        Ferris opens his study of the creative process in the blues
with a description of the area with which he is primarily concerned,
the Mississippi Delta, and of previous research there on black folklore. His main focus is on verse structure of the blues of this region and its "relation to the composition and performance of blues
by individual singers" (p. 34). As an illustration of the creative
process he describes in detail a blues session in Clarksdale, and
concludes with discussions of the important influence of recordings
on the oral tradition, and of racial repertoire. The bibliography
gives books and articles, and the discography LPs, but there is no
index.

822. LEADBITTER, Mike. Crowley, Louisiana blues: the story
        of J. D. Miller and his blues artists, with a guide to their
        music. Bexhill-on-Sea: Blues Unlimited, 1968. 30p.
        illus.
        This booklet features blues musicians who recorded for Jay
Miller (mainly on the Excello label) in the 1950s and 1960s, up to
1966, including Lightnin' Slim, Lazy Lester, Lonesome Sundown,
Slim Harpo. There are accounts of their recording careers with
Miller, their style and their recordings. There is also an account
of Miller himself and of his recording business.

823. LEADBITTER, Mike. Delta country blues. Bexhill-on-Sea:
        Blues Unlimited, 1968. 47p. illus.
        These are accounts of some of the post-war artists of the
Mississippi Delta, tracing their activities up to the time when, in
a large number of cases, they moved North, and outlining their
part in the post-war recording sessions in their areas. Included
under the Upper Delta are Howlin' Wolf, Sonny Boy Williamson
(Rice Miller), Elmore James, Willie Love and Charlie Booker; under
the Lower Delta, Dr. Ross, Ike Turner, and B. B. King. There is
also information on WDIA radio station and the beginnings of the
"Sun" label.

824. MITCHELL, George. Blow my blues away. Baton Rouge:
     Louisiana State University Press, 1971. 208p. illus.
     A well-presented series of interviews, made in the summer
of 1967, with black country blues singers in the Mississippi Delta.
These are some of the last exponents of a rapidly vanishing style
of expression, and the book sets out to document the final stages;
it also aims to present the rural Negroes of the Delta as individuals
and, through this, discover something of the course of their blues-
making. The author sets the general scene with a description of
the area, and describes briefly the setting in which each of his cast
of characters lives. The men and women interviewed describe their
lives, outlook and emotions, and the place of the blues in their existence. There are accounts of a barbecue and a church service.
The book concludes with a selection of blues verses. The evocative
photographs which appear throughout are reminiscent of Ramsey (no.
765).

825. OLSSON, Bengt. Memphis blues and jug bands. London:
     Studio Vista, 1970. 112p. illus., bibliog., discog.
     The result of research in Memphis in 1969, this is an inves-
tigation into the lives and background of the blues and jug band
musicians, including the medicine shows. Among the artists featured are Frank Stokes, Jim Jackson, Memphis Jug Band, Robert
Burse, Gus Cannon and Furry Lewis. Appendices give lists of
Brunswick recordings made in Memphis in 1929-1930, and the words
of a selection of songs recorded by Memphis musicians. No index.

826. ROWE, Mike. Chicago breakdown. London: Eddison Press,
     1973. 226p. illus., bibliog., discog.
     A well-documented and liberally illustrated history of the
Chicago blues scene of the 1940s and 1950s. Rowe has extensive
knowledge of the record industry and is particularly concerned with
the rise and fall of the companies involved with the blues, an overall framework into which he fits accounts of the careers and style
of a large number of post-war artists. He sets the scene by outlining the movement of the blues from country to city, describing
the features of the urban Chicago blues of the 1930s, the pattern of
Negro migration, the typical Chicago club scene of the period and
some of the bluesmen involved. From here the various record companies, great and small, take over, the careers of their artists being
told in relation to the company's attitudes, activities and changing
fortunes in the post-war years. Prominent on the business side are
Leonard and Phil Chess, while among the many artists the following
predominate: Muddy Waters, Little Walter, Sunnyland Slim, Howlin'
Wolf, Elmore James, Floyd Jones, Sonny Boy Williamson, Rice
Miller and Johnny Shines. Ancillary material includes a list of Chicago rhythm and blues hits, 1945-1959, and an index.

d. Collected Portraits

827. CHARTERS, Samuel. The bluesmen: the story and the mu-
     sic of the men who made the blues. New York: Oak Pub-

lications, 1967. 223p. illus., discog.

The first of a projected series of studies devoted to the male
blues singers of particular regions, this volume focuses on singers
from three Southern states--Mississippi, Alabama, and Texas--cov-
ering the period up to 1939. A survey of the relationship between
the blues and African music is a prelude to the central part of the
text, which features discussion of the blues styles of--among others--
Charley Patton, Bukka White, Son House, Skip James, Robert Johnson, Blind Lemon Jefferson, Henry Thomas and Texas Alexander.
In these studies Charters describes something of each singer's background and personality, but concentrates mainly on analysis of his
songs, making wide use of both textual and music illustrations, the
latter transcribed as closely as possible from the original recordings.
There is a list of records referred to in the text, and an index.

828. CHARTERS, Samuel. The country blues. New York: Rine-
       hart, 1959. (Repr. New York: Da Capo, 1975). 288p.
       illus.
       _____.   . London: Joseph, 1960; London: Jazz
       Book Club, 1961. 203p. illus.

This important and illuminating work was the first book-length
study of early blues artists, their background and their styles.
Charters begins with a survey of the origins and early development
of blues, the first published blues and the growing interest and involvement of the record companies. The role played by the recording industry is frequently referred to in the subsequent studies of
the major artists (which are the raison d'être of the book) from Blind
Lemon Jefferson, Lonnie Johnson, Rabbit Brown, Furry Lewis and
the Memphis Jug Band, through Leroy Carr, Robert Johnson, Blind
Willie McTell, Big Bill Broonzy and Blind Boy Fuller to Brownie
McGhee, Muddy Waters and Lightnin' Hopkins. Charters' preference
is for the "raw vitality and savage intensity" of the earlier style.
There are no music examples, but frequent quotations from blues
verses.

829. CHARTERS, Samuel. The legacy of the blues: a glimpse
       into the art and the lives of twelve great bluesmen; an in-
       formal study. London: Calder & Boyars, 1975. 192p.
       illus., discog.

The twelve living bluesmen Charters chooses each represent
a different style and mood of the blues, from early Mississippi to
urban band; they are: Big Joe Williams and J. D. Short, Bukka
White, Robert Pete Williams, Juke Boy Bonner, Snooks Eaglin,
Champion Jack Dupree, Sunnyland Slim, Mighty Joe Young, Eddie
Boyd and Memphis Slim, and Lightnin' Hopkins. All but two were
interviewed by Charters, whose portraits of their individual lives
and styles emphasizes how, in their different ways, the blues of each
man reflect the "otherness" of black America. The discography is
a list of the contents of the twelve accompanying LPs, recorded between 1962 and 1973.

830. GURALNICK, Peter. Feel like going home: portraits in
       blues and rock 'n' roll. New York: Outerbridge & Dienst-

frey, 1971. 224p. illus. , bibliog. , discog.
The object of this group of profiles is to demonstrate a progression from country blues to urban blues to rock and roll. It begins with a personal account of the author's own reaction to rock
and roll, and a brief history of blues development, outlining the contribution of early artists such as Blind Lemon Jefferson, Charley
Patton, Son House, and Robert and Tommy Johnson, and pointing out
chains of influence between and beyond them. The profiles which
follow are based mainly on interviews, and include bluesmen Muddy
Waters, Johnny Shines, Skip James, Robert Pete Williams and
Howlin' Wolf, rock and roll stars Jerry Lee Lewis and Charlie Rich,
while the crucial contribution of the record industry is represented
by pieces on Sam Phillips and the Chess family. Each artist profile
combines a sketch of the individual's life and career with an evaluation of his style and influence. No index.

831. LEADBITTER, Mike, ed. Nothing but the blues. London:
        Hanover Books, 1971. 261p. illus.
    A collection of articles of varying lengths on blues and blues
artists, reprinted from the first 50 issues of the British magazine
Blues Unlimited. The articles are arranged by geographical area--
Chicago, the South, etc.--and constitute a valuable body of research
work mainly of a biographical kind. Some recent, previously unpublished material is also included. The author and date of publication of each piece is given, but the almost incredible omission, in
a volume of this nature, of both a contents list and an index, makes
the book most difficult to use properly.

832. NAPIER, Simon A. , comp. Back woods blues: selected re-
        prints from Blues Unlimited magazine and elsewhere. Bex-
        hill-on-Sea: Blues Unlimited, 1968. 55p. illus.
    An excellent short anthology of 14 articles from the period
1962-1968, many on lesser known artists and figures. There are
biographical sketches of Jaybird Coleman, Arthur Spires, Henry
Speir (outstanding talent scout) and Babe Stovall, autobiographical
reminiscences from Fred MacDowell and Rev. Jack Harp, appreciations of Bull City Red, Texas Alexander, Snooks Eaglin, Son House,
Hattie Hart and Allen Shaw, articles on Cajun music and on the
Archive of American Folk Song at the Library of Congress, and a
substantial memoir of Muddy Waters by Paul Oliver, who also contributes two of the other articles. Other authors include Paul Garon,
Pete Welding, Charlie Gillett, David Evans, Gayle Dean Wardlow,
and the compiler.

833. STEWART-BAXTER, Derrick. Ma Rainey and the classic
        blues singers. London: Studio Vista, 1970. 112p. illus. ,
        bibliog. , discog.
    Defining the area of study as the female singers of the 1920s
whose style was influenced by vaudeville and tent shows, and whose
repertoire extended beyond the blues, the author traces the careers
of the major figures, including Mamie Smith, Rosa Henderson, Ma
Rainey, Bessie Smith, Ida Cox, Victoria Spivey, etc. , concluding
with chapters on lesser known artists and on the post-classic period.

Some comment is offered on individual styles and contributions. The bibliography is limited to books, while the discography lists original releases and microgroove reissue numbers for 36 artists. Liberally illustrated and with an index.

e. Individual Artists

PERRY BRADFORD

834. BRADFORD, Perry. Born with the blues: the true story of the pioneering blues singers and musicians in the early days of jazz. New York: Oak, 1965. 175p. illus.
A lively, colloquial autobiography by the jazz musician and song writer (1895-1970) who broke the race barrier in the recording industry when Mamie Smith recorded his "That Thing Called Love" in January, 1920, and the first recorded blues, "Crazy Blues," in August of the same year. He was a significant figure in the development of jazz in the first quarter of the century, and he presents some useful information on early jazz in New York and the early blues singers. Some allowance must be made for the local color and a certain degree of hyperbole. Numerous photographs and a selection of his early songs--texts and tunes, with piano accompaniment. Index.

BIG BILL BROONZY

835. BROONZY, William. Big Bill blues: William Broonzy's story as told to Yannick Bruynoghe; with 9 pages of halftone illustrations and 4 drawings by Paul Oliver. London: Cassell, 1955. 139p. illus., discog.
_____. _____; foreword by Charles Edward Smith. New York: Oak, 1964. 176p. illus., discog.
Big Bill's fascinating story of his life, his songs and his friends remains the only book by a male blues artist. Though he spent most of his life in Chicago and excelled in urban-oriented "good-time" music (of a type often poking fun at the rural black South) Big Bill (1893-1958) could also sing slower, powerful country blues. His memories of his life, forming the first part of the book, reflect something of the varied experience behind this--his Mississippi childhood, the Arkansas farm he kept, while living in Chicago, and the extensive touring that resulted from his discovery by white enthusiasts in the 1950s. The chapter on his songs that follows, in which he talks about the background to a selection of blues from his prolific recording career (complete texts of eleven songs are included), is a valuable insight into blues origins in black experience.
The third part of the book contains personal portraits of a number of Big Bill's fellow musicians, including Sleepy John Estes, Big Maceo Merriweather, Tampa Red, Memphis Slim, Memphis Minnie, Tommy McClennan and Washboard Sam. Smith's introduction to the 1964 edition is a worthy tribute to a fine artist and his repertoire. The original discography by Albert McCarthy is revised by Ken Harrison and Ray Asbury in the Oak edition.

LEONARD CASTON

836. TITON, Jeff., ed. From blues to pop: the autobiography
of Leonard "Baby Doo" Caston. Los Angeles: John Edwards Memorial Foundation, 1974. (Special Series, No.
4) 29p. illus.
A transcription of an interview with the blues pianist and
guitarist whose Big Three Trio (Caston, Willie Dixon and Ollie
Crawford) developed a style of singing blues songs in harmony. He
describes his life (he was born in Mississippi in 1917), his view of
the blues, and what the editor terms his "commercial aesthetic."
The text contains several music examples.

GARY DAVIS

837. DAVIS, Gary. Rev. Gary Davis: the holy blues; compiled
and edited by Stefan Grossman. New York: Robbins,
1970. 127p. illus., discog.
A collection of the words and tunes, with guitar chords, of
80 songs composed by Blind Gary Davis in the course of a long life
that began in South Carolina at the turn of the century, and ended in
1972. The "holy blues" is the term given to his unique blend of
blues and ragtime guitar styles with gospel lyrics.

W. C. HANDY

838. HANDY, W. C. Father of the blues: an autobiography; edited
by Arna Bontemps; with a foreword by Abbe Niles. New
York: Macmillan, 1941; London: Sidgwick & Jackson,
1957. 317p. illus., bibliog.
_____ . _____ . London: Jazz Book Club, 1961. 258p.
illus., bibliog.
Blues commentators prefer to think of Handy (1873-1958) as
an uncle, a godfather, or even a musically-inclined obstetrician in
the blues family tree, rather than as the father. Here the most
successful and popular of the blues composers tells of his childhood
and his acquisition of musical knowledge of a kind his strictly religious family viewed with severe disapproval. He has much to say
about his first blues and the extent to which they were developments
of the Negro folk music he heard in his youth. The text includes
musical extracts from several blues of this and later periods. The
narrative also describes his moving to Chicago and New York, his
music publishing business and his life there. There is a chronological list of his compositions, arrangements and books, and a name
index.

BLIND LEMON JEFFERSON

839. JEFFERSON, Blind Lemon. Blind Lemon Jefferson. Knuts-
ford, Cheshire: Blues World, 1970. (Blues World Booklet No. 3) 35p. discog.
A booklet containing transcriptions of the lyrics of some 60
of Blind Lemon's recordings (others appeared in Blues World, 18 on-

wards), given in matrix number order, with take and Paramount release numbers.   There is an introductory essay, "The Legacy of Blind Lemon," by Bob Groom.   Approximate recording dates are given at the end.

PETE JOHNSON

840.   MAUERER, Hans J., comp.   The Pete Johnson story.   Bremen: Printed by Humburg, 1965.   78p.   illus., discog.
A tribute to the great boogie-woogie and jazz pianist (b. 1904), including a biography by his wife (reprinted from Jazz Report magazine, 1962), an account of his career in his own words (reprinted from Jazz Journal, 1959), a collection of tributes and comments from friends and reviewers, a critical assessment by James Wertheim that includes examination of individual pieces, a selection of Johnson's letters to the compiler, 1962-1965, a discography of 78s and LP reissues, and a list of his compositions with publisher and other recorded versions.

ROBERT JOHNSON

841.   JOHNSON, Robert.   Robert Johnson, King of the Delta blues. London: Immediate Music, 1969.   61p.
A set of transcriptions of the words and melodies of all Johnson's 29 recorded blues.   The melodies are transcribed from what is sung in the first verse of the song, and are provided with guitar chords.   Unlike the Charters version (no. 842) this collection provides no extra information in the form of discographical notes or explanatory comments, and it is not chronologically arranged.   Interpretation of time signatures often differs, with Charters using 4/4 where the transcriber of this version (who signs himself J. R. M.) chooses 12/8 to allow complex rhythms to be better indicated. J. R. M. also provides transcriptions of the guitar introductions (omitted by Charters), and gives full alternative lyrics for three blues.   There are several instances of different readings of the words as Johnson sings them (e.g., "Stones in My Passway"); J. R. M. 's solutions seem generally more convincing.

842.   CHARTERS, Samuel.   Robert Johnson; with photos of Robert Johnson's Delta country by the author.   New York: Oak Publications; London: Music Sales, 1973.   87p.   illus.
The legendary Mississippi blues singer, whose 29 recordings made in San Antonio and Dallas in 1936-1937 have been highly influential, has obsessed the compiler of these transcriptions since the 1950s (see also his Country Blues, no. 828).   In his deeply felt introduction he pieces together what biographical information there is, using information gained from interviews, and provides an appreciation of Johnson's blues from the viewpoints of influence, style, and themes.   The transcriptions are grouped into the five recording sessions, and by matrix number.   The melody of each blues is given with guitar chords.   Key signatures are often changed from the originals.   Notes and comments are given with each song, and there is complete discographical information under each title.   (For some

comparisons with the transcriptions published by Immediate Music, see no. 841.)

TOMMY JOHNSON

843. EVANS, David. Tommy Johnson. London: Studio Vista, 1971. 112p. illus., bibliog., discog.

A fine biographical portrait of a centrally important figure in the Mississippi blues tradition, based on interviews with Johnson's contemporaries carried out mainly in Mississippi and Louisiana. Evans traces Johnson's life and career to his death in 1956, outlining the influences on his style, and his place in the blues tradition. The chapters concerned with his recording career include examples of song texts and commentary, with some remarks on aspects of his musical style. The concluding chapter sums up his repertoire, style and legacy. The illustrations include photographs of his contemporaries, and of buildings associated with Johnson himself. The discography lists LP reissues. No index.

LEADBELLY

844. LEDBETTER, Huddie. Leadbelly: a collection of world-famous songs; edited by John A. Lomax and Alan Lomax; Hally Wood, music editor; special note on Leadbelly's 12-string guitar by Pete Seeger. New York: Folkways, 1959. 80p.

_____. The Leadbelly legend: a collection of world-famous songs ... (Rev. and augmented ed.) New York: Folkways, 1965. 96p. illus.

A selection of 70 songs (79 in the revised edition) from Leadbelly's vast repertoire, including blues and folk songs. Melodies, texts and guitar chords are provided for each item. All the songs were transcribed from Leadbelly's recordings for Folkways Records. There is a brief introduction by Alan Lomax.

_____. The Leadbelly songbook: the ballads, blues and folk songs of Huddie Ledbetter; edited by Moses Asch and Alan Lomax. New York: Oak, 1962. 96p. illus., discog.

A further selection (with some overlapping) from Leadbelly's Folkways recordings, including, like the other anthologies, material both written and adapted by Leadbelly. The 74 songs (melodies, texts and chords) are preceded by preliminary material from Asch, Pete Seeger, Frederic Ramsey, Charles E. Smith and Woody Guthrie.

845. JONES, Max, and McCARTHY, Albert, eds. A tribute to Huddie Ledbetter. London: Jazz Music Books, 1946. 26p. discog.

The main features of this early homage to Leadbelly are a discography by Frederic Ramsey and Albert McCarthy, a portrait by Charles E. Smith (from Jazz magazine), and an account of Leadbelly performing by Frederic Ramsey. There are various record reviews, and a review of the Lomaxes' book (no. 846) by Stanley Dance.

846. LOMAX, John A., and LOMAX, Alan. Negro folk songs as sung by Lead Belly, "King of the twelve-string guitar players of the world," long-time convict in the penitentiaries of Texas and Louisiana; transcribed, selected and edited by John A. Lomax and Alan Lomax. New York: Macmillan, 1936. 242p. illus.

The Lomaxes' pioneer study/collection of the life and songs of an individual Afro-American folk artist, who, in his colorful and violent life, had amassed a songster's repertoire of unequaled variety, is one of the outstanding works in the field of Negro secular folk music. In the first part of the book Leadbelly tells his life story in his own words, with linking narrative by the editors, who then describe their experiences since their association with Leadbelly began upon his release from prison in 1934. The 48 selected songs which follow are mainly taken from discs made for the Library of Congress, the music transcriptions being the responsibility of George Herzog, who attempts in his notation to reproduce the nuances of Leadbelly's singing. The section in which the songs are grouped are: reels, work songs, hollers, blues, talkin' blues, ballads and miscellany. The song texts include Leadbelly's chanted interpolations and explanations. Each song is preceded by an editorial introduction. On black adaptation of already existing song material, as exemplified by Leadbelly, Herzog remarks, "we ought not to picture him copying a melody or picking it up indiscriminately, but rather modeling it with artistry so distinctive that the child is more pleasing than the parent." (Leadbelly died in 1949.)

BROWNIE McGHEE

847. McGHEE, Brownie. Guitar styles of Brownie McGhee; edited by Happy Traum. New York: Oak; London: Music Sales, 1971. 102p. illus.

An unusual feature of this tutor is that much of the text accompanying the transcriptions of the music of Walter "Brownie" McGhee, outstanding blues guitarist and long time partner of harmonica player Sonny Terry, is given in his own words. He also tells his life story. The transcriptions, given in conventional notation and tablature, are of complete songs, breaks, and accompaniments.

LITTLE BROTHER MONTGOMERY

848. TERKEL, Studs. Hard times: an oral history of the Great Depression. New York: Pantheon Books; London: Allen Lane The Penguin Press, 1970. 461p.

In this vivid portrait of people's lives during the Depression, and of their views in perspective, there are some appearances by musicians, including, in a section titled "The Fine and Lively Arts," Little Brother Montgomery. This same section also contains an account of some performances of Blitzstein's "The Cradle Will Rock."

849. ZUR HEIDE, Karl Gert. Deep South piano: the story of Little Brother Montgomery. London: Studio Vista, 1970. 67p. illus., discog.

An account of the life of the blues pianist up to 1940, based
on interviews with contemporaries and with Little Brother himself.
The author follows him through some of his many travels, beginning
with his leaving home in Louisiana at the age of 11, his time in
New Orleans, Florida and Mississippi, and his settling in Chicago.
The many quotations from fellow blues pianists give an idea of their
way of life and of the development of the tradition up to the outbreak
of war. There is a short post-war appendix, a section of biographical data of over a hundred musicians whose path crossed Little
Brother's before 1942 (this section is almost as long as the main
text), and a set of transcriptions of the texts of his songs given in
the discography, which lists the pre-1942 sessions in which he participated, with original issue numbers. Name index, and many photographs.

CHARLEY PATTON

850. FAHEY, John. Charley Patton. London: Studio Vista, 1970.
        112p. illus., bibliog., discog.
        Guitarist Fahey's study of this seminal figure in country blues
is an impressive musical and textual analysis of Patton's songs,
based on all but six of his recorded output. Placing his study initially in the context of general research into blues recordings, and
arguing for the validity of criticism based on this body of recorded
material, Fahey goes on, following a short biography, to prove his
case with analyses of Patton's tunes, a classification according to
scale, and a grouping into families. The results of these analyses
suggest that a predominating influence was the holler tradition.
There is also a study of the texts. Fahey establishes five categories of song, all based on transcriptions from recordings. These
transcriptions, which include virtually all of Patton's recordings, are
presented--words and tunes--in an appendix, and represent a remarkable achievement, given Patton's indistinct vocal style and the condition of some of the rarer records.

BESSIE SMITH

851. ALBERTSON, Chris. Bessie. New York: Stein & Day;
        London: Barrie & Jenkins, 1972. 253p. illus., bibliog.,
        discog.
        Feeling that previous accounts of the greatest of all female
blues singers (1894?-1937) had failed to give an accurate portrait of
her, Albertson spares no detail in a thorough, down-to-earth, occasionally unedifying (not, one suspects, only to those with "outmoded,
puritanical values") account of her life and personality, of which he
says "its candor may offend, its dispelling of myths may disillusion,
but a biographer is obligated to document his subject's whole personality" (p. 12). His impressively thorough research included
countless interviews, of which the most fruitful were with Bessie's
niece, Ruby Walker, and a scouring of the black press. The resulting biography is unfortunately very sketchy on Bessie's formative
years, but from the time of her first recording in 1923 to her death
following a car crash outside Clarksdale, Miss. (the controversial

aspects of which are well handled at the end of the story) there is
a mass of detail about her movements as a touring entertainer on
the T. O. B. A. circuit, her career as a recording artist, and her
private life. If the round of shows, recording studios, trains, parties, love affairs, drinking bouts and intermittent brawls become a
little monotonous before the end this is partly because of the lack of
good written documentation that is a problem with jazz and blues biography. We do, however, have an enormous body of recordings--
Bessie's and other classic blues singers'--that should surely play a
far more central part. Though there are general comments on
numerous individual recordings they are almost asides, and nowhere
is there any attempt to get inside the artist. Why was she so outstanding? We are no wiser.

852. MOORE, Carman. Somebody's angel child: the story of
        Bessie Smith. New York: Crowell, 1969. 121p. illus.,
        bibliog., discog.
        A straightforward biographical account, tracing Bessie's life
from her birth in Chattanooga to her death in 1937. There
are four general sections: early life, first steps to fame as a teen-
ager, rise to stardom, decline and death. Examples of the verses
of some of her songs and some music are woven into the narrative,
which is mainly concerned with recreating the character of the singer
and the events of her life, and thereby laying the way open for some
understanding of her style. There is a list of her compositions and
an index.

853. OLIVER, Paul. Bessie Smith. London: Cassell, 1959;
        New York: Barnes, 1961. (Kings of Jazz, 3) 83p. illus.,
        bibliog., discog.
        The first full-length account of the singer's life, career and
death, combining biographical information and critical appreciation.
A large number of her recordings are mentioned specifically in their
chronological context, and in many cases briefly described and evaluated. An overall assessment of her artistry emerges, as does
something of her complex personality. There is a short bibliography
of principal sources and reference works, and a selected discography
of 78s in chronological order.

ETHEL WATERS

854. WATERS, Ethel. His eye is on the sparrow: an autobiogra-
        phy (with Charles Samuels). Garden City: Doubleday,
        1951; New York: Pyramid Books, 1967. 278p. illus.
        _____. _____. London: Allen, 1951; London: Jazz
        Book Club, 1958. 260p. illus.
        A dispassionate but moving account of her life by the Negro
singer and actress who made a large number of blues and jazz recordings in the period from 1921-1940, and has been active more
recently in evangelism. The book begins by describing candidly the
conditions of her early life in Chester, Pennsylvania, and the place
of singing in her life as a child. In the account of her subsequent,
very varied career, from talent contest to New York theater, the

touring, the recording with Black Swan and others, the big dramatic successes, there are appearances by several blues and jazz artists, including Bessie Smith and Fletcher Henderson. The account concludes with her emergence to renewed success in 1950, after a long lean spell in the '40s.

855. WATERS, Ethel. To me it's wonderful; with an introduction by Eugenia Price and Joyce Blackburn. New York: Harper & Row, 1972. illus., discog.

Based on taped interviews with the former blues and jazz singer, this is an account of her participation in the Billy Graham Crusades from 1957 on. A discography of 259 items was prepared by George Finola, but the reductio ad absurdum which is given instead merely describes her recording career in very brief terms, mentioning a few selected items in connection with stages in her career.

PEETIE WHEATSTRAW

856. GARON, Paul. The Devil's son-in-law: the story of Peetie Wheatstraw and his songs. London: Studio Vista, 1971. 111p. illus., bibliog., discog.

Information on the life of Peetie Wheatstraw's (real name William Bunch) is very fragmentary, and the author pieces together what knowledge there is, relying for a great deal of his portrait of the man on the information of Peetie's colleagues, through which he is also able to sketch the daily and musical life in St. Louis and East St. Louis in the 1930s. A large part of the book is devoted to a discussion of the lyrics of many of Peetie's 160 or so songs. These are studied chronologically, so that his recording career is also outlined. There are frequent textual quotations, and a few musical examples. Though a large number of blues artists appear in the course of the book there is no index. Well illustrated.

857. PEEL, David. Oooh, well, well, its the Peetie Wheatstraw Stomps. Burlington, Ontario: Belltower Books, 1972. 26(x2)p.

This booklet aims to act as a companion to the three re-issued albums of Peetie Wheatstraw available in 1972, by providing (on the left-hand page, in red) transcriptions of the words of forty songs, from the period 1930-1937, and (on the opposite page, in black) commentary on each song. In his introduction the author exhorts listeners to listen to the songs wholeheartedly before submitting them to analysis. His own examination of each song succeeds in conveying the spirit of the song and at the same time presenting objective, informed commentary on such aspects as imagery, performance and questions of authorship. (Available from 2358 Lakeshore Road East, Burlington.)

f. Interpretative Studies

858. CHARTERS, Samuel. The poetry of the blues; with photo-

graphs by Ann Charters. New York: Oak Publications, 1963. 111p. illus., bibliog.

A wide-ranging study of the content, technique and significance of the words of blues songs. Charters sets the scene by first describing some of the outstanding features of Negro society that gave rise to the blues, before proceeding to a detailed examination of blues verses, illustrating his argument with a wealth of examples of song texts. The discussion ranges over immediacy of feeling in the blues, the dramatic potential of the blues form, poetic technique in the blues, the themes of love, travel and rootlessness, and the effects of these on the singers and their songs. Sexual imagery and social protest, or the lack thereof, are also examined. No index.

859. COOK, Bruce. Listen to the blues. New York: Scribner, 1973. 263p. illus.

This popular study fits no established category of blues writing, though it has elements of most of them: it is not a history, though several chapters follow a broad chronology from speculation on origins, through the Delta to Chicago; it is not a collection of portraits, though Cook interviewed several surviving bluesmen (particularly in rural areas) and incorporates descriptions of them; it is not a critique of blues as poetry or social expression, though, again, these subjects are touched on. It is a somewhat diffuse account of the very personal reaction of one man, who, though he tells us he discovered blues as a boy, seems to have got around to investigating it very late in the day. Thus his mistrust of previous writings and his heavy reliance on limited travel in the South and material obtained from the survivors--however outstanding they were and are--give him the air of a man arriving after the race is over. His central theme is the mutual influence of blacks and whites in American music, of which he sees blues as an outstanding example (he also devotes space to country music, rock and jazz in his pages). The book's virtue is the way it tries to nudge the reader into listening and discovering for himself. Several of Cook's ideas are interesting; many are also annoying (e.g., his superficial attitude to blues scholarship, and his attempt to replace considered criticism, born of a breadth of knowledge he clearly does not possess, by "personal emotional investment"--"proud knownothingism" one reviewer called it--in the music). The great trouble, however, with books like this, which attempt to communicate ideas in a style designed to prod the nation painlessly into consciousness at Sunday breakfast, is that this style has built into it an instant disposability. Ideas need linguistic hooks to attach themselves to the brain; when they are passed on by means of this kind of contrived colloquialism they quite simply do not survive the closing of the book.

860. KEIL, Charles. Urban blues. Chicago: University of Chicago Press, 1966. 231p. illus., bibliog. notes.

A brilliant study by a white social anthropologist of contemporary Chicago bluesmen, particularly as examples of "an expressive male role within urban lower-class Negro culture." An introduction examines studies of acculturation and kinship. The main text begins with a discussion of the exclusion of contemporary blues from general blues criticism; LeRoi Jones is seen as an exception to this, and his approach leads to a discussion of musical revitalization and increased Africanization, with the suggestion that the familiar appropriation-revitalization cycle may be entering a final stage. There follows a historical sketch of the development of blues styles. Suggesting reasons for stylistic and thematic changes, Keil demonstrates that a process of rationalization has taken place (greater technical efficiency leading, surprisingly, to increased emotional effect). He shows how a bluesman's goal of communication is affected by economic, legal and technical factors. The theme of the bluesman's role is pursued in a backstage interview with B. B. King, an analysis of a Bobby Bland stage performance, and a theoretical examination of the artist's role and the audience's response. The question of blues and group solidarity is explored as he isolates and describes "soul" components and demonstrates them in the blues. The concluding chapter explores the wider field of the future of cultural identity. Appendices discuss identity theories, an anthropological framework for music discussion, and give an annotated outline of blues styles. Index.

861. LEHMANN, Theo. Blues and trouble. Berlin: Henschelverlag, 1966. 190p. illus., discog.
A wide-ranging essay in German on the expressive nature of the blues explores such features as ambiguity, integrity, frankness, realism and superstition, and describes the characteristics of a number of outstanding blues singers. Many blues texts are quoted as illustrations, in English and German. A set of 41 complete blues song texts in English with German translations follows the essay. There are no indexes.

862. LEISER, Willie. I'm a road runner baby. Bexhill-on-Sea: Blues Unlimited, 1969. 38p. illus.
The diary of a Swiss blues enthusiast's visit to the U.S. (December, 1968 to January, 1969), and of the blues and gospel artists he met and heard perform in Chicago, Philadelphia, Washington and San Francisco.

863. MIDDLETON, Richard. Pop music and the blues: a study of the relationship and its significance. London: Gollancz, 1972. 271p. bibliog., discogs.
This outstanding study by an English critic falls into two separate but related parts. The first, on the blues, is a penetrating analysis of the way the blues relate to the black cultural experience in America; in particular (and this is what makes the book so different--previous works used blues texts as their basis) how the individual musical features of the blues each play their part in underlining the cultural function of the music as a whole. From an outline of the essential social and cultural background in which the culture clash between white and black is stressed, Middleton proceeds first to describe and analyze the basic musical ingredients of the blues, showing how these are each, in their way, expressions of the culture-clash. From here he explores in detail (and with a wealth of

illustration that suggests he is very familiar with the music) the elements characteristic of the country, city and sophisticated urban traditions from Charley Patton to Bobby Bland--constantly relating musical features to the changing situation of the Negro in America, and the attendant shifts in the web of his emotions. The second half of the book deals with the relationship of popular white music to the blues, in a much wider context than is customary: that of the relation of the white western world to non-Western culture, and the repressions characteristic of that relationship. Middleton sees the significance of pop music as being "the climax of a long attempt to come to terms with non-Western experience through the Negro and his music" (p. 127), and analyzes it on this basis, discussing the direct influence of the blues, the characteristics of rock 'n' roll, two different attempts at synthesis between Western and non-Western culture by the Beatles, Bob Dylan, rhythm and blues, soul, and "way-out" pop (Hendrix, Zappa, et al.). Each chapter is followed by suggestions for listening--which Middleton prefers the reader to do to studying musical examples, of which he gives very few. Index.

864. OLIVER, Paul. Blues fell this morning: the meaning of the blues; with a foreword by Richard Wright. London: Cassell; New York: Horizon Press, 1960; London: Jazz Book Club, 1963. 336p. bibliog., discog.
          . The meaning of the blues ... New York: Collier, 1963. 282p. bibliog., discog.
This is a penetrating exploration and explanation of the meaning and content of the blues in which, with the help of 350 textual examples, transcribed from recorded blues (mainly of the pre-1942 era), the author demonstrates how the blues provide a mirror of Negro life in America. He first examines the way various socio-economic topics are reflected in the blues (the employment situation, conditions of work, the transient work force, the significance of the railroads). Moving to more personal themes he analyzes the treatment of love, devotion, marriage and the purely sexual themes and symbols. The extent of superstition is also discussed. The later chapters are concerned with the picture of types of social evil given in the blues: slum housing, prostitution, crime, punishment and prisons, disasters natural and man-made, and disease. With a few exceptions no mention is made of specific singers; one must look to the discography of quoted blues to identify the singer of each excerpt. There is also an index of these quoted singers, plus a general index.

865. OLIVER, Paul. Conversations with the blues; illustrated with photographs by the author. London: Cassell; New York: Horizon Press, 1965; London: Jazz Book Club, 1967. 217p. illus., discog.
This revealing document is composed of extracts from recorded conversations with about 70 blues performers, made by the author during a field trip in 1960. No specific arrangement is indicated, and the text proceeds from one conversation to the next, but there is an overall chronological and geographical pattern, and each

excerpt has a title, taken from the interviewee's words. The speakers reflect on the nature of the blues and what the blues mean to
them, and describe aspects of life in the South of their youth, and
something of the life of a blues musician. We move North with the
migration, and are given a picture, chiefly from younger musicians,
of blues life in Chicago and Detroit. The main text concludes with
opinions on the relation of blues and the church, and the basic character of the blues as a means of expression. There are 80 photographs, biographical notes on the speakers, and an index.

866. OLIVER, Paul. Screening the blues: aspects of the blues
tradition. London: Cassell, 1968. 294p. bibliog.
_____ . Aspects of the blues tradition. New York: Oak
Publications, 1970. 294p. bibliog.
A thorough examination of previously little-researched aspects
of the body of recorded blues. The introduction gives a clear survey
of some broad themes: the effects of recording on blues development, the extent to which recorded blues are representative of the
blues as they were sung, and the limitations of content; the author
also identifies traditional elements in the blues. Six particular
topics are then examined in detail: the treatment of Christmas
themes; the attitude of blues singers to religion and the relation between early blues and gospel song; patterns of change and continuity
in the development and varied treatment of a particular blues--the
Forty-Fours (with musical examples); the policy blues (obscure, but
indicating to the initiated a system of betting in combinations of numbers); blues featuring a Negro hero; and finally, and in considerable
detail, the treatment of sexual themes. There are bibliographical
notes to each chapter, and indexes of titles and names.

g. Collections of Music and Texts

867. BERENDT, Joachim Ernst. Blues. Munich: Nymphenburger
Verlagshandlung, 1957. 122p. discog.
Principally intended to introduce German readers to the blues,
this is an anthology of the texts of 48 songs, in the original language and in German translations, with 27 tunes. The songs--which
range from field hollers to mid-'50s Big Bill Broonzy--are preceded
by a 26-page essay in German on the nature and influence of the
blues: the dominant mood, racial elements (African and European
influences and characteristics), sociological aspects, musical and
metrical form, themes (love, racial discrimination, etc.), the use
of double talk, the common montage type of structure, and the in-
terrelations of blues and jazz. Berendt published another book of
blues lyrics later (Schwarzer Gesang II, Munich, 1962).

868. ELLINGTON, Duke. Piano method for blues. New York:
Robbins, 1943. 44p.
Designed as a tutor, Duke's small book describes in a clear,
practical way, and with special reference to the piano, the musical
features characteristic of the blues: form and harmonic structure
(with a chart showing variations of blues form), melodic structure,

rhythmic characteristics. He also explains stylistic aspects of piano blues, such as the various bass styles, and briefly describes boogie-woogie. The numerous examples range from a few short bars to complete short pieces (by Duke), and the book ends with seven full piano adaptations of recordings by the Ellington Orchestra. (How much of the book is Duke's work, and how much Billy Strayhorn's, is not indicated.)

869. GARWOOD, Donald. Masters of instrumental blues guitar. New York: Oak Publications, 1968. 78p. illus., discog.
The techniques of various country blues artists are explained in this guide with examples of the instrumental solos to numerous songs. Chord progressions for eight-, twelve- and sixteen-bar blues are illustrated, and bass fingerpicking technique, as illustrated by Gary Davis, Frank Stokes and others, is described. Two artists are examined closely: the "songsters" Mississippi John Hurt and Mance Lipscomb; together with transcriptions of several of their songs there is analysis of their stylistic characteristics, with notes on the particular technical features of each song. Music is given in standard notation and tablature, with chord diagrams. Texts are given only for two songs by Bo Carter, illustrating vocal and instrumental integration.

870. GROSSMAN, Stefan. The country blues guitar. New York: Oak Publications, 1968. 119p. illus., discog.
The first volume in Grossman's instructional series sets the pattern for the rest. It consists of transcriptions of the words and music of blues recordings by outstanding artists. The musical accompaniment is given in conventional notation and tablature, with a detailed explanation in the introduction, notes to each song (on both historical and technical features) and photographs illustrating chord positions. Other illustrative material is there for atmosphere: some fine photographs of the artists and reproductions of contemporary advertisements. This particular volume contains 23 songs; eight are by Mississippi John Hurt, eleven are by blues artists from the Memphis area (Furry Lewis, Robert Wilkins and others), and four are from Alabama and Arkansas (including Buddy Boy Hawkins).

871. GROSSMAN, Stefan, et al. Country blues songbook, by Stefan Grossman, Stephen Calt and Hal Grossman. New York: Oak Publications, 1973. 208p. illus., bibliog. notes, discog.
A generous anthology containing 142 transcriptions (words, melodies and chord diagrams) of country blues. Approximately half were transcribed from recordings made in the 1960s and 1970s by "rediscovered" bluesmen, notably Mance Lipscomb, Bukka White, Skip James, Son House, Robert Wilkins and Mississippi John Hurt. Of the other half, transcribed from original recordings of the 1920s and 1930s, a large proportion are by Charley Patton, Robert Johnson and Blind Boy Fuller. A most interesting feature of the book is the stimulating 28-page essay by Stephen Calt, "The Country Blues as Meaning," in which he attacks blues commentators who have glamorized country blues as "existential self-expression or

poetry" and attempts a reassessment based on its functional, expedient and eclectic qualities. Neither sociological nor historical approaches get to the heart of the blues in his view; an aesthetic approach can only succeed if it abandons conventional criteria for judging art--Calt applies these and shows how unsusceptible the themes, images and form of the blues are--and approaches the blues as a performing art whose chief virtue is that it "speaks a dialect that may be more compelling and more eloquent than its own verbal statements: the rhythmic body English ..." (p. 35).

872.   GROSSMAN, Stefan. Delta blues guitar. New York: Oak
        Publications, 1969. 136p. illus., discog.
        The Mississippi Delta was one of the richest sources of country blues. The 26 records transcribed for this volume are all by Mississippi bluesmen, notably Charley Patton, Son House, Robert Johnson, Tommy Johnson, Bukka White, Fred McDowell, two Willie Brown's, and Skip James. The text of each song is given, and the accompaniments are presented in tablature and conventional notation. Each song has a prefatory note pointing out particular features.

873.   GROSSMAN, Stefan. Ragtime blues guitarists. New York:
        Oak Publications, 1970. 131p. illus., discog.
        The third of Grossman's instructional guides contains a set of transcriptions of records by bluesmen who, though they come from widely scattered areas of the South, have in common a ragtime-influenced guitar style. Eighteen of the items are songs, and three are instrumentals. Texts are given for all the songs, and the guitar accompaniments are given in both tablature and conventional notation. The four artists most prominently represented are Blind Lemon Jefferson, Blind Boy Fuller, Big Bill Broonzy and Blind Blake. Others included are Willie Moore, Blind Willie McTell, Rev. Gary Davis and white country guitarist Sam McGee.

874.   HANDY, W. C., ed. Blues: an anthology; with an introduc-
        tion by Abbe Niles; illustrations by Miguel Covarrubias.
        New York: Boni, 1926. 180p. illus., bibliog.
        _____. A treasury of the blues; complete words and mu-
        sic of 67 great songs from "Memphis Blues" to the present
        day; with an historical and critical text by Abbe Niles;
        with pictures by Miguel Covarrubias. New York: Boni,
        1949. 258p. illus., bibliog.
        _____. Blues: an anthology; complete words and music
        of 53 great songs...; revised by Jerry Silverman. New
        York: Macmillan; London: Collier-Macmillan, 1972. 224p.
        illus., bibliog.
        Though blues existed for a number of years (as far as we know) before the day in 1903 when he heard and was enthralled by a blues singer in Tutwiler, Miss., to Handy goes the credit for being the first to recognize their potential as popular songs, and the first to compose blues with an eye on their commercial value. The 1st edition of this famous anthology (14 years after the publication of his "Memphis Blues") contained 48 songs (plus two excerpts from Gershwin) in arrangements for voice and piano. The collection

embraced "not only my work but examples of the folk songs that preceded and influenced it, and the later compositions of both Negroes and whites representing the blues influence" (Handy's autobiography, no. 838, p. 210). There is considerable variation between the 1st and 3rd editions. By 1972 over a dozen of the original items have been omitted in favor of songs added in the 2nd edition, and a further five added in reproductions from sheet music. The single sequence of the 1st edition was later changed to a grouping under three heads: "the background" (folk songs, mainly arranged by Handy), "blues" (popular, commercial blues by Handy and others), and "blues-songs" (blues-influenced popular songs, mainly by Handy). Niles' introduction on textual and musical features, Handy himself, other blues "pioneers," and the influence of blues, remains little changed in the later versions. Notes on each song are collected at the back of the book, with titles, first line and name indexes.

875. JAHN, Janheinz, ed. Blues und Work Songs; übertragen und herausgegeben von Janheinz Jahn, mit Melodienotiernungen und einem Essay von Alfons Michael Dauer. Frankfurt: Fischer, 1964. 185p. bibliog., discog.
    Essays on the characteristics of blues poetry by Jahn, and of the music by Dauer, are followed by over 60 blues texts in English and German, with the tunes of 40. No indication is given of the recording or the printed source used as the basis of each transcription.

876. KRISS, Eric. Barrelhouse and boogie piano. New York: Oak Publications, 1974. 111p. illus., discog.
    This second set of transcriptions by Kriss contains 22 pieces by separate pianists, grouped by categories that are, frankly, of little help ("stomps and struts," "roll and tumble," etc.). Writing in Blues Unlimited, 116, Nov/Dec. 1975, Bob Hall and Richard Noblett suggest that a third of the musical transcriptions are inaccurate, and that the number of errors in the transcriptions of the lyrics exceeds this.

877. KRISS, Eric. Six blue-roots pianists. New York: Oak Publications, 1973. 164p. illus., bibliog., discog.
    A collection of transcriptions of 17 blues by six outstanding pianists (Jimmy Yancey, Champion Jack Dupree, Little Brother Montgomery, Speckled Red, Roosevelt Sykes and Otis Spann). An introduction describes the genesis and basis of blues piano. There is a biographical account of each pianist, a description of the character of his blues, and a note on the structure of each blues. The bibliography includes short annotations, and the discography, in two parts, lists solo performances by the six artists, and other currently available albums, arranged by label.

878. MANN, Woody. Six black blues guitarists. New York: Oak Publications, 1973. 112p. illus., discog.
    A personal selection of 28 blues records transcribed, with texts, in tablature and standard notation, and presented, like the Grossman volumes (nos. 870-873), in an instructional way. The six

musicians are: Blind Blake, Blind Willie McTell, Big Bill Broonzy, Memphis Minnie, Revs. Robert Wilkins and Gary Davis. There is a brief introduction on the life and musical style of each artist, and each song has a short historical and technical note.

879. OSTER, Harry. Living country blues. Detroit: Folklore
     Associates, 1969. 464p. illus., bibliog., discog.
     The major part of this important study and collection is de-
voted to the texts of 230 annotated country blues recorded in Louisiana between 1955 and 1961, with some transcribed melodies. They
are arranged thematically in nineteen groups--farming, drinking,
gambling, wandering, love, sex, imprisonment, etc. The notes include information on the singer, accompanist and date, remarks on
the tune and on particular aspects of the subject or form. Many of
the songs were recorded in Angola State Penitentiary. This is described in the first part of the book, which consists of chapters on
the setting of the country blues, history and definition, themes and
function, and study of the blues as poetry. Oster's main interest
lies in literary and sociological aspects of the subject. There are
sixteen photographs, and a discography of performances in the collection, a bibliography of books and articles, and a title index.

880. SACKHEIM, Eric. The blues line: a collection of blues
     lyrics; with illustrations by Jonathan Shahn. New York:
     Grossman, 1969. 500p. illus.
     An impressive, lavishly presented collection of the lyrics of
270 blues covering the period from the mid-1920s to the mid-1950s,
with a predominance of pre-war songs. Arrangement is basically
geographical under states and towns; in addition there are sections
devoted to female blues singers, piano blues artists, and to "the
1940s and 1950s." The printed arrangement of texts on the page is
designed to covey such elements as breath, pause, weight. Passages
where the accuracy of the transcription is in doubt are given in
italics. The volume concludes with a collection of quotes from
blues artists, together with quotes on similar themes from other
world literatures, in an attempt to create a "constructive dialog."
There are line drawings of 77 artists. No index, but an expanded
contents list.

881. SHIRLEY, Kay, ed. The book of the blues; annotated by
     Frank Driggs; record research by Joy Graeme; music re-
     search by Bob Hartsell. New York: Leeds Music, 1963.
     301p. discog.
     The 1930s and 1940s are particularly well represented in this
collection of 100 blues (melodies, guitar chords and texts) which includes examples of the country, classic and urban styles, as well as
some of the more sophisticated compositions of the Clarence Williams
type, and some instrumental jazz numbers, with supplied lyrics.
Notes to each song give brief comments, a list of recorded versions
(without dates), guitar and tenor banjo diagrams. Though some piano blues are included these are given with melodies and guitar
chords only. There is a title, but no artist index.

882. SILVERMAN, Jerry, ed. <u>Folk blues: 110 American folk</u>
<u>blues</u>; compiled, edited and arranged for voice, piano and
guitar by Jerry Silverman. New York: Macmillan, 1958;
New York: Oak Publications, 1968. 297p. illus., bibliog.,
discog.
An anthology of words and music divided into six groups
(work songs, love songs, etc.). The 110 songs are mainly of black
origin, though there are some white blues (Woody Guthrie, Jimmie
Rodgers). They are provided with accompaniments for piano or guitar, and there is a section of talking blues. Each song has a brief
prefatory note on its theme, with acknowledgment of the composer
if known. The editor's introduction describes the lives of Blind
Lemon Jefferson, Leadbelly, Rodgers, Guthrie and Josh White, and
explains some technical aspects of the blues style. The index of
song titles and first lines is combined with the bibliography and
discography.

11. Rhythm and Blues, Soul, Gospel

a. Rhythm and Blues

883. BROVEN, John. <u>Walking to New Orleans: the story of New</u>
<u>Orleans rhythm and blues.</u> Bexhill-on-Sea: Blues Un-
limited, 1974. 249p. illus., bibliog., discog.
Broven's book provides very welcome information on a less
well documented area of the music of New Orleans: its significance
as a center for rhythm and blues and for rock and roll. The aspects he chooses to emphasize are the record companies and the
recording careers of the various artists (around 80 of them). The
text proceeds chronologically from the late 1940s, through the rock
and roll era to the decline of the city's importance in this idiom,
and the rise in popularity of soul music in the 1960s. There is a
separate chapter on the local record scene, 1955-1963. Each broad
section contains a large number of short, separate accounts of individual artists and of the activities of record companies, for which
Broven's chief source is interview material. This method provides
plentiful biographical and historical facts, but seems to prevent the
emergence of a coherent historical outline. The author writes regularly for the British blues journal <u>Blues Unlimited</u>, which has made
outstanding contributions to our knowledge of the careers of blues
singers great and small, usually utilizing the same basic sources
as he does. At times his book resembles a pastiche of <u>BU</u> articles,
not always interrelated. All the facts are there, but he seems reluctant to assimilate them. One looks in vain, also, for any discussion of the music. The appendix includes a list of the personnel of
the major New Orleans rhythm and blues bands, and a compilation
of hit singles by New Orleans singers, 1946-1972. There is also
an album discography and an index.

884. GROIA, Philip. <u>They all sang on the corner: New York</u>

City's rhythm and blues vocal groups of the 1950s. Setauket, N.Y.: Edmond, 1973. 147p. illus., discogs.

Based on interviews, articles and a "personal listening experience that dates back to 1954," Groia's book contains an abundant supply of data on the musical activities of the black rhythm and blues groups of New York City, whose a capella singing on street corners and church stoops was very influential in the course taken by popular music. The period covered is 1947-1960, and the major part of the book is taken up with a chronologically organized account of the major groups, from the pioneers of the 1940s, such as The Ravens and The Orioles, and the groups with strong gospel roots (Dominoes, Drifters, etc.), to the peak period of the mid-'50s, featuring The Harptones, Cadillacs, Vocaleers, Solitaires and others (with discographies for a number of these). Large numbers of groups were never known outside of their locality, and Groia describes the groups of two particular areas of Harlem--115th St. and Sugar Hill. In general, though he summarizes stylistic features and hints at social aspects, he avoids close examination of the music and its function in the society from which it sprang. Index.

885. MILLAR, Bill. The Coasters. London: Star Books, 1975. 206p. illus., discog.

A similar work to the author's book on the Drifters (no. 886), this is a thoroughly researched history and study of the West Coast rhythm and blues group linked with the success of the songwriting partnership of Jerry Leiber and Mike Stoller (a list of whose songs is included).

886. MILLAR, Bill. The Drifters: the rise and fall of the black vocal group. London: Studio Vista, 1971. 112p. illus., bibliog. notes, discog.
_____. _____. New York: Macmillan, 1971. 180p. illus., bibliog. notes, discog.

A chronicle of the fortunes and changing approaches of black rhythm and blues groups in the 1950s and 1960s, with particular attention to the Drifters. The author describes first the emergence of gospel music, and its influence on post-war rhythm and blues. Beginning with the Inkspots, he traces the development of rhythm and blues groups, their initial successes, and their adaptability or otherwise to the advent of rock and roll. Discographical references are given for each record title quoted in the text, and there is a complete Drifters discography, a list of lead singers and a chronology of hit records. Many photographs, but no index.

887. PROPES, Steve. Golden oldies: a guide to '60s record collecting. Radnor, Pa.: Chilton, 1974. 240p.

Organized on the same pattern as no. 888, and aimed at the beginner in the field of record collecting, this is a listing of the most sought after rhythm and blues, soul, rock and roll, and rock 45 rpm singles from the 1960s, with short accounts of the history of each artist or group, and some comments on the scarcity of particular types of record. The artists concerned are arranged in groups ("Memphis Sound," "Folk Rock," etc.); though the contents

page does not name the minor performers there is no index. The
discographical information given is limited to record company and
number, titles and year.

888.   PROPES, Steve.   Those oldies but goodies: a guide to '50s
        record collecting.   New York: Macmillan, 1973.   192p.
        discogs.
        45 r.p.m. and 78 r.p.m. records of the 1950s having be-
come collectors' items, Propes offers advice to the collector, and
lists those recordings, in the fields of rhythm and blues (groups,
duets and individual artists), rock and roll, and rockabilly, that he
deems "the most significant and influential." Each entry for a major figure includes notes on the group's or artist's recording history, and on the rarity and value of the records, followed by a
simple discography, giving label, release numbers, titles, and year.
Other "notable" groups and individuals are treated chronologically.

889.   SCHIESEL, Jane.   The Otis Redding story.   Garden City:
        Doubleday, 1973.   143p.   discog.
        Rather slight popular biography, complete with eavesdropped
conversations, of the rhythm and blues singer from his early days
(and gospel roots) in Georgia to his untimely death in a plane crash
in 1967--a death that robbed black music of one of its leading lights.

890.   WHITBURN, Joel, comp.   Top rhythm and blues records,
        1949-1971.   Menomonee Falls, Wis.: Record Research,
        1973.   183p.   illus.
        Not a complete rhythm and blues discography, but, like no.
1340 for popular hits, a listing of best-selling records, based on
Billboard charts, (the "Rhythm and Blues" chart changed its name
to "Soul" chart in 1969).   The main listing is by artist; alongside
the title of each record there is information regarding its date of
entry to the chart, highest position, number of weeks on the chart,
label name and release number.   There is also a title index, a
chronological list of records reaching the "Number 1" position, and
an artist listing, taken from "Hot 100," for the period between November 1963 and January 1965, when the rhythm and blues chart
was not published.

b.   Soul

See also no. 1339.

891.   GARLAND, Phyl.   The sound of soul.   Chicago: Regnery,
        1969.   illus., bibliog. notes, discog.
        This informal account by a black journalist begins with an
examination of the continuity of soul elements in the black music
tradition, embracing jazz, blues and gospel, an exploration of the
reasons for this mode of expression being a jealously guarded racial
property, and a discussion of the conflicts and contradictions caused
by its rise to popular success.   The author identifies the roots of
soul music in the Negro past, and traces the lines of musical develop

ment through blues, spirituals, jazz and minstrelsy. Turning to the current scene, she interviews B. B. King and Nina Simone, gives a profile of Aretha Franklin, and describes the recording of soul music in Memphis. A section devoted to soul in jazz includes an interview with Billy Taylor, a portrait of John Coltrane, and a forecast that the future of soul will be as a functional art tied to contemporary life. The LPs in the discography are selected to illustrate the text. Index.

892. HARALAMBOS, Michael. Right on: from blues to soul in black America. London: Eddison Press, 1974. 187p. illus., bibliog., discog.

Using sociological statistics and information obtained from black radio personnel this study sets out to account for the decline in popularity of the blues among the Negro population, and the increasing appeal of soul, relating the process directly to changes in black society and culture. Examination and comparison of two urban blues styles--"downhome" Chicago style, and the modern Memphis synthesis--and the reasons for the relatively greater popularity of the latter, lead to exploration of the different support given to the blues in areas of the South, and the suggestion that strong connections exist between the function of the blues and widespread discrimination and poverty. Reasons for the decrease in the blues' popularity are sought in the characteristics, functions, attitudes and associations of the idiom, which is seen as out of harmony with the modern mood. The distinctive features of soul and its appeal for the black audience are discussed and contrasted with those of blues (e.g., attitudes to the love theme, where soul is more moralistic, virtuous, and optimistic). Changes in music and attitudes to music are related closely to social changes in the 1950s and 1960s, and the decline of the blues specifically to reaction against the Jim Crow system and associated attitudes of acceptance. Appendices discuss blues and soul vis-à-vis the black family, and possible trends. Index.

893. MORSE, David. Motown and the arrival of black music. London: Studio Vista, 1971. 110p. illus.
_____. _____. New York: Macmillan, 1971. 143p. illus.

A study of the enormously successful black commercial enterprise, the background to its development into one of the major styles and influences in contemporary popular music, the characteristic features of its gospel-based style, and its critical reception. The author also gives accounts of the music and the careers of some of Motown's most successful artists: Martha Reeves and the Vandellas, Smokey Robinson and the Miracles, the Supremes, the Temptations, and the Four Tops. A chapter is devoted to lesser known artists, and the book ends with an indication of some of the social and cultural implications of the Motown phenomenon. A large number of artists appear in the photographic illustrations. No index.

894. NICHOLAS, A. X., ed. The poetry of soul. New York:

Bantam Books, 1971. 103p. discog.

The lyrics of 43 soul songs, recorded by Aretha Franklin, Otis Redding, B. B. King, Nina Simone, James Brown, Curtis Mayfield, Sam Cooke and others, are given here, arranged in four groups as they reflect aspects of black experience. In his introduction the compiler provides a brief, politically angled historical survey of black music in the U.S., and in the context describes the genesis and character of soul music. The discography lists LPs on which the songs appear.

895. SHAW, Arnold. The world of soul: black America's contribution to the pop music scene. New York: Cowles, 1970. 306p. illus., discog.

This account traces the development of soul music from its roots in country blues, and explores the music of a large number of individuals in the blues and rhythm and blues field for details of how the sense of identification with a group evolved, and for characteristic features such as pride, social anger, and jubilant eroticism. The section on soul music itself stresses that the most immediate roots are in gospel and black church music, and illustrates this by describing the singing of Rosetta Tharpe, Mahalia Jackson and others. There are profiles of some outstanding individuals: Nina Simone, James Brown, Jimi Hendrix, Otis Redding, Aretha Franklin, Ray Charles. A final chapter discusses white imitators. The LP discography is arranged by chapter. Index.

c. Gospel Music

See also no. 806.

896. HAYES, Cedric. A discography of gospel records, 1937-1971. Copenhagen: Knudsen, 1973. 116p.

This selective discography marks the first step towards a complete listing of gospel records from 1943 on (Godrich and Dixon, no. 806, covers the period to 1942). It consists of discographies for three individual artists--Mahalia Jackson, Sister Rosetta Tharpe, and Marian Williams--and eleven groups: Caravans, Dixie Hummingbirds, Five Blind Boys of Mississippi, Gospelaires, Mighty Clouds of Joy, Soul Stirrers, Spirit of Memphis Quartet, Staple Singers, Stars of Faith, Swan Silver Tone Singers, Ward Singers. The discographical information given is personnel, location, date, matrix number, title and release number (78, EP and LP, including reissues). There is no index.

897. HEILBUT, Tony. The gospel sound: good news and bad times. New York: Simon & Schuster, 1971. 350p. illus. discog.

This first attempt at a history of 20th century black gospel music is a well-researched and enjoyable chronicle that gives a clear outline of historical development through the series of biographical profiles that form the kernel of the book, and in which we not only see the lives and careers of the principal performers, but are also

led to appreciate their style and influence. The early trailblazers
appear first--Sallie Martin, Thomas Dorsey, Ira Tucker, Mahalia
Jackson and R. H. Harris--followed by a group of outstanding pioneer
singers, including Bessie Griffin, Alex Bradford, and Dorothy Love
Coates. The author bases his accounts on interviews, and includes
the performers' own recollections, along with examples of the verses
of some of their songs, and assessment of their achievement. There
are also portraits of the Holiness Church, its role and influence, and
of the gospel life. Heilbut is deeply sympathetic to the music and
the musicians; he also clearly distinguishes between the good and indifferent. The discography lists LPs under artist or group, and
there are indexes of names and titles.

898. JACKSON, Jesse. Make a joyful noise unto the Lord! the
      life of Mahalia Jackson, queen of gospel singers. New
      York: Crowell, 1974. 160p. illus.
    A re-telling of Mahalia Jackson's story for younger readers,
using much material collected from her radio and television appearances.

899. JACKSON, Mahalia. Movin' on up; with Evan McLeod Wylie.
      New York: Hawthorn Books, 1966. 212p. illus., discog.
      _____. _____. New York: Avon Books, 1969. 217p.
      illus., discog.
    The autobiography of probably the best-known post-war gospel
singer (1911-1972), describing her childhood in New Orleans, long
musical apprenticeship in Chicago (where, among other activities,
she toured for five years with Thomas A.--formerly Georgia Tom--
Dorsey), her rise to fame with the recording "Movin' On Up" in
1946, her subsequent career as concert artist in Europe and America
and as television personality, and her involvement with the Civil
Rights movement. Among the numerous interesting features of her
story are her account of the uncompromising attitude towards secular black music common among black church people in the South,
and the way in which her own success, with its attendant commercialism and the move of gospel music from church to concert hall,
illustrates a secularization process in the music (though she herself
retains a simple, devout religious faith). Her association with the
Civil Rights movement reminds us of the important role music played
in black protest in the 1960s. The discography is a selection of LPs
with their contents.

900. MEMORIAL TRIBUTE: Mahalia Jackson, world's greatest
      gospel singer. n.p., n.d., 1972? unpaged, illus., discog.
    A commemorative booklet, including a report of Mahalia's
funeral in January 1972, reproductions of biographical liner notes by
Tom Paisley and of a contribution by Mahalia to Gospel World, and
photographs of the singer on tour, of her part in campaigns, and of
other public and personal moments. The discography is a partial
list of LPs with contents.

1. Reference Works

a. General Reference

See also no. 1158

901. CHILTON, John. Who's who of jazz: Storyville to Swing-
        street. London: Bloomsbury Book Shop, 1970. 447p.
        illus.
        _____. _____. Philadelphia: Chilton, 1972. 419p.
        illus.
        A valuable biographical dictionary, giving precise, factual in-
formation in compact form on the careers of over 1,000 jazz musicians born before 1920 in the U.S. Arrangement is alphabetical.
Entries give area of musical activity, dates of birth and death, and
details of the life and career of each individual, presented without
comment. In each entry the names of other jazz figures connected
with the artist in question are given in capital letters. In some instances a note at the end of an entry mentions film appearances,
books, and similar information. Following the main section there
is a list of band-leaders mentioned in the text.

902. DANCE, Stanley, ed. Jazz era: the 'forties; written in
        collaboration with Yannick Bruynoghe, Scoops Carry, Max
        Harrison, Hugues Panassié, John Steiner, Dickie Wells,
        Charlie Wilford. London: MacGibbon & Kee, 1961; Lon-
        don: Jazz Book Club, 1962. 252p. discogs.
        The first and only volume in an intended four-part set cover-
ing a decade each from 1920-1959, this work shows clearly how dif-
fering jazz styles--in this decade probably more than any other--ex-
isted concurrently. The main part of the book takes the form of an
annotated guide to the playing of almost 200 individual artists and
bands in both jazz and blues. Entries give some biographical information, concise critical assessment, and a selective list of record
titles with dates and label names (but no further information). Preceding the guide are an introduction by Dance, and transcriptions of
interviews with Carry and Wells.

903. FEATHER, Leonard. The encyclopedia of jazz; foreword by
        Duke Ellington. New York: Horizon Press, 1955; London:
        Barker, 1956. 260p. illus., bibliog., discog.

_____. New edition of the Encyclopedia of jazz; completely revised enlarged and brought up to date; appreciations by Duke Ellington, Benny Goodman and John Hammond. New York: Horizon Press; New York: Bonanza Books, 1960; London: Barker, 1961; London: Jazz Book Club. 1963. 527p. illus., bibliog. discog.

In 1956 and 1957 Feather published an Encyclopedia Yearbook of Jazz, and all the new material in these volumes was included in the new edition of this most useful reference work. The major part of the book is given over to a biographical dictionary of over 2,000 musicians, with details of instrument played, place and dates of birth and death, career, and, in a large number of instances, assessment of the artist's place and contribution. Also included are a historical survey, a chronology, an analysis of the musical make-up of jazz, and an assessment of jazz in American society. Following the biographies we have a description of the blindfold test, international popularity polls for 1959 and 1960, pieces on jazz overseas by various contributors, and one on jazz and classical music by Gunther Schuller. There are lists of recommended records, musicians' birthdays and birthplaces, jazz organizations, schools and booking agencies, record companies and books. In the preface to the first edition Feather acknowledges a great debt to the research of Ira Gitler.

904. FEATHER, Leonard. The encyclopedia of jazz in the sixties; foreword by John Lewis. New York: Horizon Press; New York: Bonanza Books, 1966. 312p. illus., bibliog., discog.

Continuing Feather's Encyclopedia of Jazz (no. 903), this work is arranged in much the same way, combining biographical sketches, essays, and reference information. There are some 1100 biographies of instrumentalists, singers and composers; all those included had established a reputation in jazz in the U.S. or abroad, had made contributions to jazz in the '60s and had participated in at least one LP. Entries give instrument, dates and place of birth and death, career details with emphasis on the artist's work in the '60s, and in many cases, comments on the artist's stylistic development in the period, significant influences and partnerships, etc. Some discographical information is given, often chosen by the artist. Other pieces include a selection of blindfold texts and an essay on the blues and folk scene by Pete Welding. The discography is a personal selection and the bibliography lists books published in the '60s.

905. GOLD, Robert S. A jazz lexicon. New York: Knopf, 1964. 363p. bibliog.

_____. Jazz talk. Indianapolis: Bobbs Merrill, 1975. 400p. bibliog.

An interesting dictionary of the vernacular speech of the jazz world, the individual words and short phrases which make up a peculiarly American idiom that grew out of the conditions that nurtured the development of jazz. An introduction examines the nature and purpose of jazz slang. In the dictionary itself most entries consist of an indication of the part of speech of the particular word, a note on its etymology and currency, sometimes a plain definition, but more often references to printed sources (books, articles, liner notes) which themselves attempt a definition, and examples of the word's usage. The 1975 edition updates and revises the information given in the first version.

906. JÖRGENSEN, John, and WIEDEMANN, Erik. Mosaik Jazz-lexicon. Hamburg: Mosaik, 1966. 399p. bibliog.
A good reference work with a wide coverage of individuals and no date restrictions. There are approximately 1,800 biographies of jazz musicians, singers, orchestra leaders and composers, plus a few entries under individual orchestras, and a smattering of blues and gospel singers. Each entry gives field of activity, date and place of birth (and death where relevant), and a summary of the person's professional career; for the more significant musicians there are concise comments on style and influence, and references to important recordings. There are no entries for styles, instruments or clubs.

907. KEEPNEWS, Orrin, and GRAUER, Bill. A pictorial history of jazz: people and places from New Orleans to modern jazz. New York: Crown, 1955; London: Hale, 1956; London: Spring Books, 1958. 282p. illus.
_____. _____. New ed., revised by Orrin Keepnews. New York: Crown; London: Hale, 1968. 297p. illus.
Over 700 illustrations (in the rev. ed.) make up this crowded portrait album of musicians from all periods of jazz, photographed singly and in groups, some posing, others relaxed, some bland, others intense, the majority making music, others taking a break from it. The text is kept to a minimum. Arrangement is broadly chronological, divided into twenty chapters ("New Orleans Joys," "Swing, Brother, Swing," etc.,), with some devoted entirely to individuals (Armstrong, Morton). A list of picture sources is given, and an index.

908. LANGRIDGE, Derek. Your jazz collection. London: Bingley; Hamden: Archon Books, 1970. 162p. bibliogs.
The author of this guide for the private collector and the librarian has had wide experience in each activity. The opening chapters relate the philosophy of collecting to jazz and offer guidance on collectors' aids--institutions and the various kinds of literature. Bibliographies in the text list items in the categories of material described--discographies, reference works, introductions, histories, social and musical analysis, and biographies. Half of the book is devoted to a detailed scheme for classifying and indexing both literature and recordings. Index.

909. LONGSTREET, Stephen, and DAUER, Alfons M. Knaurs Jazz-lexikon. Munich: Knaur, 1957. 324p. illus. (some col.), discog.
_____. Encyclópedie du jazz; adaption francaise de Jacques Bureau. Paris: Somogy, 1958. 320p. illus. (some col.), discog.
It is instructive to compare a concise, objective reference

work like this one with other "encyclopedic" offerings in popular music, such as Shestack (no. 609) or Roxon (no. 1338). Whereas they are almost totally concerned with individuals, Longstreet and Dauer's compass extends to dances, technical terms, jazz styles, related forms, instruments, countries. While one of the salient characteristics of entries in Shestack and Roxon is an inability to state facts plainly, Longstreet and Dauer's entries are to the point, factual, and almost wholly free of waffle. (Beyond Longstreet's effective paintings, it is not clear how he and Dauer divided the work.)

910. MARKEWICH, Reese. Bibliography of jazz and pop tunes sharing the chord progressions of other compositions. Riverdale, N.Y.: the author, 1970. 58p.
_____ . _____ . New expanded ed. New York: the author, 1974. 45p.
An alphabetical list of tune titles, with brief details of their composer and lyricist, publisher, selected "creatively interesting recordings" and show titles where appropriate. Each of these "standards" is followed by a list of other compositions based on the same chord progressions, also with details of composer, publisher and recording.

911. MARKEWICH, Reese. Jazz publicity: bibliography of names and addresses of international jazz critics and magazines. Riverdale, N.Y.: the author, 1973. 24p.
_____ . Jazz publicity II: newly revised and expanded bibliography ... New York: the author, 1974. 25p.
Dictionaries normally define "bibliography" as the history of books, their authorship and editions, or as a list of books of any author, printer, country or subject. According to this compiler it means an out-of-date address book.

912. PANASSIE, Hugues, and GAUTIER, Madeleine. Dictionnaire du jazz. Paris: Laffont, 1954. 366p. illus.
_____ . Dictionary of jazz; translated by Desmond Flower; foreword by Louis Armstrong. London: Cassell, 1956; London Jazz Book Club, 1959. 288p. illus.
_____ . Guide to jazz; translated by Desmond Flower; edited by A. A. Gurwitsch; introduction by Louis Armstrong. Boston: Houghton Mifflin, 1956. 312p. illus., discog.
Readers of Panassié's books must make some allowances for the strong personal likes and dislikes of their author, and this reference work is no exception. Panassié holds, for example, that bop is not jazz--so one does not look to his entry on the subject expecting an unprejudiced description. Nevertheless, there is much useful data, particularly in the biographies (of "true jazzmen" only), many of which include also a brief stylistic appreciation. There are also entries for bands, instruments, styles, standard tunes and technical terms, making Panassié's coverage more genuinely encyclopedic than that of most jazz reference works.

b. Bibliographies

913. HASELGROVE, J. R., and KENNINGTON, D., eds. Readers'
     guide to books on jazz. London: Library Association,
     County Libraries Section, 1960. (Readers' Guides. New
     Series, 55) 16p.
     _____. _____. 2nd ed. London: Library Association,
     County Libraries Group, 1965. (Readers' Guides. New
     Series, 83) 15p. discog.
     A short, selective bibliography, the first of its kind to be
published in Great Britain. The second edition is divided into general background (including social studies), theory, biography and
criticism, discographies and reference works, jazz literature (fiction)
and periodicals. There is also a list of fifty LPs.

914. KENNINGTON, Donald. The literature of jazz: a critical
     guide. London: Library Association, 1970; Chicago:
     American Library Association, 1971. 142p. bibliogs.
     A guide to the various kind of jazz literature: the general
musical background (with small amounts of social history), jazz histories, biographies, analysis and theory, reference sources, periodical literature, jazz and literature, and organizations. The author
describes the main features of the most important works in each
category, giving a useful overall idea of the various lines jazz writing has taken, and at the end of each chapter provides an annotated
bibliography of the books he has described, adding others in the
same category. An appendix lists jazz films, and there are author/
subject and title indexes.

915. MECKLENBURG, Carl Gregor, Herzog zu, ed. International
     jazz bibliography: jazz books from 1919 to 1968. Stras-
     bourg: Heitz, 1969. (Collection d'Etudes Musicologiques,
     49) 193p.
     The first attempt at a comprehensive listing of books on jazz
--which is here taken to include blues literature (except where blues
is a "psychological, literary and musical complex as a whole"), ragtime
literature, books on symphonic jazz or jazz-influenced light music,
and all books on jazz except poetry, fiction, primers and various
kinds of ephemera. There are 1,562 entries (not all for totally separate entities--many are reissues, translations, etc.). Arrangement
is alphabetical by author in an unbroken sequence, with full title,
imprint and collation. Reissues, new editions and translations are
all indicated as such in notes. There are eleven indexes: series,
persons, second authors, editors, authors of forewords or epilogs,
contributors and collaborators, translators, illustrators, countries,
and subjects. The latter is restricted to twelve subjects, which
makes for some long sequences of numbers; the remainder of the
index is made up of catchwords (which are often virtually equivalent
to titles).

916. MECKLENBURG, Carl Gregor, Herzog zu, ed. 1970 Supple-
     ment to International jazz bibliography, and International
     drum and percussion bibliography. Graz: Universal Edi-

tion, 1971. (Studies in Jazz Research, 3) 59, 43p.

This first supplement to no. 915 lists a further 429 titles of books and pamphlets published between 1968 and 1970, and ones missed in the initial volume. Unlike the latter, this volume is arranged in fourteen categories, including bibliographies and reference works, biographies and monographs, history, theory, discographies, blues, dance and sound recording. Indexes have been dispensed with (a dubious step: all classified bibliographies should have supporting name indexes at the very least). Of the various categories one in particular--"background literature"--begs a great many questions, especially as only eight items are listed. (The compiler does not define his terms until the second supplement.) As a mark of thanks to his contributors Mecklenburg includes after each entry the name of the person or persons who supplied the data. There is a noticeable increase in the number of queries indicating doubt as to specific items. The drum and percussion bibliography lists 358 books on all aspects of drumming in relation not only to jazz but also to dance band music, rock and roll and Latin American styles. There are also sections devoted to percussion ensemble scores and scoring (38 items), drum magazine titles (4), and practice recordings. No author index.

917. MECKLENBURG, Carl Gregor, Herzog zu, ed. 1971/72/73 Supplement to International jazz bibliography, and selective bibliography of some jazz background literature, and bibliography of two subjects previously excluded. Graz: Universal Edition, 1975. (Studies in Jazz Research, 6) 246p.

This second supplement contains new titles published between 1971 and 1973, plus details of items missed in the original volume and in the 1970 supplement. In arrangement (fifteen categories) and coverage it is very similar to its immediate predecessor, and, like that volume, again omits all indexes--an even more regrettable decision in a book of 1,302 entries. (The two new subjects are dissertations, and books on beat, rock and pop.) There is no gainsaying the enormous contribution these three volumes have made to our knowledge of jazz literature, but this second supplement in particular illustrates the great difficulties involved in compiling a bibliography very largely from information supplied by others, and doing so in an area where personal access both to the books themselves and to reference information in bibliographies is apparently limited. A great many items in this volume seem to have queries beside one category of data or another, be it date, place, publisher, or pagination. The compiler's practice is to enter all the information supplied to him, regardless of how incomplete it is, or how it contradicts data supplies by others. For all his protestations to the contrary, many of these queries could have been cleared up by reference to national bibliographies, catalogs of national or large public libraries, etc. (e.g., 602, Bernstein's Joy of Music, or 713, Oxford Companion to Music). This is not "petty" criticism, as the editor believes; the book's lack of confidence in its own data sooner or later engenders the same feeling in the user. It is to be hoped that the proposed "Chronological International Bibliography of Jazz Books," designed to succeed this volume, will correct much of this.

918.   MERRIAM, Alan P., ed.   A bibliography of jazz; with the
            assistance of Robert J. Benford.   Philadelphia: American
            Folklore Society, 1954.   (Repr. New York: Da Capo; New
            York: Kraus, 1970).   145p.
        The first book-length bibliography of jazz literature, listing
3,324 books, parts of books, and articles, arranged alphabetically by
author, with subject and periodical title indexes.   All jazz items
known to the compilers published before 1951 are included.   Each entry in the main section is followed by a code symbol indicating the
principal subject of the entry; there are thirty-two such symbols.
Following the main section there is a list of 113 magazines devoted
wholly or largely to jazz.   The subject index is based on the thirty-
two categories, and also includes jazz artists.   The index to periodicals includes place of publication.

919.   MOON, Pete, comp.   A bibliography of jazz discographies
            published since 1960; edited by Barry Witherden.   London:
            British Institute of Jazz Studies, 1969.   unpaged.
                            .   2nd ed.   South Harrow. Middx.:   Brit-
            ish Institute of Jazz Studies, 1972.   unpaged.
        This most useful mimeographed list is devoted principally to
single artist discographies.   It is arranged alphabetically by artist
with details of compiler, source and format (periodicals, books,
booklets, with dates).   There are also lists of discographies in the
pipeline, of the booklets of W. F. Van Eyle and Ernest Edwards
Jr., of the various parts of the Stan Kenton Directory, and of
discographers' addresses.   The 2nd edition contains a supplement
which includes corrections and additions, and lists of the discographies published in Musica Jazz (Milan) and Orkester Journalen (Stock-
holm).

920.   REISNER, Robert George, ed.   The literature of jazz: a
            preliminary bibliography; with an introduction by Marshall
            W. Stearns.   New York: New York Public Library, 1954.
            53p.
                        .   The literature of jazz: a selective bibliography...
            2nd ed., revised and enlarged.   New York: New York
            Public Library, 1959.   63p.
        The first version of this check list appeared at about the
same time as Merriam (no. 918) but it is a much more selective
work.   The 2nd edition has four sections: books on jazz (slightly
over 500), background books (about 100), selective magazine references in non-jazz periodicals (about 900), and an international list
of magazines devoted wholly or principally to jazz.   (The 1st edition
lists some articles in specialist journals, but these are omitted in
the 2nd.)   Within each section items are arranged alphabetically by
author, and, as there is no subject index, this makes locating material on specific subjects difficult.   The only concession the compiler makes is in annotating a biographical work if its title is not
self-explanatory.   (Fiction is also annotated.)   Full bibliographical
details are given.

c. Jazz on Film

921. MEEKER, David. Jazz in the movies: a tentative index to
the work of jazz musicians for the cinema. London:
British Film Institute, 1972. 89p. illus.
A useful annotated list of 709 films, both feature films and
shorts, alphabetically arranged by title. Coverage includes films
about jazz and blues, feature films including appearances by jazz
and blues artists, and feature films with scores by jazzmen. For
each film the information given includes country of origin, date, director and duration. The annotations frequently include personal
opinions, and, in the case of feature films with appearances by jazz
and blues artists, tend to describe and evaluate the cinematic and
aesthetic aspects of the film and merely note the musicians' contribution. There is an artist index.

922. WHANNEL, Paddy, comp. Jazz on film. London: British
Film Institute, (1962?). 9p.
A selective list of 61 films in distribution at the time of compilation. It is arranged in two sections: feature-length films and
shorts. The entries give details of director, duration, country,
date, and distributors for 16mm and 35mm where known. There
are annotations regarding the jazz musicians featured. Jazz on the
sound track only is excluded.

2. Discographies

a. General*

923. SCHLEMAN, Hilton. Rhythm on record: a who's who and
register of recorded dance music. London: Melody Maker,
1936. 334p. illus.
While the various editions of Delaunay's discography (no. 924)
mark the inauguration of the science of jazz discography in book
form, this rare item claims the distinction of having preceded Delaunay by a few months. Unlike subsequent discographies, Schleman
includes a large number of dance bands (an area not comprehensive-
ly surveyed until Rust's dance band discography, no. 936). He also
prefaces each artist or band listing with a brief biography. Arrangement is alphabetical in one sequence, with, by modern standards,
very incomplete discographical detail. (The present writer has not
seen this book. Information comes from Paul Sheatsley, "A Quarter
Century of Jazz Discography," Record Research, Feb. 1964. Curious scholars or amateurs are advised that the British Museum's
copy was destroyed by bombing, and the Library of Congress has
never had one.)

---

*This section is arranged chronologically.

924. DELAUNAY, Charles. Hot discography; forewords by Hugues
      and Lucienne Panassié and Henri Bernard. Paris: Hot
      Jazz, 1936. 271p.
      _____. _____. (New ed.) Paris: Hot Jazz, 1938.
      408p.
              . Hot discography; edited by Hot Jazz. (3rd ed.)
      New York: Commodore Music Shop, 1940. 416p.
              . Hot discographie, 1943. Paris: Collection du
      Hot Club de France, 1944. 538p.
              . New hot discography: the standard directory of
      recorded jazz, edited by Walter E. Schaap and George
      Avakian. New York: Criterion Music Corp., 1948. 608p.
              . Hot discographie encyclopédique; avec la collabora-
      tion de Kurt Mohr. Paris: Jazz Disques, 1951-1952.
      3v. (A-Hefti)
      These are the works to which all jazz discographers owe a
great debt, for it was Delaunay who established the standard pattern
of information (location, date, personnel, title, matrix and release
numbers) and recognized the significance of matrix numbers. His approach was a selective one, and his initial method was to group the
chosen artists in broad, chronologically arranged categories by
stylistic affinity. The various editions greatly expanded the amount
of information given and broadened the scope, but the approach remained selective. The attempt at a classified historical arrangement was eventually dropped, however, in favor of a single alphabetical sequence; not, apparently, through a failure of belief, but
because of the exigencies of publication in parts in Hot Discographie
Encyclopédique. (In fact, the increasing amount of jazz recordings
forced the abandonment of this edition.) It was a worthwhile experiment, offering interesting parallels with bibliographic guides, but one
more suited to a situation where all the recoverable information had
been sifted and made available. Combined with a more comprehensive approach than Delaunay's it could still have interesting results.
(Artist indexes are provided to the group arrangement.)

925. BLACKSTONE, Orin. Index to jazz. Fairfax, Va.: The
      Record Changer, 1945-1948. 4v.
      _____. _____. (2nd ed.) New Orleans: Privately
      printed, (1949). Vol. 1 A-E. 312p.
      The first general American discography shunned Delaunay's
evaluative approach, attempting to be as comprehensive as possible.
By beginning with an alphabetical artist arrangement and seeing the
project through Z, Blackstone gave us the first of the modern, would-
be definitive discographies. Much information is lacking, especially
dates and matrix numbers. The 2nd edition held promise of considerably improving this but remained unfinished. One feature of Blackstone's approach not often emulated is his preference for catalog
over matrix number order.

926. CAREY, David A., and McCARTHY, Albert J., comps. The
      directory of recorded jazz and swing music... Fording-
      bridge, Hants.: Delphic Press, 1949-1952 (Vol. 1-4);
      London: Cassell, 1955-1957 (Vols. 5, 6). 6v. (A-Long-

shaw)

_____. _____. Vols. 2-4. 2nd ed. London: Cassell,
1955-1957. (C-I).

Otherwise known as Jazz Directory, this British discography
was the most successful attempt at a broadly-based, definitive work,
when it unfortunately ceased publication in 1957 mid-way through the
letter L. Its coverage went beyond jazz to Negro spirituals, gospel
and "race" records, omitting most "commercial renderings" unless
they featured prestigious artists or soloists of merit. A large
amount of both swing and bop is included. The team was originally
a trio: Ralph Venables, responsible for white jazz research in Vol.
1, dropped out before the second volume. McCarthy's role seems to
have gradually increased, as he is the first named in Vols. 5 and 6.
Better produced than previous multi-volume discographies, the Directory gives all known discographical details, limiting its listing of
catalog numbers to American and British labels in most cases. (Because of the Directory's extensive post-1942 coverage Jepsen, when
he began publishing his Jazz Records (no. 931), began where Carey
and McCarthy had ceased, at the letter M.)

927. TRAILL, Sinclair, and LASCELLES, Gerald. Just jazz.
London: Davies, 1957. 226, 218p. illus., discog.

_____. _____. 2. London: Davies, 1958. 193, 253p.
illus., discog.

_____. _____. 3. London: Landsborough Publications,
1959. 347p. illus., discog.

_____. _____. 4. London: Souvenir Press, 1960.
128, 159p. illus., discog.

These volumes of essays on many aspects of jazz, mainly by
British writers, contain the forerunner of Cherrington and Knight's
Jazz Catalogue (no. 929). Each book contains an annual discography,
those in Volumes 1 and 2 being by Derek Coller and Eric Townley,
that in Vol. 3 by Frank Dutton and Townley, and that in Vol. 4 by
George Cherrington. (1958 thus received royal attention, as it was
also covered by McCarthy's Jazz Discography, no. 928. The Just
Jazz discographies do, however, lay more emphasis on British releases.)

928. McCARTHY, Albert J., comp. Jazz discography 1: an international discography of recorded jazz, including blues, gospel, and rhythm-and-blues for the year January-December
1958. London: Cassell, 1960. 271p.

The great difficulty in keeping up with new releases was the
chief cause of the demise of the Directory of Recorded Jazz (no.
926). Keenly aware of the need to keep abreast of this flood of
material--"it is essential to document the new issues as they appear"
(introduction)--McCarthy tried with this volume to provide complete
coverage of both new releases and U.S.A. reissues for one year.
Although he hoped to continue this endeavor it was the Jazz Catalogue
of Cherrington and Knight that successfully accomplished this for several years (no. 929). (See also Traill, no. 927.)

929. CHERRINGTON, George, and KNIGHT, Brian, comps. Jazz

catalogue: a discography of all British jazz releases, complete with full personnels and recording dates. London: Jazz Journal, 1960-1971. 10v. bibliogs.

The valuable function performed by these volumes in responding to the need to document recorded material in jazz as it appeared (rather than retrospectively--which the great increase in releases in the 1960s made an enormous task) makes it the more regrettable that no volumes have been issued since 1971. Each volume covers the releases in Britain for one particular year (those for 1968-9 being published together in 1970). Coverage includes jazz, blues and gospel music, and numerous American labels (e.g., Riverside, Blue Note, Prestige) are given. Arrangement is alphabetical by artist, with a separate section for collections at the back of each volume. Special mention should be made of the bibliographies by Colin Johnson that appeared in Vols. 2 through 7. These are particularly good for British periodical articles, although they also include material in some American journals. Vol. 1 was compiled by George Cherrington alone. With Vol. 8 the editors changed to Ralph Laing, Michael Coates and Bernard Shirley.

930. RUST, Brian. Jazz records, A-Z, 1897-1931. Hatch End, Middx.: the author, 1961. 844p.
_____. _____. 2nd ed. Hatch End, Middx, 1962. 736p.
_____. _____. Index, compiled by Richard Grandorge. Hatch End, 1963. 62p.
_____. Jazz records, A-Z, 1932-1942. Hatch End, 1965. 680p.
_____. Jazz records, 1897-1942. Rev. ed. London: Storyville Publications, 1970. 2v. 1968p.

One of the outstanding achievements in discography, this gigantic labor of love lists all known records made up to the Petrillo ban in the ragtime, jazz and swing styles, principally in the U.S. and England. Arrangement is alphabetical by artist or band as given on the label; sessions are listed chronologically with personnel and instruments, venue, date, matrix, take and issue numbers (dubbed issues are denoted by underlining). Composers' names are given for ragtime numbers. Microgroove reissues are not included unless the only issue of a title has been on microgroove. A system of abbreviation is used not only for instruments and labels, but also for vocalists and special soloists in a particular title. There are cross references for pseudonyms and notes under certain artists. The indispensable 90-page artist index in the revised edition is by the compiler's wife. (Additions and corrections appear in Storyville magazine, no. 36f.)

931. JEPSEN, Jorgen Grunnet. Jazz records: a discography. Copenhagen: Knudsen, 1963-1970. 8v. in 11.

A compilation as mammoth as Rust's (no. 930), which it continues, listing records issued from 1942 to 1962 (Vols. 5-8), to 1965 (Vols. 1-3) and to 1967 (Vol. 4). Vols. 5-8 were published first, to provide a continuation of the Jazz Directory of Carey and McCarthy which had ceased at the letter L. In Vols. 1-4 Jepsen extended the final date to include information from 1962 to the compilation time of the particular volume. Vol. 4d concludes the work, which he describes as "only the beginning." Coverage is similar to Rust's, but more international, and includes blues records in Vol. 1-3, 4a, 5-8. Gospel records, vocal ensembles (especially rhythm and blues) and "semi-jazz" are excluded. Arrangement is alphabetical by artist or band, and chronological within an artist entry. Information given includes personnel (with instruments), place, date, title, matrix number for originals only, release numbers in the order 78, EP, LP, and whether stereo. Tapes are not included. There are cross references, but there is a great need for a supplementary index.

932. BRUYNINCKX, Walter. 50 years of recorded jazz, 1917-1967. Mechelen: Privately printed, 1968- . (looseleaf sheets)
    The idea behind this production is an interesting one: Bruyninckx attempts to overcome the enormous problems posed for discographers by reissues and new releases by offering, on a subscription basis, an amendments and additions service. This is the reason for the looseleaf format, which does, however, have the disadvantage of rapidly deteriorating pages. The complete discography, A-Z by artist, is currently available, and contains full discographical information.

b. Special

933. AVAKIAN, George. Jazz from Columbia; a complete jazz catalog. New York: Columbia Records, 1956. 32p. illus.
    Put out to advertise Columbia's albums, this list of about 150 LPs and EPs is arranged in categories (swing, piano jazz, etc.), each section having a short introductory essay. The titles of each album track are given, but discographical information is confined to the album release number.

934. EVENSMO, Jan, comp. The tenor saxophonists of the period 1930-1942. Vol. 1. Oslo: Evensmo, 1969. (Jazz Solography Series) 150p.
    Separate discographies of Leon "Chu" Berry, Herschel Evans, Coleman Hawkins, Ben Webster and Lester Young for the thirteen-year period. Besides listing full details of all known recordings and broadcasts of these artists the compiler also gives notes on each solo, with durations, and critical comments.

935. RUPPLI, Michel. Prestige jazz records 1949-1969: a discography. Copenhagen: Knudsen, 1972. 399p.
    A discography listing all recordings made by Prestige Records in the areas of jazz, blues and gospel music between January 1949 and January 1970, and all reissues in the same period made by Prestige from other labels. The main section, the original Prestige recordings, is arranged in chronological order of recording ses-

sions; this is supplemented by a listing of sessions with unknown recording dates and additions. The reissues from other labels are also listed chronologically by original recording date (from 1944 to 1962), with an additional section for the 1969 reissues (ranging from 1933 to 1968). The value of these two lists is increased by various supplementary listings: of 12" LP numbers with artists and page numbers; of 12" LP French and English issues; of 45 rpm singles; and of 78 rpm, 10" LP, and 45 rpm EP issues. There is also an index of leaders. Complete discographical information is given for each session, with the addition of the engineers and supervisors.

936.   RUST, Brian. The American dance band discography, 1917-
           1942. New Rochelle: Arlington House, 1975. 2v.
           From the mould that produced his definitive Jazz Records (no. 930), and with the same zeal, painstaking accuracy and limitless patience, Rust here presents a full listing that complements both his earlier work and his dance band history (no. 1044). Complete data is given for the recordings of some 2,000 bands, with some brief biographical sketches. The black bands, well covered by Jazz Records, are omitted, as are Glenn Miller and Benny Goodman (who have their own bio-discographies, nos. 1125 and 1115). The massive index is by Mary and Victor Rust.

937.   STAGG, Tom, and CRUMP, Charlie. New Orleans, the re-
           vival: a tape and discography of Negro traditional jazz
           recorded in New Orleans or by New Orleans bands 1937-
           1972. Dublin: Bashall Eaves, 1973. 307p. illus.
           A listing by two English discographers of traditional New Orleans jazz recordings made in the period since the revival of interest was sparked (initially with some private recordings in 1937). It is basically a record of the music of New Orleans Negro musicians (including brass bands) playing in their traditional idiom. Negro musicians resident in New Orleans had to make up at least half the band for it to be included. Most of the recordings listed were made in the New Orleans area; those made elsewhere are all of New Orleans musicians, and no long-term expatriates are included. The material listed covers 78s, LPs (first releases and reissues) and unissued recordings (including private tapes and archive-held taped interviews). Approximately half the book is made up of these unissued recordings. The arrangement is alphabetical by band leader or group name (with occasional title entries for anthologies) and there are four supplementary name indexes. Information given for each session includes location, date, personnel, titles and release numbers.

c.   Discographies of Individuals

> Note: Many discographies of individual jazz musicians are issued as small leaflets. What follows is a list of the most substantial. For further information, see Moon, no. 919; and Cooper, A3.

938. BAKKER, Dick M. Billie and Teddy on microgroove, 1932-
1944. Alphen aan den Rijn: Micrography, 1975. 52p.
Building on (not duplicating) the work of Rust, Jepsen et al.,
but aiming his work at LP collectors, Bakker provides a discography
of the microgroove reissues of Billie Holiday's 181 and Teddy Wilson's 371 recordings, separately and together, for the Brunswick,
Okeh and Vocalion labels (plus Billie's 1944 Commodore recordings).
The work is laid out in the same way as earlier discographies; i.e.,
chronologically, with details of personnel, location and date. Matrix
and original 78 rpm release numbers are not given, however. Instead there are LP reissue numbers, frequently abbreviated (the
system is explained in preliminary notes). A table of equivalents
indicates the numbers of records not given after the titles. The sequence of each artist's recordings is numbered with a running number, and these are used in the indexes of musicians and titles.

939. BAKKER, Dick. Duke Ellington on microgroove, 1923-1942.
Alphen aan den Rijn: Micrography, 1974. unpaged.
The main source for this compact discography is the Massagli
set (no. 946). Bakker lists all recordings made during the period
covered (including broadcasts), regardless of the existence or otherwise of an LP reissue, but omits all matrix and original release
numbers. All known microgroove release numbers are given (fully
described in a listing at the front), along with the name of the recording unit, original record company (or broadcast, film, etc.),
date, individual titles and take numbers. Personnel are not included
in the discography itself, but are given in a table and key in the introduction. Each session has a running number (the same as in
Massagli), and each title a letter. The title index refers to the
number only.

940. COOPER, David J. Buddy Rich discography. Blackburn,
Lancs.: the author, (1974?). 48p.
A mimeographed listing of Rich's recordings from 1938 to
1973, with details of personnel, dates, locations, titles and release
numbers. Broadcasts are indicated in their chronological place,
and there are snippets of biographical information.

941. DAVIES, John R. T., and WRIGHT, Laurie. Morton's music. London: Storyville Publications, 1968. unpaged.
A discography of Morton's recordings in three sections: piano
rolls, commercial discs, and Library of Congress recordings. The
information given in the second and third sections includes name of
band, personnel, venue and date, titles, matrix and catalog numbers and notes. Microgroove reissues are indicated, but no catalog
numbers are given for them. Alternate takes are identified by a
piece of musical notation, usually comparing the same place in each
take (unless there is a variation in lyrics). The authors also give
master disposition dates for Victor and Columbia, giving original
disposition instructions, any change of intent, and the current disposition of each title.

942.   DAVIES, John R. T.   The music of Thomas "Fats" Waller
         with complete discography.   London: Jazz Journal Publi-
         cations, (1950).   26p.   illus.
         _____.   _____;   (revised by R. T. Cooke).   London:
         "Friends of Fats" (Thomas "Fats" Waller Appreciation
         Society), 1953.   40p.   illus.
    The six hundred or so recordings (including discs, film
soundtracks and radio transcriptions) made by Fats Waller between
1922 and 1943 as soloist, accompanist, session man and leader of
his own group are listed chronologically.   Full details of personnel,
date, place where known, matrix number, title and release number
are given.   Besides containing details of more sessions than the
original version the revised edition also provides frequent illuminating notes and a useful title index (a rare bird in discographies!).
Prefatory material to the first edition is by Ed Kirkeby and
"G. L. H.," and to the second edition by Andy Razaf, Floyd Levin
and Rudi Blesh.   Both editions give a list of piano roll titles.   Further revisions appeared in Storyville magazine, no. 2 on.

943.   DEMEUSY, Bertrand, et al.   Hot Lips Page; compiled by
         Bertrand Demeusy, Otto Flückiger, Jorgen Grunnet Jep-
         sen, Kurt Mohr.   Basel: Jazz Publications, 1961.   30p.
         illus.
    Based on Delauney's New Hot Discography (no. 924) this dis-
cography of jazz trumpeter Oran "Hot Lips" Page (1908-1954) includes brief biographical notes, a full listing of the recordings made
by Page with his own band, as well as details of other bands with
which he recorded (without discographical information), of personnel and of band routes, 1935-1954.

944.   JEPSEN, Jorgen Grunnet.   A discography of Louis Armstrong.
         Copenhagen: Knudsen, 1968.   3v.
         _____.   A discography of Count Basie.   Copenhagen:
         Knudsen.   1969.   2v.   [Vol. 1, 1929-1950, is by Bo
         Scherman and Carl A. Haellstrom; Vol. 2, 1951-1968, by
         Jepsen.]
         _____.   A discography of John Coltrane.   Copenhagen:
         Knudsen, 1969.   35p.
         _____.   A discography of Miles Davis.   Copenhagen:
         Knudsen, 1969.   40p.
         _____.   A discography of Dizzy Gillespie.   Copenhagen:
         Knudsen, 1969.   2v.
         _____.   A discography of Billie Holiday.   Copenhagen:
         Knudsen, 1969.   37p.
         _____.   A discography of Thelonious Monk and Bud Powell.
         Copenhagen: Knudsen, 1969.   21, 44p.
         _____.   A discography of Charlie Parker.   Copenhagen:
         Knudsen, 1968.   38p.
         _____.   A discography of Lester Young.   Copenhagen:
         Knudsen, 1968.   45p.
    In the 1950s and 1960s Jepsen compiled a quantity of indi-
vidual artist discographies, mostly consisting of a few mimeographed
sheets; a number were printed as booklets by Debut Records of

Brande, Denmark, with biographical notes by Knud Ditlevson (Armstrong, Kenton, Morton, Tatum, Lee Konitz, Fats Navarro and Clifford Brown were among the artists covered). Towards the end of the 1960s the indefatigable discographer began to produce completely revised versions of some of these, in more substantial form, and these are the Knudsen booklets listed above. (For fuller details of his other listings, see Moon, no. 919, and the International Jazz Bibliography, nos. 915-917.) Each one follows the same basic pattern: a chronological listing of the recording sessions featuring the named artist with his/her own and other bands, covering the whole career span. Full details are given: band name, personnel, location, date, matrix and take numbers, titles, original release and LP reissue numbers. There are no additional indexes.

945.　KOSTER, Piet, and BAKKER, Dick M. Charlie Parker. Vol.
　　　　1. 1940-1947. Alphen aan den Rijn: Micrography, 1974.
　　　　34p.
　　　　　　.　　　　. Vol. 2. 1948-1950. Alphen aan den
　　　　Rijn: Micrography, 1975. 36p.
　　　　The first two parts of a projected four-volume discography
of commercial releases, private recordings and broadcasts. Full
discographical information is given, including microgroove releases.
Each session is numbered, and these numbers are referred to in
the supplementary indexes of personnel and titles. Vol. 1 is deliberately designed to include all the Dial recordings. Vol. 3 is
expected to cover 1951-1954, while Vol. 4 will be devoted to details
of omissions, corrections and additions, combined indexes, and a
survey of tunes "based on the chord structures of compositions already in existence."

946.　MASSAGLI, Luciano, et al. Duke Ellington's story on records,
　　　　by Luciano Massagli, Liborio Pusateri, Giovanni M. Volonte. Milan: Musica Jazz, 1966- . 9v. (to 1975).
　　　　The nine volumes of this outstanding discography issued up to
1975 cover the period 1923-1955 and include commercial recordings,
soundtracks, concerts, radio and television performances. The major part of each booklet is devoted to a chronological listing. Complete information is given for each session: place, date, personnel,
matrix and take numbers, titles, singers where relevant, original
release and LP reissue numbers. In addition this enterprising team
provides a breakdown of the structure of each piece--the number of
bars comprising the theme, the succession of choruses and the contributions of particular soloists in order of entry. Each individual
item is identified for indexing purposes by a number denoting the
session, plus a letter for each title. Each volume has indexes of
titles (with composers), personnel (with dates of each musician's
stay in the band, and references to solos), and microgroove releases
(with contents). Vol. 9 includes additions and corrections to the
previous eight volumes. The dates covered by each volume are:
1 - 1923-31; 2 - 1932-38; 3 - 1939-42; 4 - 1943-44; 5 - 1945; 6 -
1946; 7 - 1947-50; 8 - 1951-52; 9 - 1953-55.

947.　MAUERER, Hans J. A discography of Sidney Bechet. Copenhagen: Knudsen, 1969. 83p.

A chronological listing of all Bechet's recordings, with his own and other groups, from 1921 to 1964. Full discographical details are provided (as in the Jepsen series, no. 944). Each session is given a letter A-K denoting, for example, recordings made under the direction of Clarence Williams, recordings for RCA, or Blue Note, followed by a number. These symbols, besides categorizing the recordings broadly, are the references used in the artist and title indexes (valuable additions which give Mauerer's volume the edge over Jepsen's otherwise excellent compilations).

948. PIRIE, Christopher A., and MUELLER, Siegfried. Artistry in Kenton: the bio-discography of Stan Kenton and his music. Vol. 1. Vienna: Siegfried Mueller, 1969. 289p.
_____. _____. 3rd ed. Vienna: Mueller, 1972. 289p. illus.

The joint effort of an English-Austrian team, this impressive first volume lists, with full details, all Kenton's recordings (commercial releases, broadcasts, airchecks and radio transcriptions) from 1937 to the end of November, 1953. A biographical narrative lists and comments on each session. There is also an itinerary, an alphabetical title index of first recordings, and an artist index. Comparison with Venudor and Sparke (no. 950) suggests that Pirie and Mueller include rather more material. Both volumes list arrangers.

949. SANFILIPPO, Luigi. General catalog of Duke Ellington's recorded music. Palermo: Centro Studi di Musica Contemporanea, 1964. 70p.
_____. _____. 2nd ed. Palermo: Centro Studi di Musica Contemporanea. 1966. 112p.

Lacking the immense detail of Massagli et al. (no. 946), but a useful one-volume work, this discography lists 1,472 titles, covering 1924-1965, in a chronological sequence with a title index. Full discographical details are given, including, in many cases, durations. There is also information on V-discs, films, and radio and television transcriptions.

950. VENUDOR, Pete, and SPARKE, Michael. The standard Kenton directory; compiled, edited and annotated by Pete Venudor and Michael Sparke. Vol. 1. 1937-1949. Amsterdam: Pete Venudor, 1968. 32, 20p.

A chronological discography of Kenton's various recordings, including studio recordings, sound tracks, broadcasts, airchecks. Supplementary material includes an index of all titles in the Kenton band book, whether recorded or not, and surveys of "choreographed Kentonia" and of Kenton on film.

951. WILBRAHAM, Roy. Milt Jackson: a discography and biography, including recordings made with the M.J.Q. London: the author, 1968. 40p.
_____. Jackie McLean: a discography with biography. London: the author, 1967. 16p.

_____. Charles Mingus: a biography and discography.
London: the author, 1967. 28p.
These are reliable private productions, with full chronological
discographies, short biographical introductions, and indexes of each
individual's compositions (those for Mingus and McLean being given
after the introductions).

d. The Science of Jazz Discography

952. BLACK, Douglas C. Matrix numbers: their meaning and
history. Melbourne: Australia Jazz Quarterly, (1946?)
(A. J. Q. Handbook No. 1) 23p.
A pamphlet containing a brief introduction to the significance
of matrix numbers and their usefulness to collectors, a sketch of
the connections between several recording companies in America and
England, some notes on different matrix number series employed by
various companies (including Brunswick, Columbia, Okeh, Decca and
Victor), and lists of representative matrix numbers with dates.

953. STUDIES IN JAZZ DISCOGRAPHY, 1. (Walter C. Allen,
editor). Newark: Institute of Jazz Studies, Rutgers University Extension Division, 1971. 112p. bibliog. notes.
These are the edited proceedings of three conferences--the
first two Conferences on Discographical Research (June, 1968 and
1969) and the Conference on Preservation and Extension of the Jazz
Heritage (July, 1969). The first set of proceedings contains four
papers, on discographical goals and methods, problems of dating and
of performer identification, and on jazz and social science. The
second conference is longer, including historical aspects and neglected areas of discography, archival practices of record companies,
and Negro newspapers as source materials. The third conference
ranges widely over the function of a jazz archive (the longest paper
in the volume, by Richard Allen of Tulane), the collection and preservation of material, visual aspects, jazz education and the community, and related topics. Most contributions are short, of three or
four pages.

e. Annotated Record Guides*

954. SMITH, Charles Edward. The jazz record book; with Frederic Ramsey, Charles Payne and William Russell. New
York: Smith & Durrell, 1942. 515p. bibliog.
This volume inaugurated a sparse, spasmodic, but very valuable international series of annotated guides to jazz record listening. Still of interest, it opens with a brief history of the phases
of jazz to 1942, indicating significant features. The records chosen
for short reviews are grouped in five categories: Chicago, New
York, Blues and Boogie-woogie, Bands, and Contemporary. Within

_____
*This section is arranged chronologically.

each group an artist approach is adopted, with comments on each record (full details of which are given) in turn, so that some idea of the artist's development is conveyed. (This approach is the opposite of that in the British Jazz on Record, no. 958, which concerns itself firstly with an artist's overall style and achievement, pointing to specific records to illustrate this.)

955.   JAZZ ON 78's: a guide to the many examples of classic
        jazz on Decca, Brunswick, and London 78 r.p.m. records.
        London: Decca Record Co., 1954. 83p.
        JAZZ ON LP's: a collector's guide to jazz on Decca, Bruns-
        wick, Capitol, London and Felsted long playing records.
        London: Decca Record Co., 1955. 212p.
        .   . Rev. ed. London: Decca Record Co.,
        1956. 282p.
        Record company literature on its own releases must naturally
be treated with some caution, but the writing in these anonymous
publications is good and the assessments fair. From certain similarities of phrase they appear to be the immediate predecessor of
Jazz on Record (Fox, no. 958). The 78's booklet is the first guide
to adopt the overall stylistic assessment approach (as opposed to
criticism restricted to individual records); each artist entry contains
a general estimate, followed by a list of recordings, with personnel
and date. In the LP volumes the method is similar, but the records
are listed ahead of the assessment.

956.   RAMSEY, Frederic. A guide to longplay jazz records. New
        York: Long Player Publications, 1954. 264p. illus.,
        bibliog.
        Following the pattern established by the Jazz Record Book
(no. 954), this annotated guide consists of short discussions of particular, currently available recordings of individual artists or bands.
The useful title index lists 4,000 or so separate items (there is
also an artist index). It is a tribute to Ramsey that most guides
of this type, whether using the record review or the overall stylistic
approach, have required a team (cf. Modern Jazz, no. 959, the
latest of the reviewing volumes) to do justice to their subject.

957.   HARRIS, Rex, and RUST, Brian. Recorded jazz: a critical
        guide. Harmondsworth: Penguin Books, 1958. 256p.
        Almost totally confined to traditional jazz musicians, this
guide includes biographical data and stylistic comments for each
artist or group covered, with lists of recordings on both American
and British LPs and EPs of the 1950s. Index.

958.   JAZZ ON RECORD: a critical guide, by Charles Fox, Peter
        Gammond, Alun Morgan, with additional material by Alexis
        Korner. London: Hutchinson; London: Arrow Books,
        1960. 352p. discogs.
        JAZZ ON RECORD: a critical guide to the first 50 years,
        1917-1967, by Albert McCarthy, Alun Morgan, Paul Oliver,
        Max Harrison; with additional contributions by Ronald At-
        kins... (et al.) London: Hanover Books; New York: Oak,

1968. 416p. discogs.

These are two useful practical guides for jazz and blues enthusiasts and record collectors to the "best, the most significant, or
occasionally simply the most typical recorded works of the leading
jazz and blues artists" (preface to 1968 volume). The second book
adopts a similar format to the first--a series of alphabetically arranged entries on individual artists--but contains a completely new
text. In both books individual entries give artist's dates and instrument, place him/her in the development of the music, and describe
and assess recordings and stylistic evolution with reference to the
list of microgroove issues at the end of each entry. As selection
of artists for each volume depended to a considerable extent on
recordings available at the time of writing there is a degree of variation in the artists included. The lists of available recordings,
while giving priority to English releases, is international and includes
many American labels. The deletion rate of many jazz and blues
records unfortunately means the reissue information in volumes of
this type goes very quickly out of date, but the informed comment
is of lasting value. The 1968 volume includes a second section in
which related artists (most of whom do not appear in the alphabetical
artist sequence) are grouped into 20 or so categories, and their recordings described as in Part 1. These categories include blues
from broad geographical areas, piano blues, ragtime, New Orleans
jazz, big bands, post-war pianists, progressives, spirituals and
songs. Both books have a full name index.

959. HARRISON, Max, et al. Modern jazz: the essential records;
a critical selection by Max Harrison, Alun Morgan, Ronald
Atkins, Michael James, Jack Cooke. London: Aquarius
Books, 1975. 131p.

From the mass of post-war recorded jazz five British critics
select and review what they consider the 200 best LPs, pointing out
relationships and influences, but designing their 500-600 word pieces
for independent reference. Though figures such as Parker, Coleman, Coltrane, Monk and Rollins dominate the book (especially the
first two), a large number of musicians are covered (the index lists
about 1,000 names). In his introduction Harrison states the aim as
being "to show the positive aspect of this music's diversity..."; a
little later he says: "our chief criterion has been originality."
Though there are eight, very broadly chronological categories (e.g.,
swing to bop, bop, cool, thirdstream), these are for the reader's
convenience and do not imply any particular historical viewpoints.
Each record chosen has a complete discographical heading (personnel, date, place, titles) and the latest available numbers (usually)
British and American).

3. General Books on Jazz

a. General Guides and Handbooks

960. BERENDT, Joachim. Das Jazzbuch: Entwicklung and Be-

deutung der Jazzmusik. Frankfurt: Fischer, 1953. 240p.
illus., discog.
_____. Das neue Jazzbuch... Frankfurt: Fischer, 1959.
318p. illus., discog.
_____. The new jazz book: a history and guide; trans-
lated by Dan Morgenstern. New York: Hill & Wang, 1962;
London: Owen, 1964; London: Davies; London: Jazz
Book Club, 1965. 314p. illus., discog.
_____. Das Jazzbuch: von New Orleans bis Free Jazz.
Frankfurt: Fischer, 1968. 334p. discog.
_____. Das Jazzbuch: von Jazz bis Rock... Frankfurt:
Fischer, 1973. 426p. discog.
_____. The jazz book: from New Orleans to rock and
free jazz; translated by Dan Morgenstern and Helmut and
Barbara Bredigkeit. New York: Hill, 1975. 459p.
discog.
One of the most widely-read books on jazz, this guide com-
bines the historical and analytical approach in presenting a useful
overall picture. Berendt begins by outlining the development of successive jazz styles from 1890 (ragtime), dividing the music's evolution into decades. He then proceeds with a series of profiles, incorporating biography and general assessment, of some outstanding
musicians: Buddy Bolden, Louis Armstrong, Bessie Smith, Bix
Beiderbecke, Duke Ellington, Coleman Hawkins and Lester Young,
Charlie Parker and Dizzy Gillespie, Miles Davis, plus, in the most
recent edition, John Coltrane and Ornette Coleman. These are followed by a discussion, with music examples, of the various musical
features of jazz: sound and phrasing, improvisation, arrangement,
the blues, melody, rhythm, etc. A section devoted to jazz instruments describes the developments in the use of each instrument--
brass, winds, strings, percussion--in terms of the technique and
stylistic characteristics of its principal exponents. Further chapters discuss big bands and jazz combos from the early swing era to
(in the latest edition) rock and electric jazz. The extensive discography is a selection of LPs for use in connection with the book.
Name index.

961. COLLIER, Graham. Inside jazz. London: Quartet Books,
1973. 144p. illus.
A British jazz musician gives a good introduction to the jazz
world as seen from the inside, discussing aspects of performance
(instruments, musical framework, the solo), of performers (jazzmen as people), and of the jazz environment (business matters, the
recording studio, the critic).

962. COLLIER, Graham. Jazz: a student's and teacher's guide.
Cambridge: Cambridge University Press, 1975. 167p.
illus., bibliogs., discogs.
Only time will prove the value of this textbook in education,
but it has the hallmarks of being an excellent aid: a clear style
and good layout; a balance between stressing the importance of the
individual in jazz expression and offering practical help towards understanding the music's technical basis; plenty of music examples;

sensible, realizable projects; lists of points to listen for; suggestions for further reading and listening using available material. Part 1 of the book describes and briefly evaluates the music of seven individuals: Armstrong, Ellington, Reinhardt, Parker, Davis, Brubeck and Coleman. Part 2 turns to improvisation the blues, popular song form, arranging, the big band, modes and scales, jazz composition, and contemporary trends. The appendices provide further information on some theoretical topics.

963. DANKWORTH, Avril. Jazz: an introduction to its musical basis. London, New York: Oxford University Press, 1968. 89p. bibliog., discog.
A handy short guide for laymen and students to the musical features of jazz and their development in specific styles, beginning with general technical characteristics--chords, forms, scales, rhythm and tonal effects--and showing these in use in seven periods, from the pre-jazz era to the '60s. There are many music examples, and an appendix lists some standard jazz tunes with key, composer, publisher and date. There is an index to tunes and styles.

964. ERLICH, Lillian. What jazz is all about. New York: Messner, 1962; London: Gollancz, 1963. 181p. illus., bibliog.
_____. _____. Rev. ed. New York: Messner, 1975. 255p. illus., bibliog.
An introductory chronological account of the development of jazz, beginning with African and European elements, tracing the line of evolution from the work and religious music of slavery, through minstrels, blues and ragtime to New Orleans and on through subsequent stylistic developments up to the beginning of the '60s (further in the new edition). The author combines good description of the basic musical elements at each stage of the evolution with factual accounts of significant individuals. Index.

965. FEATHER, Leonard. The book of jazz: a guide to the entire field. New York: Horizon Press, 1957; London: Barker, 1959; New York: Meridian Books, 1960; London: Jazz Book Club, 1961. 280p. bibliog. notes, discog.
_____. The book of jazz from then till now: a guide to the entire field. Rev. ed. New York: Horizon Press, 1965. 280p. bibliog. notes, discog.
The object of this book is to offer "a series of instrument-by-instrument histories enabling the reader to see each artist's role, period of impact and relative importance" (p. 6). A preliminary section discussing sources sets out to counterbalance the existing documentation, especially concerning New Orleans. It also includes a discussion of jazz and race. The second, central section, describing the role of each instrument, its development and its principal exponents, includes consideration of the voice, of big and small combos, and of arrangers. The third and fourth sections are concerned with the art of improvisation, and the future of jazz. There are references to recordings in the text, and a short list of anthology LPs. Name and title index.

966.   FOX, Charles. The jazz scene; special photography by Val-
            erie Wilmer. New York: Hamlyn, 1972. 127p. illus.
            (some col.), bibliog.
        Mainstream and modern, singers and composers, gospel and
blues, the remnant of the New Orleans tradition and the powerful
influence of rock, the big bands, the "far out," Miles Davis with a
section to himself--these are some of the many faces of jazz in
the 1960s and early 1970s that are well captured here. Valerie
Willmer's superb photography may be the most striking feature, but
it is matched by an eminently enjoyable text by Charles Fox that
combines wit and polish with shrewd and canny insight.

967.   GAMMOND, Peter, ed. The Decca book of jazz; foreword
            by Milton "Mezz" Mezzrow. London: Muller, 1958; Lon-
            don: Jazz Book Club, 1960. 431p. illus., discog.
        These 25 essays by a predominantly British team of con-
tributors cover a wide variety of subjects, including the jazz styles
of specific cities and areas (New Orleans, Harlem, Kansas City,
modern trends on both East and West Coasts), individuals (Armstrong, Ellington), pianists and vocalists, instruments (saxophone,
clarinet), white jazz of various periods, African elements, and developments in Europe. There are also two pieces on blues and one
on ragtime. Contributors include Paul Oliver, Rex Harris, Brian
Rust, Francis Newton, Sinclair Traill, Charles Fox, Gerald Lascelles,
Raymond Horricks, Alun Morgan, Benny Green, Vic Bellerby, Ernest Bornemann and Stanley Dance. There is a 79-page discography
of 78s, EPs and LPs and an index.

968.   GILLENSON, Lewis N., ed. Esquire's world of jazz; com-
            mentary by James Poling. New York: Grosset & Dunlap,
            1962; London: Barker, 1963; London: Jazz Book Club,
            1964. 224p. illus., (some col.)., discog.
        A magnificent-looking coffee-table book, chiefly noteworthy
for the many spectacular color photographs and paintings. The text
discusses several specific topics, including the nature of jazz, its
evolution, jazz giants, women in jazz, jazzmen's own views of their
art, and its future.

969.   POSTGATE, John. A plain man's guide to jazz. London:
            Hanover Books, 1973. 146p. bibliog.
        A good introduction to the basics of jazz, written in a crisp,
no-nonsense style. Having no particular axe to grind Postgate "car-
ries the torch for jazz as a whole" (preamble). His view of jazz is
that, seen from the vantage point of the 1970s, it is "an orderly
process of artistic maturation and development." The initiation begins with a bird's-eye view of jazz history, by decades, and an
identification of some broad principles common to all types of jazz,
concerning improvisation, intonation, rhythmic sense and collective
sympathy. The reader is then introduced to the characteristics of
successive styles from New Orleans to date, and, instrument by instrument, to the principal exponents of the "main stream" (defined
as the "cumulative musical idiom deriving from all styles"). This,
the core of the book, is followed by a description of some outstand-

ing singers. There is a glossary and an index. Musical comment is kept elementary, and no music examples are given (though there are some diagrams).

970. ULANOV, Barry. A handbook of jazz. New York: Viking Press, 1957. 248p. discog.
_____ . _____ ; foreword by Kingsley Amis. London: Hutchinson, 1958; London: Jazz Book Club, 1960. 204p. discog.
Though not as detailed as Berendt (no. 960)--or as long-lived--Ulanov's guidebook is designed along similar lines, catering for a possibly larger variety of approaches--historical, stylistic, instrumental, theoretical, discographical, linguistic, moral, professional, critical and biographical--in a concise introductory manner. The biographical information is provided in an appendix, which gives very brief sketches of about 500 musicians. There is also a comparative chronology of events in jazz and other 20th century arts, and an index.

971. WILLIAMS, Martin. Where's the melody? a listener's introduction to jazz. New York: Pantheon Books, 1966; New York: Minerva Press, 1967. 205p. bibliog., discogs.
_____ . _____ . (Rev. ed.) New York: Pantheon Books, 1969. 205p. bibliog., discogs.
A collection of essays on various aspects of jazz and jazz musicians, arranged to give listeners guidance on how to approach the music. The author examines the basic materials and practices as illustrated in eight recordings (a group of record reviews), describes the role of the composer-arranger, and outlines a basic record library. The second section of the book looks at four artists in their milieu: Monk, Milt Jackson, Big Joe Williams and Jimmy Giuffre. The third part comments in less detail on other artists, illustrating and elucidating themes and aspects mentioned in earlier chapters, and with a section on the avant-garde. No music examples. Index.

b. Jazz Life, including Social Aspects

See also nos. 991, 997, 998.

972. CLARKE, John Henrik, ed. Harlem, U.S.A.: the story of a city within a city. Berlin: Seven Seas Books, 1964. 361p. illus., bibliog. notes.
_____ . Harlem, U.S.A. Rev. ed. New York: Collier Books, 1971. 388p. illus., bibliog. notes.
A chapter on the music of Harlem by William R. Dixon is a personal recollection of some features of the jazz scene, mingled with regret that Harlem's taste in music has turned away from jazz.

973. HENTOFF, Nat. The jazz life. New York: Dial Press, 1961; London: Davies, 1972. 255p.
_____ . _____ . London: Panther, 1964. 221p.
A description of the world of the jazz musician. The author deals first with background aspects--the change in social acceptance

of jazz, the musician's period of apprenticeship, the extent of prejudice against white musicians and the reasons for it, drug-taking,
and the attempts to win wider recognition for jazz at the price of
lowering standards, epitomized by the Newport Jazz Festival. In
the second part he deals more immediately with the music: the
recording studio, and the character, life and life-style of various
musicians--Basie, Mingus, Lewis, Davis, Monk, Coleman--illustrat-
ing the great variety of approach among individuals and dispelling
the romantic notion of the hipster musicians.

974.   LAMBERT, Constant. Music ho! a study of music in decline.
        London: Faber, 1934. 342p.
        _____. _____. Rev. ed. London: Faber, 1937.
        342p.
        _____. _____. 3rd ed., with an introduction by Arthur
        Hutchings. London: Faber, 1966; New York: October
        House, 1967. 288p. illus.
        An English composer's lively study of the relationship of mu-
sic to 20th century life--social, political, and aesthetic. It includes
an assessment of jazz which emphasizes European and Jewish elements, and which, though dated and containing some misunderstand-
ings, is an interesting early example of the view of a "serious" composer, albeit an unusual one. It also includes chapters on symphonic jazz and film music. In general Lambert's a gloomy view of the
present and future states of music.

975.   LEONARD, Neil. Jazz and the white Americans: the accep-
        tance of a new art form. Chicago: University of Chicago
        Press, 1962; London: Jazz Book Club, 1964. 214p. bib-
        liog.
        Based on a 1960 Harvard thesis, this is a chronicle of the
swift change in taste among white Americans between the two world
wars, from heated opposition to jazz to general acceptance. Within
this framework are described the growth of commercial jazz for the
white market and its effect on the phonograph and the motion picture,
both media that provided an ever-widening audience with watered-
down versions of the original. The author examines traditional problems white people have with jazz, the gulf between a new art style
and a traditionally-minded audience, and the way in which this nar-
rows; jazz history is seen in this context as demonstrating a Hegel-
ian pattern. The appendices are devoted to definitions and critical
analyses of lyrics, bibliography includes books and articles, and
there is an index.

976.   MALCOLM X. The autobiography of Malcolm X; with the
        assistance of Alex Haley; introduction by M. S. Handler.
        New York: Grove Press, 1965. 455p. illus.
        _____. The autobiography of Malcolm X; with the as-
        sistance of Alex Haley. London: Hutchinson, 1966. 462p.
        illus.
        _____. _____. Harmondsworth: Penguin, 1968. 512p.
        The Black Muslim leader's account of his life in Boston and
Harlem in the early 1940s (before his imprisonment in 1946 and con-

version to the doctrines of Elijah Muhammad) contains interesting descriptions of big bands, particularly at the Roseland State Ball- room in Boston, and of the lindy-hop dance craze (a dance at which Malcolm X excelled and for which the bands frequently played). His acquaintanceship with bands such as Ellington's and Basie's began when he took a job as a shoeshine boy at the Roseland--"musicians never have had, anywhere, a greater shoeshine boy fan than I was" (p. 133 in Penguin ed.)--and continued during his time in Harlem, where he was acquainted with numerous jazzmen.

977. NEWTON, Francis. The jazz scene. London: Macgibbon & Kee, 1959; New York: Monthly Review Press, 1960; London: Jazz Book Club, 1960. 303p. illus., bibliog., discog.

A wide-ranging and searching study by a British critic of cultural, social, economic and musical aspects of jazz. Newton outlines the origins and development of the music, and describes the various musical styles and instruments involved, assessing the total musical achievement. The relation of jazz to other arts and to popular music is explored, prior to an examination of the eco- nomic side. Subsequent chapters range over the character and role of the jazz musician, the jazz public, and jazz as protest. There are notes to the chapters, an appendix on jazz language, a guide for further reading and an index. (Francis Newton is a pseudonym for the distinguished economic historian E. J. Hobsbawm.)

978. SHAW, Arnold. The street that never slept: New York's fabled 52nd St.; foreword by Abel Green. New York: Coward, McCann & Geoghegan, 1971. 378p. illus.

Shaw tells the story of the high spot in New York's night life in the 1930s and 1940s, where jazz and jazz clubs were among the central attractions, through a series of interviews which he fits into the potted histories of each of the most important clubs. Among the interviewees are John Hammond, Johnny Mercer, Red Norvo, Woody Herman, Mary Lou Williams, Dizzy Gillespie, Leonard Feather, and Errol Garner. Index.

c. Practical Guides to
Arranging, Composing and Improvising

979. BAKER, David. Arranging and composing for the small en- semble: jazz / r & b / jazz-rock. Chicago: Maher, 1970. 184p. illus., bibliogs., discogs.

An instruction book aimed at the requirements of the com- poser/arranger interested in small combinations in jazz, rhythm and blues and jazz-rock. It takes him through the rudiments of nomenclature and instrumentation, general rules for scoring, the construction and development of a melody, writing for a rhythm section, aspects of writing for two to six voices, and the use of the blues. There are many examples, suggested listening assign- ments, and lists of suggested bebop tunes, blues songs, and of standard jazz tunes with keys.

980.   BAKER, David. Jazz improvisation: a comprehensive meth-
        od of study for all players. Chicago: Maher, 1969. 184p.
        illus., bibliogs., discogs.
    A carefully prepared manual for both student and teacher on
the technical problems involved in jazz improvisation, dealing with
them, as Gunther Schuller remarks in his foreword, "at both the
fundamental and most sophisticated levels." An interesting feature
is the "psychological approach to communicating through an improvised solo" (Chapter XIX). Another work by Baker which, although
intended for musicians performing in any style, has particular relevance to jazz, is his four-volume Techniques of Improvisation: a
method for developing improvisational technique (based on the Lydian
chromatic concept by George Russell), Chicago, Maher, 1971. This
is a meticulously planned set of exercises using the nine Lydian
scales as a foundation.

981.   COKER, Jerry. Improvising jazz. Englewood Cliffs: Pren-
        tice-Hall, 1964. 115p.
    A practical instruction book in the basic theoretical principles
of jazz. Aimed mainly at the beginner with some technical ability
and knowledge of scales, it lays out clearly and logically the information necessary for learning the technique of improvisation, starting with the elements of a blues tune, describing the characteristics
of melody and rhythm, and progressing from these to more advanced
analysis of chord progression, swing, melody, scales, chord superimposition and functional harmony. Each chapter concludes with a
list of projects, and the text is filled with music examples. Appendices give aesthetic criteria for the evaluation of a jazz artist,
examples of left hand chord voicings and of chord progressions, and
a collection of tunes grouped according to their characteristic progressions.

982.   HARVEY, Eddie. Jazz piano. London: English Universities
        Press, 1974. (Teach Yourself Books) 161p. bibliog.
    A useful practical guide by an English teacher and composer
for the would-be jazz pianist, outlining, with a great many examples,
the principles behind jazz piano improvisation. The final chapter
presents a variety of musical material as a basis for improvisation, including several pieces by contemporary jazz composers.

983.   MEHEGAN, John. Jazz improvisation. New York: Watson-
        Guptill, 1958-1965. 4v.
    An important practical textbook, especially for the pianist.
The first volume, Tonal and Rhythmic Principles, defines the basic
elements of improvisation. Vol. 2, Jazz Rhythm and the Improvised
Line, outlines the development of jazz rhythm in five lessons, and,
with 29 transcriptions of solos from Bessie Smith to Oscar Peterson,
illustrates the evolution of the improvised line. Vol. 3, Swing and
the Early Progressive Piano Styles, dissects the styles of Teddy
Wilson, Art Tatum, Bud Powell, George Shearing and Horace Silver.
Vol. 4, Contemporary Piano Styles, uses the work of Oscar Peterson and others to illustrate contemporary technical approaches. The
volumes contain a wealth of transcribed music.

984. RUSSELL, George. The Lydian concept of tonal organization
      for improvisation. New York: Concept Publishing, 1959.
      50, 38p. illus. , discog.
      John Lewis described jazz composer and pianist Russell's
treatise as "the first contribution made by jazz to the theory of
music" (quoted by Max Harrison, no. 959, p. 98). In his introduction Russell himself calls his concept "an organization of tonal resources from which the jazz musician may draw to create his improvised lines. " The book is a step-by-step introduction to the
system, which is based on relating every type of chord to a parent
scale. A reprinted article from Jazz Review, in which Russell is
questioned by Martin Williams on Ornette Coleman and tonality, is
included. (A discussion of Russell's theories may be found in Olive
Jones, "Conversation with George Russell: a New Theory for Jazz, "
Black Perspective in Music, Spring 1974.)

985. RUSSO, William. Composing for the jazz orchestra. Chi-
      cago: University of Chicago Press, 1961. 90p.
      A concise practical textbook, based on Russo's own techniques
("pulled out of the earth, inch by inch"--preface), and covering chord
symbols, types of chords, harmonic considerations, voicing, writing
for particular instruments, writing for ensembles, and other related
topics.

986. RUSSO, William. Jazz composition and orchestration. Chi-
      cago: University of Chicago Press, 1968. 825p.
      Russo's massive expansion of his earlier volume is not only
much more detailed in its guidance, it also abandons the "tight-
lipped" approach for a more openly polemical one. Underlying his
method is the conviction that those who prophesy a black future for
jazz are merely susceptible to the influence of the clichés of fashion
("fascism in disguise"), and that what jazz requires is not further
revolutionary changes (vertical development) but "deepening and
growth"--a horizontal development in which avenues opened up by
great jazzmen are explored in much greater detail. Whereas the
examples in the earlier volume were written especially for it, the
large number incorporated here are drawn from Russo's work over
20 years with various orchestras including Kenton's, the London
Jazz Orchestra, and the Chicago Jazz Ensemble.

d. General Analytical and Critical Works

987. BORNEMANN, Ernest. A critic looks at jazz. London:
      Jazz Music Books, 1946. 53p. bibliog. notes.
      First published as a series of articles in The Record Changer,
this is a thoughtful attempt to establish new critical standards for
judging jazz, based on an anthropological approach, to apply these
firstly to the practical problem of reconciling developments in instrumentation with continuity of tradition, and secondly to a historical
survey of the evolution of Afro-American music into jazz. In his
concise survey Bornemann covers a lot of ground--African roots,
worksongs, blues, spirituals, ring shouts, minstrelsy, the emergence

of jazz and the subsequent development of swing--with due attention
to sociological and economic factors.

988.　DAUER, Alfons M.　Der Jazz: seine Ursprünge und Entwick-
　　　　lung.　Kassel: Röth, 1958.　284p.　illus., bibliog.
　　　　This is an impressive, scholarly work on the origins and development of jazz that deserves to be better known in English-speaking countries.　The textual study grows out of a set of 70 transcriptions in standard notation, given at the back of the book.　These consist not simply of melody, but of accompaniment also for songs, and
of parts for instrumental group items.　They represent the following areas: Africa, African music in America, Afro-American music
in South America and the West Indies, Creole, Afro-American music
in North America (hollers, work-songs), Afro-American religious
music, blues, and jazz (archaic, classic, Dixieland and Chicago).
A series of commentaries on each item precedes the music transcriptions.　These involve chord schemes, analysis, and include the
texts of vocal items.　The main text is an outline of the musical
evolution of jazz in which frequent references are made from the
text to the music transcriptions, and which is similar in its sections
to the groupings of the examples (there are, for example, 22 pages
on blues).　Anyone seeking a reason for the absence of an English
translation of this work need probably look no further than at Dauer's
uncompromising emphasis on African elements.　(It is worth remarking also that Dauer's research on Africa found no place in Schuller's
account of African music in Early Jazz, no. 1038.)

989.　DEER, Irving, and DEER, Harriet A., eds.　The popular
　　　　arts: a critical reader.　New York: Scribner, 1967.
　　　　356p.　bibliog.
　　　　Included in this collection of articles is one by John A.
Kouwenhorn on "Stone, Steel and Jazz," which compares American
architecture and jazz.　There is also a comparison of American
and British musicals, reprinted from the Times Literary Supplement.

990.　DE TOLEDANO, Ralph, ed.　Frontiers of jazz; foreword by
　　　　Milton Gabler.　New York: Durrell, 1947; London: Jazz
　　　　Book Club, 1966.　178p.　bibliog. notes.
　　　　―――――.　―――――.　2nd ed.　New York: Ungar, 1962.
　　　　178p.　bibliog. notes.
　　　　The sixteen articles in this collection are of a high standard
and are chosen from various journals, jazz and non-jazz, covering
1926 to 1947, with the addition of a specially written essay on directions in jazz by the editor.　The book is divided into two parts.　The
first is concerned with forms and styles, and contributors include
Abbe Niles on blues, Bill Russell on boogie-woogie, and Jean-Paul
Sartre on jazz in America.　The second contains shorter pieces on
musicians, and contributors here include Preston Jackson, Hugues
Panassié, Jelly Roll Morton, Ernst Ansermet, etc.　Among the musicians covered are King Oliver, Bunk Johnson, Morton, Sidney
Bechet, Bix Beiderbecke, Duke Ellington, Benny Goodman and James
P. Johnson.　Each piece is preceded by a short editorial note.　In-
dex.

991. FINKELSTEIN, Sidney. Jazz: a people's music; illustrated
     by Jules Halfant. New York: Citadel Press, 1948; Lon-
     don: Jazz Book Club, 1964. 278p. illus., discogs.
   The aim of this stimulating study is "to place jazz as part
of world music," to help break down the barriers between jazz and
concert music and between partisans of different types of jazz, by
outlining and judging the music in the light of its fundamental characteristics (sound, elements of blues and folk song, improvisation and
form) instead of its "popular" aspects, and by drawing attention constantly to the interrelationship of jazz and social questions. A chapter on the future of jazz goes in some detail into the use of jazz in
composed music. Index.

992. GROSSMAN, William L., and FARRELL, Jack W. The heart
     of jazz. New York: New York University Press, 1956;
     London: Vision Press, 1958. 315p. illus., bibliog. notes.
   The "heart of jazz" for these authors is the "synthesis of
Christian feeling and robust vitality" (p. 297) that characterizes the
traditional jazz of New Orleans--the form they regard as superior
to all others. In particular it is with the work of white Californian
revivalists that the authors are chiefly concerned (Lu Watters, et al.).
Index.

993. HODEIR, André. Hommes et problèmes du jazz; suivi de La
     religion du jazz. Paris: Portulan, 1954. 412p. illus.,
     discog.
   _____. Jazz; its evolution and essence; translated by David
     Noakes. New York: Grove Press; London: Secker & War-
     burg, 1956; London: Jazz Book Club, 1958. (Repr. New
     York: Da Capo, 1975). 295p. discog.
   This highly regarded, penetrating study of the elements at
the heart of jazz is aimed at the musically literate, with a bias towards modern styles. Hodeir defines five periods in the evolution of
jazz, discusses the extent of borrowing from other traditions, and
proceeds to examine and analyze the style of specific musicians: the
Hot Five, Dicky Wells, Charlie Parker, Miles Davis, and one particular piece: Ellington's "Concerto for Cootie." He also explores
basic questions of improvisation, swing, rhythm, etc., and concludes
with surveys of the influence of jazz on European music, and of the
state of contemporary jazz, at the death of Parker. (This last chapter was written especially for the English edition.) The discography
lists items discussed, referring the reader to the relevant page.
Music examples are included in the text and there is an index.

994. HODEIR, André. Toward jazz; translated by Noel Burch.
     New York: Grove Press, 1962; London: Jazz Book Club,
     1965. 224p.
   With his second volume of jazz criticism (comprising a selection of articles written between 1953 and 1959), Hodeir feels his approach to his subject is in a transitional state; he has moved away
from the objective, closely argued "book about jazz" towards the embodiment of personal attitudes in a "jazz book," or "poetic medita-
tion" (he arrived at this destination in no. 995). His principal con-

cern here is with the individual musician and his relation to the group, and though it might be hard to discern the "visionary outlook of a Nietzsche" that Hodeir says is called for, there are interesting discussions of Parker, Ellington, Basie, Carter, Tatum, Milt Jackson, Gil Evans and Monk, plus essays on jazz criticism, "group relations," and the future prospects of jazz. Music examples are included in some of the pieces, and there is an index.

995. HODEIR, André. Les mondes du jazz. Paris: Union Générale d'Editions, 1970. 384p.
————. The worlds of jazz; translated by Noël Burch. New York: Grove Press, 1972. 279p.
    A difficult, frequently obscure volume in which Hodeir rejects the direct relationship between author and reader, and the consistency of style that unifies most criticism of value (and is normally indispensable for the trust a reader develops in the author as he reads) in favor of a mélange (a hodge-podge, some might say) of stylistic experiments based on a fictionalizing technique. Imaginary characters--musicians, professors, arrangers, a Finnish jazz composer, a preacher, mock television panelists, space-travelers (to a planet called "Jazzinia"), and archeologists of some undetermined future age who unearth a copy of a Miles Davis LP--are paraded before us in a variety of assumed styles, grouped basically around two themes: the jazz musician and the composer/arranger. Hodeir's thesis seems to be that if jazz is to survive, its future lies in the hands of the jazz composer; developments after Parker are totally rejected. The tone of the book varies from whimsical to passionately outspoken--there are numerous witty passages and just as many where a weak joke has to beg for mercy--but herein is the problem for the reader: how is he to identify the author, and if he thinks he can, why should he believe him? Why, when each piece is clad in borrowed clothing, should one not laugh as much at poor Matti Jarvinen (Hodeir himself?) from Finland, or at the outbursts against musicians one takes to be Coltrane and others, as at the archeologists? Humor, satire and homiletics are all compatible only if bound together by an author's style--which is his soul.

996. JAZZFORSCHUNG/JAZZ RESEARCH, 1. Graz: Universal Edition, 1969. 203p. bibliog. notes.
    Founded in 1969, the International Society for Jazz Research is dedicated to "the systematic exploration of jazz." The first issue of its planned annual volumes contains twelve scholarly articles (eleven of them in German) by, amongst others, Gerhard Kubik, Ernest Borneman, Alfons M. Dauer and Ekkehard Jost. English summaries are included. Subsequent volumes (five have been published by 1975, including double volumes for 1971/2 and 1974-5) are similarly erudite, with a slight increase in the number of articles in English (notably by David Evans and William Ferris on aspects of the blues). The standard of writing is clearly high and the tone serious evidence of the growth in musicological interest in jazz, particularly in Germany.

997. LANG, Iain. Background of the blues. London: Workers'

Music Association, 1943. 55p.

_____. Jazz in perspective: the background of the blues.
London, New York: Hutchinson, 1947; London: Jazz Book
Club, 1957. 148p. illus., discog.
(The original edition was "an expansion of an essay written
for the first volume of Leonard Feather's Saturday Book.") The 1947
edition was an influential survey of the development of jazz from
New Orleans at the turn of the century to Kansas City in the 1930s,
showing the connections between jazz and the character of the society
out of which it grew. The concluding chapter is a pioneering study
of the blues, discussing European analogies, textual and musical
characteristics, and studying, with the help of some sixty textual
examples, variety of thematic content. A discography lists recordings of the texts quoted, and there is an index.

998.　MAROTHY, János. Music and the bourgeois, music and the
proletarian; translated from the Hungarian by Eva Róna.
Budapest: Akadémiai Kiadó, 1974. 588p. bibliog. notes.
This intense, unsmiling Marxist sociological interpretation of
bourgeois and proletarian aspects of music history includes a section
on jazz, seen in the context of "workers' folk music in world imperialism." Here, with several music examples (and reference to
printed sources that are frequently rather dated), Maróthy distinguishes
and examines types of "proletarian folk antecedents" (sea shanties,
ballads, spirituals, blues, dance music, marches), and discusses
rhythm, melody, polyphony, and other features of jazz in terms of
their "proletarian musicality." One of the central themes is the exploitation by capitalist industry of the well-springs of proletarian
creativity. It is worth pointing out that there is no discussion of
jazz developments of the 1950s or beyond, no consideration of any
possible positive contributions by the capitalist industrial system
(jazz and blues are, after all, the world's best recorded folk mu-
sics), and not a glimmer of light to show the writer actually enjoys
a single note of the music.

999.　OSTRANSKY, Leroy. The anatomy of jazz. Seattle: University of Washington Press, 1960. (Repr. Westport: Greenwood Press, 1973). 362p. illus., bibliog.
An excellent analytical introduction to jazz, particularly for
the "serious" musician (to whose world, as a composer, the author
primarily belongs). Ostransky sees himself as a conciliator of opposing factions, and states his aim as "to present jazz in its proper
perspective to those whose primary interest is in 'serious' or classical music, and to relate jazz theory to music theory in general,
... to introduce those whose primary interest is in jazz to the problems of nonjazz composers and performers by relating jazz to the
history of music in general ... [and] to indicate to jazzmen what I
believe to be their present position in music, as well as their musical responsibility to the future" (p. vii). He begins by describing
some difficulties of jazz analysis, and some past trends in jazz criticism, going on to examine various attempts at a definition of jazz
(by Paul Eduard Miller, Ulanov, Stearns and Hodeir) and to essay
one of his own (p. 45). Musical elements of jazz are discussed and

explained, with music examples, and there is a historical analysis
of jazz styles from New Orleans to the 1950s, with some thoughts
on the future. The bibliography of books and articles is very extensive, and there is an index. (The reprint lacks illustrations.)

1000.   PLEASANTS, Henry.   Death of a music? the decline of the
        European tradition and the rise of jazz.   London: Gol-
        lancz, 1961; London: Jazz Book Club, 1962.   191p.
        bibliog.
        In this challenging and frequently controversial study the two
idioms which are seen as dominating 20th century music--serious music
and jazz--are examined and contrasted.   The author begins by discussing the divorce of the contemporary composer from his audience,
contrasting this with previous eras and seeking reasons.   He explores the use made by the modern composer of his musical heritage
of harmony, melody, rhythm and orchestra, and suggests that if
these rich seams are not worked out the workings have certainly--
and mistakenly--been closed down.   The consequences for the performing musicians and the critic are considered.   This situation is
sharply contrasted with the emergence of jazz in America.   Pleasants examines the status of jazz and the serious music community's
refusal to accept it.   Discussing contrasting views of what constitutes
jazz, he attempts a definition on the basis of the relation of swing
to explicit beat.   He also explores characteristics of the musical and
suggests that a parallel situation to that of jazz exists between the
musical and opera.   No index.

1001.   PLEASANTS, Henry.   Serious music--and all that jazz! an
        adventure in music criticism.   London: Gollancz; New
        York: Simon & Schuster, 1969.   256p.
        Here Pleasants continues, up-dates and expands the argu-
ments in no. 1000, no less forcibly or controversially.   His basic
aim is to describe and explore the art/entertainment schism in contemporary music.   Continuing the search for a definition of jazz, he
describes some distinctive elements, points to the decisive African
contribution, and compares the role of a jazz performer with his
serious music counterpart.   The most important idiom in the present musical epoch is identified as Afro-American, and its emergence
is compared to the transition from Renaissance to Baroque in Europe.
Reviewing the attitude of the musical Establishment to American popular music, he takes issue with those who refuse to acknowledge its
importance.   Turning to the current state of jazz the author examines
bop and the new jazz, and points to crises similar to those experienced
by serious music.   The future is seen to lie rather in Afro-American vocal styles.   These he identifies and describes, from big band
singers on the one hand, to blues and gospel singers on the other
(and including Negro-influenced country music), through to rock.
Still in terms of the future, and pursuing his interest in musical
theater, he also examines the music of the cinema.   Index.

e. General Histories

1002. FOX, Charles. Jazz in perspective. London: B. B. C.,
1969. 88p. illus., bibliog., discog.
A useful introductory work written originally for a series
of radio broadcasts. It presents the outstanding features of jazz
history in a lucid, unsentimental fashion, concentrating above all on
the music itself as a performer's art (with many musical examples),
and also describing the background from which it sprang, and the
personalities involved. Well illustrated, and with annotations in
both bibliography and discography.

1003. HARRIS, Rex. Jazz. Harmondsworth: Penguin, 1952.
224p. bibliog.

_____. _____. 2nd ed. Harmondsworth: Penguin,
1953. 256p. bibliog.

_____. _____. 4th ed. Harmondsworth: Penguin,
1956. 272p. bibliog.

_____. The story of jazz; with an afterword and dis-
cography by Sheldon Meyer. New York: Grosset & Dunlap, 1955. 280p. discog.
A well-thumbed volume in Britain in the 1950s, where it
was the first native attempt at a coherent history, Harris' account
is very thorough on the African roots of the music, the many influences upon its genesis, and its early history. He also covers,
in his final chapter, jazz's influence on modern composers. He is,
however, a self-confessed "purist" ("if being catholic in its outlook
on jazz means accepting as jazz forms of music which are utterly
divorced from the real thing then this is a purist book"--p. 168,
2nd ed.) whose definition of true jazz excludes, inter alia, Henderson and Ellington, both of whom manifest tell-tale traces of the influence of "European orthodoxy." There is no musical analysis
("this book does not purport to be a musical textbook"--footnote on
p. 42), but plentiful historical discussion of the pioneers, black and
white. An interesting chart illustrates the origins and development
of jazz to 1950. Index. (The 1955 New York edition is an abridged
version of the Britist text.)

1004. MALSON, Lucien. Histoire du jazz. Lausanne: Editions
Rencontre, 1967. (Histoire Illustrée de la Musique, 19)
128p. illus.
A quite short but attractive pictorial history of jazz that
strikes a nice balance between historical information, critical perception and evocative illustration as it describes the antecedents of
jazz in black America, and its development from New Orleans to
the 1960s.

1005. POLILLO, Arrigo. Jazz: la vicenda e i protagonisti della
musica afro-americana. Milan: Mondadori, 1975. 782p.
illus., bibliog. notes.
This weighty tome is divided into two separate sections: a
historical account of the development of jazz from its origins to the
present, and a series of portraits of 34 outstanding individual jazz

personalities from Jelly Roll Morton to Ornette Coleman. There are no music examples, but there is a large general index.

1006.   SHAPIRO, Nat, and HENTOFF, Nat, eds. Hear me talkin' to ya: the story of jazz by the men who made it. New York: Rinehart, 1955. (Repr. New York: Dover Publications, 1966). 432p.
_____. _____. London: Davies, 1955; London: Jazz Book Club, 1967. 383p.
A unique portrait of jazz from the inside. In conversation, correspondence and interviews with the editors, and in excerpts from books and articles, 150 jazzmen describe the jazz world they know-- their lives in jazz, their fellow musicians, and the development of their own and other people's styles. Full accounts of various musicians (e. g. , Bix Beiderbecke) emerge. The arrangement of the texts is basically chronological, beginning in New Orleans and ending with the West Coast school and the Dixieland revival. In a coda a dozen musicians express what jazz means to them. There is an index of talkers and a general index.

1007.   STEARNS, Marshall, and STEARNS, Jean. Jazz dance: the story of American vernacular dance. New York: Macmillan, 1968. 464p. illus. , bibliog.
Based on material gathered from over two hundred interviews with dancers, this study charts the development and decline of American dancing to jazz rhythms, and studies various artists and styles, relating this development to jazz evolution and its economic, social and human factors. The story begins in West Africa and the West Indies, and moves through the blending processes of New Orleans, the minstrel and medicine shows, the early 20th century roadshows, to the surge of popularity, and the contribution of Tin Pan Alley and the Broadway musicals of the '20s and '30s. Here outstanding individuals are studied, together with various specialist acts and styles, and the story is pursued until popularity wanes in the mid-'40s. An epilog speculates on the future of vernacular dance. There are copious references, a long book bibliography, a list of films (by Ernest Smith), and an analysis of Afro-American dance movements in Labanotation by Nadia Chilkovsky. Index.

1008.   STEARNS, Marshall W. The story of jazz. New York: Oxford University Press, 1956; London: Sidgwick & Jackson, 1957. 367p. illus. , bibliog.
_____. _____; with an expanded bibliography and a syllabus of fifteen lectures on the history of jazz. New York: New American Library, 1958. 272p. illus. , bibliog.
The great virtue of this basic history of the development of jazz up to bop and Afro-Cuban music is that, although it eschews all detailed musical analysis, it presents a lucid historical documentation of its origins and evolution. Stearns begins with an examination of connections between jazz and West African music, describes the mingling of cultures in the New World and the comparative patterns of acculturation in the West Indies and the U. S. In Part 2 he

describes the unique New Orleans background and the emergence of
jazz, proceeding in Part 3 to study sources in the religious and
secular music of 19th century America from the Great Awakening
through work song, blues, minstrelsy and spiritual up to ragtime.
The outstanding developments in jazz itself are described in Parts
4 and 5, with further sections devoted to the use in jazz of elements
such as harmony, rhythm, etc. , and to the future of jazz and its
relation to the Negro. The bibliography is by R. G. Reisner, and
there is an index.

1009. ULANOV, Barry. A history of jazz in America. New
      York: Viking Press, 1952; London: Jazz Book Club,
      1957; London: Hutchinson, 1958. (Repr. New York:
      Da Capo, 1972). 382p.
      A balanced, detailed history, beginning with a definition of
jazz and tracing its sources and development up to bop, progressive
and cool jazz, and concluding with an evaluation based on the criteria
of freshness, profundity and skill, moulded by intuition and collective
tension. No musical analysis is attempted, and there are no music
examples or reference sources. There is a glossary of jazz words
and phrases, and an index.

f. Collected Criticism and Appreciation

1010. BALLIETT, Whitney. The sound of surprise: 46 pieces on
      jazz. New York: Dutton, 1959. 237p.
      _____. _____. London: Kimber, 1960. 254p.
      _____. _____. London: Jazz Book Club, 1962.
      254p.
      _____. _____. Harmondsworth: Penguin, 1963.
      202p.
      The first collection of Balliett's writings, these are pieces
from Saturday Review and the Reporter (1954-6), but mainly from
the New Yorker, 1957-9. They provide an interesting commentary
on jazz in the 1950s. Among artists discussed are: Ellington, The
Modern Jazz Quartet, Cootie Williams, Mingus, Red Allen, Vic
Dickenson, Ben Webster, Sid Catlett, Sidney Bechet, and Pee Wee
Russell. Index.

1011. BALLIETT, Whitney. Dinosaurs in the morning: 41 pieces
      on jazz. Philadelphia: Lippincott, 1962. 224p.
      _____. _____. Toronto: McClelland, 1962. 224p.
      _____. _____. London: Phoenix House, 1964. 224p.
      _____. _____. London: Jazz Book Club, 1965.
      224p.
      Further essays on jazz from the New Yorker, 1957-1962.
Written mainly in response to concerts and recorded performances
(of both contemporary and older material) they have more than
merely historical value; they are fine examples of literate, perceptive jazz appreciation within the somewhat restrictive confines of the
short journal article. Balliett has few axes to grind, and ranges
widely over traditional and contemporary jazz, ragtime and blues.

Most of the essays are devoted to personalities, and include interviews, portraits, descriptive and historical pieces, access to which is possible through the index.

1012. BALLIETT, Whitney. Such sweet thunder. Indianapolis: Bobbs-Merrill, 1966; London: Macdonald, 1968. 366p.
A collection of 49 enjoyable articles on jazz written for the New Yorker between 1962 and 1966. They are arranged chronologically, with an index, and cover critical discussions of musicians and reviews of records, performances and festivals.

1013. BALLIETT, Whitney. Ecstasy at the Onion: thirty-one pieces on jazz. Indianapolis: Bobbs-Merrill, 1971. 284p.
More good jazz appreciation from the New Yorker. This particular collection, from the period 1967-1971, includes a diary of jazz at Newport, Monterey, and in New York, a sequence of five pieces on Duke Ellington, a selection of seven critical reviews, and portraits of selected jazz personalities of the time, including Ray Charles, Elvin Jones, the Modern Jazz Quartet, Red Norvo, Bobby Short and Charles Mingus. There is an index. With Balliett's other volumes of articles and reviews this forms an impressive, perceptive chronicle of the jazz scene from the early 1950s to the beginning of the 1970s.

1014. CERULLI, Dom, et al. The jazz word; (edited by) Dom Cerulli, Burt Korall, Mort Nasatir. New York: Ballantine, 1960. 240p. illus.
————. ————. London: Dobson, 1962. 192p.
————. ————. London: Jazz Book Club, 1963. 192p.
A potpourri of previously published jazz writings of the late 1950s--liner notes, newspaper and magazine articles, press releases --plus some original material. The most substantial pieces are by Mercer Ellington, by Gary Kramer on narcotics in jazz, and by George Russell on jazz's future. There is also a group of articles on Ella Fitzgerald, four on blues (featuring Big Bill Broonzy, Billie Holiday, Lester Young and Charlie Parker), a section on jazz and poetry, another on humor in jazz, and a selection of jazz slang. No index.

1015. CONDON, Eddie, and GEHMANN, Richard, eds. Eddie Condon's treasury of jazz. New York: Dial Press, 1956. 488p.
————. ————. London: Davies, 1957. 510p.
An anthology of articles from the period 1946-1955 by a host of writers, including Nat Hentoff, Whitney Balliett, Leonard Feather, Marshall Stearns, Ralph Gleason, John Hammond, etc. Most seem to take a greater interest in the life habits and style of the musicians than in their music. The fifth section contains eight short stories on jazz themes.

1016. ELLISON, Ralph. Shadow and act. New York: Random

House, 1964; London: Secker & Warburg, 1967. 317p.
_____. _____. New York: New American Library,
1966. 302p.
     This collection of essays by an outstanding Negro novelist
and lecturer includes a section of seven highly perceptive pieces
from the period 1955 to 1964 on "Sound and the Mainstream," which
are primarily concerned with jazz and blues. The first is a humorous description of juxtaposed musical traditions and practices, centered on (un)neighbourly habits in an apartment block. The second
focuses on Minton's, the New York club that was the cradle of bop
in the 1940s, assessing its significance in particular as a venue for
the all-important jam sessions. The third essay is a profile of the
art of Mahalia Jackson, and the fourth an appreciation of Charlie
Parker. This is followed by an account of guitarist Charlie Christian, and by a recollection of the past style of Jimmy Rushing and
his present approach (1958). The final musical essay is a review
of LeRoi Jones' Blues People (no. 689), in which Ellison takes issue with Jones' view of the relations between blues, the American
Negro and American culture at large.

1017.   ESQUIRE'S JAZZ BOOK; edited by Paul Eduard Miller (1947
          ed. by Ernest Anderson); introduction by Arnold Gingrich.
          New York: Smith & Durrell, 1944, 1947; New York:
          Barnes, 1945-1946. 4v. illus., discogs.
          _____; edited by Paul Eduard Miller, and (for England)
          by Ralph Venables. London: Davies, 1947. 184p. illus.
     The English edition is a selection of the best articles from
the first three American yearbooks, covering individuals, cities,
styles, and an "analysis of the art of jazz" by Miller. The originals
also contain several bio-discographies.

1018.   GLEASON, Ralph. Jam sessions: an anthology of jazz.
          New York: Putnam, 1958. 319p. illus., bibliog.
          _____. _____. London: Davies; London: Jazz Book
          Club, 1961. 253p. illus., bibliog.
     An anthology of thirty-five pieces on jazz by musicians and
critics, chosen mainly from journals and books of the 1940s and '50s.
There are six main sections: the background of jazz (blues, spir-
ituals, New Orleans jazz, by Leadbelly, Sterling Brown, Jelly Roll
Morton); the growth of the jazz culture; the jazz revival (including
Bunk Johnson on himself); some jazz personalities (Fats Waller,
Earl Hines, Dizzy Gillespie, Django Reinhardt, Nat King Cole and
Erroll Garner); modern jazz (including a piece by Henry Pleasants);
and a miscellany. The selective discography is annotated. No in-
dex.

1019.   GREEN, Benny. Drums in my ears. London: Davis-
          Poynter, 1973. 188p.
     One of the most enjoyable and stimulating of jazz journalists,
Londoner Benny Green (who began his career as a jazz musician) is
also one of the most outspoken. He admits to having axes to grind,
and from the evidence of this anthology of his articles he also wields
them powerfully, as when he attacks the music of the Modern Jazz

Quartet and Dave Brubeck. A Shavian love of battle is tempered by a Shavian wit (the "studied gloom" of the MJQ is likened to that of "four eminent Victorians who have just heard about 'The Origin of Species'"). He has strong preferences, and they range from George Lewis and Bix Beiderbecke through Armstrong, Ellington and Tatum to Young, Parker and Gillespie, all of whom are featured. The articles cover the period 1958-1970 and are chosen from Green's criticism for various British newspapers and journals. They are arranged in broad groups (saxophonists, singers, father figures, avant garde, etc.) and are mostly occasioned by performances or recordings by individual musicians. One group is devoted also to musical comedy. No index.

1020.   HENTOFF, Nat, and McCARTHY, Albert J., eds. Jazz: new perspectives on the history of jazz by twelve of the world's foremost jazz critics and scholars. New York: Rinehart, 1959; London: Cassell, 1960; New York: Grove Press, 1961; London: Jazz Book Club. 1962 (Repr. New York: Da Capo, 1974). 387p. illus., bibliog., discog.
      This collection of specially commissioned essays is one of the most rewarding of critical anthologies on jazz. The articles belong in five categories: general historical (Ernest Bornemann on jazz roots, Hentoff on jazz at mid-century); regional studies (New Orleans, by Charles Edward Smith, Chicago by John Steiner, and Kansas City by Franklin S. Driggs); studies of individuals (Jelly Roll Morton, by Martin Williams; Duke Ellington, by Gunther Schuller; and Charlie Parker, by Max Harrison); studies of jazz styles (Hsio Wen Shih on big bands, Martin Williams on bebop, and McCarthy on the re-emergence of traditional jazz); and on related genres (blues, by Paul Oliver; ragtime, by Guy Waterman; and boogie-woogie, by Max Harrison). The extensive discography of 78s and LPs is arranged in parallel subject groups. Some essays have music examples, and there is an index.

1021.   JAMES, Burnett. Essays on jazz. London: Sidgwick & Jackson, 1961; London: Jazz Book Club, 1962. 205p.
      These ten essays are based on material originally published in the British jazz periodical, Jazz Monthly. Eschewing analysis, they are good examples of the most common kind of jazz appreciation--general critical assessment of the style of individual jazz musicians. To the normal equipment of the jazz critic James adds a valuable dimension, with his extensive knowledge of art music. The individuals are Billie Holiday, Lester Young, King Oliver, Bix Beiderbecke, Oscar Peterson, Johnny Hodges and Duke Ellington (two pieces, one on "Such Sweet Thunder"). Two more general essays consider improvisation, and the rights and wrongs of "Swinging Bach."

1022.   NANRY, Charles, ed. American music: from Storyville to Woodstock; with a foreword by Irving Louis Horowitz. New Brunswick: Transaction Books, 1972. 290p. bibliog. notes.
      These thirteen essays on aspects of jazz and rock and roll

are mainly papers given at a conference on "Jazz and All That Sociology" at Rutgers University. All center around the "sociohistorical process that shaped ... American music," examining how jazz and rock reflect changes in American life and society. The contributors are: Morroe Berger, Neil Leonard (twice), Howard S. Becker, Nat Hentoff, Robert A. Stebbins, Richard A. Peterson, the editor, Christopher White, Robert R. Faulkner (an excerpt from his book, no. 1307), Howard Junker, Jon Landau and I. L. Horowitz.

1023.   WILLIAMS, Martin, ed.   The art of jazz: essays on the nature and development of jazz.   New York: Oxford University Press, 1959; London: Cassell, 1960.   248p.   illus.
   ————.   ————.   London: Jazz Book Club, 1962. 248p.
   A collection of 21 essays on a variety of jazz and blues musicians and styles, ranging from ragtime to bop.   Among the individuals covered are Morton, Oliver, James P. Johnson, Beiderbecke, Ellington, Billie Holiday, Tatum, Christian, the Modern Jazz Quartet, blues singers Sonny Terry and Bessie Smith, and boogie pianists Lofton, Yancey and Lewis.   Contributors include Marshall Stearns, George and Al Avakian, Paul Oliver, William Russell, Ernest Ansermet and Max Harrison.   The essays for the most part appeared originally in various journals between 1948 and 1958.   There are also some reprinted liner notes.   Introductory notes precede each article, and there are some music examples.   Index.

1024.   WILLIAMS, Martin, ed.   Jazz panorama: from the pages of "The Jazz Review."   New York: Crowell-Collier, 1962. 318p.   illus.
   ————.   ————.   London: Jazz Book Club, 1965. 318p.
   The Jazz Review aimed, in Williams' words, "to discuss jazz as if it were a music, an important music with an important heritage" (introduction).   These 39 contributions--historical essays, extended record reviews, personal recollections, interviews and analyses--are devoted in the main to a variety of outstanding individual musicians, from Jelly Roll Morton and King Oliver, via James P. Johnson, Don Redman, Louis Armstrong, Jimmie Lunceford, Stan Getz, Miles Davis, Sonny Rollins and numerous others up to Ornette Coleman, Ray Charles and Lightnin' Hopkins.   Contributors include both critics and musicians, and all but one are American.   Besides the editor, who contributes eight, there are two pieces each by Nat Hentoff, Frank Driggs, Dick Katz, Mait Edey, Gunther Schuller and Julian Cannonball Adderley.   Several include music examples.   No index is provided.

4.   History and Criticism
of Specific Periods

a.   To 1940

1025.   BLESH, Rudi.   Shining trumpets: a history of jazz.   New

        York: Knopf, 1946; London: Cassell, 1949. 365p.
        illus., discog.
        ————. ————. 2nd rev. and enlarged ed. New
        York: Knopf, 1958. (Repr. New York: Da Capo, 1975).
        410p. illus., discog.
        ————. ————. 4th (i.e. 2nd) rev. and enlarged ed.
        London: Cassell, 1958. 369p. illus., discog.

A pioneer scholarly study of early jazz which is still considered controversial because of the author's view that jazz's potential remained unexplored after about 1926, and his over-emphasis on New Orleans as the birthplace of the music. Blesh divides his history into a study of the origins of jazz and a detailed outline of its history up to the rise of swing. In the first part he discusses African root elements in jazz, the development of secular and sacred Negro music in the American South, and the character and influence of the blues. In Book 2 he traces the course of traditional jazz from New Orleans through classic jazz, Chicago jazz, and the Golden Age of recorded jazz, up to swing. There are many valuable analyses of performances by New Orleans jazzmen, with transcriptions of forty-seven musical examples referred to in the text collected at the back of the book, together with nine appendices, a list of records cited and an index.

1026.   BLESH, Rudi. This is jazz: a series of lectures given at
        the San Francisco Museum of Art. San Francisco: the
        author, 1943. 36p. bibliog. notes, discog.
        ————. ————. London: Jazz Music Books, 1945.
        34p. bibliog. notes, discog.

More exactly titled "This is hot jazz," Blesh's lectures provide a concise outline of the development and essential characteristics of New Orleans jazz, a passionate advocacy of its greatness and originality, and a stern critique of all other types (white imitations, Chicago-based styles, big band jazz--for all of which he has little liking). The authoritative historical descriptions and musical analysis--and the highly personal view of subsequent jazz development--reappear in expanded form in Shining Trumpets (no. 1025).

1027.   GOFFIN, Robert. Aux frontières du jazz; préface de
        Pierre MacOrlan. Paris: Editions du Sagittaire, 1932.
        356p. illus.

The Belgian writer Robert Goffin occupies a distinguished place among jazz critics in being the first to see in jazz a significant contribution to music and to publish his thoughts in book form. This he achieved without visiting America. Reflecting, in the opening pages of a later book (no. 1028), on his earlier achievement, Goffin remarks: "I am proud to think that I was the first in the world to draw the distinction technically between hot and commercial jazz. I even had the audacity ... to dedicate my book to Louis Armstrong, 'the real King of Jazz,' explaining that Paul Whiteman had been wrapped in an unmerited mantle. My book was not translated because of its decidedly uncompromising attitude..." (1946 ed., p. 2).

1028. GOFFIN, Robert. Jazz: from the Congo to the Metropoli-
       tan; introduced by Arnold Gingrich. Garden City: Double-
       day, 1944. (Repr. New York: Da Capo, 1975). 254p.
       bibliog.
       _____. Histoire du jazz. Montreal: Parizeau, 1945.
       337p.
       _____. Jazz: from Congo to Swing. London: Musicians
       Press, 1946. 273p. illus., bibliog., discog.
       This first of Goffin's books to appear in English (in a trans-
lation by Walter Schaap and Leonard Feather) was an influential historical survey in which Goffin maintained his clear distinction between commercial jazz and genuine, spontaneous music. His account
of the rise and development of jazz from New Orleans to the mid-
1940s includes perceptive discussion of many outstanding musicians,
with separate chapters on Louis Armstrong and Benny Goodman.
His confident view of the future foresees the development of individual jazz styles on every continent. In Sidney Finkelstein's view
(no. 991, p. 6), Goffin regarded jazz in the same light as he viewed
aesthetic experiments in Paris such as Dada, and gave it a "left-
handed compliment" by praising it, then saying "music has no need
of the intelligence." No index. (The London edition incorporates
revisions made in the 1945 French text. The original French text,
of which the 1944 edition was a translation, was apparently not published.)

1029. HADLOCK, Richard. Jazz masters of the twenties. New
       York: Macmillan, 1965; London: Collier-Macmillan,
       1966. 255p. illus., bibliogs., discogs.
       A study of the musical output in the 1920s of Louis Arm-
strong, Earl Hines, Bix Beiderbecke, the Chicagoans (Goodman,
etc.), Fats Waller and James P. Johnson, Jack Teagarden, Fletcher
Henderson and Don Redman, Bessie Smith, and Eddie Lang. The
author examines the development of each musician's style through
his recordings, and describes and assesses the influence and importance of each in jazz evolution. Each chapter has a selected
reading list and discography. No index.

1030. HOBSON, Wilder. American jazz music. New York: Nor-
       ton, 1939; London: Dent, 1940. 230p. illus.
       _____. _____. (Rev. ed.). London: Dent, 1941;
       London: Jazz Book Club, 1956. 227p. illus., discog.
       Hobson's perceptive critical study of jazz up to the swing
era is one of the best of the early attempts to define "the distinctive musical qualities of this music in itself" (p. 18). Part historical, part analytical, the book first examines the origins of jazz,
isolates and discusses particular technical features (tone color,
rhythm, etc.), and assesses the exponents of commercial and concert
jazz. Three chapters are devoted to the spread of jazz from South
to North and its development in Chicago and New York. There is
also a discussion of the swing style of the 1930s. The final chapter
lists and describes 30 selected records suggesting the development
of jazz as outlined in the book. The later English editions contain
a list of discographical references for these. Index.

1031.   McCARTHY, Albert. The trumpet in jazz. London: Citizen Press, (1945?). 82p. discog.
   A booklet tracing the evolution of the role of the jazz trumpeter through examination of the recordings of various individuals, from Louis Armstrong and New Orleans musicians to the soloists of the swing era.

1032.   MENDL, R. W. S. The appeal of jazz. London: Philip Allan, 1927. 186p.
   The "first book about jazz to be published in Great Britain" (preface) is of little but historic interest. Its subject is not jazz at all, but dance music and its place in the European concert tradition. Mendl's knowledge of American black music goes no further than spirituals and his examples are confined to ragtime (Irving Berlin version), the Charleston, a smattering of Paul Whiteman and George Gershwin, and Vincent Youman's "No, No, Nanette." Even these are outnumbered by references to European classical composers.

1033.   OSGOOD, Henry O. So this is jazz. Boston: Little, Brown, 1926. 258p. illus.
   It is customary to denigrate this first book-length attempt (in English) at a history and appreciation of jazz because it concentrates on the concert jazz of Paul Whiteman, the piano of Zez Confrey, etc., to the total exclusion of King Oliver and Jelly Roll Morton, to name but two. This verdict is plainly correct, but three points are worth making: (i) it was a widely read and oft-quoted book in its day; (ii) it does give a detailed portrait of Whiteman, Grofé and Gershwin, among others (including a first-hand account of the first performance of "Rhapsody in Blue"). (iii) there are other things in the book--e. g., a discussion of the origin of the word "jazz," and an account of black folk music. There are several music examples in the text, and there are indexes of general subjects and of popular music titles mentioned.

1034.   PANASSIE, Hugues. Le jazz hot; présenté par Louis Armstrong; préface par Eugène Marsan. Paris: Correa, 1934. 432p. illus., discog.
   _____. Hot jazz: the guide to swing music; translated by Lyle and Eleanor Dowling; especially revised by the author for the English language edition. New York: Witmark; London: Cassell, 1936. 363p. discog.
   Writing eight years after his pioneer volume of jazz criticism appeared, Panassié belittled some of his earlier judgments of certain black musicians: "I made the mistake of judging (them) unconsciously by standards acquired from the white instrumentalists" (preface to The Real Jazz, no. 1035). There were mitigating circumstances, however: records of these musicians were very hard to find. Despite such errors of judgment Panassié's book occupies a proud place; the 1936 translation was the first serious attempt to come to critical grips with jazz to be published in English, and its appearance was most welcome. "I doubt," remarks Langridge (no. 908, p. 57), "if any other book has been so effective in arousing enthusiasm for the music. If the spirit rather than the letter is ac-

cepted as the prime factor in this function, I can think of many worse introductions to the subject even today. "

1035.   PANASSIE, Hugues. The real jazz; translated by Anne
        Sorelle Williams; adapted for American publication by
        Charles Edward Smith. New York: Smith & Durrell,
        1942. 326p. discog.
        _____.   . Rev. and enlarged ed. New York:
        Barnes, 1960; London: Jazz Book Club, 1967. 284p.
        discog.
        _____. La véritable musique de jazz. Paris: Laffont,
        1946. 304p. illus., discog.
        _____.   . Ed. revue et augmentée. Paris:
        Laffont, 1952. 254p. discog.
        In its presentation this second volume of Panassié's criti-
cism to appear in English (the translator worked from a manuscript
badly damaged in wartime transit from France to America) is similar to the first, with the bulk of the book devoted to general stylistic
examination and assessment of musicians in groups by instrument
(trumpeters, saxophonists, guitarists, and so on). The difference
is that "I did not realise until some years after the publication of
my first book that, from the point of view of jazz, most white musicians were inferior to colored musicians" (preface). Besides having a respectful ear for only a few white jazzmen, Panassié has no
liking at all for contemporary jazz movements--"be-bop music is not
jazz" (p. 73). The revised edition contains a selected list of LPs,
reflecting his preferences. No index.

1036.   RAMSEY, Fredric, and SMITH, Charles Edward, eds.
        Jazzmen. New York: Harcourt, Brace, 1939; London:
        Sidgwick & Jackson, 1957; London: Jazz Book Club,
        1958. (Repr. St. Clair Shores, Mich.: Scholarly Press,
        1972). 360p. illus.
        A landmark in jazz criticism, combining the contributions
of nine critics into an outstanding historical and analytical survey.
The text is divided into four sections: New Orleans (chapters by
William Russell, Stephen W. Smith, and the editors), Chicago (E.
Simms Campbell, Russell, E. J. Nichols and the second editor),
New York (Wilder Hobson and Otis Ferguson), and finally "Hot jazz
today" (Hobson and the editors, with a chapter on collecting by
Stephen Smith and a discussion of early jazz criticism by R. P.
Dodge). The story of each period is told mainly through the career
and work of the outstanding individuals. Contributors combine history with critical assessment, adding to their specialist knowledge
from a central pool of information obtained by interview. The
standard of writing is high, and there is a general and a music index. No music examples.

1037.   SARGEANT, Winthrop. Jazz hot and hybrid. New York:
        Arrow, 1938. 234p.
        _____.   . New and enlarged ed. New York:
        Dutton, 1946; London: Jazz Book Club, 1959. 287p.
        bibliog.

_____. Jazz: a history. New York: McGraw-Hill, 1964. 287p. bibliog.

_____. Jazz hot and hybrid. 3rd. ed. New York: Da Capo, 1975. 302p. illus., bibliog.

The first attempt to approach jazz with the tools of musical analysis and to define, describe and explain its musical make-up. Illustrating his argument with frequent musical examples, Sargeant analyzes jazz rhythm and melody, scalar structures and the derivation and development of the blues scale, harmony and--though too early to take advantage of the coming research--African influences. He also considers the jazz orchestra, and musical form, concluding with an examination of jazz as a fine art. The extensive bibliography in the later editions lists books and articles. Index.

1038. SCHULLER, Gunther. Early jazz: its roots and musical development. New York: Oxford University Press, 1968. 401p. bibliog. notes, discog.

This unique work--the first of a projected two-volume set-- attempts a detailed analysis of jazz up to the big band era, combining a scholarly musicological approach with the subjective reactions of an "engaged listener." Schuller begins by examining the origins of the various characteristic musical features--rhythm, form, harmony, melody, timbre and improvisation--discussing African and European elements, and by describing the first emergence of jazz as a distinct music. He then assesses the work of Louis Armstrong and Jelly Roll Morton, and various virtuoso performers of the 1920s (including Bix Beiderbecke, Bessie Smith, Harlem pianists such as James P. Johnson and Fats Waller, and clarinettists Sidney Bechet and Johnny Dodds). The final chapters are concerned with the formation of the big bands and the origins and early development of the Ellington style. There are frequent music examples, a glossary, selected LP discography, and an index. An appendix contains the transcript of an interview with George Morrison.

1039. STEWART, Rex. Jazz masters of the thirties. New York: Macmillan; London: Collier-Macmillan, 1972. 223p. illus.

Rex Stewart (1907-1967) concluded a distinguished career as a cornetist (with Ellington and Henderson among others) by writing pieces for various journals. This volume comprises a selection of these--so whatever their merits as enjoyable, miscellaneous portraits of musicians of the 1930s (and the 1920s, too, for several articles stretch well back there) they cannot by any leap of the imagination be thought of as a thorough, coordinated account of the leading musicians of the decade. (To be fair to Stewart, he did not live to prepare his pieces for publication in book form; the series editor-- whose book on the 1960s (no. 1059) is also a collection of reprinted essays--must take responsibility for evidently deciding that these writings constitute a balanced biographical and critical portrait of the major figures.) Stewart's writing is cheerful, easy-going, with a heavy reliance on anecdotes from his own experience; he knew all the musicians he talks about, and it is this first-hand knowledge which is the book's redeeming feature. A central section on member of Ellington's orchestra (among them Joe Nanton and Harry Carney) is flanked on one side by profiles of Jean Goldkette's band, and of Henderson, Armstrong, Jimmy Harrison, Hawkins and Norvo, and on the other by John Kirby, Sid Catlett, Benny Carter and Art Tatum. Since Basie is missing an appreciation of him by Hsio Wen Shih is included in an appendix, where is also found a portrait of Stewart himself by Francis Thorne. No index.

b. Swing and Dance Bands

1040.   DANCE, Stanley. The world of swing. New York: Scribner, 1974. 436p. illus., discog.
    A series of interviews with 40 musicians of the swing era, originally published in various journals between 1962 and 1971. Supplementary material includes a list of bands in Harlem theaters by Walter C. Allen and Jerry Valburn. Index.

1041.   FERNETT, Gene. Swing out: great Negro dance bands. Midland, Mich.: Pendell, 1970. 176p. illus.
    A collection of mostly short but informative accounts of twenty-five Negro jazz band leaders and their bands from Fate Marable to Dizzy Gillespie. All the bands had some measure of commercial success, included influential musicians or played in a style that caused the band to make a significant contribution, and made several records. The author focuses his attention on the leader and his career; he also notes the most important of the musicians who played with him, characterizes the style of the band, and gives a brief account of their activities. The book is illustrated with over a hundred photographs; there is an index of these, but no general index. There is also a list of the dates and places of birth of fifty-four musicians, and a list of theme songs.

1042.   McCARTHY, Albert. Big band jazz. London: Barrie & Jenkins, 1974. 360p. illus., bibliog., discog.
    This handsomely illustrated volume describes the development of big band jazz in terms of the individuals involved. The sequence of chapters moves from the early syncopated bands of James Reese Europe, Wilbur Sweatman and others, and the early pioneers in Chicago and New York, through the "first flowering" with Fletcher Henderson, McKinney's Cotton Pickers and Luis Russell, the territory bands (the longest, most detailed chapter, divided into regions), and the white bands to the swing era itself, culminating in an extended portrait of Duke Ellington and his orchestra, and a consideration of the reasons for the decline of the big bands. Each chapter is filled with factual information on individuals and bands, accompanied by informed but rather generalized description and assessment. Particularly in the early chapters and in that on the territory bands McCarthy introduces numerous lesser-known figures, not only giving a fuller portrait of big band jazz in the important centers, but also drawing attention to the great amount of this kind of music that was performed all over the country. The enormous name index is preceded by a detailed list of references, in which disco-

graphical (LP) and bibliographical (books and articles) information is
divided according to the chapters in the book.

1043.   McCARTHY, Albert.   The dance band era: the dancing
        decades from ragtime to swing, 1910-1950.   London:
        Studio Vista; Philadelphia: Chilton, 1971.   176p.   illus.,
        bibliog., discog.
        More than half of this liberally illustrated volume is devoted
to British and European dance bands.   These give an idea of the extensive invasion of American styles and fashions, but are chiefly concerned with the European response.   Several chapters in the chronological sequence are devoted to the American scene--to the formative
years in the 1910s and the social dance craze, to the 1920s (especially the bands of Paul Whiteman, Jean Goldkette, and Ben Pollack),
to the 1930s (Glen Gray and the Case Loma Orchestra, Guy Lombardo, and Isham Jones and several others), and very briefly, to
Benny Goodman.

1044.   RUST, Brian.   The dance bands.   London: Allan, 1972;
        New Rochelle: Arlington House, 1974.   160p.   illus.
        Like McCarthy (no. 1043), Rust is a connoisseur of the
dance bands, with a particular interest in British bands, and his
book, too, is liberally illustrated.   Rust's account, however, does
not divide the American and British scenes quite so sharply, preferring to pass to and fro across the Atlantic more frequently, to
illustrate parallels, influences and changing fashions.   His detailed
historical text, which he describes as "an account of a fascinating
facet of entertainment during an era that had a character all of its
own, seen against the background of world events" (p. 7), contains
plentiful biographical information on individuals and bands in the period from 1910 to the early 1940s.   Index.

1045.   SIMON, George.   The big bands; with a foreword by Frank
        Sinatra.   New York: Macmillan, 1967.   537p.   illus.
        _____.   _____.   Rev. ed.   New York: Macmillan;
        London: Collier-Macmillan, 1971.   584p.   illus., discog.
        The standard work on the bands of the 1930s and 1940s;
written in an informal, columnist's style, it is a rich source of information for the big band era.   The 1971 edition contains four parts.
The first surveys in general terms the life-style and contributions
of various groups of people and institutions making up the world of
big bands--the leaders, musicians, and vocalists, the businessmen,
the media, etc.   Part 2 consists of portraits of seventy-two bands.
Part 3 looks at musicians in other bands under eight group headings,
such as "arranging leaders," "piano-playing leaders," briefly describes the work of a further 100 bandleaders and lists a further
144.   In Part 4 Simon examines the contemporary scene, with interviews conducted in 1971 with seven major figures of the swing era:
Basie, Goodman, Herman, James, Kenton, Lombardo and Shaw.
There is a selective LP discography and a name index.

1046.   SIMON, George.   Simon says: the sights and sounds of the
        swing era, 1935-1955.   New Rochelle: Arlington House,

1971. 491p. illus.
Another useful source of information on swing, this volume
contains a selection from Simon's writings for Metronome magazine
between 1935 and 1955. It includes interviews with band leaders, a
long section of band reviews with ratings, extracts from a fictional
jazz society columnist's diary, histories of five bands, a chapter on
Bix Beiderbecke and Bunny Berigan, interviews with singers (Sinatra,
Dinah Shore, Peggy Lee, Ella Fitzgerald, Mahalia Jackson and others) and with composers and arrangers. An appendix contains a
listing of Metronome band reviews, 1935-46. Index.

1047. SPECHT, Paul L. How they became name bands: the
modern technique of a dance band maestro. New York:
Fine Arts Publications, 1941. 175p. illus.
The leader of the first dance band to broadcast reflects on
his experience from 1920-1940, and, with the help of anecdotes,
gives advice on how to have a successful band. He is assisted in
this by some reproduced letters from a number of top band leaders.
He also gives his own account of some early jazz band days. There
is a chapter on some of the pioneer radio band leaders, including
Specht, by Ken Farnsworth.

c. Bebop and After

1048. GITLER, Ira. Jazz masters of the forties. New York:
Macmillan, 1966; New York: Collier Books, 1974. 290p.
illus., discogs.
A biographical and critical guide to the outstanding musicians of the bebop era: Charlie Parker, Dizzy Gillespie, Bud
Powell, J. J. Johnson, Oscar Pettiford, Kenny Clarke and Max
Roach, Dexter Gordon, Lennie Tristano and Lee Konitz, Tadd Dam-
eron, and, in less detail, some disciples. Gitler combines biographical information (beyond the boundaries of the decade), character portrayal and general critical assessment of each major figure
in a lucid narrative. Selected LP discographies close each chapter
and there is an index.

1049. GOLDBERG, Joe. Jazz masters of the fifties. New York:
Macmillan; London: Collier-Macmillan, 1965. 246p.
discogs.
A collection of well-written chapters on outstanding musicians
who came to prominence in the 1950s, giving general outlines of
their careers, personalities, the influences upon them, their approach
to music, and their contribution. Included are Gerry Mulligan, Thelonious Monk, Art Blakey, Miles Davis, Sonny Rollins, the Modern
Jazz Quartet, Charlie Mingus, Paul Desmond, Ray Charles, John
Coltrane, Cecil Taylor and Ornette Coleman. There are short discographies at the end of each chapter. No index.

1050. HORRICKS, Raymond, et al. These jazzmen of our time.
London: Gollancz, 1959. 236p. illus.
The sixteen contemporary musicians whose profiles are

drawn in this collection of essays are: Thelonious Monk, Miles
Davis, J. J. Johnson, Gerry Mulligan, Bud Powell, Gil Evans, Milt
Jackson, John Lewis, Max Roach, Art Blakey, Jimmy Giuffre, Dave
Brubeck, Charles Mingus, Gigi Gryce, Sonny Rollins and Quincy
Jones. Horricks himself is responsible for half of the portraits
(which usually combine biographical detail and some critical appre-
ciation), the other authors being Alun Morgan, Max Harrison,
Charles Fox, Benny Green, Ed Michel, Nat Hentoff, and Martin
Williams. Index.

1051. JAMES, Michael. Ten modern jazzmen: an appraisal of
        the recorded work of ten modern jazzmen. London:
        Cassell, 1960. 146p. illus.
        The ten concerned in this collection of interpretative essays
are: Charlie Parker, Dizzy Gillespie, Bud Powell, Miles Davis,
Stan Getz, Thelonious Monk, Gerry Mulligan, John Lewis, Lee Konitz
and Wardell Gray.

1052. JONES, LeRoi. Black music. New York: Morrow, 1967.
        221p. illus. , discog.
        A collection of twenty-eight articles and reviews written be-
tween 1959 and 1967 on aspects of modern jazz; they include pieces
reprinted from Down Beat, Kulcher, liner notes, and one piece published here for the first time. They focus attention in particular on
the playing of various jazz musicians: Thelonious Monk, Roy Haynes,
Sonny Rollins, John Coltrane, Cecil Taylor, Archie Shepp, etc. A
vigorous advocate of the music, Jones sees it constantly against a
sociological and philosophical background, and in the context of the
whole of black American life. He attacks with power, too, as in
the first chapter, "Jazz and the White Critic. "

1053. JOST, Ekkehard. Free jazz. Graz: Universal Edition,
        1974. (Studies in Jazz Research, 4) 214p. bibliog. ,
        discog.
        A welcome attempt at a musical analysis of the stylistic
directions taken by a number of outstanding figures from the jazz
world of the 1960s and 1970s. The author feels that the sociological approach predominant in jazz literature has obscured, rather
than illuminated, the variety of musical principles in free jazz, and
his book sets out to correct this. The musicians examined are:
Coltrane, Mingus, Coleman, Taylor, Shepp, Ayler, Cherry, the
Chicago-based Association for the Advancement of Creative Musicians
(Richard Abrams et al.), and Sun Ra. The text, in excellent English,
contains many music examples.

1054. KOFSKY, Frank. Black nationalism and the revolution in
        music. New York: Pathfinder Press, 1970. 280p.
        illus. , bibliog. notes, discog.
        A powerfully argued exposition of the connection between
the social situation and outlook of black people and avant-garde jazz.
An aggressive, penetrating introduction examines the reasons put
forward by white jazz idealogues for the white cultural and commercial exploitation of black artists, contesting them in three areas of

discussion: the distinctively Negro quality of jazz, the relationship of the black community to jazz, and jazz's social content. The main text begins with a condemnation of the attitude of jazz critics to black nationalism and jazz, an assessment of Jones' Blues People (no. 689), and an account of Establishment hostility to black musicians. The second part of the book deals with its main theme: modern jazz as the musical representation of the Negro's disaffiliation from white civilization. Kofsky isolates the musical trends expressing this, in particular the music of Coltrane, Coleman and Taylor. A large section is devoted to Coltrane--to an analysis of his music and influence. The argument for his central importance is reinforced by an assessment of Albert Ayler and an account of his influence on rock musicians. Part 3 of the book describes the innovations of Coltrane's drummer, Elvin Jones, and contains interviews with pianist McCoy Tyner and Coltrane himself. Part 4 relates the revolution in jazz to the career of Malcolm X. There are notes to the text, with a guide to Coltrane's recordings, but the book lacks an index.

1055. McRAE, Barry. The jazz cataclysm. London: Dent; South
        Brunswick, N. J.: A. S. Barnes, 1967. 184p. discog.
        A perceptive critical survey of the developments in jazz from the "Cool" movement to the free form of the late 1960s. The author does not mask his personal taste, which strongly favors trends from bop on, but is antagonistic to "cool" jazz, which is seen as producing jazz "divested of its life blood." Developments of the 1950s and 1960s are shown as continuing and building on the basic jazz foundation. Particular attention is paid to Sonny Rollins, John Coltrane, and Ornette Coleman. Index.

1056. MALSON, Lucien. Histoire du jazz moderne. Paris: La
        Table Ronde, 1961. 258p.
        A good historical survey of developments in jazz from World War II to the late 1950s. Scrupulously avoiding mythology and anecdote, and using biographical detail only to illuminate a discussion, Malson provides a lucid interpretive account of stylistic movements, individual contributions and the exploitation of particular instruments. Each of the four sections is dominated by a small group of musicians--bebop by Gillespie, Parker and Monk; cool by Getz, Davis, Mulligan and Lewis; the continuation of 1930s "middle jazz" by Basie; and the "period of synthesis" (1954 on) by Clifford Brown and Coltrane--but large numbers of other individual musicians are also considered. All are listed in the index, which also gives their dates. There is a glossary.

1057. MECKLENBURG, Carl Gregor, Herzog zu, and SCHECK,
        Waldemar. Die Theorie des Blues im modernen Jazz.
        Strasbourg: Heitz, 1963. (Collection d'Etudes Musicol-
        ogiques, 45) 131p. bibliog., discog.
        A technical analysis of the elements of blues--intonation, blue notes, blues tonality, form, rhythm, ornamentation, content-- and of their role in modern instrumental jazz. The book contains 64 music examples in all, 16 of these in the appendix, which contains transcriptions and thematic analyses of various jazz solos.

1058.   SPELLMAN, A. B.   Four lives in the bebop business.
            New York: Pantheon Books; London: MacGibbon & Kee,
            1967; New York: Schocken, 1970.   241p.
         Based on taped interviews and incorporating many verbatim
quotations, these are separate accounts of the lives and careers of
three prominent jazz musicians of the 1960s: Cecil Taylor, Ornette
Coleman, and Jackie McLean--and one lesser-known figure: Herbie
Nichols.   Some early biographical data is given, but the emphasis
is on the professional career of each musician, his opinions, stylistic development and musical contribution.   Other prominent figures
to appear include Charlie Parker, John Coltrane, Miles Davis and
Thelonious Monk.   Index.

1059.   WILLIAMS, Martin.   Jazz masters in transition, 1957-69.
            New York: Macmillan; London: Collier-Macmillan, 1970.
            288p.   illus.
         A mirror of jazz activity in a decade of change, when "jazz
moved from one era to another."   These 87 pieces were all written
by Williams during the period covered, for a variety of journals
(specialist and non-specialist); brought together they create a kaleido-
scopic picture of a constantly shifting scene in which stars, new and
not so new, wax and wane, are lost and rediscovered.   They are
chronologically arranged and include "reviews, interviews, brief profiles and narrations of such events as rehearsals, recording dates,
television tapings, and evenings in night clubs" (preface).   An index
would not have been amiss.   (Cf. comments on the use of second-
hand material in this series in the entry for Stewart, no. 1039.)

1060.   WILMER, Valerie.   Jazz people.   London: Allison & Bus-
            by; Indianapolis: Bobbs-Merrill, 1971.   167p.   illus.
         This book is based on interviews with fourteen contemporary
black jazz musicians: Art Farmer, Cecil Taylor, Eddie Lockjaw
Davis, Thelonious Monk, Billy Higgins, Jimmy Heath, Randy Weston,
Babs Gonzales, Clark Terry, Jackie McLean, Buck Clayton, Howard
McGhee, Joe Turner and Archie Shepp.   The author links quotations
from the artists with her own commentary to provide a profile of
each artist's style, opinions and approach to music.   The text is
illustrated with her own photographs.   Index.

1061.   WILSON, John S.   Jazz: the transition years, 1940-1960.
            New York: Appleton-Century-Crofts, 1966.   185p.   illus.,
            discog.
         Wilson, whose jazz criticism for the New York Times is
consistently enjoyable and well-informed, here provides a clear historical survey of trends in jazz in "two explosive decades" and of
the musicians involved.   His view of the period is one of contrasting
movements in thought and practice (he perhaps does not make quite
clear enough that many of these were contemporaneous), each with
outstanding exponents.   Five processes based on changing attitudes
are outlined: revolution (bop, from its antecedents such as Eldridge
and Christian to Parker and Gillespie); reaction (the cool jazz of
Getz, early Mulligan and Davis); re-evaluation (a return towards the
roots characteristic of Horace Silver, bluesmen like Lightnin' Hop-

kins and Ray Charles, musicians with emotional power like Coltrane); intellectualization (from Kenton to Brubeck and the Modern Jazz Quartet); reacceptance (the revivalists). There are also chapters on jazz around the world, and jazz and the mass audience. Index.

5. Regions

a. New Orleans

1062. BUERKLE, Jack V., and BARKER, Danny. Bourbon Street Black: the New Orleans black jazzman. New York: Oxford University Press, 1973. 244p. illus., bibliog. notes.

Bourbon Street Black is a "semi-community of New Orleans musicians, their relatives, peers, friends, and general supporters" (p. 41); commitment to music characterizes the group, which numbers about 400 jazzmen. Sociologist Buerkle (with what contribution from the great banjo player Barker is not made clear) applies sociological study methods to the lives of these contemporary musicians (the average age is about 50) who play predominantly, but not solely, in the traditional New Orleans style. Fifty-one musicians from Local 496 of the American Federation of Musicians were studied, and quotations (frequently unidentified) of their responses to interview questions are organized, with slices of socio-historical background, into chapters on specific subjects, such as their apprenticeship as musicians, the work of the union, attitudes to racial questions in a jazz context ("slightly more than half of them see no difference between white and black music," p. 116), the influence of social class, the effects of travel and of night work, the role of the church and religion, and attitudes to deviant behavior. From this the musicians emerge as basically conventional, average working men. What this tells us about jazz itself, many years after it packed its bags and left home, is open to question. Index.

1063. CHARTERS, Samuel. Jazz: New Orleans, 1885-1957: an index to the Negro musicians of New Orleans. Belleville, N.J.: W. C. Allen, 1958; London: Jazz Journal, 1959. 168p. illus., discog.
_____. Jazz: New Orleans, 1885-1963 ... Rev. ed. New York: Oak Publications, 1963. 173p. illus., discog.

A collection of biographies of over 200 musicians who played in New Orleans between 1885 and 1931. No effort is made to follow the careers of the musicians who left New Orleans and lived permanently elsewhere, and no musicians coming on the scene after 1931 are included. The book is divided into periods (1885-1899, 1899-1919, etc.); under each period heading there is a general introduction, followed by the biographies, which give details of instrument played, dates of birth and death, and information on the artist's life and musical career; some details of the brass bands and orchestral groups of the period are also provided. The discography lists the recordings made in the 1920s, and the revival recordings of the 1950s and 1960s. There are many contemporary illustrations, and indexes of musicians, bands, halls and tune titles.

1064.　COLYER, Ken. New Orleans and back. Delph, Yorks: Brooks & Pratt for the author, n. d. (1968?). 40p.
British jazzman's account of a visit to New Orleans as a merchant seaman (in the 1950s?), and of the various jazz personalities he met and the bands he heard.

1065.　FRENCH QUARTER INTERVIEWS. New Orleans: Vagabond Press, 1969. 96p. illus.
Among the nine interviews with contemporary personalities of the French Quarter in New Orleans is one with the curator of the Jazz Museum, Danny Barker.

1066.　LONGSTREET, Stephen. Sportin' house: a history of New Orleans sinners and the birth of jazz. Los Angeles: Sherbourne Press, 1965. 293p. illus.
Inclined more than somewhat to sensationalization and to fancifulness, this description of the ingredients that went to make up life in New Orleans--especially the brothel life of Storyville--in the early days of jazz is illustrated by the author's own drawings and watercolors.

1067.　MARTINEZ, Raymond J. Portraits of New Orleans jazz: miscellaneous notes. New Orleans: Hope Publications, 1971. 63p. illus., bibliog.
A miscellany of short pieces on various aspects of the development of jazz in New Orleans, including Congo Square, Storyville, New Orleans funerals, and five influential individuals--Gottschalk, Armstrong, Oliver, Morton, and George McCullum. A chapter on the "Mardi Gras Indians" is written by Fin Wilhelmson. The text is illustrated from the collections of the New Orleans Jazz Museum, and concludes with a list of almost 1,000 "jazz greats."

1068.　ROCKMORE, Noel. Preservation Hall portraits: paintings by Noel Rockmore; text by Larry Borenstein and Bill Russell. Baton Rouge: Louisiana State University Press, 1968. unpaged, illus.
Reproductions in black and white of a hundred or so paintings of traditional New Orleans jazz musicians, who play or have played at Preservation Hall in the city. Somber, often filled with pathos, but totally unsentimental and very dignified, the portraits are Rockmore's attempt to capture "the funereal feeling that permeates New Orleans creativity." They are accompanied by accurate biographical texts for each artist. In addition to the main sequence of over fifty portraits there are others of the members of the Eureka Brass Band, a miscellany, and a conversation between Rockmore and Bill Russell.

1069.　ROSE, Al, and SOUCHON, Edmond. New Orleans jazz: a

family album.   Baton Rouge: Louisiana State University
Press, 1967. 304p. illus.

Illustrated with over 500 photographs, this impressive portrait of the city and of the exponents of traditional New Orleans jazz
from its early stages to the present includes brief biographical
sketches of around 1,000 musicians, with indication of instruments,
dates of birth and death, and career outlines.   These are followed
by sections on the jazz and brass bands, with dates, personnel and
instruments, and on the various locations where jazz could and can
be found, afloat and on land, around the Crescent City.   Name index.

1070.   TALLANT, Robert.   Voodoo in New Orleans.   New York:
Macmillan, 1946.   247p.   bibliog.
_____.   _____.   New York: Collier Books, 1962.
252p.   bibliog.

Voodoo is frequently referred to in studies of jazz pre-
history, particularly in connection with Congo Square, New Orleans.
Tallant is not centrally concerned with music, but his very detailed
history of the cult, much of it concerned with Marie Laveau, makes
numerous references to music in voodoo practice.   An article by
Susan Cavin, "Missing Women: on the Voodoo Trail to Jazz" (Journal
of Jazz Studies, Vol. 3, No. 1, Fall 1975), draws considerably on
Tallant's book to suggest some new hypotheses in the discussion of
the voodoo-jazz relationship, in particular the central role played
by women in the cult.

1071.   WILLIAMS, Martin.   Jazz masters of New Orleans.   New
York: Macmillan; London: Collier-Macmillan, 1967.
287p.   illus., bibliogs., discogs.

Jazz musicians whose styles were formed in New Orleans
between the 1890s and the 1920s are the focus of attention in these
profiles.   Nine chapters are centered on individuals: Buddy Bolden,
Jelly Roll Morton, Joe Oliver, Sidney Bechet, Louis Armstrong,
Zutty Singleton, Kid Ory, Bunk Johnson and Red Allen, and two on
bands: the Original Dixieland Jazz Band and the New Orleans
Rhythm Kings.   The author combines biographical data with musical
assessment based on recordings.   With the exception of Armstrong,
whose early career only is included, there are accounts of the subsequent careers of those who left New Orleans.   The first chapter,
on Bolden, includes material on the character of New Orleans, and
each other chapter covers the careers of other musicians, as well
as the one named.   Discographical and bibliographical notes follow
each chapter, and there is an index.

b.   Elsewhere

1072.   CHARTERS, Samuel B., and KUNSTADT, Leonard.   Jazz:
a history of the New York scene.   New York: Doubleday,
1962.   382p.   illus., bibliog., discog.

This first-rate, well-documented history of jazz in New York
from the turn of the century to the late 1950s, with particular attention to the first thirty years, is the result of Kunstadt's painstaking

research (organized and written up by Charters), and makes a powerful case for the central importance of New York in jazz history.
Much information comes from contemporary printed sources--news-
paper announcements and reports, articles, leaflets, reviews, etc.
The detailed, eminently readable narrative describes and examines
the contribution of outstanding individuals and the characteristics of
developing trends, beginning with the syncopated dance music of Jim
Europe in the early 1900s. The richness of the New York's jazz
history is impressively unfolded: ragtime; the first visits of New
Orleans bands (Keppard, ODJB); the Negro military bands of World
War I; Perry Bradford and the first recorded blues by a black artist
(Mamie Smith) in 1920; the subsequent blues craze, centered around
female artists; the musical revues, with Florence Mills, and their
influence on jazz; the progress of jazz from vaudeville novelty to
"respectability" with Paul Whiteman on the one hand, and the creation of a distinctive New York style with Fletcher Henderson and
Don Redman on the other; the development of the jazz ensemble with
Duke Ellington and Clarence Williams; the swing era (Jimmie Lunceford, Chick Webb, Benny Goodman, et al.); the piano of Fats Waller
and James P. Johnson; the rise of bebop (Dizzy Gillespie, Charlie
Parker, Thelonious Monk). An appendix describes recordings available in 1962, and there is a good index.

1073. RAMSEY, Frederic. Chicago documentary: portrait of a
jazz era. London: Jazz Music Books, 1944. 32p.
A sketch of jazz in Chicago in the 1920s, presented as the
script of a dramatized sound documentary, with parts for narrator,
numerous jazz personalities (whose utterances are based on interview
material garnered during the preparation of the pioneering Jazzmen,
no. 1036), the voice of the "Chicago Defender," and with specified
music excerpts.

1074. RUSSELL, Rose. Jazz style in Kansas City and the Southwest. Berkeley: University of California Press, 1971.
292p. illus., bibliog., discog.
Before Russell's book appeared Kansas City's significance in
the development of jazz had not been well covered in writing on the
1930s; what he terms the "last incubating place in the superheated
culture of the black ghettoes where jazz flowered" (introduction) had
been overshadowed by New Orleans, Chicago and New York. His
well-researched account does, however, acknowledge the pioneer efforts of Frank Driggs (published mainly in Jazz Review, and Hentoff
and McCarthy's Jazz, no. 1020). As a prelude to his discussion of
the musicians of the Southwest Russell describes in vivid terms the
social background of Prendergast's Kansas City (politics and night
life) against which the jazz style developed (and which caused such
problems in later years for Parker, to take an outstanding example).
He also devotes some space to Southwestern blues and ragtime performers (notably Leadbelly), before considering at length the style
and influence of the territorial bands (orchestras based in outlying
areas) in which Basie and others began their careers. Discussion
of individual bands and artists begins with Buster Smith and Bennie
Moten and includes Jack Teagarden and the Texas school, Basie,

Lester Young, Andy Kirk, Harlan Leonard, Jay McShann, Charlie Parker. There are also chapters on bebop (the great legacy of Kansas City), and Kansas City pianists, string, percussion and wind players. The terms in which features of the style and contribution of these players are discussed are broadly descriptive rather than analytical. A good deal of biographical data is incorporated. There are 80 photographs and extensive notes to the text. The discography lists available LPs and the bibliography books and articles. There is also an index.

6. Jazz Musicians

a. Collected Profiles

1075.   BLESH, Rudi. Combo: USA; eight lives in jazz. Philadelphia: Chilton, 1971. 240p. illus., bibliog., discog.
Evocative, admittedly subjective biographical portraits of eight outstanding jazz artists: Louis Armstrong, Sidney Bechet, Jack Teagarden, Lester Young, Billie Holiday, Gene Krupa, Charlie Christian and Eubie Blake. The chapters on Krupa and Blake contain material obtained first-hand from each musician; that on Christian uses conversations with novelist Ralph Ellison. The discography is confined to LPs, and there is a general and a music index.

1076.   FEATHER, Leonard. From Satchmo to Miles. New York: Stein & Day, 1972; London: Quartet Books, 1974. 258p. illus.
A series of portraits of thirteen individuals Feather considers to have played a particularly important part in the development and advancement of jazz. The pieces themselves were all previously published in various journals and booklets between 1951 and 1972, and are described by the author as "portraits of human beings first, analyses of musicians or musical history only peripherally if at all." The thirteen are: Louis Armstrong, Duke Ellington, Billie Holiday, Ella Fitzgerald, Count Basie, Lester Young, Charlie Parker, Dizzy Gillespie, Norman Granz, Oscar Peterson, Ray Charles, Don Ellis and Miles Davis.

1077.   GREEN, Benny. The reluctant art: five studies in the growth of jazz. London: MacGibbon & Kee, 1962; London: Jazz Book Club, 1964. 191p.
————. The reluctant art: the growth of jazz. New York: Horizon Press, 1963. 191p.
These are perceptive studies of Bix Beiderbecke, Benny Goodman, Lester Young, Billie Holiday, Charlie Parker--chosen as musicians whose contribution in some way altered the course of jazz. The rapid, largely independent technical evolution of this music has led, in Green's view, to its having become an art form almost in spite of itself.

1078.   MALSON, Lucien. Les maîtres du jazz. Paris: Presses
        Universitaires de France, 1952. (Que sais-je? 548)
        127p.

_____. _____. 2e. ed. Paris: P. U. F. , 1955.
127p.

_____. _____. 6e. ed. Paris: P. U. F. , 1972.
127p.

In a series renowned for illuminating corners of human experience and creativity in a concise, approachable and at the same
time penetrating way, this volume comes well up to standard.   The
six editions have seen various changes of content without any increase in the volume of text.   Each contains a series of interpretative essays, remarkably full of insight, on the musical pilgrimage
of outstanding jazzmen.   The nine featured in the 6th edition are
King Oliver, Louis Armstrong, Sidney Bechet, Duke Ellington, Lester Young, Charlie Parker, Thelonious Monk, Miles Davis and John
Coltrane.   There are no music examples, but frequent references to
titles of recordings.

1079.   SHAPIRO, Nat, and HENTOFF, Nat, eds.   The jazz makers.
        New York: Rinehart, 1957; London: Davies, 1958; New
        York: Grove Press, 1958.   368p.   illus., bibliog. notes.
        These are 21 biographical and critical studies, by George
Avakian, Leonard Feather, George Hoefer, Orrin Keepnews, Bill
Simon, Charles Edward Smith, John S. Wilson, and the editors.
Each contributor was left free to choose a biographical or an analy-
tical approach (or a combination of the two), but "the main goal for
all was to try to communicate something of the personality of each
of these jazz makers" (preface).   The 21, democratically chosen,
musicians are: Morton, Baby Dodds, Armstrong, Teagarden, Hines,
Beiderbecke, Pee Wee Russell, Bessie Smith, Waller, Tatum,
Hawkins, Goodman, Ellington, Parker, Henderson, Basie, Young,
Billie Holiday, Eldridge, Christian and Gillespie.   Index.

1080.   WILLIAMS, Martin.   The jazz tradition.   New York: Ox-
        ford University Press, 1970.   232p.   discog.
        A collection of fifteen perceptive essays on individual jazz
musicians (mostly revised versions of articles written between 1959
and 1967), with an introductory chapter on the significance of jazz.
The author examines a selection of individual recordings by each
artist, analyzing them stylistically but without musical examples.
His coverage extends from Jelly Roll Morton to Ornette Coleman,
taking in Armstrong, Beiderbecke, Hawkins, Billie Holiday, Ellington, Basie, and Young, Parker, Monk, Lewis, Rollins, Silver,
Davis and Coltrane along the way.   The discographical notes give
details of the recordings referred to in the text.   No index.

b.   Individuals

Note: for discographies of individual musicians see H. 2. c.

LOUIS ARMSTRONG

1081. ARMSTRONG, Louis. Louis Armstrong, a self-portrait:
the interview by Richard Meryman. New York: Eakins
Press, 1971. 59p. illus.

In an uninterrupted sequence of clearly recalled memoirs
and candid opinions Louis describes his life up to his second departure from Chicago to New York in 1928--a colorful portrait of
his New Orleans childhood (waifs' home, honky-tonks, riverboats),
of the jazz scene in Chicago with Joe Oliver and in New York with
Fletcher Henderson. From the point where he began to play less
for fellow-musicians and more to please the public he describes only
a few isolated events in his life, dwelling instead on less glamorous
aspects of an entertainer's life as he sees it, the way he survived
(lessons learned from others, and the careful, almost obsessive
practical principles of daily life), and his (mainly critical) view of
contemporary musicians. A large portion of the interview was published in Life magazine in April, 1966.

1082. ARMSTRONG, Louis. Satchmo: my life in New Orleans.
New York: Prentice-Hall, 1954; London: Jazz Book
Club, 1957. 240p. illus.
_____. _____. London: Davies, 1955. 215p. illus.
_____. _____. New York: New American Library,
1961. 191p. illus.

Louis' own account, written as he would have spoken it, of
his early life and career in New Orleans (where he was born in
1900) is a valuable description, not only of his own background, but
also of the kind of existence experienced by many New Orleans jazz
artists. The story is taken to Louis' departure for Chicago in 1922,
and his debut there with King Oliver. (Louis died in 1971.)

1083. ARMSTRONG, Louis. Swing that music; with an introduction by Rudy Vallée; music section edited by Horace Gerlach ... London: Longmans, Green, 1937. 144p. illus.,
discogs.

Louis' first autobiography was also the first book-length account of a black jazz musician's life, and as such, despite any doubts
over the extent of Louis' authorship, is an interesting document.
His picture of his first 36 years describes in lively, colloquial style,
his New Orleans childhood and youth, his time with King Oliver and
Fletcher Henderson in Chicago and New York, and the European tours
of the early 1930s. The music section contains a description of elements of Louis's playing, and ten musical fold-outs--an original song
(called "Swing That Music," penned by Louis and Gerlach) and individual improvisations by nine outstanding swing musicians, including
Goodman, Tommy Dorsey, Joe Venuti, Bud Freeman, Red Norvo and
Louis himself.

1084. JONES, Max, and CHILTON, John. Louis: the Louis Armstrong story, 1900-1971. London: Studio Vista; Boston:
Little, Brown, 1971. 256p. illus.

An expansion of no. 1085, containing some new, some revised and some identical material. The main feature is Max Jones' biographical portrait, in which a picture of the much-traveled ambassador of jazz and an outline of the outstanding aspects of his musical contribution in lead playing and singing precede the chronological account. Louis' own statements play a large part in the biography, which describes in detail his early life in New Orleans, and his rise to the top in Chicago and New York. Developments in his style are noted, and his style of life is also described, with discussion of the questions of drugs and racialism. The later years are less thoroughly covered. "Satchmo Says," a section in Louis' own words, is reprinted from no. 1085, as are the film list and John Chilton's itinerary, with additions. The latter's useful chapter on Louis' recordings is an expanded assessment of the developments in his style and of public reaction. There are no references to sources in the text, but many photographs. Index.

1085.   JONES, Max, et al. Salute to Satchmo, by Max Jones, John
            Chilton, Leonard Feather. London: IPC, 1970. 155p.
            illus., bibliog., discog.
        This homage to Louis, on his seventieth birthday, begins with a short tribute by Feather, and a letter from Louis. The main text is an appreciation of the man, public reaction to him, his personality, style and something of his life, by Max Jones. There is also a summary of his life and attitudes in Louis' own words. John Chilton contributes an itinerary, an outline of his recording career and a list of LPs available in Britain. There is also a selection of tributes by other musicians, a list of films and an index.

1086.   McCARTHY, Albert J. Louis Armstrong. London: Cas-
            sell, 1960. New York: Barnes, 1961. (Kings of Jazz,
            5) 86p. illus., discog.
        An objective account and assessment of Louis' career and stylistic development up to 1959, with close attention to the playing of his middle years. His early life and musical activities in New Orleans are briefly told, followed by an account of his rise to greatness in the '20s. The author isolates from a selection of recorded titles the characteristics of his playing which marked his increasing mastery. Accounts of Louis the virtuoso, 1930-35, and the jazz star and entertainer, 1935-47, deliberately consider his playing over this period in some detail, attempting to explain and evaluate the change in style to that of an international performer, which has troubled many admirers. The book ends with a chapter on the All Stars, with quotations from contemporaries. The selected LP discography is chronologically arranged.

1087.   PANASSIE, Hugues. Louis Armstrong. Paris: Nouvelles
            Editions Latines, 1969. 220p. illus., discog.
            _____. Louis Armstrong; photograph collections by Jack
            Bradley. New York: Scribner, 1971. 148p. illus.
        Panassié's tribute to his long time friend and idol is in three parts. The first is a biographical narrative, the second a general description of Louis' style, and the third (and longest) a chronological survey and discography of Louis' recordings from 1923 to 1968. There is no index, but the photographs are nice.

COUNT BASIE

1088.   HORRICKS, Raymond. Count Basie and his orchestra: its
           music and musicians; with a discography by Alun Morgan.
           London: Gollancz; New York: Citadel Press, 1957; Lon-
           don: Jazz Book Club, 1958. (Repr. Westport: Negro
           Universities Press, 1971). 320p. illus., discog.
     Horricks views the Basie band as the sum of its individual
parts and sets out in this illuminating study to describe what these
parts were, and what contribution they made to the workings of the
whole. The book opens, fittingly, with the Count himself--a portrait
of "the more human side of Basie as a leader" (p. 7)--followed by
a full account of the evolution and development of the musical style
of the band over its first 20 years. These more general views give
way to specific studies: of Basie as a pianist, of the style and contribution of nine principal sidemen from 1936 to 1950 (including Buck
Clayton, Dicky Wells, Lester Young and Jimmy Rushing) and ten
from the 1950s. These are interspersed with biographical sketches
of 22 band members from the first period and 14 from the second.
The discography gives full details of all recordings on which Basie
himself plays, plus a representative selection of recordings by band
members not featuring the Count.

BIX BEIDERBECKE

1089.   BERTON, Ralph. Remembering Bix: a memoir of the jazz
           age. New York: Harper & Row, 1974. 428p. illus.,
           bibliog. notes.
     One would normally expect to learn a lot about Bix Beider-
becke (1903-1931) from a 400-page book with his name in the title.
But in this case one would be wrong. Berton's contribution to jazz
literature turns out to be an interminable, rambling account of a
period in 1924 when, through his elder brother Vic Berton, the drummer who recorded with the Wolverines in 1924 and 1927, the author
was able to hero-worship from close quarters. In effect, his main
interest is in the doings of the Berton family (which turn out to be
instantly forgettable as he recounts them), with Bix, more often than
not, a little out on the sidelines. (For the record, Berton was 13
at the time, but--as they say--big for his age.)

1090.   JAMES, Burnett. Bix Beiderbecke. London: Cassell,
           1959. (Kings of Jazz, 4) 90p. illus., discog.
           _____.   _____.   New York: Barnes, 1961. (...)
           88p. illus., discog.
     James's account contains a brief biographical sketch, fol-
lowed by a considered, objective appreciation of Bix's style and
achievement, with reference to his recordings. The selected discography lists by title all microgroove collections released in Britain,
and gives a breakdown with full personnel and dates of those currently available. No index.

1091.   SUDHALTER, Richard M., and EVANS, Philip R. Bix:
           man and legend; with William Dean-Myatt. New Rochelle:
           Arlington House; London: Quartet Books, 1974. 512p.

illus., discog.

"Writing anything new about Bix Beiderbecke is almost an impossible task," wrote Brian Rust in a 1960s liner note; far from impossible in fact, as is emphatically demonstrated by this fine biography, which sets out to present a factual account of the life of this legendary early white jazzman, to set his personality and his musical ability clearly in the context of time and place, and to examine and assess his achievement. Meticulously researched, immensely detailed and well written in a style combining "the reportage and quotation techniques of journalism," re-created conversation, and technical discussion of many of Bix's recordings, the book is the product of 15 years' combined research. The story of the unassuming young man with the formidable natural talent is told without sentiment, but with deep respect: his boyhood in Iowa, his obsession with music, the progress of his short career from bands on Iowan river steamers, odd jobs (and many influences) in Chicago, the formation of the Wolverines and their recordings, to his membership of the Goldkette and the Whiteman orchestra, culminating in his physical and psychological decline, attributable to alcoholism, and his death in New York in 1931, aged 28. The bulk of the information given came from innumerable contacts with friends and colleagues. Some traditional anecdotes about Bix are confirmed, others repudiated by being simply omitted. On the often debated topic of the quality of the music played by the Whiteman orchestra, the authors bring musical assessment to support their argument that there should be no single absolute standard for judging jazz, and that as a popular music orchestra with a strong jazz element its formula worked well. Bix's growing fascination with the piano, and with contemporary European art music, is seen as a significant development. A unique feature of the book is the 56-page "diary" of Bix's life. The comprehensive 78 rpm discography includes music notation to differentiate takes. It is followed by an essay on Bix's use of the third valve, and by an index of people, places and tunes.

1092. WAREING, Charles, and GARLICK, George. Bugles for Beiderbecke. London: Sidgwick & Jackson, 1958; London: Jazz Book Club, 1960. 333p. discog.

An admittedly subjective biography and assessment. The first part is devoted to an account of Bix's life and career. In Part 2 the authors consider the musician, the influence upon him and his own influence, his artistry, the character of his compositions, and his partnership with Frankie Trumbauer. The third part is a comprehensive discography. No index.

HOAGY CARMICHAEL

1093. CARMICHAEL, Hoagy. The stardust road. New York: Rinehart, 1946; London: Musicians Press, 1947. 156p. illus.

In his first autobiography the songwriter, singer and pianist (b. 1899) mixes humor, surrealist fancy, and fictional techniques in an account of his life up to the death of his friend and idol, Bix Beiderbecke. It is more an attempt to recapture the spirit of a par-

ticular time and place than a conscientious effort to hand down facts
--the time being the 1920s and the place, mainly, the Indiana University campus at Bloomington, where jazz and the comic talents of
his friend William Moenckhaus have an equal fascination for Hoagy.

1094.   CARMICHAEL, Hoagy.   Sometimes I wonder: the story of
         Hoagy Carmichael; with Stephen Longstreet.   New York:
         Farrar, Straus & Giroux, 1965.   London: Redman, 1966.
         313p.   illus.
         In his second autobiography Carmichael re-covers some of
the earlier ground (association with Bix Beiderbecke, etc.), and
continues the story on into the 1950s, with many encounters with individuals from the worlds of jazz, popular song and film.

LEE COLLINS

1095.   COLLINS, Lee.   Oh, didn't he ramble: the life story of
         Lee Collins, as told to Mary Collins; edited by Frank J.
         Gillis and John W. Miner.   Urbana: University of Illinois
         Press, 1974.   159p.   illus., bibliog., discog.
         Trumpeter Lee Collins (1901-1960) began writing and dictat-
ing his recollections of the people, places and events in his life in
1943.   John W. Miner started the editing of the material in 1959,
but following Collins' death the manuscript lay fallow for several
years, until Gillis undertook and completed the work.   Like Armstrong, to whom he is often compared (and whom he followed in
King Oliver's band in Chicago in 1924), Collins was a native of New
Orleans, and the first chapters are devoted to his childhood and
early years there--a colorful account of the apprenticeship and early
career of a jazz musician.   Brief portraits of New Orleans musicians
with whom he played are included.   The following chapters describe
his life from 1929, when he finally settled in Chicago, with accounts
of his two European tours of 1951 and 1954.   His health had not
been very good, and during the second tour he became seriously ill.
His active musical life ceased, and the last pages describe his
struggle with illness in his last years.   The discography includes
a list of commercial releases (by Brian Rust) and private recordings
(by Gillis).   Index.

JOHN COLTRANE

1096.   THOMAS, J. C.   Chasin' the Trane: the music and mys-
         tique of John Coltrane.   Garden City: Doubleday, 1975.
         252p.   illus., discog.
         The aim of this biographical portrait is not only to describe
the great saxophonist's life and career from his birth in North Carolina in 1926 to his death in Huntington, Long Island, in 1967, but,
as he crossed the lives of others--musicians, friends, admirers--
to see him as they saw him, and to show how wide and how deep
was his influence as a musician and as a man.   Using techniques
not unlike those in film documentaries, Thomas continually introduces
into the narrative the comments, recollections and assessments of a
large number of individuals who knew Coltrane at particular times;

in this way the story is deftly moved forward and, as Coltrane and his music change and develop, we see also how far-reaching for many of these people was the effect of knowing or hearing him. The narrative itself mixes a plentiful supply of matter-of-fact detail with passages in which the author attempts to feel his way into his subject's thought processes, and others where he assesses him more objectively. We begin to see Coltrane as one of that small number who are able single-mindedly to pursue an ideal, with the necessary willingness to change that that involves, and at the same time possess a breadth of vision that responds with empathy to the wider world; the result is a music in which technical frontiers are continually extended in a search for a way to speak with the greatest possible compassion for humanity. The discography is a complete list of Coltrane's commercial readings, with personnel, titles and release numbers. There is no index, unfortunately.

EDDIE CONDON

1097.　CONDON, Eddie, and O'NEAL, Hank. The Eddie Condon
　　　　　scrapbook of jazz. New York: St. Martin's Press, 1973;
　　　　　London: Hale, 1974. unpaged, illus.
　　　　Condon's own album of mementos of his fellow musicians, his family and himself--photographs, clippings, posters, cartoons, letters--is presented with entertaining comments and reminiscences. "Oh yes," he says in his introduction, "this book is just for fun," and many unpublished photographs, mostly informal, make a genial addition to the iconography of jazz jamming and conviviality.

1098.　CONDON, Eddie. We called it music: a generation of jazz;
　　　　　narration by Thomas Sugrue. New York: Holt, 1947.
　　　　　(Repr. Westport: Greenwood Press, 1970). 341p. illus.,
　　　　　discog.
　　　　　　　　　　　.　　　　　. London: Davies, 1948; London: Jazz
　　　　Book Club, 1956. 287p. illus., discog.
　　　　An autobiographical account by the jazz guitarist and bandleader (1905-1973) reconstructing the events, the personalities, the conversations and the atmosphere of the jazz world in Chicago and New York in the 1920s and 1930s. Numerous musicians make an appearance. The story is interspersed with "narratives" describing the development and filling in some biographical details about Condon. The extensive Condon discography is by John Swingel. Name index.

MILES DAVIS

1099.　COLE, Bill. Miles Davis: a musical biography. New
　　　　　York: Morrow, 1974. 256p. bibliog., discog.
　　　　The course taken by the musical career of Miles Davis (b. 1926), the succession of musicians who played with him, and the musical influences upon him are charted in the biographical section of this study, which includes only essential information on his life outside music. The discussion of Davis' style that follows is an examination and assessment of his musical idiosyncrasies that at-

tempts also to interpret his "total musical mind." References are made to the appendix, which contains thirteen transcriptions of Davis' playing, spanning twenty years, from "Jeru" (1949) to "Sanctuary" (1969). Though Cole is deeply admiring of much of Davis' musical achievement he regrets the idiom Davis has adopted in the 1970s, the commercialism, and the emphasis on non-musical aspects of his performance, but sees these as the natural result of the difficulties of trying to develop the African-American musical tradition in contemporary America. The excellent bibliography includes books and articles, and there is a general index.

1100.   JAMES, Michael. Miles Davis. London: Cassell; New
            York: Barnes, 1961. (Kings of Jazz, 9) 90p. illus.,
            discog.
        A clear account of Davis' musical development, based on a study of his recordings. Such career details as are necessary to understand this development are given, with little other biographical data. The author describes and assesses Davis' evolving style from his earliest recordings in 1945 with Charlie Parker up to 1959, pointing out both his strengths and his weaknesses. The selected bibliography is chosen to illustrate the text. No index.

JOHNNY DODDS

1101.   LAMBERT, G. E. Johnny Dodds. London: Cassell; New
            York: Barnes, 1971. (Kings of Jazz, 10) 89p. illus.,
            discog.
        A brief biographical sketch of the clarinettist (1892-1940) is followed by a description of Dodds' role in his recordings with King Oliver, Louis Armstrong's Hot Five and Hot Seven, his own Washboard Band, and at other sessions, and by an assessment of his contribution to jazz. The selected discography lists 78s and microgroove recordings. No index.

WARREN "BABY" DODDS

1102.   DODDS, Warren "Baby." The Baby Dodds story, as told to
            Larry Gara. Los Angeles: Contemporary Press, 1959.
            109p. illus.
        Autobiography of the New Orleans drummer (1894-1959), edited from taped accounts recorded in 1953, describing his life and early career in New Orleans to the New Orleans revival of the '40s. His descriptions of playing with Louis Armstrong, King Oliver, Jelly Roll Morton and Bunk Johnson are a prominent feature of the book. Other subjects include the life of a musician in New Orleans, the features of the New Orleans style, and the role of the drummer. Index.

ERIC DOLPHY

1103.   SIMOSKO, Vladimir, and TEPPERMAN, Barry. Eric Dolphy:
            a musical biography and discography. Washington: Smithsonian Institution Press, 1974. 132p. illus., bibliog.,

discog.

This nicely produced volume on the music of Eric Dolphy (1928-1964) opens with an essay by Simosko that attempts to evaluate his music and his position in jazz. The musical biography that follows (also by Simosko) charts Dolphy's musical development through the evidence of his recordings, placing it in the wider context of the course taken by his career. The discography (mainly by Tepperman) lists all Dolphy's known recordings in any form (including broadcasts), with his own and other groups. Arrangement is chronological, with complete discographical detail (personnel, date, place, titles and release numbers for each session) clearly laid out. Abbreviations after each item heard by the compilers indicate whether Dolphy plays a solo. Notes to each session mention the source of the information. There is also a list of composer credits.

DORSEY BROTHERS

1104. SANDFORD, Herb. Tommy and Jimmy: the Dorsey years.
New Rochelle: Arlington House; London: Ian Allan,
1972. 305p. illus.

Sandford knew both Dorseys well from the 1920s on, and his liberally illustrated book, which confines itself to their careers and distinct personalities, and to describing the world of the swing band, contains anecdotes, personal recollections (his own and various bandsmen's) and plentiful background detail. He describes the brothers' beginnings with the Goldkette and Whiteman orchestras, the period of their own band, the break-up of the partnership, and the careers of their separate organizations--particularly Tommy's--to the twilight of the swing era in the later 1940s. (Reunion took place in the early 1950s. Tommy died in 1956 and Jimmy in 1957.) The author makes little attempt at assessment or critical appraisal, though he does include a series of general reflections on swing, on jazz musicians, writers and singers, and on that perennial obsession--Bix. There is a list of outstanding musicians who worked with the Dorseys, a 1935 itinerary, and an index.

DUKE ELLINGTON

1105. ELLINGTON, Edward Kennedy. Music is my mistress.
Garden City: Doubleday, 1973; London: Allen, 1974.
522p. illus., bibliog., discog.

In Duke's urbane and sanguine, pleasant but curiously uninspiring memoirs of his life and career from his childhood in Washington to his foreign tours of the 1960s and early 1970s, one is sorely disappointed if one looks for an inside picture of how some of the greatest jazz was created. Duke's views on music are expressed in free verse, which informs us that it is "the oldest entity ... is eternal ... is divine ... is a cedar," and that "without music I may feel blind, atrophied, incomplete, inexistent" (p. 218-9). Which is not very informative. But then, from one who had already given so much how dare we ask for more? Characteristically, about half the book is devoted to thumb-nail, anecdotal portraits of around 100 fellow-musicians, many of them members of his orchestra; to each

Duke is unfailingly loyal and generous. Self-examination is mainly
reserved for an epilog, in which Duke is interviewed by an anonymous interviewer and, while answering the practical questions,
slides out of the others with practiced grace--and refers them mostly
to God. Supplementary material includes a full list of the many
honors he received, and a catalog of his compositions in copyright
order. (Born in 1899, Duke died in 1974, shortly after the British
edition of his book was published.)

1106. DANCE, Stanley. The world of Duke Ellington. New York:
　　　　Scribner, 1970. 311p. illus. , discog.
　　　　　　　　.　　　　　. London: Macmillan, 1971. 301p.
　　　　illus. , discog.
　　　　A portrait of the man, his approach to music, and his en-
tourage, based on a series of interviews with Ellington and his musicians made during the '60s. Three interviews with Ellington (1962-
3) and part of a press conference in Calcutta in 1963 begin the book,
followed by interviews with three people close to him: Billy Strayhorn, Mercer Ellington and Thomas L. Whaley. Twenty-six musicians
were also interviewed, and these, supplemented often by the author's
accounts of their careers and musicianship, are arranged in the order
in which the musicians joined the band. There are also descriptions
of five outstanding events: the Monterey Festival (1961), the two
Sacred Concerts (1965 and 1968), the Latin American tour (a journal,
1968), and the seventieth birthday celebrations at the White House
(1969). The discography is selective, and there is also a chronology
of his life and an index.

1107. GAMMOND, Peter, ed. Duke Ellington: his life and music;
　　　　foreword by Hugues Panassié. London: Phoenix House;
　　　　New York: Roy, 1958; London: Jazz Book Club, 1959.
　　　　256p. illus. , discog.
　　　　The 15 contributors to this volume are almost all British,
and their essays include impressions of Ellington the man, examinations of his recordings over four decades, discussions of his piano
playing, of his orchestral suites, and of his composer's art, biographical sketches of his musicians, and a detailed, chronological
discography.

1108. LAMBERT, G. E. Duke Ellington. London: Cassell, 1959.
　　　　(Kings of Jazz, 1) 90p. illus. , bibliog. , discog.
　　　　　　　　.　　　　　. New York: Barnes, 1961. (...)
　　　　88p. illus.
　　　　Divided into two sections this introduction provides a biographical sketch up to 1958, and an assessment of Ellington's musical achievement to the same date. The latter takes the form of
an examination of the recordings in chronological order, noting
changes in the band personnel, and how Ellington used these to advantage. Many of the recordings are described in detail, with special attention to Ellington's understanding of his band and its potential, and to the nature of his music. The selected discography includes 78s, EPs and LPs.

1109.   ULANOV, Barry. Duke Ellington. New York: Creative
          Age Press, 1946; London: Musicians Press, 1947. 322p.
          illus., discog.
        This first book-length biography of Ellington attempts, in
addition to providing a readable account of Duke's career up to
"Black, Brown and Beige" (1944), "to delineate the atmosphere and
conditions of the jazz world" (introduction). General descriptive
comments on Duke's major recordings appear in their chronological
context.

POPS FOSTER

1110.   FOSTER, Pops. Pops Foster: the autobiography of a New
          Orleans jazzman as told to Tom Stoppard; introduction by
          Bertram Turetzky; interchapters by Ross Russell; dis-
          cography by Brian Rust. Berkeley: University of Cali-
          fornia Press, 1971. 208p. illus., bibliog., discog.
        Told in a colloquial style as transcribed from a series of
recorded interviews, this account of his life by the famous string
bass player (1892-1969) whose career spanned seventy years is particularly valuable for the information on New Orleans. Written with
specific desire to "straighten a lot of things out" about early jazz,
it describes, after his early life on a Louisiana plantation, the music and musicians in New Orleans from 1899-1919. Following his
departure from New Orleans Foster played on the riverboats. During Prohibition, when the style of the music began to change, he
played mainly in St. Louis, moving on to New York in 1929. The
last chapters describe his life in New York, and his travels with
Louis Armstrong. The introduction describes and assesses his
technique, and each chapter is preceded by a short section filling
in historical detail. There is a chronology of the groups with whom
he played, a selected list of available LPs, a comprehensive discography, a brief bibliography and an index.

PETE FOUNTAIN

1111.   FOUNTAIN, Pete. A closer walk: the Pete Fountain story;
          with Bill Neely. Chicago: Regnery, 1972. 202p. illus.,
          discog.
        Ghosted autobiography of the New Orleans-born white clari-
nettist (b. 1930) who achieved fame on the Lawrence Welk television
show in the 1950s, and returned to New Orleans to breathe life into
the performance of jazz there, particularly in Dixieland and swing
era combo styles.

DIZZY GILLESPIE

1112.   JAMES, Michael. Dizzy Gillespie. London: Cassell, 1959.
          (King of Jazz, 2) 89p. illus., discog.
          _____. New York: Barnes, 1961. (...)
          86p. illus., discog.
        A combination of biography and assessment. The author
traces Gillespie's life up to 1957 (he was born in 1917), at the same

time describing the development of his style and the influences on
him.   Particular attention is paid to his recordings; taking them in
their context in Gillespie's development, the author builds up an objective appreciation of the artist's role in a changing tradition, and
his innovatory brilliance.   The discography is a selective listing
chosen to complement the text; it covers 1939-1957.

BABS GONZALES

1113.   GONZALES, Babs. I paid my dues: good times--no bread.
         East Orange: Expubidence Publishing Corp. , 1967. 160p.
         discog.
         "A story of jazz" is how the cover describes these racy
recollections by the bebop singer, adding--with a greater degree of
accuracy--"and some of its followers, shyster agents, hustlers,
pimps and prostitutes. " Though many jazz stars of the 1940s and
1950s make brief appearances they come low down the credits, and
Babs himself prefers to recount his extra-musical activities.

BENNY GOODMAN

1114.   GOODMAN, Benny, and KOLODIN, Irving. The kingdom of
         swing. New York: Stackpole; London: Allen, 1939.
         (Repr. New York: Ungar, 1961). 263p. illus.
         Autobiography, with Kolodin's collaboration, covering Good-
man's life and early career from his birth in 1909 up to 1939.
Goodman's presentation of the world of jazz implied in the book has
been described by Benny Green (no. 1077), as "the jazz life seen
through the imbecile prism of a Hollywood musical. " Kolodin contributes an "interpolation" entitled "Swing is Here, " which describes
the characteristics of the style.

1115.   CONNOR, D. Russell, and HICKS, Warren W. B. G.--off
         the record: a bio-discography. Fairless Hills, Pa.:
         Gaildonna Publishers, 1958. 305p. illus.
         _____ . B. G. on the record: a bio-discography of
         Benny Goodman. New Rochelle: Arlington House, 1969.
         691p. illus.
         The second of these two volumes is an extension and revi-
sion of the first, and is a very good example of an integrated bio-
discography.   Beginning with Goodman joining Pollack's band in
1925, aged 16, and covering his career up to 1968, it provides a
chronological discography of all Goodman's recordings, issued and
unissued, private and commercial, and links details of these recording events with a biographical commentary, concentrating chiefly on
Goodman's professional life, his engagements, associates, etc.   The
authors also give critical evaluation.   There are lists of addenda
and of records falsely attributed to Goodman, indexes to radio and
television programs, films, etc. , to artists and arrangers, and to
tune titles.

COLEMAN HAWKINS

1116.   McCARTHY, Albert J. Coleman Hawkins. London: Cassell, 1963. (Kings of Jazz, 12) 89p. illus., discog.
A brief biographical sketch of Hawkins' life from his birth in 1904 (he died in 1969) is followed by a study of his recordings in three sections, 1924-1939, 1939-1949, and 1950-1962. In this the development of his tenor saxophone style is traced from his earliest recorded solos, a considerable number of titles from his prolific output being quoted to illustrate points. The discography is a list of recommended LPs.

FLETCHER HENDERSON

1117.   ALLEN, Walter C. Hendersonia: the music of Fletcher Henderson and his musicians; a bio-discography. Highland Park, N.J.: Walter C. Allen, 1973. (Jazz Monographs No. 4) 651p. illus., bibliog.
An admirable, devotedly detailed compilation of information on the musical activities of Henderson (1898-1952) and his sidemen, by one of the doyens of the art of bio-discography. Segments of biographical and discographical material are arranged side by side in chapters that cover anything from a few months to several years in Henderson's career. Each of the main chapters contains biographical text (dealing with the activities of a whole group of musicians, and drawing freely on contemporary journal and newspaper reports), an itinerary of engagement dates, and a discography of the period covered by the chapter. The discographies include all known recordings featuring Henderson as performer or conductor, and all the sessions at which the musicians were almost entirely Henderson sidemen at the time. Meticulous attention is given to discographical detail: artist credit (as on the record), date, location, personnel (with notes and comments), matrix and take number, title, composer credit, arranger, vocalist, identification of soloists, tempo, all known release numbers including microgroove reissues--all these are given. Other features include a chapter devoted to a descriptive catalogue of Henderson's arrangements (an "orch-ography"), a chronological list of his compositions, rosters of his musicians and vocalists (with biographical notes), and indexes of places in the itineraries, names and subjects, tune titles, and catalogue numbers.

BILLIE HOLIDAY

1118.   HOLIDAY, Billie. Lady sings the blues; with William Dufty. New York: Doubleday, 1956. 250p. illus., discog.
_____. _____. London: Barrie Books, 1958. 226p. illus.
_____. _____. New York: Popular Library, 1958. 192p.
_____. _____. New York: Lancer Books, 1965. 191p.
_____. _____. London: Barrie & Jenkins, 1973. 234p. illus., discog.

_____ . _____ . London: Sphere Books, 1973. 188p.
Told in a popular style (which Glenn Coulter in Cambridge
Review, 1956, called a "racy, side-of-the-mouth idiom"), but moving
nevertheless, this personal story of one of the greatest jazz singers
(1915-1959) describes her early life and checkered career, and
many of the figures in the jazz world of the late 1930s and 1940s.
Written three years before her death it speaks frankly of the many
personal problems which beset her, but does not greatly enlighten
us on what constituted her unique musical ability.   The excellent
discography in the 1973 Barrie and Jenkins edition is by Albert Mc-
Carthy.

1119.   CHILTON, John.   Billie's blues: a survey of Billie Holi-
         day's career, 1933-1959; foreword by Buck Clayton.   Lon-
         don: Quartet Books; New York: Stein & Day, 1975.
         259p.   illus. , bibliog.
         Billie Holiday's tragic personal story, more likely than any
other in jazz history to send writers scampering after emotive epi-
thets, is told here in a dispassionate, unsentimental way by Londoner
John Chilton, who, having collected a large quantity of the fragmentary recollections of her friends and associates from printed sources
and personal contacts, pieces them together and allows them to speak
for themselves.   Indications of the diligence of the author's research
are provided by the bibliography, which includes approximately 600
magazine and newspaper references to Billie Holiday, spanning 1933-
1974, and the list of acknowledgments, which gives 96 names.   Part
2 of the book is given over to a chronological review of Billie's recording career.   Here, though there is no close analysis, Chilton
makes perceptive comments on features of her singing and also provides insights into the alchemy by which great artists turn private
pain into the raw material for their art.

1120.   KUEHL, Linda, and SCHOKERT, Ellie.   Billie Holiday re-
         membered.   New York: New York Jazz Museum, 1973.
         20p.
         Billie is briefly recollected by approximately 60 people.

MAX KAMINSKY

1121.   KAMINSKY, Max.   My life in jazz; with V. E. Hughes.
         New York: Harper & Row, 1963; London: Deutsch,
         1964.   242p.
         In Kaminsky's long career as a jazz trumpeter (he was born
in 1908), he played with a great many illustrious names, including
Louis Armstrong, the Dorseys, Artie Shaw, and the personal portraits of these and other musicians are an interesting feature of his
autobiography.   Perhaps more memorable, however, is the picture
which emerges of the day-to-day existence of jazz musicians, in
Chicago especially, and, at the other end of the scale, the demands
and impressions of world-touring.   Index.

GEORGE LEWIS

1122.   STUART, Jay Allison. Call him George. London: Peter
        Davies, 1961; London: Jazz Book Club, 1963. 285p.
        illus.
        FAIRBAIRN, Ann. _____ . (New ed.) New York:
        Crown, 1969. 303p. illus.
        (Both of these authors' names are pseudonyms for Dorothy
Tait.) A nicely written biography of the outstanding New Orleans
clarinettist George Lewis (1900-1968), based largely on information
from Lewis himself, whose memory is described as "tenacious and
almost photographic," while as a man he "preferred silence to talk,
and truth above all else." The account of New Orleans is particularly interesting. The 1969 edition takes in Lewis' death.

WINGY MANONE

1123.   MANONE, Wingy, and VANDERVOORT, Paul. Trumpet on
        the wing; foreword by Bing Crosby. New York: Double-
        day, 1948. 256p. illus., discog.
        _____ . _____ . London: Jazz Book Club, 1964.
        256p. discog.
        Born in New Orleans of Italian descent in 1904, Joe "Wingy"
Manone lost an arm in a childhood accident--hence his nickname--
but makes very light of that hardship in this buoyant, colloquial autobiography that covers his life from New Orleans through his early
career in St. Louis, New York and Chicago, and rise to prominence
in the swing era, to his migration to the West Coast (where he was
a resident comedian/musician for a Hollywood group centering on
Bing Crosby, and where he featured in several films) and subsequent
activity there.

MEZZ MEZZROW

1124.   MEZZROW, Milton "Mezz," and WOLFE, Bernard. Really
        the blues. New York: Random House, 1946; London:
        Musicians Press, 1947. 388p.
        _____ . _____ . New ed. London: Secker & War-
        burg, 1957; London: Jazz Book Club, 1959. 388p.
        _____ . _____ . New York: Transworld, 1961. 381p.
        _____ . _____ . New York: New American Library,
        1964. 320p.
        _____ . _____ . Garden City: Doubleday, 1972. 348p.
        Though not noted as an outstanding jazz performer, clarinet-
tist Mezz Mezzrow (1899-1972) provided the stimulus for many great
jazz recordings, and, with this ghosted autobiography, created considerable interest in the music and in the jazz life. Written in a
colloquial style, it contains many interesting accounts of jazz in
Chicago and New York in the 1920s and 1930s, as well as graphic
descriptions of Mezzrow's own experience with drugs and in prison.
Supplementary material includes a glossary of jazz word slang, appendices on the characteristics of New Orleans and Chicago styles
and on the recordings Mezzrow made under Panassié's supervision

in 1938, and an index. There is also a translation of the four
pages of text that give a recreated dialogue between marijuana smok-
ers in Harlem.

GLENN MILLER

1125. FLOWER, John. Moonlight serenade: a bio-discography of
the Glenn Miller Civilian Band. New Rochelle: Arlington House, 1972. 554p. illus.
    With this fine reference work, the product of ten years'
work and much combined effort among enthusiasts, Glenn Miller
joins the select band of jazzmen whose careers have been fully
chronicled by interweaving biography and discography (Goodman and
Henderson being other examples). Here we have a detailed diary of
the Glenn Miller Orchestra's strenuous schedule from 1935 to Sept.
1942 (when Miller joined the army), noting changing personnel and
quoting excerpts from contemporary press reviews and reports;
slotted into this sequence is a full catalog of all commercial recordings and broadcasts. Complete discographical information is given
for the recordings, plus the names of arrangers, vocalists, composers, lyricists and instrumental soloists. For the broadcasts
Flower gives date, precise location, type of show, announcer and
tune titles, and notes, if the broadcast was commercially released,
the matrix and release numbers, and the timing of the item. Ancillary material includes a considerable list of addenda and errata, an
index of tune titles, and an index of personnel.

1126. SIMON, George T. Glenn Miller and his orchestra. New
York: Crowell; London: W. H. Allen, 1974. 473p.
illus., discog.
    The enduring popularity of Miller's music naturally creates
a desire for greater knowledge about the man himself. This Simon
(whom Miller once asked to be his biographer) provides in an entertaining, extremely detailed biography, for which he supplemented
personal knowledge, gained from long personal and professional association with Miller (he was editor of Metronome magazine, and also
Miller's first drummer), with information obtained from a very
large number of interviews. He divides Miller's life into four: the
early years from birth in 1904 to 1935; "The Band that Failed,"
1935-1938; "The Band that Made It" (1938-1942); and the American
Armed Forces band, from 1942 to his death in December, 1944.
Simon has little to say about Miller's music and does not attempt
to explore the reasons for its continued appeal. He is more concerned to give a candid, accurate portrait of Miller's complex char-
acter--of a man, it turns out, who allowed few people to get close
to him, and who, though often respected, was rarely liked. A musician beset by a sense of inferiority, as a band leader he had a
cold, business-like attitude and a strong taste for discipline which
only infrequently permitted warmth and kindness to any but his wife.

CHARLES MINGUS

1127. MINGUS, Charlie. Beneath the underdog: his world as

composed by Mingus; edited by Nel King. New York: Knopf; London: Weidenfeld & Nicolson, 1971. 365p.

A highly charged and highly individual autobiography of the bassist (b. 1922), apparently written over a twenty-year period, and owing its final form, one imagines, to its editor. The candid, self-analytical narrative reads like fiction, and is made objective by the use of the third person ("Charles, my boy"). Three themes predominate: sex, music, and blackness. Mingus' attitudes to his own life vary from profound guilt to exultant self-inflation. Among the other jazz personalities in his life Fats Navarro made a deep impression. The book concludes with Mingus voluntarily committed to a psychiatric ward in Bellevue Hospital.

JELLY ROLL MORTON

1128. LOMAX, Alan. Mister Jelly Roll: the fortunes of Jelly Roll Morton, New Orleans Creole and "inventor of jazz." New York: Duell, Sloan & Pearce; New York: Grosset & Dunlap, 1950. 318p. illus., discog.
_____. _____. London: Cassell, 1952. 296p. illus., discog.
_____. _____. New York: Grove Press, 1956. 302p. discog.
_____. _____. London: Pan Books, 1959. 253p. illus.
_____. _____. 2nd ed. Berkeley, London: University of California Press, 1973. 318p. illus., discog.

This classic of jazz literature was based on Lomax's interviews with Morton (1885-1941) at the Library of Congress in 1938, and is told for the most part in Morton's own words. It describes his early life in New Orleans (an evocative portrait of the city, of Storyville, of the musicians, and of Jelly Roll himself), and his subsequent travels and way of life, including his time in Chicago, California, New York, and Washington. In between chapters there are interludes in which Lomax fills in the background and ties some threads together, largely from interviews with Morton's contemporaries. A section in Mabel Morton's own words describes Jelly Roll and their life together, ending with his final trip to California. His last days are described in his correspondence with Mabel. There are appendices on his tunes, with a chronological list of his compositions and his recordings, and a selection of his music. No index. The illustrated editions contain drawings by David Stone Martin.

1129. WILLIAMS, Martin. Jelly Roll Morton. London: Cassell, 1962. (Kings of Jazz, 11) 88p. illus., bibliog. notes, discog.
_____. _____. New York: Barnes, 1963. (...) 85p. illus., bibliog. notes, discog.

A brief biography precedes a study of Morton's music, which opens with an introduction on the roots of his style, followed by chapters on the piano solos, the orchestra recordings prior to the Red Hot Peppers, the duets, trios and quartets, and finally the

Peppers recordings. Individual records are closely studied. No index.

KING OLIVER

1130.   ALLEN, Walter C., and RUST, Brian A. L. King Joe
        Oliver. Belleville, N.J.: Allen, 1955. 162p. discog.
        _____. _____. London: Jazz Book Club, 1957; London: Sidgwick & Jackson, 1958. 224p. illus., bibliog., discog.
        The high quality of its research marks this bio-discography out as one of the outstanding works of the kind separating biography from discography. The biographical section of some forty pages is followed by an assessment of Oliver's character, influence and compositions, and by an immense discography occupying 98 pages and representing a complete account of Oliver's recordings. Arrangement is chronological, and all known information on personnel, location, date, composer, matrix and catalog numbers and soloists is given for each number. An appendix is devoted to the Oliver orchestra itinerary, 1934-35. There are indexes of recorded titles, musicians, catalog numbers and rarities.

1131.   WILLIAMS, Martin. King Oliver. London: Cassell, 1960;
        New York: Barnes, 1961. (Kings of Jazz, 8) 89p.
        illus., discog.
        An introductory work in two sections: a biography of Oliver's life (1885-1938) and a discussion of his recordings. The first describes Oliver's early career in New Orleans and the influences on him there; the years in Chicago, California and New York, and his death are narrated in stark outline. In the second part Williams makes a critical examination of Oliver's three bands: the Creole Jazz Band, the Dixie Syncopators, and his Orchestra for the 1929-30 Victor recordings, analyzing several titles closely. He also discusses Oliver's own style of playing, and his technique as an accompanist. No index.

ORIGINAL DIXIELAND JAZZ BAND

1132.   BRUNN, H. O. The story of the Original Dixieland Jazz
        Band. Baton Rouge: Louisiana State University Press,
        1960; London: Sidgwick & Jackson, London: Jazz Book
        Club, 1963. 268p. illus.
        A somewhat controversial account of the formation of the white band that made the first jazz record in 1917, and of the rise and fall of its fame. The author describes Nick La Rocca's beginnings in New Orleans, the ragtime bands he played in and the ODJB in embryo there, the move to Chicago, and the further development of their style. The climax of the book is the band's success in New York in 1917, the first recordings and broadcasts, and the London visit. The subsequent change in public taste and the band's fall from grace are also described. Based mainly on material from La Rocca, the book is marred by a virtually total disregard of any Negro influence in New Orleans and Chicago, and the author's contention

that jazz was "created" by the ODJB. An appendix gives a chronological personnel table, 1915-1938. Index.

CHARLIE PARKER

1133.   HARRISON, Max. Charlie Parker. London: Cassell, 1960.
            (Kings of Jazz, 6) 88p. illus., bibliog. notes, discog.
                        .   . New York: Barnes, 1961. (...)
            84p.   illus., bibliog. notes, discog.
            A short biographical account of Parker's life (1920-1955),
incorporating critical commentary on his style and influence in the
biographical narrative. The resulting sharp contrast between the
chaos of his life and the "wild, impassioned beauty" of the music
Parker created out of this turmoil is handled with understanding.
The selective discography lists outstanding titles in chronological
order, with personnel.

1134.   MORGENSTERN, Dan, et al. Bird and Diz: a bibliography;
            edited by Dan Morgenstern, Ira Gitler and Jack Bradley.
            New York: New York Jazz Museum, 1973. 19p.
            The separate sections for Parker and Gillespie each list
books about them, discographies, books with significant sections,
and articles (1947-1971 for Parker, 1945-1973 for Gillespie).

1135.   REISNER, R. G. Bird: the legend of Charlie Parker. New
            York: Bonanza Books; New York: Citadel Press, 1962;
            London: MacGibbon & Kee, 1963; London: Jazz Book
            Club, 1965. 256p. illus., discog.
            Eighty people who knew Parker, or had significant contact
with him, give their recollections in interviews with the author.
Most are jazz musicians, though there are also members of his
family, critics, a poet, a disc jockey and a composer (Varèse).
Some describe incidents and encounters, others the various sides of
Parker's personality. Reisner contributes his own recollections,
and these open the book. There is also a chronology, a detailed
discography by Erik Wiedemann, and an index.

1136.   RUSSELL, Ross. Bird lives: the high life and hard times
            of Charlie (Yardbird) Parker. New York: Charterhouse,
            1973. 404p. illus., bibliog., discog.
                        . Bird lives! London: Quartet Books, 1973.
            404p. illus., bibliog., discog.
            An outstanding biography, rich in insight into Parker as a
man and as a musician. As proprieter of Dial Records, for whom
Parker made some of his most famous recordings, Russell knew
"Bird" and many other bop musicians. To this experience he adds
a great familiarity with the life of musicians in Kansas City (Parker's birthplace and where he learnt his jazz), and a mass of information, patiently accumulated from countless interviews. The har-
rowing, unforgettable story of Parker's life that results is finely
told, especially as it gets to the heart, not only of his complex character, but of his creativity. The intensity with which all Bird's un-
dertakings were performed and his complete removal from conventiona

behavior are seen as indispensable to his creative processes. The technical knowledge and accomplishment behind his creative achievement are shown to have been painfully, but single-mindedly, won. The supreme irony of Parker's life, however, was that at this very same time in Kansas City--in order to be a part of this world where he would leave his mark--he acquired a lifestyle of excess, and it was this that destroyed him so early. The question of the contribution or otherwise of heroin addiction to Parker's music is explored by Russell, while its destructive personal effects are everywhere apparent in his adult life. Though detailed musical analysis is not attempted, Russell describes numerous performances, stresses the influence of the blues, and pays particular attention to the daily details of playing this music at this time. Some music examples are included. The story ends in a legal tangle over Parker's body and estate, a suitably mundane response from a world he rejected.

BUDDY RICH

1137. BALLIETT, Whitney. Super drummer: a profile of Buddy Rich; with photographs by Fred Seligo. Indianapolis: Bobbs-Merrill, 1968. 138p. illus.
  First published in the New Yorker, this profile of the virtuoso jazz drummer and band leader is described as "an attempt to capture in words and photographs the sound and sight and feel of his skills." Balliett describes a day spent with Rich, in which he accompanies him to a concert given by the Rich band at a New York prison, and subsequently engages him in conversation about life and music. The photos catch him at informal moments on the road, backstage, and at home.

ARTIE SHAW

1138. SHAW, Artie. The trouble with Cinderella: an outline of identity. New York: Farrar, Straus & Young, 1952. 394p.

_____.   _____. London: Jarrolds, 1955. 379p. illus.

_____.   _____. New York: Collier, 1963. 352p.
  Autobiography of the big band leader and clarinettist (b. 1910). Including a certain amount of biographical material, it is basically a self-portrait of the personality and attitudes of a very articulate musician--Shaw calls it a "sort of inventory"--that stands apart from most jazz artists' accounts of themselves. No index.

1139. BLANDFORD, Edmund L. Artie Shaw: a bio-discography. Hastings, Sussex: Castle Books, 1973. 229p. illus., discog.
  A factual biographical account of Shaw's career as one of the outstanding white bandleaders of the swing era. The author draws heavily on contemporary articles in Metronome, Down Beat and Melody Maker and on the books by Kaminsky and by Shaw himself. He does not attempt to examine the music. The discography, following the biography, lists all known recordings, including air-

checks, by Shaw as sideman and bandleader from 1928 to 1954. No index.

WILLIE "THE LION" SMITH

1140. SMITH, Willie "The Lion." Music on my mind: the memoirs of an American pianist; with George Hoefer; foreword by Duke Ellington. Garden City: Doubleday, 1964; London: MacGibbon & Kee, 1965; London: Jazz Book Club, 1966. (Repr. New York: Da Capo, 1975). 318p. bibliog. notes, discog.

A colloquially told autobiography of the stride pianist and composer (1897-1973), covering his upbringing and musical career, particularly in New York, and including a large number of anecdotes concerning jazz musicians. Four "interludes" by Hoefer fill in historical and biographical background. The notes and references include the Lion's European itinerary in 1949-50, a list of his compositions with publication details and name of lyricist, and a discography for 1920-1961. Index.

JACK TEAGARDEN

1141. SMITH, Jay D., and GUTTRIDGE, Len. Jack Teagarden: the story of a jazz maverick. London: Cassell, 1960; London: Jazz Book Club, 1962. 208p. illus., discog.

A popular biography of the outstanding white trombonist and singer (1905-1964), describing his fluctuating professional and personal fortunes, and his many associations with other jazz musicians, up to the late 1950s. The tone is light, with much reliance on re-created conversations. The discography is a selected chronological listing of individual recordings, made between 1928 and 1958, with personnel and LP/EP issue numbers (American and British); no details of 78s are given. Index.

FATS WALLER

1142. FOX, Charles. Fats Waller. London: Cassell, 1960. (Kings of Jazz, 7) 89p. illus., bibliog. notes, discog. _____ . _____ . New York: Barnes, 1961. (...) 87p. illus., bibliog. notes, discog.

A short concise biography, incorporating some perceptive critical assessment of Waller's style and approach to music, as seen through his recordings. The inimitable personality comes across clearly and affectionately. The discography is limited to a listing of Waller's records available at the time of compilation in Britain (Cassell) or in the U.S. (Barnes). No index.

1143. KIRKEBY, W. T., "Ed." Ain't misbehavin': the story of Fats Waller; in collaboration with Duncan P. Schiedt and Sinclair Traill. London: Davies, 1966; London: Jazz Book Club, 1967. 248p. illus., discog.

Kirkeby was Waller's manager from 1937 to Fats' death in 1943, and his biography concludes with a personal account of these

six years.   Prior to that he describes in detail the course of Fats'
life from his birth in Harlem in 1904.   Numerous compositions are
mentioned, without scrutiny.   There is no index, but a good, selective discography, with full details of personnel, matrix and catalog
numbers for each title, by the Storyville team (John R. T. Davies
and others).

DICKY WELLS

1144.   WELLS, Dicky.   The night people: reminiscences of a jazz-
          man; as told to Stanley Dance; foreword by Count Basie.
          Boston: Crescendo; London: Hale, 1971.   118p.   illus.
          Black trombonist Wells' informal, assorted recollections
describe the day-to-day ups and downs of the jazz musician's life as
he experienced them in a long career (he was born in 1909) that included work with--among others--Fletcher Henderson, Count Basie
and Ray Charles; many jazzmen, both great and small, are featured
in the incidents he relates.   Basie himself observes that in Wells'
narrative style (he presumably spoke into Dance's tape recorder)
"you can find translations of some of those talking phrases he spe-
cializes in. "   (French critic André Hodeir analyzes and praises
Wells' playing in no. 993, but finds him in the 1950s in Paris a
much diminished figure.   Wells replies in his book that his poor performance was caused by heavy drinking at the time.)   Beside an index there is a glossary of colloquial terms used.

1. General Reference Works

1145.   ARMITAGE, Andrew D. and TUDOR, Dean.   <u>Annual index
         to popular music record reviews, 1972.</u>   Metuchen:
         Scarecrow Press, 1973.   467p.   bibliog.
      The first in a projected series (with the hope of retrospec-
tive compilations covering 1947-1971), this useful work, listing 3,679
recordings and their reviews, is aimed principally at American librarians as a selection tool in the area of popular music.   The field
covered is mainly the year's output of LPs on American and European
labels of music in the American vernacular tradition (including British jazz and rock groups); also included are folk, ethnic, stage,
band, and popular religious music and humor.   Thirty-five American, Canadian and reviewing journals, both general and specialized,
were chosen.   The index is divided into twelve sections: rock,
mood-pop, folk, ethnic, jazz, blues, rhythm and blues, religion,
show and stage, band and humor.   Each section is introduced by
comments on the current state of the particular art; these are followed by the year's outstanding records (based on reviewers' opinions) and by a full list of the releases in the genre.   Entries are
arranged alphabetically by artist, and consist of item number, artist,
title, record and tape release numbers, price, country of origin (if
outside the U.S.A.--in the case of American releases no foreign
release numbers are given), and lists of journals where a review
appeared, with full reference, number of words, and evaluation (a
numerical system, based on the reviewer's overall assessment).
There is also a partly annotated bibliography, a directory of record
labels, an artist and anthology index.   Not only is the book a useful tool for tracing reviews, its evaluation system makes it a good
selection guide in itself.

1146.   THE ASCAP BIOGRAPHICAL DICTIONARY of composers,
         authors and publishers; 1966 ed., compiled and edited by
         the Lynn Farnol Group, Inc.   New York: American So-
         ciety of Composers, Authors and Publishers, 1966.   845p.
      ASCAP was founded in 1914 to protect the performing rights
of its members, who, by 1966, numbered over 10,000.   This 3rd
edition of a useful, generally accurate source book provides biographical information on 5,238 members, both past and present.   Most
are, or were, active in the popular music field, particularly the
musical stage and screen, but some art music composers are in-

cluded. Entries give name, activity, dates, career outline and a representative list of works, and of stage and screen credits. There is a separate list of publishers who are members.

1147. BURTON, Jack. The blue book of Tin Pan Alley: a human interest anthology of American popular music. Watkins Glen, N.Y.: Century House, 1950. 520p. illus., discogs.

_____. _____: a human interest encyclopedia of American popular music. Expanded new ed. Watkins Glen, N.Y.: Century House, 1962. 2v. illus., discogs. This reference guide is sometimes considered the "Bible" of its subject, one assumes by people who wish to imply that holy writ is incomplete and generally unreliable, even if wide-ranging and well-meaning. The part most often referred to--the listing of 20th century popular composers and their songs--begins towards the end of Vol. 1 (prior to that we have a historical survey of the period 1776-1900, which is informative and entertaining, but totally unlike an encyclopedia in approach). From here on Burton adopts a decade-by-decade approach, grouping song composers in the decade when they first attained popularity. Following an introductory note to each period composers are dealt with chronologically, with accounts of their careers and listings of their songs by copyright date. Lyricists, cast members and song titles are included for shows, and there are notes of recordings, with artists' names and release numbers. Unfortunately, use of the book suggests too many errors of fact, and a great many omissions. For example, as Martin Power of London, author of an as yet unpublished index of American popular music, 1920-1929, has pointed out (in correspondence with the present writer), the listing of Ray Henderson's work in the 1920s represents barely half of Henderson's published output in this period. The supplementary material in the 1965 edition includes a list of post-1950 additions to the original composer listings, and new listings for composers covering 1950-1965. Each volume has a composer and lyricist index, but there is no title index.

1148. BURTON, Jack. The index of American popular music: thousands of titles cross-referenced to our basic anthologies of popular song. Watkins Glen, N.Y.: Century House, 1957. unpaged.
When Burton's Blue Books (nos. 1147, 1251, 1263) were published the publishers excused themselves from providing title indexes on the grounds of cost and space. In due course they relented, and the resulting index is indispensable to the set. It is an alphabetical song title index referring the user to the appropriate page in Burton's three Blue Books, and, in addition, to Larry Freeman's The Melody Lingers On (Century House, 1951), which describes the stories behind the numerous popular songs.

1149. CHIPMAN, John H., comp. Index to top-hit tunes (1900-1950); with a foreword by Arthur Fiedler. Boston: Humphries, 1962. 249p. bibliog.
A useful quick-reference index containing over 3,000 popular

song titles, alphabetically arranged, and giving key, composer and lyricist, publisher and date, with film or show title where relevant. All titles included sold over 100,000 copies of sheet music or records, and all are "originally or typically American popular music." The titles are also given in chronological arrangement, and there is a list of pre-1900 songs still in the popular repertory.

1150. DICHTER, Harry, and SHAPIRO, Elliott. Early American sheet music: its lure and its lore, 1768-1889; including a directory of early American music publishers. New York: Bowker, 1941. 287p. illus., bibliog.
        A book by collectors for collectors, but useful to many without such aspirations, this reliable work has no intention of being a complete bibliography, but aims instead, by parading the choicest items of popular music in subject groups to show their great diversity, and by giving close attention to bibliographic detail, to communicate the compilers' fascination with their subject. A cross-section of items is presented in broad chronological periods, sub-divided into categories such as topic (fires, railroads, Indian items, tobacco, etc.), type (early music, college, minstrel etc.) or individual song ("Dixie," "Home Sweet Home," etc.). Earliest known editions of each item are given. Arrangement in each section is by title, with complete transcription of the title page, pagination, plate mark, notes on illustrations and any other pertinent matter. Most sections have "muted" introductory notes. The directory of publishers is alphabetically arranged, and gives changes of imprint and address. Part 3 lists by state lithographers and artists working in American sheet music before 1870. There are 32 plates of unusual items, and there is an all-in-one index.

1151. EWEN, David, ed. American popular songs from the Revolutionary War to the present. New York: Random House, 1966. 507p. discog.
        Ewen describes this reference volume as "the first attempt to provide a comprehensive alphabetical guide to the songs Americans have sung and loved down the years" (introduction). It lists over 3,600 songs by title, including "standards," songs of historical, social or political interest, songs popular in their day though since forgotten, and rock and roll songs. Jazz and folk songs are excluded. Each entry gives the name of the lyricist and the composer, the performance history of the song, and its inclusion in stage or screen productions. There are also entries for 300 musicals, 140 composers and 140 lyricists, with cross references to the relevant songs. Supplementary lists give the biggest song successes in chronological order; the best sellers from 1919 to 1966, arranged by artist, with label and date; and performers, with a selection of their best known songs. A glance at Shapiro (no. 1161) or Mattfeld (no. 17) is sufficient to show that Ewen's coverage is far from comprehensive, but his comments are generally informative.

1152. EWEN, David. Great men of American popular song: the history of the American popular song told through the lives ... of its foremost composers and lyricists. Engle-

wood Cliffs: Prentice-Hall, 1970.
_____. _____. Rev. and enlarged ed. Englewood
Cliffs: Prentice-Hall, 1972. 404p.
Basically a series of biographical portraits of 30 outstanding individual composers or "teams," from Billings to Dylan, through which Ewen attempts to describe the changing and evolving style of popular song. A clear majority are 20th century, and most of these are associated with the musical stage or film. There is biographical and career detail, background information on individual songs, some attention to musical characteristics, and an attempt to relate the portraits to the development of particular song types--war songs, Negro songs, show songs, etc.--and to the development of the lyric. Index.

1153. EWEN, David. Men of popular music. Chicago: Ziff-
Davis, 1944. 213p. illus., bibliog., discog.
Through the careers and achievements of fifteen representative figures from the musical, jazz and blues Ewen sets out to trace the main lines of the 20th century development of popular music up to the 1940s. The fifteen are King Oliver, Irving Berlin, Louis Armstrong, W. C. Handy, Meade Lux Lewis, Duke Ellington, Paul Whiteman, and Ferde Grofé, George Gershwin, Jerome Kern, Richard Rodgers and Lorenz Hart, Cole Porter, Benny Goodman and Raymond Scott. There is biographical information, and description of the personality, style and contribution of each figure.

1154. EWEN, David. Popular American composers from Revolutionary times to the present: a biographical and critical
guide. New York: Wilson, 1962. 217p. illus., bibliogs.
_____. _____. 1st supplement. New York: Wilson,
1972. 121p. illus., bibliogs.
This selective biographical dictionary provides accounts of 130 composers from Billings to André Previn; about one-third of this number were living at the time of compilation, and most of these were interviewed by the compiler. Selection is based mainly on popular success, productiveness and significant contributions to popular music, but the book includes composers of familiar art songs and of popular instrumental and concert music as well as those from Tin Pan Alley. Arrangement is alphabetical, and each entry includes biographical data and information on musical output, with some assessment of the style and contribution of the composer. A portrait is included wherever possible, and there are references to relevant literature after each entry. The main section is supplemented by a chronological list of composers with dates, revised to the second printing (1966), and there is an index of titles and first lines, with indication of the composer. The supplement updates the biographies of those represented in the first volume who remained productive, and adds biographies of a further 31, including some from the musical theater, but rather more from rock and country music.

1155. FULD, James J. American popular music (reference book),
1875-1950. Philadelphia: Musical Americana, 1955.

94p. illus.

_____. Supplement to American popular music (reference book), 1875-1950. Philadelphia: Musical Americana, 1956. 9p.

A very selective, descriptive bibliography of the first editions of between 200 and 300 pieces of popular music, mainly songs, (forming the groundwork for the American material included in no. 1156). Basing his choice on contemporary familiarity, the compiler includes a wide range of music: "patriotic songs, love songs, waltzes, blues, rags, jazz, military songs, ballads, novelty items, college songs, Hawaiian melodies, cowboy songs, folk music, Negro spirituals, marches, instrumental pieces, children's songs." Arrangement is alphabetical by title in one sequence, and precise bibliographical descriptions of each item are given--not only composer, lyricist and date, but also details of the song cover (a number of which are illustrated), plate marks, etc. There is a chronological and a general index. The supplement contains corrections.

1156. FULD, James J. The book of world-famous music: classical, popular and folk; foreword by William Lichtenwanger. New York: Crown, 1966. 564p.
_____. _____. Rev. and enlarged edition. New York: Crown, 1971. 688p. bibliog.

The fruit of over 30 years' devoted collecting and sleuthing, this impressive achievement in descriptive bibliography includes in its scope a great many American popular and folk items, especially from the musical theater, and besides being useful for collector, musician and librarian, is greatly enjoyable for the casual browser. Fuld's primary aim is to describe the first printed edition of each piece of music included; having traced the melody back to its source, he extracts all information he can. Arrangement is alphabetical by title (there is a general index). Musical incipits are given for almost every item, followed by name of composer (and lyricist), copyright date, full bibliographic description, location in library or private collection, further information and comments, and brief biographical details. In theory at least, a whole volume could be devoted to music in any of the three categories in the title; nevertheless, Fuld's "fair sample of well-known melodies" is very catholic, even though a personal choice. His heaven for musical immortals clearly has many mansions; one hopes that the neighbors will not quarrel.

1157. GAMMOND, Peter, and CLAYTON, Peter. A guide to popular music. London: Phoenix House, 1960. 274p. illus., bibliogs.
_____. Dictionary of popular music. New York: Philosophical Library, 1961. 274p. illus., bibliogs.

The compilers of this dictionary-style reference book express their conviction that "popular music needs a Grove." Certainly, much pruning had to be done to enable such a vast subject to be encompassed in one slim volume, but nevertheless the result contains much useful information. Coverage is international, from the 18th century to date, with generous American representation. Most

space is given to individual composers of the "best of light music"
--operetta and musical and musical comedy, popular song, jazz (in
general, jazz musicians are excluded, though jazz styles and terms
are featured). These entries give biographical data and selected
works (usually show titles with selected songs); critical comment is
generally avoided. Lyricists and singers are not included. Other
subjects covered are: musical genres (blues, folk music), instruments (history, description, exponents), terms, notable individual
songs, dance, theaters, societies, some show titles. Entries are
balanced and authoritative. As a bonus we are given a chronological
index of musical productions of stage and screen from 1725 to 1960.

1158.   KINKLE, Roger D.   The complete encyclopedia of popular
         music and jazz, 1900-1950.   New Rochelle: Arlington
         House, 1974. 4v. bibliog. , discogs.
              The value of this massive compendium of information on the
         worlds of jazz, popular song, musical theater and film, radio and
         television music lies not in any great originality--much of the infor-
         mation is available, often in greater detail (e. g. Chilton, no. 901,
         for biographies of early jazzmen)--but in the sheer convenience of
         having so much reference data brought together in one book. Volume
         1 is devoted to chronological listings of: a) Broadway musicals,
         each with details of opening date, number of performances, leading
         performers, composer and lyricist; b) popular songs from 1909, ar-
         ranged alphabetically by title under each year (year of popularity
         rather than copyright), with authors' names; c) movie musicals, with
         credits; and d) representative 78 rpm and LP recordings from 1927 on.
         Volumes 2 and 3 form a biographical dictionary of "all artists whose
         importance warranted it," including "singers, orchestra leaders,
         musicians, arrangers, composers and lyricists to popular music
         and/or jazz. " Although the cut-off date for an established artist to
         be included is 1950, the careers of those who continued beyond that
         date are followed through to their deaths or to 1973, as appropriate.
         The biographies, which are particularly plentiful in the field of popu-
         lar song, contain very general critical assessment. (These are oc-
         casionally of an irritating kind; e. g. , the description of Blind Lemon
         Jefferson as "one of the better male blues singers"; one might also
         question the total omission of Robert Johnson--the criteria become
         wobbly hereabouts.) Very selective discographies follow the entry
         of each recording artist, and composer entries have selective lists
         of works. Volume 4 contains a plethora of appendices: Down Beat
         and Metronome poll winners; a time chart of release dates for 19
         major record labels; Academy Award winners and nominees; musical
         listings of nine major record labels including Victor, Bluebird and
         Okeh; a very short bibliography; indexes of names, musicals and
         song titles. One small carp: the wholeness implied in the title is
         a feature of very few human achievements.

1159.   RUST, Brian.   The complete entertainment discography,
         from the mid-1890s to 1942, by Brian Rust, with Allen
         G. Debus.   New Rochelle: Arlington House, 1973.   677p.
         illus.
              Similar in design to Rust's Jazz Records (no. 930), this im-

pressive compilation provides discographical details of recordings made by entertainers--individuals and vocal groups--up to the Petrillo ban. Under the banner of entertainment are included popular singers (Bing Crosby, Johnny Marvin), minstrel show artists (Al Jolson), vaudevillians (Bert Williams), film stars (Judy Garland), radio personalities (Vaughn de Leath), straight actors and actresses (Sarah Bernhardt, Orson Welles) and comedians (Will Rogers). Jazz, blues and gospel artists are excluded, as are commercial dance bands (covered in another Rust volume, no. 936). Most recordings are songs, but there are some instrumentals, and various examples of speech--humorous, descriptive and dramatic. All artists are either American by birth, or "of such stature that they are as well-known in America as in their own countries." Arrangement is alphabetical by artist, and each individual listing is preceded by a biographical note giving details, titles of films and stage shows, etc. The discographical information includes accompanist (names of individuals or of band), location, date, matrix number, title (with stage show or film title where relevant), and original release number. There are no supplementary indexes.

1160. RUST, Brian, comp. The Victor master book. Vol. 2
         (1925-1936); with indexes by Malcolm Shaw and Nevil
         Skrimshire. Hatch End, Middlesex: the author, 1969;
         Stanhope, N. J.: Walter C. Allen, 1970. 776p.
     This fine discography lists in matrix number order the recordings made by the Victor Company (merged with RCA in 1929) from the first electric recordings to 1936, when a new system of matrix numbers was introduced. (The compiler hopes to produce companion volumes covering the acoustic period of Eldridge R. Johnson's famous company--the pioneers of the flat, lateral-cut disc--covering 1901-1935, and the years up to the Petrillo ban, 1935-1942.) All domestic black-label recordings are included, but Red Seal classical records are omitted, as the book is aimed at collectors of popular music. All Bluebirds, from 1933 to 1936, are listed. A large cross-section of the popular music of the period is represented--dance music, jazz, blues, hillbilly, cowboy, humorous, popular vocal, light orchestral--making the book valuable not only as a reference source for the recording careers of large numbers of popular musicians, but also as a mirror of the tastes of the age. The discography itself, proceeding by matrix numbers, is frequently but not entirely chronological. It provides details of the performer's name, the personnel of smaller groups, instrumentation, vocalists, location, matrix and take numbers, titles, dates and catalogue numbers. A numerical listing of catalog numbers following the main discography provides the corresponding matrix numbers. Two first-class indexes of titles and artists complement the text (the former includes some 14,000 individual titles).

1161. SHAPIRO, Nat. Popular music: an annotated index of Amer
         ican popular songs. New York: Adrian Press, 1964-
         1973. 6v.
     Shapiro's aim in this substantial reference work is "to set down in permanent and practical form a selective, annotated list of

the significant popular songs of our time" (introduction). Musicians, scholars, librarians and enthusiastic amateurs alike are indebted to him for his diligent industry. The chronologically-arranged index, which covers published music from the areas of musical theater and film, popular song, jazz, blues, folk, country music and rock for the period 1920-1969, is spread over the six volumes as follows: Vol. 1, 1950-59; Vol. 2, 1940-49; Vol. 3, 1960-64; Vol. 4, 1930-39; Vol. 5, 1920-29; Vol. 6, 1965-69. Shapiro proceeds a year at a time, listing titles alphabetically with details of composer, lyricist and publisher, and notes concerning who introduced the item or recorded it, whether it was adapted from a foreign source, etc. Each volume has a current list of publishers' addresses and a title index. The absence of composer indexes is unfortunate. Shapiro's description of his work as a "comprehensive selective documentation" is a bit obscure, but his criteria are clearly stated--each item must either have achieved a substantial degree of popular acceptance, or have been exposed to the public in especially noteworthy circumstances, or else have been accepted and given important performances by influential musical and dramatic artists (p. x). He is, in effect, quite selective. Martin Power (see entry for no. 1147) suggests that for the 1920s there were approximately 1,000 more popular titles published than Shapiro includes.

1162. TUDOR, Dean, and TUDOR, Nancy, comps. Popular music periodicals index, 1973. Metuchen: Scarecrow Press, 1974. 338p.
    Intended as a companion to Armitage and Tudor (no. 1145), this is the equally welcome first volume in a projected series of annual indexes of articles in popular music periodicals. Forty-seven English-language periodicals from U.S.A., Great Britain and Canada are included (and a further 19 selectively treated). The central section is an alphabetical subject index which lists articles on individual artists (each of whom is categorized in a musical style) and on broader subjects, including musical genres (blues, gospel, country, jazz, ragtime, rock, soul, etc.), geographical areas, instruments, concerts and festivals, record companies and non-musical activities. The entries for the articles give author's name, title, periodical title, date of issue, pagination and collation. Complementing this main sequence is an alphabetical author index, which also includes full details of each article.

2. Social and Cultural Studies

1163. BRAUN, D. Duane. Toward a theory of popular culture: the sociology and history of American music and dance, 1920-1968. Ann Arbor: Ann Arbor Publishers, 1969. 165p. bibliog. notes.
    A combined history and socio-historical analysis of American popular music and dance from jazz to rock and roll. Braun traces the innovations over this period, examines the causes (which

he ascribes to individual creativity, cultural preconditions, and society's attitude to life), and finds that the occurrence of innovations
is higher in periods of peace and prosperity. He also stresses the
importance of a correct understanding of popular culture. Bibliographic references follow each chapter. No index.

1164. HALL, Stuart, and WHANNEL, Paddy. The popular arts.
      London: Hutchinson Educational, 1964. 480p. illus.,
      bibliog., discog.
      An interesting study of the contents and forms of mass
communication in the 1950s and 1960s, in which the authors search
out the educational relevance of the popular arts and mass media.
Written from a British viewpoint, it makes frequent use of popular
music, jazz and blues as illustrations. One chapter is devoted to
a presentation of the blues as a folk art transformed into a popular
art, and of Billie Holiday as a popular blues singer. The chapter
on teenage entertainments describes the interplay between authentic
self-expression and commercially provided fashions and emotions as
illustrated by pop music, and surveys the changes in pop music
styles. A possible curriculum for the study of the music is outlined.

1165. NYE, Russell. The unembarrassed muse: the popular arts
      in America. New York: Dial Press, 1970. 497p. bib-
      liog.
      A scholarly study of commercial entertainment that views
music in the context of the popular arts in general. Four chapters
are on specifically musical subjects: Chapter 6 encompasses the
musical theater from minstrelsy through vaudeville to musical comedy; Chapters 13-15 attempt a concise survey of popular music from
the 17th century to date (Chapter 13 covering popular song up to the
1920s, Chapter 14 being devoted chiefly to jazz, and Chapter 15 outlining the development of country music, rhythm and blues, and rock
and roll). Coverage is inevitably rather sketchy, but there are interesting observations.

1166. SELDES, Gilbert. The seven lively arts. New York:
      Harper, 1924. 398p. illus.
      _____ . _____ . 2nd ed. New York: Sagamore Press,
      1957. 306p.
      Seldes' book was in the forefront of an attempt in the 1920s
to gain critical acceptance for the popular arts, including popular
song, ragtime, jazz and musical theater, each of which is discussed
here. One of his central arguments is that "the greatest art is
likely to be that in which an uncorrupted sensibility is worked by a
creative intelligence" (p. 99, 2nd ed.)--which leads him to prefer
Paul Whiteman's version of jazz to that of black musicians. Although, in one of the self-critical interpolations inserted by Seldes
in the 1957 edition, he regrets his myopia, his original view reflected contemporary feeling. (In another interpolation he refers to
his discussion of jazz as "only of antiquarian interest.") There is
no index, but the names of Irving Berlin, George Gershwin, Al Jolson, Jerome Kern and Florenz Ziegfeld occur quite frequently.

3. Historical Works

1167.   EWEN, David. Panorama of American popular music.
        Englewood Cliffs: Prentice-Hall, 1957. 365p.
        Ewen tackles an enormous subject with a laudably catholic
approach, but at no more than an introductory level, diluting information available elsewhere. His coverage encompasses national
songs, folk music, spirituals, minstrelsy, vaudeville, blues, ragtime,
jazz, and the many styles of musical stage presentation of the 20th
century. One misses the historian's feeling for interactions, for
fruitful juxtapositions, for the significance of the particular (which is
very different from giving odd morsels of minor information). It is
essentially a book for bedtime, when Ewen's bland style and lack of
anything incisive to say may aid slumber. Index.

1168.   GILBERT, Douglas. Lost chords: the diverting story of
        American popular songs. Garden City: Doubleday,
        Doran, 1942. (Repr. New York: Cooper Square, 1971).
        377p.
        Gilbert describes his lively, enjoyable, articulate book as
an examination of popular song as a "social expression in the lives
of our people" (foreword); he refrains from any discussion of musical features, believing "its interpretation often an impertinence
... words are the thought and the feelings of the times of a song."
In his coverage of numerous songwriters from the 1860s to 1940 he
deliberately excludes Stephen Foster, spirituals and folk songs.
There are numerous excerpts from song texts, and there is a general and a title index.

1169.   GOLDBERG, Isaac. Tin Pan Alley: a chronicle of the
        American popular music racket. New York: Day, 1930.
        341p. illus.
        _____. Tin Pan Alley: a chronicle of American popu-
        lar music; introduced by George Gershwin; with a supple-
        ment by Edward Jablonski. New York: Ungar, 1961.
        371p. illus.
        Goldberg's breezy, not totally accurate history has advan-
tages that come from close acquaintance with the popular music industry. Tracing the American popular tradition back to William
Billings, he follows the developing genre through minstrelsy, and
the white variety shows of the second half of the 19th century, deals
in detail with the rise of the popular music industry in the late 19th
and early 20th centuries, and considers the relationship of ragtime
and jazz to this commercial world. One chapter is devoted to Sousa,
De Koven and Herbert. Other notable composers, performers and
lyricists appear throughout the story, with examples of lyrics, and--
less frequently--music. The author concedes a shallowness in much
of the music, but defends the existence of the Alley as a necessary
complement to serious music. The 1961 supplement describes some
of the changes and developments from swing music to rock and roll.
Index.

1170. LEVY, Lester S. Grace notes in American history: popu-
       lar sheet music from 1820 to 1900. Norman: University
       of Oklahoma Press, 1967. 410p. illus. (some col.),
       bibliog.
           Illustrated with 94 plates of sheet music covers, four of
which are in color, and containing also the melodies and texts of a
large number of these, this informative study of the "grace notes"
of American 19th century history--the popular songs which reported,
interpreted and retold contemporary events--describes the background
of a selection of social and historical happenings that were illustrated in song; it shows not only how important a position popular
song occupied in the communication of news and opinions, but also
what a variety of purpose and character it exhibited. Concentrating
mainly on day-by-day happenings and leaving the high and low spots
of history out of account, the author divides the songs into those
illustrating mores, and those concerned with history. He produces
a backcloth of selective social phenomena and historical events that
inspired songs, including contemporary heroes, figures of ridicule,
social movements, female dress, drinking and temperance, Presidents and Presidential candidates, transport, Indians, disasters,
and the Civil War. Apart from brief comments on the composers,
the music itself is not discussed. There is a detailed bibliography
of sources, and an index.

1171. SPAETH, Sigmund. A history of popular music in America.
       New York: Random House, 1948. 729p. bibliog.
           A detailed, informative history, beginning with the second
half of the 18th century and continuing, with a chapter on 1800-1859
and one on each subsequent decade, up to the 1940s. Outstanding
song-writers figure prominently, but there is a wealth of information also about lesser known figures, and a plethora of song titles,
with dates of publication. An appendix contains a listing of several
hundred additional song titles covering 1770-1948, arranged under
year of publication. Index to titles, composers and performers.

1172. WHITCOMB, Ian. After the ball. London: Allen Lane,
       The Penguin Press, 1972; Harmondsworth: Penguin; New
       York: Simon & Schuster, 1973; Baltimore: Penguin,
       1974. 311p.
           This witty, entertaining history of developments in the forms
and fashions of popular music is written by a one-time British rock
and roll star (also a university history graduate) who, through his
own version of the story up to the swing era, remains fascinated
but detached, and then, in the section on rock and roll, takes a personal role in the action as he describes his own experiences of stardom. The first half of the book covers developments in the style
and business of popular music with its attendant historical and social
associations, from ragtime through the various dance crazes of the
1910s, the expansion of Tin Pan Alley, the rise and influence of
jazz, technological progress in the shape of the phonograph and the
talkie, to the swing era. Part 3 looks at the American invasion of
British popular music, and Part 4 describes rock and roll. This
is a vast canvas, and in filling it Whitcomb avoids mere recitation

of facts and conveys a clear outline of changes in and interactions between the musical, social and business worlds. There is a good deal of factual information of many kinds, but it is conveyed in a style that makes its assimilation effortless. Whitcomb rarely pauses to comment or analyze; his commentary is implied very often in the way he states his facts and tells his anecdotes. This is the one problem: his jaunty style and keen eye for the potentially amusing angle sooner or later blur all value distinctions; topics of greater or lesser significance are described using the same approach, so that the various kinds of vernacular music featured are all reduced to the mean level of Tin Pan Alley, and the best songwriters to that of the navvy.

1173. WITMARK, Isidore, and GOLDBERG, Isaac. From ragtime to swingtime: the story of the House of Witmark. New York: Furman, 1939. 480p. illus.

In the early days of Tin Pan Alley, before the century turned, few publishing concerns could rival that of the Witmarks for energy and enterprise. Isidore Witmark, founder and driving force of the firm, tells how it began in the early 1880s as the youthful venture of himself and two of his brothers (all under age). In their early history they were twice pioneers in popular song publishing: in capitalizing on contemporary events in choosing song subjects, and in actively persuading singers to sing the firm's songs. Isidore also makes clear how closely the firm was connected with the musical stage, in particular with the music of Victor Herbert and George M. Cohan, and with minstrelsy (brother Julius was a celebrated child prodigy of minstrel show and other presentations). It is a rich portrait of the popular music scene in New York in the 1890s and early 1900s--of the ragtime pioneers, of a host of music and stage personalities, of Negro musicians and songwriters, of early sound recording, and of the problems of copyright. The firm was taken over by Warner Bros. in 1928. An appendix lists some of the firm's publications--operettas, opera and musical comedy numbers, song successes, etc.--and there is an index.

4. Studies of Words and Music

1174. SPAETH, Sigmund. The facts of life in popular song. New York: Whittlesey House, 1934. 148p.

Many ill-informed pen-pushers have mocked the lyrics of popular songs, but when Spaeth sets off on a fun-poking romp it is not always the irony that lingers so much as his intimate knowledge of all the nooks and crannies of Tin Pan Alley. The opening chapter, which gives the book its title, is concerned to send up suggestive qualities in song lyrics. The following chapters cover such topics as songs with titles and lyrics borrowed from literary works, the tradition of bad grammar, liberties with rhyme, the school of self-pity, nostalgia, songs of home, of love, of nature. These show "varying degrees of absurdity, frankness, pathos, maudlin sentimen-

tality," but sometimes also "straightforward honesty" (p. 144).
Spaeth's conclusion is of interest; he notes that, however insincere
and cheap many songs may seem, they do reflect a people's language,
and may be a "fairly accurate summary of our manners and customs,
our language and our general standards" (p. 147).

1175. WILDER, Alec. American popular song: the great innovators, 1900-1950; edited and with an introduction by
James T. Maher. New York: Oxford University Press,
1972. 536p.
Wilder, himself a songwriter with a long experience of the
world of popular song, adds a new dimension to its study with an
in-depth examination of the music of a number of popular composers.
Combining tools of musical analysis with strong personal tastes he
does not hesitate to express, and with a lively tone and style, he
sets out, from an extensive study of the sheet music, to explore
"the precise nature of the musical characteristics ... that distinguished the emergent native song of the 1890s, and its familial successors up to the middle of the present century." Wilder's particular concern is innovation, and his major area of exploration--Broad-
way having been more receptive to innovation than Tin Pan Alley--
is the body of song created by eleven musical theater composers
(though the songs are analyzed for their musical, not theatrical
qualities). The eleven are: Jerome Kern, Irving Berlin, George
Gershwin, Richard Rodgers, Cole Porter, Harold Arlen, Vincent
Youmans, Arthur Schwartz, Burton Lane, Hugh Martin and Vernon
Duke. These detailed, illuminating studies are followed by an examination of some non-theatrical songs by twelve "great craftsmen,"
who include Hoagy Carmichael, Harry Warren, Duke Ellington and
Richard Whiting, and by a concluding chapter on some sixty outstanding songs by other composers. Throughout the book Wilder
makes plentiful use of music examples (with the exception of one
chapter, whose subject declined to grant permission). Being concerned exclusively with musical features he does not quote lyrics.
There are indexes of composers and song titles.

1176. WILK, Max. They're playing our song: from Jerome Kern
to Stephen Sondheim--the stories behind the words and
music of two generations. New York: Atheneum, 1973.
295p.
Popular songwriters and lyricists talk divertingly, appreci-
atively and with a great fund of anecdotes about one another (and a
little more guardedly about themselves) in the interviews which form
the kernel of a series of 21 portraits of both the quick and the dead.
Some biographical information, accounts of influences and partnerships, background stories to songs and shows, character facets,
comic incidents, occasional forays into questions of technique, of
creative processes, and of the eternal enigma--what makes a hit
song; these are the main ingredients. A deal of mutual admiration
and adulation is apparent in the ranks, together with a certain un-
willingness to attempt critical assessment. The composers represented are: Jerome Kern, Vincent Youmans, Richard Rodgers, Richard Whiting, Harry Warren, Harold Arlen, Jule Styne, Saul Chaplin,

Frank Loesser, Stephen Sondheim and Irving Berlin; and the lyricists:
Dorothy Fields, Lorenz Hart, Oscar Hammerstein, Ira Gershwin,
Leo Robin, Betty Comden, Johnny Mercer, Sammy Cahn and E. Y.
Harburg. The team of Bert Kalmar and Harry Ruby is also included.
No index.

5. Collections with Historical Narrative

1177. GELLER, James J. Famous songs and their stories. New
York: Macaulay, 1931. 248p.
Each of the 55 popular songs presented here with piano accompaniment is preceded by a two-page, informal, often a little sentimental, but still valuable account of its genesis. The songs come
from the period 1870-1912, are mostly of American origin, and all
attained a considerable popularity. Included are "After the Ball,"
"In the Good Old Summertime," and "Little Annie Rooney."

1178. LEVY, Lester S. Flashes of merriment: a century of humorous songs in America, 1805-1905. Norman: University of Oklahoma Press, 1971. 370p. illus., bibliog.
Taste in humor changes more noticeably than taste in melody,
and Levy admits the humor of 19th century popular song "would not
on first hearing snare many of today's sophisticates." Nevertheless
it is with the distinctly period flavor of the verses to many of the
songs, rather than musical features, that he is chiefly concerned--
though his book includes a generous amount of music in the form of
complete songs following each chapter. Ten groups of songs are
described. They include comic stories set to music, dialect songs,
nonsense songs, songs about drink, etc. Levy looks at each, not
too seriously, "trying to tickle any funny-bones that may be exposed,"
and sketching portraits of singers and songwriters where relevant.
One of the splendid features of the book is the number and quality of
the song covers that are reproduced (mainly, one assumes, from the
author's own large collection). Index.

1179. LOESSER, Arthur, comp. Humor in American song; arrangements by Alfred Kugel; illustrated by Samuel M.
Adler. New York: Howell, Soskin, 1942. 315p. illus.
An anthology of 99 humorous popular and folk songs from
the public domain, in arrangements for voice and piano. The 18th
and 19th century material is gathered into 12 groups, which include
Appalachian folk songs, Revolutionary songs, minstrel, army and
college songs, dialect songs and barber shop ballads. Each group
is introduced by the editor, who, both here and in his 20-page introduction, adopts a rather serious tone. The humor is left to stand
for itself.

1180. LUTHER, Frank. Americans and their songs. New York:
Harper, 1942. 323p.
In as entertaining a way as any to demonstrate the links be-

tween America's heritage of folk and popular songs and the country's history Luther provides an informal historical narrative in 25 chronological sections, covering 1620-1900, illustrating the text with the words and music of 124 songs (and the texts of many more) of both white and black races, including both sacred and secular material. Most of the tunes are given in harmony. There is a chronological listing of the most widely sung tunes, and an index of names and titles.

1181.   SPAETH, Sigmund. Read 'em and weep: the songs you forgot to remember. Garden City: Doubleday, Page, 1926. 267p. illus.
_____. Read 'em and weep: a treasury of American songs; the songs you forgot to remember ...; foreword by Richard Rodgers. New and rev. ed. New York: Arco, 1945, 1959. 248p. illus.
        Comment, music and song texts are judiciously balanced in this light-hearted but informative excursion through the fertile pastures of popular and folk songs from the second half of the 18th century to 1925. Spaeth's main concern is with the more ephemeral music-hall type of song, but he also includes some better-known items that have passed into tradition. There are words and tunes of some 200 songs in all, in eight chronological chapters, with entertaining introductions to each item that mingle sarcasm, nostalgia and information, and footnotes that are not intended to add anything to scholarship. A title index and a small selection of decorated song covers complete the volume.

1182.   SPAETH, Sigmund. Weep some more, my lady. Garden City: Doubleday, Page, 1927. 268p. illus.
        A sequel to no. 1181, this volume contains a comparable number of items, and, like its predecessor, is regarded by its compiler as representing a commentary--in this case a slightly less mocking one--on American ways and foibles. Presentation is similar, but a chronological order is abandoned in favor of groups showing a common theme (love, temperance), mode of expression (self-pity, moralizing, comedy), or origin (English influence, Negro or pseudo-Negro material). There are rather more examples of the decorated covers illustrating the text, and there is an index of titles.

6.   National Songs

1183.   ELSON, Louis C. The national music of America and its sources. Boston: Page, 1900. 326p. illus.
_____.   . New rev. ed. Boston: Page, 1924. (Repr. Detroit: Gale Research Co. , 1974). 338p. illus. , bibliog. notes.
        Sonneck, whose own impeccable researches into several national songs were models of accuracy, refers on various occasions in his Report (no. 1187) to Elson's work, criticizing it (pp. 104-5)

on numerous counts, and adding, "nor does the amount of his original
critical research rise above what may be expected from a book plainly designed and written in a style to satisfy the popular demand for
more or less verified facts on our national songs." Elsewhere he
calls the book "widespread" (p. 54), a nice description of the opening chapters, in which Elson embarks on a general historical outline
of the developments in musical life and composition from the Pilgrims. Following this he turns his attention to particular songs
("Yankee Doodle," "Hail Columbia," "Star Spangled Banner") and
groups of songs (sea songs, Civil War songs, and folk songs--by
which Elson means Stephen Foster). Index.

1184.   FILBY, P. W., and HOWARD, Edward G., comps. Star-
        spangled books: books, sheet music, newspapers, manu-
        scripts, and persons associated with "The Star-Spangled
        Banner." Baltimore: Maryland Historical Society, 1972.
        175p. illus.
        A whole exhibition and subsequently a whole book devoted to
just one song--whatever significance posterity has bestowed on it,
relevant or otherwise--sounds excessive. But what this detailed
catalog achieves--which was presumably also an aim of the society's
exhibit of 1969--is to freeze time for a moment and investigate a
cross-section of human activity, centering round one particular artistic product, and to show just how many people were necessary to its
creation. That this product of a momentary confluence was later
elevated to function as a means of demonstrating national homage is,
in a sense, irrelevant--though it heightens interest in the proceedings. One hundred and seventy items are fully described in the catalog, encompassing printed manuscript and music items. The
abundant prefatory material includes a "dramatis personae" of soldiers, printers, publishers, and Francis Scott Key, some historical
background, a history of the writing and printing of the poem, an
analysis of the text, and an examination of the song that provided
the tune. Besides a general index, there are indexes of printers
and publishers.

1185.   KOBBE, Gustav. Famous American songs. New York:
        Crowell, 1906. 168p. illus.
        Accounts of the background and the authors of a selected
number of songs wholly or partially originating in America: "Home,
Sweet Home" (words by John Howard Payne), "Old Folks at Home"
(Foster), "Dixie" (Emmett), "Ben Bolt" (Thomas Dunn English and
Nelson Kneass), "Star Spangled Banner," "Yankee Doodle," "Hail
Columbia," "America," and some war songs.

1186.   MULLER, Joseph, comp. The Star Spangled Banner:
        words and music issued between 1814-1864; an annotated
        bibliographical list with notices of the different versions
        .... New York: Baker, 1935. 223p. illus.
        This expert bibliography by an ardent collector is confined
to editions of the song in sheet music form. These are arranged
in chronological order and the bibliographic details are accompanied
by lengthy, knowledgeable annotations. An introduction, outlining

the song's history from the English origins of the tune to the 20th century, is followed by an essay on the Carr family of pioneer American publishers. The numerous fine illustrations include portraits and facsimiles, and there is an index.

1187.   SONNECK, Oscar George Theodore. Report on "The Star Spangled Banner," "Hail Columbia," "America," "Yankee Doodle." Washington: Government Printing Office, 1909. (Repr. New York: Dover Publications, 1972). 255p. illus., bibliog.

This report on America's national songs, prepared for the Librarian of Congress, is described by Sonneck as "not a history of the subject, such as one would write for popular consumption. Rather, in this report data are collected, eliminated or verified; popular theories founded on these data analyzed, their refutation or acceptance is suggested, and, of course, some theories of my own are offered for critical consideration" (prefatory note). Making extensive use of contemporary documents Sonneck discusses the British antecedents and the American history of "Star Spangled Banner," identifies the author of "Hail Columbia" as Joseph Hopkinson, and the composer probably as Philip Phile, and briefly discusses Samuel F. Smith, author of "America." "Yankee Doodle" had been a favorite among the inventors of implausible theories, and Sonneck describes, analyzes and eliminates 16 of these suggestions as to its origin. Many facsimiles of autographs and early editions illustrate the text.

1188.   SONNECK, Oscar George Theodore. The Star Spangled Banner; (rev. and enlarged from the "Report" on the above and other airs, issued in 1909). Washington: Government Printing Office, 1914. (Repr. New York: Da Capo, 1969). 114p. illus., bibliog.

Prepared for the centenary of Key's song, this is a considerably expanded version of the chapter in no. 1187. The 1909 Report had "stimulated a revival of interest," and a 'lively controversy arose as to whether or not John Stafford Smith composed 'To Anacreon in Heaven'" (preface). Taking the question of the British antecedent first, Sonneck makes a meticulous examination of the evidence, and of existing theories, before concluding that Smith (1750-1836) did indeed compose the celebrated tune, to words by one Ralph Tomlinson which had made their earliest known appearance in print in 1778 (facsimiles of this and many other relevant items are given in the appendix). An equally detailed examination of the history of Key's poem follows.

7.   War Songs--The Civil War

1189.   GLASS, Paul, ed. Singing soldiers (the spirit of the sixties): a history of the Civil War in song; selections and historical commentary by Paul Glass; musical arrangements for piano and guitar by Louis C. Singer; foreword

by John Hope Franklin. New York: Grosset & Dunlap, 1968. 300p. illus., bibliog.
A generous anthology of 105 songs, a "unique amalgam of Negro and White spirituals, gospel tunes, minstrel songs, foreign folk songs, and Stephen Collins Foster melodies" (introduction). There are five groups: general historical and political background, army life and conditions, fighting, personal aspects (home and loved ones), and memories. Each song has a short preamble giving concise background information.

1190.   HEAPS, Willard A., and HEAPS, Porter W. The singing
        sixties: the spirit of Civil War days drawn from the mu-
        sic of the times. Norman: University of Oklahoma
        Press, 1960. 423p. illus., bibliog.
The authors of this fine study-collection state in their preface that their aim is "to arrange a representative number of these war songs in a way which will illustrate the human as well as the historical and contemporary elements involved in the conflict." The words of a large number of popular songs from both North and South are grouped by subject (e.g., conscription, soldier's life, battle, folks at home), with a linking commentary. A poignant chapter on the aftermath of the strife concludes the book. The range and power of the songs emerges clearly; but only a limited number of tunes are included, the music being considered more dated and less resilient than the verse. The bibliography includes song books, and books of poems, with and without music. Index.

1191.   SILBER, Irwin, ed. Songs of the Civil War; compiled and
        edited by Irwin Silber; piano and guitar arrangements by
        Jerry Silverman. New York: Columbia University Press,
        1960. 385p. illus., bibliog., discog.
From a vast heritage of popular song bequeathed by the Civil War, as represented in contemporary sheet music and songsters, the compiler has selected about a hundred items for this anthology, using criteria such as popularity, enduring musical value, and historical significance. They are grouped in broad categories: marching and inspirational songs of the Union; the same of the Confederacy; songs of Abraham Lincoln; sentimental war songs; songs the soldiers sang; songs of battles and campaigns; Negro spirituals, abolitionist songs, songs of the Negro soldier; dialect, minstrel and comic songs; post-war songs. Each section is preceded by general remarks on the development and character of the particular category, and specific details of the composition and popularity of each item. Original lyrics are usually preserved, but the musical accompaniments have been re-arranged. Guitar chords are also given. There is a list of sources for each song, and a 223-item bibliography of anthologies, monographs, songsters, periodicals, histories and LP recordings. There are also title, first line and general indexes.

8. Bands and Their Music

1192.   BERGER, Kenneth, ed. Band encyclopedia. Evansville,
         Ind. : Band Associates, 1960. 613p. illus. , bibliog. ,
         discog.
         An American bandman's bible, incorporating revised versions
of the author's Band Bibliography, Band Discography, and Bandmen,
all separately published earlier. Though international in scope it
has a pronounced U.S. bias. The various sections of the book are:
a band dictionary (organization and terms); a biographical directory
of bandmen dead and alive; a bibliography of books, articles and
theses arranged in one author sequence with a subject index; a discography of commercial recordings in two parts--albums and singles,
each arranged by title with name indexes; a directory of related
trades (publishers, instrument makers); a listing of municipal, industrial and other professional bands, arranged by state and town;
a listing of college and university bands by institution; and a directory of non-U.S. bands.

1193.   BERNARD, Kenneth A. Lincoln and the music of the Civil
         War. Caldwell, Idaho: Caxton Printers, 1966. 333p.
         illus. , bibliog.
         One may be excused for enquiring why, if Lincoln was "one
of our most unmusical Presidents," a whole, meticulously thorough
study is needed to demonstrate it. This unpromising soil, however,
proves quite fertile. Music crossed Lincoln's path a great deal,
and the musical pageant of the war is made apparent in the story
of this association. Band music is to the fore, and there are illustrations of the various forms it took. A chain of inspiration is
noted from the battlefield to music to President to battlefield. Unfortunately the wood is somewhat obscured by the trees, or rather
by the musically uninteresting vegetation of the President's life that
keeps growing up. No music is actually included. Index.

1194.   BRIDGES, Glenn. Pioneers in brass. Detroit: Sherwood
         Publications, 1965. 113p. illus. , discogs.
         Quite thorough biographical portraits of 59 American band
celebrities from the 19th and early 20th centuries. Fourteen were
trombonists, and all began as instrumentalists, though many became conductors and composers. Included are David Wallis Reeves,
Alessandro Liberati, Jules Levy, Arthur Pryor and Herbert L.
Clarke. There is a portrait of each individual, and, for several,
a list of recordings made on cylinder or disc.

1195.   DARLINGTON, Marwood. Irish Orpheus: the life of Patrick
         S. Gilmore, bandmaster extraordinary. Philadelphia:
         Olivier-Nancy-Klein, 1950. 135p. illus.
         A popular biography of the career of the Irish-born band-
leader (1829-1892) who dominated the military band scene in America
in the second half of the 19th century. Darlington gives a fair idea
of Gilmore's popularity but does not attempt to examine or evaluate
his contribution. No index or list of sources.

1196.   GOLDMAN, Richard Franko. The band's music. New York,
         London: Pitman, 1939. 442p.
         "This book endeavors to provide a set of reasonably useful
program notes for the repertory of the present day American concert band" (preface). The music listed and briefly described is almost exclusively in the form of transcriptions of works for orchestra or piano. Of the 131 composers whose music is featured 13
are American: Dudley Buck, Bainbridge Crist, George Gershwin,
Edwin Franko Goldman, Ferdinand Grofé, Henry Hadley, Victor Herbert, Karl King, Mayhew Lake, Edward MacDowell, Ethelbert Nevin,
John Philip Sousa and Ernest S. Williams.

1197.   GOLDMAN, Richard Franko. The concert band. New York:
         Rinehart, 1946. 246p. illus., bibliog.
         With the authority of personal and paternal experience Gold-
man presents here a historical and theoretical survey of the development and instrumentation of the concert band (a concert-giving ensemble of wind and percussion instruments performing music mainly
taken from the orchestral repertoire). The origins and functions of
the band in Europe and America are described, and the characteristic types and composition of the modern band outlined. Detailed
theoretical discussion embraces questions of instrumentation, the
function of individual instruments, and problems of arrangement and
transcription. There is a review of original band music and of the
role of the bandmaster.

1198.   GOLDMAN, Richard Franko. The wind band: its literature
         and technique. Boston: Allyn and Bacon, 1961. (Repr.
         Westport: Greenwood Press, 1974). 286p. illus., bib-
         liog.
         More up-to-date, and containing more specifically American
information than The Concert Band, though organized along very similar lines, this is a combined history, contemporary survey and
practical handbook of the wind band that takes into its compass people, trends, techniques and music. A short survey of European
origins is followed by an account of the development of band music
in the United States from Revolutionary times to 1960, emphasizing
the contribution of some outstanding individuals (Patrick Gilmore,
Sousa, Victor Herbert and the writer's father, Edwin Franko Gilmore, who did much to broaden the scope of band music, and kept
in close touch with the contemporary musical scene). A survey of
the contemporary composition and repertoire of professional, school
and industrial bands precedes examination of technical questions such
as instrumentation, arranging and scoring, a detailed discussion of
the repertoire (European and American), and practical suggestions.

1199.   LORD, Francis A. and WISE, Arthur. Bands and drummer
         boys of the Civil War. New York: Yoseloff, 1966.
         237p. illus., bibliog., discog.
         An interesting and well-researched account of the role of
military bands on both sides in the Civil War. The authors describe
the organization, dates and contribution of Federal regimental and
brigade bands, fife and drum corps, buglers and boy musicians.

Bands were equally valuable to the Confederate cause, and this is also clearly portrayed, though less information is available to researchers. There are sections on uniforms and instruments, and on the musicians' part in camp life and at the front. The chapters on the music played by bands on both sides are sadly rather short (though other works cover this). Bugle calls are given individual treatment, and there are musical examples of these. Perhaps the most interesting part of the book is the rich collection of 350 contemporary photographs and drawings. The bibliography lists primary and secondary sources, while the discography is limited to LPs. Index.

1200.　SCHWARTZ, Harry Wayne. Bands of America. Garden City: Doubleday, 1957. (Repr. New York: Da Capo Press, 1975). 320p. illus.

An informative, reliable history that focuses mainly on the careers and achievements of outstanding band leaders from the eccentric but practical Frenchman, Antoine Jullien (that "splendid, bold, dazzlingly successful humbug") in 1853/4 to the year following World War I. The late 19th century is dominated by Gilmore, and the next period by Sousa; we also get good accounts of Alessandro Liberati, Frederick Innes, Thomas Preston Brooke, and frequent mention of such figures as David Wallis Reeves, Arthur Pryor and Jules Levy. Index.

JOHN PHILIP SOUSA

1201.　SOUSA, John Philip. Marching along: recollections of men, women and music. Boston: Hale, Cushman and Flint, 1928. 384p. illus.

Jovial, anecdotal, modestly written autobiography that demonstrates some of the factors that made Sousa (1854-1932) the outstanding figure he was in popular music--his benign but very determined personality, his arrival at a key point in the development of the wind band, his aim in music (simplicity and good entertainment). He traces his triumphant career as band leader and composer from childhood, early apprenticeship with theater orchestras, through the key period (1880-1892) as conductor of the Marine Band, to his formation of his own concert band, and its unstoppable success story in America and Europe. The narrative ends with his discharge from the Navy after World War I (he had enlisted, aged 62, to train bandmen); following this he describes some of his attitudes to music and musical life in general, and in America in particular, and tells something of his approach to composition.

1202.　SOUSA, John Philip. Through the year with Sousa: excerpts from the operas, marches, miscellaneous compositions, novels, letters, magazine articles, songs, sayings and rhymes of John Philip Sousa. New York: Crowell, 1910. 209p.

Is today a bad day? Do you feel that all is, after all, not for the best in the best of all possible worlds? Then turn to today's date in the genial March King's compendium and you will find there an epigram, an anecdote, a few sentences from a novel or a letter, or a snatch of music (facsimile of original MS)--for JPS was nothing if not versatile--guaranteed to dispel the clouds of darkness. Perhaps now you can compose a platitude-a-day yourself and present it to the waiting world.

1203.   BERGER, Kenneth. The March King and his band: the story of John Philip Sousa. New York: Exposition Press, 1957. 95p. illus. , discog.
Not intended as a full biography, this slim volume sets out to clarify some points relating to Sousa's life and career (points he himself was not always clear about), and to take the story beyond the time Sousa wrote his autobiography, to cover the last years of his life. In the appendices are a list of works, a band roster, and a discography arranged by title, giving composer, record company name and catalog number, and year of release.

1204.   BIERLEY, Paul E.   John Philip Sousa: American phenomenon. New York: Appleton-Century-Crofts, 1973. 261p. illus. , bibliog.
The first full-length biography of Sousa, detailed, informative, and as soundly researched as the author's bibliography (no. 1205). Bierley deliberately refrains from any attempt at musical analysis, and even without that the accumulation of information is impressive. Possibly awareness of the lack of any thorough preceding study lies behind his tendency to adulation and the lack of a really objective assessment. The book opens with a parade of Sousa's general accomplishments--a tactic usually reserved for conclusions--and continues with a series of sections (biography, character, philosophy of music) in which the ploy of separating biographical detail from sketches of personality and professional attitudes deprives the reader of the advantages of overall impression given by more conventional biographical approaches. There is also a detailed portrait of the Sousa band, and a chapter devoted to Sousa memorials. Not only is fluency forfeited by method, but there is little attempt to place Sousa in the context of the American band tradition, and to indicate something of his debt to others. Appendices list Sousa's works (including literary output), and give details of the Sousa family, and of Sousa's residences. Index.

1205.   BIERLEY, Paul E.   John Philip Sousa: a descriptive catalog of his works. Urbana: University of Illinois Press, 1973. 177p. illus. , bibliog.
An excellent work, the product of ten years' painstaking research. The 500 or so musical and literary works catalogued are a reminder of the variety of Sousa's output, and contradict the stereotype of him as a writer of marches, outstanding as these were and remain. Following the introduction, which summarizes Sousa's life and significance, and gives brief details of the compilers task and method, the catalogue itself is divided according to categories of work, e.g., operettas, marches, suites, songs, waltzes, overtures, arrangements and transcriptions, literary works. Within each section the works are arranged alphabetically by title; each title is

followed by a detailed note describing circumstances of composition, inspiration, etc. The catalogue description of each work gives details of the manuscript (type of score, number of pages, date and place of composition, location), publisher, and copyright entry. The section of literary works lists books, and a hundred articles and letters to journals. Synopses of the novel plots are given, and summaries of the content of the other literary works. Appendices give lists of Sousa's compositions in chronological order, and of publishers. There are no indexes, a lapse in an otherwise impressive work.

1206. SMART, James R. , comp. The Sousa Band: a discography. Washington: Library of Congress, 1970. 123p.

Sousa himself had little use for the phonograph and recorded only a handful of times, but his band made a large number of recordings--first on cylinder, then on disc--under Arthur Pryor and others, between 1890 and 1931. This careful discography lists them all (plus some records by the U. S. Marine Band in 1890-1892, and by the Philadelphia Rapid Transit Co. Band under Sousa himself in 1926), with as much discographical detail as the Recorded Sound Division of the Library of Congress can muster. In the case of pre-1900 recordings this amounts to little more than the title of each item, but information gets fuller as we move into the 20th century, and we have catalog and matrix numbers, dates, composers, and notes on soloists. Arrangement in each section (cylinders; discs grouped under record companies) is alphabetical by title. Smart includes a general introduction, and historical commentary within the discography itself; 1, 052 items are listed in all. The appendix includes a chronological list of Victor sessions, complementing the alphabetical title list for this largest of the groups, and indexes of soloists, composers, and conductors.

1207. WHITE, William Carter. A history of military music in America. New York: Exposition Press, 1944. 272p. illus.

Though he gives biographical sketches of 21 outstanding individuals from the military band world of the 19th and 20th centuries, the author, himself a bandmaster, deals more with the plain facts of the development of the bands and their activities from the Continental Army through the Civil War up to 1941. He describes the bands of particular regions (New England, New York, Pennsylvania) from the late 18th to the late 19th centuries, differentiates between the bands of the navy and the regular army, portrays some famous individual bands past and present, discusses the teaching of military music in schools, and surveys the developments in the use of musical instruments. There are over 80 illustrations of bands, individuals and instruments.

9. 19th Century Composers
of Popular Song

STEPHEN FOSTER

1208.   FOSTER, Morrison. My brother Stephen. Indianapolis:
Hollenbeck Press for the Foster Hall Collection, 1932.
55p. illus.
   Stephen Foster's elder brother Morrison (1823-1904) wrote
this early biographical sketch for his collection, Biography, Songs
and Musical Compositions of Stephen C. Foster (Pittsburgh: Percy
F. Smith, 1896). Though short, and containing nothing ungentle,
Morrison's account of the family background, and of Stephen's life
(1826-1864) and character is an important source, and relates some
specific incidents connected with music.

1209.   FULD, James J. A pictorial bibliography of the first editions of Stephen C. Foster. Philadelphia: Musical Americana, 1957. 25, (181)p. illus. ·
   Continuing and enlarging upon the work of Whittlesey and
Sonneck (no. 1214), and of Foster Hall (whose Reproductions of the
Songs, Compositions and Arrangements by Stephen Collins Foster
was published in 1933), Fuld's book is a handsomely produced bibliographic checklist, complete with full page reproductions of the
covers of 204 Foster compositions. Each edition listed is believed
to be the first, or the earliest known. The bibliography, by title,
gives publisher, address, notes, and the location of the copy (mainly
Library of Congress). Several of the reproductions which follow are
in color, some are illustrated, and some include music. Fuld's
work lacks the supplementary indexes provided by Whittlesey and
Sonneck.

1210.   HOWARD, John Tasker. Stephen Foster: America's trouba-
dour. New York: Crowell, 1934. 445p. bibliog.
   _____ . _____ . New ed. New York: Crowell, 1953.
433p. bibliog. notes.
   The advantage Howard had over Milligan (no. 1211) in the
writing of what has become the standard biography of Foster was
the material made available to him by Joseph Kirby Lilly, the retired pharmaceutical manufacturer whose private collection of Fos-
teriana went to found Foster Hall. Howard is generous in his thanks,
remarking in the preface to the new edition that "no biographer has
ever had so much handed him on a silver platter as was handed me
by Foster Hall. " As one would expect, therefore, this is a well-
documented and dispassionate document of Foster's life. The 1953
edition contains various items of new information, including some
concerning Foster's last days. The section of the final chapter describing the many Foster memorials was rewritten for this edition.
In the appendices are a chronology of the Foster family and of
Stephen's life, lists of his published works and of the authors of his
song texts, followed by a good index. Though Howard makes some
general comments on features of Foster's music he does not attempt
any detailed investigation or assessment.

1211.   MILLIGAN, Harold Vincent. Stephen Collins Foster: a bi-
        ography of America's folk-song composer. New York:
        Schirmer, 1920. 116p. illus.
        This first independent biography of Foster is a balanced,
impartial account. Milligan is wary of the myths that had become
attached to Foster's life, and treats them with circumspection.
Though he had fewer sources than Howard (no. 1210) he did have
access to family documents and made some discoveries of his own,
including information on Foster's last days from the lyricist George
Cooper. His handling of Foster's death is praised by Howard (p.
306) for its avoidance of the lurid. Milligan's attitude to Foster
(whose songs, like Elson [no. 21], he views as folk songs) is that
his early environment was not conducive to true musical culture.
His songs present a paradox: was his a great gift that remained
basically uncultivated, or a mediocre one that produced a few isolated miniature masterpieces?

1212.   MORNEWECK, Evelyn Foster. Chronicles of Stephen Fos-
        ter's family. Pittsburgh: University of Pittsburgh Press,
        for the Foster Hall Collection, 1944. 2v. 767p. illus.
        Mrs. Morneweck (a niece of Stephen Foster) makes only
modest claims for her book--"a compilation of notes and letters
and personal recollections"--which are shown to be a considerable
understatement by the contents of this rich collection. A large variety of documents--correspondence, written reminiscences, extracts
from newspapers, etc.--is presented, with a lively linking narrative,
depicting the history of the Foster family, in which Stephen, though
late on the scene, is eventually the central, but not the dominating
figure (his mother is that--at least for him). The first two sections
chronicle the family saga in Pittsburgh and Allegheny from 1814
(twelve years before Stephen's birth) to 1845. From this we get a
good picture of Stephen's childhood background, especially significant
being his mother's series of third person recollections, fitting exactly what Gilbert Chase called "the urbanized frontier" and "the
cultural dualism of [Foster's] background." The largest section,
1845-54, covers the most fruitful period of Stephen's life--his first
successful songs, his decision to compose full-time, his marriage
(and its deterioration) and his spreading fame. The circumstances
of the composition of some songs are outlined, and there are significant documents relating to "the Ethiopian business." The final
section featuring Stephen alive, 1855-1864, begins with his mother's
death; this, and other family tragedies, hasten his own decline and
degeneration (told without sentimentality), culminating in his death
in New York, his massive talent still present, but his inspiration
all but totally departed. The devotion of brother Morrison to
Stephen's memory is shown in the last section. Included in the
various appendices is an account of the numerous memorials and
tributes (not all appropriate), compiled by Fletcher Hodges. Detailed index.

1213.   WALTERS, Raymond. Stephen Foster: youth's golden
        gleam; a sketch of his life and background in Cincinnati,
        1846-1850. Princeton: Princeton University Press;

London: Oxford University Press, 1936. 160p. illus.,
bibliog. notes.

Foster called the period when, between the ages of 20 and
23, he worked in Cincinnati as a bookkeeper for a steamboat commission firm, the happiest in his life. In this documentation of
these years, which the author deems of vital importance in the shap-
ing of Foster's genius, Walters makes extensive use of local records to draw a picture of Cincinnati at this time, of the life on the
wharfs, of Negro music, and of Foster's own life, the significant
influences upon him, and his creative achievements.

1214. WHITTLESEY, Walter R., and SONNECK, O. G. Catalogue
of first editions of Stephen C. Foster (1826-1864). Washington, D. C.: Library of Congress, 1915. (Repr. New
York: Da Capo, 1971). 79p.
Sonneck himself described bibliography as "the handmaiden
of history," and here he and Whittlesey served all Foster scholars
and afficionados finely with an exact, detailed catalog of all Foster
editions that could be traced in the Library of Congress at the time.
(Fifteen songs mentioned by Morrison Foster in 1896 could not be
found, but some others came to light.) The editions are described
in one alphabetical title sequence, with full transcriptions of each
title page, details of date, pagination and size, the first line of the
song text, and plentiful descriptive notes. There are also indexes
of authors, publishers and first lines. (For a continuation of Foster
bibliography, see James J. Fuld, no. 1209.)

CHARLES K. HARRIS

1215. HARRIS, Charles K. After the ball: forty years of melody;
an autobiography. New York: Frank-Maurice, 1926.
376p. illus.
"After the Ball" (copyrighted in 1892) sold more copies than
any previous popular song. Its history appears in its creator's story
of his life from 1886 to 1926 (he was born in Poughkeepsie in 1867
and died in New York in 1930), in which he describes how he became a songwriter, his various publishing, song-plugging and vaudeville activities, and the world of the infant Tin Pan Alley.

GEORGE F. ROOT

1216. ROOT, George F. The story of a musical life: an auto-
biography. Cincinnati: Church, 1891. (Repr. New York:
AMS Press, 1973). 206p. illus.
Best remembered for his Civil War songs ("Battle Cry of
Freedom," "Tramp, Tramp, Tramp," etc.), Root was very influential in the field of music education, and also active in music publishing. His account of his life (he was born in Massachusetts in 1820
and died in 1895) is aptly titled, for it all revolved around music.
Most significant are the accounts of the Normal Institute in New
York and elsewhere, which he founded in 1853 with William Bradbury
(with Lowell Mason a faculty member), and of the music conventions
for teachers, in which he became increasingly involved. Composition

was less important than education, but he does give some account of how he began composing, and of his own view of his music. Chapter II contains information on the writing of some of his Civil War songs, and of incidents connected with them.

10. The Genteel Tradition

JOHN HILL HEWITT

1217. HEWITT, John Hill. Shadows on the wall; or, Glimpses of the past: a retrospect of the past fifty years ... Baltimore: Turnbull, 1877. (Repr. New York: AMS Press, 1971). 249p.

Hewitt (1801-1890), the eldest son of English composer James Hewitt, who came to America in 1792, led a varied life as composer (mainly of ballads such as "Minstrel's Return from the War," but also oratorios), poet and journalist. Besides describing episodes in his own life, which included a military training at West Point, experiences with failed theater groups in the South, active newspaper work in Baltimore, Washington, Savannah and elsewhere (for music alone could not earn a livelihood), and a return to Baltimore at the end of the Civil War, where he became one of the city's characters, Hewitt has many anecdotes concerning contemporary figures, including musicians (e. g., Heinrich). He also gives the texts of numerous poems, and recounts the tale of the poetry contest in which he was awarded first prize ahead of Edgar Allan Poe.

HUTCHINSON FAMILY

1218. HUTCHINSON, John W. Story of the Hutchinsons (Tribe of Jesse); compiled and edited by Charles E. Mann; with an introduction by Frederick Douglass. Boston: Lee & Shepard, 1896. 2v.

The singing Hutchinson family from New Hampshire--five members of a family of 14 surviving children--traveled widely in America from the 1840s on, and pioneered a style of family group singing that was frequently imitated. John Hutchinson (1821-1908) was the organizing and driving force behind the group, whose curious repertoire, mingling the sentimental, the sanctimonious, and the gently humorous, and espousal of the causes of temperance and abolitionism won them widespread fame both in America and England. His volumes are filled with details of the 19th century version of one-night stands that constituted much of the group's life, of the associations formed and friendships made, of the public reception of their performances, and of the family's own history.

1219. BRINK, Carol. Harps in the wind: the story of the singing Hutchinsons. New York: Macmillan, 1947. 312p. illus.

A sympathetic biography of the Hutchinson family group, based very largely on John Hutchinson's account. The author attempts to view them in the context of their age and environment, to show how they "vibrated to every popular breeze," and to avoid a 20th century temptation to ridicule. Though the book has something of the air of a novel, we are assured the Hutchinsons "did not need to be fictionalized." The conversations included are apparently quoted verbatim from written accounts or based on reports of those who heard them. The author includes accounts of the group's involvement with temperance and abolitionism, and adds a list of some of the songs they performed (many of which they also wrote).

1220. JORDAN, Philip D. Singin' Yankees. Minneapolis: University of Minnesota Press, 1946. 305p. illus.

This is a highly enjoyable chronicle of the Hutchinson family, the flowing narrative of which is apparently distilled from the fruits of many years' research in diaries, letters, scrapbooks, newspapers, songbooks and other contemporary documents. No references are made to any of these in the text, which, like Brink's account (no. 1219), is filled with recreated conversations; as in that book, one must believe these to be as near the real thing as time, and memory will permit (even an oral historian with a tape recorder could not have improved on sprightly 83-year-old John's remarks at his wedding in 1905 to a widow over 30 years younger). Numerous examples of song texts from the group's repertoire are included in the narrative, and there is an index.

HENRY RUSSELL

1221. RUSSELL, Henry. Cheer! boys, cheer! memories of men and music. London: Macqueen, 1895. 276p. illus.

Composer of sentimental and rousing popular songs ("Woodman, Spare that Tree," "A Life on the Ocean Wave"), Russell (1812-1900) was a cheery, egotistical English showman, who spent the years from 1833 to 1841 in the U.S. (he was based at Rochester, where he was a church organist) and did much to foster the style of song that was an intrinsic part of the genteel tradition. His "rambling recollections of a long life" cover extensively the American period of this "oldest of living English entertainers" and "disciple of melody," as he described himself in 1895. Many of his perennials were written in America, and there are various accounts of how well they were received (Russell was his own promoter, singing the songs himself at his entertainments—a factor in his success that has been contrasted with the personal tragedy of Stephen Foster). Russell's travels brought him into contact with black music, and we find, for example, this account of Negro psalm singing in Vicksburg: "When the minister gave out his own version of the Psalm, the choir commenced singing so rapidly that the original tune absolutely ceased to exist—in fact, the fine old psalm tune became thoroughly transformed into a kind of Negro melody" (p. 85). A visit among Indians with George Catlin was not so happy, Russell finding their songs "hideous noises."

11. Popular Music of the Stage and Screen

a. Reference Works and Histories

1222.   EWEN, David. Complete book of the American musical
         theater: a guide to more than 300 productions of the
         American musical theatre from "The Black Crook" (1866)
         to the present, with plot, production history, stars,
         songs, composers, librettists, and lyricists. New York:
         Holt, 1958. 447p. illus.
         _____. _____. Rev. ed. New York: Holt, 1959.
         447p. illus.
         _____. New complete book of the American musical
         theater. New York: Holt, Rinehart & Winston, 1970.
         800p. illus.
         A vast, though far from encyclopedic, reference work,
whose coverage includes extravaganzas, burlesque, operettas, comic
operas, revues and musical comedies (but not opera) by American
composers (American being interpreted as including many non-native
composers). The main section consists of a series of alphabetically
arranged entries on selected individual composers, giving biographical details and a show-by-show listing, with description, synopsis
and general comments. The appendices provide information on other
significant individuals and shows, a chronological table of all musical productions mentioned in the book, and a list of outstanding
songs. (For fuller lists of songs, casts, etc., one must look elsewhere, e.g., the appendix to Green, no. 1256, or Lewine and Simon, no. 1259.)

1223.   EWEN, David. The story of America's musical theater.
         Philadelphia: Chilton, 1961. 268p.
         _____. _____. Rev. ed. New York: Chilton,
         1968. 278p.
         A history of the production of stage musicals in America
from the earliest 18th century ballad operas to "Man of La Mancha."
Aimed at the layman, and outlining circumstances of the composition
of many works, basic plot and salient characteristics, the book attempts no detailed analysis, and contains no additional material such
as illustrations.

1224.   LUBBOCK, Mark. The complete book of light opera; with
         an American section by David Ewen. London: Putnam;
         New York: Appleton-Century-Crofts, 1962. 953p. illus.
         The "American section" of this reference work contains ac-
counts of 85 operettas and musical comedies by 33 composers, from
"Robin Hood" (1890, Reginald De Koven) to "Bye Bye Birdie" (1960,
Charles Strouse). Shows are grouped by composer, and each entry
provides authors' names, details of the first production, a list of
the principal characters, plot synopsis, and a general summary of
the show's features. There are none of the selected music examples
that illustrate the main part of the book. An appendix lists London
productions of American musicals from 1891 to 1961, and there is
an index.

1225.   MARKS, Edward B. They all had glamour: from the
         Swedish Nightingale to the naked lady. New York: Mess-
         ner, 1944. (Repr. Westport: Greenwood Press, 1972).
         448p. illus.
         Marks' second volume is a series of portraits from the vari-
ous types of late 19th century musical stage entertainment--pictur-
esque accounts first of the "Black Crook" (1866), the Kiralfy brothers, opera bouffe, English opera comique, Edward E. Rice's "Evan-
geline" (1874), and troupes of family entertainers. The center of
the stage is occupied by outstanding operatic sopranos, from Mme.
Malibran to Minnie Hawk. (All are European with the exception of
Clara Louise Kellogg.) Also featured in a very varied bill of fare
are mid-century glamor girls such as Lola Montez. More valuable
perhaps are the multitude of lists: a roll of honor, with biographical
sketches of over 200 singers, actors, writers, composers and lyricists of the 19th and 20th centuries; the repertoires of various operatic and concert stars, and of popular entertainers (including the
Hutchinson Family, Tony Pastor, Williams and Walker); favorite
minstrel songs, arranged under the troupe that sang them; old-time
ballads, grouped under composers with comments (an impressive list
including Cole and Johnson, Bland, Dave Braham, De Koven, George
Cooper, Paul Dresser, Will S. Hays, Victor Herbert, Richard Stahl,
etc.); a glossary of old-time colloquialisms, and an index.

1226.   MARKS, Edward B. They all sang: from Tony Pastor to
         Rudy Vallée; as told to Abbott J. Liebling. New York:
         Viking Press, 1934. 321p. illus.
         These colorful memoirs of a prominent music publisher,
who first published popular songs in 1894, provide a breezy behind-
the-scenes account of the popular music and musical theater business in New York in the late 19th and 20th centuries. Beginning
in the 1890s, Marks tells of his early days as a publisher, describes
his association with burlesque and minstrel shows, the rise of ragtime, the entertainment team of Bert Williams and George Walker,
and the arrival of the phonograph. Songwriters James J. Walker,
Reginald De Koven, Paul Dresser and others appear in the early
1900s, together with the lavish musical comedy of Florenz Ziegfeld
and Victor Herbert, vaudeville, and the fledgling motion picture.
World War I and the advent of radio also have their effects on popular song. The appendix provides some interesting lists: of 1,545
titles of songs "outstanding in my memory," with the year, the songwriter and the artist (a great many of these are from the 19th century); of famous names in minstrelsy, and in variety and vaudeville,
with their roles; and of locations in "high and low life in old New
York," with addresses and descriptions. There are also indexes of
names and subjects, and of songs.

1227.   MATES, Julian. The American musical stage before 1800.
         New Brunswick: Rutgers University Press, 1962. 331p.
         illus., bibliog.
         Contrary to the customary practice of regarding the second
half of the 19th century as the starting time for the American musical, Mates sets the date back over seventy years, suggesting that

the late 18th century lyric stage contains the seeds of the 20th century musical comedy. Taking as a focal point the production of William Dunlap and Benjamin Carr's "The Archers" at the John Street Theatre, New York, in 1796, he examines the various elements making up the 18th century theater, illustrating its essentially lyric character. A description of related forms of entertainment (concert life, circuses, etc.) establishes the cultural context, and is followed by accounts of the workings of the theater (seasons, facilities, stage equipment), of the practical aspects of theater music, of the theatrical companies (in particular the singing actors performing in "The Archers"), and of the repertory (notably the assortment of musical entertainments, from serious opera to extravaganza). Assessments of various librettists and composers, including Dunlap and Carr, and a detailed inspection of the production of "The Archers" and of 18th and 20th century critical reaction conclude a scholarly study, which also has 67 pages of footnotes, a bibliography of books, plays, periodicals, pamphlets and manuscripts, and an index.

1228. SMITH, Cecil. Musical comedy in America. New York: Theatre Arts Books, 1950. 374p. illus.

An informative, witty and sympathetic history of the Broadway musical stage that is particularly interesting for its account of the various forms prevalent in the second half of the 19th century. The author's objectives are stated in his foreword: to describe "what the various entertainments were like, how they looked and sounded, who was in them, and why they made people laugh or cry ... "; "to treat the works on their own level and in their own terms"; and to examine works and groups of works "within the historical continuity that led to musical comedy as we know it today." This he does in a historical survey in three parts. Part 1 (1864-1907) describes the development of burlesque and of the variety show, with particular attention to the shows of Edward E. Rice, and to Nate Salsbury's "The Brook" (1879), described collectively as "the germinal cell out of which musical comedy grew" (by arranging the typical materials of the variety show upon the framework of a plot). Part II (1908-1925) covers operetta, vaudeville and revue of the pre- and post war years, and Part III (1926-1950) the "civilization of the revue," as musical comedy in its modern sense appears and develops.

b. Negroes on the Musical Stage

See also no. 667.

1229. CHARTERS, Ann. Nobody: the story of Bert Williams. New York: Macmillan; London: Collier-Macmillan, 1970. 157p. illus., discog.

A biographical and critical study of the famous black vaudeville comedian and songwriter (1875-1922) whose stage career ranged from medicine and minstrel shows of the 1890s, through Negro musical comedies and the Ziegfeld Follies to the jazz reviews of the early 1920s. The team of Bert Williams and George Walker not only introduced the cakewalk to the world, but also produced and headed the cast in a number of black musical productions (e.g., "In Dahomey," 1902, "Bandana Land," 1907) with music by Will Marion Cook. After Walker's death in 1911 Williams embarked on a successful career on the white stage; he also made recordings estimated to have sold "in the hundreds of thousands" (Langston Hughes, no. 1232, p. 58). But the particular interest of Ann Charters is not so much with his success as with the tragic irony of a situation in which an outstanding Negro entertainer was forced to don blackface --and in doing so to degrade his own race--in order to succeed. She sees his career as "the story of a man neatly trapped by the prejudice and intolerance of his times," and explores his life from this angle. In the course of the book the sheet music of ten songs, some by Williams himself, is reproduced.

1230. FLETCHER, Tom. The Tom Fletcher story: 100 years of the Negro in show business! New York: Burdge, 1954. 337p. illus.
   Tom Fletcher's long personal involvement with black musical activity (especially the musical stage) began with a minstrel show at the age of 15 (he was born in 1875) and ended only with his death, as his book went to press. His own experiences as singer, manager and agent form the framework of the book, but it is rather for the performers that he knew and the events he witnessed that it is most valuable. Particularly rich in detail is his informal account of the period from the late 1890s to the emergence of the jazz age; among the people and events described at first-hand are minstrels James A. Bland, Billy Kersands and Sam Lucas, the cakewalk craze, the ragtime and coon songs of actor-songwriter Ernest Hogan and others, Will Marion Cook's New York Syncopated Orchestra, the singing of Florence Mills, Sissle and Blake's "Shuffle Along," William C. Handy, the team of Williams and Walker, the orchestra of James Europe, and the dancing of Bill "Bojangles" Robinson. There is, unfortunately, no index.

1231. HATCH, James V. Black image on the American stage: a bibliography of plays and musicals, 1770-1970. New York: Drama Book Specialists, 1971. 162p.
   A chronologically arranged bibliography of over 2,000 stage presentations including musicals, revues and operas (but not minstrel shows). Two of four criteria apply to each item: it must contain at least one black character; have been written by a black author; be on a black theme; have been written and produced in America between 1867 and 1970. There are sections for pre-1800, the 19th century (dated and undated), and each decade of the 20th century. Arrangement is by author within each period, and entries include title, genre, date, publisher and library location. Unproduced items and pieces existing only in transcript are included. There are author and title indexes, but there is no short cut to the musical items.

1232. HUGHES, Langston, and MELTZER, Milton. Black magic: a pictorial history of the Negro in American entertainment. Englewood Cliffs: Prentice-Hall, 1967. 375p. illus.

With its many fascinating illustrations, this wide-ranging account, covering all manner of entertainment from circus to opera, is a valuable general record of achievement. In the period up to the 20th century, music and dance predominate, from the instruments of Africa and the kinds of plantation entertainment, to blackface minstrelsy, the early musicals, and the vaudeville entertainment of Bert Williams and George Walker. The panorama of the 20th century which spans drama, films and television, also includes jazz, blues, songwriters, Negro musicals, spirituals, concert composers, performers (from Marian Anderson to Leontyne Price), gospel singers, the Apollo Theatre and nightclubs. Index.

1233.   ISAACS, Edith J. R.   The Negro in the American theatre. New York: Theatre Arts, 1947. (Repr. College Park, Md.: McGrath, 1968). 143p. illus.

The importance of music and dance in the history of the Negro on the American stage is reflected in Edith Isaacs' short historical survey, which, though mainly concerned with spoken drama, gives due prominence to singers, composers and dancers, particularly in the earlier chapters. A preliminary survey to 1890 includes a brief account of the minstrel show, while the "middle distance," as she terms the period 1890-1917, is dominated by the Negro musical comedy of Bob Cole, J. Rosamond Johnson and Will Marion Cook, and the performing of Bert Williams, to whom particular attention is given. Blues and spirituals are briefly considered before the author moves on to the 1920s, which feature Sissle and Blake's "Shuffle Along," the singing of Florence Mills and the dancing of Bill Robinson. In the 1930s two significant events in the musical theater involve Negro performers, "Four Saints in Three Acts" (Thomson-Stein) and "Porgy and Bess" (Gershwin). Much of the historical matter is rather sketchily presented, and the influence of Alain Locke is readily apparent in the author's tendency not to accept things as they were but to look constantly for the seeds of a future when Negroes will produce theatrical or operatic masterpieces in the white tradition. The lack of an index is unfortunate (even in the reprint!), but the illustrations are excellent.

1234.   KIMBALL, Robert, and BOLCOM, William.   Reminiscing with Sissle and Blake. New York: Viking Press, 1973. 254p. illus., discog.

With this fine pictorial and textual record of the careers and achievements of two very prominent figures in the story of the black contribution to the musical theater the authors seek deliberately to correct an imbalance in traditional views, which have lauded the considerable achievements of Rodgers and Hammerstein, Berlin and Porter, etc., while neglecting not only Sissle and Blake (whose "Shuffle Along," 1921, is fully documented here) but also Bob Cole, Will Marion Cook, Andy Razaf and others. The book reconstructs the careers of Noble Sissle (1889-1975) and Eubie Blake (b. 1883) separately and together, up to the unsuccessful "Shuffle Along" revival of 1952. The 1920s are naturally the main focus of attention.

Large numbers of contemporary photographs and posters are reproduced, complemented by a text composed of the recollections of the two protagonists, press cuttings, sundry documents, and linking narrative by the authors. The appendices are described as "an attempt to catalogue the immense output of Sissle and Blake, as a team, separately, and as collaborators with other writers." They include a chronological list of their songs and productions, an alphabetical list of the songs, a selected list of Blake's piano rags and semiclassics, a piano rollography, an "exploratory" discography of Sissle, Blake and James Reese Europe, their mentor, and a list of Sissle and Blake films.

1235. ROWLAND, Mabel, ed. Bert Williams, son of laughter: a symposium of tribute to the man and his work, by his friends and associates; with a preface by David Belasco. New York: The English Crafters, 1923. 218p. illus.
An anthology of recollections and anecdotes of Williams, arranged to form a biography of his life and career, including his celebrated partnership with George Walker, his Broadway success, the cakewalk craze, and his spell in the "Follies." Among the contributors are Bide Dudley, Alex Rogers, Rennold Wolf, Ada Patterson, Ring Lardner, Heywood Broun, George LeMaire, E. F. Albee and George Cohan. Williams' own and his wife's reminiscences are included also.

c. Minstrelsy

1236. DALY, John Jay. A song in his heart; introduction by Harry F. Byrd; illustrated by Marion L. Larer. Philadelphia: Winston, 1951. 102p. illus.
Daly's short biography of the Negro minstrel composer James A. Bland (1854-1911), whom tradition credits with seven hundred songs, pays most attention to his childhood and youth in Philadelphia and Washington. Using material apparently gathered from boyhood friends in their old age he describes, with fictional techniques, Bland's early obsession with music, his popularity as an entertainer in the Washington area, while a student at Howard University, his first songs, and the composition of "Carry Me Back to Old Virginny." The account of his subsequent career with Haverly's Colored Minstrels, his visits to England and his popularity there, the decline of his reputation in the 1900s as vaudeville usurped minstrelsy, and his death in poverty, is clear in outline, but tantalizing in the sparseness of detail. Also included is the music of eight of the best-known songs (more of which are given in The James A. Bland Album of Outstanding Songs ... compiled, edited and arranged by Charles Haywood, New York, Marks, 1946).

1237. GALBREATH, Charles Burleigh. Daniel Decatur Emmett, author of "Dixie." Columbus, O.: Fred J. Heer, 1914. 66p. illus.
Galbreath, who knew Emmett (1815-1904) towards the end of the minstrel composer's life, describes his main aim as being "to

fix for all time his title to the authorship of this famous melody";
with this in view he gives an account of the composition of "Dixie"
(with a manuscript facsimile), its reception, and its becoming the
national song of the Confederacy.   He also relates the alternate
claims to authorship of the song and summarizes the evidence.   Before and during these affairs he provides a biographical outline of
Emmett's career.   Other material includes texts of other songs to
the "Dixie" tune, some excerpts from Emmett's manuscript books
of unpublished material, a list of his "walk-arounds," and an index.

1238.   NATHAN, Hans.   Dan Emmett and the rise of early Negro
        minstrelsy.   Norman: University of Oklahoma Press,
        1962.   496p.   illus. , bibliog.
        A splendid, deeply researched study, combining a biography
of Emmett, one of the most versatile figures in early blackface minstrelsy, and an account of the origins and development of the early
shows, with a study and collection of the music.   Beginning with a
discussion of the theme of the Negro in 18th century English song,
and of Negro impersonation in Dibdin and in the early Republic,
Nathan proceeds to study in detail the development of the minstrel
groups in 19th century America, the tunes and the dances, and uses
Emmett's surviving MSS. to trace his career.   The music of the
shows receives particular attention, and the music anthology contains
selections from Emmett's songs, tunes and walk-arounds, and from
other minstrel material of the 1840s, with several banjo tunes.
Texts and tunes are provided, with piano accompaniment.   There are
general and title indexes.

1239.   PASKMAN, Dailey, and SPAETH, Sigmund.   "Gentlemen,
        be seated!" a parade of the old-time minstrels; with a
        foreword by Daniel Frohman.   Garden City: Doubleday,
        1928.   247p.   illus.
        Dailey Paskman had long experience of theater and radio
(including broadcasting minstrel shows) and this informal portrait,
with its songs, illustrations and dialogue, allows the reader to get
a close-up view of the minstrel show as it was typically performed.
The main components of the book are descriptions of the different
elements making up the first and second parts of a show (the first
involving the trio of Interlocutor, Tambo and Bones; the second being
less formulated, more like a revue), selections of the music and
words of 21 minstrel songs arranged for voice and piano, examples
of some typical humor, and--the central feature--a "working model"
of the first part of the show, with dialogue and more songs, followed
by an "afterpiece" (an "Africanization" of J. M. Morton's Box and
Cox, by E. Byron Christy).   The many illustrations include photographs, playbills and drawings.   Background information of a restricted kind is included on the development of minstrelsy, on centers
of performance, and on performers, and there are indexes of songs
and personalities.

1240.   RICE, Edward Le Roy.   Monarchs of minstrelsy from "Dad-
        dy" Rice to date.   New York: Kenny, 1911.   366p.   illus.
        Rice's crowded portrait gallery of mostly long-forgotten per-

formers provides a window on the world of everyday minstrelsy.
An account of the first minstrels--Thomas Dartmouth Rice, the Virginia Minstrels, Dan Emmett, etc. --is merely prefatory to the informally arranged biographies of 1,000 or so performers who filled
the minstrel ranks. The biographical data given, which concentrates
on the role each played in minstrel shows, was obtained from the individuals themselves, and/or from records in the New York Clipper
and the Dramatic Mirror. There are illustrations for about half the
cast, and indexes at the front to both illustrations and text.

1241. ROURKE, Constance. American humor: a study of the na-
        tional character. New York: Harcourt, Brace, 1931.
        324p. bibliog.

        _____. _____. New York: Doubleday, 1953. 253p.
        bibliog.
        This classic study, based on popular culture and literature
of the 19th and early 20th centuries, includes a chapter on humor in
blackface minstrelsy, in which Miss Rourke considers in particular
Negro sources of inspiration for Rice and Emmett (including spirituals), and the kinds of comedy in the shows themselves.

1242. SIMOND, Ike. Old Slack's reminiscence and pocket history
        of the colored profession from 1865 to 1891. Chicago,
        1891. 33p.

        _____. _____; (with a preface by Francis Lee Utley
        and an introduction by Robert C. Toll). Bowling Green:
        Bowling Green University Popular Press, 1974. 123p.
        bibliog.
        These recollections of a one-time black minstrel constitute
a significant document on black minstrelsy. As Toll remarks, "Even
though the careers of black minstrels are obviously of great importance, little has been written about them in the standard treatments
of minstrelsy" (p. xxvi). What was written was mostly second-hand
(e.g., Tom Fletcher, no. 1230), but Simond was a black minstrel
by profession for over 20 years, and knew many of the players he
mentions in his pamphlet, which is basically a list of people, places
and events. The 1974 edition includes a bibliography of black minstrel songsters, a chronology of the major dates in black minstrelsy,
and an index.

1243. TOLL, Robert C. Blacking up: the minstrel show in nine-
        teenth-century America. New York: Oxford University
        Press, 1974. illus., bibliog.
        This outstanding social and historical analysis of the origins
and development of minstrelsy seeks the reason for the existence and
popularity of the institution in the performer-audience relationship in
the 19th century; using surviving sources, such as songsters, joke-
books, etc. (song texts provide frequent illumination), the author
demonstrates how the minstrel show created and reflected popular
thought and feeling, particularly vis-à-vis questions of race and
slavery. The social and theatrical context of the early 19th century
is examined first, to show how minstrelsy emerged as the first entertainment institution created in response to the desire for a common

man's culture, which itself grew out of growing urbanization, the need for a substitute for folk culture, and the anti-elitist sentiments this audience directed at all the arts. Tracing the evolution of the minstrel show, Toll examines the reasons for its popularity, and analyzes the sources of its material, drawing attention to the clear presence of elements--all showing great vitality--of music, dance and folklore borrowed from the Negro (which marks the introduction of Negro culture, however caricatured, into popular culture). Minstrelsy's antebellum image of the Negro is scrutinized--in particular its ambivalent approach to slavery--as a revealing point in the evolution of stereotypes, in which minstrelsy reflected and shaped opinion. The place of sentimental songs in this process, and in the idealization of the plantation is described. A different type of sentimental song, the war song, emerged as one effect on minstrelsy of the Civil War. The post-war period saw a change to a format marked by more lavish presentation and a decrease in Negro portrayal, which eventually led to whiteface minstrelsy. The social commentary of this form is examined. The final chapters describe the advent and effect of black minstrelsy, which marked a turning point in the history of black entertainment. In discussing its content, Toll pays particular attention to the rejuvenating effects on the idiom of Afro-American music, as interpreted, at last, by Afro-Americans.

1244. WITTKE, Carl. Tambo and bones: a history of the American minstrel stage. Durham, N.C.: Duke University Press, 1930. (Repr. Westport: Greenwood Press, 1969). 269p. bibliog. notes
    The first full-length study of minstrelsy, this account describes its origins, the early shows of the 1840s and 1850s, the period of prosperity up to 1860, and the decline. Wittke also examines the technique of the minstrel show, and traces the careers of some of the leading figures: Emmett, Christy, etc. Index.

d. Burlesque, Vaudeville, Revue

1245. BARAL, Robert. Revue: the great Broadway period; introduction by Robert J. Landry. New York: Fleet Press, 1962. 296p. illus.
    The exotic, glamorous world of revue--successor to burlesque and one of the predecessors of the musical comedy--provided a stage for the talents of many songwriters (Gershwin, Berlin, Kern, Romberg, Henderson, etc.). Baral's history embraces a period extending from the turn of the century to the 1950s, but concentrates on the greatest period, the 1920s, describing the year-by-year progress of various outstanding revues (Ziegfeld's Follies, the shows at the Shuberts' Winter Garden, the Greenwich Village Follies, George White's Scandals, the Music Box revues, and Earl Carroll's Varieties). Other "hits and flops" of Broadway from 1920 to 1939 are also described, as are eight revues of 1940s-1950s. An appendix gives the casts and credits of over 180 shows, 1903-1945.

1246. CARTER, Randolph. The world of Flo Ziegfeld. New York: Praeger; London: Elek, 1974. 176p. illus. (some col.) bibliog.

Master theatrical showman of the first thirty years of the century, great glorifier of American girlhood, Ziegfeld (1868-1932) had little personal feeling for music and inspired a hearty dislike in numerous musicians, but his long succession of opulent shows, musicals (e. g. , "Show Boat," "Rosalie") and revues, particularly "Follies" (1907-1931), used music by many popular composers, including Victor Herbert, Sigmund Romberg, Rudolf Friml, Jerome Kern, Irving Berlin, George Gershwin, as well as his regulars, Dane Stamper, Louis Hitsch and Raymond Hubbell. Many popular standards were first heard in the context of a lavish Ziegfeld spectacular. Carter's liberally illustrated biographical portrait includes a selection of the superb designs of Joseph Urban for " Follies" and other shows.

1247. FARNSWORTH, Marjorie. The Ziegfeld Follies; with an introduction by Billie Burke Ziegfeld. New York: Putnam; London: Davies, 1956. 194p. illus.

Framing it with an outline of Ziegfeld's own career, the author presents a chronologically-arranged portrait gallery of the stars (particularly the girls) of his "Follies" from 1907 to 1931. There is little about the music which had so integral a part--nothing about composers, a very little about lyricists (brief portraits of Gene Buck and Ring Lardner)--except insofar as the stars themselves were also singers. Among the many girls whose lives, careers and appearances are described (often with a tinge of irony) are Nora Bayes, Lillian Lorraine, Fanny Brice, Marilyn Miller and Helen Morgan. Men take a back seat, though singer-comedians Bert Williams and Eddie Cantor are included. Index.

1248. GILBERT, Douglas. American vaudeville: its life and times. New York: Whittlesey House, 1940. (Repr. New York: Dover Publications, 1963). 428p. illus.

Vaudeville's lifespan as a popular theatrical entertainment covered 50 years, from 1881, when Tony Pastor first began to present "respectable" variety shows, combining comedy, dance, song and sketches, to 1930; in that time this "Irish stew of acts" (Whitcomb, no. 1172, p. 15) gave countless opportunities to singers, dancers and instrumentalists to perform, and to songwriters to publicize their wares. The appendix in Gilbert's very lively, entertaining history is an alphabetical list of acts, and it is interesting to see just how many were musical. Names such as the Six Brown Brothers (comedy saxophone act), Drummond-Staley and Belle-Birbeck (musical blacksmiths)--and what became, one wonders, of Elsie Boehhm, "female baritone"?--are forgotten, but were as vital a part of vaudeville as more famous musical names such as George M. Cohan and Sophie Tucker. Though he quotes numerous song texts and gives occasional music examples, Gilbert does not lay particular stress on music; his focus is rather on the theatrical aspects of performers' routines, and on the background world of impresarios and managers such as Edward Albee and B. F. Keith. Nevertheless, a

considerable amount of information about the role of music is turned
up as the author converts his research into contemporary sources into zestful narrative. Index.

1249. LAURIE, Joe. Vaudeville; from the honky-tonks to the
        Palace. New York: Holt, 1953. 561p.
        Laurie's breezy history, covering the period from the turn
of the century to the 1930s, takes account of the place of music in
vaudeville. In his first section, which takes the form of letters from
a fictitious vaudevillean called Lefty, there is a chapter on music
(pp. 60-74) which describes its place and the different musical acts,
and another (pp. 75-80) on singers--quartets and soloists--with lists
of names. Also featured are blackface acts--how they differed from
earlier minstrels--and the role of the Negro in vaudeville. In the
second part of the book, on individual promoters and impresarios,
there are portraits of Tony Pastor and the Hammersteins among
others.

e. Broadway Musical Comedy

1250. BERNSTEIN, Leonard. The joy of music. New York:
        Simon & Schuster, 1959; London: Weidenfeld & Nicolson,
        1960. 303p.
        _____. _____. New York: New American Library,
        1967. 299p.
        This miscellany of Bernstein's writings contains several
items of American interest: two entertaining "imaginary conversations," one with a Broadway producer on the relative merits of
symphonies and musicals in America, and the second with a "professional manager" on the subject of Gershwin tunes; and two "Omni-
bus" television scripts on jazz and the musical. These each contain
music examples.

1251. BURTON, Jack. The blue book of Broadway musicals.
        Watkins Glen: Century House, 1952. 320p. illus.,
        discog.
        _____. _____; with additions by Larry Freeman.
        Watkins Glen: Century House, 1969. 327p. illus.,
        discog.
        The main part of this reference volume in the Blue Books
series, covers the 1,500 or so musicals and operettas performed
on Broadway up to 1951. These are divided into five chronological
periods of a decade each, preceded by a survey of the pre-1900 era.
In each section there is a short introduction, followed by a listing
of the shows chronologically under composer. Following the title
and date of each show there is a note on the lyricist, cast, etc.,
and a list of the songs in the order they appear. Revivals are also
listed, and there is a discography of albums available in 1951. The
index of musicals includes numbers of performances. The supplement in the 1969 edition covers 1951-1969 in the same style, with a
separate index. (For general comments on the Burton books, see
no. 1147. For the title index, see no. 1148.)

1252.   DUNN, Don. The making of "No, No, Nanette." Secaucus:
        Citadel Press, 1972. 335p. illus.
        Vincent Youman's musical comedy, first produced in 1925,
re-surfaced in 1971 on a wave of nostalgia and enjoyed a very successful revival. Dunn's jaunty, colloquial account of this revival,
which starred Ruby Keeler and was directed by the 75-year-old
Busby Berkeley, relates the story of the original production, gives
informal portraits of the co-producers of the revival (Harold Rigby
and Cyma Rubin), surveys the lives and careers of Berkeley and
Keeler (and Al Jolson), and describes the various stages leading up
to the 1971 production. Seeking out all dramatic situations and con-
frontations behind the scenes, Dunn draws a very interesting portrait
of the mix of theatrical flair and big business ethics that is Broadway.

1253.   ENGEL, Lehman. The American musical theater: a con-
        sideration. New York: CBS, 1967. 236p. illus., bib-
        liog., discog.
        _____. _____. Rev. ed. New York: Macmillan,
        1975. 266p. illus., bibliog., discog.
        Illustrated with a large number of photographs from the 1870s
to the 1950s, this study by an experienced professional of the musical
stage begins with an examination of the origins of the musical in 19th
century music hall, minstrel show and European operetta, and of its
first steps towards individuality with Victor Herbert, Sigmund Romberg, Jerome Kern, etc. The role of the revue in its evolution is
also considered. To illustrate the character of the musical at its
most distinctive the author discusses eleven outstanding shows from
the period 1940-1957, analyzing aspects of the music and the libretto.
A chapter is devoted to the Broadway operas of Gershwin, Blitzstein,
Gian Carlo Menotti and Frank Loesser, and the final section considers a miscellany of topics, including the ensemble, the orchestra,
the critic, the role of recordings. There are lists of recorded
shows, published librettos and vocal scores, and a short book bibliography. Index.

1254.   ENGEL, Lehman. This bright day: an autobiography. New
        York: Macmillan, 1974. 366p. illus.
        The autobiography of a distinguished figure in the American
musical theater, as director and conductor. Engel (b. 1910) describes his Mississippi childhood, musical apprenticeship, and early
experiences in New York. His account of the changing fortunes that
marked the following years affords behind-the-scenes glimpses into
the production of various Broadway shows, and demonstrates the tireless energy that has characterized his particular contribution.

1255.   GREEN, Stanley. Ring bells! Sing songs! Broadway mu-
        sicals of the 1930s; introduction by Brooks Atkinson.
        New Rochelle: Arlington House, 1971. 385p. illus.,
        bibliog., discog.
        Though still largely in the market of escapist entertainment,
the musical theater of the 1930s reflected something of the change in
America's mood and condition following the Depression, supplying, in

Green's words, "a lighthearted, satirical, yet basically optimistic view of a sorely troubled country and world." Green charts the progress of the musical to a more mature vehicle for expression with a spirited, well illustrated historical account of the decade, filled with enjoyment of its subject. Each year has a chapter to itself, and each of the 175 musical productions is described--plot summary, stars, reception, general features--from "Strike Up the Band" (Gershwin) to "DuBarry Was a Lady" (Porter). The music itself does not feature prominently in the narrative. Full reference details of all 175 shows, including song titles and numbers of performances, are given in a long section of casts and credits, which is followed by details of London productions and of film versions. The discography is limited to LPs, and there is a general index.

1256. GREEN, Stanley. The world of musical comedy: the story of the American musical stage as told through the careers of its foremost composers and lyricists; foreword by Deems Taylor. New York: Ziff-Davis, 1960; New York: Barnes; London: Yoseloff, 1962. 391p. illus.
_____. _____. New York: Grosset & Dunlap, 1962. 397p. illus.
_____. _____. Rev. ed. South Brunswick: Barnes, 1968. 541p. illus.
_____. _____. 3rd. ed., rev. and enlarged. South Brunswick: Barnes, 1974. 556p. illus.

One of the most reliable and knowledgeable writers on the musical comedy, Green succeeds well in outlining the development of the genre in America through the careers of outstanding individuals and partnerships, beginning with Victor Herbert. The 1968 edition includes 52 individuals, from George M. Cohan, Rudolf Friml and Otto Harbach through the Gershwins, Vincent Youmans, Howard Dietz and Arthur Schwartz, Kurt Weill to Frank Loesser, Stephen Sondheim, John Kander and Fred Ebb. Green describes each of their works, with the story of the original production, and picks out major characteristics. Attention is also paid to performers, and there is a section on "promising talents." There are numerous good illustrations, and the most useful appendix gives a chronological listing of the shows of each composer covered, with details of opening dates, theaters, number of performances, full credits, principal songs and notes of recordings (original cast and others). The index includes names, shows and song titles.

1257. GUERNSEY, Otis L., ed. Playwrights, lyricists, composers on the theater: the inside story of a decade of theater in articles and comments by its authors, selected from their own publication, "The Dramatists Guild Quarterly"; drawings by Tom Funk. New York: Dodd, Mead, 1974. 435p. illus.

Section 2 of this collection of pieces from 1964 to 1974 is devoted to theater lyrics, and includes the reflections of Stephen Sondheim and Richard Rodgers, plus an anthology of "memorable lyric moments on Broadway" in which Broadway authors name their favorite lyrics and lyricists. Section 3, "on theater music," includes an interview with Jerry Herman, a symposium of seven viewpoints (Richard Rodgers, Jules Styne, Jerry Bock, E. Y. Harburg, George Abbott, Micki Grant and Harvey Schmidt), a piece by John Kander on adaptation, and a discussion between Al Carmines, Nancy Ford and Jeff Sweet.

1258. LAUFE, Abe. Broadway's greatest musicals. New York: Funk & Wagnalls, 1969. 465p. bibliog.
———. ; illustrated ed. New York: Funk & Wagnalls, 1970. 481p. illus., bibliog.
———. ; (new ed.) New York: Funk & Wagnalls, 1973. 502p. illus., bibliog.
A detailed history from 1884 to the 1970s. Laufe divides the period covered into lengths of five to ten years and deals in turn with each show which ran for 500 or more performances. Some sections are devoted entirely to outstanding shows: "Show Boat," "Oklahoma!," "South Pacific," "My Fair Lady." He gives background information on the show's history, with description of the production, plot sources and outline, comment on outstanding songs, description of critical reception, details of the run, and of the careers of the performers as they appear. The main focus of attention is theatrical history and economics. A long appendix gives production details of shows in descending order of number of performances. Indexes of names and titles.

1259. LEWINE, Richard, and SIMON, Alfred. Songs of the American theater: a comprehensive listing of more than 12,000 songs, including selected titles from film and television productions; introduction by Stephen Sondheim. New York: Dodd, Mead, 1973. 820p.
The bulk of this impressive reference work is an alphabetical title list of songs from Broadway and off-Broadway shows from 1925 through 1971; also included are 300 pre-1925 songs (Victor Herbert et al.), and songs for films and television by theater composers and lyricists. Designed to answer specific questions of the "who wrote that song?" and "what show did it come from?" variety, this list provides under each song title the names of composer and lyricist, the show title, and the year it opened. (Browsers in this section may be afforded all kinds of interesting insights into musical theater history.) Supporting the main section is an alphabetical show listing, giving date, number of performances, credits, all song titles, and noting the existence of a complete vocal score and/or vocal selections, and of a recording. There is also a chronological list of productions and an index of composers and lyricists. (A previous compilation by the same authors, Encyclopedia of Theatre Music, 1900-1960, New York, Random House, 1961, is a 247-page work on very similar lines to this later one, listing over 4,000 songs, with a separate section for songs from films.)

1260. SALEM, James M. A guide to critical reviews. Part 2: The musical from Rodgers-and-Hart to Lerner-and-Loewe. Metuchen: Scarecrow Press, 1967. 353p.
A chronologically arranged bibliography of reviews in Amer-

ican and Canadian periodicals (and the New York Times) of Broadway musicals from 1920/21 to 1964/65. The terminus post quem is Rodgers' and Hart's first collective show ("Poor Little Ritz Girl"), and from that point to the 1927/28 season only musicals by selected composers and lyricists are included. From 1928/29 on all musicals that opened on Broadway are listed. Operettas are excluded. The bibliography is arranged by seasons, and alphabetically by title within each season. Following each title the number of performances is indicated, and there is a listing of individuals responsible for book, music, lyrics, staging, sets, costumes, and choreography. The date of the opening is followed by the list of reviews, with full references. In addition to a list of long run musicals in descending order there are four indexes: of authors, composers, lyricists; of directors, designers, choreographers; of original works and authors; and of titles. The exhaustive indexes make this a useful work not only for review details, but also for basic information about Broadway musicals.

1261.   STAGG, Jerry. The brothers Shubert. New York: Random House, 1968. 431p. illus.
        Between 1901 and 1954 Sam, J. J. and Lee Shubert staged over 500 productions, including many musical ones. These dominating figures on the New York theatrical scene were particularly involved with the careers of Sigmund Romberg and Al Jolson. Stagg's lengthy biography of all three impresarios and wheeler-dealers bursts with theatrical lore and is redolent of 20th century New York theater life. There is an ancillary list of Shubert-produced musicals and plays in New York City, giving titles, theater, date and producer. Index.

1262.   TUMBUSCH, Tom. Guide to Broadway musical theatre; with additional research and compilation by Marty Tumbusch; foreword by Richard Rodgers. New York: Richards Rosen Press, 1972. (The Theatre Student Series) 224p. illus.
        Designed to help would-be producers select a musical for performance, and at the same time providing reference information for students of musical theater, this work gives detailed outlines of 114 Broadway shows: title, composer and lyricist, original work upon which the show was based (if any), opening date, number of performances, agent, publisher, recordings, plot digest, musical numbers, instrumentation, casting, scenes and sets, period and costumes, choreography, lighting and special effects, and notes. The main section is supported by a comprehensive list of shows generally available in January, 1971, and other lists of shows not generally available (with advice on the securing of production rights), and of operettas and light operas. There is a combined name and title index. (A further book by Tumbusch is entitled Complete Production Guide to Modern Musical Theatre, New York, Richards Rosen Press, 1969.)

f. Film Musicals

1263. BURTON, Jack. The blue book of Hollywood musicals: songs from the sound tracks and the stars who sang them since the birth of the talkies a quarter-century ago. Watkins Glen: Century House, 1953. 296p. illus., discog.

This work covers 1927-1952, and includes about 3,000 musicals, feature films, westerns and full-length cartoons with songs, and also some foreign films with American writers or stars. The films are arranged in 25 chronological sections, each with a short introduction on the films of the period, followed by a listing of the films by category, alphabetically by title within each group. Following each title a short note gives studio, stars, director, and songwriter, and a list of the songs. There is a short album and LP discography, a list of the foremost stars with dates of birth and film debut and a title index.

1264. FORDIN, Hugh. The world of entertainment! Hollywood's greatest musicals. Garden City: Doubleday, 1975. 566p. illus.

Two things about this otherwise interesting book are regrettable: the title makes no mention of the fact that the main subject is producer and lyricist Arthur Freed (1894-1973) and there is, amazingly enough in a book so studded with names, no index whatsoever. With the help of "the words, remarks, criticism and documented facts transcribed from over five hundred hours of recorded tapes of those who made Freed's films under his guidance" (p. viii), and with a great many photographs, largely from Freed's own collection, Fordin reconstructs the story behind the many successful musicals produced by Freed, or under his auspices, for MGM, from "The Wizard of Oz" (1939), on which he was associate producer, through "Lady Be Good," "Easter Parade," "On the Town," "Annie Get Your Gun," "Singin' in the Rain," "Brigadoon" and numerous others (46 altogether), to "Light in the Piazza" (1962). He is hardly ever concerned to evaluate, but rather chronicles in as much detail as possible the events and people involved in the genesis, scripting and shooting of these pictures. Besides Freed himself, prominent roles are played by members of the so-called "Freed Unit"--"a handful of highly talented and highly efficient people" (p. 89)--who included Roger Edens, Lela Simone, and Kay Thompson. Freed was largely responsible for the successful film careers of Fred Astaire, Gene Kelly and Judy Garland among others, and they appear frequently also. The concluding filmography provides complete credits for all Freed productions in alphabetical order, along with song titles, composers and lyricists and running time.

1265. KOBAL, John. Gotta sing gotta dance: a pictorial history of film musicals. London: Hamlyn, 1970. 319p. illus., bibliog.

Text is subservient to illustration in Kobal's chronicle, which concerns itself with cinematic rather than musical aspects of the history of the film musical. The story from the first sound pictures to the 1960s is told in terms of stars, directors and successful formulae:

in the 1920s early stars such as Bebe Daniels and Bessie Love, pioneer directors Ernst Lubitsch, King Vidor and Rouben Mamoulian; in the 1930s Busby Berkeley, Fred Astaire and full supporting cast; in the 1940s directors like Vincente Minnelli, lyricist-turned-producer Arthur Freed, stars Betty Grable, Alice Faye, Gene Kelly, Judy Garland. The 1950s and 1960s get shorter shrift, the laurels going without reserve to "Sweet Charity." Many notables were interviewed by the author, and the results are quoted at length. But the splendid photographs steal the show. Text and illustrations are both indexed.

1266. KREUGER, Miles, ed. The movie musical from Vitaphone to 42nd Street, as reported in a great fan magazine. New York: Dover Publications, 1975. 367p. illus.

The pages reproduced here--articles on the infant screen musical selected from the monthly fan magazine Photoplay from 1926 to 1933--may evoke a nostalgic response in the 1970s, but they were compiled originally with no thought of the morrow; rather, their aim was to supply as much information as possible to meet the public interest in the daily developments in the industry. It is, nevertheless, a particularly happy event for a scholar when he finds a source of information that is also very good light reading. Photoplay provides that felicitous combination by virtue of the great amount of information its pages contain--reviews of virtually every musical film with cast and production details, progress reports on the making of individual pictures, biographical sketches, articles on developing cinematic techniques; all this and glamorous photographs, beguiling ads and gossip column items too. The editor provides brief introductions to each year covered, noting overall trends, as well as indexes of film titles and persons.

1267. TAYLOR, John Russell, and JACKSON, Arthur. The Hollywood musical. London: Secker & Warburg; New York: McGraw-Hill, 1971. 278p. illus. (some col.)

A combined study (by Taylor) and reference guide (by Jackson). In 90 pages Taylor outlines the major points in the origin and development of the film musical, and looks in turn at the composers, stars, and directors, with a revue of trends in the 1960s. Jackson's guide consists of an alphabetical filmography, listing 275 films, with details of studio, date, duration, stars, producer, director, composer, musical director, etc., and a list of the songs with indication of who sang them. There is a name index with biographical and career data for over 1,000 individuals, and a song index which lists some 2,750 songs and refers the reader to the film title index which follows. This lists 1,437 titles, with studio and date, those in the main index being in bold type.

1268. VALLANCE, Tom. The American musical. London: Zwemmer; New York: Barnes, 1970. 192p. illus.

An alphabetical directory containing 509 entries for names associated with Hollywood musicals, including actors, singers, dancers, composers, lyricists, producers, directors, and some subjects (e.g., composers on the screen). Entries for persons list their main achievements in the musical, give a minimum of biographical data, and list the musical films with which the artist was associated. These include comedies, westerns, and dramas in which song and dance were important. Some notable songs are listed after the film title for singer and composer entries. Some of the illustrations are in color, and there is a film title index.

g. Individual Composers & Lyricists for Stage and Screen Musicals

HAROLD ARLEN

1269.   JABLONSKI, Edward. Harold Arlen: happy with the blues. Garden City: Doubleday, 1961. 286p. illus., discog.
The most extensive biographical portrait of Arlen (b. 1905), one of the truly outstanding popular song writers, Jablonski's account gives details of his childhood background (he was the son of a cantor in Buffalo), his early career as a singer and the influence of the jazz bands, his collaboration with lyricist Ted Koehler for the Cotton Club revues of the late 1920s and early 1930s (the birthplace of the classic "Stormy Weather"), with E. Y. Harburg (a partnership that included "The Wizard of Oz" (1933), "Bloomer Girl" (1944) and "Jamaica" (1957)), with Johnny Mercer on "St. Louis Woman" (1946) and Truman Capote on "House of Flowers" (1954), concluding with the blues opera, "Free and Easy" (1959). Arlen, though basically a shy man, apparently cooperated willingly with the author in the provision and checking of biographical detail; on questions of creation, however, he cannot have been so forthcoming, and hence Jablonski falls short of really capturing his subject. He attempts little assessment other than the fairly general, but provides us with a complete list of Arlen's compositions, chronologically arranged, with show credits, and a selected discography of collections, film and show scores, individual interpretations, and Arlen's own recordings. Armed with some of these, and the perspicacity of Alec Wilder (no. 1175), we may probe a little ourselves, or merely enjoy.

IRVING BERLIN

1270.   FREEDLAND, Michael. Irving Berlin. London, New York: Allen, 1974. 307p. illus.
————————. New York: Stein & Day, 1974. 224p. illus.
As the only book-length biography of Berlin (b. 1888) to cover his entire career (though, as Freedland points out, in 1973, aged 85, Berlin was still producing songs regularly) this is the most detailed chronological account of his life that is available. (Writing in England, one may suppose the author to have been rather less open to the pressure that apparently stopped other attempts.) Freedland writes in an unpretentious, uncomplicated way that suits the show business side of this most remarkable of American success

stories, but, as is often the case with popular biographies, is unable to raise his writing above the commonplace to handle the critical points in Berlin's life. The existence of each one of us is lived at many levels, and however much a biographer respects his subject's privacy (and Berlin's reserve about his private life is clearly a difficulty) he does him no service by implying that he is an exception to this rule. Many biographers of composers bring their subjects to life through their music; Freedland does not attempt this (his prose is not designed for it); "his is above all a show business story," he says (p. ix). Though his research into the show business world is clearly thorough, Freedland does not have the close familiarity with it enjoyed by Woollcott (no. 1271) to enable him to recapture the atmosphere.

1270a. JAY, Dave. The Irving Berlin songography, 1907-1966. New Rochelle: Arlington House, 1969. 172p.
    A somewhat idiosyncratic chronological listing of Berlin's songs and their recordings, the value of which is undermined by the absence of a title index. Jay proceeds a year at a time, giving titles alphabetically under each year, with occasional (sometimes subjective) explanatory notes and comments, but without any attempt to provide publishing details. The discographical information that follows many of the titles includes artist, record label and number, and playing speed. Recordings included in LP albums of Berlin songs appear in a section at the end, arranged alphabetically by artist (hence titles can appear in more than one place--another good reason for having a title index). For each of Berlin's shows there is a note, followed by a listing of song titles and by album listings. Stage and screen versions are entered under the year they appeared. While the book is clearly the result of much diligent research, poor organization and inadequate indexing (there is no name index either) considerably reduce its usefulness.

1271. WOOLLCOTT, Alexander. The story of Irving Berlin. New York: Putnam, 1925. 237p. illus.
    As a drama critic Woollcott (cf. no. 711) was renowned for his devastating attacks and his ability to make or destroy reputations. To Irving Berlin in this first biography he is kind without being patronizing, frank about his limitations without displaying his own critical weaponry. He views the story he relates, of Berlin's rise from a busker in the Bowery to the "Music Box Revues" of the 1920s, as illustrating the "rhythm of history"--American history in microcosm. Berlin's East Side background is his "Vulgate," acting as his principle source of inspiration. Less than half of Berlin's life is covered--the phrase "studied discourtesy of a premature obituary" is quoted on p. 222--but these formative years are full of interest, and Woollcott's knowledge of the show business world of the early 20th century adds conviction, as well as allowing him to make parallels, point out crossing and diverging paths, and set Berlin in a clear context of time and place. The book concludes with a chronological title list of Berlin's songs and shows, 1907-1924.

SAMMY CAHN

1272.   CAHN, Sammy. I should care: the Sammy Cahn story.
New York: Arbor House, 1974. 318p. illus.
An easy-going autobiography by the lyricist (b. 1913) of
many stage and screen shows, and of such popular standards as
"Three Coins in the Fountain," "Call Me Irresponsible," with plentiful anecdotal information on the background to his shows and songs,
and on his many acquaintances on Broadway and in Hollywood.

REGINALD DE KOVEN

1273.   DE KOVEN, Mrs. Reginald. A musician and his wife.
New York: Harper, 1926. 259p. illus.
The principal source of information on the life of Reginald
De Koven (1859-1920), Connecticut-born, Oxford-educated composer
of light operas such as "The Begum" (1887) and "Robin Hood" (1889).
The book is firstly an autobiography (Mrs. De Koven, née Anna Far-
well, wrote several novels and historical biographies), and its au-
thor gives a full account of her own background. Plenty of space is
allotted also to details of the couple's social life in Europe and
America.

VERNON DUKE

1274.   DUKE, Vernon. Passport to Paris. Boston: Little, Brown,
1955. 502p. illus.
"Schizophrenic" is a popular word to describe the musical
personality of Vernon Duke (1903-1969), musical comedy composer
and creator of " April in Paris" and "I Can't Get Started With You,"
otherwise known as Vladimir Dukelsky, composer of symphonies,
concertos and ballets. He himself, in this entertaining, if a little
self-indulgent, autobiography, sees the first signs of this tendency
emerging on his initial arrival in America from his native Russia in
1921. A lengthy stay in Europe in the mid-'20s produced acquaintanceship with Diaghilev and Prokofiev, but his career did not blossom
until after his return to the U.S. in 1929. Before then he already
knew the Gershwins, and his portrait of them is keenly observed, as
is the whole world of musical theater and revue in New York in the
1930s. Meanwhile his alter ego moved in "serious" circles, showing
the same observancy (Varèse is described as having "superbly
chiseled strong features and a bomb thrower's manner"). The climax of the story--and of Duke's career--is the writing and production of "Cabin in the Sky" (1940), starring Ethel Waters.

GEORGE AND IRA GERSHWIN

1275.   GERSHWIN, Ira. Lyrics on several occasions: a selection
of stage and screen lyrics. New York: Knopf, 1959.
362p.
_____. _____. New York: Viking Press, 1973.
371p.
Described by an acquaintance as playing "the tortoise to

George's hare," Ira Gershwin (b. 1896) is acknowledged as a master
of the art of lyric-writing. Although the book is basically a selection of his lyrics (about 100 of them are included, written to music
by brother George, Jerome Kern, Harold Arlen, Vincent Youmans,
Kurt Weill and others), the notes and comments he himself appends
to each lyric--"technical, digressive, autobiographical, ruminative,
skippable, long, short..."--give it added value, as an inside view
of musical theater, as an illuminating, if rather self-effacing, account of the creation of popular music, and as a self-portrait. The
lyrics were selected to give a cross-section of the practice of lyric-
writing; some are famous, but many are less well-known. They
are grouped into 19 categories, with full details of the show they
were written for, the date, the composer, the tempo, the original
performer, and the situation in which the song is sung. The lyric
itself is followed by the commentary. There are title and general
indexes.

1276.   ARMITAGE, Merle, ed.   George Gershwin.   London, New
            York: Longmans, Green, 1938.   252p.   illus., discog.
        Of the 38 pieces in this collection twelve were reprinted
from various other published sources (including two by Gershwin himself), and the remainder were written specially for the volume.
Armitage encouraged each person invited to "cover whatever aspects
of the life, work or personality of George Gershwin they knew best"
(preface). All were friends or acquaintances and all were celebrated
in their own right. Most of the pieces are based on personal recollections, moving from these to general appreciation of Gershwin's
achievement. Among the contributors are Ira Gershwin, Paul Whiteman, Ferde Grofé, DuBose Heyward, Rouben Mamoulian, Arnold
Schoenberg, Albert Sendrey (the celebrated description of a Gersh-
win-Schoenberg tennis game), Isaac Goldberg, S. N. Behrman and
Olin Downes.

1277.   ARMITAGE, Merle.   George Gershwin: man and legend;
            with a note on the author by John Charles Thomas.   New
            York: Duell, Sloan and Pearce, 1958.   188p.   illus.,
            bibliog., discog.
        Armitage's second Gershwin volume is all his own. It is
an assembly of personal recollection and critical--or rather, uncrit-
ical--assessment that remains of interest chiefly because of the
enormously wide range of Armitage's own activities and acquaint-
ances--impresario, art collector, book designer, writer, producer--
and his close contact with Gershwin during the last years of the
composer's life, a combination that allows him to place Gershwin
in a cultural and historical context. His involvement with "Porgy
and Bess"--he produced the first staging after Gershwin's death--
is described, and there is a historical account, with a chronological
table, of the various productions of the opera to 1956. Other material includes a portrait of Gershwin the man, a survey of critical
attitudes, and some sketches of outstanding contemporaries. There
are also listings of Gershwin's work in various categories.

1278.   BEHRMAN, S. N.   People in a diary; a memoir.   Boston:

Little, Brown, 1972. 338p. illus.

These richly evocative and entertaining memoirs of the theatrical and literary worlds of America and England, drawn from diaries kept over a long period, contain an affectionate portrait of George and Ira Gershwin. Drawing on an abundant harvest of anecdotes, Behrman conveys something of the excitment George generated in these "Gershwin years," sketches the brothers' contrasting personalities (Ira's altruism, diffidence and gentle humor, George's vitality, his "quality of joy," his self-absorption born of total sincerity) with a discerning eye, and adds his own account of George's final illness.

1279.   DURHAM, Frank. DuBose Heyward: the man who wrote
        "Porgy." Columbia: University of South Carolina Press,
        1954. 152p. illus.
        An account of the life of the writer from Charleston, S. C.,
whose novel "Porgy" formed the basis of "the first indisputable
masterpiece of the American lyric theater" (Chase, no. 25). In his
account of Heyward's early life the writer draws attention to his
familiarity with the Charleston waterfront and the life of the stevedores. Heyward's progress as a writer is carefully examined,
reaching a high point with "Porgy" in 1925. The genesis of the
novel (from an item in a Charleston paper) and its gradual emergence are described, along with an assessment of Heyward's achievement--what Durham sees as his fatalism, his grasp of racial psychology, but his lack of realism and tendency to stereotype analysis.
The adaptation of "Porgy" for stage precedes the intervention of
George Gershwin, first in 1926, and again, to more lasting effect,
in 1932. The story of their collaboration, with Ira Gershwin making
three, is told in the ninth chapter. There is also an account of
Heyward's stage adaptation of his novel "Mamba's Daughters," in
which Ethel Waters took the leading role.

1280.   EWEN, David. A journey to greatness: the life and music
        of George Gershwin. New York: Holt, 1956. 384p.
        illus., bibliog., discog.

        _____.   _____. London: Allen, 1956. 255p. illus.,
        _____. George Gershwin: his journey to greatness.
        Englewood Cliffs: Prentice-Hall, 1970. 354p. illus.
        Though subsequent authorities have drawn attention to errors
of fact in both versions of Ewen's book (cf. Schwartz, no. 1285,
p. 374) it is a generally enjoyable biography, covering Gershwin's
life and career from his birth in Brooklyn in 1898 to his untimely
death in California in 1937, and including accounts of the composition
and reception of his major works, with generalized comment on the
music itself. The 1970 edition is described as "completely rewritten."

1281.   GOLDBERG, Isaac. George Gershwin: a study in American music. New York: Simon & Schuster, 1931. 305p.
        illus.

        _____.   _____; supplemented by Edith Garson; with a
        foreword and discography by Alan Dashiell. New York:

Ungar, 1958. 287p. illus., discog.

This first biography of Gershwin, expanded from three articles for Ladies Home Journal (1931), was written with the composer's approval and support (when he could be caught, "on the wing," as Goldberg puts it). It traces Gershwin's life and career up to his arrival in Hollywood and his "Second Rhapsody." There is a good portrait of his personality, life-style and milieu, with some music examples and comments on stylistic aspects of his music, but no detailed study. The role of jazz in his music is examined in the concluding chapter of the first edition. Goldberg's style is informal, occasionally flippant, something that Edith Garson in her supplement covering the years to Gershwin's death does not attempt to copy.

1282.   JABLONSKI, Edward, and STEWART, Lawrence D. The Gershwin years; with an introduction by Carl Van Vechten. Garden City: Doubleday, 1958. 313p. illus. _____. _____. 2nd ed. Garden City: Doubleday, 1973; London: Robson, 1974. illus., bibliog., discog.

Text and illustrations complement each other nicely in this, the most soundly conceived and executed of the Gershwin biographies; there is a suitable sense of style and movement, and a reasonable objectivity that also embraces warmth and understanding and does not force the authors to cold, clinical judgments against their inclinations. What they achieve is not only a quite detailed biographical account of the lives (public lives mainly) and careers of both George and Ira, with special attention to their collaborative efforts, but also a portrait of their time and their milieu. They make little attempt, beyond general comments, to scrutinize the music, or to examine the Gershwins in a musical and literary context, though the genesis and reception of each work is described, particularly "Porgy and Bess." The second edition contains some new material but, in the authors' words, "does not drastically revise our original view of the Gershwins: George, the Jazz Age Meteor, and Ira, the contemplative craftsman." Ira receives more attention than is often the case, and following the account of George's death in 1937 there is a probing portrait of his life after 1937, his work and his personality. The appendix contains a wealth of information: a chronological list of George and Ira's published works, an "informal" discography (with Kay Swift), which describes the recordings considered outstanding, a discussion of the literature on the Gershwins, and a description of the Gershwin archives. There is also an index.

1283.   KIMBALL, Robert, and SIMON, Alfred. The Gershwins; designed by Bea Feitler. New York: Atheneum, 1973. 292p. illus. (some col.), bibliog., discog.

A magnificent collection of Gershwiniana, this lavishly-produced volume presents the success story of George and Ira Gershwin exhibition-style in a well-constructed combination of complementary pictures and text. John S. Wilson provides an overall biographical portrait in his introduction. The main text of the volume juxtaposes biographical narrative with a variety of primary and secondary material--diary entries, letters, Ira's lyrics, recollections of friends

and colleagues. The fascinating array of illustrations includes
formal and informal photographs of the brothers, their circle and
their shows, posters, programs, manuscript and printed music,
drawings and paintings. Valuable supplementary material includes
a chronology of Gershwin shows, with production dates and song
titles, an alphabetical listing of songs, with collaborators, show
titles and dates, a discography (by Miles Kreuger) of 78s and LP reissues, a piano rollography (by Michael Montgomery), and a book
bibliography. No index.

1284. PAYNE, Robert. Gershwin. New York: Pyramid Books,
       1960. 157p. illus.
              .   . London: Hale, 1962. 128p. illus.,
              bibliog. , discog.
       A short biographical portrait, giving a fairly objective as-
sessment of Gershwin's character and life-style--Payne sees him as
a mirror of his age--and describing the qualities and characteristics
of his music in general terms, in its biographical context. Payne
sees the "Concerto in F" and "Porgy and Bess" as the height of
Gershwin's achievement, and regards most of his song output as of
much lesser value. He also emphasizes what he sees as the influence of Jewish traditional music on Gershwin, without getting down
to details. The English edition has a select discography of British
recordings, compiled by Peter Watt.

1285. SCHWARTZ, Charles. Gershwin: his life and music. New
       York: Bobbs-Merrill, 1973; London: Abelard-Schuman,
       1974. 428p. illus., bibliog. , discog.
       Aiming for objectivity and accuracy Schwartz wrote his
weighty biography "in the hope of bringing Gershwin's life and music
into better focus" (prologue); or, in other words, to demonstrate his
mere mortality, which the author does with an accumulation of not
always very flattering detail from the whole of Gershwin's life that
builds into the portrait of a "living, breathing, striving, plotting
mass of contradictions. " The rather leaden-footed chronicle, however, with its addiction to minutiae, is ill-suited to its subject, and
for all Schwartz's attempt at reassessment the essence of Gershwin
the composer escapes the narrow mesh, even though the man may be
caught. Clearly, much of the detail gathered is of value; other portions, though initially arresting, are less likely to be rewarding in
the long-term. (Gershwin frequented prostitutes--so did Schubert.
Are we expected to think less of Gershwin, and does it make any
difference to the music of either?) Besides describing the genesis
of each work for stage or concert hall Schwartz also provides general critical assessment of the work and its place in Gershwin's
development, without attempting close inspection of any individual
songs. (Appendix I is devoted to reflections on some special features of Gershwin's music, especially his "Jewishisms, " and all
use of music example is confined to illustrating these remarks.)
There are copious notes to the text, and, in the other appendices,
a chronological list of Gershwin's compositions, a list of films based
on his work, a selected discography of 78s and LPs, and a massive,
though still selected bibliography, with occasional annotations. There
is also a combined index.

1286.   SCHWARTZ, Charles.   George Gershwin: a selective bib-
        liography and discography.   Detroit: Information Co-
        ordinators for the College Music Society, 1974.   (Bib-
        liographies in American Music, No. 1) 118p.   illus.
        "Because of the amplitude of the material on Gershwin," the
compiler states, "a 'complete' Gershwin bibliography is probably not
realizable."   This selection of 654 items (books, parts of books,
articles, reviews, one or two dissertations) is virtually identical with
that in Schwartz's biography of Gershwin (no. 1285), except that
there it occupied 26 pages, whereas here, with the addition of cross
references, it is extended to cover 68.   The material is arranged
in one alphabetical sequence by author (or title).   Many items have
brief annotations.   No indexes have been added to facilitate location
of information on particular shows, compositions, etc.   The discography, also substantially the same as that in the biography, is
highly selective, and is designed to serve "a wholly practical function, notwithstanding the inherent subjectivity of choice."   Hence,
though a few 78s are given, the list is mainly confined to LPs.   The
"serious" works get preferential treatment, with extensive lists of
mainly contemporary recordings.   These are followed by details of
26 recorded collections, mostly of songs, devoted entirely to Gershwin, and by seven versions of musicals.   This is moderately helpful
but of greater value, as far as the songs are concerned, would be
a song-by-song listing, with a selection of recorded versions.   Useful though the volume is, a question mark must be placed against the
value, indeed the ethics, of the separate publication of material already available.

OSCAR HAMMERSTEIN II

1287.   HAMMERSTEIN, Oscar, II.   Lyrics.   New York: Simon &
        Schuster, 1949.   215p.
        Hammerstein (1895-1960) prefaces his selection of 71 song
lyrics with a fascinating introduction in which he discusses at some
length the function of the lyric in musical theater, and explains
practical aspects of lyric writing.   "Embryo lyric writers should
learn it by heart," enthused a Notes reviewer, and indeed it gives
an excellent idea of Hammerstein's professional craftsmanship.
The lyrics themselves come from shows written with Rodgers, Kern,
and Romberg, as well as songs to music by Georges Bizet.   Composer
Jerry Bock's reaction to the book (in Guernsey, no. 1257) is pertinent: 'I'll never forget my surprised disappointment.... Those
sensitive, romantic, sweetly singing treasures became dry, academic
curiosities, awkward to the eye where once they soared to the ear.
Lyrics should be heard, not seen."

VICTOR HERBERT

1288.   KAYE, Joseph.   Victor Herbert: the biography of America's
        greatest composer of romantic music.   New York: G.
        Howard Watt, 1931.   271p.   illus.
        An informal biography of the best-known composer of light
opera for the American stage.   Born in Ireland, Herbert (1859-

1924) studied in Europe and came to America in 1886 as an outstanding cellist, pursuing his career at the Metropolitan, with Theodore Thomas, and with the New York Philharmonic. His versatile career, though chiefly centered on composition, also involved--as Kaye narrates--succeeding Gilmore as bandmaster, and conducting, among others, the Pittsburgh Symphony Orchestra (1898-1904). Kaye's account is chiefly concerned with Herbert's operettas, and in this it is detailed, a little gossipy but not too fulsome. Far less informative than Waters (no. 1289), he does describe the openings and receptions of Herbert's shows, but does not fully succeed in relating Herbert himself to the musical and theatrical context of the time. The appendix contains a classified list of published compositions, and there is an index.

1289. WATERS, Edward N. Victor Herbert: a life in music. New York: Macmillan, 1955. 653p. illus., bibliog. notes.

Splendidly thorough research is evident on every page of this immensely detailed biography, which is also, by dint of Waters' mastery of his material, a very enjoyable document. Each of Herbert's various activities receives its full due, with particular attention, quite naturally, to his work for the musical stage (including his two attempts at grand opera). Besides fully reporting the critical reception of each of Herbert's works, both for stage and for orchestra, Waters also discusses each himself. The huge number of notes to the chapters, many referring to newspaper sources, bear witness to the amount of research that went into the book's making. Yet, in the final analysis, the author concedes he finds his man elusive--"he was a bundle of contrasts and extremes, serious and gay, jolly and sad, and almost any description of him may be true" (p. 561)--and adds a final chapter to re-cap on some of his outstanding characteristics and achievements that may have got swamped in historical details. Index.

JEROME KERN

1290. EWEN, David. The world of Jerome Kern: a biography. New York: Holt, 1960. 178p. illus., discog.

Alec Wilder, whose analysis and appraisal of Kern (1885-1945) in his American Popular Song (no. 1175) is required reading, talks of Kern's "pure uncontrived" melodies "which have become as intrinsic a part of the American ethos as Stephen Foster songs." This prolific lyrical talent of Jerome Kern enriched the Broadway musical stage from the first decade of the century to the end of the 1930s, and produced in "Show Boat" a show often regarded as epoch-making for the history of the musical in the way that music is used as one ingredient--with local color, greater depth of character, etc. --serving the overall purpose embodied in a strong story. Ewen's straightforward, unpretentious biography makes such points in the course of the narrative, which relates Kern's life from childhood in New York City, where his musical ability developed early, his apprenticeship in London and New York, his first successes, marriage, progress to Broadway pre-eminence, and work for Hollywood, up to his death. The many sides of his character, including love of games and jokes, are brought out. There is general assessment of each show, with some comment on individual songs. Useful appendices provide a chronological list of stage productions, with credits and song titles, a selection of Broadway productions with interpolated Kern songs, Kern's scores for motion pictures, instrumental music, a title list of his "greatest songs," and a selected LP discography, with artists. Index.

COLE PORTER

1291. PORTER, Cole. 103 lyrics; selected with an introduction and commentary by Fred Lounsberry. New York: Random House, 1954. 224p.

The ordeal by fire of isolated exposure on the printed page makes the wings of a good many song lyrics melt like those of Icarus, but Porter's survive it quite well, their emotional ambivalence coming clearly across. The compiler, who advises us to read them slowly, groups his selection in 20 categories (each with an introduction), arranged to stress the "alternation between devil and divine" which he sees as of basic importance. No references are made to the particular context of a song in a show; each stands alone. Besides forecasting characteristics to look out for (e.g., mixing of opposites), the compiler has a number of interesting things to say in his preambles, including (before he awards his own laurels to "I Concentrate on You") some observations on Porter's use of intelligence in the cause of love.

1292. EELLS, George. The life that late he led: a biography of Cole Porter. New York: Putnam; London: Allen, 1967. 383p. illus.

————. ————. New York: Berkeley Medallion Books, 1972. 447p. illus.

If, as Mark Twain observed, "biographies are but the clothes and buttons of the man," Eells is an excellent tailor, and dresses his friend immaculately, as befits him, all buttons fastened. The facts of Porter's public life and career are chronicled in faithful detail, with plentiful anecdotes; there is a clear portrait of the social milieu in which he moved, and interesting information on the genesis and critical reception of each show. Eells is tolerant of the unrelenting hedonism, makes no attempt to belittle the man because of his social snobbishness, and is quick to point to kindness, warmth and professional humility. But clothes do not make the man, and although we see his courage in the face of physical adversity, and glimpse his perceptive wit in the delightful Hollywood diary of 1935/6, in the last analysis there is a vacuum at the book's heart, a yawning gulf between the dapper man portrayed by Eells and the composer of such sensitivity to emotional moods. Critic John Lahr, in a memorable review (London Magazine, Nov. 1967), remarked that the author "never sees the work--as Porter did--as the real expression of his personality." Hence, "the bon vivant ... seems rather silly and sad without the weight of his rich musical imagination." A handy appendix provides a show-by-show list of Porter's work for theater and film, with production details, including cast and song titles. Index.

1293. HUBLER, Richard G. The Cole Porter story, as told to Richard Hubler; with an introduction by Arthur Schwartz. Cleveland: World Publishing Co., 1965. 140p. illus., bibliog.

Porter's life story in his own words, as recorded in a series of interviews in 1954, forms about a third of this study, and takes us up to "Kiss Me Kate" (1948). Porter subsequently refused to sanction publication of his account, but after his death in 1964 Hubler published it with the addition of several chapters of his own. One of these brings the narrative up to 1964, and others describe and discuss the man and his work, including his method of composition, and assess his position and contribution. A bibliography lists Porter's songs registered for copyright in alphabetical order, with publisher and date. No index.

1294. KIMBALL, Robert, ed. Cole; [with] biographical essay by Brendan Gill. New York: Holt, Rinehart & Winston, 1971; London: Joseph, 1972. 283p. illus., discog.

The impressive result of some painstaking research, this is a presentation in words and pictures of Porter's life (1892-1964), life-style and work as a lyricist. A hugely enjoyable book for the browser, it is also a source book for biographical or literary study. The main ingredients are contemporary photographs and documents, and many examples of Porter's lyrics, arranged in decades (1910-1950) with a minimum of linking narrative. Porter's more than typically pleasurable way of life, from Yale to Europe, to Hollywood, New York and Williamstown, Mass., is seen in a mass of photographs of himself, his wife and acquaintances, while his stage and screen work is generously represented in illustrations of the shows and their stars. The large selection of lyrics (200 in all) is divided according to the show. Accompanying material includes quotations from Porter and others, reproductions of letters, notes and some music MSS, and commentary. In the appendices are a chronology of all his songs and productions, and an alphabetical list of songs, with indication of the shows for which they were written, and references to those lyrics included in the text. The discography lists 78s and LPs of original cast recordings from 1916 to 1958. The lack of an index is unfortunate.

RICHARD RODGERS

1295. RODGERS, Richard. Musical stages: an autobiography. New York: Random House, 1975. 341p. illus.

Far too few composers of any kind of music have even started out to write their own life stories for us, the public, to be anything but pleased and thankful that Rodgers accomplished his. It is a craftsman's story, dignified, level-headed, unemotional, businesslike. He tells us the facts of his life and career, from his birth in New York in 1902, as he recalls them. He is proud of his achievement, which he sees in fairly uncomplicated, practical terms, and if he is restrained on the subject of the emotional content of his music, its sources and its effects, there is plenty of evidence of his cool professionalism in the snippets about songwriting, about particular songs, and particular shows. It is good, too, to have his accounts of Hart and Hammerstein, and of the backgrounds of the shows that these and others, briefer partnerships produced. Index.

1296. EWEN, David. Richard Rodgers. New York: Holt, 1957.
        378p. illus., bibliog., discog.
        It sometimes seems that authors who begin biographies with general assessments of the character and significance of their subject (as Ewen does here) do so because they fear an assessment at the end might be disagreed with by the reader in the light of his reading; placed at the front it is more likely the reader will have forgotten it. Not that there is anything especially probing in Ewen's summary or in his book as a whole; it is an easy-going, readable, quite detailed account of Rodgers' life and career up to "Cinderella" (for TV in 1957), with plentiful information on his method of working, and on the background and reception of his shows. Nothing is overblown--Ewen knows a Rodgers tune is almost always recognizable as such--but Rodgers himself remains enigmatic. Robert Russell Bennett, composer and arranger of distinction, is quoted as saying, "He is a man with a beautiful warmth somewhere deep in his blood." Too deep for this biographer. Lorenz Hart, whose partnership with Rodgers began in 1920 and ended with his death in 1943, is treated somewhat moralizingly, his disintegration contrasted with Rodgers' all-round aptitude for success. It speaks volumes for most writing on Broadway that the success stories have all been chronicled, while an infinitely more rewarding subject, biographically speaking, like Hart, has hitherto been neglected. Ancillary material includes a chronology of stage productions, movie scores and other material.

1297. GREEN, Stanley. The Rodgers and Hammerstein story.
        New York: Day, 1963. 187p. illus., bibliog.
                .   . London: Allen, 1963. 170p. illus.
        A serviceable biography of the professional careers of Rodgers and Hammerstein that aims to focus attention on their outlooks and attitudes as expressed through their musicals. The first part of the book is a parallel biography, in which their early, almost entirely separate careers are described in such a way that one may see what each was accomplishing at a particular time. The second part deals with their successful partnership, from "Oklahoma!" to "Sound of Music." Green's critical commentary is straightforward and intelligent, without attempting detailed examination. An appendix lists the shows resulting from the partnership, with songs and casts.

1298. RODGERS AND HAMMERSTEIN FACT BOOK. New York:
        Richard Rodgers and Oscar Hammerstein II, 1955. 678p.
        illus., bibliogs., discog.
                . Supplement. New York: Lynn Farnol Group,
        1959-1961. 2v.
        RICHARD RODGERS FACT BOOK WITH SUPPLEMENT.

New York: Lynn Farnol Group, 1968. 582, 77p. illus., bibliogs., discog.

Each of these two large, accurate reference compilations contains full details of all Rodgers and Hammerstein productions for stage, screen, radio and television, including production credits, cast details, plot synopses, list of musical numbers, etc. An interesting feature is the section following each show devoted to excerpts from contemporary reviews (not all favorable) and references to other relevant articles. The shift of emphasis between 1955 and 1968 means that the sections in the first volume given over to Rodgers' and Hammerstein's productions independent of each other (with biographical note, and chronological listings of shows with full details) are reduced in the later volume to one for Rodgers only, before and after the Hammerstein partnership. In other respects the two volumes are very similar in design. The 1963 volume extends coverage to 1967 (Hammerstein died in 1960) and generally enlarges the review sections. Both volumes have extensive bibliographies, that in the first volume including letters to the press and articles by and about Rodgers and Hammerstein (many of which are quoted). The appendices in both include alphabetical lists of productions and of songs, all Hammerstein's independent work being omitted in 1968.

1299.   TAYLOR, Deems. Some enchanted evenings: the story of Rodgers and Hammerstein. New York: Harper, 1953. 244p. illus.

Conscious of a lack of dramatic tension in his narrative of the careers of Rodgers and Hammerstein to 1953, Taylor remarks at one point that "a tale of such almost uninterrupted success is bound to possess a certain degree of monotony." Nevertheless, there is plenty of interest in the many productions they were independently and jointly involved in, conveyed with a lightness of tone that is occasionally weighted for an insight, a portrait, or a flash of humor. The biographical chronicle is presented in three parts: Rodgers' career up to 1942, in particular the long, fruitful partnership with Lorenz Hart; Hammerstein's career to the same date; and their collaboration from "Oklahoma!" to "The King and I." Part 4, a portrait of Rodgers and Hammerstein in 1953, includes a description of their methods of working, a brief comparison of Hammerstein and Hart, and an examination, with some examples, of the features of Rodgers' music.

SIGMUND ROMBERG

1300.   ARNOLD, Elliott. Deep in my heart: a story based on the life of Sigmund Romberg. New York: Duell, Sloan and Pearce, 1949. 511p.

Novelist Arnold's fictionalized account of the life of the prolific operetta composer (1889-1951), whose rich lyrical talent imbued a number of his 60 shows with remarkable longevity, is backed up by an impressive amount of supplementary material--a chronological list of shows with first performance details, titles of numbers and publishers, an alphabetical list of Romberg's songs with show title, and a chronological index of his life. The book describes his early life in Hungary, arrival in the U.S. in 1909 (where he worked first in a pencil factory before becoming in due course a staff composer at the Winter Gardens Theatre for producer J. J. Shubert), and his subsequent Broadway career, which, from "The Whirl of the World" (1914) to "Up in Central Park" (1948), included such perennial favorites as "Blossom Time" (1921), "The Student Prince" (1924), "Desert Song" (1926), and "New Moon" (1928).

HARRY B. SMITH

1301. SMITH, Harry B. First nights and first editions. Boston: Little, Brown, 1931. 325p. illus.

These reminiscences of a "theatrical journeyman's experiences" make an enjoyable autobiography from the story of a stage-struck youth who went on to write over 300 plays and the words for 6,000 songs. Smith (1860-1936) has a line in ironic understatement that is refreshing, turning this also on himself ("this chronicle lacks a serious purpose and seems to contain nothing that can influence the human race in its struggle towards perfection," p. 299). His career, which encompassed the librettos for De Koven's "The Begum" and "Robin Hood" in the 1880s, lyrics for Weber and Fields productions, for Ziegfeld Follies, and for Romberg and Berlin in the 1910s and 1920s (and hence involved him in operetta, revue and musical comedy) gave him an intimate, extensive knowledge of the musical stage and popular song world of New York. He was also a bibliophile (hence the book's title) with a particular interest in Napoleon. There are indexes of both names and plays.

STEPHEN SONDHEIM

1302. ZADAN, Craig. Sondheim & Co. New York: Macmillan, 1974. 279p. illus., discog.

One might call this volume, in which Sondheim's eight Broadway shows (three with his lyrics, five with his music and lyrics) are described and discussed in the words of those most closely involved, an experiment in Broadway oral history. A full behind-the-scenes history of the growth of each show and the contribution of each principal participant is constructed out of the personal account and opinions of the main protagonists themselves, who express their views (in transcriptions of taped interviews) quite candidly about each other, and on aspects of the writing, casting, production and reception. Sondheim himself (b. 1930) is the central figure, both talked about and talking, but also featured prominently are Arthur Laurents, Harold Prince, David Merrick, Burt Shevelove, Flora Roberts, Michael Bennett and Leonard Bernstein, as well as members of the casts of each production. The author acts as a reporter, linking the excerpts from his interviews and commenting little himself. There are also nine short chapters devoted to the craft of the musical theater: production, libretto and lyric writing, publishing, musical direction, casting, staging, orchestrating, and producing an original cast recording; these are also compiled from interview material. Appendices provide full details of Sondheim productions and cast albums, and there is an index.

HARRY WARREN

1303. THOMAS, Tony. <u>Harry Warren and the Hollywood musical;</u>
       foreword by Bing Crosby. Secaucus: Citadel Press,
       1975. 344p. illus.

This sumptuously produced volume is a fitting record in
words, music and photographs of the long and distinguished career
of Harry Warren (b. 1893), one of the great composers of American popular song--and also probably the least well-known outside
the music industry. In his opening pages Thomas points out the
unique importance of Warren in the history of the film musical:
in a 25-year period, 1932-1957, he composed continuously for each
of the major studios making musicals, producing approximately 250
songs (his total output exceeds 400, as the catalog at the end of the
book shows), 50 of which have become popular standards (e.g.,
"Lullaby of Broadway," "I Only Have Eyes For You"). The lack of
recognition is, in Warren's own words, his only regret in a full,
successful life. The early, uncertain career of this self-taught musician, born in Brooklyn of Italian parents, is recorded in Part 1,
which also describes his time as a song plugger and his work for
Broadway up to 1932. Parts 2-5 are devoted to the films Warren
worked on for the four studios: Warner (1932-1939), Fox (1939-
1944), MGM (1944-1952) and Paramount (1952-1957). Taking each
film in turn, Thomas gives background information, summarizes the
plot, describes something of the function and character of the songs,
and often includes Warren's own enlightening comments on a range
of subjects from particular songs, or working with other Hollywood
personalities, to the role--and treatment--of a Hollywood songwriter.
There are frequent snatches of the melody and lyrics of individual
songs in the text, and each of the five sections of the book is followed by the complete music of a number of songs (25 altogether).
Most of the large number of illustrations are stills from movies.
The catalog includes names of lyricists and publishers. Index.

KURT WEILL

1304. WEILL, Kurt. <u>Ausgewählte Schriften</u>; herausgegeben und
       mit einem Vorwort von David Drew. Frankfurt: Suhr-
       kamp, 1975. 239p. illus., bibliog. notes.

Collaborator with Bertolt Brecht on the celebrated "Dreigro-
schenoper" (1928), Kurt Weill (1900-1950) came to the U.S. in 1935
and remained till he died. During these 15 years he wrote a number of musicals for Broadway (including "Lady in the Dark," 1941,
with Moss Hart and Ira Gershwin, and "Love Life," 1947, with
Alan Jay Lerner) that caused dismay and consternation in "serious"
music circles in Europe and America, but which reveal him, in
Stanley Green's words, as "a complete man of the theatre" (no.
1256). All but three of the examples of his prose writings in this
selection were written in Europe. The three are significant, however, for an understanding of his attitude to the musical stage.
They consist of: (i) a consideration of opera in America; (ii) an account of his connection with the "Lunch Time Follies," a war-time
entertainment for factories, etc.; and (iii) a short quote from an in-

terview, in which Weill expresses the view that opera had run its course, and that its replacement was musical theater.

1305. DREW, David, ed. Über Kurt Weill. Frankfurt: Suhr-
    kamp, 1975. 186p.
    This collection of critical responses to Weill includes eight pieces (all in German translations) of particular relevance to his Broadway years (1935-1950). German conductor and musicologist Paul Bekker writes on the Broadway version (called "The Eternal Road") of Weill's "Der Weg der Verheissung," the original cause of Weill's coming to America; Marc Blitzstein discusses "Johnny Johnson" (1936); a letter to Weill from one George Maynard is concerned with "Knickerbocker Holiday" (1938); Mary McCarthy describes the season, 1943-44, that included "One Touch of Venus"; Elliott Carter, writing about the same show, is one of the few notable musicians to discuss Weill in print in the 1940s; John Gassner reviews "Love Life" (1948); Langston Hughes describes his collaboration with Weill on "Street Scene" (1947); and Maxwell Anderson (who collaborated on "Knickerbocker Holiday" and "Lost in the Stars," 1949) pays tribute to Weill shortly after the composer's death. Apart from these few examples most of the appraisal of Weill's Broadway career was left to Broadway critics, whose writings the editor compares unfavorably with the natural simplicity and warmth of Hughes' tribute. The ed-itor himself, in his fine introduction (printed in English in the Times Literary Supplement, Oct. 3 & 10, 1975), discusses at length the various critical attitudes to Weill, declaring a "full and just ap-praisal" of his Broadway work will only be possible "when his ear-lier work has been fully reappraised and not before."

h. Music for Films

1306. EISLER, Hanns. Composing for the films. New York:
    Oxford University Press, 1947; London: Dobson, 1951.
    165p.
    German composer Hanns Eisler (1898-1962), who had col-laborated with Bertolt Brecht in 1929-1933, lived in the U.S. for ten years, 1938-1948, during which time he wrote scores for a num-ber of Hollywood films ("The 400 Million," "Hangmen Also Die," "The Forgotten Village") and, from 1940-1943, directed the Film Music Project of the New School for Social Research, whose objec-tive was to study the application of modern musical techniques to film music. This book is the result of his American experience, "an account of theoretical and practical experiences with cinema music" (introduction). Eisler's highly developed critical standards and uncompromising attitude towards "industrialized culture" lead to a critical, generally pessimistic but constantly stimulating view of film music as shackled by the commercial ideology of the industry. Nevertheless, accepting the limitations, he tries to see how a com-poser can function best, and to identify aesthetic potentialities. Hav-ing caustically outlined some "prejudices and bad habits" (leitmotifs, clichés, etc.) he discusses, with specific examples, the dramatur-gical functions of film music, going on to suggest the possibilities

offered by new musical resources. The social function of film music and aesthetic issues are also examined, before he turns to practical aspects of the film production process affecting the composer.
The suggestions for improving the situation that conclude the main
text are the result of his Film Music Project experience, which is
fully described in the appendix.

1307.   FAULKNER, Robert R. Hollywood studio musicians: their
         work and careers in the recording industry. Chicago:
         Aldine Atherton, 1971. 218p. bibliog. notes.
         This sociological study explores the position of the free-
lance professional musician (creative artist) within the film world
structure (commercial mass entertainment), and his attitudes towards it, in particular the degree of acceptance and alienation. Following description of the procedures involving musicians in film production, and the divisions of studio labor, the author uses interview
material to illustrate and discuss the dilemma musicians face when
choosing a commercial career (youthful aspirations, and the idea of
comparative failure with regard to artistic fulfillment in a concert
milieu), and their positive and negative responses to the job and its
routines, particularly the degree to which they consider their skill
is fully exploited and their professional dignity maintained. The hir-
ing structure, and musicians' business perspectives--with associated
fears and constraints--are also discussed.

1308.   KORNGOLD, Luzi. Erich Wolfgang Korngold: ein Lebens-
         bild. Vienna: Lafite, 1967. (Österreichische Kompon-
         isten des XX. Jahrhunderts, 10) 111p. illus.
         A biographical portrait by his wife, of the Austrian-born
composer (1897-1957) who astonished European music circles as a
child prodigy--a second Mozart--but who, in the post-war years,
was derided critically in his homeland. Korngold composed the music for 18 Hollywood films between 1936 and 1946, living permanently in California from 1938. In her account of her husband's involvement with Hollywood, which began in 1934 with the arrangement of
Mendelssohn's music for Max Reinhardt's "Midsummer Night's
Dream," Mrs. Korngold has much of interest to say about the early
pressures exerted upon Korngold by Hollywood, about his initial
fears and reluctance (especially over "Robin Hood," 1938), the virtually ideal working arrangement he obtained, his general approach
to film composition, the appeal of its operatic qualities, and something of his technique. Of the films that followed "Robin Hood"
("Sea Hawk," "King's Row," etc.) she says very little, giving the
impression that Korngold regarded his work as bread-and-butter,
and recalling the delight she felt when, at the end of the war, he
returned to composing concert music. (This image of the return of
peace releasing his creativity would appeal to artistic European minds
who had experienced the pain of a homeland destroyed by war, and
who had never quite accepted the optimism of Hollywood, and its
ability to reduce all art to dollars and cents when necessary; but it
ignores the fact, made clear by Tony Thomas in his section on Korngold in no. 1315--in which he makes considerable use of Mrs. Korngold's recollections--that Korngold drew heavily on his film scores

for these later works. Korngold, like many others, thought highly of
his music for the screen.) A list of works is included.

1309. LIMBACHER, James L., comp. Film music: from violins
        to video. Metuchen: Scarecrow Press, 1974. 835p.
        bibliog. (p. 190-1), discog.
        A mighty, dual-purpose volume on the background music to
films, combining between two covers the roles of anthology and reference work. In the first part there are 50 short articles on aspects
of film music by 32 individuals closely connected with the musical
side of the industry (including Elmer Bernstein, David Raksin and
Miklos Rozsa). These are reprinted from various sources, covering 1946 to 1971, and are grouped in subject sections such as "the
early days," "scoring the dramatic film," and "classical music on
the screen." The main part of the book is the large, impressive
international index of film composers and their music. This is divided into four parts: (i) an alphabetical list of film titles with release dates, acting as an index to (ii), in which film titles are listed
under their release year (1908-1972) with composers' names; (iii) a
composer listing, with film titles listed chronologically under each
name; (iv) a discography of 78s, 45s and LPs, arranged by title,
with label and release numbers. This is a tremendous achievement,
which shows all the signs of being definitive. The books concludes
with an index to Part 1.

1310. LONDON, Kurt. Film music: a summary of the charac-
        teristic features of its history, aesthetics, technique; and
        possible developments; translated by Eric S. Bensinger;
        with a foreword by Constant Lambert. London: Faber,
        1936. (Repr. New York: Arno Press, 1970). 280p.
        illus.
        Although it does not consider the American film at all, being
chiefly concerned with the history of technical features involving music in Europe, London's classic early history says much about the
function of film music and the various associated problems as they
appeared in the 1930s that has some application to America. He
himself considers the American film at the time to be more notable
for its visual than for its musical effects.

1311. McCARTY, Clifford. Film composers in America: a check-
        list of their work; foreword by Lawrence Morton. Glen-
        dale: J. Valentine, 1953. (Repr. New York: Da Capo,
        1972). 193p.
        Though largely superseded by Limbacher (no. 1309), this
checklist of background music to films is still of value; not only does
it include under a composer films in which he acted as musical director or orchestrator, it also provides the names of arrangers,
collaborators, composers of additional material, etc. Furthermore,
comparison with Limbacher for the period up to 1953 suggests that
many of the listings under individual names do not exactly correspond. McCarty's coverage is much smaller, however, including
only 163 composers in a work encompassing feature films, documentaries, shorts and cartoons from 1911 to 1953. Arrangement is

alphabetical by composer, and chronological under each name; an abbreviation for the producing organization follows each film title. There is an index of orchestrators, arrangers and adaptors, a title index of over 5,000 titles, and a list of Academy Award winners. The reprint edition updates the latter to 1972 (one of its few minor additions).

1312.   MANVELL, Roger, and HUNTLEY, John. The technique of film music; with the guidance of the following Committee appointed by the British Film Academy: William Alwyn (Chairman), Ken Cameron, Muir Mathieson, Basil Wright. London: Focal Press, 1957. 299p. illus. , bibliog. , discog.

_____.   . Rev. and enlarged by Richard Arnell and Peter Day. London: Focal Press, 1975. 310p. illus. , bibliog.

This impressive historical and technical survey of the use of music in films, particularly those made in the U.S. and in Britain, has a specific objective: "to help resolve the comparative lack of understanding of music by film-makers and the lack of a proper recognition of the art and craft of film-making by many composers" (introduction--William Alwyn). The authors show first how music for silent films grew out of incidental theater music, and how the first principles of film music composition were developed up to 1935. The central section of the book explores the techniques involved, first in "realistic" music--music that is an integral part of the action of a film--and second in "functional" music. Various types of "functional" music are isolated and examined, with illustrations: music for types of action, for places and periods, for tension, comedy and emotion. This section includes an attempt to reproduce on the printed page the way music links with visual effects in scenes from three films: "Louisiana Story" (music by Virgil Thomson), "Julius Caesar" (Miklos Rozsa) and the British "Odd Man Out" (Alwyn). Musical notation, photographic stills, and short descriptions of the action are juxtaposed effectively, but the authors admit the techniques to do this adequately have not been evolved. Concluding the survey are accounts of the function of the music director, and some composers' viewpoints (including David Raksin, Hugo Friedhofer, Rozsa, Max Steiner, Aaron Copland). In the appendix an "outline history of film music" provides details of film titles and composers for 1895-1955. The discography is an extensive selection of recordings in composer order, with many annotations. The 2nd edition, besides updating the 1st, omits the discography, expands the bibliography, adds sections on the underground and pop music, increases the numbers of composers' points of view, and discusses some post-1955 films. Index.

1313.   PALMER, Christopher. Miklos Rozsa: a sketch of his life and work; with a foreword by Eugene Ormandy. London: Breitkopf & Härtel, 1975. 78p. illus.

A short but excellent introduction to the music of the Hungarian composer (b. Budapest, 1907) who came to the U.S. in 1940 and whose career as a composer for the screen includes over 80 film scores. Rozsa's compositions also include numerous pieces in the art music tradition, and, following a biographical sketch and a general "perspective," Palmer discusses virtually all of these. In his section on the film music he confines himself to the major scores, from "Thief of Bagdad" (1940) and "Jungle Book" (1942) through "Spellbound" (1945), "Madame Bovary" (1949) and "Quo Vadis" (1951) to "Julius Caesar" (1953), "Ben Hur" (1959) and "El Cid" (1960). (A full-scale study of the film music is evidently in preparation, and is an event to look forward to.) Forty-four music examples accompany the text; these are collected together at the back, preceding the photographic illustrations, the list of concert works, and the filmography.

1314. SMOLIAN, Steven, comp. A handbook of film, theater, and television music on record, 1948-1969. New York: The Record Undertaker, 1970. 2v.

In need of updating, but still useful, this specialized LP discography is described by the compiler as not definitive but "a gathering of available information." Its scope includes film background music. The first of the two 64-page booklets is a tabulated listing, arranged by show title; for each show information is given on category (sound track, television musical, original cast recording, etc.), date (year of release or premiere), title and composer, label, issue (earliest date traced for release of recording), and cut-out (i.e., deletion) date. The second volume is a listing of this information by label, with a composer index.

1315. THOMAS, Tony. Music for the movies. New York: Barnes; London: Tantivy Press, 1973. 270p. illus., discog.

This excellent book tells the story of film background music from the 1930s on in a series of detailed portraits and informal assessments of outstanding Hollywood film music composers; they are grouped according to common characteristics, and include Victor Young, John Green, and Alfred Newman; Dimitri Tiomkin, Franz Waxman, Bronislau Kaper and Miklos Rozsa; Max Steiner and Erich Korngold; Bernard Herrmann, Hugo Friedhofer and David Raksin; George Antheil, Virgil Thomson, Aaron Copland, Alex North and Elmer Bernstein; Henry Mancini, Leonard Rosenman, Jerry Goldsmith and Lalo Schifrin. Much of the information came from interviews, conducted by the author over a period of years as a broadcaster with the Canadian Broadcasting Company. There are also examples of composers' writings on their trade (e.g., Rozsa). Supplementary material includes a discography of film music on records, arranged by composer, a list of each composer's film scores, with dates and the name of the film corporation, and an index.

i. Stars and Personalities of the Musical Stage and Screen

FRED ASTAIRE

1316. ASTAIRE, Fred. Steps in time. New York: Harper, 1959; London: Heinemann, 1960. 338p. illus.

Astaire's gentlemanly and, as one would expect, sprightly autobiography describes the course of a long and distinguished career in stage and film musicals, from his partnership with his sister Adele--which included Gershwin's "Lady Be Good" (1924) and "Funny Face" (1927), and which ended with Howard Dietz and Arthur Schwartz's "Band Wagon" in 1931--to the film of Cole Porter's "Silk Stockings" (1957). As the first to sing numerous famous songs by Gershwin, Berlin, etc., Astaire occupies a central place in the history of popular song--and his importance as a singer has been recognized by Berlin among others--but in his own story song is secondary to anecdotes involving production, his co-partners, and--above all-- dance. He declines to be drawn into any discussion even of this, however: "I just dance," he concludes, disarmingly. There is a list of shows, and an index of names.

1317. GREEN, Stanley, and GOLDBLATT, Burt. Starring Fred
        Astaire. New York: Dodd, Mead, 1973. 501p. illus.,
        discog.
        A richly illustrated album of Astaire's distinguished stage
and film career with full details of the shows in which he was involved. A biographical account to 1933 is followed by a chronological list of stage shows with authors' names, cast, musical numbers, opening date and number of performances. The main part of the book is devoted to descriptions of 35 movies, from "Dancing Lady" (1933) to "Midas Run" (1969), including four with no featured singing or dancing. For each film the authors give background details, plot, an account of the critical reception and comprehensive production information. Supplementary material includes a list of radio and television appearances, a discography of 78s, 45s and LPs from 1923 to 1971, a chronological table of Astaire's career, a list of 21 songs with his music, and an index.

GEORGE M. COHAN

1318. MOREHOUSE, Ward. George M. Cohan, prince of the
        American theater. Philadelphia: Lippincott, 1943.
        (Repr. Westport: Greenwood Press, 1971). 240p. illus.
        Stanley Green (no. 1256) brackets Cohan (1878-1942) with
Victor Herbert, calling them "the two most important creative figures of the American musical stage during the first decade of the twentieth century" (p. 25). In contrast to Herbert, Cohan epitomized the new century--confident, energetic, fast-moving--and this was the basis of his popularity. Morehouse's biography, itself breezy and energetic, describes how the composer of such popular standards as "Mary's a Grand Old Name" and "Give My Regards to Broadway" came from a family of vaudevilleans, and traces his career from "The Four Cohans" to first Broadway success ("Little Johnny Jones," 1904) and subsequent versatile Broadway-centered existence as composer and lyricist, actor, playwright and producer. Morehouse sets out "to tell this story against the ever-changing background of the New York and American stage for a half century and more" (foreword), paying less attention to details of Cohan's personal life and to describing the

nature of his creative talent. Cohan himself wrote an autobiography (Twenty Years on Broadway and the Years It Took to Get There: the true story of a trouper's life from the cradle to the 'closed shop.' New York: Harper, 1925. 264p. illus.), in which he was mainly concerned with his early life in vaudeville. Morehouse declares "its easy informality, its somewhat self-conscious, frequently apologetic, chip-on-the-shoulder style was certainly Cohan all the way" (p. 170).

JUDY GARLAND

1319. DEANS, Mickey. Weep no more, my lady, by Mickey Deans and Ann Pinchot. New York: Hawthorn Books, 1972. 247p. illus.
_____. Weep no more, my lady: an intimate biography of Judy Garland, by Mickey Deans, her last husband, and Ann Pinchot. London: Allen, 1972. 238p. illus.
_____. _____. St. Albans: Mayflower Books, 1973. 221p. illus.
Chiefly concerned with their relatively short life together, in the months before Judy Garland's death in London in 1969, Deans' personal portrait is enlightening for the account it contains of the way the singer looked back on her career, particularly her "bondage" to MGM ("I was born at the age of twelve on the MGM lot"), and the role played by her mother.

1320. FRANK, Gerold. Judy. New York: Harper & Row; London: Allen, 1975. 654p. illus.
Of the crop of books on Judy Garland (1922-1969) that appeared in 1975 (see Appendix), Frank's biography is by far the most comprehensive. While others relied heavily on press cuttings, etc., he was fortunate enough to have access to family papers and correspondence, and to have enjoyed the confidence of Judy's immediate family and of several husbands (among whom Sid Luft was the most forthcoming). In addition, Frank was commissioned to assist Judy to write her own story, a project which never materialized. The massively detailed, unsentimentally told story is compulsive reading, and a memorable impression is left of the many facets and contradictions of her personality--and of its remarkable power over others --though it is perhaps a pity that Frank elected to enliven his narrative with recaptured conversations (it appears his informants can even remember which four-letter words they used and when), which inevitably lend the book a quasi-fictional air. There is a good deal about her relationship with her family and with the film studios, and something of the complex interconnections between her private and public personalities comes across. The book is, however, a little short on perceptive appreciation of what made her singing and performing so outstanding. Index.

ETHEL MERMAN

1321. MERMAN, Ethel. Don't call me madam. London: Allen, 1955. 215p. illus.

_____ . Who could ask for anything more; as told to Pete
Martin. Garden City: Doubleday, 1955. 252p. illus.
As irrepressible in prose as she ever was on stage or
screen, Ethel Merman (b. 1909) the author has at her disposal an
apparently bottomless reservoir of anecdotes and jokes to describe
her life and career. Though she is very fond of a digression one
may follow her through her colorful versions of numerous outstanding Broadway and Hollywood musicals in which she starred, including "Girl Crazy" (Gershwin), "Anything Goes," "Panama Hattie,"
"Red Hot and Blue," "DuBarry Was a Lady" (Porter), "Annie Get
Your Gun" and "Call Me Madam" (Berlin).

12. Popular Song Entertainers

1322.   BARNES, Ken. Sinatra and the great song stylists; with
        contributions from Stan Britt, Arthur Jackson, Fred Del-
        lar and Chris Ellis. London: Ian Allan, 1972. 192p.
        illus.
A knowledgeable team of British writers presents a series of
portraits of popular singers from Al Jolson to Andy Williams. A
short historical account of the development of popular song precedes
the first, most substantial group--"the great individualists"--which
includes Jolson, Louis Armstrong, Bing Crosby, Ella Fitzgerald,
Judy Garland, Frank Sinatra, Peggy Lee, Nat King Cole, Doris
Day, Mel Torme, Sarah Vaughan and Tony Bennett. Mainly biographical, these portraits also offer general comments on the singer's
style and contribution, and lists of recommended recordings. Considerably briefer are the profiles that follow: of 18 male and female artists from Sophie Tucker to Rosemary Clooney, grouped under the heading "style and personality"; of seven performers from
the area where jazz and popular song overlap (including Mildred
Bailey and Jimmy Rushing); of vocal groups (an overall view); and
of six male ballad singers. The concluding portraits of Perry Como
and Andy Williams are longer, and again have recommended recordings. Index.

1323.   PLEASANTS, Henry. The great American popular singers.
        New York: Simon & Schuster; London: Gollancz, 1974.
        384p. illus.
A landmark in the critical appreciation of popular singers,
this study combines the tools of art and popular music criticism to
dispel the clouds of critical doubt surrounding the singers, arising
from their categorization as "popular," and to show them as un-
questionably worthy of greater acceptance on the basis of their artistry. The author presents a series of 22 portraits of singers he
regards as most innovative and influential in the Afro-American
idiom. In his introduction he establishes the principal area of
achievement--in relating singing to language--and directs his study
deliberately at song technique, as more important in this field than
type of song. A chapter on the art of the popular singer relates

their aims and accomplishments to exponents of Italian "bel canto" (who also accepted song "as a lyrical extension of speech"), stresses the significance of the microphone, and points to various differences between popular and classical singers. The portraits themselves, covering all main categories of popular music, are of Al Jolson, Bessie Smith, Ethel Waters, Louis Armstrong, Jimmie Rodgers, Bing Crosby, Mildred Bailey, Billie Holiday, Ella Fitzgerald, Frank Sinatra, Mahalia Jackson, Nat King Cole, Hank Williams, Ray Charles, Elvis Presley, Judy Garland, Johnny Cash, B. B. King, Aretha Franklin, Ethel Merman, Peggy Lee and Barbra Streisand. They are eloquent studies that combine character portrayal and some biographical detail with astute analysis and assessment of stylistic characteristics and achievement. No discographical information is given, unfortunately, but there is an index.

NAT KING COLE

1324.   COLE, Maria. Nat King Cole: an intimate biography, by Maria Cole, with Louie Robinson. New York: Morrow, 1971; London: W. H. Allen, 1972. illus., discog.
An affectionate personal portrait of the jazz pianist and popular singer (1919-1965) is drawn here by his widow, who, with recreated conservations, outlines a general picture of his character and of their life together, narrates the main events in his life and career, and recalls some of the ways in which he encountered racial prejudice. The 20-page discography is a chronological title listing from 1943 to 1964, with album release numbers.

BING CROSBY

1325.   CROSBY, Bing. Call me lucky; as told to Pete Martin. New York: Simon & Schuster, 1953. 344p. illus.
_____ . Call me lucky. London: Muller, 1953. 253p. illus.
Fine as light reading, with its wealth of funny stories, Bing's autobiography does not give a very clear outline of his career. His days in Hollywood form the background to most of the anecdotes, but there is some mention of his time with Paul Whiteman, featuring Mildred Bailey, Bix Beiderbecke, Eddie Lang and Joe Venuti. Index.

1326.   BASSETT, John, et al. The Bing Crosby mini-discography, 1926-1974, by John Bassett, Leslie Gaylor and Bert Bishop. (2nd ed.) Cwmbran: International Crosby Circle, 1974. 40p.
BASSETT, John, and BISHOP, Bert. The Bing Crosby LP-ography; (with an introduction by Bing Crosby). Cwmbran: International Crosby Circle, 1973. 81p.
BISHOP, A. S., and BASSETT, J. D. The A-Z of Bing Crosby: (a title listing). Cwmbran: International Crosby Circle, 1971. unpaged.
These three useful volumes, produced by members of the British-based International Crosby Circle, are largely complementary,

the first and the third being particularly interdependent. The first edition of the mini-discography was compiled by Frank Murphy and Jean-Paul Frerault. This revised version lists Bing's recordings, from "I've Got the Girl" in October 1926 to "We Love Old St. Mary's" in December 1973, in strict date order, with matrix numbers and alternate takes. The reason for the designation "mini" is that personnel are not listed; this information must be sought in the "A-Z," which also serves as a title index to the mini-discography.

The LP-ography is basically an alphabetical label-by-label listing of 300 or so LPs and their contents, preference being given to U.K. releases. Under each label name the albums are arranged in catalogue number order, with all the songs on each album listed under the album title. No extra information--date, location, personnel--is given, nor any indication of whether the LP is an original or a reissue. The "A-Z" can supply some details of personnel and the year of recording of the individual songs. The main list is supported by a simplified version, giving just issue numbers, and by an alphabetical index of album titles. (There is no song title index, and to discover the whereabouts of a particular song one must refer to the "A-Z" to ascertain a date, then to the mini-discography to discover a number; where this number and the catalogue number are one and the same, one can refer to the LP-ography to reveal the album title.)

The function of the "A-Z"-title index to each of Bing's commercially issued recordings is largely that of an adjunct to the other two. Following each song title the year the record was mastered is given, followed by the name of the musical accompanist (solo or band), and, in parentheses, the vocal accompanist. In this and the other volumes the compilers adopt the unconventional practice of making definite and indefinite articles count for filing purposes. (All three publications are available to members of the International Crosby Circle from the Secretary, Reg Bristo, 7, Greenmeadow Close, Cwmbran, Gwent, Wales. Another Circle publication, The Road to Bing Crosby, is being planned.)

1327. CROSBY, Ted, and CROSBY, Larry. Bing. Los Angeles: Bolton Printing Co., 1937. 205p. illus.
CROSBY, Ted. The story of Bing Crosby; with a foreword by Bob Hope. Cleveland: World, 1946. 239p. illus., discog.

The second of these two biographies is described as a revised edition of the first. Without any disrespect to Bing (b. 1904), his fellow-traveler Bob Hope virtually steals this particular show with a splendid little preface. Bing's brother Ted's affectionately drawn biography describes his rise to celebrity and his career to 1937. A preliminary note declares: "some of the names and places mentioned in this book are fictitious, and any resemblance to actual people or places is purely accidental,"--but "all incidents are true" saith Bing in his own preamble.

SAMMY DAVIS JR.

1328. DAVIS, Sammy. Yes, I can: the story of Sammy Davis

Jr. , by Sammy Davis Jr. , and Jane and Burt Boyar.
New York: Farrar, Straus & Giroux; London: Cassell,
1965. 612p. illus.
————————. ————————. New York: Pocket Books, 1966.
626p. illus.
Powerful personal story of the singer (b. 1925), vividly portraying the problems of being black in the show business world.
Written in the style of a fast-moving novel, with a strong reliance
on recreated conversations, it is an evocative self-portrait, which
includes appearances by many other figures in the film and musical
world.

LENA HORNE

1329. HORNE, Lena, and SCHICKEL, Richard. Lena. Garden
City: Doubleday, 1965; London: Deutsch, 1966. 300p.
illus.
————————. ————————. New York: New American Library,
1966. 224p. illus.
Autobiography of the singer and actress (b. 1917), covering
her childhood in Brooklyn and various Southern cities, her first engagement at the Cotton Club (1933), tours with Noble Sissle (1935-6),
leading role in Lew Leslie's "Blackbirds of 1939," discovery by
MGM's Roger Edens, first films ("Cabin in the Sky," "Stormy Weather") and subsequent career up to her involvement with the Civil
Rights movement in 1963.

AL JOLSON

1330. FREEDLAND, Michael. Jolson. London: Allen, 1972.
318p. illus.
————————. ————————. New York: Stein & Day, 1972. 256p.
illus.
Staggeringly successful in his lifetime (1886-1950), Jolson's
reputation since his death as a singer of lasting appeal has dwindled
and been left increasingly to devotees. Examination of the kind begun by Henry Pleasants (no. 1323) could do much to rekindle it.
This easy-going biography, while it conveys a good deal of information and has clearly been long-researched, offers the fruits of the
author's labors in a presentation that neither asks nor expects any
effort by the reader, and contributes little to our knowledge of, for
instance, Jolson's use of the blackface tradition, or the sources of
his style. Much of the text reads rather like fiction (Jolson seems
to be stuck with this kind of treatment--cf. Sieben, no. 1333) and
there is such minimal attention to other things going on in the popular music world that the uninitiated might imagine Jolson was the
"world's greatest entertainer" because he was the only one. Index.

1331. JAY, Dave. Jolsonography; written, compiled, annotated
and published by Dave Jay. Washington: Big Time Press,
(1966). 320p. illus. , bibliog. , discogs.
————————. Jolsonography: the world's greatest reference
book on the world's greatest entertainer; written, compiled

and annotated by Dave Jay. 2nd ed. Bournemouth: Barrie Anderton, 1974. 284p. illus., bibliog., discogs.

Of the first edition the compiler states: "For the first time, something of excellence and integrity, something worthy of Jolson has been written of him, even if I had to write it myself"; and indeed the colossal amount of detailed information here on the products of Jolson's career as singer, songwriter, stage personality, film actor, etc. bears witness to the compiler's zeal and lifelong devotion to his subject. There are ten sections: a chronological discography with full details; a second, "simplified" discography arranged by label series, including private releases and providing plentiful historical notes on each label (a title index is supplied for this section); a miscellaneous discography of Jolson's professional associates, of songs mentioning his name, of imitations of the Jolson style, and of "Mammy" songs; a "stageography" listing all the Broadway shows in which Jolson appeared, with details of performers and songs, and short discographies of other versions of famous items; a "screenography" performing the same service for motion pictures in which Jolson appeared and/or sang; a "radiography" listing songs sung by Jolson on his own and other radio programs; a "songography" detailing all songs written in full or in part by Jolson, with information on co-writers and recordings; a "sheet-music-ography" cataloging all sheet music bearing Jolson's name and/or picture; a bibliography of books, part of books, whole magazines, articles, portraits, obituaries and news items; and a "factography" chronicling, year by year, the significant events in Jolson's life. The illustrations (tipped-in Xerox reproductions of photos and record labels) are the least successful ingredient in a remarkable work, which would have benefitted from more extensive indexing. The second edition is described as complete as to known material up to April 1969. (Jay died in October 1969.) (It is available from 70 Southcote Road, Bournemouth, Hants., England.)

1332. JOLSON, Harry. Mistah Jolson; as told to Alban Emley. Hollywood: House-Warren, 1957. 257p. illus.

The autobiographical reminiscences of Al Jolson's elder brother (born Hirsch Yoelson), whom he partnered in vaudeville acts at the beginning of his career (1901-1905). Harry Jolson later had a career as an individual vaudeville and minstrel performer.

1333. SIEBEN, Pearl. The immortal Jolson: his life and times. New York: Fell, 1962. 231p.

Rather superficial show-biz biography of Jolson's life and career that makes little attempt to examine the nature of his achievement or the reasons for his magnetic appeal. That much-traveled fly-on-the-wall who feeds the conversations of heroes to their biographers worked overtime here, and enables the author to do some rudimentary psychologizing ("his ego was gargantuan, but behind it was an inferiority complex that made the ego minute by comparison.")

FRANK SINATRA

1334. HAINSWORTH, Brian. Songs by Sinatra. Bramhope, Leeds: the author, 1973. 92p.

A discography listing all known Sinatra recordings "from his earliest sessions with Harry James to his final session for Reprise" (in October, 1970--shortly before the "retirement"). Arrangement is chronological, and information given for each date includes place, accompanying orchestra, arranger where known, titles (including un-issued material), matrix numbers, 78 rpm label name and release numbers, and major LP reissue/issue labels and numbers. No sup-plementary indexes.

1335. KAHN, E. J. The voice: the story of an American phe-nomenon (Frank Sinatra). New York: Harper; London: Musicians Press, 1947. 125p. illus.

A description of Sinatra's life-style and the "Sinatra-mania" of the time, describing his unique place in the entertainment world of the 1940s. Generally subjective in approach, and with little bio-graphical detail or musical comment, the text is based on articles for the New Yorker, Oct. and Nov., 1946.

1336. LONSTEIN, Albert I., and MARINO, Vito R. The compleat Sinatra: discography, filmography, television appear-ances, motion picture appearances, radio appearances, concert appearances, stage appearances. Monroe, N.Y.: Library Research Associates, 1970. 383p. illus.

Sinatra is probably the supreme example of the versatility of the 20th century entertainer, as is demonstrated in these detailed records of his activities in the seven different contexts listed in the title. The first eight chapters are bio-discographical, each chapter relating to a phase in Sinatra's career from 1939 to 1970, each with a short biographical summary and a full discography (orchestra, personnel, date, place, matrix, title, release number). These are followed by: chronologies of TV appearances with lists of songs performed, and of film appearances, with full credits, usually a synopsis, and a general assessment of the movie; a list of airchecks; a title listing of songs recorded, with names of composers and lyri-cists; an album listing with contents; a sample list of concerts; a list of names of orchestral arrangers, composers, soloists, vocal-ists and groups with whom Sinatra worked; various addenda. Un-fortunately, an otherwise excellent compilation is marred by being unnecessarily difficult to use. The various title and name lists are just that, not indexes--there are no proper indexes. The contents page lacks page numbers, and there are no running heads for the various sections. So locating pieces of information becomes rather a matter of luck or stubborn perseverance.

1337. SHAW, Arnold. Sinatra: twentieth century romantic. New York: Holt, Rinehart & Winston, 1968. 371p. illus. _____. Sinatra: retreat of the romantic. London: Allen, 1968. 392p. illus.

An enjoyable biography of Sinatra the star, describing his

career from discovery by Harry James and Tommy Dorsey to his 50th birthday, Dec., 1965. Shaw approaches his subject with a knowledge of the development of popular culture and sets Sinatra clearly in this context, chronicling the divergences of his career in a readable manner, and concentrating on the public figure, without attempting to analyze style or musical contribution. Appendices are devoted to an outline of his career as a recording artist, with a list of his most recorded songs, and a brief assessment, and to a filmography.

13. Rock and Roll, and Rock

a. Reference Works

1338.   ROXON, Lillian. Rock encyclopedia. New York: Grosset & Dunlap, 1969. 611p. illus., discogs.
   The entries in this work cover groups, individuals, styles and "sounds" from the rock music world in the U.S. and U.K., and include some influential figures from blues, folk and gospel music. Unfortunately the compiler prefers impressionistic prose to all those boring facts one normally looks for in encyclopedias, and while there are some career data for individuals and groups they take a back seat to picturesque description and very generalized evaluation. Each entry does, however, have a list of record titles and dates, divided into albums and singles (without label names and numbers). Each song title included in the album is listed. There are some cross references. An appendix lists top albums and singles for 1949-1968, and Billboard's Number 1 each week from 1950 to 1967.

1339.   STAMBLER, Irwin. Encyclopedia of pop, rock and soul. New York: St. Martin's Press, 1975. 609p. illus., bibliog.
   Similar in style and design to Stambler and Landon's folk and country encyclopedia (no. 610), this reference book is largely devoted to the careers of 500 individuals and groups from the 1960s and 1970s. More general topics of commercial, technical or stylistic interest are also included, and there are essays on the development of popular music styles by Stambler, Johnny Otis, and Michael Ochs. Entries are concise, with some general evaluative judgments but an emphasis on easily digestible facts.

1340.   WHITBURN, Joel, comp. Record research; compiled from Billboard Magazine's "Hot 100" charts, 1955-1969. Menomonee Falls, Wis.: Record Research, 1970. unpaged.
   _____. _____. Supplement. Menomonee Falls, Wis.: Record Research, 1971. unpaged.
   _____. (These two volumes reprinted as: Top pop records 1955-1970: facts about 9800 recordings listed in Billboard's "Hot 100" charts ... Detroit: Gale Research Co., 1972. unpaged.)

        _____. Top pop records, 1940-1955. Menomonee Falls,
Wis.: Record Research, 1973. 88p.
        _____. Top pop records, 1955-1972. Menomonee Falls,
Wis.: Record Research, 1973. 416p. illus.

As a reliable record of which music "singles" were popular
at a given time, and as a guide to their comparative popularity,
Billboard's weekly charts are invaluable. What Whitburn does in
these volumes is to reorganize the Billboard information into an
alphabetical artist listing. His first two volumes cover the period
from the inauguration of the "Hot 100" (initially "Top 100") chart
at the start of the rock and roll era to the end of the 1960s, and
include hit records by about 2,500 artists. Under each artist's
name information is given in five columns: date the record entered
the chart, highest position reached, total number of weeks in the
chart, record title, label name and number. The last volume listed
above, covering 1955-1972, expands the number of artists to 2,735
(the total number of records is over 11,000). The information regarding date of entry, etc., of each record is presented in the same
way, but this volume improves on its predecessor by providing a
title index, cross-referenced to the artist's name, and a chronological list of "Number 1" hits. The volume covering 1940-1955 also
has these additional features. This embraces the period covered by
Billboard's "Best Selling Singles" charts, the forerunner of the "Hot
100." In all it contains 1,700 hit records by 400 artists. (The
chronological approach to the popular hits is adopted by H. Kandy
Rohde in her The Gold of Rock and Roll, 1955-1967, New York:
Arbor House, 1970. 352p. illus., bibliog.)

1341. WOOD, Graham. An A-Z of rock and roll. London: Studio
      Vista, 1971. 128p. illus.

A biographical dictionary of 91 American and British rock
and roll stars (individuals and groups) who came to prominence in
the period 1955-1961. The entries give straightforward, factual accounts of their careers, with some information on outstanding recordings, but generally no evaluation. There are illustrations for
each. Also included are lists of major U.S. films of the period
featuring rock and roll performers, and of million-selling records.

b. Recordings

1342. ESCOTT, Colin, and HAWKINS, Martin. Catalyst: the
      Sun Records story. London: Aquarius Books, 1975.
      173p. illus., bibliog., discog.

Sam Phillips' "Sun" label, on which appeared the first records of Elvis Presley, Carl Perkins, Jerry Lee Lewis and Johnny
Cash, occupies an important place in the early development of rock
music, particularly with the style of "rockabilly"--the commercial
mingling of hillbilly with rhythm and blues. This history aims "to
use a study of Sun--its distinctive sound, its artists and its market
--as a starting point for wider study of the environment that spawned
popular music as we know it today" (foreword). Because of Presley's importance in bringing a black approach to country music the

story of his association with Sun Records (founded in 1952) in 1954-5 is told first, after which the authors describe Phillips' initial recording ventures from 1950, his involvement with blues, his turning away toward country styles, and his subsequent success with rockabilly and later with the "Memphis Sound." In the appendices are numerical lists of all records on each of Phillips' labels, including singles and LPs, and short biographical sketches of artists and personalities in the story. Index.

1343. ESCOTT, Colin, and HAWKINS, Martin. The Sun session file. Ashford, Kent: the authors, 1973-1974. 6v.
With these mimeographed volumes the authors perform a valuable service in listing the entire recordings made on Sam Phillips' "Sun" and "Phillips International" labels of Memphis from 1950 on. The areas covered by each volume are: 1) Jerry Lee Lewis and Billy Lee Riley; 2) Johnny Cash, Carl Perkins and country artists; 3) Elvis Presley, Roy Orbison and rock artists; 4) blues; 5) Charlie Rich, Carl Mann; 6) miscellany and index. In addition to discographical information there are numerous articles and interviews. The set is intended to supplement the same authors' book on the "Sun" label (no. 1342), and none of this information is duplicated there.

1344. GILLETT, Charlie. Making tracks: Atlantic Records and the growth of a multi-billion-dollar industry. New York: Dutton; London: Allen, 1975. 305p. illus., bibliog.
Though much lighter in weight than Gillett's Sound of the City (no. 1350) this is in some ways a complementary study, as it sets out to meet and describe some of the people responsible for the history of post-war popular music recorded in the earlier volume. One reason Gillett chose Atlantic for this purpose was the enduring quality of much of the company's management. The story of how Atlantic Records grew from modest, independent beginnings in 1947 as a jazz, and later rhythm and blues, label to a fully-fledged popular music industry (taken over by Warner Bros.) emerges through numerous interviews with significant people such as founders Herb Abramson and Ahmet Ertegun, arranger Jesse Stone, songwriters Jerry Leiber and Mike Stoller, producer Rick Hall, and, most important, vice-president Jerry Wexler. The chronology is not Gillett's primary concern, however; what interests him most is the area where business and music overlap, and this motivates his probing into the various activities. Index.

1345. HIRSCH, Paul. The structure of the popular music industry: the filtering process by which records are presented for public consumption. Ann Arbor: Institute of Social Research of the University of Michigan, (1970?). 72p. bibliog. notes.
A socio-economic investigation of the preselection system in the record industry, whereby oversupply of material is reduced before the consumer is involved in selection himself. The organization of the industry is examined, and broken down into six stages of creation, filtration and consumption, from the artist to the public; all this before popular acclaim is possible.

1346.   VERNON, Paul. The Sun legend. London: Steve Lane, 1969. 64p. illus.

Though lacking the detail of the Escott & Hawkins volumes (no. 1343), this is a good short guide to the records issued by the Sun Record Company, with which Elvis Presley, Carl Perkins and Johnny Cash first recorded. There is an introductory history of Sun, 1953-1966, followed by a numerical listing of the singles, with artist's name, title, and matrix number for each, some notes, and an artist index. There are also listings of EPs and LPs, with titles of all tracks, and some biographical notes.

1347.   WILLIAMS, Richard. Out of his head: the sound of Phil Spector. New York: Outerbridge & Lazard; New York: Dutton, 1972. 206p. illus., discog.

A lively account of the career of one of the most innovatory and influential producers of pop music records in the 1960s, whose celebrated "Spector Sound" was an individual concoction with strong roots in rhythm and blues and in gospel music. Williams' outline focuses particularly on the Phillies label (1961-1966), for which Spector produced hit songs by the black female groups, the Crystals and the Ronettes, and the white Righteous Brothers. The discography includes date of entry into Billboard's "Hot 100," and the highest position reached. There is also a list of songs by Spector, alone and in collaboration, and an index of names and titles.

c.   Histories and Other Studies

1348.   BELZ, Carl. The story of rock. New York: Oxford University Press, 1969. 256p. illus., discog.
         .   . 2nd ed. New York: Oxford University Press, 1972. 286p. illus., bibliog., discog.

Based on a view of rock as a folk art, this is a sober chronological survey, examining the origins of rock, the style and influences of a succession of rock artists from the early 1950s to the late 1960s, and relating the music to the media. Belz deals in detail with outstanding figures, such as Presley, Dylan, the Beatles, but attempts no musical analysis. The discography is a selected list of singles from 1953 to 1963. The 2nd edition contains a bibliographic essay. Index.

1349.   COHN, Nik. Pop from the beginning. London: Weidenfeld & Nicolson, 1969. 238p. illus.
         . Rock from the beginning. New York: Stein & Day, 1969. 256p. illus.
         . Awopbopaloobop alopbamboom: pop from the beginning. London: Paladin, 1970. 244p. illus.

Chatty in style and streaked with jargon, but generally objective in approach, this general, chronological survey by an English critic of the emergence of rock and roll, and the development of rock in the U.S. and Britain up to 1967 concentrates on portraits of musicians and of their public image; Cohn also describes the influence of American artists on English rock and vice versa. Index.

1350.   GILLETT, Charlie. The sound of the city: the rise of
         rock and roll. New York: Outerbridge & Dienstfrey,
         1970; New York: Dell, 1972. 375p. bibliog., discog.
         _____.   _____. London: Souvenir Press; London:
         Sphere Books, 1971. 387p. bibliog., discog.
         This well-researched and clearly presented account of the
origins, emergence and development of rock is based on a detailed
study of the intricate, fluctuating relationships and interactions in
the triangle of recording industry/artist/audience. Basing his account on the hit records of the period, the author describes first
the emergence and development of rock and roll in the period 1954-
1958. In this he outlines the progression from insipid popular music to a virile new style by a process of interaction between major
and minor companies, majority and minority audiences, and artists
able to fuse elements from different styles. Following this, he
delves further back and describes the development of the music out
of which rock and roll sprang--the rhythm and blues and gospel
sounds of 1945-1956. The course taken by blues after the emergence
of rock and roll and up to 1969 is also described. Gillett concludes
with a study of the music that evolved from rock and roll. There
are examples of lyrics but not of music. A chronological list of
hit singles, a selection of anthology albums, a bibliography of background book material and periodical titles, and an index complete
the book.

1351.   GOLDSTEIN, Richard, ed. The poetry of rock. New York:
         Bantam Books, 1969. 147p. illus.
         A collection of some 70 rock music lyrics from Chuck Berry
to the Doors. The editor's introduction picks out some of their
principal characteristics, and he also prefaces many of the lyrics
with comments on individual artists and writers.

1352.   HALL, Douglas Kent, and CLARK, Sue C. Rock: a world
         bold as love; photographed and edited by Douglas Kent
         Hall from interviews by Sue C. Clark. New York:
         Cowles, 1970. 192p. illus.
         A collection of photographs and excerpts from interviews
with artists from the worlds of rock, blues, gospel and soul, carried out in the second half of 1969. The interviewees reflect on
music in general, on particular styles, and on mutual influences.
Other subjects include the influence of blues, gospel music, rock and
roll, performing at festivals, television, audiences and, last but not
least, themselves. Index of artists.

1353.   HOPKINS, Jerry. Festival! the book of American music
         celebrations; text by Jerry Hopkins; photographs by Jim
         Marshall ... New York: Macmillan; London: Collier-
         Macmillan, 1970. 191p. illus.
         Twelve festivals are described and illustrated, including
Woodstock, Newport, Monterey and Berkeley, and covering rock,
blues, jazz, folk, country and western, fiddling and bluegrass. The
photographs, which form a substantial part of the book, are largely
informal and include both artists and audience. The text describes

the history and development of festivals, especially those of the 1960s, and gives an account of individual events. Text and illustrations are not arranged so as to illuminate each other, and there is no index.

1354.   HOPKINS, Jerry. The rock story. New York: New American Library, 1970. 222p. illus., discog.

An informative and readable chronicle of rock from 1954 to 1968, with a brief outline of its roots. In Part 1 the author combines accounts of the major developments and descriptions of the principal protagonists with background material on the performing and recording industry, anecdotes on a variety of individuals and discussion of some related subjects, e.g., press and public reaction. The second part looks at some specific aspects of the musical scene and industry in the late 1960s: the making of an Aretha Franklin hit, economic questions, the role of the radio stations, the fans, male and female, three different types of idol, touring, and an account of the rise and decline of Buffalo Springfield. There is an LP discography, arranged by chapters, but no index.

1355.   JAHN, Mike. Rock: from Elvis Presley to the Rolling Stones. New York: Quadrangle, 1973. 326p. illus., bibliog. notes, discog.

Sometime rock critic for the New York Times, Jahn attempts, in his own words, "a complete overview of the rock age; a chronology which views the whole matter from a slight distance and reports on it as a whole" (p. ix). Generally dispassionate and (thankfully) unostentatious in approach, it is an informative year-by-year summary of musical developments from 1955 through 1969, with particular attention to the "key years" of 1956, 1957, 1964, 1965 and 1966. All the major individuals and groups are included, usually at one particular point in the chronology. Jahn's accent is on features on their recordings and their performances (with basic career details), rather than on the sensationalism and hyperbole of the day-to-day rock scene. Some thoughts on social implications are gathered together in the final chapter. There is a selective discography of recommended LPs, and an index.

1356.   LAING, Dave. The sound of our time. London: Sheed & Ward, 1969; Chicago: Quadrangle Books, 1970. 138p. bibliog.

A perceptive study of popular music of the 1950s and 1960s and its relation to society. The first part is concerned with the role of the technical and commercial media in the development of popular music in the 20th century, and the second with the rise of pop music on both sides of the Atlantic. Part 3 examines various artists, including the Beatles, Rolling Stones, Cream and Bob Dylan, and Part 4 presents some socio-philosophical lines for further study. No index.

1357.   MARCUS, Greil, ed. Rock and roll will stand. Boston: Beacon Press, 1969. 182p. discogs.

A collection of 21 pieces by seven West Coast writers, originally published in various journals about 1968. Some are retrospective, some analytical, and some are attempts to recapture the feeling of the music with words. The political background of Berkeley, 1968 is apparent, but the overriding importance of the music itself, words and music, is stressed. Several pieces are devoted to individual artists. The book as a whole aims to set out arguments for the lasting artistic value of the music.

1358. MELTZER, R. The aesthetics of rock. New York: Something Else Press, 1970. 346p. illus., bibliog. notes.
An attempt to describe rock music through a "parallel artistic effort" rather than by studying it "from without." Add to the complex thought trains that this effort produces in the author an apparent compulsion to draw on a philosophy major's heritage, and you have a difficult book that does not always stay close to its subject. There is no music, but there are many examples of lyrics.

1359. SCHAFER, William J. Rock music: where it's been, what it means, where it's going. Minneapolis: Augsburg, 1972. 128p. illus., bibliog., discog.
Taking a few steps back from the mythology of the subject, Schafer attempts a dispassionate discussion of rock's history and social significance. There are three main sections: a historical summary, tracing the development of rock from the blues to the Beatles, and noting broad trends; an examination of extra-musical features of the phenomenon (rock as language, as rebellion, as mythology, and so on); and a speculation on the future. Specifically musical features are not discussed.

1360. SHAW, Arnold. Rock revolution. New York: Crowell-Collier, 1969. 215p. illus., discog.
_____. _____. New York: Paperback Library, 1971. 251p. illus., discog.
A broadly chronological account of the sources and development of rock music, written from a background of experience in the music industry. The preliminary chapters describe the change in the role of the recording studio. Shaw then traces the rise of rock and roll in Presley and Haley, discusses sources in blues and rhythm and blues, and influential figures. His attention is focused subsequently on individuals, styles and trends of the 1960s: Bob Dylan, the Beatles and British groups, soul, and different styles of East and West Coast rock. There is a glossary, a selected discography related to each chapter, and an index.

1361. WISE, Herbert H., ed. Professional rock and roll. New York: Amsco; New York: Collier; London: Collier-Macmillan, 1967. 94p. illus., discog.
A collection of pieces by fifteen "experts," aiming to provide elementary practical information for the uninitiated on aspects of the performing of rock music. Subjects covered include forming a band, instruments and equipment, lead singing, touring, reading music, managers, agents and publishers.

d. Collections of Rock Criticism

1362. CHRISTGAU, Robert. Any old way you choose it: rock and other pop music, 1967-1973. Baltimore: Penguin, 1973. 330p.

With the exception of an autobiographical introduction on how he became a rock critic (and what sort of a rock critic he became), the pieces in Christgau's anthology are all reprinted from magazines (Esquire, Village Voice, Newsday, New York Times). They portray many different sides of the rock scene, with an emphasis on the stars, seen through the eyes of one who describes himself (p. 9) as being of a "polemical temperament." Index.

1363. EISEN, Jonathan, ed. The age of rock: sounds of the American cultural revolution; a reader. New York: Random House, 1969. 388p. illus.

An anthology of 30 articles and extracts from books, all originally published elsewhere, mostly between 1966 and 1968. Arrangement is broadly chronological by subject matter, progressing from articles on the rise of rock and roll and on Elvin Presley through to the music of the Doors in 1968. Many of the articles are on individual musicians and groups (Beatles, Rolling Stones, Frank Zappa, Bob Dylan), and there is also coverage of aspects of the rock music industry in the 1960s. Critics include Alan Aldridge, Wilfred Mellers, R. Meltzer and Frank Kofsky. Index.

1364. EISEN, Jonathan, ed. The age of rock, 2: sights and sounds of the American cultural revolution. New York: Random House, 1970. 339p. illus.

A second miscellany of rock literature of the 1960s, containing 42 pieces in all, including album notes and reprints from various journals. Its coverage extends from music and musicians to more general aspects of rock culture. No index.

1365. FONG-TORRES, Ben, ed. The Rolling Stone rock 'n' roll reader. New York: Bantam Books, 1974. 783p.

A generous selection of about 130 items, mainly on rock music, from the doyen of West Coast rock journals, covering 1967 to 1972. The bulk of the anthology consists of articles (short features, interviews and longer profiles) devoted to bands or individual performers. These include the Byrds, the Doors, Dylan, Hendrix, Jefferson Airplane, Janis Joplin, Captain Beefheart, Blood, Sweat and Tears, and others. There are also pieces on festivals, radio, and rock as a business. No index.

1366. LANDAU, Jon. It's too late to stop now: a rock and roll journal. San Francisco: Straight Arrow Books, 1972. 227p. discog.

A collection of pieces written between 1967 and 1972 (mostly quite short and consisting basically of reviews of records and live performances) by one of the more thoughtful rock critics, who admits that in the period covered his writing changed from a polemical style to one of increasing detachment. His underlying theme is a "search for the source behind the music, the search for continuity in all of the musician's/artist's work" (p. 14). The reviews of individuals are divided into "white rock" and "black rock," and these are set off by more general pieces. Landau's "growing estrangement" is seen in his last piece, "Confessions of an Aging Rock Critic."

1367. WILLIAMS, Paul. Outlaw blues: a book of rock music.
       New York: Dutton, 1969. 191p. illus., bibliog., dis-
       cog.
       A selection of material drawn largely from the magazine
Crawdaddy, which Williams founded and edited. The articles cover
1966 to 1968.

e. Collected Profiles

1368. LYDON, Michael. Rock folk: portraits from the rock 'n'
       roll pantheon. New York: Dial, 1971. 199p. illus.
       These profiles, which first appeared in various journals and
newspapers between 1968 and 1971, are devoted to a very heterogeneous group of seven rock and blues figures: Chuck Berry, Carl
Perkins, B. B. King, Smokey Robinson, Janis Joplin, the Grateful
Dead, and the Rolling Stones. Some biographical data are normally
included, but mainly the author uses interview material, combined
with his own impressions of performances, to catch something of
the aura surrounding the artists, and to explore the relation between
them, their work and their world.

1369. MARCUS, Greil. Mystery train: images of America in
       rock and roll music. New York: Dutton, 1975. 313p.
       Six portraits from a wide range of American popular music:
Harmonica Frank, Robert Johnson, The Band, Sly Stone, Randy Newman, Elvis Presley.

1370. RIVELLI, Pauline, and LEVIN, Robert, eds. Rock giants.
       New York: World Publishing Co., 1970. 125p. illus.
       A selection of articles on rock and rock artists, that ap-
peared originally in Jazz and Pop magazine between 1967 and 1970.
There are nine interviews, and among those interviewed are Frank
Zappa, Randy Newman, Eric Clapton, Creedence Clearwater Revival
and Canned Heat. There are articles on censorship, Jefferson Airplane, racial integration in rock, Gary Burton. Contributors include
Frank Kofsky, Richard Williams, John Szwed. No index.

1371. ROLLING STONE. The Rolling Stone interviews; compiled
       by the editors of Rolling Stone. New York: Warner
       Paperback Library, 1971. 465p. illus.
       _____. The Rolling Stone interviews. Vol. 2. Edited
       and with an introduction by Ben Fong-Torres. New
       York: Warner Paperback Library, 1973. 430p.
       A selection of the best interviews, mainly with rock mu-
sicians, that appeared in Rolling Stone between 1967 and 1972, aimed
"at filling those spaces between the musical notes, at etching in the

background behind the music the artists put forth." The seventeen interviewees in Vol. 1 include Mike Bloomfield, Frank Zappa, Booker T and the MG's, Chuck Berry, Jim Morrison, Phil Spector, Bob Dylan, Robbie Robertson, John Fogarty, Little Richard, David Crosby and Grace Slick with Paul Kantner. Among the fifteen in Vol. 2. are Dylan again, B. B. King, Roger McGuinn, Leon Russell, Stephen Stills, Country Joe McDonald, Johnny Otis, Joe Smith, Marvin Gaye and Paul Simon. A number of British musicians are also featured.

1372. SOMMA, Robert, ed. No one waved good-bye: a casualty report on rock and roll. New York: Outerbridge & Dienstfrey, 1971; London: Charisma Books, 1972. 121p. illus.

Of fairly peripheral interest, the ten pieces in this collection--mostly by rock journalists--muse in various ways upon the premature deaths of Janis Joplin, Jimi Hendrix, Brian Jones of the Rolling Stones, and Brian Epstein, Beatles manager. Several are reprinted from newspapers (those by Craig McGregor, Jon Landau, George Frazier and Al Aronowitz); others appear here for the first time, the longest being a conversation between Danny Fields and Jeff Nesin. Other writers are Neil Louison, Lou Reed, Lillian Roxon and Richard Meltzer. The main concern is life-style, rather than death-style; music comes nowhere.

f. Individuals and Groups

BOB DYLAN

1373. DYLAN, Bob. Writings and drawings. New York: Knopf; London: Cape, 1973. 315p. illus.

This handsomely produced volume contains the words to approximately 190 copyrighted songs (1962-1972) by Bob Dylan, plus a selection of poems, liner notes and other writings. They are arranged, album by album, in a basically chronological order from "Bob Dylan" to "New Morning." Each album has a separate section, in which Dylan's own songs on the album (usually all of them) are followed by other songs of his dating from around the same time (these are frequently available in recorded form only on what are euphemistically called "collectors' items"). One section, called "From 'Blonde on Blonde' to 'John Wesley Harding'," in fact contains items recorded with The Band in 1967 on the celebrated "Basement Tape" (released commercially in 1975). Though the transcriptions are faithful to the recordings most of the time, attentive listeners will notice discrepancies. The index to the volume is unusually good, containing not only titles but first lines and key phrases.

1374. GRAY, Michael. Song and dance man: the art of Bob Dylan. London: Hart-Davis, 1972; New York: Dutton, 1973. 336p. illus., bibliog. notes, discog.

This challengingly original book--one of the few outstanding volumes on the popular music of the 1960s--employs the tools of literary criticism in an ambitious attempt to explain the various sources of Dylan's inspiration and poetic technique, and his recreation of these in an art that expresses a very contemporary, yet universal, vision of life. Gray admits a literary bias in his own background, and although musical features crop up occasionally (and he is at pains to stress the complementary nature of words and music in Dylan) it is with literary and cultural questions that he is mainly occupied. Dylan is treated from the outset as an outstandingly significant figure in the expressive arts. An exploration of his roots occupies the first chapters: the folk tradition of Yankee, Southern poor white, cowboy, and black; the English literary tradition from Bunyan to Lawrence and Eliot via Donne, Blake and Browning; the rock and roll tradition of Chuck Berry, Elvis Presley and Buddy Holly. Here Gray seeks constantly to show not just influence on Dylan, but his distilling of these disparate elements into new art --whose achievement, like Bunyan's, is the restoration of the strengths of popular culture to the culture of the midstream. The roots established, Gray gives a detailed literary analysis of Dylan's imagery (especially in "Blonde on Blonde") and use of cliché. There are many lighter moments, as in a diverting exposé of various crackpot interpretations of Dylan's songs (more plausible ones such as mysticism and drugs are accorded more serious discussion). Gray's command of irony is perhaps less successful when it occurs close to objective analysis; here it sometimes seems trendily facetious and dismissive, and leads to gratuitous insults for things and persons he dislikes. A remarkable book, nevertheless, which includes an annotated list of official and unofficial Dylan albums.

1375. McGREGOR, Craig, ed. Bob Dylan: a retrospective. New York: Morrow, 1972. 407p. illus.
A generous helping of Dylan appraisal and appreciation by a variety of writers, mostly reprinted from newspapers and journals. The 40 or so pieces are arranged chronologically (1961-1971), an order which conveys an idea of the lines of development and changing attitude taken by critical writings on Dylan. The most substantial items are by Nat Hentoff (1964), Ralph J. Gleason (1966), Ellen Willis (1967), Jon Landau (1968) and Wilfrid Mellers (a specially commissioned piece); there are also several interviews: with Nora Ephron and Susan Edmiston (1965); with Joseph Haas (1965); with Nat Hentoff for Playboy (1966); with an anonymous reporter in Austin, Texas (1965); with John Cohen and Happy Traum for Sing Out! (1968); with Jann Wenner for Rolling Stone (1970); and with A. J. Weberman (1971).

1376. PICKERING, Stephen, ed. Dylan: a commemoration; assistant editor, Scott Sullivan. Berkeley: Book People, 1971. 62p. illus.
A collection of articles, essays and reviews, produced in a newspaper format, focusing on what Pickering sees as the religious and existentialist basis of Dylan's songs. Most of the material is by Pickering himself (including detailed reviews of several of Dylan's LPs), whose uncontrollable habit it is to introduce his favorite philosophers (no poets or musicians here) and quote them out of context.

(Kierkegaard, William James, Martin Buber, and Friedrich Nietz-sche are among those competing to translate Dylan's utterances into statements of universal significance--thereby generally divesting them of their otherwise considerable force and appeal.) Besides the editor, other contributors include Gil Turner, T. Mike Walker, Paul J. Robbins (interview with Dylan, 1965), Louis Morgan and Jerry Yudelson.

1377. PICKERING, Stephen. Praxis one: existence, men and realities. Berkeley: Book People, 1971. 152p. illus., bibliog.

Pickering's second volume of essays and articles is, in his view, about the "awakening of the I-Thou consciousness in man and woman." Bob Dylan is not the only guinea pig, but he is the main one. This time the Judaic aspect of Dylan's religiosity--as Pickering sees it--comes further to the fore, and he is described as having "a quasi-perennial philosophy rooted in the Jewish mystical tradition," and a "hasidic existentialism"; he is a "Judaic universal moralist." Those who view Dylan differently might find Pickering's extensive, though selective, bibliography of newspaper and magazine articles covering 1961 to 1971 of greater value. The large number of photographs in this and the earlier volume are often of interest, too. Contributors include Scott Sullivan, Jerry Yudelson, David Meltzer and Elia Katz.

1378. SCADUTO, Anthony. Bob Dylan. New York: Grosset & Dunlap, London: Allen; London: Abacus, 1972. 280p. illus., discog.

_____. _____. New York: New American Library, 1973. 351p.

Given the inherent difficulties in obtaining and verifying plausible biographical information on Dylan, Scaduto's is a creditable piece of detective work. It is, he says, "the result of hundreds of hours of conversations with those who knew [Dylan], loved him, sometimes hated him, often feared him, and usually needed him" (preface). Dylan himself provided "personal information that was surprising from so secretive a man." In addition to details of Dylan's life, there is some comment and evaluation of his recordings in their context.

JERRY GARCIA

1379. REICH, Charles, and WENNER, Jann. Garcia: the Rolling Stone interview; plus a Stoned Sunday rap, with Jerry, Charles and Mountain Girl. San Francisco: Straight Arrow Books, 1972. 254p. illus.

These are the transcripts of conversations between Jerry Garcia of the Grateful Dead, his wife, the editor of Rolling Stone (Wenner), and the law professor and author of The Greening of America (Reich), held at Garcia's home in the summer of 1970, and published--conversational warts and all--with a minimum of editing in 1971 in Rolling Stone. Some time later Reich returned for the "Stoned Sunday Rap," which is published here for the first time.

Reich's interest lies mainly in the cultural significance and philosophical undertones of 1960s rock, and puts some fairly abstruse questions, which Garcia does his best to answer. This puts some strain on the basically chronological approach Wenner tries to establish, but he keeps trying, and succeeds in eliciting quite a lot about the group's formation and career, and about Garcia's attitude to music and other rock artists.

JIMI HENDRIX

1380. KNIGHT, Curtis. Jimi: an intimate biography of Jimi Hendrix. New York: Praeger; London: Allen, 1974. 223p. illus., discog.
As leader of the group with which Hendrix (1942-1970) made his first recordings in New York in 1965, Knight had first-hand knowledge of his life-style and of his musicianship in a still formative stage. Like Hendrix, his parentage was a mixture of Negro and Indian. His detailed biography draws on material from Hendrix himself as well as from numerous friends and associates. From one who seems to have understood him, musically speaking, the musical content is rather generalized and unrevealing. The human portrait is clearer, with Hendrix, who talks about life in spiritual terms while living it physically to excess, a complex, enigmatic figure. The discography, by John McKeller, lists commercial recordings and bootlegs. Index.

1381. WELCH, Chris. Hendrix: a biography. London: Ocean Books, 1972; New York: Flash Books, 1973. 104p. illus., discog.
This composite, extensively illustrated portrait by a writer for Melody Maker draws its material mainly from interviews with Hendrix himself and a number of associates. A short outline of Hendrix's career is followed by the personal recollections of Chas Chandler (his co-manager, who took him to England), Noel Redding, bass guitarist with the Jimi Hendrix Experience, two road managers, and various others. Welch assesses Hendrix's music in general terms, and also pieces together an account of his death in London in 1970.

BUDDY HOLLY

1382. LAING, Dave. Buddy Holly. London: Studio Vista, 1971. 111p. illus., discog.
———. ———. New York: Macmillan, 1971. 144p. illus., discog.
An account of the development of the style of Buddy Holly (1936-1958) and a study of his recordings. Laing traces the formative influences on his style from country music through rockabilly to rock and roll. Details of his career are given in Chapters 1 and 2 (particularly the latter), following which the author proceeds with a guide to the records, examining first the Crickets' recordings and the solo records of 1957-1958 under such headings as lyrics, vocals, instrumental work and rhythm section. He also looks at the records

with string backings, 1958-59, the posthumous releases, and the work of the Crickets, 1959-65. Finally, he assesses Holly's influence on rock. The discography lists single releases with full discographical details, groups his songs chronologically, and gives some albums. There are contemporary photographs of many of the major figures in the story. No index.

JEFFERSON AIRPLANE

1383.   GLEASON, Ralph J. The Jefferson Airplane and the San Francisco sound. New York: Ballantine Books, 1969. 340p. illus.
Partly reprinted from the San Francisco Chronicle, Gleason's material includes an 80-page survey of developments in rock music in San Francisco from 1965 to 1969, interviews with the individual members of the Jefferson Airplane, producer-manager Bill Graham, and Jerry Garcia, and a roster of San Francisco bands.

JANIS JOPLIN

1384.   FRIEDMAN, Myra. Buried alive: the biography of Janis Joplin. New York: Morrow, 1974; London: Allen, 1974. 333p. illus.
The author was Janis Joplin's press agent, and her candid portrait of the singer's life and life-style (she was born in Texas in 1943, and died in 1970 in Los Angeles) draws extensively on this experience, and on interview material. Gnawing away obsessively at the problem of the singer's unconventionality and general boorishness, she returns with monotonous regularity to the trusty triumvirate of sex, drink and drugs. The occasional descriptions of Joplin's singing usually come back to sex, too.

JIM MORRISON

1385.   JAHN, Mike. Jim Morrison and the Doors: an unauthorized book. New York: Grosset & Dunlap, 1969. 95p. illus.
Low on information, poor as entertainment, and not very handsome as wallpaper, this is a none-too-glorious little exercise in rock journalese that attempts in its portrait of a moderate group to match their inflated posturing with inflated prose. (Morrison himself died of a heart attack in Paris in 1971, aged 28.)

ELVIS PRESLEY

1386.   HOPKINS, Jerry. Elvis: a biography. New York: Simon & Schuster, 1971; London: Open Gate Books, 1972. 448p. illus., discog.
An objective popular biography of Presley's life and career up to 1971. Descriptions and accounts from a large number of contemporaries and associates from all periods of his life illuminate the narrative, which begins with an account of his childhood in Tupelo, Miss. (where he was born in 1935), his school career and first recordings for the "Sun" label. In the story of his rise to fame the

figure of Col. Tom Parker plays an increasingly dominant role. Throughout this account, and that of Presley's army service and subsequent life-style, career and eventual marriage, the author focuses attention on details of his life, personality and behavior, and on public reaction. His recordings are mentioned in their context, sometimes with brief descriptions, but without any attempt to explore musical aspects of his style, appeal and achievement. The discography lists singles, EPs and LPs chronologically in separate sections. There is also a list of films, but no index.

PAUL SIMON

1387. LEIGH, Spencer. Paul Simon now and then. Liverpool: Raven Books, 1973. 110p. illus., bibliog., discog.

A "companion to Paul Simon's music," written to help redress the balance in rock literature, tilted the way of Bob Dylan for far too long. As a chronicle of Simon's recording career it is useful--there is mention of almost every recorded song in chronological sequence--but comment on the songs and on Simon's style is generally superficial. The biographical background is sketchy, and there is no musical description or objective assessment. The author makes liberal use of quotations from interviews and articles (all of which are listed in a glossary), but his own rather maladroit style is ill-fitted to so stylish a subject. There is a useful discography, and a listing of sheet music.

FRANK ZAPPA

1388. WALLEY, David. No commercial potential: the saga of Frank Zappa and the Mothers of Invention. New York: Dutton, 1972. 184p. illus., bibliog., discog.

A portrait of the life, life-style and recordings of the "prime iconoclast" whose music is described by Eric Salzman as "born out of a kind of pop-Dada mixture of rock, jazz, classical modern (even atonal expression), camp and nostalgia, parody and protest, as well as a strong sense of music theater" (no. 266, p. 190).

APPENDIX

As was noted in the Preface, the Appendix does not constitute an attempt to render the bibliography as a whole comprehensive, but is rather intended to point out other material of interest encountered during the preparation of the book. It includes a small number of items (some twenty in all) that I should like to have included in the main text, but which I have not seen. There are also one or two books which were published in the latter part of 1975, and which would be included in a future supplement.

In its main divisions (Sections A, B, C, etc.) the Appendix follows those of the bibliography.

A: GENERAL AND REFERENCE

Reference and Historical Works

A 1 BARNES, Edwin N. C. American music: from Plymouth Rock to Tin Pan Alley. Washington: Music Education Publications, 1936.

A 2 BURK, Cassie, et al. America's musical heritage, by Cassie Burk, Virginia Meierhoffer, Claude Anderson Phillips. Chicago: Laidlaw, 1942.

A 3 COOPER, David Edwin. International bibliography of discographies: classical music and jazz and blues, 1962-1972; a reference book for record collectors, dealers and libraries; with a preface by Guy A. Marco. Littleton, Col.: Libraries Unlimited, 1975.

A 4 DESPARD, Mabel H. The music of the United States, its sources and its history: a short outline. New York: Muirhead, 1936.

A 5 KAUFMANN, Helen L. From Jehovah to jazz: music in

America from psalmody to the present day. New York: Dodd, Mead, 1937.

A 6   KINSCELLA, Hazel Gertrude. History sings: backgrounds of American music. Lincoln, Neb.: University Publishing Co., 1940.

A 7   LANDOWSKI, Wanda Alice L. La musique américaine. Paris: Horay, 1952.

A 8   LAVIGNAC, Albert. Music and musicians; translated by William Marchant; edited, with additions on music in America, by H. E. Krehbiel. New York: Holt, 1899. (4th ed. New York: Holt, 1903.)

A 9   McCALL, Adeline. Music in America; assisted by Margaret Lee Maaske. (Library Extension Publications, Vol. 10 No. 3) Chapel Hill: University of North Carolina Press, 1944.

A 10   MARROCCO, W. Thomas, and GLEASON, Harold, comps. Music in America: an anthology from the landing of the Pilgrims to the close of the Civil War, 1620-1865; with historical and analytical notes. New York: Norton, 1964.

A 11   MOORE, John W. A dictionary of musical information, containing also a vocabulary of musical terms, and a list of modern musical works published in the United States from 1640 to 1875. Boston: Ditson, 1876.

A 12   MOSES, Julian Morton. Collectors' guide to American recordings, 1895-1925; foreword by Giuseppe de Luca. New York: American Record Collectors' Exchange, 1949.

A 13   OVERMYER, Grace. Famous American composers; illustrated by Constance Joan Naar. New York: Crowell, 1944.

A 14   SAMINSKY, L. Living music of the Americas. New York: Howell, Soskin, 1949.

A 15   SIMPSON, Eugene E. America's position in music. Boston: Four Seas, 1920.

A 16   SONNECK, O. G. Miscellaneous studies in the history of music. New York: Macmillan, 1921. (Includes a chapter on music in America)

Church Music

A 17   GAY, Julius. Church music in Farmington in the olden time: an historical address... Hartford: Case, Lockwood and Brainard, 1891.

A 18 GOODSPEED, E. J. A full history of the wonderful career
of Moody and Sankey, in Great Britain and America...
New York: Goodspeed, 1876. (Repr. New York: AMS
Press, 1973.)

A 19 HATFIELD, Edwin F. The poets of the church: a series of
biographical sketches of hymn-writers with notes on their
hymns. New York: Randolph, 1884.

A 20 KELPIUS, Johannes. The diarium of Magister Johannes
Kelpius; with annotations by Julius Friedrich Sachse.
Lancaster, Pa.: New Era Printing Co., 1917.

A 21 KRIEBEL, Howard Wiegner. The Schwenkfelders in Penn-
sylvania: a historical sketch; illustrated by Julius F.
Sachse. Lancaster, Pa.: New Era Printing Co., 1904.
(Repr. New York: AMS Press, 1971.)

A 22 LLOYD'S Church Musicians' Directory (1910): the blue book
of church musicians in America; compiled by Rev. Frederic E. J. Lloyd. Vol. 1. Chicago: Ritzmann, Brookes,
1910.

A 23 SEIPT, Allen Anders. Schwenkfelder hymnology and the
sources of the first Schwenkfelder hymn-book printed in
America. Philadelphia: Americana Germanica Press,
1909.

A 24 SWEET, Charles Filkins. A champion of the cross; being
the life of John Henry Hopkins... New York: Pott, 1894.
(Repr. New York: AMS Press, 1971.) (Hymn composer,
1820-1891.)

Musical Life

A 25 ANDRUS, Helen Josephine. A century of music in Poughkeepsie, 1802-1911. Poughkeepsie: F. B. Howard, 1912.

A 26 APTHORP, William Foster. By the way; being a collection
of short essays on music and art in general, taken from
the program-books of the Boston Symphony Orchestra...
Boston: Copeland & Day, 1898.

A 27 ARMSBY, Leonora. We shall have music. San Francisco:
Pisani, 1960. (The San Francisco Symphony Orchestra.)

A 28 BARNES, William H., and GAMMONS, Edward B. Two centuries of American organ building. Glen Rock, N.J.:
Fischer, 1970.

A 29 CAMPBELL, Jane. Old Philadelphia music; written for the
City Historical Society of Philadelphia, and read by her at

the meeting of May 8th, 1907. Philadelphia: The Society, 1926.

A 30 FOOTE, Henry Wilder. Musical life in Boston in the eight-eenth century. Worcester, Mass.: American Antiquarian Society, 1940. (Repr. from the Proceedings of the Society, October, 1939.)

A 31 FRANK, Leonie C. Musical life in early Cincinnati. Cin-cinnati: Ruter Press, 1932.

A 32 FREDRICKS, Jessica M. California composers: biograph-ical notes. San Francisco: California Federation of Mu-sic Clubs, 1934.

A 33 FURLONG, William B. Season with Solti: a year in the life of the Chicago Symphony Orchestra. New York: Macmillan, 1974.

A 34 GOOD, Marian Bigler. Some musical backgrounds of Penn-sylvania. Carrolltown, Pa.: Carrolltown News Press, 1932.

A 35 HALE, Philip. Philip Hale's Boston Symphony programme notes; historical, critical and descriptive comment on mu-sic and composers; edited by John N. Burk; with an intro-duction by Lawrence Gilman. Garden City: Doubleday, 1935.

A 36 HOWE, Mabel Almy, comp. Music publishers in New York City before 1850. New York: New York Public Library, 1917.

A 37 HUGHBANKS, Leroy. Talking wax; or, The story of the phonograph, simply told for general readers. New York: Hobson Book Press, 1945.

A 38 KREHBIEL, H. E. Reviews of the New York musical sea-sons 1885-1890, containing programmes of noteworthy oc-currences, with numerous criticisms. New York: Lon-don: Novello, Ewer, 1886-1890. 5v.

A 39 LIGHTFOOT, Robert M., and WILLIS, Thomas. The Chi-cago Symphony Orchestra; photos by Robert M. Lightfoot III; text by Thomas Willis. Chicago: Rand McNally, 1974.

A 40 MADEIRA, Louis C. Annals of music in Philadelphia and history of the Musical Fund Society from its organization in 1820 to the year 1858; edited by Philip H. Goepp. Phila-delphia: Lippincott, 1896. (Repr. New York: Da Capo, 1973.)

A 41 MAHAN, Katherine. Showboats to soft shoes: a century of

music development in Columbus, Ga., 1828-1928. Columbus, Ga.: Columbus Office Supply, 1969.

A 42 MENCKEN, H. L. H. L. Mencken on music: a selection of
his writings on music, together with an account of H. L.
Mencken's musical life and a history of the Saturday Night
Club, by Louis Cheslock. New York: Knopf, 1961.

A 43 REINBACH, Edna. Music and musicians in Kansas. Topeka:
Kansas State Historical Society, 1930.

A 44 SAMAROFF STOKOWSKI, Olga. An American musician's
story. New York: Norton, 1939. (The wife of Leopold
Stokowski; a noted concert pianist and teacher, 1882-1948.)

A 45 SEWALL, Samuel. Diary; edited by Mark Van Doren. New
York: Macy-Masius, 1927. (An abridgment of the three
volumes published in Collections of the Massachusetts Historical Society, 1878-1882. Sewall's account contains
references to musical activity in and around Boston in the
late 17th and early 18th centuries.)

A 46 SPALDING, Walter Raymond. Music at Harvard: a historical review of men and events. New York: Coward-Mc-
Cann, 1935.

A 47 STANDISH, L. W. The Old Stoughton Musical Society.
Stoughton, Mass., 1929.

A 48 THOMAS, Margaret F. Musical Alabama. Montgomery:
Paragon Press, 1925.

Opera and Operatic Life

A 49 BLOOMFIELD, Arthur J. 50 years of the San Francisco
opera. San Francisco: San Francisco Book Co., 1972.

A 50 BLUM, Daniel. A pictorial treasury of opera in America.
New York: Greenberg, 1954.

A 51 DAVIS, Ronald L. Opera in Chicago. New York: Appleton-
Century, 1966.

A 52 EATON, Quaintance. The miracle of the Met: an informal
history of the Metropolitan Opera, 1883-1967. New York:
Meredith Press, 1968.

A 53 GRAF, Herbert. Producing opera for America. Zurich:
Atlantis, 1961.

A 54 HACKETT, Karleton. The beginning of grand opera in Chicago (1850-1859). Chicago: Laurentian Publishers, 1913.

A 55   MAPLESON, James Henry.   The Mapleson memoirs, 1848-
         1888.   New York: Belford, Clarke; London: Remington,
         1888.   2v.

A 56   MOORE, Edward C.   Forty years of opera in Chicago.   New
         York: Liveright, 1930.

A 57   MOSES, Montrose J.   The life of Heinrich Conried.   New
         York: Crowell, 1916.

A 58   RUSSELL, Henry.   The passing show.   Boston: Little,
         Brown, 1926.   (Impresario, 1871-1937, son of Henry
         Russell, no. 1221.)

Some General Works on the Theater

A 59   BROWN, T. Allston.   History of the American stage, con-
         taining biographical sketches of nearly every member of the
         profession that has appeared on the American stage, from
         1733 to 1870.   New York: Dick & Fitzgerald, 1870.

A 60   BROWN, T. Allston.   A history of the New York stage from
         the first performance in 1732 to 1901.   New York: Dodd,
         Mead, 1903.   3v.

A 61   DUNLAP, William.   A history of the American theatre.   New
         York: Harper, 1832; London: Bentley, 1833.

A 62   IRELAND, Joseph N.   Records of the New York stage, from
         1750 to 1860.   New York: Morrell, 1866-1867.   (Repr.
         New York: Franklin, 1968.)

A 63   ODELL, George C. D.   Annals of the New York stage.   New
         York: Columbia University Press, 1927-1949.   15v.

A 64   STRATMAN, Carl J.   Bibliography of the American theater,
         excluding New York City.   Chicago: Loyola University
         Press, 1965.

B: MUSIC TO 1800

A 65   EAMES, Wilberforce.   A list of editions of the "Bay Psalm
         Book," or New England version of the psalms.   New York,
         1885.

A 66   FISHER, William Arms.   Ye olde New England psalm tunes
         (1620-1820); with historical sketch, biographical notes, and
         hints on performance.   Boston: Ditson, 1930.

A 67   GILMAN, Samuel.   Memories of a New England village choir;
       with occasional reflections.   By a member.   Boston:
       Goodrich, 1829.   (Supposedly Atkinson, N. H.)

A 68   GOLDMAN, Richard Franko, and SMITH, Roger, eds.   Land-
       marks of early American music, 1760-1800: a collection
       of thirty-two compositions, compiled, arranged, and edited
       for orchestra or band, or smaller instrumental groups, or
       mixed chorus...   New York: Schirmer, 1943.   (Repr.
       New York: AMS Press, 1974.)

A 69   STAPLES, Samuel E.   The ancient psalmody and hymnology
       of New England.   Worcester, Mass.: Jillson, 1880.

C: THE CULTIVATED TRADITION
IN THE 19TH CENTURY

A 70   D(IDIMUS), H(enry).   Biography of Louis Moreau Gottschalk,
       the American pianist and composer.   Philadelphia: Dea-
       con & Peterson, 1853.

A 71   FINCK, Henry T.   My adventures in the golden age of music.
       New York: Funk & Wagnalls, 1926.

A 72   FREER, Eleanor Everest.   Recollections and reflections of
       an American composer.   New York: Musical Advance Pub-
       lishing Co., 1929.

A 73   THOMPSON, Vance.   The life of Ethelbert Nevin, from his
       letters and his wife's memories.   Boston: Boston Music
       Co., 1913.

D: THE CULTIVATED TRADITION
IN THE 20TH CENTURY

A 74   APPLETON, Jon H., and PERERA, Ronald C., eds.   The
       development and practice of electronic music.   Englewood
       Cliffs: Prentice-Hall, 1975.   (Contains an extensive bib-
       liography on the theory and practice of electronic music
       inside and outside of the United States.)

A 75   BOARDMAN, Herbert R.   Henry Hadley, ambassador of
       harmony.   Emory University, Ga.: Banner Press, 1932.

A 76   EWEN, David.   Leonard Bernstein: a biography for young
       people.   Philadelphia: Chilton, 1960.   Rev. ed., Phila-
       delphia: Chilton; London: Allen, 1967.

A 77   THE FOUR SUITS: Benjamin Patterson, Philip Corner, Ali-
son Knowles, Tomas Schmit.   New York: Something Else
Press, 1965.

A 78   HIGGINS, Dick.   Computers for the arts.   Somerville, Mass.:
Abyss Publications, 1970.

A 79   KRENEK, Ernst.   Exploring music: essays.   London: Calder
& Boyars; New York: October House, 1966.

A 80   KRENEK, Ernst.   Music here and now; translated by Barthold
Fles.   New York: Russell & Russell, 1967.

A 81   MARTENS, Frederick H.   Leo Ornstein: the man, his ideas,
his work.   New York: Breitkopf & Härtel, 1918.

A 82   MYERS, Rollo H., ed.   Twentieth century music.   London:
Calder, 1960.   (Includes section on U.S.A. by Robert
Layton.)

A 83   ROSSI, Nick, and CHOATE, Robert.   Music of our time: an
anthology of works of selected contemporary composers of
the 20th century.   Boston: Crescendo, 1970.   (Collection
of criticism.)

A 84   SLONIMSKY, Nicolas.   Music since 1900.   New York: Norton,
1937.   4th ed., New York: Scribner, 1971; London: Cassell, 1972.   (Descriptive chronology.)

A 85   TEFFT, Lulu Sanford.   Little intimate stories of Charles
Wakefield Cadman.   Hollywood: David Graham Fischer,
1926.

A 86   TENNEY, James.   Meta (+) Hodos: a phenomenology of
twentieth century musical materials and an approach to the
study of form.   New Orleans: Inter-American Institute
for Musical Research of Tulane University, 1964.

A 87   YOUNG, La Monte, ed.   An anthology of chance operations,
by George Brecht (et al.)...   Bronx: Young & MacLow,
1963.

E: MUSIC OF THE AMERICAN INDIAN

A 88   CATLIN, George.   Letters and notes on the manners, customs and condition of the North American Indians; written
during eight years' travel amongst the wildest tribes...
London: Tosswill & Myers; New York: Wiley & Putnam,
1841.

A 89   DENSMORE, Frances.   Cheyenne and Arapaho music.   Los
       Angeles: Southwest Museum, 1936.

A 90   DENSMORE, Frances.   Music of Santo Domingo Pueblo, New
       Mexico.   Los Angeles: Southwest Museum, 1938.

A 91   DENSMORE, Frances.   Music of the Indians of British Colum-
       bia.   (Bureau of American Ethnology, Anthropological Pa-
       pers, No. 27.) Washington: Government Printing Office,
       1943.   (Repr. New York: Da Capo. 1972.)

A 92   FLETCHER, Alice Cunningham.   The Hako: a Pawnee cere-
       mony; assisted by James R. Murie; music transcribed by
       Edwin B. Tracy.   (Bureau of American Ethnology, 22nd
       Annual Report, 1900-1901, pp. 5-372.) Washington: Gov-
       ernment Printing Office, 1904.

A 93   MATTHEWS, Washington.   Navaho myths, prayers, and songs
       with texts and translations; edited by Pliny Earle Goddard.
       (Publications in American Archaeology and Ethnology, Vol.
       5, No. 2.) Berkeley: University of California, 1907.

A 94   MOONEY, James.   The ghost-dance religion and the Sioux
       outbreak of 1890.   (Bureau of American Ethnology, 14th
       Annual Report, 1892-1893, pp. 641-1136.) Washington:
       Government Printing Office, 1896.   (Includes transcrip-
       tions.)

F: FOLK MUSIC

A 95   BOATRIGHT, Mody C.   Gib Morgan, minstrel of the oil
       fields.   (Publications of the Texas Folk-Lore Society, No.
       20.) Austin: Texas Folk-Lore Society, 1945.

A 96   CAMBIARE, Celestin Pierre.   East Tennessee and Western
       Virginia mountain ballads.   London: Mitre Press, 1934.

A 97   CHAPPELL, Louis W.   Folk-songs of Roanoke and the Albe-
       marle.   Morgantown, W. Va.: Ballad Press, 1939.

A 98   CHRISTESON, R. P., comp.   The old-time fiddler's reper-
       tory: 245 traditional tunes.   Columbia: University of
       Missouri Press, 1973.

A 99   COMBS, Josiah, comp.   Folk-songs from the Kentucky high-
       lands; with piano accompaniments by Keith Mixson.   New
       York: Schirmer, 1939.

A 100 COX, John Harrington.   Folk-songs, mainly from West Vir-

ginia; introductory essay and supplementary references by
Herbert Halpert... New York: National Service Bureau,
1939.

A 101   COX, John Harrington. Traditional ballads mainly from
West Virginia; introductory essay and supplementary
references by Herbert Halpert... New York: National
Service Bureau, 1939.

A 102   DA SILVA, Owen, ed. Mission music of California: a collection of old California mission hymns and masses,
transcribed and edited by Owen da Silva; accompaniments
and chirography by Arthur M. Bienbar; mission sketches
by Paul A. Moore; with an introduction by John Steven
McGroarty. Los Angeles: Lewis, 1941.

A 103   DUNSON, Josh, and RAIM, Ethel, eds. Anthology of American folk music; musical transcriptions by Ethel Raim;
interviews with Moses Asch and Frank Walker. New
York: Oak Publications, 1973. (Companion to Folkways
Records' three-volume record anthology.)

A 104   ECKSTORM, Fannie Hardy, and SMYTH, Mary Winslow,
comps. Minstrelsy of Maine: folk-songs and ballads of
the woods and the coast. Boston: Houghton Mifflin, 1927.

A 105   FINGER, Charles J., comp. Sailor chanties and cowboy
songs. Girard, Kan.: Haldeman-Julius, 1923.

A 106   GLASS, Paul, and SINGER, Louis C., comps. Songs of
forest and river folk: folk songs, ballads, historical
songs... New York: Grosset & Dunlap, 1967.

A 107   GLASS, Paul, and SINGER, Louis C., comps. Songs of
hill and mountain folk: ballads, historical songs and folk
songs... New York: Grosset & Dunlap, 1967.

A 108   GLASS, Paul, and SINGER, Louis C., comps. Songs of
the sea: chanteys, historical songs, ballads... New
York: Grosset & Dunlap, 1966.

A 109   GLASS, Paul, and SINGER, Louis C., comps. Songs of
the West: ballads, topical songs, folk songs... New
York: Grosset & Dunlap, 1966.

A 110   GLASS, Paul, and SINGER, Louis C., comps. Songs of
town and city folk: folk songs, composed songs, ballads... New York: Grosset & Dunlap, 1967.

A 111   GRAY, Roland Palmer, comp. Songs and ballads of the
Maine lumberjacks, with other songs from Maine. Cambridge, Mass.: Harvard University Press, 1924.

A 112 GUTHRIE, Woody. Ballads of Sacco and Vanzetti; commissioned by Moses Asch, 1945... New York: Oak Publications, 1960.

A 113 HARLOW, Frederick Pease. Chanteying aboard American ships. Barre, Mass.: Barre Gazette, 1962.

A 114 HENRY, Mellinger Edward, comp. Folk-songs from the Southern Highlands. New York: Augustin, 1938.

A 115 HENRY, Mellinger Edward, comp. Songs sung in the Southern Appalachians, many of them illustrating ballads in the making. London: Mitre Press, 1934.

A 116 HUGHES, Robert, and STURGES, Edith B., comps. Songs from the hills of Vermont, sung by James and Mary Atwood and Aunt Jenny Knapp... New York: Schirmer, 1919.

A 117 KORSON, George. Black rock: mining folklore of the Pennsylvania Dutch. Baltimore: Johns Hopkins Press, 1960. (Includes music of a sample of folk songs and ballads.)

A 118 LINSCOTT, E. H., comp. Folk songs of Old New England; with an introduction by James M. Carpenter. New York: Macmillan, 1939.

A 119 McGILL, Josephine, comp. Folk songs of the Kentucky mountains: twenty traditional ballads and other English folk-songs, notated from the singing of the Kentucky mountain people and arranged with piano accompaniment; introductory note by H. E. Krehbiel. New York: Boosey, 1917.

A 120 POUND, Louise. Folk-song of Nebraska and the central West: a syllabus. (Publications of the Nebraska Academy of Sciences, Vol. IX, No. 3.) Lincoln, Neb.: Nebraska Academy of Sciences, 1915.

A 121 THOMAS, Jean. Devil's ditties; being stories of the Kentucky mountain folk, with the songs they sing. Chicago: Hatfield, 1931.

A 122 THOMAS, Jean. The singin' fiddler of Lost Hope Hollow. New York: Dutton, 1938. (About Jilson Setters.)

A 123 WHEELER, Mary, comp. Kentucky mountain folk-songs; the words and melodies collected by Mary Wheeler; the pianoforte accompaniments by Clara Gregory Bridge; with an introduction by Edgar Stillman Kelley. Boston: Boston Music Co., 1937.

A 124   WHITE, John I. Git along little dogies: songs and song-
makers of the American West. Urbana: University of
Illinois Press, 1975.

A 125   WYMAN, Loraine, and BROCKWAY, Howard, comps.
Twenty Kentucky mountain songs... Boston: Ditson,
1920.

Country Music

A 126   CASH, Johnny. Man in black. Grand Rapids: Zondervan,
1975.

A 127   CYPORYN, Dennis, comp. The bluegrass songbook. New
York: Macmillan, 1972.

A 128   GENNETT Records of Old Time Tunes: a catalog reprint.
(Special Series, No. 6.) Los Angeles: John Edwards
Memorial Foundation, 1975.

A 129   GRISSIM, John. Country music: white man's blues. New
York: Paperback Library, 1970.

A 130   LONGWORTH, Mike. Martin guitars: a history. Knolls,
N.J.: Colonial Press, 1975.

A 131   LORD, Bobby. Hit the glory road! Nashville: Broadman
Press, 1969. (Folk and country singers.)

A 132   MALONE, Bill C., and McCULLOH, Judith, eds. Stars
of country music: Uncle Dave Macon to Johnny Rodriguez.
Urbana: University of Illinois Press, 1975.

A 133   SCHLAPPI, Elizabeth, comp. Roy Acuff and his Smoky
Mountain Boys: discography. Cheswold, Del.: Disc
Collector Publications, 1966.

A 134   SHELDON, Ruth. Hubbin' it: the life of Bob Wills. Kingsport, Te.: Kingsport Press, 1938.

A 135   TRIBE, Ivan M., and MORRIS, John W. Molly O'Day,
Lynn Davis, and the Cumberland Mountain Folks: a bio-
discography. (Special Series, No. 7.) Los Angeles:
John Edwards Memorial Foundation, 1975.

Instructional Books

A 136   KRASSEN, Miles. Appalachian fiddle. New York: Oak
Publications, 1973. (Includes transcriptions.)

A 137   RITCHIE, Jean. The dulcimer book; being a book about the three-stringed Appalachian dulcimer, including some ways of tuning and playing... New York: Oak Publications, 1963.

A 138 ROSENBAUM, Art. Old-time mountain banjo: an instruction method for playing the old-time five-string mountain banjo based on the styles of the traditional banjo-pickers. New York: Oak Publications, 1968.

A 139 SCRUGGS, Earl. Earl Scruggs and the 5-string banjo. New York: Peer, 1968.

A 140 SEEGER, Pete. How to play the 5-string banjo. New York: People's Songs, 1948.

A 141 SILVERMAN, Jerry. The flat-picker's guitar guide: an advanced instruction manual and song book. New York: Oak Publications, 1966.

A 142 TAUSSIG, Harry. Folk style autoharp: an instruction method for playing the autoharp and accompanying folk songs. New York: Oak Publications, 1967.

A 143 TAUSSIG, Harry. Instrumental techniques of American folk guitar. Laguna Beach, Ca.: Traditional Stringed Instruments, 1965.

A 144 TRAUM, Happy. Finger-picking styles for guitar. New York: Oak Publications, 1966.

G: BLACK MUSIC

General Reference and Histories

A 145 CALIFORNIA. State College, San Diego. Library. Afro-American bibliography: list of the books, documents, and periodicals on black-American culture located in San Diego State College Library; compiled by Andrew Szabo. San Diego, 1970.

A 146 THE CHICAGO Afro-American Union Analytic Catalog: an index to materials on the Afro-American in the principal libraries of Chicago. Boston: G. K. Hall, 1972. 5v.

A 147 DE LERMA, Dominique-René. The black American musical heritage: a preliminary bibliography. (Explorations in Music Librarianship, No. 3.) n.p., 1969.

A 148 LAWRENZ, Marguerite Martha. Bibliography and index of

Negro music. Detroit: Board of Education of the City of Detroit, 1969.

A 149 MILLER, Elizabeth W. The Negro in America: a bibliography; with a foreword by Thomas F. Pettigrew. Cambridge, Mass.: Harvard University Press, 1966.

A 150 NEW YORK PUBLIC LIBRARY. Schomburg Collection of Negro Literature and History. Dictionary catalog. Boston: G. K. Hall, 1962. 9v. 1st supplement. Boston: Hall, 1967. 2nd supplement. Boston: Hall, 1972.

A 151 RUBLOWSKY, John. Black music in America. New York: Basic Books, 1971. (Chiefly for schools.)

Personalities in Black Music
(See also Popular Music Personalities, A 267-283)

A 152 DOBRIN, Arnold. Voices of joy, voices of freedom: Ethel Waters, Sammy Davis, Jr., Marian Anderson, Paul Robeson, Lena Horne. New York: Coward, McCann & Geoghegan, 1972.

A 153 EMBREE, Edwin R. 13 against the odds. New York: Viking Press, 1944. (Includes Marian Anderson, Paul Robeson and William Grant Still.)

A 154 GRAHAM, Shirley. Paul Robeson, citizen of the world; foreword by Carl Van Doren. New York: Messner, 1946.

A 155 NEWMAN, Shirlee P. Marian Anderson: lady from Philadelphia. Philadelphia: Westminster Press, 1965.

A 156 ROBESON, Eslanda Goode. Paul Robeson, Negro. New York, London: Harper, 1930. (By Robeson's wife.)

A 157 STEVENSON, Janet. Marian Anderson: singing to the world. Chicago: Encyclopaedia Britannica Press, 1963.

The African Heritage

A 158 CARRINGTON, John F. Talking drums of Africa. London: Carey Kingsgate Press, 1949. (Repr. New York: Negro Universities Press, 1969.)

A 159 DIETZ, Betty Warner, and OLATUNJI, Michael Babatunde. Musical instruments of Africa: their nature, use and place in the life of a deeply musical people; illustrated by Richard M. Powers. New York: Day, 1965.

A 160   MERRIAM, Alan P.   African music on LP: an annotated
         discography.   Evanston: Northwestern University Press,
         1970.

A 161   LA MUSIQUE AFRICAINE: réunion de Yanoundé (Cameroun),
         23-27 février 1970; organisée par l'Unesco.   Paris: La
         Revue Musicale, 1972.

A 162   TRACEY, Hugh.   Chopi musicians: their music, poetry and
         instruments.   London, New York: Oxford University
         Press, 1948.

         _____.   _____; with a new introduction.   London, New
         York: Oxford University Press, 1970.

Black Musical Life in the Slave Era

A 163   DAVIES, Samuel.   Letters from the Rev. Samuel Davies
         &c. shewing the state of religion in Virginia, particularly
         among the Negroes...   London: Printed by R. Pardon,
         1757.

A 164   FITHIAN, Philip Vickers.   Journal and letters, 1767-1774...;
         edited for the Princeton Historical Association by John
         Rogers Williams.   Princeton: University Library, 1900-
         1934.   2v.

A 165   HARRISON, William P., ed.   The gospel among the slaves:
         a short account of missionary operations among the Afri-
         can slaves of the Southern states; compiled from original
         sources. Nashville: Publishing House of the M. E. Church,
         South, 1893.

A 166   HEARN, Lafcadio.   American miscellany: articles and
         stories now first collected by Albert Mordell.   New York:
         Dodd, Mead, 1924.   2v.

A 167   HUNGERFORD, James.   The old plantation, and what I
         gathered there in an autumn month.   New York: Harper,
         1859.   (Includes music and texts of two slave song.)

A 168   JONES, Charles C.   The religious instruction of the Ne-
         groes in the United States.   Savannah: Purse, 1842.
         (Repr. New York: Kraus; New York: Negro Universities
         Press, 1969; Freeport: Books for Libraries Press,
         1971.)

A 169   SVININ, Paul.   Picturesque United States of America, 1811,
         1812, 1813; being a memoir on Paul Svinin, Russian dip-
         lomatic officer, artist, and author, containing copious
         excerpts from his account of his travels...   by Avrahm
         Yarmolinsky; introduction by R. T. H. Halsey.   New

York: Rudge, 1930. (Includes account of singing at AME church, Philadelphia.)

Folk Music, Spirituals, Ragtime and Blues

A 170   BERENDT, Joachim Ernst, and KNESEBECK, Paridam von dem, comps. Spirituals: geistliche Lieder der Neger Amerikas; Originaltexte, Melodien und Übertragungen. Munich: Nymphenburger Verlagshandlung, 1955.

A 171   BREMAN, Paul, comp. Blues, en andere wereldlijke volksmuziek van de Noordamerikaanse neger. Den Haag: Servire, 1961.

A 172   BREMAN, Paul, comp. Spirituals: Noordamerikaanse geestelijke volksliederen. Den Haag: Servire, 1959.

A 173   BURLEIGH, Harry T., comp. Negro spirituals; arranged for solo voice. New York: Ricordi, 1917-1928. 2v.

A 174   CHARTERS, Ann, comp. Ragtime songbook: songs of the ragtime era by Scott Joplin, Hughie Cannon, Ben Harney, Will Marion Cook, Alex Rogers and others; with historical notes concerning the songs and times. New York: Oak Publications, 1965.

A 175   CURTIS, Natalie, comp. The Hampton series of Negro folk songs; recorded by Natalie Curtis-Burlin. New York: Schirmer, 1918-1919. 4v. (20 songs arranged for male quartet.)

A 176   FISHER, William Arms, comp. Seventy Negro spirituals. Boston: Ditson, 1926.

A 177   GLOVER, Tony. Blues harp: an instruction method for playing the blues harmonica. New York: Oak Publications, 1965.

A 178   HOARE, Ian, et al. The soul book. London: Eyre Methuen, 1975.

A 179   KENNEDY, R. Emmet. Black cameos; decorations by Edward Laroque Tinker. New York: Boni, 1924. (Repr. Freeport: Books for Libraries Press, 1970.) (Includes melodies of 17 spirituals.)

A 180   KING, B. B. B. B. King: the blues, the wellspring of today's American popular music, and its greatest performer, B. B. King, in an unusual and beautiful collection of articles, music, lyrics, photos and quotes...; music editor, Harvey Vinson. New York: Amsco, 1970.

A 181   LESTER, Julius, and SEEGER, Pete. The 12-string guitar as played by Leadbelly: an instruction manual. New York: Oak Publications, 1965.

A 182   LYDON, Michael. Boogie lightning. New York: Dial Press, 1974.

A 183   McCUTCHEON, Lynn Ellis. Rhythm and blues: an experience and adventure in its origin and development. Arlington, Va.: Beatty, 1971.

A 184   PAPARELLI, Frank. The blues and how to play 'em: a piano method book. New York: Leeds Music, 1942.

A 185   PAPARELLI, Frank. Leeds' eight to the bar: boogie woogie piano method book in all its styles. New York: Leeds Music, 1941.

A 186   PRICE, Sammy. Boogie-woogie land: an album of selected boogie-woogie favorites, old and new... New York: Marks, 1944.

A 187   SILVERMAN, Jerry. The art of the folk blues guitar: an instruction manual. New York: Oak Publications, 1964.

A 188   WALLASCHEK, Richard. Primitive music: an inquiry into the origin and development of music, songs, instruments, dances, and pantomimes of savage races. London, New York: Longmans Green, 1893.

A 189   WHEELER, Mary, comp. Roustabout songs: a collection of Ohio river valley songs; words and melodies... arranged by William J. Reddick; with an introduction by Irvin S. Cobb. New York: Remick, 1939.

A 190   WHEELER, Mary, comp. Steamboatin' days: folk songs of the river packet era. Baton Rouge: Louisiana State University Press, 1944. (Unaccompanied Negro melodies.)

H: JAZZ

A 191   BARTSCH, Ernst. Neger, Jazz und tiefer Süden. Leipzig: Brockhaus, 1956.

A 192   BELLOCQ, E. J. Storyville portraits: photographs from the New Orleans red light district, circa 1912; reproduced from prints made by Lee Friedlander; preface by Lee Friedlander; edited by John Szarkowski. New York: Museum of Modern Art, 1970.

A 193   BERENDT, Joachim Ernst. Der Jazz: eine zeitkritische
         Studie. Stuttgart: Deutsche Verlags-Anstalt, 1950.

A 194   BERENDT, Joachim Ernst. Jazz optisch. Munich:
         Nymphenburger Verlagshandlung, 1954.

A 195   BERENDT, Joachim Ernst. Variationen über Jazz: Auf-
         sätze. Munich: Nymphenburger Verlagshandlung, 1956.

A 196   CASTELLI, Vittorio, et al. The Bix bands, by Vittorio
         Castelli, Evert Kaleveld and Liborio Pusateri. Milan:
         Raretone, 1972.

A 197   COEUROY, André, and SCHAEFFNER, André. Le jazz.
         Paris: C. Aveline, 1926.

A 198   DAUER, Alfons. Jazz, die magische Musik: ein Leitfaden
         durch den Jazz. Bremen: Schünemann, 1961.

A 199   DEXTER, Dave. Jazz cavalcade: the inside story of jazz;
         with a foreword by Orson Welles. New York: Criterion,
         1946.

A 200   DEXTER, Dave. The jazz story, from the '90s to the '60s;
         with a foreword by Woody Herman. Englewood Cliffs:
         Prentice-Hall, 1964.

A 201   EDWARDS, Ernie. Big bands discography. Whittier, Ca.:
         Jazz Discographies Unlimited, 1965-1968. 7v.

A 202   FEATHER, Leonard. Inside be-bop. New York: Robbins,
         1949.

A 203   FERNETT, Gene. Thousand golden horns: the exciting age
         of America's greatest dance bands. Midland, Mich.:
         Pendell, 1966.

A 204   FRANCIS, André. Jazz. Paris: Editions du Seuil, 1958.

         _____ . _____ ; translated and revised by Martin Wil-
         liams. New York: Grove Press, 1960.

A 205   GLEASON, Ralph. Celebrating the Duke. Boston: Little,
         Brown, 1975.

A 206   GOFFIN, Robert. Louis Armstrong, le roi du jazz. Paris:
         Seghers, 1947.

         _____ . Horn of plenty: the story of Louis Armstrong;
         translated from the French by James F. Bezou. New
         York: Allen, Towne & Heath, 1947.

A 207   GÖTZE, Werner. Dizzy Gillespie: ein Porträt. Wetzlar:
         Pegasus Verlag, 1960.

A 208 GREEN, Benny. Blame it on my youth. London: Mac-Gibbon & Kee, 1967.

A 209 HARRIS, Rex. Enjoying jazz. London: Phoenix House; New York: Roy, 1960; London: Jazz Book Club, 1961. Rev. ed., London: Phoenix House, 1963.

A 210 LARKIN, Philip. All what jazz: a record diary, 1961-68. London: Faber; New York: St. Martin's Press, 1970. (Articles from the "Daily Telegraph.")

A 211 LEYDI, Roberto. Sarah Vaughan. Milan: Ricordi, 1961.

A 212 MELLERS, Wilfrid. Caliban reborn: renewal in twentieth-century music. New York: Harper & Row, 1967; London: Gollancz, 1968. (Includes a chapter on "parallel lines in jazz and pop.")

A 213 MORGAN, Alun, and HORRICKS, Raymond. Modern jazz: a survey of developments since 1939; with a foreword by Don Rendell. London: Gollancz, 1956.

A 214 PANASSIE, Hugues. Histoire des disques swing enregistrés à New York par Tommy Ladnier, Mezz Mezzrow, Frank Newton... Geneva: Grasset, 1944.

A 215 PANASSIE, Hugues. Quand Mezzrow enregistre: histoire des disques de Milton Mezzrow et Tommy Ladnier; préface de Milton Mezzrow. Paris: Laffont, 1952.

A 216 PAUL, Elliot. That crazy American music. Indianapolis: Bobbs-Merrill, 1957.

_____. _____: the story of North American jazz. London: Muller, 1957.

A 217 PRESTON, Denis. Mood indigo. Egham: Citizen Press, 1946.

A 218 REISNER, Robert G. The jazz titans, including "The parlance of hip"; with short biographical sketches and brief discographies... Garden City: Doubleday, 1960.

A 219 ROSENKRANTZ, Timme. Swing photo album 1939; a revised reissue of photographs... Lowestoft: Scorpion Press, 1964.

A 220 SIMPKINS, Cuthbert Ormond. Coltrane: a biography. New York: Herndon House, 1975.

A 221 STOCK, Dennis. Jazz street: photos by Dennis Stock; with an introduction and commentary by Nat Hentoff. Garden City: Doubleday; London: Deutsch, 1960.

A 222 TANNER, Paul, and GEROW, Maurice. A study of jazz.
Dubuque: Brown, 1964.

_____. _____. 2nd ed. Dubuque: Brown, 1973.
(A versatile guide for use in schools and colleges. Includes a number of scores.)

A 223 TRAILL, Sinclair, ed. Concerning jazz. London: Faber,
1957; London: Jazz Book Club, 1958.

A 224 TRAILL, Sinclair, ed. Play that music: a guide to playing jazz. London: Faber, 1956; London: Jazz Book
Club, 1958.

A 225 WALKER, Leo. The wonderful era of the great dance bands.
Berkeley, Ca.: Howell-North, 1965; Garden City: Doubleday, 1972.

A 226 WHITEMAN, Paul, and LIEBER, Leslie. How to be a bandleader. New York: R. M. McBride, 1941.

A 227 WHITEMAN, Paul, and McBRIDE, Mary Margaret. Jazz.
New York: J. H. Sears, 1926.

A 228 WILLIAMSON, Ken, ed. This is jazz. London: Newnes,
1960; London: Jazz Book Club, 1961.

A 229 WILSON, John S. The collector's jazz: modern. Philadelphia: Lippincott, 1959.

A 230 WILSON, John S. The collector's jazz: traditional and
swing. Philadelphia: Lippincott, 1958.

I: POPULAR CURRENTS

General

A 231 ALLAN, Francis D., comp. Allan's lone star ballads: a
collection of Southern patriotic songs, made during Confederate times. Galveston: Sawyer, 1874. (Repr. New
York: Franklin, 1970.) (Texts only.)

A 232 ASCAP. 40 years of hit tunes. New York: Ascap, 1956.

_____. Ascap hit tunes. New York: Ascap, 1967.

A 233   AUSTIN, William W. "Susanna," "Jeanie" and the "Old folks at home": the songs of Stephen C. Foster from his time to ours. New York: Macmillan, 1975.

A 234   CLAGHORN, Charles Eugene. The mocking bird: the life and diary of its author, Septimus Winner. Philadelphia: Magee Press, 1937.

A 235   DACHS, David. Anything goes: the world of popular music. Indianapolis: Bobbs-Merrill, 1964.

A 236   DAMON, S. Foster, ed. Series of old American songs, reproduced in facsimile from original or early editions in the Harris Collection of American Poetry and Plays, Brown University; with brief annotations. Providence: Brown University Library, 1936.

A 237   DOLPH, Edward Arthur, comp. "Sound off!" soldier songs from Yankee Doodle to Parley Voo; music arranged by Philip Egner; illustrated by Lawrence Schick; foreword by Peter B. Kyne. New York: Cosmopolitan Book Corp., 1929.

           _____. "Sound off!" soldier songs from the Revolution to World War II... New York: Farrar & Rinehart, 1942.

A 238   EWEN, David. History of popular music. New York: Barnes & Noble, 1961.

A 239   GREEN, Abel. Inside stuff on how to write popular songs; with endorsement-introduction by Paul Whiteman. New York: Paul Whiteman Publications, 1927.

A 240   MARCUSE, Maxwell F. Tin Pan Alley in gaslight: saga of the songs that made the gray nineties "gay." Watkins Glen, N.Y.: Century House, 1959.

A 241   MEYER, Hazel. The gold in Tin Pan Alley. Philadelphia: Lippincott, 1958.

A 242   NILES, John Jacob, comp. Singing soldiers; illustrated by Margaret Thorniley Williamson. New York: Scribner, 1927.

A 243   NILES, John Jacob, et al., comps. The songs my mother never taught me, according to John J. "Jack" Niles, Douglas S. "Doug" Moore and A. A. "Wally" Wallgren. New York: Macaulay, 1929. (Mainly World War I songs.)

A 244   RUBLOWSKY, John. Popular music. New York: Basic Books, 1967.

A 245   STAMBLER, Irwin. Guitar years: pop music from country and western to hard rock. Garden City: Doubleday, 1970.

A 246   TATHAM, David. The lure of the striped pig: the illustration of popular music in America, 1820-1870. Barre, Mass.: Imprint Society, 1973.

Popular Music of the Stage and Screen

A 247   ASCAP. 30 years of motion picture music: the big Hollywood hits from 1928-1958. New York: Ascap, 1958.

A 248   BRANEN, Jeff, and JOHNSON, Frederick G. How to stage a minstrel show: a manual for the amateur burnt cork director... Chicago: Denison, 1921.

A 249   CANTOR, Eddie, and FREEDMAN, David. Ziegfeld, the great glorifier. New York: A. H. King, 1934.

A 250   DAY, Charles H. Fun in black; or, Sketches of minstrel life...; with the origin of minstrelsy, by Col. T. Allston Brown. New York: De Witt, 1874.

A 251   DIETZ, Howard. Dancing in the dark. New York: Quadrangle, 1974; New York: Bantam Books, 1976. (Original ed. withdrawn from sale; new ed. omits one chapter.)

A 252   ENGEL, Lehman. Planning and producing the musical show. New York: Crown, 1957. Rev. ed., New York: Crown, 1966.

A 253   GRAHAM, Philip. Showboats: the history of an American institution. Austin: University of Texas Press, 1951.

A 254   GREEN, Abel, and LAURIE, Joe. Show biz, from vaude to video. New York: Holt, 1951.

A 255   HAGEN, Earle. Scoring for films: a complete text. New York: Criterion Music Corp., 1971.

A 256   HARE, Walter Ben. The minstrel encyclopedia. Boston: Baker, 1921.

A 257   HOFMANN, Charles. Sounds for silents; foreword by Lillian Gish. New York: DBS Publications, 1970.

A 258   KNOWLES, Eleanor. The films of Jeanette MacDonald and Nelson Eddy. South Brunswick, N.J.: A. S. Barnes, 1974.

A 259   LONGOLIUS, Christian. George Gershwin. Berlin: Hesse, 1959.

A 260   McVAY, J. Douglas. The musical film. London: Zwem-
        mer; New York: Barnes, 1967.

A 261   PURDY, Claire Lee. Victor Herbert, American music
        master. New York: Messner, 1945.

A 262   RAPEE, Erno. Encyclopedia of music for films. New
        York: Belwin, 1925. (Repr. New York: Arno Press,
        1970.)

A 263   RUSHMORE, Robert. The life of George Gershwin. New
        York: Crowell-Collier, 1966.

A 264   SCHOORL, Bob. George Gershwin: van Broadway tot
        Carnegie-Hall. Amsterdam: Strengholt, 1952.

A 265   THOMAS, Lawrence B. The MGM years; with an introduc-
        tion by Sidney Skolsky and a commentary on soundtrack
        recording by Jesse Kaye. New York: Columbia House,
        1972.

A 266   WEBBER, Malcolm. Medicine show; illustrated by L. P.
        Harting. Caldwell, Id.: Caxton Printers, 1941.

Popular Music Personalities

A 267   ANDERTON, Barrie. Sonny boy! the world of Al Jolson.
        London: Jupiter Books, 1975.

A 268   BAILEY, Pearl. The raw Pearl. New York: Harcourt,
        Brace & World, 1968; New York: Pocket Books, 1969.

A 269   BAILEY, Pearl. Talking to myself. New York: Harcourt,
        Brace, Jovanovich, 1971.

A 270   CANTOR, Eddie. My life is in your hands; as told to David
        Freedman. New York: Harper, 1928.

        _____ .   ; with a new chapter... New York:
        Blue Ribbon Books, 1932.

A 271   CASTLE, Irene. Castles in the air; as told to Bob and
        Wanda Duncan. Garden City: Doubleday, 1958.

A 272   DAHL, David, and KEHOE, Barry. Young Judy. New
        York: Mason, Charter, 1975.

A 273   DiORIO, Al. Little girl lost: the life and hard times of
        Judy Garland. New Rochelle: Arlington House, 1973;
        London: Robson, 1975.

A 274   DOUGLAS-HOME, Robin. Sinatra. London: Joseph; New
        York: Grosset & Dunlap, 1962.

A 275 EDWARDS, Anne. Judy Garland: a biography. New York: Simon & Schuster; London: Constable, 1975.

A 276 FINCH, Christopher. Rainbow: the stormy life of Judy Garland. New York: Grosset & Dunlap; London: Joseph, 1975.

A 277 HORNE, Lena. In person, Lena Horne; as told to Helen Arstein and Carlton Moss. New York: Greenberg, 1950.

A 278 KITT, Eartha. Thursday's child. New York: Duell, Sloan & Pearce, 1956; London: Cassell, 1957; London: Landsborough Publications, 1958.

A 279 MIZE, J. T. H. Bing Crosby and the Bing Crosby style: Crosbyana thru biography, photography, discography. Chicago: Who is Who in Music, 1946.

A 280 SHAW, Arnold. Belafonte: an unauthorized biography. Philadelphia: Chilton; New York: Pyramid Books, 1960.

A 281 TUCKER, Sophie. Some of these days: an autobiography; (written in collaboration with Dorothy Giles.) London: Hammond, 1948.

A 282 ULANOV, Barry. The incredible Crosby. New York: McGraw-Hill, 1948.

A 283 VALLEE, Rudy. Vagabond dreams come true. New York: Dutton, 1930.

Rock, Rock and Roll, Pop

A 284 CHIPMAN, Bruce L., ed. Hardening rock: an organic anthology of the adolescence of rock and roll; with an appreciative essay by X. J. Kennedy. Boston: Little, Brown, 1972.

A 285 DALTON, David. Janis. New York: Simon & Schuster, 1971.

A 286 DYLAN, Bob. Approximately complete works. Amsterdam: De Bezige Bij, Thomas Rap, 1970. (Song texts.)

A 287 DYLAN, Bob. Tarantula. New York: Macmillan; London: MacGibbon & Kee, 1971.

A 288 FREDERICKS, Vic, ed. Who's who in rock 'n roll: facts, fotos and fan gossip about the performers in the world of rock 'n roll. New York: Fell, 1958.

A 289 GABREE, John. The world of rock. Greenwich, Ct.: Fawcett Publications, 1968.

A 290   GOLDMAN, Albert. Freakshow: the rocksoulbluesjazzsick-
jewblackhumorsexpoppsych gig and other scenes from the
counter-culture. New York: Atheneum, 1971.

A 291   GOLDSTEIN, Richard. Goldstein's greatest hits: a book
mostly about rock 'n' roll. Englewood Cliffs: Prentice-
Hall, 1970.

A 292   HALLOWELL, John. Inside Creedence. New York: Bantam Books, 1971.

A 293   HARRISON, Hank. The Dead book: a social history of the
Grateful Dead. New York: Links Books, 1973.

A 294   KRAMER, Daniel. Bob Dylan. New York: Citadel Press,
1967. (Photographs.)

A 295   LANDAU, Deborah. Janis Joplin: her life and times.
New York: Paperback Library, 1971.

A 296   MABEY, Richard. The pop process. London: Hutchinson
Educational, 1969. (Mostly about Great Britain.)

A 297   MARKS, J. Rock and other four-letter words: music of
the electric generation. New York: Bantam Books,
1968.

A 298   MILLER, William Robert. The world of pop music and
jazz. (Christian Encounters) St. Louis: Concordia
Publishing House, 1965.

A 299   PENNEBAKER, D. A. Bob Dylan, don't look back. New
York: Ballantine Books, 1968.

A 300   REDD, Lawrence N. Rock is rhythm and blues: the impact of mass media. East Lansing: Michigan State University Press, 1974.

A 301   RIBAKOVE, Sy, and RIBAKOVE, Barbara. Folk-rock: the
Bob Dylan story. New York: Dell, 1966.

A 302   THOMPSON, Toby. Positively main street: an unorthodox
view of Bob Dylan. New York: Coward-McCann, 1971.

INDEX

Note: The numbers in this index are item, not page, references. The letter A before a number denotes that the item will be found in the Appendix.

Abbey, Henry E. 148
Abbott, George 1257
Abolitionist songs 732, 1218
Abrahams, Roger D. 420, 463, 500, 657, 658, 754, 763
Abrams, Richard 685, 1053
Abramson, Herb 1344
Abravanel, Maurice 372
Acuff, Roy 608, 633, A133
Adams, E. F. 517
Adams, John Quincy 42
Adams, Russell L. 702
Adderley, Julian ("Cannonball") 685, 1024
Adgate, Andrew 41, 210
Adler, Samuel M. 1179
Adomian, Lan 746
African Methodist Episcopal Church 729, 740, 741
African music 342, 423, 426, 427, 447, 548, 607, 659, 674, 677, 680-682, 685, 690, 693-695, 697-699, 712-728, 756, 757, 759, 761, 770, 789, 794, 817, 967, 987, 988, 1003, 1007, 1008, 1025, 1037, 1038, 1232, A157-A162
Aikin, Jesse B. 532, 535
Ailey, Alvin 686
Ainsworth, Henry 66, 186, 187
Alabama 491, 529, 569, 644, 645, 745, 776, 827, 870, A48
  Birmingham 743, 744
  Selma 743
Albee, Edward F. 1235, 1248
Albertson, Chris 851
Alcott Family 324

Aldrich, Richard 105, 106, 114, 374
Aldridge, Alan 1363
Alexander, Texas 827, 832
Allan, Francis D. A231
Allen, Duane 71
Allen, Henry ("Red") 1010, 1071
Allen, Jules Verne 558
Allen, Rev. Richard 698, 702, 729, 741
Allen, Richard B. 953
Allen, Una L. 237
Allen, Walter C. 953, 1040, 1117, 1130
Allen, William Francis 7, 757, 758, 768, 792
Almanac Singers 581
Alwyn, William 1312
American Federation of Musicians 365, 1062
"American Folk Music Occasional" 646, 754
American Indian music 21, 22, 25, 26, 28, 37, 102, 120, 121, 384-419, 424-427, 429, 431, 435, 447, 678, 1221, A88-A94, A102
Amerson, Rich 745
Ames, Mrs. L. D. 510
Ames, Russell 436
Amis, Kingsley 970
Amish hymns 482
Amorosi, Nicholas 397
Amram, David 299
Anderson, Donna K. 321
Anderson, Ernest 1017

Psalmody 20, 22, 28, 29, 38,
  51, 57, 61, 62, 66, 68, 100,
  180-201, 204, 211, 214, A5,
  A65-A69
Purdy, Claire Lee A261
Puritans 28, 57, 63, 66, 100,
  180-192, 194, 196
Pusateri, Liborio 946, A196

Quarles, Benjamin 654, 669

Rabaud, Henri 96a
Radio 141, 360, 369, 370, 372,
  373, 376, 608, 609, 611, 618,
  620-622, 633, 635, 823, 892,
  1047, 1115, 1132, 1158, 1159,
  1226, 1298, 1331, 1336, 1354,
  1365
Ragtime 5, 12, 25-27, 29, 30,
  37, 259, 667, 682, 691, 692,
  694, 697, 701, 799-804, 837,
  873, 930, 958, 964, 967,
  1008, 1011, 1020, 1023, 1032,
  1072, 1074, 1155, 1162, 1166,
  1167, 1169, 1172, 1226, 1230,
  A174
Railroad songs 429, 454, 457,
  493, 503, 511, 565, 571, 572,
  586, 612, 636, 767
Raim, Ethel 742, 743, A103
Rainey, Gertrude ("Ma") 46,
  833
Raksin, David 1309, 1312,
  1315
Ralston, J. K. 508
Rambo, Dottie 71
Ramsey, Frederic 765, 766,
  824, 844, 845, 954, 956,
  1036, 1073
Randall, James Ryder 168
Randolph, Vance 499
Rapee, Erno A262
Rathbun, Frederic G. 774
Rau, Albert G. 84
Rauschenberg, Robert 273
Ravens, The 884
Ravenscroft, Thomas 188
Razaf, Andy 942, 1234
Read, Daniel 11, 38, 522
Read, Oliver 177, 179
Record guides 253, 887, 888,

954-959, A12, A229, A230
Records and recording 94, 175,
  360, 365, 370, 518, 545,
  568, 571, 612, 614, 615,
  618, 632, 635, 646, 649,
  679, 683, 813, 822, 823,
  826, 828, 830, 834, 883,
  893, 961, 1132, 1145, 1162,
  1342-1347, 1350, 1354,
  1360, A214, A215
  See also Discographies,
    Phonograph
Redd, Lawrence N. A300
Reddick, William J. A189
Redding, Noel 1381
Redding, Otis 889, 894, 895
Redman, Don 1024, 1029, 1072
Redway, Virginia Larkin 110
Reed, Blind Alfred 617
Reed, Lou 1372
Reeder, Barbara 699
Reese, Gustave 40
Reeves, David Wallis 1194,
  1200
Reeves, Goebel 613
Reeves, Martha, and the Van-
  dellas 893
Regular singing 64, 66, 181,
  193-200
Reich, Charles 1379
Reich, Steve 275, 283, 342
Reinagle, Alexander 41, 116,
  117, 210
Reinbach, Edna A43
Reinhardt, Django 962, 1018
Reinhardt, Max 1308
Reis, Claire R. 45, 291, 296
Reisner, Robert George 920,
  1008, 1135, A218
Religious folk music (including
  white spirituals, folk hymns)
  25, 29, 66, 87, 193, 434,
  439, 457, 458, 470, 489,
  493, 499, 502, 503, 521-557,
  693, 729, 741, 759, 781, 793,
  794, 1189
Reno, Don 623, 626
Reuss, Richard A. 599
Revitt, Paul J. 550
Revivalism and its music 62,
  65, 76, 536, 539-541, 549,
  559, 741
Revolutionary War songs 436,